The Society of the Sacred Heart in the World of Its Times
1865 -2000

Monique Luirard

The Society of the Sacred Heart in the World of Its Times
1865 -2000

Preface by Clare Pratt
Past Superior General

Translated by
Frances Gimber

Society of the Sacred Heart
Saint Louis, Missouri

The Society of the Sacred Heart in the World of Its Times 1865 -2000

Copyright © 2016 Society of the Sacred Heart
Author: Monique Luirard
Translated by Frances Gimber

All rights reserved. No part of this book may be used or reproduced by any means, graphic, electronic, or mechanical, including photocopying, recording, taping or by any information storage retrieval system without the written permission of the publisher except in the case of brief quotations embodied in critical articles and reviews.

Translated from the original French:
La Société du Sacré-Cœur dans le monde de son temps 1865-2000
Presses Universitaires du Septentrion, 2009
Villeneuve d'Ascq
France

iUniverse books may be ordered through booksellers or by contacting:

iUniverse
1663 Liberty Drive
Bloomington, IN 47403
www.iuniverse.com
1-800-Authors (1-800-288-4677)

Because of the dynamic nature of the Internet, any web addresses or links contained in this book may have changed since publication and may no longer be valid. The views expressed in this work are solely those of the author and do not necessarily reflect the views of the publisher, and the publisher hereby disclaims any responsibility for them.

ISBN: 978-1-4917-8305-4 (sc)
ISBN: 978-1-4917-8306-1 (e)

Print information available on the last page.

iUniverse rev. date: 03/29/2016

TABLE OF CONTENTS

Acknowledgements xiii
List of Illustrations xv
Preface xvii
Introduction xxi

First Part
The Vitality of the Society of the Sacred Heart 1865-1909

Chapter I
A Religious Congregation in Full Flower 5
   Rapid progress 5
   Reasons for Success: a Roman Congregation 8
   Contribution of the Society of the Sacred Heart to
   Ultramontane Devotion 9
      Affirmation of Devotion to the Sacred Heart 9
      The Society of the Sacred Heart and Marian Devotion 13
   The Society of the Sacred Heart and the Holy See 21

Chapter II
A Portrait of the Society of the Sacred Heart 31
   Social Composition: Choir Religious and Coadjutrix Sisters 31
   The Force of Numbers 33
      Increase in Numbers 33
      Entrance into Religious Life 34
      Reasons for a Choice 35
   To Live and Die in the Society of the Sacred Heart 39
   Geographic Extension 45
   Consequences of Development 52
      Redistribution of Forces 52
      Gradual Adaptation to Local Conditions 54

Chapter III
The Ups and Downs of Mission 61
   Journey to the Heart of Raging Elements 62
   Natural Dangers 66

Religious Life and Geopolitics 70
   The Civil War in the United States 70
   Liberalism and National Unity in Europe 74
      Unification of Italy 74
      Spain from Monarchy to Republic 76
   1870-1871: A Disastrous War 78
      The Terrible Year 79
      In the Heart of Paris under Siege 81
      Revolutionary Troubles 83
      New Apostolic Activities 87
      Consequences of the Defeat 89
The Fight against Catholics in Germany: Consequences of the
Kulturkampf 90
At the Heart of Political Disturbances in Latin America 94

Chapter IV
Passion for the Education of Youth 99
   The Educational Principles of the Society of the Sacred Heart 99
      Uniform Teaching 99
      Education Based on Solid Studies. 101
      Glorify the Heart of Jesus through Education 106
      Personalized Education 112
   Diversification of Educational Works 115
      Boarding Schools 116
      Day Schools 127
      Education among the Working Class 129
      Cultural and Educative Identity in the School of Charity 139
   Follow-up Projects 143
      Alumnae Associations of the Sacred Heart 143
      Retreat Work 148

Chapter V
Consolidation of the Society of the Sacred Heart 153
   The Work of Consolidation 154
      Putting in Order and Taking Hold 154
      Government and Fidelity to the "Primitive" Spirit 156
      Originality of Several Governmental Practices 159
   Renewed Relationship to the Founder 168
   Portrait of the Model Religious of the Sacred Heart 174

Chapter VI
The Shock of the Expulsions 193
   Faced with Legislation for "the Defense of the Republic" 193
   Modalities of Withdrawal 201
   An Intransigent Attitude: Causes and Consequence 207

SECOND PART
INTERNATIONALIZATION OF THE SOCIETY OF THE SACRED HEART
1909-1957

Chapter I
A New Departure 217
   A Generalate Full of Promise 217
   "Continuing Blessed Mother Barat's Work on Other Shores" 220
   Living Religious Life Elsewhere 230
   Reaffirmation of Unity 237

Chapter II
The Great War and the Religious of the Sacred Heart 243
   Harbingers of Confrontation in the Dark Days of Summer 1914 243
   Aspects of a Four-year War 250
   The Return to France 258
   The Days Following the Armistice 260

Chapter III
Tradition, Evolution and Modern Life 273
   The Society of the Sacred Heart in the Years between the Wars 273
      Effects of Social and Economic Transformation 273
      Apostolic Mission and Cloister 280
   Old and New Fields of Apostolate 282
      Appearance of Sacred Heart University Colleges 283
      Studies in Europe 286
      Life in the Institutions 294
      Development of Normal Schools 297
   Access to New Cultural Worlds 298
      Flowering of the Work in Japan 298
      Entry into China 302
      Congo 305
      India 311

Chapter IV
Persecutions and Extreme Ideologies 315
   Revolutions in Latin America 315
   Political Crisis and Civil War in Spain 323
      The Second Republic 323
      From National Movement to Civil War 326
   The Sacred Heart in Germany and Austria under Nazism 337

Chapter V
The Dark Years of World War II 365
   Concerns of the Motherhouse 365
   March toward Catastrophe 367
      Campaign in the East 368
      War in the West and the Collapse of France 369
      Great Britain's Resistance 371
      Life in North America 373
   The Sacred Heart and the Swastika: Life in Hitler's Europe 374
   Reversal: toward the Liberation of Europe. 393
   War in the Far East 398
      Prelude: the China Incidents 398
      From Pearl Harbor to Hiroshima 398

Chapter VI
From Chaos to Reconstruction 405
   The Traces of War 405
   Foreign Occupation 411
   Renewal of the Central Government 413
   A New Geopolitical Context 415
      The Cold War and the Iron and Bamboo Curtains 415
      Nationalism and the Rise of the Third World 429
   Prudent Openness 434
   Affirmation of Devotion to the Sacred Heart 440

THIRD PART
THE SOCIETY OF THE SACRED HEART REFOUNDED
1958-2000

Chapter I
Innovation or Renewal 1958-1967 455
   New Waves 455
      "The times are changing" 455
      Independence and National Politics 457

    Missionary expansion 462
        Favorable Context 462
        New Methods for the Mission 463
        New Places for Mission 465
  The Beginning of the Reform 474
    The Shock of the Council 475
    A Transitional General Congregation 476
        A Different Climate 477
        The Beginning of Renewal 479
  Expectations of the Religious of the Sacred Heart 488
    Troubles, Fears and Hopes 489
    Eddies, Revolt and Protests 495
    Widespread Desire for Change 497

Chapter II
From One World to Another 507
  The Shock of the Special Chapter 507
  The Orientations of the Chapter 528

Chapter III
The Opening 1968-1970 535
  Reception of the Special Chapter 535
  Setting up New Governmental Structures 540
  The Kaski Research 548
  Unity, Charity and Government 550
  The Chapter of 1970 555
    Careful Preparation 555
        The Lima Assembly 555
        Preparation of the Chapter in the Provinces 557
    The Work and Decisions of the Chapter 559

Chapter IV
Turbulence 571
  Varied Pathways 571
  The Crisis of Authority 574
  Major Changes 577
    Returning to the Family 577
    Religious Life and Appearance 578
    Apostolic Activities and Community Life 584
        Education and Sacred Heart Schools 584
        New Apostolates 590
        "Insertions" 591

    New Forms of Community Life 599
    New Ways of Expressing Sacred Heart Spirituality 606

Chapter V
Great Hopes 621
    Another Kind of Governance: Collegial Government 621
        Community of Government 623
        Knowing the Provinces Better 627
    Challenges and Tensions 632
        The Causes of Conflict 632
        Malaise and Sorrow: the Case of the House in Florence 641
    The Chapter of 1976 646
    Human Maturity and Formation 650
        The Need for a Fresh Start 650
        A Case in Point 655
    Peace Returns 662
        A New Approach to Education 662
        Toward New Constitutions 666
        The Chapter of 1982 669

Chapter VI
The Return to "Ordinary Time" 675
    Re-appropriation of the Identifying Characteristics 676
        Approbation of the Constitutions 676
        The International Education Commission 682
        Poverty and Financial Management 684
        Towards Uniform Formation 686
        Separation of the House in Florence 688
    The Weight of Politics 693
        A New International Situation 693
        General Chapter of 1988: the Political Dimension 695
        The Collapse of Bipolarity 700
        Politics and the Society of the Sacred Heart 703
    Refocusing Regarding Government 707
        From a Central Team to General Council 707
        Development of Administrative Structures and New Foundations 709
        Communication in the Society 710
            Visits 711
            Relations between the Provinces and the Motherhouse 714
            Other Modes of Communication 716
            The International Commission for Justice and Peace 718

    Another Mode of Development 719
        Reduced Numbers 720
        Aspects of Demographic Decline 720
        New Spaces, Contrasts and New Faces 723
        One Mission and Many Apostolates 727
    Return to the Source 731
        The Unexpected Canonization of Philippine Duchesne 732
        The Bicentenary of the Society of the Sacred Heart 734
Conclusion 739
Sources and Bibliography 745
Index 753

ACKNOWLEDGEMENTS

This work could not have come to completion without the support of the Society of the Sacred Heart. I would like to express my gratitude to Patricia García de Quevedo and Clare Pratt, superiors general of the Society. The former, in 2000, welcomed the idea of this "History of the Society of the Sacred Heart in the World of Its Times." The latter assigned me the task of carrying it forward.

The motherhouse and the provinces have facilitated the task. I wish to thank especially Margaret Phelan, general archivist. Archivists and provincial secretaries have been a great help: Frances Gimber in St. Louis, Missouri; Mary Coke (+) at Roehampton; Jeanine Zech and Clotilde Meeûs in Brussels; Anne Leonard in Rome, then in Montreal; Claude Brahamsha in Cairo; Maryvonne Duclaux in Poitiers; Tanaka Tsutako in Tokyo; Marta Elena Mejía in Medellín; Blanca de Sivatte in Barcelona; Concepción Santamaría in Madrid. Francisca Tamayo, who had contributed to my research when she was secretary general, guided me in Peru, as did Patricia García de Quevedo in Mexico. Both enabled me to enter into the culture and the life of these two provinces.

My thanks are due also to those provincials who passed on to the religious the questionnaires I sent them and who have thus augmented the archives of their province by asking for the reminiscences of their sisters. I am grateful especially to Ysabel Lorthiois, Geneviève Mousset and Hélène Carré (+), who translated the documents that came from Spain, Colombia and Chile.

Finally, I wish to thank all those who have supported this project by their prayer, the interviews and responses they have given me, the time they have given to it and the confidence they have shown me. These encounters have been important moments during which I received a great deal. Moreover, it is to the thousands of women, living or not, who entered the Society of the Sacred Heart to glorify the Heart of Christ and to follow Saint Madeleine Sophie that I would like to dedicate this history, which is theirs.

Monique Luirard

Translator's note:

This English version owes a great deal to the careful editing of Dorothea Hewlett in Auckland, New Zealand, and Patricia Cannon Willis of Sequim, Washington, U.S.A., to whom the translator is immensely grateful. Thanks are due also for her support to Kathleen Conan, superior general, and to Carolyn Osiek, archivist of the United States-Canada Province, for her assistance.

Since publishing the original French version of this work, the author, Monique Luirard, RSCJ, has died. The translation is dedicated to her memory in gratitude.

LIST OF ILLUSTRATIONS

01 Statue of Saint Madeleine Sophie Barat by Enrico Quattrini
   Erected in St. Peter's Basilica, Rome, 12 September 1934
02 Chapel of the Motherhouse, Paris, Boulevard des Invalides
03 Children's Uniforms, watercolor
   1. Calais, 1868-1874: black dress, velvet shoulder straps, straw hat trimmed with blue ribbons
   2. Roehampton, 1870: winter, black dress
   3. Roehampton, 1870: summer, yellow dress, blue sash
   9. Conflans, 1872: winter, black dress; summer, blue and white checked dress with collar
   10. Beauvais, 1870: light coffee colored dress with pelerine and straw hat trimmed with white ribbons, blue tie
   11. Beauvais, 1873: straw hat; grey alpaca dress, shoulder straps and bodice, blue tie
   12. Santa Rufina, Rome, 1870: yellow wool mousseline in honor of the Pope
04 Students of Montpellier, 1880-1890, wearing the ribbon of distinction; others, the medal of the Children of Mary
05 Centenary album presented to Mother Digby by the Vicariate of England and Ireland, 21 November 1900
06 Convent of the Sacred Heart, Roehampton, England, before 1940
07 Convent in Heliopolis, Egypt
08 Pupils' dining room, Sault-au-Récollet, Montréal
09 Student dormitory, Les Anglais, Lyons
10 Science laboratory in the boarding school, the Cerro, Havana
11 Students' monthly outing, boarding school, Tijuca, Rio de Janeiro
12 Departure of Belgian religious for the Congo in 1927
13 Day school, Kalina, Congo, 1933
14 Mission at Kipako, Congo, 1933
15 Chamartín, Madrid, after the fire, 11 May 1931

Monique Luirard

16 Convent in Shanghai
17 Young Chinese religious, postulants, novices and aspirants in Shanghai, 1947
18 Arrival in Miami of the religious who left Cuba in 1961
19 Boarding School, Lindthout, Brussels, 1949
20 Pontifical Mass at Blumenthal, Netherlands, 1949-1950. Students are wearing white veils.
21 Manhattanville College of the Sacred Heart, New York, 1950
22 Audience with Pope Pius XII of *grandes pensionnaires* of the Trinità dei Monti, 1958
23 Religious of Rose Bay, Sydney, fishing at the end of the garden
24 Pupils' dormitory, Haregaon, India
25 Religion class in Marathi in the parish, Haregaon
26 Dispensary in Upper Egypt
27 Hope Rural School for Mexican and Caribbean immigrants, Indiantown, Florida
28 School children, Huacullani, Bolivia, 1976-1979
29 Women's literacy class, Huacullani
30 Literacy class for men, Myky people, Brazil
31 Art class for children of Sankocho, Tokyo
32 Kindergarten, Guadalajara, Mexico
33 A community house, Redfern, Sydney, Australia
34 Chapel of the retreat center, Paju-Si, Korea
35 Clare Pratt, after her election as superior general, lighting the founder's candle in the oratory of St. Madeleine Sophie, Amiens, 7 August 2000.
A tradition in the Society: since 1865 each newly elected superior general lights a candle that belonged to the founder.

PREFACE

It is with gratitude and admiration that I write a few words to present this history of the Society of the Sacred Heart from the death of its founder, Madeleine Sophie Barat, in 1865, to its bicentenary in 2000. There exist histories of some of the provinces or regional groups of countries where the Society is located, but this is the first time that a history of the entire congregation has been written, and it is a most impressive work.

Monique Luirard combines the research methods and analytical skills of a professional historian with the "inside experience" of being a Religious of the Sacred Heart, a combination of "head" and "heart" that gives the book a quality that is very satisfying.

I think it can be said that at some point in the life of every person a desire awakens to know something of one's family genealogy, the history of one's ancestors, perhaps out of curiosity, but also as a help to greater self-understanding. The same can be said of a religious congregation, of which the history provides both the foundation and an inspiration for each new generation. For the Society of the Sacred Heart, the directive of the Second Vatican Council (1962-1965) to renew religious life by a "simultaneous process" of adapting to the changed conditions of the time, while returning to the original inspiration of the founder, was an invitation to recover or to discover for the first time documentation of our history that was hitherto unknown or undisseminated.

Phil Kilroy, in her *Madeleine Sophie Barat: a Life*, presented the founder as a woman of her time, an extraordinary woman who was at the helm for the first sixty-five years of the congregation's life and who became a saint by living fully the ideal with which she was inspired when barely twenty-one years of age. This book, *The Society of the Sacred Heart in the World of Its Times*, can be considered its sequel. Its focus, however, is not one person but the thousands of Religious of the Sacred Heart living the same ideal on five continents over the course of one hundred and thirty-five years.

Monique Luirard

The years following Sophie Barat's death have been divided into three parts: 1865 to 1909, 1909 to 1957 and 1958 to 2000. The third part is nearly half the book; this in itself is understandable. The semi-cloister and uniformity of life and apostolate prior to Vatican II are less complex and easier to narrate than the explosion of experimentation and diversification of apostolic responses to local needs that the Council unleashed. That being said, the second part includes the international expansion due to the expulsions from France (and from China), two world wars, as well as violence and political unrest (for example, Spain and Mexico), and a number of natural disasters (such as the 1923 earthquake in Japan), all of which affected the Society, despite its cloistered life.

There are some threads woven throughout the history of the Society of the Sacred Heart that I think are particularly significant. From the beginning, the vision was a universal one, and *internationality* has been an integral dimension of the Society since 1818, when Philippine Duchesne left France to bring the love of the Heart of Jesus to America. Another name for it is the *sens du corps*, a characteristic of the Society from the beginning, nurtured by Madeleine Sophie's relational manner, which became the hallmark of future government and was instrumental in instilling in the hearts of religious of every generation *a deep love of the congregation*. Symbolic of this affection, which we often speak of as the *cor unum*, is the extraordinary fact that when the expulsions occurred in France (1904-1909), not one of the professed religious, most of whom were French, chose to leave the congregation rather than be sent to another country. The *sens du corps* was stronger than national loyalty.

Another thread is the commitment to repair the torn fabric of society through the work of *education*. Even when the religious could not leave the property, where the convent, boarding school and poor school were all located, they were ingenious in inventing ways to address the needs that could not be addressed by the institutions or in assuring an educative dimension to situations forced on them by such events as war, occupation or epidemic. Once cloister was eliminated and the religious were able to go out, they went with the heart of an educator.

One thread that can be detected throughout is the evolution of political consciousness within the Society, from a stance of refraining to speak of anything political (wise in the early days of the Society and helped by the rule of silence) to recognizing in the General Chapter of 1988 "the political dimension of our apostolic life." The more the Society has become inculturated, the more our life has become intertwined with the lives and struggles of others.

The Society of the Sacred Heart in the World of Its Times 1865 -2000

What is striking in reading page after page of horrific events touching our lives, such as war, persecution and natural disasters, is that thousands of Religious of the Sacred Heart continued to live their daily lives: people entered, received the habit, made their vows, taught their classes, cooked for hundreds, cared for the wounded, sheltered refugees and orphans and managed to have a life of prayer. Perhaps it was/is the solid *contemplative dimension* of the RSCJ vocation, shaken for a time with the elimination of monastic structures, but subsequently deepened and strengthened, that explains the serenity and equanimity of many Religious of the Sacred Heart in the face of unprecedented challenges.

Giving color and texture to this tapestry that is the Society of the Sacred Heart is its *raison d'être*: the communication by word, deed and example of the *love of God for each human being*, the discovery in each one of that same love that may be hidden from sight.

Discovering the treasure that is hidden in another reminds me of some words of Madeleine Sophie that I think are appropriate here: "*Il y a des sources qui restent inconnues. Enlevez un peu de terre et aussitôt vous verrez apparaître une eau claire et limpide.*" [There are springs that remain hidden. Remove a bit of the soil and soon you will see clear, clean water appear.] In this book Monique Luirard has done a great work of clearing the earth away from the sources that have always been there but until now have been inaccessible to us.

I think that the Society, along with its ever expanding circle of lay friends and colleagues, former students and associates, will welcome this book. It is a great contribution to our "family history," as well as to the history of women religious in the nineteenth and twentieth centuries. It is interesting, often riveting, and inspiring.

Clare Pratt, RSCJ
Superior General
Rome, Italy
3 July 2008, 20th Anniversary
of the Canonization of Philippine Duchesne

INTRODUCTION

The Society of the Sacred Heart is a congregation that appeared in France in 1800 and since has brought together several thousand women of different ages, cultures, languages and nationalities, all united in the desire to follow Christ. What set them on this path, then and now, and why? The answer varies with each person and acquires new expression throughout one's life, but all answers are unified in the project conceived at the end of the eighteenth century by Sophie Barat, who was canonized in 1925.

On the occasion of the Second Vatican Council the Church rediscovered the importance of charisms in the Christian world and asked religious congregations to return to their spiritual sources. For the Society of the Sacred Heart, the founding charism is that of a French woman who was born in Burgundy under the reign of Louis XVI and who died in the last years of the Second Empire. In her youth Sophie Barat had experienced that the love of God, of which the Sacred Heart of Jesus is a symbol, could give meaning to her life and to that of women who had and would have the same experience. The love given freely by God could not be kept for oneself, but once known, it must be transmitted, offered to everyone.

To glorify the Heart of Jesus is a goal that may be expressed in various ways of life. Sophie Barat owed her personality and character to her birth, to her temperament and to an exceptional education for a girl of her time. She understood that in a country in which Revolution had destroyed traditional institutions and certain social structures, glorification of the Heart of Jesus could be accomplished by religious whose service in the Church was the education of young women. For her, it was thanks to well-formed women that society could achieve or regain stability. Sophie Barat had an intuition that a religious institute could thus contribute to the remaking of a social fabric attentive to family life, founded on a strong Christian life and on a faith supported by reason. This project worked out in the context of France immediately had a broader value; to educate young women was to form adorers of the Heart of Jesus able to show forth the love of Christ to the very ends of the earth.

A founding charism evolves according to the human societies in which it takes shape. Even during the lifetime of Mother Barat, the initial intuition found progressively new and attractive expressions, depending on social needs that had been identified but also on the aptitudes of those who had entered the Society. A religious body was being constructed little by little. Founded on a close alliance of contemplation and action, the Society of the Sacred Heart developed a "mixed" style of life. It took its governmental structures from the Society of Jesus, among others. Thanks to its founder, who was superior general for almost sixty years, it created and gave life to institutions capable of supporting the apostolic life of religious called to serve in countries with diverse political regimes and social and cultural organization.

The history of a group reflects the ideology or the stance of the one who is carrying it out. For a long time the history of the Society of the Sacred Heart was that of its superiors general, and everything that took place within it harked back to their style, their administration and the type of councilor they were able to invite. Examination proves that the superiors general of the congregation have been remarkable women, and they have been surrounded by equally gifted religious. The Society is Ignatian; its structure is pyramidal, founded on obedience and on a close relationship between the head and the members, or rather between the members and the "Center," an expression that only recently has fallen into disuse. But its history is also that of the women of many backgrounds who have entered and whose unique mission of glorifying the Heart of Christ was expressed in multiple activities. Some of them were gifted with vast literary, scientific or artistic culture. A few, charged with high level responsibilities, have been superiors general, members of general councils, vicars or provincials, local superiors. Most have lived their vocation in obscure tasks in distant mission posts, sometimes very far from their birth place. All have been Religious of the Sacred Heart, animated by the concern to discover and manifest the love of the Heart of Christ. The charism of Sophie Barat and her congregation has given meaning and relish to their task as educators in the service of people whose life situations were changing as a result of mutations in the world at large.

To give the sweep of one hundred fifty years of the history of a congregation is to try to discover how a religious body lives and evolves. It is to try to perceive how the means and the structure emerge that permit the expression and adaptation of its apostolic work. But it is also to preserve the memory of the religious who have given it life through their fidelity to their vows in "one heart and one mind." It is to recall that religious life is not disconnected from the political, economic and social climate and that Religious of the Sacred Heart throughout the world have always had to take that climate into account in creating and developing their apostolic works. All the events, major and minor, they have lived through, all the religious, political, economic and social change they have had to confront have influenced their world view in one way or another. Global, national and local history have roles to play in this narrative, for they have shaped the women who entered the Society of the Sacred Heart and have given a tonality to the Society, even though for a long time there was a vigilant effort to keep politics outside of the life of the community. This history of the Society of the Sacred Heart, from the death of the founder to the celebration of its bicentennial, aims at discovering how a congregation of apostolic life maintains and transforms itself, faithful to its origins, attentive to the signs of the times and desirous of glorifying the Heart of Jesus in the heart of the world.

First Part

THE VITALITY OF THE SOCIETY OF THE SACRED HEART
1865-1909

The Society of the Sacred Heart in the World of Its Times 1865-2000

On the twenty-fifth of May, 1865, feast of the Ascension, Madeleine Sophie Barat, founder of the Society of the Sacred Heart, died. She had been elected superior general for life in 1806, when she was only twenty-six years old. She had directed the congregation from that date, sometimes in the face of grave crises that she had been able to surmount without yielding in the essentials. In 1864 she had expressed the desire to give up her charge, but she was dissuaded. Nevertheless, she had prepared for her succession in naming a vicar general, Mother Joséphine Gœtz, who was destined to replace her. The succession, therefore, was easy. The religious in Detroit, United States, expressed the general sentiment of the Society when they wrote: "[Mother Barat] left us in the care of a Mother who is already known and loved and who became doubly dear to us because chosen by her."[1] For Joséphine Gœtz was surely "the one [Mother Barat] had herself chosen."[2]

Because of this choice the Society supposed that the new superior general would exercise her charge for a long time, as she was only forty-seven years old. It was expected also that she would travel; for the houses of the Sacred Heart, except those around Paris, had not had visits from the Mother General for about fifteen years. Certainly Mother Barat had followed their progress closely by means of the abundant correspondence she maintained, writing many business letters as well as letters of spiritual advice; however, the time had come for day-to-day management and for regular visits by the superior general herself, not just by her assistants.

Mother Gœtz had already fulfilled responsibilities that had acquainted her with many members of the Society, both in France and abroad: She had been mistress of novices at Conflans for seventeen years; then from 1864, mistress of probation, the period of preparation for full membership in the Society of the Sacred Heart, which brought together religious of all nationalities at the motherhouse. Her spiritual gifts were well known: she was austere, but above all her humility was proverbial and placed her in a direct line with the founder, whose humility was practically the only virtue remembered.[3] She was also one of those "learned saints" (*saintes savantes*) whom Mother Barat had desired. A solitary worker, Joséphine Gœtz needed long periods of quiet work and reflection. Gifted with powers of solid thought and a logical mind, she had read and annotated the *Summa* of Saint Thomas Aquinas. In this regard she was ahead of her time, for

---

[1] *Lettres annuelles*, 1865, p. 119.
[2] *Lettres annuelles*, 1865, p. 124, Rochester.
[3] Cécile de Cassini, one of Mother Barat's first companions, died at the age of ninety, shortly after Sophie. When asked for her recollections of the founder, she answered, "I remember only one thing about Mother Barat, that she was as humble as dust!"

neo-Thomism had not yet become the basis of seminary formation, and the reading of that text was neither current nor widespread.[4]

The news of Sophie Barat's death – learned only in the middle of June 1865 in Louisiana and in mid-July in Santiago, Chile, for cable was rarely used at that time –[5] saddened all the Religious of the Sacred Heart and those associated with them. However, it was not unexpected, since Mother Barat, born 12 December 1779, in Joigny in today's department of Yonne, was eighty-five years old. As an alumna, intending no irony, remarked in her letter of condolence: "Mother Barat could no longer follow on earth her children scattered to all the corners of the globe; the spread of the Society of the Sacred Heart has assumed such proportions that only from heaven could the founder direct the progress of her work that is so valuable for the world."[6] Humanly speaking, the time had come for Mother Barat to hand over her charge. She left a fully alive congregation that had developed rapidly, if we remember that it was only on 21 November 1800, in the private chapel of a Paris townhouse in the Rue de Touraine, that the young Sophie Barat had consecrated herself to the Sacred Heart.

---

[4] In 1879 the encyclical *Aeterni Patris* restored in the teaching of the Church "the Christian manner of philosophizing, of which the teaching of Saint Thomas must remain…the model and the rule."

[5] On the other hand, the election of Mother Lehon in 1874 was known in Detroit in less than a week by means of the cable *Atlantis*.

[6] *Lettres annuelles*, I. 1865, p. LXII.

Chapter I

A Religious Congregation in Full Flower

At the end of the period of the Directory, Sophie Barat had the intuition to gather adorers of the Heart of Jesus and to form "hundreds, thousands of adorers."[7] This desire coincided with plans developed in exile by a group of young priests, the Fathers of the Sacred Heart. These young men, desirous of reviving the vision of the Society of Jesus, had gathered around Léonor de Tournély. He had died in Vienna in 1796,[8] hoping to create a women's branch of his congregation, consecrated to the Sacred Heart and dedicated to the education of young women. His successor, Joseph Varin, upon returning to France in 1800, sought to consolidate the Fathers of the Sacred Heart by joining them to the Fathers of the Faith and, at the same time, to found the congregation of women. He made the acquaintance of Sophie Barat, about whom he knew only that she wanted to become a religious and that, guided by her elder brother Louis, she possessed an exceptional education for a young woman of her time. She seemed suitable to support the project he had in mind. Sophie Barat made her first religious consecration in Paris a few months later.

Rapid progress

In the fall of 1801, an educational institution was founded in Amiens in Picardy. The first community increased little by little, accepting young women attracted to religious life as well as former nuns exiled from their monasteries by the Revolution. This coexistence was not without certain

---

[7] Pauline Perdrau, *Les loisirs de l'Abbaye*, vol. 1, pp. 423-424.
[8] In 1868 the Society of the Sacred Heart made a foundation in Vienna, where Father de Tournély had predicted that "the work of the Sacred Heart would exist" (*Lettres annuelles*, 1867-1868, p. 49). His body was buried later in the chapel of the house at Rennweg in Vienna.

risks, for religious formed before monastic vows had been forbidden by the *Constituante* were doubtless more interested in reviving community life and in the educational aim of the congregation than in consecration to the Sacred Heart and its Ignatian structure. The type of "mixed life" was new enough not to be accepted unanimously at first; but after overcoming a severe crisis, the new congregation began to flourish.[9]

The First Empire had shown some good will toward religious congregations of women; it permitted their foundation or reestablishment on condition that they had some social benefit: care of the sick or education of youth. The Association of Ladies of Christian Instruction – as the Society was known at first – saw its legal existence recognized by a decree signed by Napoleon I in 1807; at that time it already possessed four houses. Thanks to a change in the political regime, the new congregation was able to achieve recognition.

Under the Restoration the institute could identify itself as the Society of the Sacred Heart, whereas it had not been possible to use that title earlier because of the counterrevolutionary connotation of the symbol of the Sacred Heart at the time of the wars in the Vendée. The inauguration of a boarding school in Paris and the transfer there of the generalate, called the "motherhouse," in 1816, gave the Society new impetus and helped it build a reputation based on the quality of its works. That reputation was solidified by the acquisition in 1825 of the Hôtel Biron in the Rue de Varenne. The Society of the Sacred Heart took advantage of a law of 1825 that permitted religious congregations to obtain legal existence: it was authorized by a royal ordinance dated 22 April 1827. This step undoubtedly facilitated expansion by giving financial stability and political and administrative support.[10]

While the Society pursued its expansion in France, it began rapidly to extend its mission to the rest of the world. On 8 February 1818, Philippine Duchesne with four companions set out for Louisiana and a few months later settled in Missouri, the base from which the Society of the Sacred Heart developed in the United States. In the spring of the same year, 1818, negotiations were underway for a foundation in Chambéry, at that time a city in the Kingdom of Sardinia. From Turin, where it opened a house in 1822, the Society spread to the Italian peninsula. Six years later, when the Constitutions had finally been approved by Pope Leo XII, the congregation was called to Rome. The Revolution of 1830 occasioned the entry into Switzerland. Other houses were opened in Piedmont, in northern Italian principalities, in the Papal States and in the Italian possessions in Austria.

---

[9] See Phil Kilroy, *Madeleine Sophie Barat, a Life*.

[10] Later on, the Society was authorized again at the beginning of the Second Empire on the occasion of modifications to its Constitutions, or Rule.

The Society of the Sacred Heart in the World of Its Times 1865-2000

The Society of the Sacred Heart reached into Belgium in 1836, a few years after that country achieved independence. It opened its first houses in the British Isles at the beginning of the 1840's. The Emancipation Act of 1829 had freed Catholics in Great Britain and was beginning to bear fruit. From 1833 on, the Tractarian Movement, called the Oxford Movement, had sought to free the Anglican Church from the control of the State. Through the activity of John Keble, Edward Pusey and John Henry Newman, it had called for a renewal of study in the Church. It was after the last of Newman's *Tracts for the Times*, in which he wrote that the "second spring" of the Church would come about in part through education, that the Society of the Sacred Heart settled, in 1842, in Roscrea, Ireland, and at Berrymead in England. The congregation founded houses in Polish Galicia in 1843, in Spain, and in Styria in 1846, in Holland in 1848, in the Kingdom of Prussia in 1851 and in 1857 opened others in the Rhineland and in Greater Poland. At the same time development continued in the United States and in France. In 1842, the Society went to Algiers and to Canada. In 1853 and in 1858 it reached Latin America, through the foundations in Chile and in Cuba.

At the death of the founder, therefore, the Society of the Sacred Heart had already spread "to the ends of the earth," as Sophie Barat had wished.[11] It had arrived rapidly at a specific religious identity. As a congregation that had received from the Society of Jesus, not only its governmental structure, but also its spiritual framework and its nature as an institute of apostolic life, it aimed at the glorification of the Heart of Jesus. The Society of the Sacred Heart had also experienced a remarkable growth in numbers in a very short period of time: it already had 3539 members, of whom 1277 lived outside of France. It was divided into seventeen vicariates and vice-vicariates that did not necessarily coincide with national boundaries. Belgium, Holland and Prussia, with relatively few houses, were joined together. Cuba depended on the northeastern United States. The vicariate of eastern France, besides the houses in Lorraine, Alsace and Franche-Comté, included Riedenburg, a house near Bregenz in the Tyrol, from which the Society spread to Austria and Bavaria. The Society profited by changes in national borders to bring together in one vicariate houses of the same country formerly included in a broader unit. It showed a certain audacity in uniting in the vice-vicariate of Poland the houses of Posen and Lemberg, located in regions controlled respectively by Prussia and Austria at a time when Poland no longer existed as an independent entity.

---

[11] Pauline Perdrau, *Loisirs*, vol. 1, p. 424.

Monique Luirard

Reasons for Success: a Roman Congregation

The Society of the Sacred Heart did not owe its rapid development to favors from governments, although some did give aid. Louis XVIII, for example, made a financial contribution to the acquisition of the Hôtel Biron in Paris. In Latin America some countries opened their frontiers to the Society in exchange for its contribution to the training of local teachers. The authorization, not financial help, granted by states like Spain and Austria required the Society to conform to certain clearly stated principles. Moreover, it was during the July Monarchy, which showed no interest in the Society, that the congregation fled France. Finally, links of the Society with certain conservative governments sometimes had severe consequences, as some houses had to be closed following the victory of liberal parties, as in Switzerland and Italy.

It was rather to the founder and her first companions that the Society owed the establishment of a solid educational work. Sophie Barat welcomed at the same time the aspirations of young girls and of women of all ages to religious life and answered a social need, that of the education of girls, which she linked to the glorification of the Heart of Jesus; that is what was new. The "little Society" of the Sacred Heart – as Madeleine Sophie loved to call it – benefited from an original internal structure, well adapted to the times and capable of aiding its expansion. Mother Barat wanted to form a religious society of women whose rules and spirit would be adapted to the needs of the times. Although she had to accept cloister in the end in order to allow the members of the Society to be recognized as religious, she did not want her daughters to be constrained by religious exercises, such as recitation of the Office, which were not suited to the rhythm of life in a school. She adopted also, on the model of the Society of Jesus, the structure of a congregation understood as a single body governed by a superior general. When the Holy See approved the Constitutions of the Society of the Sacred Heart, it granted the Society a cardinal protector. This measure, unfavorably viewed by the French episcopate, contributed to the creation of a special link between the congregation and the Vatican. It did not prevent serious conflicts with bishops, chiefly the archbishop of Paris; but it gave the Society of the Sacred Heart real autonomy with regard to the local Ordinary, although bishops were always treated with deep respect by superiors general and by communities. Above all, the Society of the Sacred Heart appeared to be in perfect accord with the evolution in French Catholicism that turned towards Rome. Its ultramontane orientation manifested itself as much by its contribution to a new type of devotion as in original relations with the Holy See.

Contribution of the Society of the Sacred Heart to Ultramontane Devotion

Theological and spiritual changes in the course of the first half of the nineteenth century affected the Catholic world and contributed to modifications in the manner of speaking of the mystery of God and expressing faith in Jesus Christ. While the Society of the Sacred Heart drew profit in this respect from a flourishing ecclesial milieu, it also contributed to making it possible. The Society was one of the means by which the theological, spiritual and pastoral innovations of the time were spread. Making its appearance in 1800, it was the first of the numerous congregations founded to honor the Heart of Christ; and it participated in the development of an affective, celebratory devotion.

Affirmation of Devotion to the Sacred Heart

Devotion to the Sacred Heart is often presented as one of the principal aspects of ultramontane Catholicism. As Monsignor d'Hulst, the first rector of the *Institut catholique*, put it, "The nineteenth century was the century of the Sacred Heart." Strongly contested earlier by the Jansenists as well as by different anti-mystical currents in Catholicism, this devotion had profited by different developments, in political and social culture as well as in the religious. Its success is doubtless to be seen in relation to the current rediscovery of Jesus Christ, which counterbalanced a preponderant theocentrism in the expression of belief. Christology restored to honor ancient works like *The Imitation of Christ*, the success of which was considerable. The devotion allowed for the revival of the intuitions of the great French spiritual teachers of the seventeenth century, who were attached to the person of Jesus and who had demonstrated that in Jesus Christ God was fully manifest. Therefore, in order to take the Incarnation seriously and to be Christian, one must go to Jesus, discover in contemplation of the Gospel his way of loving God and human beings, study "the interior dispositions of his Heart in order to unite and conform ourselves to them."[12]

The return to Jesus manifested itself in and through devotion to Christ suffering in his Passion. "Holy Hour," the practice recommended by Margaret Mary Alacoque,[13] spread, thanks to the efforts of a Jesuit who resided at Paray-le-Monial, Father Debrosse. He established it in 1829.

---

[12] *Abridged Plan of the Institute*, V, and *Constitutions*, 2nd Part, Chapter Two, XI.
[13] It was during a holy hour in 1806 that Philippine Duchesne felt that she was destined for a mission to the Native Americans.

Devotion to the Sacred Heart in popular forms was spread through the images of the Heart of Christ. These doubtless reproduced those that Margaret Mary had painted or those the Jesuits had used at the beginning of the eighteenth century in publications that made known the content of the revelations with which the Visitandine of Paray-le-Monial had been gifted.

The images that the Society of the Sacred Heart was diffusing often had as their purpose to ward off evils. The religious had the custom of pasting on the doors and walls of their houses small stamps bearing the inscriptions, "Cease, the Heart of Jesus is here!" or "Cease, the Heart of Jesus is with me!" These served to protect against lightning, to turn aside an epidemic, a fire, a flood or a popular revolution, as well as to prevent an evil intruder from entering their houses.[14] It happened also that during epidemics or wars the religious distributed images or scapulars of the Sacred Heart to their neighbors, members of their households, even to neighboring doctors. These objects, considered capable of warding off contagion, were called scapulars "of preservation."[15]

The cult of the Sacred Heart formed part of the Eucharistic renewal that took place during the nineteenth century. For the fervent faithful, the following of Christ involved adoration of the Blessed Sacrament under different forms: prayer before the Blessed Sacrament exposed, Benediction or night adoration. Theologians placed strong emphasis again on the Real Presence. In 1848 Father Boone and the Countess de Meeûs founded the Association of Perpetual Adoration. In Spain, Father Rubio originated Guards of Honor, which Religious of the Sacred Heart adopted and popularized in different countries. Very early Mother Barat had linked devotion to the Sacred Heart with Eucharistic devotion, hardly distinguishing between adoration of the Eucharist and adoration of the Sacred Heart. Therefore, her daughters had directed their pupils and persons with whom they were connected toward reception of the Eucharist as much as toward adoration of the Blessed Sacrament. They contributed thus to the encouragement of frequent Communion, which the public in general accepted with great difficulty.

The Society of the Sacred Heart sought to make it understood that God is love and, to borrow an expression of Lacordaire, to go beyond that "difficult Christianity that never arrives at love but remains only rules."[16] Like many others at the time, the Society tried to show that God is always

---

[14] Thus the Trinità defended itself at the time of the Revolution in 1848, which forced Pius IX to leave Rome, and likewise the religious of Sarriá in Spain, when the royalty fell in 1866.

[15] *Lettres annuelles*, 1872-1873, p. 173.

[16] Letter to Paul Rencker, 11 May 1846, in *Les plus belles lettres de Lacordaire* (ed. Pierre Gombert), p. 106.

ready to pardon and that those who recognize their powerlessness are guilty if they refuse to turn to Jesus Christ. In the religious education of both young people and adults, the religious insisted on childlike confidence as the means of touching the heart of God, whose fatherhood Jesus had revealed. The stress on the love of God, on God's goodness and mercy, manifested in Jesus Christ, symbolized by the Heart of Jesus, was the purpose the congregation proposed for itself from the beginning. To quote a friend of the Society, Monsignor Gaston de Ségur, it was a question, "of making the Lord loved and better served;" for how can one love without serving? The Society contributed to this end by popularizing the theological and spiritual discourses of the *magisterium* and by encouraging a renewed and demanding religious practice. As one Religious of the Sacred Heart, Mother de Neuville, put it one day, it was not a question of forming pious persons but Christians.

The Society of the Sacred Heart, following the lead of the founder, was not called to a bland spirituality but to real devotion; it continued to be characterized by a certain severity, even dolorism, the stress often being on reparation. The practices initiated at Paray-le-Monial, for example, the Office of the Sacred Heart on the first Friday of the month, were in use in the Society, but they were not its purpose. For Mother Barat reparation was not to be found in supplemental religious exercises but in the execution of daily duties, that is, for the religious by their participation in the transformation of persons and of the world through education.[17] In the same spirit, in 1844, Father François-Xavier Gautrelet, a Jesuit, had founded the "Apostleship of Prayer," which proposed the offering of daily work and frequent communion for the salvation of sinners. Religious of the Sacred Heart introduced this work in their establishments and contributed to making known *The Messenger of the Heart of Jesus*, the magazine launched in 1861 by Father Henry Ramière. The Apostleship of Prayer was at the origin of different movements supported by the congregation, such as consecration of families to the Sacred Heart and the Eucharistic Crusade of Children, ancestor of the Eucharistic Movement of Young People.

Shortly before the death of Mother Barat the devotion to the Sacred Heart finally triumphed, when the Church took note of its spread in the Catholic world. The feast of the Sacred Heart had been permitted in 1765, but it was not prescribed. In 1856 Pius IX extended it to the universal Church at the request of the French bishops assembled in Paris for the baptism of the Prince Imperial. In 1864 Margaret Mary Alacoque was beatified. Although the spirituality sustained and practiced in the Society of the Sacred Heart found its source in the school of spirituality of Bérulle rather than

---

[17] Françoise Greffe, "*Réparation et vie apostolique: la Société du Sacré-Cœur*," Claude de la Colombière, Paris, Médiasèvres, pp. 91-101.

that of Paray-le-Monial, the *Abridged Plan of the Institute* made reference to the devotion to the Sacred Heart of which France had been the cradle. "So suitable to touch the hearts of sinners and to reanimate the fervor of just persons," the devotion spread by the Visitandine had contributed, "not only to rendering to this divine Heart the worship of love and of adoration due to it for so many reasons," but also to "reanimating the torch of faith and the sacred fire of charity, which impiety was trying to extinguish in all hearts."[18] Henceforth, reticence with regard to the devotion to the Sacred Heart disappeared. It is true that some Catholics did not care for it, but they dared not argue with it on the grounds that it was an "innovation." The fact remains that Mother Barat had asked the Sacred Congregation of Rites in 1853 for permission to use the Mass *Egredimini*, which exposed "the inward life of the Sacred Heart with all its expressions of itself, with its tenderness, its splendors and the glow of its sanctuary fire,"[19] and which thus incited to conformity to the interior virtues of Christ. The Mass *Miserebitur*, which the Society had been using up to that time, inspired by Paray, highlighted only one of the effects of that charity, that manifested in the course of the Passion.[20]

On the occasion of the beatification of Margaret Mary Alacoque, numerous houses of the Sacred Heart were given pictures or statues in which Jesus was pointing to his heart.[21] These works served a devotional purpose. The artists interpreted the divine mystery in such a way as to appeal to the senses of the faithful. Works that sought to transmit to the believer the profound meaning of the love of Christ favored a mystical relationship to God, while contributing to the glorification of the Heart of Christ. In Rome at the Trinità dei Monti painters of the Nazarean movement created pictures known for playing a role in the conversion of some who saw them. In 1858, Philippe Veit painted a *Sacred Heart* that adorned the chapel of the same name. Contemplation of this work facilitated the going over of Anglicans to Roman Catholicism, and the chapel was often used for baptisms following conversions of Jews or for the abjurations of Protestants.

After the war of 1870 devotion to the Sacred Heart tended to become national in France. From 1873 on, numerous dioceses in Europe and America, even whole countries, were consecrated to the Sacred Heart. The director of the project of the National Vow had asked Mother Gœtz for

---

[18] *Abridged Plan* § 2 and 1.
[19] Janet Erskine Stuart, *The Society of the Sacred Heart*, London, 1924, p. 48.
[20] Brigitte Combier, *Voix et regards. Approches historiques de la liturgie et de la spiritualité dans la Société du Sacré-Cœur*, Paris, 1985.
[21] On 12 September 1857, the Sacred Congregation of Rites forbade displaying in churches images of the Sacred Heart in which the person of the Savior was not portrayed.

the cooperation of all the Children of Mary of the World in the pilgrimages that prayed for "the salvation of Rome and of France"[22] and that ended up in Paray-le-Monial. They were extremely effective in their support. The British national pilgrimage, which gathered 1300 persons of all social classes from all the British Isles, was organized by a committee directed by members of the British aristocracy, among whom was Lord Walter Kerr, son of the Marchioness of Lothian, president of the Children of Mary of Roehampton.[23] Mother Gœtz took part in the homage rendered to the Sacred Heart in the city of Paray-le-Monial by giving the gift of a "very beautiful medieval liturgical vessel bearing a commemorative inscription."[24]

Not everyone devoted to the Sacred Heart had the means to go to Burgundy. Some had to be content to gather in local or national pilgrimage sites. Devotion to the Sacred Heart thus reanimated earlier pilgrimages while conserving the memory of those who originated them. These vast popular assemblies linked to consecration to the Sacred Heart were the occasion of a kind of mission that united religious and lay people in a real renewal of the life of faith. The Religious of the Sacred Heart sought to associate with this devotion the patron saints of the dioceses or of the countries where they were living. In Ireland, for example, banners and statues of St. Patrick were solemnly carried in procession in the houses of the congregation on the day of the consecration of the island to the Sacred Heart. In Armagh, an illumination in the form of a shamrock was placed on the altar, attracting a large crowd, for, as one religious wrote, "the patriotic devotion to the trefoil is well known; the very sight of this symbolic leaf speaks to every Irish heart."[25]

The Society of the Sacred Heart and Marian Devotion

The Society of the Sacred Heart played a role also in Marian devotion. In line with the spirituality developed by Bérulle and his disciples, the *Abridged Plan of the Institute* began with the following invocation: "In the name and for the glory of the Sacred Hearts of Jesus and of Mary," further specified by paragraph IV: "The object of this Society is, therefore, to glorify the Sacred Heart of Jesus, by labouring for the salvation and perfection of its

---

[22] The reference is to the refrain of a hymn that was popular for a long time: "God of mercy, triumphant God, save Rome and France in the name of the Sacred Heart." In the twentieth century after the Lateran Treaty, only "Save France" was sung. Mother Gœtz loved this hymn and asked the students of the Trinità to sing it for her during one of her visits to Rome.
[23] *Lettres annuelles*, 1873-1874, pp. 99-101.
[24] *Lettres annuelles*, 1873-1874, p. 4.
[25] *Lettres annuelles*, 1872-1873, pp. 102-107.

members through the imitation of the virtues of which this Divine Heart is the centre and model [….] The Society proposes also to honour with particular devotion the most Holy Heart of Mary, which was so perfectly conformed in everything to the adorable Heart of Jesus her Divine Son." In the boarding schools and free schools, Religious of the Sacred Heart created sodalities of Children of Mary according to the model of the Marian associations existing in Jesuit institutions. Mother Barat and her first companions honored especially the feasts of the Virgin Mary. That of Our Lady of Sorrows, instituted by Pius VII in commemoration of and reparation for the misdeeds of the French Revolution, was in special favor. Mother Anna de Rousier had inculcated the devotion in her Piedmontese novices, in particular in Mother Christine Gazelli di Rossano, who was sometimes regarded in the Society as "fanatically devoted to the Blessed Virgin." Mother Barat also had particular devotion to Our Lady of Sorrows, and at the time of the grave crisis of 1839 she decided to consecrate the Society to *Maria addolorata*.[26] In moments of great difficulty successive superiors general have done the same.[27]

At times Religious of the Sacred Heart have had to become accustomed to forms of devotion to Mary that might have been a bit surprising. In Cuba, for example, Mother Tommasini asked a coadjutrix sister one day what her employment was: "She answered very seriously, 'I am in charge of Our Lady's wigs.' And seeing my stupefaction, she continued, 'Oh, Mother, I assure you, it is no sinecure: on each feast of Our Lady I have to change the wig according to the type and color of her outfit.' I asked to see the trousseau of wigs, and the sister took me to admire the magnificent blond curls, the bands of jet, hair pieces of all possible shades, in all styles imaginable."[28] These wigs had been made with hair donated by women who offered them to the Madonna for the return or cure or conversion of members of their families.

The Society of the Sacred Heart contributed, perhaps accidentally, to this triumphal Marian devotion by introducing to the Church a devotion that had its origin in the Society, that of *Mater Admirabilis*. A fresco representing the Virgin in the Temple decorates a corridor of the Roman

---

[26] It was traditional in the Society of the Sacred Heart to repeat this consecration every year on the 15th of September. In her letter of 16 July 1949, Mother de Lescure wrote that what Saint Madeleine Sophie "had understood about the sorrowful soul of the Blessed Virgin and what she asked of her for each of her daughters…was the meaning of the Cross…and effective union with Jesus crucified" (*Circular letters of V.R.M. de Lescure*, p.55).

[27] Thus, Mother Digby acted in 1904, Mother Vicente in the summer of 1939 and Mother Bultó in 1967.

[28] *Mémoires de la R.M. Tommasini*, pp. 273-274.

convent, the Trinità dei Monti. It was painted in 1844 by Pauline Perdrau, a young artist, a postulant at the Trinità, who was taking courses in a studio of a member of the Nazarean movement, Maximilian Seitz. The image is that of a young woman, seated on a simple chair, at her feet a work basket with an open book laid on top. Young Mary, in an attitude of peaceful serenity, holds a spindle in her lap; she is dressed in pink and a single blond curl escapes from under her veil. Near her is a distaff with wool ready to be spun. One foot on a footstool, the young woman is meditating, eyes lowered "keeping all things in her heart." A lily in a vase near her chair gave the picture the name of "Madonna of the Lily," which Mother Perdrau often used. A Basilian abbess, Mother Makrina Mieczystawska, who was staying at the Trinità at the time, named the Madonna *Mater Admirabilis*. Pope Pius IX, who particularly loved the image, took up the name when he blessed the fresco on 20 October 1846. From 1849, a pontifical brief allowed the celebration of a Mass for the feast of *Mater Admirabilis* on 20 October. Pauline Perdrau's work of art rapidly became popular in Rome, where it was credited with obtaining cures and conversions. Soldiers of the French Expeditionary Force proclaimed themselves "*Sons of Mater.*"

The boarders of the Trinità had immediately fallen in love with this picture. "She is our age, this *virginella*, and no other one is," they said. Certainly the painting itself was rather indifferent, but it was much more its significance that struck visitors. Mother Barat loved it: "Your little Blessed Virgin is not at all bad," she told Pauline Perdrau. "In going to the tribune, I often make a detour to gaze at her. She attracts me; she is the age of our children and she speaks to me of the young people to whom I have devoted my life."[29] The devotion to *Mater Admirabilis* was special to the boarders, who had been the first to honor it by coming to lay flowers before the fresco, taking up the invocation from one of the litanies of the Blessed Virgin, "the flower of the field." It was "a tender devotion in keeping with the needs of their age,"[30] a devotion recognized as "that of young Christian women sheltered in religious houses as the young Mary was in the Temple of Jerusalem."[31] The fresco represented a young woman awaiting what life is going to disclose, ready to welcome God's plan, both active and contemplative. This attitude was the one the founder of the Sacred Heart wished for her religious and the young women they were to educate. "What youth! What purity in that beautiful head! One fears to disturb her, one hardly dares to fix one's eyes on her: it seems that she is blushing from

---

[29] Pauline Perdrau, *Loisirs*, vol. 2, p. 18.
[30] *Lettres annuelles*, 1863-1866, p. 43.
[31] Pauline Perdrau, *Loisirs*, vol. 1 p. 247.

being caught in her devout meditation, but one stays for a long time in contemplation before her! She inspires prayer, pious reverie and the gentlest calm." Thus was she described by Hermine de Clock in 1867.[32]

The devotion became general after Mother Barat decided to consecrate the Paris motherhouse to *Mater Admirabilis*. The superior general had a picture of *Mater*, "like the one at the Trinità," placed on the wall of the choir of the chapel, and "to complete the illusion, had paintings done that reproduced the mosaics of the blessed corridor." This consecration and Mother Barat's visible devotion to *Mater* caused the religious, even the most cautious, to follow suit. Mother Desmarquest, assistant general in charge of the probation, was not exactly taken by this "Blessed Virgin in a pink dress," as she called her. However, she added a visit of fifteen minutes to *Mater* to the daily schedule of the probanists. In Poitiers, the community gathered daily in the oratory of *Mater* to recite the Litany of the Blessed Virgin and a prayer for the pope composed in 1848.

The devotion spread throughout the world, promoted by pictures, statues, holy cards and medals.[33] Mother Cahier, secretary general of the Society, sent all the houses a picture of the Roman fresco,[34] which was rapidly copied by painters or by Religious of the Sacred Heart. The Trinità dei Monti sent copies of the fresco to all the houses that asked for it. Mother Perdrau, who left Rome in 1846, never again saw her work. In the houses to which she was sent, she made copies, keeping the figure of Mary as in the original, but changing the background, which often reproduced the panorama she had before her eyes. The painting she did for the house at Layrac was very up to date, since it depicted a train crossing a viaduct![35] The pictures were placed in oratories already in existence or in chapels specially built, often in neo-Gothic style, and solemnly blessed. Outside of Paris, the first houses to possess one of these copies were Montpellier and Laval, thanks to the efforts of Mothers de Mandon and de Quatrebarbes. At the death of Mother Barat every house of the Sacred Heart had an image of *Mater*.

---

[32] Related by Chantal de Clock, RSCJ.

[33] The first medal was cast in Rome, in 1848, for those pupils who had remained at the Trinità during the Revolution. On the reverse, it had the inscription "I am the flower of the field and the lily of the valley."

[34] Copyists corrected some of the faults of proportion of the original. When the fresco at the Trinità was restored recently, the decision was made to go back to the original work.

[35] At the end of her sojourn in Paris about 1872, she had the idea of painting the Blessed Virgin at Ephesus, called also *Mater in the House of John*. She showed a sketch of it to Mother Gœtz and executed it in Marseille in 1878. She reproduced this work several times; however, it never had the same appeal as the Roman fresco.

From the start devotion to *Mater* was popular, both within the Society of the Sacred Heart and outside. Pupils visited her shrine constantly, even during recreation. At Besançon the littlest boarders used to write to the Blessed Virgin: "Often there were fantastic zigzags on the page. When asked what they meant, the children replied: 'Oh! Our Lady will know how to read them!'" From the beginning of the 1850's, on days of high *congé* when the children were free of all school obligations, little theatricals in honor of *Mater* were presented, scenes or *tableaux vivants* or dialogues.[36] The first took place at the Rue de Varenne. Mother Prévost, the superior, was so fond of them that she offered to play the role of the prophetess Anna in these plays representing different episodes in the life of Mary. She obtained the services of a Belgian composer who composed choral pieces in the style of Lully, and she provided costumes and stage decorations. Some boarding schools, like those in Vienna and Valparaiso in Chile, and some day schools, like Philadelphia and New Orleans, were placed under the patronage of *Mater*. In Austria a special charitable association, called Association of *Mater Admirabilis*, had for a patron the Archduchess Marguerite, niece of Emperor Franz Josef.[37] The latter made a sizable donation toward the construction of a church dedicated to *Mater* in Vienna.

The spread of the devotion to *Mater* coincided with the proclamation of the cult of the Immaculate Conception. Mother Gazelli had the custom of the lily procession – originally from the house in Turin – introduced in the boarding schools along with the offering that each pupil made on the occasion: "O Mary, I give thee the lily of my heart; be thou its guardian forever." From 1854 onward this procession was held on December 8 and honored in one celebration the Immaculate Conception and the "Virgin of the Lily." The same year the Vatican granted indulgences to those who prayed to *Mater Admirabilis* in Rome. Three years later these indulgences were extended to all the houses of the Sacred Heart, on condition that the title of *Mater Admirabilis* was given to another picture or statue of the Virgin if the house could not procure a copy of the original fresco. In Natchitoches, Louisiana, a chapel, originally dedicated to the Immaculate Conception, was subsequently consecrated to *Mater* with the approval of the local bishop. At the Sacred Heart First Communions and confirmations were often held in *Mater's* chapel. In Santiago, Chile, ceremonies of first vows took place there on 20 October. Many young women wanted to enter the Society as postulants on that date. It is a fact that many said they owed their vocation to *Mater*, having seen the fresco in Rome or having discovered her in reproductions.

---

[36] These were reproduced in vellum and illuminated.
[37] When she married the Prince of Wurtemberg, she was offered a miniature of *Mater*.

Even though it was sustained by religious congregations consecrated to the Virgin, like the Marists, who spread it in Louisiana, or the Assumptionists, the new devotion sometimes awakened reservations in the clergy. On 8 December 1867, Mother Shannon consecrated the day school in New Orleans to *Mater Admirabilis*, designated as queen and mistress of the house. "This title, not well understood at first, was labeled exaggerated by ecclesiastics; and when the children said, 'We go to the house of *Mater Admirabilis*,' they were often reprimanded: 'Say rather that you go to the Sacred Heart.' Little by little prejudice was overcome and the devotion spread among the families and clergy of the city." Besides, the Religious of the Sacred Heart were vigilant to avoid competing with older, better known Marian devotions. In Mexico in 1887 when placing a statue of *Mater* in a little oratory, they said they did not wish to prejudice devotion to Our Lady of Guadalupe. Through reproductions of the fresco at the Trinità and through the medals and statues distributed, the devotion reached countries where the Society of the Sacred Heart had no establishments, like Bosnia, China and Japan, where almost 1100 medals were sent in 1865.

Through the pupils the new devotion spread among families and parishes. Alumnae came to the convent on their wedding day to place their bouquets on the altar of *Mater*. In Latin America they made *Mater* known to the indigenous peoples who lived on their lands. Near Amiens there was a kind of combination workroom and convent that housed 600 orphans; it was placed under the name of *Mater*. In the South of France shrines of *Mater,* erected by priests and religious who had seen the fresco in Rome, attracted pilgrims. At the request of Father d'Alzon a shrine to *Mater* was built at Notre-Dame du Bouquet, about twenty kilometers from Alès. A pilgrimage under the direction of the Assumptionists drew crowds to the gigantic statue of *Mater* that dominated the plain.[38]

The devotion found echoes in every milieu. Because of the fame of Mother Makrina, after July 1846, Polish *émigrés* in Rome donated the funds to have the corridor where the fresco was located transformed into a chapel. Illustrious Polish writers, like Adam Mickiewicz and Cyprian Norwid, were attracted by the image and came often to the Trinità to contemplate it. Norwid, who was poet, sculptor and painter, wrote about *Mater Admirabilis*, "The Queen with the Colors of Poland," or "The Queen of the Crown of Poland," in a poem entitled "*Légende.*"[39] Other donors

---

[38] The names of the pupils of the school at Montpellier were inscribed on the back of Mary's chair.

[39] "Behold the Queen on her throne in the colors of the nation. On her left, the distaff, Martha

known and unknown contributed to the sometimes sumptuous enrichment of the oratory of *Mater*, which received jewels, silver hearts, relics, altar vessels and ornaments for the fresco itself.[40] A little Polish girl brought her toys after her cure. Princess Clementine of Orleans gave an embroidery that she had done herself. Princess Marie-Antoinette de Bourbon gave a rug decorated with the fleur-de-lys that she and her mother had made. Associating devotion to *Mater* to that of the Sacred Heart, the queen of Saxony offered a reliquary containing a bone of Blessed Margaret Mary Alacoque.[41] As the religious of the Trinità noted in 1867, "We often find numerous *ex-voto* on her altar. Often we do not know the name of the donor and the reason for the offering, but we know about a sufficient number of miracles to increase our filial confidence in Mary who is always so prompt to assist those who call upon her. Traffic is incessant to the chapel of our august protectress, and even in winter we see her altar covered with bouquets left there by pious faithful."

The chapel in Rome became a popular center of Catholic devotion and attracted pilgrims. A princess of Wurtemberg, whose father was a Protestant, asked to make her First Communion there, as did many converts, among whom were former Anglicans prepared by Cardinal Manning. The archbishop of Westminster looked on the chapel of Mater as his cathedral. Archbishop Lavigerie baptized an Arab and a Kabylian there on 9 January 1870. Converted Jews came frequently. In June 1872, after making their First Communion at the Vatican, the Spanish *infantas*, accompanied by their mother, Queen Isabella II, visited *Mater* to make their act of consecration to her. In November 1887, young Thérèse Martin [Saint Thérèse of Lisieux] went to the Trinità, in the company of her sister Céline and their father, to pray to *Mater* during their pilgrimage to Rome so that Thérèse could obtain the pope's permission to enter Carmel in spite of her youth. Don Bosco, future founder of the Salesians, celebrated one of his first Masses in the chapel, as did many young priests of many nationalities.

> On her right those lilies that do not spin but are more beautiful than Solomon in all his glory, Mary
> The Queen of the crown of Poland spins the thread of the active life toward Mary
> And she has arrived at spinning half
> And she rests in thought
> And the lilies lean on their stems to the left towards the distaff
> And they are thoughtful like the spinner in the fullness of bloom
> And the open book is turned over as if it is time for reading" (information supplied by Aline Merdas, RSCJ).

[40] The first *ex-voto* had been given on 20 June 1846 by an English Jesuit from the Roman College who was cured after invoking *Mater*.

[41] *Lettres annuelles*, 1863-1866, p. XXIV.

Father Libermann of the Congregation of the Holy Heart of Mary also came to celebrate Mass at *Mater*.

During the Council of 1870, the chapel of *Mater* was particularly sought out by priests who wished to say their Masses there. A religious of the time, Mother Sacripante, has left a picturesque account:

> Our Mother fears that *Mater Admirabilis* is going to lose her simplicity, for she is always being reproduced, complimented and admired. She sees that priests are vying with one another to say Mass at her altar: they have to make a reservation two weeks in advance. Twelve Masses a day at the altar of the admirable Mother has become the norm, sometimes more. Yesterday there were fifteen. Before 4:30 a.m. the sacristan goes down, expecting to arrive before these priests; she finds two of them vesting at the same time. She looks at them with a smile: "But, Fathers, only one of you can say Mass at a time." "That's all right," was the response, "I'll serve my friend's Mass vested so as to begin my own Mass as soon as he has finished." The sacristan informs him that a bishop has an appointment for five o'clock. The poor priest was almost in tears, as he took off his amice, which he had been in such a hurry to put on. "Maybe he'll be late," he said. He waited a little while to see if there would be an empty slot he could take; but as there was no interruption, finally he had to go down to the church.[42]

Pilgrims used to climb the stairs to *Mater* on their knees and kiss the floor of the little shrine.

The popularity of the devotion united rich and poor, religious and lay persons. In the oratory at Manhattanville, New York, "Several lamps burn continually for particular intentions: a journey someone wants to place under Mary's protection, the success of an undertaking, domestic troubles another hopes to see resolved through her intercession...."[43] Everywhere *Mater Admirabilis* was recognized for the same powers. She obtained physical and spiritual cures,[44] about which Religious of the Sacred Heart knew the details. It was above all returns to the faith and to religious practice that were recorded when persons had been placed under *Mater*'s influence or had worn her medal. *Mater Admirabilis* was also reputed to have warded off epidemics and to have unfailingly supported many Religious of the Sacred Heart in their daily life.

A Jesuit, Father Fessard, who became an apostle of *Mater* as far away as China, proclaimed at Quimper in 1865: "*Mater Admirabilis* is a gift given to

---

[42] Prov. Arch. France. Letter of 25 June 1870.
[43] *Lettres annuelles*, 1863-1866, p. 110.
[44] The first cure on record was that of Father Blampin, 7 November 1846.

the Sacred Heart." The same year the Litany to *Mater*, the work of Father Monnin, appeared. In 1883 Pope Leo XIII granted the Society the privilege of a proper Mass, based on that of the purity of Mary. In time the Society learned to integrate devotion to *Mater* into its spirituality and advisedly to make use of it in apostolic activity. Triumphal feasts were celebrated in Rome on the occasion of the golden jubilee of *Mater* in 1894. They brought together Religious of the Sacred Heart and their acquaintances from around the world in thanksgiving. In 1949 Mother de Lescure presented *Mater Admirabilis* as "the jewel of the Society."[45] A few years later, Mother Sabine de Valon composed Litanies to *Mater*. Down to our day the chapel of *Mater* remains a place of special devotion for Religious of the Sacred Heart and their alumnae/i: a place where they exhibit *ex-voto* plaques thanking for graces received, decorations awarded and photographs;[46] a place where they come on their wedding day or soon after to confide their home to the Virgin Mary.

The Society of the Sacred Heart and the Holy See

The Society of the Sacred Heart was ultramontane in the posture it assumed regarding the papacy. Sophie Barat had been raised with respect for the Holy See; her brother Louis had revoked his oath of fidelity to the state church when he learned that the Civil Constitution of the Clergy had been condemned by the Church. The links the Society had formed with the Society of Jesus also contributed doubtless to its good reputation in Rome. Granted a cardinal protector in 1827, the congregation enjoyed more independence than others regarding the local hierarchy. The crisis of 1839, during which the Society barely escaped ruin, only found a solution when the Vatican intervened decisively with an order to return to the primitive text of the Constitutions.

The relations of the Society of the Sacred Heart and the episcopacy were peaceful from then on. Bishops appreciated the apostolate of the congregation and the respect that all its members showed them on every occasion. They often sought to introduce the religious into their dioceses, suggesting that they did not look askance at the presence of the Society and that they believed the religious could further their policies. However, there were misunderstandings: the most serious one developed in Cuba.

In 1866 the new bishop of Havana, Jacinto María Martínez y Sáez, created difficulties for the Religious of the Sacred Heart. "Maybe he was ill

---

[45] *Circular Letters of V.R.M. de Lescure*, p. 53.
[46] Empress Michiko herself observed the tradition. On the occasion of her visit to the Trinità she left a photograph of Japan's imperial couple.

disposed on account of malevolent suspicions. He not only refused to allow ours [our religious] to follow their ceremonial, but he could not accept the relationship of this house with a superior general who lived abroad." Neither did he want the formation of young religious to take place outside of his diocese. Bishop Martínez was a Spanish Capuchin, hostile to exempt orders. His nationalist mind was further embittered by the fact that the convent in Havana belonged to a vicariate in the United States.[47] Upon his arrival in Havana, he determined that the Religious of the Sacred Heart were established in Spanish territory without permission or royal sanction, a condition contrary to the laws of the West Indies. The life of the nuns in Havana was seriously disturbed by this hostile attitude, for the bishop withdrew the permission for acts of worship in the school, such as Sunday Mass, Benediction of the Blessed Sacrament and Holy Week services. He also forbade the Jesuit who served as their chaplain to hear the nuns' confessions. An Irish coadjutrix sister who did not speak Spanish, Anne Leveau, died without the sacraments, because the confessor assigned to the convent spoke neither English nor French.

While traveling in Europe, Bishop Martinez refused to meet with Mother Gœtz [superior general] and tried to win the Sacred Congregation to his cause by formulating different sorts of accusations against the Society of the Sacred Heart, of whose life style and works he disapproved. In consequence, Mother Gœtz advised Rome that the Society was prepared to leave Cuba if there was a not a change of viewpoint. The cardinal protector tried to settle the differences, writing to the motherhouse:

> The Holy Father, having received the request for the authorization of the suppression of the two houses of the Society in Cuba, does not give his approval to this measure, which would deprive the country of the spiritual benefits it is receiving at the moment in common with other countries where your religious institute is established. A school that, according to the bishop's letter, educates 150 pupils and enjoys the confidence and esteem of the public itself refutes successfully any assertion made by the bishop in his famous letter. His Holiness has expressed himself in a most benevolent manner on the subject of the Institute of the Sacred Heart. He is in accord with the religious who live in Cuba and reminds them that we must be ready for any and all sacrifices. However, the Congregation for Bishops and Regulars will write again to his Excellency, the bishop, asking him in the name of the Holy Father to show every possible attention towards the religious and to facilitate every means of fulfilling

---

[47] *Vie de la Révérende Mère Hardey*, pp. 277-280, and Louise Callan, *The Society of the Sacred Heart in North America*, New York, 1937, p. 564.

the prescriptions of their Constitutions, approved by the Holy See, and that he conform also to the established usages and customs. The Holy Father counts also on the religious for their part to try to correspond with the wishes of the bishop in whatever does not affect the fundamental laws of the institute.[48]

The motherhouse obtained from the Spanish government a royal decree, dated 29 January 1867, regularizing their situation in the island, but the interview Mother Hardey, the vicar, requested in 1868 was stormy. She obtained some permissions for the house of Sancto Spiritu but none for Havana. Appeasement resulted on account of the troubled political situation that Spain and Cuba were experiencing. Bishop Martínez was recalled to his country. An opportune change of superior in the house of Havana also helped in the reopening of relations with the diocese.[49] Bishop Serrano y Diez, named to the See of Havana in 1876, placed his diocese under the protection of the Sacred Heart as soon as he arrived.

The good rapport between the Holy See and the Society of the Sacred Heart was sustained by the mutual confidence Mother Barat established with successive popes. She had met them all, and they admired her. Certain papal visits are recorded in the annals, for example, that of Gregory XVI to the Trinità on 29 October 1832. As Mother Barat was ill, he went to visit her in her room, whispering a few words in Italian. Because of her illness, the room was heated; the pope who suffered from the heat shortened his visit. Friendly contacts were established also between the founder and Pius IX. The popes appreciated the apostolic work of the congregation and deemed the Society of the Sacred Heart sufficiently trustworthy to call it to Rome. Besides, it was in order to respond to a desire of Gregory XVI that Mother Barat had envisaged the transfer of the motherhouse from Paris to Rome and had thus unleashed the crisis in 1839, which had repercussions on relations between France and the Holy See.

The houses of the Sacred Heart in Rome, the Trinità, Santa Rufina and the Villa Lante, often received visits from popes, who used to come in the course of an outing in the city without necessarily announcing their arrival. The practice was to ring a special bell, not unlike a fire alarm, to warn the religious![50] These visits were, of course, the great events of the year and

---

[48] *Archives Bulletin*, No. 23, 9 February 2002, article by Raquel Perez, RSCJ.
[49] *Vie de la T.R.M. Gœtz*, pp. 296-297. The health of the superior of Havana had deteriorated following these events and she was sent back to the United States.
[50] Maud Monahan, *Life and Letters of Janet Erskine Stuart*, p. 297. Mother Stuart comments thus on this ancient custom in a letter of 8 May 1910: "Impressive to receive in this way the one whom Saint Catherine [of Siena] called the sweet Christ on earth!"

accounts of them were sent to the whole Society. The slightest comment, even the most banal, of the Sovereign Pontiff was recorded reverently and reproduced. Papal visits took a ritual form: a guard came at the last minute to announce the arrival of the pope, and the nuns had just enough time to have the students put on their veils and gloves and form ranks. The pope entered the house, went to pray in the chapel, during which time the nuns' choir sang a hymn. Then the ceremony of kissing the feet took place in the sacristy; all the religious and the pupils of the boarding school, sometimes those of the free school as well, took part. The religious always marveled at the consideration of the pope in having his shoe cleaned before the ceremony! The first medallion – a student outstanding for her character, grades and conduct – delivered a little speech of welcome. Sometimes the children recited a poem for the occasion. Then the pope visited the house and examined the students' work, after which he walked in the garden with them.

Pius IX was a familiar figure at the Trinità, to which he paid an annual visit after 1855. He was among acquaintances there, for several nuns in the community were related to him. In 1864 Mother Baviera, charged with the poor school for a long time, died. Like Pius IX she was originally from Sinigaglia and descended from a family connected with the Mastai; she was the goddaughter of Pius IX's mother. She always had a short conversation with the pope. He would ask also for the sister of one of his good friends, Albertine de Mérode, whose vocation to the Sacred Heart he had encouraged. As for the families of the boarders, they were related to both the lay and clerical members of the papal court and to many cardinals. The pope, therefore, referred to certain details of their family life and called their relatives by their first names.

The houses of the Sacred Heart and the Vatican used to exchange gifts. Popes sent boxes of candies elegantly presented and fruit from the gardens. The most ordinary olives were pronounced especially succulent because they came from the Vatican, and they formed the centerpiece of the nuns' dinner. Pontifical gifts were occasionally huge. On 14 January 1864, Pius IX gave the boarders an enormous cake from Siena, the circumference of which was two meters, sixty-four centimeters and on which "were painted the cardinal virtues, the emblems of our holy religion, interspersed with related verses of Holy Scripture and psalms." One hopes that the cake was as delicious as it was instructive! In January 1872 the Trinità received an enormous *jardinière*, two stories high, measuring almost three meters high and five around; it took five porters to carry it. It contained flowers but above all a variety of fruits that graced the table of the houses in Paris also, for a young religious took some samples with her when she went there.

On 31 December 1872, the Villa Lante witnessed the arrival of "a bouquet in the middle of which was a throne decorated with ivy surmounted by a bouquet of white camellias, roses and Spanish jasmine; three branches in the form of candelabra issued from the base, each holding three baskets of violets, pansies and rosebuds." Later the community received fruit preserves, then a large pastry serpent, inscribed on its scales: "Long live Pius IX." The pope commented that "this serpent would have tempted Adam." Finally, thirty bottles of Bordeaux appeared accompanied by a tray of various fruits. The gifts of Leo XIII were equally impressive by their surprising character: a swordfish five meters long, a deer, a calf. The pope, who must have been a gourmet and liked hearty dishes, asked each time that the cook save a portion for him! On the other hand, he did not ask to share an enormous *panettone*, decorated with angels holding musical instruments, which arrived at the Trinità in a cart.

There were also more pious offerings: statues of the Blessed Virgin, spiritual books in different languages, religious articles and rosaries. The Society displayed and sent around photographs of the pope received from the Vatican. It contributed thus to the establishment of a certain cult of the personality of the pope by making him known, but also by attributing importance to objects he had touched. In the course of an audience an assistant general offered Pius IX a skull cap made by one of the religious. He understood what was expected: he placed it on his head and then gave it back to his visitors. It was a gift to be sent to Mother Gœtz. History does not record what she did with it.

The pope, on his part, received medals, bouquets of artificial flowers and feathers, particularly admired at this era, chair covers embroidered by the pupils, for his birthday or for no particular occasion. One of the most curious gifts doubtless was that which Mother de Causans, superior of the Trinità, sent to Pius IX in July 1860. It was a porcelain terrine, blue Sèvres with gold stars: "She took care to put in it a cream cheese that prepared a surprise for the Holy Father, that of finding in the bottom the image of Mater perfectly painted with all the colors of the original." This gift appeared on the papal table on the occasion of a reception for prelates of the court and created a sensation, as one can easily understand!

The Society of the Sacred Heart not only saw in the pope the head of the Church, but always supported the claims of the Holy See to temporal power. At the time of the successive enlargements of the kingdom of Piedmont, a part of Italy after 1861, the Society was a victim of the liberalization imposed by the new authorities, whose anticlerical policies exacted a heavy price from religious congregations, above all those considered to be close to the Society of Jesus. The "Roman question" became crucial at the end of Mother Barat's life. From 1849 French troops guaranteed the sovereignty of the pope by their presence in Rome. In 1862 Napoleon III had put pressure on the Italian government to stop the troops of Garibaldi at Aspromonte. Two years later the September Convention provided for the establishment of the capital of Italy in Florence. King Victor Emmanuel I pledged not to attack papal territory and to prevent with force any attack "from the outside" launched against the States of the Church. In exchange the French troops were to evacuate Rome in two years, which they did. But when Garibaldi turned his volunteers loose on Rome in 1867, Napoleon III had the city occupied once more, and the French troops made common cause with the pontifical army at Mentana on 3 November. As Billault, the French minister of the interior, remarked, "If the French flag had not overshadowed the tiara, the tiara would have been trodden underfoot."[51]

From 1860 on, royalists, nobles and peasants alike, especially those from the West of France, began to mobilize to defend the threatened pope. The most convinced among them decided to reinforce his protection by joining the pontifical Zouaves. Preceded by their white flag with the emblem of the Sacred Heart, they took part in the victory that followed the bloody battle of Mentana, but they suffered heavy losses. At Quimper, Saint-Brieuc, Nantes and Rennes, many of the pupils had brothers, cousins, even a father among the papal Zouaves. When she learned that her father had left for Italy, a boarder at Quimper, Melanie de B., age eleven, cried, "How imprudent, we are seven children.... No, no, I'm happy, it's for a beautiful cause!"[52]

The boarding schools and free schools of the Sacred Heart, the Children of Mary sodalities, all mobilized to give financial support to the raising of regiments of Zouaves. The children paid by their little sacrifices for the maintenance of one or several papal Zouaves, estimated at three hundred francs per person. At Quimper, they gave their jewelry and medals and gold and silver thimbles. The smallest added holy cards so that the pope would have something with which to reward the men. The little boys at Marmoutier, all under twelve years old, wrote to Pius IX offering him the rewards for "good marks" that they usually transformed into clothes, shirts and caps, which they really needed.[53] In Canada, Bishop Bourget of Montréal had fabric sent to the sodalists of the Sault-au-Récollet for uniforms for the Zouaves; the pupils spent their recreation making the uniforms. In St. John, New Brunswick, in 1868, there were collections to support the pontifical cause.[54] Letters from the

---

51 Noël Blayau, *Billault, ministre de Napoléon III, d'après ses papiers personnels*, Paris, Klincksieck, 1969, p. 336.
52 *Lettres annuelles*, 1866-1867, VI, p. 25.
53 *Lettres annuelles*, 1868-1869, p. 231.
54 *Lettres annuelles*, 1867-1868, p. 10.

Vatican, sometimes signed by the pope, recognized their efforts. Angèle de la Bégassière entered the novitiate at Conflans on 11 September 1867, explaining "Since I cannot be a Zouave or a Jesuit, I will be a Religious of the Sacred Heart."[55]

The defense of the pontifical cause found its place in the pedagogy of the Sacred Heart. In Graz and at Riedenburg, the boarders were organized into a "Militia of the Holy Father." In Bordeaux there was a "crusade of papal Zouaves." In Nantes the boarders were named "Zouaves of duty and of silence." In Besançon, practices, that is, efforts, having a chivalrous character earned ranks in the pontifical army. In Lemberg the boarding school was introduced to the Nuncio as a battalion of papal Zouaves.

There were multiple means of aiding the Holy See. One consisted in explaining the fundamental rightness of the pontifical cause. The Religious of the Sacred Heart informed their students of the sufferings endured by Pius IX and readily presented him as a martyr and victim of the powers of darkness. They were firm adherents to the dogma of papal infallibility, which the French bishops did not uniformly affirm and which caused a schism in Germany. On 10 May 1870, Mother Gœtz made "the promise of filial and absolute submission to Holy Church and to its august head."[56] She expressed an opinion widely held when she said: "The unity of authority in Catholicism maintains its primitive purity. Rome is its center; we submit without rationalizing to the decisions coming from there."[57]

Religious of the Sacred Heart echoed the desires of the pope, no matter what they were. Mother Gœtz undertook to convey to the Children of Mary of the World Pius IX's concern to combat luxurious fashions in female dress, the indecency of which he also criticized.

> Our beloved Pius IX himself appeals to your faith and to your love. He asks that women who by their social position and their reputation are most capable of exercising a happy influence join in seconding his views in a matter that appears to him not less important than the defense of his threatened states: the suppression of unbridled luxury that brings with it the ruin of families and corrupt and unregulated social mores. It is to women that he speaks for their own salvation, first of all, and to safeguard the future of the whole of Christian society: it is they, in effect, who make and unmake fashion and fashion governs the world. Why not join in making fashionable propriety, modesty and simplicity instead of frivolous, bizarre and ruinous conformity? If all or a great number of distinguished

---

[55] *Religieuses du Sacré-Cœur*, vol. 3, p. 161.
[56] *Lettres de la T.R.M. Gœtz*, 4 July 1870, *édition complète pour les Supérieures*, p. 121.
[57] *Vie de la T.R.M. Gœtz*, p. 179.

and virtuous women agreed among themselves to strictly forbid certain unsuitable adornment, many others would follow their example and would no longer dare to call attention to themselves by scandalous fashions.[58]

The crinoline, introduced in Paris by the Empress Eugénie, an old pupil of Paris, came under general attack. However, Mother Gœtz had the tact to write to superiors only, telling them to let the Children of Mary know about rules for hairstyles considered improper for church if they judged it advisable, keeping in mind possible reactions of the members.[59]

Another way of supporting the Vatican was financial. The Society of the Sacred Heart was particularly generous in sending Peter's Pence, which the superior general or her assistants always took to the Vatican at the beginning of the year. Large gifts of money or religious objects or works of art were offered on other occasions. The pupils were encouraged to participate in collections according to their means. The sums collected were presented very carefully in different containers designed to hide the contents: heart-shaped boxes, cloth flowers with a purse in the center. The gifts were presented, with a list of students who had contributed, by Religious of the Sacred Heart or alumnae who profited from a journey to Rome and an audience to make the offering. The effort intensified after September 1870, when Pius IX decided to remain in the Vatican. The youngest boarders at Manhattanville wrote to the pope inviting him to come to America and stay at the Sacred Heart: "We will sell our toys to provide for your comfort,"[60] they added.

The Society's character as an ultramontane congregation undoubtedly contributed to the interest in it manifested by bishops and ecclesiastics of the same tendency. They flocked to its houses. When they came to Rome for an *ad limina* visit or other celebration, they visited the Roman houses, especially the Trinità. This influx was spectacular in 1867 at the time of the eighteenth centenary of the death of Saint Peter. One reads in the house journal on Pentecost, "Our Mothers kissed as many as twenty-six episcopal rings." On 29 June Masses began at one o'clock in the morning, and 120 priests succeeded one another until six thirty. The eve and the day of the feast of the Sacred Heart, 162 Masses took place from four in the morning until one in the afternoon. The accounts emphasize the honor to the houses and, by extension, to the whole Society and do not mention the overwork imposed on portresses, sacristans and those members of the community who, no doubt, had to be present to these crowds, above all when the bishops arrived in the church or in *Mater*'s chapel.

[58] *Lettres de la T.R.M. Gœtz*, 18 February 1868, p. 77.
[59] *Lettres de la T.R.M. Gœtz*, p. 74.
[60] *Enfants de Marie*, vol. 2, p. 73.

Since the bonds between the Sacred Heart and the Vatican were so close, the campaign of disparagement produced at the death of Mother Barat is astonishing. Rumors in the course of the summer of 1865 spread the idea that "the largest part of the Society was seeking to isolate itself from the influence of the Papacy." A letter from the Vatican, signed by Pius IX, recalled that "every human institution must perfect itself, and you have need of improvement on two points. First, the superior general must reside in Rome. Moreover, there must be a little more openness of heart with regard to the Holy See."[61] The secretary of state, Cardinal Antonelli, calmed the affair and appeased the pope, who appreciated the simplicity of Mother Gœtz when she visited him. Superiors general needed a great deal of prudence to act in such a context.

The relations between the Society of the Sacred Heart and the Holy See during the last years of the reign of Pius IX and subsequently were cordial, even warm. Superiors general accepted foundations in Mexico and in Argentina at the request of the papacy because there was a service to the Church to provide, to affirm the presence of Catholicism in the face of a Protestant menace.[62] In 1894 the General Congregation decided that, when a person sought entrance into the Society, "her attention would be called to the inviolable attachment that the Society professes to the Holy Roman Catholic Church, its complete submission to the direction of our most Holy Father the Pope, according to what our Constitutions require us to inculcate in our pupils."[63] The popes willingly granted audiences to Religious of the Sacred Heart and their students. As nieces and great-nieces of Pius IX and Leo XIII were educated at the Trinità, occasions of visits to the Vatican, including to the Holy Father's private apartments, were frequent. As for Benedict XV, he was the son, brother and uncle of alumnae of the Sacred Heart. During all these pontificates Religious of the Sacred Heart were welcomed at the Vatican and often received special favors from the prelates charged with protocol or from members of the Curia.

Madeleine Sophie Barat wished to be seen as a respectful daughter of the Church. In a moment of grave crisis, she affirmed: "My compass will be Peter, the Vicar of Jesus Christ; we cannot be mistaken if we follow in this wake; therefore, rather die than ever leave it...."[64] This submission could

---

[61] *Annales de la Société du Sacré Cœur, second généralat.* Cited by Margaret Williams, *Joséphine Gœtz: a Woman of Reflection, 1817-1874*, pp. 36-37.

[62] The house at Valparaiso was founded in 1870 in what was then the chief commercial center of Chile, at the request of Pius IX, who wished the Society of the Sacred Heart to contribute to the struggle against "Protestant and anti-religious influence" (*Lettres annuelles,* 1864-1866, p. 323).

[63] Gen. Arch., Society of the Sacred Heart, C I C 3, Box 11.

[64] *Lettres aux Supérieures*, vol. 3, p. 82, to Mother Hardey, 15 June 1841.

have been costly, but she maintained it. In less disturbed epochs, those who succeeded her operated in the same way. Recognized and appreciated by the Holy See, the Society of the Sacred Heart received advantages and drew to itself persons for whom the authority of the pope was not at issue. They confided their children to the Society to be educated. In the case of young girls and women discerning their vocation, they entered the institute to follow Jesus Christ there. All this contributed to an expansion that would prove remarkable and fruitful.

Chapter II

A Portrait of the Society of the Sacred Heart

Because its spirituality harmonized with one gaining recognition in the Catholic Church, the Society of the Sacred Heart showed promise of development. Still, it needed enough members to support its missions. Apostolic service demanded both religious and personal qualities, including generosity. It required also that young women come to join the congregation.

Social Composition: Choir Religious and Coadjutrix Sisters

Like the majority of religious congregations, the Society of the Sacred Heart included coadjutrix sisters. In 1865 there were 1591. Because they, like the choir religious, were members of the Society and equally "spouses of the Sacred Heart," the *Abridged Plan of the Institute* distinguishes the two groups only by function: the coadjutrix were to be employed in temporal care and the choir nuns were destined for teaching.[1] The same attitudes looked for in future choir religious were sought in those who offered themselves to be coadjutrix sisters, "with the exception of the education and talents necessary for the education of youth, which were to be replaced by knowledge of domestic service, or at least good will and aptitude for learning such skills."[2] During preparation for their final commitment, like the others, they had to seek perfection, according to the norms of the Institute.[3] They received the same treatment as the choir religious in terms of funerals and burials.[4] There were differences, however. The time given to morning meditation was half that of the choir religious,[5] and their employments exempted them from

---

[1] *Constitutions*, § VII.
[2] *Const.* § XX.
[3] *Const.* Second Part, Chapters III, XI.
[4] *Const.* Chapter VI, II.
[5] *Const.* Summary of the Constitutions, III.

the recitation of the Office of the Blessed Virgin.[6] The youngest skipped the daily walk in the garden that young choir religious had to take, because their work often took them out of doors. Finally, their recreations took place "around baskets of mending"[7] or tubs of vegetables to peel. They slept in a dormitory and in the refectory they sat at their own tables.

The Constitutions stipulated:

> Their state of life is all the more to be prized as removing them more effectually from the occasions and danger of self-love, vain self-esteem and dissipation of mind, to which those are exposed who are engaged in study; and it should be the more dear to them because as it is humble, laborious and obscure, it renders them more like Jesus Christ their Spouse, Who chose to pass the first thirty years of His earthly life in obscurity and labor. It is thus that attaching themselves lovingly to the humble and laborious offices of their state of life, through love of Jesus Christ, they will find themselves united in a most especial manner with the sentiments and affections of His Divine Heart.[8]

This spirituality of Nazareth manifested in their "humble and hidden tasks"[9] was meant to inspire "a secret satisfaction and a sort of envy" in the other members of the community.

For their employments the coadjutrix sisters might be sent to the school where they took care of the maintenance of the building. They also helped the children with their personal care, making their beds and accompanying them to the lavatory and baths. Those with proper training could also be teachers in the free schools for the poor and in the orphanages. Their daily religious life was the responsibility of the local assistant, who was charged with their spiritual direction. The choir novices helped them in some employments.[10]

Recruitment of the coadjutrix sisters was part of the reason for this specificity in formation and assignments. Sisters came from a working class milieu, from families of artisans, urban workers and country people. Accustomed very early to manual work, many had been maids, chambermaids or domestic staff. How did they end up at the Sacred Heart? Sometimes "providentially," as the death notices relate: they had seen a Religious of the Sacred Heart in a dream and afterwards recognized the habit. Sometimes they had accompanied their mistress when she became a

---

[6] *Const.* V.
[7] Jeanne de Charry, *Histoire des Constitutions…seconde partie*, vol. 1, p. 285.
[8] *Constitutions*, Second Part, Chapters III, XIII.
[9] *Const.* § XI.
[10] *Const.* § XX.

boarder or a postulant. Often they came because the priest who was guiding them indicated that a certain house of the Society would welcome them.[11]

As the Society of the Sacred Heart developed, the distinctions between choir and coadjutrix religious increased, without anyone's knowing exactly at what moment the changes took place. A reference in the ceremonial indicates that, in Rome, at the profession of obedience to the cardinal protector, the choir nuns kissed his hand, while the sisters kissed the hem of his cloak. The sisters were not always admitted to the ceremony of the kissing of the feet when the pope came to visit, doubtless for lack of time. Sisters were called to make a final commitment at the end of many years, on average between ten and fifteen years after their first vows, while choir religious were admitted to final vows after about five years. Another indication of the separation between the two classes is found in the obituary notices. While those of the choir religious are often quite detailed, those of the coadjutrix sisters are brief summaries and sometimes do not even give their dates of birth and their family names. Many sisters could neither read nor write, reflecting the poverty of instruction for women of the working class during the nineteenth century. In the Society, with regard to the sisters, the paragraph of the Constitutions that specified that they should desire knowledge only of what the spirit of the institute and the tasks confided to them demanded was followed to the letter. Since their tasks were material, why would they be given an education when they had had none before?

The sisters' illiteracy could make daily life difficult especially when someone transferred from another order to the Society of the Sacred Heart. An Irish woman, Catherine McCarthy, who had been a Brigittine, "never understood the Rule [of the Sacred Heart] perfectly, but she served the Lord piously there and made herself useful as a seamstress until the age of seventy."[12] The inability to read caused other problems when a sister was sent to a foreign country or when the language of the house changed. In 1867 German became the common language at Blumenthal in Netherlands: a choir religious had to do the reading and prepare the meditation in French for Sister Geneviève Beauquesne who could not read.

The Force of Numbers

Increase in Numbers

The death of Mother Barat did not put a stop to the growth of the

---

[11] Frequently this was the situation; it continued to be so in the first half of the twentieth century in Poland and in Spain.
[12] *Lettres annuelles*, 1872-1873, p. 104.

congregation. Between 1865 and the end of the century, the number of Religious of the Sacred Heart increased one and a half times, both categories taken together. While the number of choir nuns tripled, the increase in the number of coadjutrix sisters was more modest. Stable or increasing slightly until 1885, it fell in 1887, and until 1895, its growth was parallel to that of the choir religious. The increase stagnated in the following years, then sharply declined in 1902. This trend demonstrates that, until the 1880's, in recruiting sisters the Society respected the norm decreed by Mother Barat that the number of sisters be set at one third of the number of choir nuns. Then, during the following decade, that balance was no longer maintained. Consequently, from 1894 on, the general congregations required that the proportion be strictly observed so as not to weaken the body of the institute: "Our Society will be characterized by the mission of the majority of its members; what would be the mission of the Society if the coadjutrix sisters were in the majority?" The decline in numbers at the beginning of the twentieth century resulted from a policy of the superior general. When Mother Digby chose to leave France, she decided not to keep in the Society those sisters who had not yet made final vows. She sent them back to their families or found them employment. She was afraid that they would not be able to acclimatize themselves in countries where they could not speak the language and perhaps not even understand it.

Entrance into Religious Life

In a religious congregation the noviceship is a time of discernment, in the course of which a person decides to continue on or to return to the world. At the Sacred Heart, the number of future choir religious increased spectacularly between 1881 and 1893. The novitiate at Conflans was so crowded that new novitiates were opened in Lyons and Bordeaux.[13] Successively, two superiors general, Mothers Lehon and von Sartorius, asked for careful oversight of recruits, following the requirement of the Constitutions: "It does not suffice that a person has been our pupil in order to warrant acceptance, nor that her confessor recommends her; her qualifications must merit it."[14] The subsequent decrease in the number of novices may be the consequence of the hardening of anti-religious policy in France. Some candidates did not have the courage to enter religious life in a time of uncertainty. Also, superiors or vicars may have proposed

---

[13] Gen. Arch. C I C 3, Box 11, Report of Mother Digby, 1895. The families of the postulants were unhappy with this decision.

[14] Gen. Arch. C I C 3, Box 11, 30 August 1890.

that they postpone their entrance until the situation was healthier.[15] After the closing of French houses in 1904, the need for the French candidates to go to Italy or Belgium for their noviceship could have limited their number.

The case of coadjutrix novices is different. After 1874 the members of the general congregations noted that many sisters lacked generosity and respect for superiors and for the choir religious. This shortcoming was attributed to their early formation and to the fact that they were not properly guided in their spiritual life,[16] the assistants being too occupied with the management of the house. The formation of the sisters could well have been problematic, for it took place only in the house where they entered; and often during their noviceship, they were overworked. It was decided, therefore, to bring them together in a regional novitiate. Attention to the qualifications of the recruits and even limitation of entrances in the vicariates where the coadjutrix sisters were too numerous were recommended.

In its recruitment policy the Society of the Sacred Heart was not unusual among religious orders of that day. Women flocked to religious congregations in the nineteenth century and gave a feminine tone to the Church in France; one could characterize that religious world as "a women's Catholicism."[17] The world-wide numbers grew as much in international congregations as in diocesan institutes, increasing sharply until around 1860, then leveling off and even diminishing. At the Sacred Heart, the leveling off did not take place until after 1894. Further, the Society's recruitment remained steady, while that of other French congregations fell off. Doubtless the multinational character of the Society of the Sacred Heart, which saw women of different nationalities enter every year, contributed to evening out the flow of postulants that fluctuated wildly among congregations whose recruits came from a single nation or region.

Reasons for a Choice

Why so many young and not so young women wished to join the Society of the Sacred Heart is hard to know today. Doubtless, the driving motive was spiritual, that each woman wanted to follow Jesus Christ and to serve her

---

[15] . After the separation of church and state in France, there was a decline in the numbers of priestly ordinations.
[16] Gen. Arch. C I C 3, Box 9.
[17] Claude Langlois, *Le catholicisme au féminin. Les congrégations françaises à supérieure générale au XIXème siècle*, Paris. 1984.

neighbor in an institute whose the charism suited her. Obituary notices indicate rare cases in which one or both parents so encouraged the vocation that one wonders sometimes whether the parent was not realizing through the daughter a desire for religious life that he/she had experienced in youth. On the other hand, for the majority of postulants the family put obstacles in their way or imposed a shorter or longer delay for reconsideration. For some, entrance brought with it a break with family, often when the father was not a Catholic.

In the nineteenth century the over-all condition of women and of Catholic lay people offered few choices other than religious life for devout young women with an ardent desire to serve others, but who did not see themselves doing so in marriage or single life. In an era when women, married or single, were not free to exert influence on their own, religious life was a means of having an effect in the Church and in the civic sphere. As a congregation dedicated to education, the Society of the Sacred Heart was able to attract women who chose not to apply their skills in secular schools or who did not believe they could fulfill their aspirations there. Religious life gave them the possibility, difficult to imagine elsewhere, of assuming responsibilities, exercising initiative and holding offices.

Other reasons could have weighed in favor of religious life at the Sacred Heart; space limits their mention. The development of congregations in France must be understood as increasing the number of women choosing single life. This phenomenon should not be exaggerated, but entry into religion for women, like priesthood for men, played a role in demographic balancing. As birth control was not practiced or, when practiced, depended on unreliable methods, families who had to worry about preserving their family property could see the advantages in entrance into the convent.

Mother Barat had foreseen that postulants could be allowed to enter without dowries, perhaps attracting some candidates to her congregation in France and elsewhere. At the time of her visit to South America, Mother Stuart realized that Chileans had entered the Sacred Heart after failing to meet the requirements of other congregations; she wrote that: "Some bishops have said to me that because we do not insist on a dowry, we receive applications from women with less sturdy vocations."[18] Since education in that era depended on socio-economic status, particularly wealth, it is understandable that, at the general congregation of 1910, Mother Digby wanted the vicars to monitor that issue, linking it to the character of the apostolic mission:

> Watch carefully not to accept young women of too little means. Those who come from such families have not themselves received a sufficiently

---

[18] Gen. Arch. C I A 5 d, Box 6.

rigorous early education, and we must not disappoint the hopes of parents who, in confiding their children to us, count on seeing them well brought up.[19]

While entering at the Sacred Heart without a dowry, coadjutrix postulants at least brought a trousseau.[20] Rosario Jaque, who presented herself in 1865 in Talca, Chile, had claimed as her inheritance only a cow that had long since disappeared in the *Cordillera* of the Andes. She eventually arrived at the convent on horseback, accompanied by her brother and leading the recently found cow by a rope![21] At the end of the century, maybe to test good will, superiors required coadjutrix postulants to bring with them the price of a return ticket, in case the trial of their vocation was not successful.

Religious congregations offered some status as coadjutrix members to devout women without education who were obliged to earn their living. In the convent they performed the same tasks they would have performed, had they remained at home or gone into service. Religious life conferred on them otherwise unobtainable social and material benefits; at the time that so many joined as sisters, the Western world was experiencing a serious economic crisis. We will never know whether this crisis played a role, consciously or not, in the choice of religious life. However, the members of the general congregations thought then that the coadjutrix sisters had envisaged their entrance into religious life as a means of professional placement, in which they did not run the risk of dismissal, and that they considered "the convent a good place where they could end their days in peace."[22]

The consummate quandary was that the coadjutrix sisters were religious, but in many houses of the Sacred Heart there was concern, especially about their participation in domestic work and their behavior towards the other religious. Conscious of this problem, the Society of the Sacred Heart reviewed their case. Certainly the coadjutrix sisters took on menial and obscure work, but often they were given painful tasks. From 1884 on, the members of the general congregation recommended hiring lay persons for the kitchen and the laundry, for they could easily be dismissed if they did not perform. Recourse to paying wages in a religious congregation was neither common nor a given, but it provided

---

[19] Gen. Arch. C I C 3, Box 12, 15 August 1910, p. 12.
[20] *Religieuses du Sacré-Cœur*, vol. 2, p. 289. Delphine Martigny arrived from Rome with her brother, who said to Mother Barat: "Here is my sister's trousseau. You see, Mother, we are not rich, but we must not be stingier with the good Lord than we would be with men."
[21] *Lettres annuelles*, 1906-1908, p. 419.
[22] Gen. Arch. C I C 3, Box 11, 30 August 1895.

better clarification of the status and vocation of the coadjutrix members. In 1904, the general congregation decided that, before their *prise d'habit*, coadjutrix postulants would be required to sign a document by which they acknowledged that they had no right to compensation if they left the Society. This practice, which the bishop of London, Ontario, in Canada had suggested, was imposed after a former Canadian sister had made an appeal to Rome to obtain compensation for the work she had done while she was a member of the Society. Subsequently, the same action was required of future choir religious as well.

Some superiors were already seeking to lighten the work of the sisters. At St. Charles, United States, Mother Du Mont taught music during school vacation, and with the proceeds from the lessons, she "hired women to help our sisters with the heavy work."[23] An unusual step, both as an exception and as a source of hidden income, it was a sign that superiors thought that in conscience they ought to alleviate the work of the sisters. At Roehampton, Mother Thunder, when she was assistant, had the custom of saying to the sisters: "We want not workers but good religious."[24] Doubtless she was not the only one to think that way.

Shedding light on the social and economic dimensions of the choice of a religious congregation[25] counterbalances a view of religious life that emphasizes only the sacrifices it entails. Certainly the vows imposed renunciation; but religious life also gave women, and not only the founders, the opportunity to develop their personal and intellectual gifts and to make use of them. Overemphasis on humility, especially a badly misunderstood interpretation of it, could lead us to forget that religious life was a place of advancement and self-affirmation and, for a significant number of religious, of authority. In the Society of the Sacred Heart, religious virtue could be combined with boldness and with the assurance of the communities' independence of other controlling forces, including the ecclesiastical. The development of apostolic works required management skills in leaders, which businesses might well envy. As elsewhere no doubt, it was necessary to guard against the religious' becoming too accustomed to being in charge.

The houses of the Sacred Heart, boarding schools as well as free schools and orphanages, were the seedbeds of vocations. Certainly alumnae helped to enrich other orders and even founded some; but familiarity, acquaintance with the customs in honor at the Sacred Heart, apprenticeship

---

[23] *Lettres annuelles,* 1906-1908, p. 99. Mother Du Mont was a German, born in Cologne in 1843, who spent most of her religious life in Canada and the United States. She became superior at Saint Charles in 1891.

[24] *Life of R.M. Rose Thunder,* p. 24.

[25] See Yvonne Turin, *Femmes et religieuses au XIXe siècle. Le féminisme en religion,* Paris 1989.

in the spiritual life and attachment to their teachers led many into the novitiates of the congregation. Usually, a few years after a boarding school opened, the entrance of its first alumnae was recorded. Mother Barat noted that she worried when such and such a house did not produce any recruits. The schools had a double responsibility: to educate the young and to provide for the future of the institute.

To Live and Die in the Society of the Sacred Heart

Towards the end of the 1840's, the Society of the Sacred Heart began to collect information on its members, adopting the interest in statistics just becoming widespread among administrators. These data for internal use appeared in the *Catalogues*, which gave the name and age of the religious by category – choir religious and coadjutrix sisters – and their stage of religious life – novice, aspirant,[26] professed of fewer or more than ten years. On the other hand, the catalog did not mention nationality. Entrance into religious life meant that one had cut ties with one's background, including one's country, since the religious was to live the mission wherever she was sent. Her new bonds were to supersede all others. This practice was common to all congregations, for both men and women. In the Society of the Sacred Heart, it was never the custom to take a new religious name.[27] Soon, the Society began remembering its members by documenting their lives in some detail in the *Lettres annuelles*. These publications, which collected accounts of the activities of each house and recorded significant events, also contained what in the Society are called *"notices,"* biographies written shortly after the death of the religious. These always give a minute description of the last days of the deceased and are more or less complete in giving other types of information.[28] They tell us the age of religious at entrance and at death. From this twofold source we can document demographic aspects of religious life at the Sacred Heart.

A sampling was taken of the religious who died between 1867 and 1872 and between 1895 and 1905. For the first, the average age at entrance into religious life was twenty-five and a half, whereas one might have imagined

---

[26] Aspirant was the title given to a religious who had made first vows and was awaiting her final commitment.

[27] Some of the first companions of the founder had changed their first name out of devotion to a particular saint. Mother Barat's feast was kept on the feast of Saint Mary Magdalen, even though she was always called Sophie. But Madeleine was one of her names, and she had great devotion to Mary Magdalen.

[28] Mother Digby asked that only what was edifying in the life of the religious be included, ignoring the rest.

that girls were entering sooner, moving directly from the school to the novitiate. This timing corresponded, at least in France, to the law, since the Civil Code had set twenty-five as the age of majority.[29] A few religious may have entered at fourteen or fifteen; but the age groups most commonly represented were the twenty-, twenty-one- and twenty-two-year-olds, who made up 43.2% of those who entered before coming of age. A young woman entered at the Sacred Heart, therefore, at the age when she was pondering her future,[30] not at a particularly precocious age but at the age at which normally mature young women thought about their life choices. It appears that at the Sacred Heart the average age of entrance was slightly older than elsewhere. At the end of the century, a sample of similar size reveals that the average age at entrance was twenty-four.

Historical studies have shown that in general, over the course of the nineteenth century, candidates for religious life followed similar behavior patterns and that the average age of those entering a congregation varied according to the its chief apostolate. These studies show that coadjutrix sisters entered earlier than choir religious. By all accounts, it appears that at the Sacred Heart the average age at entrance was about the same for the two categories of postulants. We cannot know whether failed marriage plans resulted in such relatively late entrances. Most parents, although aware of their daughter's vocation, hoped that she would take her place in the world, and they rounded up potential suitors. Some of these young women suffered from such a forced social life, but this practice also provided an opportunity for realistic reflection on the kind of life they wanted to lead.

The first sample examined shows that 20% of the religious who died just after 1865 had entered the Sacred Heart between ages twenty-six and thirty-five; 5% between thirty-five and forty-two; 2.3% after forty-five, the oldest at fifty-three. Even though the Constitutions wanted postulants to be no younger than fifteen and no older than thirty, the Society never set inflexible age limits for entrance, preferring to judge case by case and welcoming, in addition to those from other institutes,[31] women who had remained single for a long time, caring for a home or aged parents or younger brothers and sisters, replacing a mother who died young – as was common at the time – and also widows. Among the latter one might mention Hélène Boznanska, who died at Lemberg in 1868; Mother de

---

[29] Until that age young people had to obtain their parents' permission to marry or to enter religious life.

[30] Odile Arnold, *Le corps et l'âme. La vie des religieuses au XIXe siècle*. Paris, Le Seuil, 1984, p. 362. See also Claude Langlois, *Le catholicisme au féminin*....

[31] There was an effort to limit the number of transfers from one order to another, however, for they required permission of the Holy See.

Barges, *née* Constance de Pombo, who entered at Conflans, having placed her only son at the military academy of Toledo, and who died at Chamartín in Spain in 1867; and Maria del Pilar de la Cerda, widow of the Duke of Veragua, who had been a lady-in-waiting to Queen Isabella II and who died in 1872. The work and the obedience required by religious life were not necessarily easy for these women who had led a life in the world. Two religious who served as assistants general, Mothers Jeanne de Lavigerie and Helen Rumbold, entered the Society as widows. The first had no children, but the second had a son who died young; it was said that she always kept a lock of his hair.

In the 1860's, the average age at death in the Society was forty-five. That figure may seem surprising, but it corresponds roughly to the average lifespan in France in the nineteenth century.[32] It is true that religious were not subject to the most frequent cause of death for lay women, childbirth, but they were victims of the periodic epidemics that affected many convents in both Europe and America. Within the Society, the age of death varied considerably. Deaths among those under thirty-five were particularly notable: they constituted 31.6%. They wore out younger than laywomen who had remained in the home, for religious life demanded work in difficult conditions, and not only in newly-established houses and mission countries. But those with resistance died in old age, older than many lay people, the oldest dying at eighty-five and beyond like the founder. However, at the Sacred Heart, only 8% lived to be older than seventy-five.

Mortality among apostolic religious was higher than among contemplatives. It is true that Religious of the Sacred Heart lived a semi-cloistered life, but their apostolate imposed on them a pace like that of hospital sisters or others who exercised their apostolate outside their houses. At the Sacred Heart religious remained active to the very limits of their strength; even the elderly religious could handle study hall surveillance. Besides, when one said of a religious that she was "quite worn out," that meant she was already at death's door! The ideal was to end one's life with "one's weapons in one's hand."[33] Many achieved that ideal in the full sense of the term. The notice of one coadjutrix sister reported that her superior met her in the corridor with a broom in her hand; finding her "quite worn out," the superior sent her to the infirmary right away. She went there obediently and died a few days later.

---

[32] Life expectancy for women changed from forty years and six months between 1861 and 1865 to forty-three years and four months between 1877 and 1881.
[33] Louise Callan, *The Society of the Sacred Heart in North America*, p. 531, letter of 30 January 1863, from Mother Barat to Mother Shannon: "A religious of the Sacred Heart ought to die with her weapons in her hand, if God leaves her the strength."

Between 1870 and 1900, the yearly average number of deaths increased steadily.[34] With more than seven thousand members by the end of the century, the increase was not surprising. It posed a question, however, that came up at every general congregation. From 1874 on, the fact that the average length of life at the Sacred Heart was forty-three years and three months caused concern that "this number ranked near the bottom among professionals." Consequently, proposals were made to lighten the work load, to dispense class mistresses from the recitation of the Office, "if it is recognized that that exercise is incompatible with teaching, as is said of men;" to limit surveillances, private lessons and division of classes, even when that provided better follow-up of the children; to make recreations times of real relaxation; to avoid imposing on the coadjutrix sisters work that was too tiring; to provide for more frequent changes of climate; and to name good "mistresses of health."[35] Ten years later it was proposed that one class each week be cut in order to give the teachers a day of rest. In 1890, it was suggested that the religious not be required to stay up at night to compose plays for school feasts, that provision be made for exercise for young nuns and that they be sent outdoors to say their beads or make their examen.[36] These measures, wise though they were, seem not to have been implemented, because the recommendations were later repeated in much the same terms. Even so, at the beginning of the twentieth century, the average age of death rose to fifty-five, a success undeniable in relation to the earlier statistics and a sign, possibly, that there was progress in medical care in houses of the Sacred Heart.

The death of young religious was rightly a cause of worry. Mother Barat, in her letters, often expressed sadness at the number of deaths of those from whom much had been expected. She complained about their weak constitutions and regretted that young religious could no longer take on the heavy loads that her first companions had managed. It is difficult to know if health was less robust then than at the time of the foundation. But the early deaths are explained by a variety of causes; the most frequent was tuberculosis, for which there was no known treatment except a change of climate and better diet. The contagious nature of the disease was not understood, since the sick continued to live in the communities and remained in contact with the pupils, even after their first hemoptysis. In

---

[34]

1870-1874	1875-1879	1880-1884	1885-1889	1890-1894	1895-1899
80	88	93	106	118	125

[35] Gen. Arch. C I C 3, Box 9.

[36] Gen. Arch. C I C 3, Box 10. "Examen" was a spiritual practice that one performed twice daily.

this regard, religious congregations took as few precautions as the general public. There is another reason for the deaths of young religious: adaptation to conventual life, to its rhythms and its obligations in sharp contrast to those of the "world" weakened some new religious and made them vulnerable to illness. Fortunately, many regained strength in a relatively short time.

On the other hand, another element in the Society's recruitment methods must be taken into account. While the Constitutions provided that to be admitted into the congregation, a person's "health must be good, and she must be free from any disease or notable infirmity that would unfit her for the works or labours of the Society,"[37] vicars and mistresses of novices bypassed this provision when they thought that the candidate had the potential for interior life, believing that the time lived in the Society, even though brief, would give her a chance to glorify the Heart of Jesus "by working at her own perfection and for the sanctification of others."[38] Novices who realized that they were afflicted with tuberculosis sometimes hesitated to inform the mistress of novices for fear of being sent home, not always the result. And yet the Society of the Sacred Heart enrolled enough new candidates to be able to apply the rule. A premature death, of either a pupil or a young religious, was considered a grace since it freed her from a dangerous and sinful world. Mother Lehon, acknowledging receipt of a letter from Mother de Pichon, then superior at Montpellier, which had announced two deaths in the community, wrote:

> You are sending your daughters to heaven, two by two. That's too much generosity. I know that they were already ill when they arrived at your house. It is always an honor to die at the Sacred Heart, and it seems to me that it is an assurance of Paradise as the Jesuits say. Let us give to the good God and to his service every day that he allows us; a single half-hour well spent carries the weight of eternal glory and merits gratitude.[39]

At the time of her visit to Saint Michael's in the United States, Mother Digby referred with humor to the losses about which she had just learned, saying, "Our Lord is trying us: he is fishing for pearls!"[40] The death of a young religious was not always as shocking then as we would consider it today.

---

[37] *Constitutions*, First Part: Of the Choice of Suitable Subjects for the Society; Chapter I, Of the Admission of Subjects, N° IV, 5.
[38] *Const.*, First Part, Chapter I, N° VI.
[39] *Vie de la Très Révérende Mère Lehon*, pp. 321-322, and *Vie de la R.M. de Pichon*, p. 160.
[40] Gen. Arch. C I A 5, Box 6, February 1899.

In 1884, the general congregation nevertheless called for greater strictness regarding the health of postulants and reminded the Society that deafness, defective vision and nervous breakdowns were reasons for refusing admission.[41] Six years later Mother Lehon insisted that a medical examination be made in case of doubt. In addition, during the noviceship superiors would determine whether the future religious had the stamina to live a cloistered life and to rise at the hour prescribed by rule, thereby avoiding too many exceptions.[42] But even though the religious believed that the seven and a half hours of sleep provided for in the Constitutions were sufficient, and though this was confirmed by the medical establishment, many young nuns had difficulty in getting accustomed to this rhythm of life.

Mortality in religious congregations regulated growth but was also traumatic, as death is in any group. Other circumstances regulated growth: departures, voluntary or not. From the general archives of the Sacred Heart we can establish the annual figure of departures during the second half of the nineteenth century, distinguishing between professed and aspirants. Departures of professed were very few, only seventy-six, of whom four-fifths were choir religious. The case of aspirants, religious to whom the Society was not yet committed, is quite different. There were proportionally more departures among coadjutrix aspirants than among the choir nuns.

The general congregations did not note the departures of religious before 1894. In 1895, Mother Digby indicated that the only dispensations from vows with which she had to deal as vicar general concerned religious suffering from mental illness. We can presume that not every departure was linked to this condition. Between 1844 and 1895, the annual average of departures represented 12.32% of entrances. During Mother Digby's generalate, it rose to 22%.[43] As well as sending away coadjutrix aspirants, the superior general decided on a strict recruitment policy, in contrast with the one in effect earlier.[44] Some houses had kept on for a long time, "through charity," some religious who lacked the necessary maturity for final vows.

The Society of the Sacred Heart formed a vibrant body. In 1865, the oldest religious was eighty-eight years old, and the youngest novice was sixteen. Those over sixty-five represented 3.86% of the whole, and those under twenty-five equaled 11.79%. The religious between twenty-five and

---

[41] C I C 3, Box 10.
[42] Box 11.
[43] Mary Quinlan, *Mabel Digby, Janet Erskine Stuart*, 1982, pp. 110-111.
[44] First vows were not "temporary" but committed the person making them for life. The Society, on the other hand, was committed to the person only after final vows.

forty-five made up almost 60% of the congregation.[45] This age pyramid, in which those under sixty-five constituted 96.6%, practically the whole body, reveals a youthful congregation. With three hundred and ninety novices, the future was bright. In 1899, the oldest religious reached ninety, while the youngest novice was eighteen. The average age, which in 1865 was thirty-nine, had moved to forty-three. On the other hand, the "mode," which in 1865 had been thirty-six and a half was now twenty-nine, an indication of increased entrances into the congregation. 90.66% of the religious were under sixty, and the Society counted four hundred seventy-five novices.

Geographic Extension

To her great regret, Mother Barat had never been able to fulfill all the requests she received for foundations. Those who succeeded her also had to refuse many proposals, but with growing numbers they could begin new foundations, completing a network already begun in some countries and introducing the congregation into new countries. Still, they paid attention to local politics, often postponing development in unsettled regions.

There were few new foundations in France. While the Society of the Sacred Heart had about forty houses spread throughout the country, only nine new houses were opened between 1865 and the end of the century. Most of those were in the southern half of the country: in addition to Annonay, reopened in 1890, Avignon was founded in 1869 and Pau in 1873. The capital of Béarn enjoyed a mild climate that had attracted a British colony. The city welcomed, for longer or shorter stays, a population from northern Europe and from Spain, drawn by an appealing social life and the proximity of Lourdes. The house became a restful haven for the religious of France, and Mother Gœtz benefited from it at the end of her life. But the religious also developed an apostolate among the tourists and political refugees. The house of Le Mans reopened in 1874. The acquisition, in 1894, of Mother Barat's birthplace established the Society in Joigny. The beatification process then in progress attracted attention to the Burgundian origin of the founder; her home in Joigny would become a place of pilgrimage and an opportunity to return to the source.

The Society spread in Europe, at first in the countries where it already had houses. In Belgium, foundations were made at Bois l'Évêque, near Liège, in 1865, and at Ixelles, in the Brussels suburbs, in 1889. In the Netherlands, the Society founded a house at Bennebroek in 1895. In England, the acquisition of seven acres of land on the banks of the Thames at Wandsworth and the opening of Hammersmith prompted the

---

[45] Those forty-five to sixty-five represented almost one fourth of the religious.

creation of a normal school and a day school in the London area, then in the capital itself. Founded in 1877 and in 1899, the houses in Brighton and Carlisle saw the Society spread towards both the South and the North of the country. The Society established a foundation in Scotland in Aberdeen in 1895.[46]

In the Austro-Hungarian Empire foundations were made first in the capitals, Vienna, Prague and Budapest, between 1868 and 1883. The fourth house in this group opened at Terlan in 1886. It had no external apostolate but was designed to welcome area religious for convalescence; too isolated, it soon closed. Through imperial generosity a house opened at Pressbaum in 1892, planned as a place for vacations and a novitiate for Austrians. Archduchess Valérie, a close friend of the superior in Vienna, persuaded her father, Emperor Franz-Josef, to make a gift of his hunting lodge.[47] Finally the house of Zbylitowska Gora in Galicia was opened in 1902.

In Mediterranean countries, the Society waited for political conditions to improve before thinking about extension. In Spain the return of the monarchy allowed expansion in a country where vocations began to flock to the Society. In 1875 and 1876, the Sacred Heart established houses in Zaragoza and Bilbao, then opened two new houses in Madrid in 1877 and 1884. Godella, near Valencia, was founded in 1892, and in 1902, the opening of a house in Palma gave access to the Balearic Islands. After Italian unity, decreasing anti-clericalism allowed a foundation in the Kingdom of Naples, then one in Florence in 1881 and a reopened house in Turin two years later. The gift of a large property in Avigliana occasioned the opening of a house at the foot of Sacra San Michele in 1889. Other foundations were made in Venice in 1896 and at Peschiera in the lakes region in 1901.

European expansion strengthened older foundations and marked the return to regions that the Society had had to flee at the time of the 1848 Revolution. The Society spread even more in America after 1865.[48] It had

---

[46] The Catholic hierarchy had been reestablished in Scotland in 1878, but *Propaganda Fide* continued to be in charge of the Church until 1907. The Society of the Sacred Heart contributed to the establishment of religious life in the country.

[47] The emperor offered this property in compensation for the damages to the house in Vienna caused by official constructions.

[48] The Society of the Sacred Heart had been in America since 30 May 1818, the day Philippine Duchesne and her four companions disembarked in New Orleans. There for the first time Mother Duchesne saw Native Americans at the door of the Ursuline convent where the Sacred Heart nuns were staying. In August 1818, they had arrived in Missouri and had opened the first free school for girls west of the Mississippi River.

well-rooted houses in Louisiana, New York and the Great Lakes regions. Foundations had profited from the increased population due to European immigration to the United States and the economic development that affected commerce from the cotton-growing South to the manufacturing cities of the North and Midwest. Alumnae had contributed to the expansion of the Sacred Heart by inviting their former educators to the areas where they had settled after marriage; often they helped to finance the foundation. Some houses had had to close as a result of yellow fever epidemics or devastating floods. After 1851 when vicariates were established, American-born religious were placed in charge of them. In 1860, 15% of the Religious of the Sacred Heart lived in the United States. Twenty schools were educating 3562 pupils, half of whom were in free schools and the Indian school in St Marys, Kansas, where the nuns had followed the Potawatomi when the government forced the tribe to move west.

The end of the Civil War occasioned the reorganization of the vicariates of North America. In Canada, where it had been called by Bishop Bourget in 1842, the Society contributed to affirming Catholics in their faith, as the bishop had hoped. The autonomy of the Canadian vicariate preceded the British North American Act, which in 1867 created the Confederation of Canada, operating from then on with a parliamentary system and an independent government. The Act had recognized the establishment of religious schools.

In the United States the Society demonstrated an impressive dynamism.[49] Expansion in the Midwest and the West followed a shift of the population, linked to increased immigration and the development of new means of communication. The house at St Marys, Kansas, was closed in July 1879, a sign of changes in the political and social climate of the Midwest. After a fire in their boarding school, the Jesuits wanted to leave the area, but the Religious of the Sacred Heart offered to sell them their house so that the people would not be without religious support. Thus, the nuns left the Potawatomi territory. In their school the mixture of Native American girls and the daughters of pioneers had had its ups and downs. The presence of the Sacred Heart in Indian Territory, which Philippine Duchesne dreamed of, had to be sought in other ways.

Foundations increased in the North, the Midwest and then the West of the United States following the vanishing frontier, filling out the original network. In the Northeast, the Society founded long-lasting houses in

---

[49] Except in Louisiana where the ruin of the South prevented the opening of a new house in New Orleans until the end of the 1880s. A day school had been opened there in 1867.

Monique Luirard

Philadelphia, Cincinnati, Boston, Providence and Grosse Pointe, near Detroit. Other foundations proved not so viable: Rosecroft in Maryland lasted only two years; its sparsely populated location was deemed too remote to attract enough pupils.[50] Atlantic City, lacking space, was closed in 1900 after seven years. Between 1872 and 1882 houses opened at Maryville in Saint Louis, in Chicago and in Omaha. In 1901 a day school began in Saint Joseph, Missouri. The Sacred Heart went to California, to San Francisco in 1887 and to Menlo Park in 1898.

The houses in the Caribbean were attached to the vicariate of Louisiana. The *Diputación*, the legislative body of the country, invited the Society to Puerto Rico in 1880. A contract specified the conditions of its establishment: Puerto Rican authorities would take the responsibility of furnishing scholastic equipment, would cover the financial deficit if the school did not have forty boarders, would pay the transportation costs of the religious needed for the boarding school and would furnish the land and the building.[51] Inspections of Sacred Heart schools would not be made.

While the financial arrangements specified in the contract met some resistance in the legislature, attacks by the liberals against the "Jesuitesses" were muted, thanks to the intervention of the governor general of the island. Such hostility concerned more than religion. The islanders, of whatever political persuasion, differed as to the type of education to develop. Even those who wanted to offer quality education to young girls thought that household management should be its core. Opposition fell away when an exhibit of their handiwork showed that at the Sacred Heart the children were also taught sewing and embroidery![52]

Mexico had achieved independence in 1821. The first decades of the Republic were troubled by civil war and by the aggression of the United States, which resulted in the loss of large territories. In 1863, France intervened, in the name of Latin solidarity, hoping to build an empire that conformed to the philosophy of Saint-Simon and able to oppose the United States and confer status on the Central American countries that were still being exploited. This step led to offering the crown to Archduke Maximilian of Austria. But after the end of its Civil War, the United States supported the Mexican insurgents. French troops left Mexico in February 1867, and Emperor Maximilian was captured and shot that June.

---

50   Gen. Arch. C I C 3, Box 9, General Congregation of 1874.
51   In fact the government of the island went beyond and equipped the chapel and the community's quarters as well. The expectation was to have eighty pupils.
52   Marie-Louise Martinez, in *Southward, Ho!*, pp. 125-126.

In 1859, the bishop of Mexico, in exile in New York, had suggested to the Sacred Heart that they establish a house in his country. Fortunately, Mother Barat did not jump into this adventure at that moment when Mexico was at the point of becoming a French satellite. Moreover, presidents of the Mexican Republic had set up a liberal regime that claimed to want to reform the church, all the while using the kind of patronage that Spain used to exercise absolute control over the Catholic Church, control that went far beyond the "right to nominate" candidates for ecclesiastical offices. Under the presidency of Benito Juarez, the Constitution of 1857 had separated Church and State, abolishing tithes, requiring priests to take a loyalty oath, forbidding public officials to take part in religious services and selling church property. About 1873, Mother Gœtz refused to make a foundation in Mexico because the political situation of the country seemed to her to be very unstable:

> The president of the Catholic Society writes that she can obtain a government decree in our favor, but even if it is granted, we run the risk of seeing that decree annulled by another one. Besides, to be in this country as an exception to the rule banning other religious orders could create a troublesome situation.[53]

Mother Lehon waited until 1883 to authorize preliminary explorations.

When Mothers Moran and Tommasini left for Mexico in order to visit a proposed site, the Society had long been known in Mexico. Mexicans had attended boarding schools of the Society in Europe, Havana and the United States and had entered novitiates at Conflans and in Cuba. But the two travelers found it hard to know whether or not the Society was wanted in the country: "One single fact is clear: we have enemies, but it is impossible to put one's finger on them."[54] Finally, after having made contact for three months with alumnae of the Sacred Heart and having acted with prudence worthy of secret agents, the visitors thought it better not to accept the place in question. They suggested to the superior general either that she give up the idea of a foundation in Mexico or that she start explorations anew.

After much hesitation, Mother Lehon agreed to open a house in Mexico City, which admitted the first pupils, boarders and older students, in October.[55] The work began without publicity because of a hostile campaign in the press, which stirred up nationalist sentiments on the pretext of

---

[53] *Vie de la R.M. Stanislas Tommasini*, p. 398.
[54] *Tommasini*, p. 412.
[55] The founders were Mothers Tommasini and Moran and Sister Saint Pierre. In 1884 Marie Emilie Jamay and Mothers Murphy and O'Reilly arrived.

Mother Moran's American nationality. In April 1885, the first stone of the new school was laid in Calle Tlaxpana. The congregation of the Children of Mary was established on 8 December 1886. The first women's retreat was held the same year. The free school began functioning in 1889. In 1884 a coadjutrix postulant, Concepción Ortega, had taken the habit in Mexico.

In June 1885, the Society of the Sacred Heart opened a house in Guanajuato, a mining town in the center of the country, to which it had been invited by María Antonia del Moral de Jiménez, who provided the building. A boarding school and a day school were begun. The bishop of San Luis Potosí invited the Society to his city in July 1887, and a third foundation was made in Guadalajara in 1895. The free school, opened in Guanajuato in 1885, was the first such establishment in Mexico. At the time it arrived in the country the Society was largely assisted by the alumnae, who had already begun to spread devotion to the Sacred Heart where they lived; they donated the needed property, took upon themselves the costs of foundation[56] and introduced the Society to networks of their friends. A vice-vicariate of Mexico was created in 1885. It included the house of Grand Coteau for ten years from 1888 on and then Puerto Rico between 1907 and 1911.

The Vatican urged the Society of the Sacred Heart to make a foundation in Mexico and to remain there because it would help nurture a Mexican Catholicism firmly in support of the Pope. In spite of the petty annoyances that it had to endure, it benefitted from several winning cards. Second Empire politics ended in Mexico with the death of Emperor Maximilian, but since then a current of Francophile sentiment remained among the Mexican upper classes, perhaps as a way to balance the influence of Spain. Moreover, the Religious of the Sacred Heart led the kind of semi-cloistered life that seemed appropriate to Mexican Catholics, and they arrived in the country at the moment when President Porfirio Diaz was discreetly initiating a political reversal later known as *Pax Porfiriato*. It consisted of encouraging economic development in the country in cooperation with foreigners, but also of creating a new type of education for young girls. The president wanted to make of Mexico City a Latin American Paris, its traces still visible in the city monuments. It is possible that his wife, Carmen Romero Rubio, who was a Child of Mary and sister of a member of the landed gentry who was a *hacendado* and defender of the Church, encouraged him to seek reconciliation with the clergy, without altogether losing face. Although Porfirio Diaz did not send a pearl necklace to the boarding school in Mexico City to reward the most gossipy student,

---

[56] Gen. Arch. C I C 3, Box 11, General Congregation of 1895.

as Mother Tommasini's memoirs would have us believe,[57] his sister-in-law and his wife did attend the Prize Day, as did both conservatives and liberals. Carmen Romero Rubio de Díaz presented exquisite pieces of needlework as rewards for the children, among whom was one of her nieces.[58] Other dignitaries of the regime, like former President Gonzáles, who was governor of Guanajato, helped the Society. As daughters of politicians of every political stripe, including those of the fiercest liberals, were pupils of the Sacred Heart, it would have been difficult to close their school.

In South America, the Society of the Sacred Heart continued to spread in Chile, and from there it expanded into neighboring countries. Foundations were made in Lima in 1876 and in Buenos Aires in 1880. After the death of Mother du Rousier, the vicariate of Chile added Almagro in 1884 and a day school in Santiago in 1885. Both the governments of Chile and Peru were interested in normal schools to provide teacher training. Thanks to developments in South America, the scope of establishments directed by the Society broadened. As the Chilean press observed at the death of Mother du Rousier in 1880: "The government entrusted her with the direction of the normal school, with the result that Reverend Mother du Rousier has educated all the school teachers of the country; thus she has directly and efficaciously built primary education" in Chile. However, in Peru this mission took on an even larger scale. A normal school for young women was created in Lima by a decree of 27 July 1876, signed by President Manuel Pardo. The religious, who were from France, England, the United States, Cuba, Mexico and Chile, took possession, in March 1878, of the former convent of San Pedro, which had belonged to the Jesuits. There were sixteen students to begin with. A boarding school was soon opened that year in the same building that housed a free school for three hundred pupils, which served as a demonstration school for the teachers in training. The first Peruvian vocations were those of Clemencia Almandoz and Guadalupe Alvarez, who entered as coadjutrix sisters, and Agueda Delgado, the first choir religious from the boarding school. In 1888 the novitiate for the choir nuns was transferred to Santiago, Chile.[59]

A new setting opened up for the Society of the Sacred Heart in 1880 with a foundation in Timaru in New Zealand. Religious from Maryville in Saint Louis took charge of it. Developments in ocean travel shortened the voyage, enabling such a distant foundation. In May 1882, the first house in Australia was opened in Sydney by religious from England

---

[57] *Vie de la R.M. Tommasini*, p. 435.
[58] Muriel Cameron, "Mexico," *Southward, Ho!*, pp. 134-136. The author draws on: María Teresa Guevara, *Historia de la Sociedad del Sagrado Corazón en Iberoamerica*.
[59] Margarita Recavarren, *Raices y horizonte*, Lima 2003, p. 25.

who traveled through the Suez Canal. Having left England on 1 April 1882, they arrived on 9 May. Five years later a house[60] was opened in Melbourne. In the next few years, day schools and a house in Wellington were opened. Both the urging of the Marist and Benedictine fathers and repeated appeals from local bishops facilitated the establishment of the Religious of the Sacred Heart in Oceania. In Sydney, the Hughes family, whose daughters had known the Sacred Heart in Europe, offered invaluable assistance to the religious in finding a property.[61] In 1888, Timaru split off from the western vicariate of the United States as did Rose Bay in Sydney from Roehampton; the three houses of Oceania then formed a vice-vicariate.

Consequences of Development

Redistribution of Forces

At the end of the nineteenth century 43.7% of the Religious of the Sacred Heart still lived in France; 27.13% lived in other European countries, where numbers had doubled since 1865. Of the latter group, Italy had the greater number, followed by Spain, where numbers had more than tripled. The most spectacular growth, however, was in the vicariate of Austria, where numbers had risen six-fold since 1865, as a consequence of both the arrival of religious obliged to leave the German Empire and the success of its apostolic works.

Elsewhere development was tied to the political and social circumstances of the country. In Ireland, the number of Religious of the Sacred Heart was limited by the distressed situation of the island. Many Irish women, forced to emigrate in order to escape the famine and poverty, met the Society of the Sacred Heart in the United States where they sought to enter. But the political chaos in Ireland can also explain its lack of growth. Was it really possible to govern from England a vicariate including both Ireland and England when sentiment in favor of independence was a growing force? Did the Society not risk appearing to be composed of "foreigners" at a moment when the local hierarchy was encouraging the creation of an educational system independent of Great Britain? In 1872,

---

[60] Gen. Arch., C I C 3, Box 11, General Congregation of 1890.

[61] Two members of the Hughes family, Susan and Maria, entered the Society. Their father donated his house at Kincoppal. A chapter in *Enfants de Marie*, vol. 2, was dedicated to Elizabeth Hughes. It recalls how young Elizabeth, who had been a boarder at Conflans, asked Leo XIII, during an audience that took place in 1880, to send the Sacred Heart to Australia where she was returning with her family (p. 170).

the vicar envisioned forming a vicariate or vice-vicariate of the houses in Ireland and transferring the novitiate of Roehampton to Ireland or at least opening an Irish novitiate. None of these plans materialized then.[62] Two Irish women who insisted that the Society in Ireland be governed by England no longer were sent to Austria and Argentina. Yet, in England, after a difficult start, the Society of the Sacred Heart was beginning to lose its French image and to take root in its new social and cultural environment. Some of its new religious had their first contact with the congregation on the continent, especially in Italy. The number of religious in England more than tripled, largely because the vicar, Mother Mabel Digby, opened new houses, discovered new modes of education and became known to the British, Catholics and non-Catholics alike.

Outside of Europe, there were only 733 Religious of the Sacred Heart in 1866. By 1899 there were 2156. 1202 religious – 22.85% of the total – lived in North America and on its nearby islands. South America counted 5.74% of the whole. The number of Religious of the Sacred Heart had doubled in the United States, tripled in Canada, quadrupled in Chile. Development was particularly impressive in Mexico, where there were already 202 religious, after only fifteen years in the country.

This expansion in Europe and the Americas was supported by France, whose novitiates sent out missionaries,[63] probably the reason that foundations in France barely increased. But the other European vicariates also sent religious to the missions or to established vicariates. Outside of Europe, transfers took place from vicariate to vicariate, from country to country, depending on available personnel or on religious who volunteered for the missions. Thus were the founder's wishes fulfilled: she had always tried to set up foundations with nuns drawn from different houses. Reality prevailed, however, especially with regard to language.

Shortly after Bishop Polding of New Holland [Australia], had asked for nuns to found a house in Sydney, Mother Barat had written: "As the national language is English, if we had a house in Ireland or in England, in which we had many religious, they would make these foundations."[64] In fact, it was a Belgian, Mother Fébronie Vercruysse, who went from Brighton, where she had spent many years, to make the foundation in Sydney on 8 May 1882. That Australia was a British colony did not matter. The motherhouse always sent a multinational group but one more or less fluent in the country's language. New Zealand was also a British colony, but religious from Chicago and Maryville in Saint Louis established the Society

---

[62] Mary Quinlan, *Mabel Digby*…, p. 35.
[63] Gen. Arch. C I C 3, Box 11, General Congregation of 1895.
[64] Madeleine Sophie Barat, *Lettres aux Supérieures*, vol.III, p. 99, 13 January 1842.

there in 1880. Did Mother Lehon think she ought to console that vicariate for the loss of the Indian school in St. Marys, Kansas, by giving them the opportunity to settle among the Maori? All the same, the language issue came up often in the Society. At the time of her visit to Louisiana, when asked to define a "mission," Mother Digby stated that for her to go to a mission meant to go to a country whose language one did not understand.[65] That was certainly the case for the greater number of "missionaries."

Gradual Adaptation to Local Conditions

Arrival in a new country calls for efforts to grasp its culture. Sending Jeanne de Lavigerie to Peru in 1879, Mother Lehon gave her advice that is still useful:

> Become as Peruvian as any Peruvian; learn and speak the language as perfectly as possible, so that you could be taken for a native of the country. In anything external, look like your sisters; let nothing seem foreign. Be slow to judge, even slower to criticize, and slower still to blame, so as never to arrive at the last two. Adopt the local customs, ways of doing things, and try not to do things in the French manner. Forget your country enough so that you never allow your sacrifice to be tarnished by regrets, annoyances, dreams of shores other than the ones to which you have been transplanted....[66]

In a congregation in which internationality was increasing with its foundations, preserving unity became an issue. In all the vicariates outside of France, and especially in those farthest away, the Religious of the Sacred Heart worked to maintain the bonds that united them to the "center" of the Society. A religious sent to Chile wrote, just before the death of Mother Barat:

> The charity, the peace, the recollection, in a word, the religious spirit that reigns in this holy house has made such a deep impression on me that I can only thank the divine Master for having called me to this blessed Society, which creates such union, such closeness, even in the farthest countries, that one could believe oneself to be at the center. Your principles, your every desire, are so much in force here that I might think that I was still near you, if I did not remember the huge ocean that separates us.[67]

---

[65] Gen. Arch. C I A 5 d, Box 6, February 1899.
[66] *Vie de la R.M. Jeanne de Lavigerie*, p. 55.
[67] Madeleine d'Ernemont, *La vie voyageuse et missionnaire de la R.M. du Rousier*, p. 169.

Even so, national characteristics appeared, and some of them amused the Europeans. Mother Digby smiled when she heard herself addressed as "Madam President" by the children of the free school at Manhattanville!

Community life had to be structured to suit religious of different nationalities. At Grand Coteau, in the beginning of the 1880's, Mother Tommasini had spiritual reading of fifteen minutes each in French, English and Spanish, so that everyone had to learn a language other than her own. Language was crucial for a long time. In Galicia, for example, sermons and lectures were given in Polish, but reading in French was maintained for those religious who were not Polish. In 1897 on the occasion of her visit to Lemberg, Mother Digby asked the superior to try to become more Polish. That vicariate lacked competence in the local language, both in teaching and in the life of the community. In 1898, the vicar, Mother Anna von Schaffgotsch, observed that too few classes were given in Polish.

The geographic expansion of the Society of the Sacred Heart could have led to modifications of its own governmental structures. That did not happen, but the expansion of vicariates outside of Europe did affect the central government. For example, Mother Aloysia Hardey, one of the earliest American religious, became assistant general in 1871. But globally the direction of the Society remained in the hands of Europeans, especially the French. Although from the death of Mother Gœtz until 1946, the superior general was never a French woman, her council included a majority of French religious. Some of the assistants general, French or not, could apprise the general council about countries where they had served or visited. By her presence in Paris Mother Hardey strengthened the bonds of the United States religious with the motherhouse. It was she who arranged for young religious who spoke French to make their probation at the motherhouse.[68]

New foundations adopted their own administrative structures independent of their vicariates, a practice that promoted hands-on management of communities and institutions, with communication enabled by reports of *visitatrices*, religious appointed as visitors. But it was essential for the superior general to travel outside of Europe. Mother Digby was the first to visit North America. That she was English-speaking facilitated this trip, at least in the United States.

From this time on, the Society of the Sacred Heart had to take into account the political, social and economic evolution of cultures throughout the world. For Cuba, Puerto Rico and Mexico, little understanding of local

---

[68] Religious from South America were later sent to France for the same reason. Mother Stuart decided that nuns from Australia and New Zealand should have the same advantage.

conditions flowed from the United States vicariates that administered them. But the international character of the congregation, expressed in the multinational make-up of communities, was not understood any better in Europe. When they were not natives of the country, the religious seemed to be foreigners. Language contributed to this misunderstanding; therefore in response, the motherhouse recommended that foreign religious spend their vacations in language study. They needed also to know the history of the country, whether of its recently cast off colonial past or its continuing domination by an occupying power, and recognize its geopolitical ambitions. As soon as the Society began to grow in Spain, many Spaniards were sent to Latin America.[69] We cannot know whether they sometimes suffered in countries where long Spanish domination had yielded to a much-relished independence or whether their sisters there found their presence difficult to accept.

The Society also had to come to terms with political changes that affected its apostolic works. At the end of the nineteenth century, for example, politically liberal Chile adopted an impartial schools policy. Freemasons established "free" high schools there, and secular boarding schools opened as well.[70] In Peru between 1899 and 1904, liberal members in the Chamber of Deputies questioned whether nuns should run a state normal school, particularly one on the same property as a private, religious school.[71]

How fast should expansion proceed? Mother Stuart, who visited South America in 1901, felt that growth had been too rapid in Chile: six houses in twenty-five years, all in need of support from abroad. But were the religious from Europe or North America really in a position to take charge? They often found the South Americans' excitability disconcerting. In order to "maintain a high level of religious spirit in the communities" Mother Stuart thought the Society must continue to send foreign religious to South America, but carefully chosen women: "Europeans who are devoted, fairly broad-minded, tactful and above all love the mission do a great deal of good and give much edification, but those who do not blend in and who show a sense of superiority, of contempt for the character and customs of the country and a desire to make everything European, these harm rather than strengthen the bonds with the Center of the Society."[72]

Recruitment also caused concern. Mother Barat had always asked founders to open a novitiate right away. But forty years after the foundation

---

[69] The first Spanish religious sent to South America was Isabel Plandiura, who arrived in Chile in 1853. She lived there for fifty-three years until her death (*Lettres annuelles*, 1906-1908, vol. 2, p. 409).

[70] Gen. Arch. C I A 5, Box 6, Visit of Mother Stuart in South America, pp. 1-2.

[71] M. Recavarren, *Raices...*, pp. 34-35.

[72] Visit of Mother Stuart, p. 8.

in Chile Mother Stuart observed that applicants had been admitted too easily and in time had shown themselves to be "lacking in virtue, ability or health." She asked, therefore, for reversal of this policy and even that a way be found to dismiss subjects whom she described as unsuitable. Did the religious exercise poor judgment or did postulants misunderstand religious life in the Society of the Sacred Heart? Upon her arrival in Chile Mother du Rousier had discovered that apostolic life did not attract postulants. Was it the style of spirituality in Chile that led people to contemplative orders, or was it that they did not perceive the contemplative dimension of apostolic religious life in the Society of the Sacred Heart?

Early formation was another cause for concern, linked to that of first assignments of religious after the noviceship. For a long time, a small number of novitiates sufficed. A common novitiate serving several vicariates in the same country, even in several countries, seemed advisable: novices came together from different countries just as members of the Society could serve outside their native country. But this policy met opposition in some places. The Polish choir postulants were sent to Riedenburg. Poles found it strange to send them to a German language novitiate at a time when Poland was partially occupied by the Second Reich and by Austria.[73] Political issues then prompted the creation of novitiates by country, in Europe as well as in America. In Canada because of military and cultural clashes between the English- and French-speaking, and in Peru because of the defeat suffered in the war of the Pacific, vocations were lost because French-Canadian families did not want their daughters to make their noviceship in the United States or Peruvian families, in Chile. At the request of the Canadian hierarchy, who wished to preserve the independence of *"la belle province"* [Québec] and to call attention to the new independence of the former colony, a novitiate was opened at Sault-au-Récollet in 1876.[74]

The General Congregation of 1895 addressed the question of national or international novitiates. If the diversity of languages called for the creation of national novitiates in the new vicariates, what about assignments of the religious afterwards? Should they be left in their own country or in the vicariate from which they came? In the latter case, "unity

---

[73] Mother de Montalembert, when she was vicar in Austria, decided to send the Polish novices into a "neutral" country. She chose Belgium, thinking that the climate of Italy would be too difficult for natives of Northern Europe. She always had a special interest in the Polish whom her father, Count de Montalembert, had supported at the time of the insurrections they mounted against Russia and in particular against Czar Nicholas I.

[74] In 1899, a common novitiate for Canada and the United States was established at Kenwood.

would soon be compromised; national or local spirit would replace the apostolic spirit that must reign at the Sacred Heart; the 'primitive spirit' would no longer keep us on the path traced by our first Mothers."[75] The decision was to remain faithful to the principle of mobility, while finding case by case solutions.

Who should be in charge? Was there no confidence in the religious of the new vicariates? Even if there was agreement in principle, practice did not always follow. The offices of vicar, superior and mistress of novices were entrusted to Europeans for a long time, giving the impression of a return to the past. When Mother Digby visited the United States, she decided to place the Kenwood novitiate in the hands of a young Irish religious, Mother Gertrude Bodkin, whom she herself had formed. Mother Bodkin had remarkable gifts, but her nomination did not meet with unanimous approval at first in the United States, where many religious did not understand why it was difficult to find a mistress of novices in a country where the Society had been since 1818!

Politics sometimes forced the Society of the Sacred Heart to adapt its religious life style to requirements of the country. This became a major issue in Mexico. If the nuns wished to stay, they had to accept not wearing the religious habit, not having Mass in their houses, not opening a novitiate for choir religious[76] and not having their right to accept pupils recognized by the State. Even though their presence was tacitly accepted, the religious were not exempt from searches. On 10 April 1885, one of them showed courage and presence of mind. The superior in Mexico City, who had been warned in advance by "friends" that a search was imminent, gave these instructions: "As soon as you hear five strokes of the bell, take off your caps, fold them up and put them in your pockets along with your veils, your crosses and beads. Then disperse silently; don't let them find more than two of you together…." As the writer of the report commented, the pockets were as big as drawers! The superior "had all her religious put on secular clothes, as she did; she then sent the children to their own classrooms with their teachers, and she went calmly and cheerfully to greet the authorities." Going through the house, the visitors met some children and asked them to sing the liveliest song they knew.

---

[75] Gen. Arch. C I C 3, Box 11.
[76] The novices were sent at first to Grand Coteau. When she became vicar, Mother de Lavigerie decided to send them to France. The long, expensive voyage, which their families had to pay for, seemed to her an excellent test of their vocations. The novitiate for the coadjutrix sisters was at San Luis Potosí.

These children stopped their singing, and forming two lines with their three disguised teachers, curtsied politely.... A little farther on, the gentlemen saw one of the nuns seated at a piano, playing a piece that an aspirant was trying to sing, even though she had no voice at all. One of the inspectors said, "Ah, these are the older girls; carry on, Mesdemoiselles." They stood up, made a respectful bow and sat down at the piano, stifling their laughter.... Farther on, an embroidery lesson so occupied "three ladies" that they did not even notice that someone had entered the hall.[77]

The Society of the Sacred Heart confronted a situation of which it had had no previous experience. Shortly after the house visit of 27 December 1885, the judge who had ordered it allowed his daughter, a day pupil at the Sacred Heart, to spend the night there in order "to receive Communion with greater recollection" on 1 January 1886. The Minister of the Interior sent Christmas wishes to the superior, and the chief of police came to pay a friendly visit. Should we characterize this as a "farce?"[78] It was in any case a way of life that called for the religious to face an undeclared policy with tact and steady nerves. While other religious orders had been sent away or were forbidden to come, the Society was allowed to remain in Mexico because it fulfilled a social role; it accepted the goals of the government and, while safeguarding its own objectives, respected the provisions of the Constitution of the country.[79] Mexico was the first scene of an unusual strategy, which annoyed the religious but offered a new framework in which to carry out religious life and apostolic activity.

---

[77] Gen. Arch. C III 2, no date.
[78] Louise Callan, *The Society of the Sacred Heart...*, p. 582.
[79] The vicars were accustomed to put on secular dress when they crossed the border. On the other hand, when she traveled in Mexico, Mother Digby kept her religious habit without attracting any unfavorable reaction on the part of the authorities, who were quite pleased to have her come.

Chapter III

THE UPS AND DOWNS OF MISSION

In order to glorify the Heart of Christ even to the ends of the earth, Religious of the Sacred Heart had to be ready to leave everything. They knew that they could be gone for good.[1] However, everywhere they went, they found the familiar customs of religious life that the founder had hoped for, allowing them to live the mission without too much adaptation. They would find a tabernacle wherever they went and, as Archbishop Richard said pithily to Jeanne de Lavigerie in 1878: "The Jesus of Peru is just as good as the Jesus of France!" Even so, leaving one's country called for generosity and trust, in the first place because one had to "sacrifice" family and country:

> A gunshot used to announce that the steamer was leaving Le Havre. This signal never failed to cause an emotional reaction; and when for the first time a person leaves what she loves best, when she sees the shore of her native land receding, not knowing whether she will ever see it again, her heart tightens involuntarily; but when the sacrifice is made for the Lord, mingled with this natural feeling is joy from on high: the joy of giving to God everything one has to give.[2]

If the biographer of Mother von Sartorius had not had the experience herself, she had certainly heard about it. Most of the religious sent to the missions died in a country that they had truly made their own.

---

[1] A religious had little chance of seeing her country again, unless she was not able to tolerate the climate or if she was called to another mission.
[2] *Vie de la T. R.M. de Sartorius*, p. 147.

Monique Luirard

Journey to the Heart of Raging Elements.

Reaching distant countries demanded courage, even daring; the long trips meant putting up with uncomfortable transportation. In an era when most people, especially women, traveled from need rather than for pleasure, religious joined the select few who could see lands usually known only from books. Transatlantic crossings offered the sight of icebergs and whales and in the southern seas the contemplation of fabulous sunsets, like the one Mother Stuart described in 1913:

> We have got into a trade-wind, the S.E....This trade-wind has a curious trick of blowing round holes through the clouds, through which one sees blue or stars by night. One evening there was a great mass of grey clouds driving westward, and driven into all sorts of shapes, and at one moment part of it rose up with the shape of an immense monstrance of old silver of the late renaissance type, blown out into a crown of cherubs and clouds, and the wind blew a round hole right in the middle of it, and – think of it! – the setting sun came down exactly there, and seemed to rest in that towering monstrance over the horizon, with the foot of the monstrance on the sea. It was a splendid Benediction of the Blessed Sacrament![3]

As Juliette de Landresse summarized it, writing about the *cordillera* of the Andes, about islands that seemed to rise up out of the ocean, about flying fish that surrounded the ship: "Two eyes are too few to admire all this."[4]

In the second half of the nineteenth century, maritime transport had not yet improved enough to be rapid and comfortable, and it could still be dangerous. In September 1863, for example, the ship carrying the superior of Halifax to New York struck a rock, ripping a hole in its hull. Mother Bowler and her companion reached a village near the shipwreck in an oxcart.[5] Three years later, six coadjutrix sisters, who had left New York for Louisiana, were shipwrecked off the coast of South Carolina. Their unruffled behavior garnered the admiration of the captain who said: "At least, here are some women who remain calm and don't scream!" They left the ship in heavy seas by means of a rope ladder, which other passengers, both men and women, refused to use! Moving from island to island, they finally reached the shore and continued their journey by train, thanks to the generosity of their companions in misfortune, for they had no money.[6]

---

[3]   M. Monahan, *Life and Letters...*, 21 November 1913, p. 429, ed. 1946.
[4]   *Lettres annuelles*, supp. 1947-1952, p. 170.
[5]   *Lettres annuelles*, 1863-1866, pp. 139-140.
[6]   *Lettres annuelles*, 1863-1866, pp. 157-158.

Contrary winds delayed crossings. In 1866 the sailing vessel bringing Mother Susannah Boudreau from the United States to France was so late that Mother Gœtz, who had to leave for Spain, could not wait for her. Intercontinental transport was not the only problem. It took several days to reach Cuba from the United States, and the crossing could be perilous. The traveler could also meet unforeseen events. In 1916 the journey from Australia to Japan took a month. After a stop in Brisbane, for some mysterious reason, the ship in which Mother Sheldon was traveling left earlier than scheduled. She and her companion joined it by launch and were hoisted aboard in a basket; when they appeared in the dining room, the passengers broke out in cheers![7]

As steam navigation became widespread, it took less time to reach the southern hemisphere. The long voyages had kept Mother Barat from sending her daughters to the Antipodes. Mother Lehon agreed to foundations in New Zealand and Australia when the Suez Canal cut short the crossing from Europe by six weeks. If long voyages allowed time for prayer and work and even time to write a book, as Mother Stuart did during her world tour, in the long run, they were a strain. On 19 August 1898, on entering the estuary of the St. Lawrence, Mother Digby "went on deck, happy to see land again, affirming that she never would have believed how much pleasure the sight of it one day would give her!"[8]

Improved navigation did not tame the elements. When in October 1884 Mother von Sartorius left for Louisiana, the crossing that ordinarily took ten days lasted two weeks because of heavy weather. The ship "fought against waves that struck its sides right and left. No one could stand up; even the men hardly went on deck. One had to hold on to something all the time." As some Marist fathers were traveling on the same ship, the nuns had looked forward to some spiritual conversation and daily Mass. There was neither. All the passengers succumbed to seasickness, which kept them in their cabins. Mother von Sartorius did not even have the strength to open her suitcase to get out her medicine. On the eve of All Saints' Day in order to prepare them for the next day's feast, she went into the cabin where two of her companions were stretched out in their berths; she heard a timid voice say, "Mother couldn't you come at another time?" Mediterranean voyages were not any calmer, and on more than one occasion, the vicar of the South of France met with storms on the way to Algiers.

Overland travel was also dangerous. In Chile, the route between Santiago and Concepción was picturesque but perilous. In February 1866 when Mother du Rousier accompanied five religious to Concepción,

---

[7] Arch. Province of Japan, Biography of R.M. Sheldon.
[8] Gen. Arch. C I A 5, Box 6.

Monique Luirard

> ...going rapidly around a mountain, one of the horses, badly handled, fell and dragged the head carriage into the gully. The same thing would have happened to our Mothers if a huge hole had not stopped their carriage: the driver jumped from his seat, opened the door and saved the travelers from certain danger. Water routes were no safer: our Mothers had to spend eleven hours, two aboard ship and nine wading without ever seeing their berths! On the Lontué, a bamboo bridge made just as unpleasant a path: suddenly, the bridge rippled, frightening them. A herd of oxen, meant to follow them below, lowed loudly, announcing that they had no wish whatsoever to cross the stream. Like the animals, the travelers, whether they liked it or not, had to cross a few gushing streams on stepping stones. One of them, Madame Camille Vacherot, unsure of her balance, slipped into the water and had to take refuge in one of the native's huts to dry her shoes.[9]

In 1901, local people tried to persuade Mothers Stuart and de Lavigerie not to try to visit the house in Colorado [Colombia] in the winter because the roads were impassable. They left anyway but "the horses and the carriage got stuck so deeply in the mud that one wondered how they would get out. A little farther along, the road became so bad that the two men who accompanied us had to use their *lazo*, a rope attached to the carriage shaft, to pull the carriage out of the mire." They crossed a river on horseback, covered by rubber cloaks that made them look like mounted knights. In 1907 the founders arrived in Bogotá on mule back.

To avoid such difficulties the motherhouse refused to consider foundations in places so isolated as to endanger the physical as well as the spiritual health of the religious. Mother Lehon refused a foundation in Antioquia, New Grenada, when she learned that it took four days on horseback to reach the spot. She had been promised, moreover, that a surgeon would accompany the religious to care for them in case of a fall![10]

Almost everywhere the railway eased communication. But at the beginning of the period, some lines were incomplete, and one still had to travel in a carriage drawn by twelve to sixteen mules to go from Madrid to Andalusia. Travelers met derailments caused, for example, by torrential rains, like the ones Mother Lehon experienced in the Alps at about the same time. The comfort of travel by train had improved by the end of the century. When Mother Digby visited Canada in 1898, between Montréal and Halifax she had a private compartment at the rear of the car giving her and her companions solitude for work and prayer: "Real beds allow

---

[9] Gen. Arch. C I A 5, Box 6, p. 177.
[10] *Vie de la T.R.M. Lehon*, pp. 307-308.

for refreshing sleep, so this trip, though long, is not tiring, except when the train is unusually jerky."[11]

In spite of the humor evident in the accounts, the travel narratives, designed to be read in community, often painted these adventures as a long series of somewhat diabolical dangers, from which the travelers were saved by the protection of the Heart of Jesus and the prayers of their sisters. The religious underwent storms and typhoons with renewed energy drawn from faith and stout confidence in God, proven amid and despite threats on all sides. But not every distant land was beset with pitfalls. Mother du Rousier reminded people that the apostolate in South America was not carried on in the heart of a virgin forest: "Those who aspire to the missions sometimes have a very erroneous idea of the trials that await them. In Chile, for example, they have nothing to fear from snakes; they will not sleep on buffalo skins; they will not live entirely on potatoes, corn and rice."[12]

For elderly women or those in frail health to cross a turbulent ocean or torrential river in a tiny vessel was a real trial. Mother du Rousier suffered from seasickness. For her to avoid a second crossing less than a year after her return to Chile, the motherhouse proposed that she should not take part in the General Congregation of 1865 but send her vote for the new superior general by mail. On these expeditions, many Religious of the Sacred Heart showed strength of character and sportsmanlike qualities that they had had no occasion to make use of in Europe. They appeared to be true "adventurers," manifesting anew the spirit that had animated the pioneers of earlier generations. Mother Stuart, who had ridden horses from childhood, was certainly happy to ride in South America.

Some of the young or not so young enjoyed journeys to new countries. Mother Nicholl, Mother du Rousier's traveling companion in Chile in 1874, wrote: "I was delighted to have a better look at a land in which human art has not destroyed natural beauty or made travel too easy. The grandeur of the landscape prevented my suffering from heat or fatigue, for I was all eyes, missing nothing, so Mother laughed at me, asking from time to time if I were seeing everything. I found everything charming," she wrote, "the sight of the neat farms, often surrounded by a pretty garden," the local costumes, the sombreros, the brightly colored ponchos, the ostrich feather parasols, the weapons made from precious metals. "Their whole ensemble is so picturesque." At stopping points, she picked "flowers worthy of a royal salon." Even the desert plains had "a wild brilliance" that she liked.[13]

---

[11] Gen. Arch. C I A 5 d, Box 6. Mother Digby had a heart condition, and during her journey in America every effort was made to spare her fatigue.
[12] *Vie de la R.M. de Lavigerie*, p. 68.
[13] Madeleine d'Ernemont, *La vie voyageuse...*, pp. 188-189 and 193-194.

Unusual scenes made the long trip especially enjoyable. On the banks of the Rio Claro, the two travelers saw a man crossing the river with his wife on his back: "The wife was a large woman, the crossing long and the current strong, and the man who was leaning on a stout stick had only one arm to hold his Dulcinea. Little by little he let her slip until she seemed to be seated on the water; she wasn't worried, but upon reaching the shore, she shook the water from her clothes, content with herself and her husband." Faced with this spectacle Mother du Rousier remarked to her young companion, "Our Lord, who likes to give us pleasure in small things, sent this amusing scene just for her, for in all her travels she had never seen anything like it!"[14]

The lands of the South did not have a monopoly on the beautiful landscapes. Henrietta Kerr, sent to Rome at the end of her noviceship, described for her father the route she had followed between Nice and Florence. The trip lasted more than thirty hours: "It was very tiring," she admitted, "but the route is so beautiful. We saw the Corniche to perfection during the night. The moon was splendid, the sea wild with brilliant flashes of light, all truly magnificent. The waves looked like silver crowns…. How beautiful it was! I do not regret at all the long hours in the coach. I would have been sorry to miss all that."[15] Mother de Lavigerie believed that "teaching nuns ought to develop their abilities by every means and learn from the great book of nature." Therefore, when she crossed the ocean, she spent evenings scrutinizing the heavens to find the constellations indicated on sky maps lent by the captain.[16]

Natural Dangers

Once they reached their destination, the religious sometimes had to adjust to a climate against which they had hardly any means of protection. Mother Barat had hesitated to send her daughters to Cuba, for people had told her that Europeans could not fight yellow fever. The religious also had to face catastrophes, both natural and man-made, that could cause havoc and even death. We must recognize, however, that though the Society of the Sacred Heart had to suffer many losses, it rarely had to mourn loss of life. A few examples from the *Annual Letters* will suffice.

In 1871, for seven nights in a row, the nuns in Chicago could claim that they were reading and writing by the sole light of the fire that destroyed twenty thousand houses in the city. Hurricanes occasionally rampaged the Caribbean. On 22 October 1865, in Cuba after one storm, "A brilliant sun

---

[14] M. d'Ernemont, p. 194.
[15] John Morris, *Life of Mother Henrietta Kerr*, 2 December 1865, pp. 135-136.
[16] *Vie de R.M. de Lavigerie*, p. 178.

lighted the scene of desolation visible everywhere: we saw trees overturned or shorn of leaves; our courtyards were full of all kinds of debris, and this sad spectacle was only a small gauge of the immense losses caused by the hurricane."[17] These events occurred regularly, of course, with greater or lesser damage to the houses. Fires caused by lightning destroyed buildings, but fortunately they were not usually of the magnitude of the one that totally destroyed the Sault-au-Récollet in Canada, in 1929, without, however, any loss of life.

Locust invasions ruined harvests and could have deadly consequences for the population. In Saint Joseph, Missouri, in the United States, at the beginning of the 1870's, the scourge recurred over several years and reduced the number of boarders from families who had lost their crops. The house in Algiers suffered from these invasions several times. The religious described the spectacle they witnessed in May 1866, when clouds of locusts, driven by the simoom winds from the desert, landed on the plains. A plague of locusts caused a food shortage that became a famine the next year, following the earthquake that affected the Mitidja plain. In 1867, described as "the year of death," an exceptional drought, coupled with a double epidemic of cholera and typhus, killed nearly a million people in Algeria. The families of students of the school camped for a long time in temporary tents.

The religious did not worry about earthquakes when there were just a few inconsequential tremors. But some seismic events caused panic. In Concepción in Chile during the night of 23 July 1898, "One would have said a giant was playing ball with our house, which rose and fell. From all the dislocated walls, stones, earth, and plaster rained down from the shifting walls. This frightening quake was followed by a second, then deadly silence. Everyone was horrified! Then came screams, tears, upset." The damage was major. Pupils and adults experienced a shock that the narrator described thus:

> Our children were very good. At the first quake they all ran to their *surveillantes*. One of them, a timid sort, cried, "For pity's sake, children, wait for a minute so I can get dressed." One little one, putting her arms around the nun's neck, said "Oh! No, we must die together!" and the others all added, "Yes, yes!" They dressed in a hurry; given the circumstances no one looked. There were similar scenes in the older girls' dormitory. The mistress general was corralled and swept along by her charges; she made three trips around the dormitory in her nightgown before she could get dressed. Mother X, another dormitory good

---

[17] *Lettres annuelles*, 1863-1866, p. 126.

shepherd, had a rain of plaster in her bed, but she had been in training when there were huge earthquakes in Valparaiso, so she was less upset and calmly gathered her terrified little lambs, barefoot in their nightgowns, into her alcove. She looked tenderly at these frightened lambs and saw one she did not recognize at first: it was the mistress general!

After another quake,

> Everyone ran out of doors to avoid being buried under the falling walls; panic ensued; children prayed, wept, made promises. The calmer ones tried to soothe the others saying: "What can happen to us in a house of the Sacred Heart? Our Lord will protect us. We are much safer here than with our parents." A little before midnight, Reverend Mother, whose calm quieted both nuns and children, gave everyone a hot drink and gave permission to spend the rest of the night wherever they wished. The children stayed in the study hall; some religious began their meditation in the chapel; others watched the door; the less hardy tried to sleep on the floor with a chair for a pillow. Tall Mother Z. lay down on the long table in the sewing room, and the Mother Assistant commented: "At the first jolt, she will flip over like an omelet!" Poor little Mother D. was dying of fear and kept repeating in her fright: "If it were not for my vocation, I would leave on the first boat...." We found fervent Mother L. on the step of the altar before the tabernacle in her dressing gown. In her left hand she held her lantern; with the right she was striking her breast while repeating, "Holy, holy, holy, Lord God of Hosts!" We could have added: "Lord God of earthquakes!'" When the earth calmed down and we did too, we had to laugh at our outfits: some were barefoot; some in skirts all askew; most in nightgowns covered with a shawl....

The narrator, who had an exceptional talent for description and a remarkable sense of humor, concludes as follows: "We are sure there were many conversions. Concepción is another Babylon, in great need of returning to the Lord. Pray for the city."[18]

---

[18] Gen. Arch. C I A 5 d, Box 6. A particularly severe earthquake was registered on 24 January 1939, in Concepción, rendering the Sacred Heart convent uninhabitable. There were two victims among the coadjutrix sisters, one a young professed; they were buried under the rubble. For three months the community "camped out." They were aided by the efforts of the Society, which sent help from everywhere. Little by little activity with the children was resumed, and after six months they organized a preliminary camp for five boarders. They had to rebuild the entire building (*Lettres annuelles*, supp. 1951-1954, biography of Mother Sara Fernandes, pp. 108-109). A year later

The earthquake that struck San Francisco in 1906 "was a terrifying event: walls cracked and caved in, buildings and houses collapsed; the ground, roiling like a furious sea, respected and spared nothing." The fire that followed added to the catastrophe:

> The darkened sun seemed the color of blood, its rays ominous with fire and flames everywhere. Explosions of dynamite came one after another, ceaselessly; distress and misery were rife; we were seized with a double disaster and death seemed inevitable. The violent shocks had broken all the water mains in the city, and the only man who knew exactly where they were all located, the fire chief, had been one of the first victims.[19]

The nuns took refuge with the Little Sisters of the Poor, witnessing the devastation on the way there. The eldest and weakest of the community were sent to Menlo Park. Because the convent escaped destruction, the religious were eventually able to return, and for the rest of the siege they sheltered emergency patients. But the earthquake brought about a change that would have taken place anyway, because the original location was not a good choice for a day school. The Sacred Heart later opened its doors in one of the most attractive sections of San Francisco, "with a magnificent view of the bay and the Golden Gate." During the same period, Vesuvius attracted lovers of great natural spectacles by its rumblings and its jets of flame. From Naples, which it spared, one saw "the air shimmer with electricity. Continual lightning bolts illumined the dark sky, and a reddish fog surrounded us; ash rained on the city, burying it under a thick, grey layer; the air was so laden with sulfur that it was hard to breathe." On Holy Thursday, 1906, the darkness became "so thick that one could hardly distinguish nearby objects."[20] The community of Portici, which took refuge in Naples, was finally dispersed and the boarding school was not re-opened.

Whether they were sent to lands near or far away, the religious had to be ready to put up with living conditions that could be rough. While some foundations had been carefully prepared by those who invited the nuns – to the point that the beds were turned down, the nightstands provided with water, soap and towels, the pantry fully supplied for several days and dinner ready on the stove in the kitchen –[21] other places had next to nothing. In Seville the convent handed over to the religious had been used for a long

---

another earthquake struck the coastline of Peru. The house in Lima, shaken by the quake of 24 May 1940, had to be closed momentarily. At Chorrillos the damage was severe but only material.

[19] *Lettres annuelles*, 1906-1908, pp. 182-183.
[20] *Lettres annuelles*, pp. 138-139.
[21] *Lettres annuelles*, 1863-1866, p. 175. That was the case in Concepción.

time as a refuge for about a hundred families. The nuns had to comb the whole place to make sure that the inhabitants were not still there. "We had only one table for many uses: refectory table, ironing board, etc. As for chairs, we had to carry them from the cells to the refectory, for there was only one for each person.... When Mother Gœtz went to visit them a few months later, the religious had only three little lanterns, "by whose light they could barely see the piles of wood chips that clogged the passageways."[22]

However, as Mother du Rousier clearly recognized, more than material privations, "the sacrifice of homeland, of dear ones, of the customs of one's country weighed the most heavily." One had also "to adapt to other ways of doing things and to the different characteristics of the children."[23] That was the price of apostolic work. The "missionaries" knew that their sisters supported them. European communities tried to share in their leave-taking. If the religious did not stop at Calais, the students went up to the top floor of the house to wave to them as the train went by.[24] In Bordeaux, the embarkation point for Latin America, the children sang the *Ave Maris Stella* and the hymn *Amour et sacrifice* during Mass, in harmony with what one guessed were the sentiments of those departing.[25]

Religious Life and Geopolitics

Some descriptions could suggest that religious life is led in a world apart, quite beyond global or national affairs. On the contrary, a religious congregation is always affected by the politics of the countries in which it functions. The Society of the Sacred Heart had to face wars or events less drastic but nonetheless important in the life of a given region. After 1865, a new, less conservative political climate developed: the Institute had to take it fully into account or lose touch with the times.

The Civil War in the United States

The last years of Mother Barat's generalate were overshadowed by the Civil War. The founder had even postponed the general congregation, hoping the war would end and the vicars of the United States could leave for Europe. When the congregation finally took place in 1864, the war was not completely over, but military operations were on the decline, and it was clear that the Union had prevailed.

---

[22] *Vie de la T.R.M. Gœtz*, p. 284.
[23] *Vie de la R.M. de Lavigerie*, p. 68.
[24] *Vie de la R.M. Nerincx*, p. 35.
[25] *Vie de la R.M. de Pichon*, p. 135.

Since the election of Abraham Lincoln, Mother Shannon, vicar in Louisiana, had foreseen the Civil War, which broke out on 12 April 1861. She had written then to Mother Barat: "The election of a president favorable to the abolition of slavery causes us to fear a revolt of the Blacks. Separation of the North and the South is inevitable. I am referring to a dangerous political situation, Very Reverend Mother, in order to ask your prayer for our dear country. Until March we will be in a state of anxious uncertainty." The houses in the northern States and the Indian mission in Kansas were not endangered during the war; but the coadjutrix sisters found their workload increased because of conscription, which caused a dearth of workmen and artisans.[26]

Louisiana, on the other hand, experienced utter upheaval. Communications were cut off, and the religious lived in fear because they were Southerners, either by birth or by their convictions or sympathies. The boarding schools lost pupils; despite dwindling resources, the religious had to provide for large communities and to assure crop production on plantations where slave labor could no longer be counted on. When Union troops appeared at St. Michael's in 1862, they knew that they were not in friendly territory, but they were received courteously, and they protected the house when neighboring properties were being pillaged.[27] In western Louisiana, Grand Coteau and Natchitoches suffered from lack of food and water.[28] The vicar, who had joined them by crossing the war zone, helped them by recovering foodstuffs that soldiers had confiscated. "Fires and pillaging had reduced the wealthiest families to poverty; the slaves had become the masters and people accustomed to luxurious living thought themselves fortunate when, to feed their children, they could glean in the abandoned camps a few husks of corn left by the horses."[29] At the time of the emancipation of the slaves in January 1863, the Sacred Heart houses had managed to keep their work force.[30] But families who had lost their slaves and their property could no longer pay their children's fees. At St. Michael's, lacking the wherewithal for new supplies, the religious had to make habits out of chapel cloaks and shoes from leftover pieces of cloth or carpet.

---

[26] *Lettres annuelles*, 1906-1908, p. 65.

[27] *Lettres annuelles*, pp. 116-117. General Banks, who had taken command of the Gulf region in December 1862, had a daughter in the boarding school in New York. He took care of the mail for the religious at Grand Coteau and gave them news of the North. He also sent them supplies of foodstuffs.

[28] *Lettres annuelles*, 1863-1866, pp. 159-160, and 1905-1907, p. 308. The Jesuits had been a great help.

[29] Arch. Jeanne de Charry. *Rapport de la Mère Gœtz*.

[30] Only one woman had left St. Michael's after the Emancipation Act.

At war's end, the convents of the Sacred Heart survived intact. But the Southern way of life, its economy based on slavery, had to be remade. Many lives had been lost. Families had been displaced. Others lost social position, their children required "to share their misery and their privations," or to transfer from the boarding school to the free school. After the surrender of General Lee,

> the social and political structure fell apart; blacks, fully enfranchised, did not understand their rights, rights now denied their former masters; all the public offices were in the hands of greedy and unscrupulous carpetbaggers from the North or of freed slaves. Many prominent Southern families were reduced to indigence; sorrow and mourning filled all hearts. Survivors found their properties devastated, their resources destroyed and their wives and children deprived of everything. Many saw the little that remained to them eaten up by debts contracted before the war, which at the time had appeared insignificant; young men on whom the future had smiled had to resign themselves to a life of poverty and manual labor.[31]

Compassionate in the face of this depressed economy, the Religious of the Sacred Heart had to support both young and old as they faced a threatening future.

Misery was widespread among white people. Young upper class women made long journeys on foot to attend the meetings of the Children of Mary, for there were no horses or carriages. In Natchitoches,

> Two young persons, who had left the boarding school because of their parents' poverty, came to see us and expressed their fervent wish to return to the convent. "Mother,'" said one of them, addressing the superior, "we want to make an arrangement with you; Papa wants to pay our fees but he cannot. We would like to help him this way: I have a little plot that I have cultivated myself, and it will produce a hundred fifty barrels of corn, if I can keep the flooding river away from it. Would you think, Mother, of accepting these hundred fifty barrels of corn in payment of my fees?" The other one said, "I can count on fifty barrels, may I make the same arrangement with you, Mother?" These dear children went home happy with Reverend Mother's answer.[32]

To the hardships of war were added floods and bad harvests, making it difficult for St. Michael's and Natchitoches to carry on: "We are afraid

---

[31] *Vie de la R.M. Shannon.*
[32] *Lettres annuelles,* 1867-1868, IV, p. 18.

that under the circumstances, most of our pupils will be unable to return to us after vacation. The harvests this year have been completely lost; the cotton, the only resource in this part of the country, has been destroyed by caterpillars. Our hearts are heavy with our inability to assuage all this misery; we can scarcely relieve the suffering of others when we too are experiencing the effects of these disasters."[33]

Salaries now had to be paid to the farm workers. Convents of the Sacred Heart, ruined by the war, lacked the means to pay their former slaves, now their employees. Mother Shannon, with no money for wages, much less raises, had suggested that they look for better jobs elsewhere, but there were none to be found. She then proposed to exchange their labor for food, clothing and lodging. A contract, a symbol of the new order, was drawn up: thirteen former slaves signed it, evidence that the nuns had already discreetly provided them with basic skills.[34]

To prepare the boarders for a life in which manual work would play a large part, at least for the moment, the religious modified the curriculum.

> We judged that it would be better to initiate the students into the new style of life to which Providence destined them by teaching them to do the work formerly left to the slaves. Divided into groups with a religious at the head of each, they are learning all kinds of manual skills and housekeeping, taking care of the dormitories, the refectory, the kitchen, dishwashing and laundry. Some have even asked to learn how the dairy works. These tasks did not replace class periods but rather the time formerly set aside for piano lessons and music and art. The children brought energy and courage to these novel occupations, as their mothers are doing in the midst of the severest reverses of fortune.[35]

Cancelling courses in *arts d'agrément* [accomplishments] was a discreet way of helping the families since the cost of these lessons was not included in the board and tuition fees.

The Civil War left the United States badly shaken. Even in the North the nuns had to practice prudence to make sure that political passions did not affect the life of the school. At the time of the assassination of President Lincoln in 1865, Mother Hardey, so as not to wound the sensibilities of boarders from the South, forbade Manhattanville students to wear black armbands, and she reproved "inexperienced" religious who

---

[33] *Lettres annuelles*, 1867-1868, IV, p. 18.
[34] Louise Callan, *The Society of the Sacred Heart...*, p. 539.
[35] *Lettres annuelles*, Grand Coteau, 1863-1866. Quoted by Callan, p.525.

showed "excessive" patriotism.[36] In Louisiana, the Civil War caused such a decline in enrollment that the house in Natchitoches was closed in 1876. By 1899 Grand Coteau still had not regained the number of students it had had *ante bellum*.[37]

Liberalism and National Unity in Europe

In Germany, the Society of the Sacred Heart experienced few problems during the struggles to unify the country. The Society had only one house there, Marienthal near Munster. After the affair of the Danish duchies, Bismarck succeeded in spinning off Austria and reorganizing northern Germany under the authority of Prussia. Brief fighting ended, on 3 July 1866, with the Prussian victory at Sadowa and resulted in the disappearance of the last traces of the Holy Roman Empire. At Blumenthal, in the Netherlands, clashes among boarders from different regions of Germany, some pro-Prussian, others pro-Austrian, might have arisen. In southern Europe, on the other hand, repercussions from unification or liberal reform provoked anxiety.

Unification of Italy

Italian unification, led by Piedmont, ended with the establishment of a liberal regime that had clearly anti-clerical aims: the Society of the Sacred Heart had already paid its price in 1848. In June 1859, after the French-aided victories at Magenta and Solferino, Piedmont annexed central Italy. The houses of the Society in Loretto, Sant'Elpidio, Perugia, Parma and Milan were closed between 1859 and 1862. At the death of Mother Barat, the Sacred Heart still had in Italy its three houses in Rome and the convent in Padua, the fate of which was uncertain; the house had been confiscated in 1863, but the Society had been granted the use of it for twenty years.[38] The boarding school in Chambéry had been reopened, because in exchange for its participation in the movement for Italian unity, in 1860, France had obtained jurisdiction over Nice and Savoy and had decided by imperial decree to reinstate the rights of religious congregations there. From then on, alumnae of Turin sent their daughters there,[39] as a way of expressing their loyalty to the Society that had educated them and instilled in them their hostility to the policies of the Italian state.

---

[36] *Vie de la R.M. Hardey*, p. 235.
[37] *Lettres annuelles*, 1906-1908, p. 315.
[38] Gen. Arch. C I C 3, Box 10.
[39] *Lettres annuelles*, 1866-1867.

After Sadowa, the Veneto, ceded by the Austrians to Napoleon III, was promptly ceded back to Italy. The Jesuits were expelled. The superior in Padua, Mother Bentivoglio, managed to save her house when, in March 1867, a popular uprising, orchestrated by Garibaldi, resulted in the suppression of many religious orders. A decree of suppression was addressed to her, but on 21 November 1867, royal officials

> conferred for a long time with Reverend Mother, then we were all sent for to sign a declaration that stated that we were resolved to continue to live together as we had been doing up to now. This formality caused some hilarity among us and seemed to convince our visitors that no one wanted a change.

Mother Bentivoglio demanded that the following be entered into the act of suppression: "Nevertheless, all these ladies, having declared their wish to live together as before, the boarding school will remain as it is, directed by the same mistresses and in the same manner."[40] Her presence of mind resulted in no loss of students and the continuation of the establishment on the same basis as before. At the same time, Garibaldi was fomenting troubles in Rome. At Santa Rufina, in the course of encounters in the Trastevere between insurgents and pontifical troops, reinforced by the French of the division of Failly, a bomb broke the chapel windows and bullets entered the house, but no one was hurt.

The French character of the convent of the Trinità dei Monti preserved it when Rome ceased to belong to the Pope. On 3 October 1870, the Trinità was invaded by the *Bersaglieri* [marksmen] who were searching for Papal Zouaves or boarders who could have been "daughters of Zouaves." This house search was repudiated by the authorities who came to the convent to apologize. The bonds between the Religious of the Sacred Heart and the Holy See were well-known, but no one wished to make trouble with France. After the closing of many convents in Rome and the expulsion of their members, the Villa Lante received some Camaldolese nuns and opened its gardens to some contemplatives whose new shelter was especially cramped. The City of Rome sought to take over parts of the Santa Rufina and Villa Lante properties, their fate remaining uncertain for years. In 1880 the Villa Lante was left in the care of a few religious who maintained the school and the orphanage. The novitiate was transferred to Florence. Only in 1891 was the Society of the Sacred Heart able to assert its rights to the Villa Lante. In 1883 the Italian state expelled the community at Padua, with the exception of

---

[40] *Lettres annuelles*, 1866-1868, p. 11.

the thirteen religious who had been there at the time of the annexation. The Society then purchased another house there in order to continue its work.[41]

Spain from Monarchy to Republic

Dynastic succession troubled the history of Spain during the whole of the nineteenth century. Deprived of a male heir, Ferdinand VII had decided in 1833, in a pragmatic move, to pass the throne to his daughter Isabel, provoking a rebellion already brewing in favor of his brother Carlos and his descendants. The "Carlists," while invoking respect for the Salic Law, defended traditionalism and absolutism. Some houses of the Sacred Heart educated children of the Carlists. Montigny received nieces of "Carlos V." Riedenburg educated two princesses of Parma, one of whom married the new pretender in March 1863;[42] Pau accepted the couple's daughter. But the three daughters of Isabel II, Pilar, Paz and Eulalie, were brought up in Paris at the Rue de Varenne[43] after their mother's exile. The Sacred Heart did not appear to take sides.

Queen Isabel II accepted a liberal constitution in 1854 and left power to O'Donnell and Narváez, inflicting on Carlists and republicans severe restraints. An insurrection in September 1866 enabled General Juan Prim to take power and overthrow the queen. Isabel II took refuge in France, where she was warmly welcomed by the imperial couple. She left such terrible memories in her country that when Mother Gœtz visited Seville, she had a narrow escape, because the crowd believed that the superior general of the Sacred Heart was the famous Sister Patrocinio, said to have secretly influenced the queen! An interim republic had been installed in September 1868, but the republican regime, proclaimed in 1873, lasted only two years. The provinces where the Sacred Heart was established were prey to insurrections and fighting among rival factions, especially at the beginning and end of the period.

In 1866, many Jesuits and Oratorians had to leave Spain, by their own choice or under pressure from local juntas. Many of them settled in France, where the convents of the Sacred Heart rallied to come to their aid.[44] In

---

[41] Gen. Arch. C I C 3, Box 10.
[42] Mother Barat had sent some small things to be given to her as a gift when she left school. She wrote in her own hand the name of the princess for whom they were destined. *Lettres annuelles,* 1863-1865, p. 51.
[43] Their brother Alfonso, the future Alfonso XII, was a student at the Collège Stanislas. He came to get his sisters when the war was beginning. He said then to the Religious of the Sacred Heart how much he envied the Prince Imperial who had already received his baptism of fire!
[44] Rennes offered shoes to one hundred fifty Jesuit refugees in Brittany, and Toulouse gave them shirts and also fruits and vegetables. *Vie de la Mère Fornier*

Spain the intensity of the troubles varied according to region. In Catalonia, where there were many republicans, the religious at Sarriá saw fires burning in parts of Barcelona, but the new government protected them. They began to look for a house where they could take refuge with their children if the situation became critical. When a statute was passed outlawing convents of women not dedicated to education or charity, the nuns of Sarriá worried about having to offer hospitality to other religious expelled from their convents, but that did not happen.[45] Fearing sudden expulsion in Madrid, Mother Goetz had prepared for withdrawal to Bordeaux. The parents of the pupils got together; the families of the poor school promised to riot if the religious were expelled. The nuns lived in uncertainty: "For the moment we appear calm...but everything around us is terribly upset. What fills [the students] with fear and distress is the freedom of worship introduced into this country that is so attached to its traditional religious beliefs."[46] The boarding school at Chamartín included many children whose families had lost their positions, another cause of pain. In Seville Catholic worship became privatized; the ringing of bells was forbidden and the Sacred Heart chapel was seized by the city; however, as a special favor, the nuns were allowed to enter the chapel by a secret door with hidden keys. A popular insurrection, inflamed by rioters from Malaga, broke out in the city at the end of May; the Sacred Heart, flying the French flag, served as a refuge for citizens at a loss for housing as a result of the widespread fighting. It sheltered children and women from poor areas whose husbands had joined the rebels. Sister Encarnación took care of them. The house also received some Trinitarians driven out of their convent with their pupils, abandoned children. This crowd exhausted the convent's supplies but added to the Sacred Heart's good reputation in the area. The house did not burn, but the chapel was destroyed and had to be rebuilt. In January 1874, when the town of Sarriá was occupied by republicans, there was a battle with heavy artillery, grenades and bayonets between republicans and government troops. At the Sacred Heart, while there was some material damage, the children were safe in a refectory in the basement during the fighting.

The French character of the Sacred Heart congregation had different consequences in different places. At Sarriá, this character, which the members of the municipal council "assumed of everyone," was a source of mistrust.[47] The house had had difficulty in obtaining official approval

---

de Mairard, pp. 73-74. In Catalonia Jesuits went into hiding but continued to exercise their ministry at Sarriá. *Lettres annuelles*, 1867-1868, p. 80.
[45] *Lettres annuelles*, pp. 75-77.
[46] *Lettres annuelles*, pp. 91-92.
[47] *Lettres annuelles*, p. 73.

and was at the mercy of local authorities. In Seville, on the other hand, the Sacred Heart benefitted from the presence of the French consul, who had helped the superior when the chapel furnishings were being inventoried. When officials announced to them that they were to be expelled, the religious answered, "If we were driven out of Spain, we would go to live elsewhere. We would not lose out, they would!"[48] But when the Republic was proclaimed in May 1873, the superiors of the houses in Spain displayed the French flag.[49] In Seville, recourse to the French and Belgian ambassadors kept the Sacred Heart chapel from being put up for auction.

Everywhere the Religious of the Sacred Heart could count on the support of the local people. Women of Sarriá answered with verbal attacks those republicans who made threatening speeches. The nuns in Seville were well regarded, thanks to their free school. "Although the fathers of several of the children were revolutionaries and irreligious, they appreciated the care lavished on their daughters: The mistress general of the poor school was very well known in the area."[50]

1870-1871: A Disastrous War

On more than one occasion, Religious of the Sacred Heart had experienced wars and expulsions. However, the Franco-Prussian War of 1870 affected the government of the Society. Headquartered in Paris, it suffered from events as they unfolded there.

Napoleon III had always avoided a confrontation with Prussia, one probably inevitable after Sadowa. Bismarck finally forced the test of strength when he sought a victory to rally the Germans of the South and a pretext for proposing a Hohenzollern as candidate for the throne of Spain. But the war, declared on 18 July 1870 by Napoleon III, set France against all the German states. Nothing foretold defeat. France had a hardened army ready for war, and the rest of Europe had decided not to join the conflict. As everyone was "greatly worried about Germany,"[51] Mother Gœtz had the novitiate of Marienthal transferred to Jette in Belgium. The boarding schools at both Marienthal and Blumenthal were closed, but the religious and boarders of Lorraine were sent only as far away as the Ardennes and Picardy.

Although the French army lacked neither ardor nor heroism, it could not withstand the German forces, superior in numbers, perfectly organized,

---

[48] *Lettres annuelles*, p. 98.
[49] *Lettres annuelles*, 1872-1874, p. 122.
[50] *Lettres annuelles*, 1867-1868, pp. 95-96.
[51] *Lettres annuelles*, p. 114.

better equipped, disciplined and united, even though composed of men from seven different countries. Mobilization in France dragged, and the decision of Emperor Napoleon III not to cross the Rhine put the French on the defensive. From the first battles, the lack of information on the belligerents' movements and real losses, the emperor's hesitant strategy, the errors or mistakes of some of his generals resulted in defeat. The first setbacks at Wissembourg, Froeschwiller, Reichshoffen and Forbach at the beginning of August gave Alsace to the Germans and opened the Moselle to them. At the end of a four-day battle at Gravelotte on the outskirts of Metz, General Bazaine found himself forced into Metz, 18 August 1870. France's finest army was trapped in this stronghold, not in communication with Paris either by railroad or telegraph. MacMahon's army, which had tried to liberate Metz, was surrounded at Sedan. On 2 September 1870, Napoleon III was taken prisoner with his whole army. Two days later a popular uprising in Paris denounced the defenseless imperial regime and the Republic was proclaimed.

The Terrible Year[52]

The houses in Lorraine and Alsace felt the consequences of the war at once. Emergency wards were organized at Montigny and Metz. Mother Gœtz gave orders to reduce the size of the communities and to send the children home. Now many German families, who had perhaps thought the war would be over in a single battle, had left their children in France. The German boarders at Montigny had to be evacuated through Charleville, and those at Nancy found the return too difficult. On the other hand, the evacuation of the Swiss pupils went smoothly. The religious from Charleville, Nancy and Besançon went to Paris and to the South of France; they endured exhausting overland journeys because the trains were reserved for the troops. In October 1870, the superior at Kientzheim sent the novices to Switzerland. In the rest of France, the nuns prepared for war, not imagining that they would see its horrors; and they obtained residence permits for the German religious.

The disasters of the first defeats spread alarm that soon became panic. Montigny, in the hands of three caretakers,[53] took wounded from any country into its emergency ward. An artillery post was installed along the convent walls. Three hundred soldiers occupied the school. "As time

---

[52] In France, this title of a poem of Victor Hugo has become a byword to describe the year 1870-1871.

[53] They sheltered a family: "They even entrusted their cow to us, a real treasure in these difficult times."

passed, our situation became more difficult. We might have been able to grow accustomed to all the privations, the rumbling of cannon day and night, but the blockade was another kind of mental anguish: contradictory rumors and advice, the failure of even the best founded hopes, led from uncertainty to anguish."[54] The religious fell ill, victims of malnutrition. Around them wounded soldiers and civilians succumbed to typhus and smallpox. The surrender of Metz, 29 October 1870, traumatized the citizenry who questioned why the authorities had not been able to prevent the disaster. One of the assistants general, Mother Desoudin, was born in Metz: "For a long time she could not believe the news of the surrender, expecting it to be denied; but when she had to face the fact, her Lorraine daughter's heart felt deep bitterness."[55] Far from their country, French religious felt the defeat. Mother du Rousier wrote: "We are suffering from our own safety. Oh! May the Lord appear to help us!"[56]

Montigny escaped being requisitioned, thanks to the brother of a Prussian general who suggested reopening the school. The house in Metz was occupied but "the abundant rations [of the soldiers] strengthened our poor wounded and relieved much misery around us. Besides, we must be fair to our German guests; they were always very polite, very reserved, and when they received from their chiefs orders to depart, they left us with as much regret as gratitude." In Nancy, the suburban house that was to receive victims of contagious diseases was not seized. The one on Rue Stanislas lodged twenty Bavarian religious after the German army left. In the Ardennes, Charleville was able to evacuate its pupils to Brussels and Liège, but the house was bombed. In the North of France, General Faidherbe preserved Lille and Calais from invasion, but did not succeed in closing the route from Paris. German troops crossed Picardy in November 1870 and stationed themselves in Amiens until July 1871 without harming the "*Berceau*." In Franche-Comté, neighbors supplied food to the nuns bereft of everything. The house in Bourges, which had been on the point of being transformed into a barracks, sheltered military supplies, then was turned into a hospital.

Leon Gambetta presided over the Republican counterattack organized from Tours. At Marmoutier, an English committee, perhaps at the suggestion of the superior, Mother Mabel Digby, undertook the care of those wounded in the nearby fighting. Then the Germans occupied Rougemont, where they used the classroom desks as horse troughs. The First French Army of the Loire, in which former Papal Zouaves were

---

[54] *Lettres annuelles*, 1870-1871, II, p. 3.
[55] *Vie de la R.M. Juliette Desoudin*, p. 166.
[56] Madeleine d'Ernemont, p. 186.

engaged in large numbers fighting under the emblem of the Sacred Heart, recaptured Orleans. After the surrender of Metz, the German forces crossed the Loire. A second army of the Loire commanded by General Chanzy regrouped, but after the battle of Le Mans it could only slow down the retreat and avoid defeat. The Prussians did not occupy Laval. A general armistice stopped the fighting on 28 January 1871.

In the Heart of Paris under Siege

When German troops surrounded the capital on 18 September 1870, the communities and the students were dispersed. The boarders of the Rue de Varenne left in small groups; the novices and the religious of Conflans went to Brittany, the orphans either to Paris or to Picardy; a dozen professed remained to guard the house. At the announcement of surrender, those surrounding Mother Gœtz begged her to leave Paris. She refused at first; but upon learning that Pius IX, while visiting Santa Rufina, had exclaimed: "When a storm is brewing, the pilot takes precautions," and that the general of the Jesuits had ordered his provincials to leave Paris, she went to Laval on 6 September 1870, with Mother Desoudin and the secretary general, Mother Dufour, leaving Mother Lehon in Paris. Mother Peacock had proposed that she come to Halifax,[57] and Mother Hardey had written to her: "Who knows whether Divine Providence has not caused all these troubles in Europe in order to give you a sign that it is his will that you visit your houses in America!"[58] But Mother Gœtz did not want to leave France.[59] Mother Lehon proposed that the religious leave Paris before the siege took effect if they thought they could not handle the pressure. The treasurer general, Mother Bulliat, went to Marmoutier. As Conflans was in the line of fire, those remaining there took refuge in Paris on 14 September, leaving the house in the care of a neighbor, one of Mother Barat's relatives, and of a servant. In December a small colony was able to return, as the convent was turned into a military hospital.

The blockade of Paris began on 19 September. The nuns on the Rue de Varenne were panic-stricken to hear the *Marseillaise* sung under their windows. In the context of the invasion, it had once again become a revolutionary anthem. On 29 September 1870, the cannon sounded for the first time. For five months the population of Paris was subjected to cannon fire at the rate of sixteen shots per minute. Mother Lehon wrote to Mother

---

[57] M. Williams, *Josephine Gœtz*, p. 50.
[58] *Vie de la R.M. Hardey*, p. 294.
[59] However, on 27 April 1871, she accepted with gratitude financial aid from Mothers Hardey and Shannon.

Gœtz, every other day, letters that reached her by balloon, if the winds were favorable and storms had not destroyed the balloons. Messages from Mother Gœtz came by carrier pigeon, whose arrival was uncertain.[60] The religious of Paris were "separated from the world."[61]

The *sorties* of the French troops, made arduous by a particularly bad winter, failed to shake off the enemy. In the city, the people suffered acutely: "After three and a half months of siege, the food supply began to fail, those in charge of provisions had long since been replacing butter with tallow, had reduced the ration of horsemeat to thirty grams, of black bread to three hundred grams containing unexpected ingredients, even string; even so resources quickly dwindled." The hardships of the siege were felt unequally by different groups. Religious communities that lived somewhat self-sufficiently were better provided for than some other city-dwellers. Although the Rue de Varenne had supplies, it had to feed a community that, even though smaller, still counted about fifty persons, to aid struggling families and to provide soup for a crowd of poor people. The supplies lasted longer than anyone had foreseen and enabled the religious to come to the aid of other communities, among them the Helpers of the Holy Souls. But still people remembered dishes of inedible nettles. On one occasion, a shell accidentally hit a cow, a butcher was able to carve it in secret, and the community had meat every day for a week.[62] There were no visitors, no mail. "It was a life of prayer, of work and of union."[63]

At the time of the first bombardments in January 1871, Mother Lehon had a dormitory and a chapel set up in the cellar. The bombs caused significant damage but no loss of life. She decided then to send the religious of the Rue de Varenne to families or friends. Mother Lehon wrote:

> One develops little by little habits that one believes one cannot get along without in food or lodging; and, behold, the siege puts an end to everything. Instead of being alone in a quite comfortable cell, with all the necessary furniture, one is encamped in a cellar, seven or eight persons in a poor room, with no space even to put a chair, and one gets along very well, all the same.[64]

---

[60] Her first letter arrived only on 21 November. Out of seventeen or eighteen letters, only one reached its destination.
[61] *Lettres annuelles*, 1869-1871.
[62] *Lettres annuelles*, 1906-1908, pp. 97-98.
[63] *Vie de la T.R.M. Lehon*, p. 249.
[64] *Vie...Lehon*, pp. 258-259.

Revolutionary Troubles

At the announcement of the first defeats, spontaneous and unorganized disturbances arose in various cities of France. The Sacred Heart did not suffer from any of these, but many convents of contemplatives were broken into. More serious troubles broke out after the surrender of Sedan. The people demanded a "levy *en masse*," [universal conscription] as in 1792; believing they had been deceived by the authorities, they wanted scapegoats. The rise of religious indifference or rejection of the Church resulted in searching for them among male religious. In Perpignan, Aix-en-Provence and Marseille, the Jesuit residences were attacked and some of the priests imprisoned. In those cities the Sacred Heart remained undamaged, but there were serious incidents in Lyons.

On 4 September, when the Republic was proclaimed, the red flag flew over City Hall in Lyons. "The authorities claimed to be powerless while armed troops guarded the convents, particularly, against threats of pillage and death." This time convents of the Sacred Heart were targeted. *Les Anglais*, protected by its neighbors, was not invaded; but precautions were taken to secure valuable objects and to disperse most of the religious, who left for Avignon, Chambéry and Montfleury. Foreseeing a siege, military authorities wanted to build battlements in walls around the property, but the installation of an emergency ward saved them. The house on Rue Boissac was visited by the National Guard who thought they would find a subterranean passageway communicating with the Jesuit residence. But this inspection forestalled the excesses and violations suffered by the nearby convent of the Poor Clares. At La Ferrandière, on the other hand, the searches fell just short of that kind of violence.

When the Jesuits were arrested, the religious of La Ferrandière, who had begun their retreat at *Les Anglais*, immediately returned to their house on 7 September in mismatched secular clothes:

> Their trip had its dangers: forced twice to get down from their carriage and go into a guardroom, they were examined minutely, surrounded by sinister looking men armed with every kind of weapon. Close inspection of their packets, especially their office books, soon identified them, leading to vague threats against religious communities.

They got away quite frightened. La Ferrandière was invaded by three hundred demonstrators: one of them pursued one of the nuns, who was carrying a packet of clothing, yelling, "Do not hide anything from the Republic!" The demonstrators were looking for subterranean passages, supplies of arms and "treasure." The next day, at the suggestion of the archdiocese, the novices were sent to Montpellier. After a second house search, the convent was left in the hands of a few caretakers.

The disturbances reached the capital after the signing of the armistice, and a revolution, the "Commune," broke out on 18 March 1871. It was the patriotic reaction of working class people who had suffered from the siege and who refused to stop fighting; it was looked upon as a "reign of terror," which it was in some ways. On 3 April 1871, the Commune decreed the separation of Church and State, the suppression of the budget for worship services and the nationalization of the property of religious congregations. In Paris a third of the parish churches were forbidden to hold services and 40% of the schools conducted by religious were secularized.

The Thiers government, which had taken refuge at Versailles, made the decision to lay siege to the city. When she learned of it, Mother Gœtz wrote to Mother Lehon: "It would be better to lose everything than to endanger our nuns."[65] She asked that the communities of the motherhouse and of the Rue de Varenne, which had both returned after the armistice, be sent to safety. Mother Lehon refused to leave, answering on 26 March: "I have already lived through several revolutions; I am not afraid, I am Belgian, I am calm, I am old; it seems to me that I have all the qualities necessary to stay in the house."[66] But she sent the most vulnerable religious and the sick to Conflans, which was located outside the zone occupied by the Prussian army but protected by its proximity, and she found hiding places for the archives and valuables.[67] Mrs. Ellen Blunt, mother of a former student, suggested that she place the motherhouse under the protection of the United States; the American flag flew over the *Maison des Anges* on the Boulevard des Invalides.

From the beginning of the second siege of Paris, the *Communards* took hostages from among the middle class and the clergy. The motherhouse then served as a refuge for members of the archdiocesan administration who came secretly to celebrate Mass and to hold meetings. When she learned of the arrest of members of the clergy, Mother Gœtz ordered Mother Lehon to join her in Laval, for she feared that religious women would also be arrested. After a house search that could have been worse but for her presence of mind, Mother Lehon sent out of the city a few religious who had difficulty obtaining passes and getting past the guarded exits. She herself left Paris on 16 April. Mother Perdrau, Mother Langlet, who was

---

[65] P. Perdrau, *Les loisirs...*, vol. 1, p. 573.
[66] *Vie de la T.R.M. Lehon*, p. 262.
[67] She was aided by an Alsatian who, having become German after the defeat, obtained passports and could conceal the domestics.

too ill to move, four sisters and four servants stayed at the Rue de Varenne. A few caretakers occupied the motherhouse.

The school on the Rue de Babylone continued to function throughout the Commune, serving three hundred and fifty pupils. "Everything is going on as usual," wrote the mistress general, Mother Esther Saingéry, "I could even say: everything is better than usual; one feels that the Master is in charge; the children are docile and much calmer." Actually she had not been bothered, although in the neighborhood,

> delegates of the Commune, the red scarf on their shoulders, were chasing sisters from their schools and inaugurating their own instruction, its program thus: first exercise: *Marseillaise* recited, second exercise: *Marseillaise* written out, third exercise: *Marseillaise* sung. It was not necessary to go further since the Commune had passed an emergency measure suppressing spelling.[68]

The *Communards* were probably not all such ignoramuses as this description suggests but, as Mother Perdrau wrote to Mother Gœtz, "What is being done, according to your wishes, for the dear friends of the Savior puts – I do not say a cordon of safety – but a divine shield around our houses. The bread we distribute does marvels; everyone around us says that we should not go to so much trouble, that they will take less than we are giving."[69]

The repression of the *Communards* by the troops from Versailles, under the mocking eyes of the Germans, was bloody. In the neighborhood of the Invalides the troops from Versailles were greeted as saviors. "At the shadows of the *Communards* passing at the end of the Rue de Bourgogne, our men from Versailles yelled: 'Ah! Scoundrels, ah! Rascals! We must beat them!'" Mother Perdrau kept them from building battlements in the walls of the motherhouse: "No, Madam, we will safeguard your house, nothing else." The gardens of the motherhouse and of the Rue de Varenne were filled, nevertheless, with munitions of all sorts, and red flags taken from the *Communards* floated in the trees. On 24 May 1871, fires broke out in the city. Mother Perdrau noted in her journal: "The sun tries in vain to pierce the thick red cloud that hovers over Babylon on fire. Our courtyard is covered with charred papers. Ash and dust fly around and descend on us like a light, bad-smelling rain." From Conflans Mother de la Guibourgère wrote to Mother Lehon:"

---

[68] Gen. Arch. C I A 2 d, Box I, "Account of the principal facts of what took place in our three Paris houses from January to August 1871," p. 25.

[69] *Le peintre de Mater admirabilis*..., p. 73.

> Staring at the fiery crater we thought we were looking at Vesuvius; deafened by cannon and machine gun fire we imagined we were hearing the prolonged rumble of those frightful storms where one thunderclap does not wait for the next but repeats itself like an echo; our souls, in anguish at the thought of the victims of the fire and the bullets, cry to the Lord for mercy.

The air was too smoke filled to breathe. That same day Archbishop Darboy of Paris was one of the first hostages shot by the *Communards*. Of the eighty-two hostages executed sixteen were ecclesiastics, among whom was a Jesuit, Father Olivaint, the former director of the Children of Mary of Paris, from then on considered a martyr for the faith by the Society of the Sacred Heart.

The end of the Commune was welcomed with relief. Mother Perdrau wrote:

> What calm after the Commune and its horrors. I thought I was dreaming; I could not get used to living without danger: I have to tell myself consciously that I can leave a letter on my desk; write one without putting it half-finished in my pocket; leave the chalice in the sacristy; hear the chaotic noises on the boulevard without fear. Nothing can make one appreciate the simultaneously strong and gentle feeling of safety than having lived for some time with misery and terror night and day.

It is true that in Paris the Religious of the Sacred Heart had lived for a long time "expecting death at any moment."[70] The *Communards* had heavy losses, with at least twenty thousand killed or wounded. Former students returning to the Rue de Varenne told the nuns that they had to step over corpses. The Paris houses were not damaged, on account, it was thought, of Mother Barat's intercession, as Mother de la Guibourgère wrote to Mother Gœtz:

> If the Sacred Heart has come through this terrible crisis without misfortune, how can we ever express our thanks for a miracle that surpasses those of Gideon, of Daniel and the rest? Our beloved Mother Foundress has obtained from the Heart of Our Lord salvation from a thousand dangers. Therefore, she is powerful and Jesus gives in when she intercedes.

---

[70] Fearing arrest, they used to go to bed partially dressed.

The Commune had also been proclaimed in Lyons, Marseille, Toulouse, Bordeaux and Grenoble. In Marseille, the religious on Rue des Dominicaines, alarmed by the pillage of several convents and by the demonstrations of bands of "patriots," took refuge in the house of Saint Joseph. Over the top of the wall they saw some "heads covered in hideous red caps," but they were only "curious but unarmed people!"[71]

Mother Gœtz returned to Paris on 6 July 1871. She never referred to the war in her circular letters, content to speak only of "the terrible crisis we are going through," but on 9 May 1872, she alluded to it indirectly: "May he [the divine Heart] be blessed for the providential, almost miraculous, preservation of our houses amid the calamities that surrounded them."[72] At the beginning of the war she had placed the fate of the houses "in Our Lord's hands" and on 6 September 1870, had named the Blessed Virgin the guardian of the Paris houses. As a chaplain of the army of Versailles said to one of the nuns: "France must be saved by the Sacred Heart; how then in view of the future would the Society that bears this name not be fully protected?"[73] The congregation echoed the same sentiment in the face of its providential preservation.

New Apostolic Activities

At the beginning of the war a Jesuit had said to the religious at Layrac: "At this time of France's misfortunes, we must reverse them by continual prayer joined to sacrifice. Our soldiers are giving the blood in their veins; the families, their tears; we, at least, give our hearts' blood by the constant sacrifice of ourselves." The war brought the religious in direct contact with suffering and death.

The superiors proved their strength in defending their houses against the French or German authorities, yielding only as a last resort. To hold on to their houses, they tried to have emergency hospitals set up in the free schools where the nuns continued to instruct pupils. In occupied cities, as factories ceased to operate, many young girls went to school in the hope of having a noon meal. Religious of the Sacred Heart prepared the hospital rooms and made hundreds of mattresses. The students made bandages for the wounded. Doctors and civilian and military nurses and male religious and seminarians ran the hospitals. Sometimes the nuns were involved in the

---

[71] *Lettres annuelles*, IV, pp. 11-12.
[72] *Circulaires de la T.R.M. Gœtz*, p. 131.
[73] Gen. Arch. C I A 2 d, Box I, "Account of the principal facts of what took place in our three Paris houses from January to August 1871," p. 1. The preceding quotations from Mothers Perdrau and de la Guibourgère come from the same source.

management or care; they prepared the most seriously wounded for death. They accepted everyone: soldiers separated from their units wandering in search of shelter and food, sick who arrived at all hours of the day and night. "We lacked everything, beds, linen; what our good sisters laundered with care froze instead of drying, and we could not relieve those poor people who were eaten up by vermin."[74] In Brittany the boarders, seeing that the coadjutrix sisters were overworked, undertook to make their own beds. In an era when operations were performed without anesthesia and when postoperative problems were rife, the nuns witnessed unheard of suffering. As the sick were attacked by typhoid fever, typhus and smallpox, contagion killed community members.

Some of the wounded were taught to read and write. In Paris, they were taught catechism by means of large pictures, probably the ones used in the school. The men were encouraged to fulfill their religious duties, and the nuns assisted at innumerable "returns." At Quimper

> Everything took place as it would in a family: a religious would arrive in a cotton nightcap, wrapped in an old bathrobe or camp blanket, carrying a cup of *tisane* to calm a coughing fit. Central to it all was confession. An eager young corporal took the first step. He went to confession and was so happy about it that it touched everyone's heart; he came to share his joy with Reverend Mother saying, "My superior, I must have a souvenir of this event, for at home no one will want to believe it." Sometimes we had to temper the zeal of these neophytes and remind a junior officer, who was getting ready to send his men to the confessional in rank order, that this religious act, however important it may be, must be free! A Gascon spent several days seated near his bed, head in hands, sighing deeply, and when asked why, he replied, "You see, Sister, confession needs to be thought about; one does not go to it as one does to a wedding!" Grace triumphed; trembling, he took his place on the bench waiting for confession. One of ours who was in the ward at that moment, touched by his emotion, encouraged his good resolutions and made him feel better with a little glass of sweet wine, which gave him back his courage.[75]

One wonders whether such creativity surfaced everywhere. Knowing that confession can be a battle, this religious had impulsively given wine to the wounded man, just as soldiers were given wine before an attack! Many soldiers, practicing Catholics, said the Rosary and went to pray in the chapel. In Nantes, they divided up the hours of adoration before the

---

[74] *Lettres annuelles*, 1869-1871, p. 32.
[75] *Lettres annuelles*, pp. 14-15.

Blessed Sacrament, for "the divine captain must not be left without his sentry." A young corporal was out walking with one of the priests. "Oh! Pardon, Father," he exclaimed, looking at his watch. "It's my hour for sentry duty; I have to go."

The Religious of the Sacred Heart discovered the real world from which cloister kept them apart. They became aware of the diversity of French society, of which the army was a mirror.[76] Their behavior had its reward. At Laval, 1 January 1871, a good soldier gave part of his meager savings to buy three oranges. "Take them," he said, "one for the superior general, one for the superior of the house and one for the sister who takes care of me."[77] After the war, all the houses received touching letters from the survivors or their families. Many wounded owed their lives to the emergency wards of the Sacred Heart. In Moulins, the mother assistant, unseen, overheard this exchange: "Tell me, do you agree that this hospital has the best nursing in all of France?" "Do you mean in all of Europe?" "No," answered a third, "It is a house where we are welcomed with kindness, cared for with kindness, and they do it better than the best!"[78] Clearly, the wounded were apprehensive about being sent to other hospitals.

During the occupation the Religious of the Sacred Heart sometimes had to let Protestants use their chapel. They cared for the enemy who generally treated them with respect; discovering many Catholics among them, they understood that beyond differences of nationality was a common faith. The Society felt the effects of the war beyond France. At Marienthal, the pupils worked for the wounded Germans. At Posen there were thousands of French prisoners in a camp. Smallpox that broke out there claimed two victims among the Religious of the Sacred Heart.

Consequences of the Defeat

The peace was signed in Frankfurt on 10 May 1871. France had to pay an indemnity of five billion gold francs, but, most important, she had to cede Alsace and part of Lorraine "[which had] become France's ransom."[79] This annexation was tempered by interim measures. Citizens could opt for French nationality until 10 October 1872. In Alsace, "everyone is in mourning" and Metz was "almost a desert."[80] How did Mother Gœtz,

---

[76] *Lettres annuelles*, p. 32, "Corsicans, Arabs, Blacks are assembled under our roof and, in spite of this diversity of races [*sic*] live in good understanding, while the work of their salvation takes place without interruption."
[77] *Lettres annuelles*, p. 41.
[78] *Lettres annuelles*, p. 47.
[79] *Lettres annuelles*, 1870-1872, II, p. 14.
[80] *Lettres annuelles*, II, p. 14.

originally from Sélestat, feel? We do not know; but we can guess that this woman who, in leaving Paris, had already experienced abandoning three communities under siege, was deeply pained by the fate of her native province. The terms of the peace treaty caused changes in the vicariate of the East. The novitiate in Kientzheim was transferred to Conflans. The nuns agonized at "seeing this beautiful province snatched away from France." For a long time the superior at Kientzheim, Mother Voitot, "refused to believe that the Queen of Heaven, who had so many shrines there in her honor, could abandon it to the enemies of her Son."[81]

The "option" did not concern the religious, but it affected many families who did not wish to live in the Reich or see their sons serve in the German army. In Metz, the superior organized a retreat for the Children of Mary before the dispersal. As a consequence of relocation, the boarding schools of Nancy, Besançon and several cities in the interior of France gained pupils. In the summer of 1873 the German armies left France. The new border was located about fifteen kilometers from Metz and Montigny.

The Fight against Catholics in Germany: Consequences of the Kulturkampf

A tragic fate hung over the German houses, or those that had become German, by virtue of Bismarck's stand against those forces, among them the Catholic Church, which he judged hostile to the unification of Germany under the hegemony of Prussia. "The Combat for Civilization," the fight against the Church in Germany, was based on the May Laws, developed between 1873 and 1875 and completed in 1878. But beginning in 1872, this battle was preceded by the expulsion of the Jesuits and the suppression of congregations judged to be a part of a "black international:" the Holy Ghost Fathers, the Redemptorists and the Vincentians. Only one congregation of women was associated with them, the Society of the Sacred Heart, which was banished from the Reich 20 May 1873.

The charge against it was "Jesuitism," which, "through the Religious of the Sacred Heart infiltrates families; it is they who, by their influence on young people, receive large subsidies for the court of Rome." They were called "Jesuitesses," because of their origin, their way of practicing obedience and their submission to Rome. The result of the education they give "cannot be other than loyalty in all things conforming to the demands of the Company of Jesus, the wasting away of the self, of one's own judgment and will."[82] The fact

---

[81] *Vie de la R.M. Voitot*, p. 61.
[82] *Lettres annuelles*, 1872-1873, p. 73 and following. As a document presented to the federal council of Prussia specified, "with regard to orders of women,

that the motherhouse was established in Paris was not in itself an additional charge. In any case, its establishment in Rome would not have been any more advantageous under the circumstances! When Mother von Sartorius, who was superior at Marienthal, received the notice of the decree of banishment, she said, "If it is on account of devotion and filial submission to the Holy Roman Church and to the Pope, vicar of Jesus Christ, that the Society of the Sacred Heart is banished, Gentlemen, it is our badge of honor."[83]

After the Jesuits were expelled, the Religious of the Sacred Heart anticipated the same step, preceded by many annoyances. The schools were inspected to check whether they were using books edited by Jesuits and whether instruction was in German. The nuns' correspondence was monitored, somewhat ineptly, it seems, since Mother von Sartorius received a letter that had on the torn envelope the following comment: "In spite of all our efforts, we cannot get rid of the mice."[84] She was obliged to send her mail through Holland and Belgium.

All the houses in Germany had to close. Montigny was rented to the Sisters of Charity of Saint Barbara; the one in Posen was sold to a family of friends. Small communities of three or four choir nuns and a few sisters stayed on after some negotiations in Metz, Montigny and Kientzheim. These were elderly or infirm religious for whom returning to France was not possible; they lived in a nearby building. The hundred and eighty who were expelled were sent to Blumenthal, Prague, Lemberg, Conflans or Jette, where their boarding pupils followed them. The orphans of Kientzheim were placed in families or sent to Besançon. These closings had both cultural and economic consequences. The teaching of Polish was forbidden little by little in the region around Posen. The closing of the boarding schools impoverished the regions affected by it.[85]

> those consecrated only to the ascetic life or those whose chief occupation is works of mercy have not been considered, even though ideas borrowed from the Jesuits are not excluded from these orders, but their influence is confined to narrower circles and, consequently, does not pose an imminent danger. But when the instruction and education of young girls is the end of their association, orders of women seem particularly apt to follow the tendencies of the order of the Jesuits: their activity being directed towards persons whose age renders them easily susceptible to harmful influences, and with regard to future family life, it is evident that the state has a notable interest in taking charge of this education."

[83] P. Perdrau, *Les loisirs...*, p. 649.
[84] *Vie de la T.R.M. de Sartorius*, p. 91.
[85] Article of 19 June 1873, excerpt from a German language newspaper. Communicated by Marie-Thérèse Houdoy, RSCJ.

In the annexed provinces banishment was seen as bullying the Catholic minority of the Reich. In Poland the primate, Ledochowski, decided to officially consecrate his dioceses of Posen and Guesen to the Sacred Heart on 8 December 1872.[86] In October 1872, the religious at Kientzheim received from the clergy of Alsace an address that was at once a vigorous protest and an expression of gratitude for the work of the congregation in Alsace:

> Noble ladies, may we be permitted to demonstrate the very poignant sorrow that the decree of suppression of the illustrious house of Kientzheim causes us. Your sad but glorious departure into exile afflicts Catholic Alsace beyond all telling. For thirty-three years the Sacred Heart has been a beacon of virtue, of knowledge and of charity for our province and the adjoining countries; in return, deception, anger, hatred against Christ and his Church escalate their fury to its fullest extent in exiling you like criminals against the State! They make a crime of right, of charity, of fidelity, of religion, and this crime is called "hostile intrigues: *Vaakgafafo!*" We repeat our protest against these assaults and sacrilegious confiscations, and united in attachment to the martyr of the Vatican, to the Company of Jesus and to the Sacred Heart, with love and fidelity for the Church; we defy the efforts of hell. – Noble ladies, at this moment, inexpressible sadness seizes our souls; our hearts are filled with tears at the thought that the hour of separation has come. As Aeneas carried from the ruins of his homeland his dearest treasures, his old father and his forbidden household gods, you carry with you the beautiful example, the knowledge, the tears of the hundreds of orphans and the blessings of weeping Alsace. Please accept, noble ladies, with our respect, our deep sympathy and our homage.[87]

The alumnae of Germany rose up in protest against the exile of the Sacred Heart; those of Great Britain sent their protest to Countess Nesselrode.[88] Mother von Sartorius addressed a letter to the governor of Westphalia in which she wrote: "We are leaving but protesting loudly and solemnly against the law that banishes us, against the manner in which it has been executed in our regard and against the violation of our rights. We are leaving our beloved country where we leave parents, brothers,

---

[86] Condemned for his hostility to Bismarck's policies, deprived of state subsidies that supplemented his income, victim of various confiscations, he was imprisoned, forbidden to celebrate Mass and deposed in February 1874. He had to abandon his see and take refuge in Rome.

[87] *Lettres annuelles*, 1873-1874, pp. 129-130.

[88] *Vie de la T.R.M. de Sartorius*, pp. 104-106 and *Enfants de Marie*, vol. 1, p. 60.

sisters, friends, benefactors; we are leaving without bitterness towards those who impose this hard necessity upon us, but with feelings of deep sorrow."[89] This letter was signed also by the assistant at Marienthal, Mother Elisabeth von Zur-Mehlen. The withdrawal took place calmly and tactfully.[90]

There was a certain falling off in German strictures at the end of the century. Emperor William II took over the Reich and Bismarck resigned, making an end of the *Kulturkampf,* which had gradually fallen into disuse. When the Reichstag authorized expelled religious congregations to take up some of their activities again, Mother Pauline Simons reopened the free school and the workroom at Montigny and accepted some day pupils. In 1895, a German boarding school was permitted, and in October 1904 a class in domestic science was opened. The community composed of Germans and French formed part of the vicariate of Austria. Soon fifteen pupils of French nationality were received at Kientzheim.

The Franco-Prussian War could have had an unfortunate aftermath in the communities.[91] Mother Gœtz asked that communities avoid all references to the events:

> I wish to call to mind a duty that the circulars and admonitions of our venerated Mother mentioned many times in various circumstances: that of excluding from our recreations, our relations with one another and with outsiders anything of a patriotic sentiment that could alter, even from afar, perfect union of minds and hearts; to this end our holy Rule forbids communication of news received from outside, conversations about politics, harmful criticism and unkind allusions to the customs of different nations.[92]

---

[89] *Vie de la T.R.M. de Sartorius,* pp. 108-110.

[90] Some German religious passed through Paris. Mother Gœtz heard the coachmen, who witnessed the warm welcome they received, cry out: "Look what happy people these nuns are. Our government will have to call back the Germans, and we will come back to get them and take them to Germany!"(M. Williams, *The Society of the Sacred Heart…,* p. 57).

[91] The life of Mother Louise du Mont, at the motherhouse during the war of 1870, was not easy, for "in spite of the reserve, discretion and charity that reigned in the community, many actions and accounts could not fail to offend her as a German" (*Lettres annuelles,* 1906-1908, p. 98).

[92] *Circulaires de la T.R.M. Lehon,* 1 October 1872, pp. 130-140. An exception was made for whatever concerned the papacy.

Already in 1870, Mother von Sartorius, who had an Alsatian in her community at Blumenthal, had forbidden mention of the events taking place. It is true that Mother Gœtz' recommendation did not contribute to the development of the political awareness of the religious; but in setting a precedent, she allowed communities to get through wars and political conflicts in the most peaceable way possible.

At the Heart of Political Disturbances in Latin America

The Society of the Sacred Heart had arrived in Latin America only after wars of independence had divided the continent into about twenty countries. Because decolonization had not led immediately to sovereignty, the states born of the dismantling of the Spanish empire were often unstable. In addition, the United States and Europe were greatly interested in the mineral wealth of the Latin American countries.

After the death of Mother Barat, a conflict arose between Chileans and Spaniards, resulting in the blockade of the port of Valparaiso. When the superior of Concepción, Mother McNally, was recalled to Santiago, she could only avoid crossing the Andes thanks to the British consul, who recommended his compatriot to the captain of an English frigate stationed in the harbor of Valparaiso. As a special favor, this captain obtained from the Spanish admiral free passage, and a Spanish gunboat transported the traveler from the Chilean steamship to an English frigate that took her ashore.[93]

Between 1879 and 1883, Chile, Peru and Bolivia clashed over possession of the nitrate mines of Atacama. In 1880, the Chilean fleet blocked Lima. The superior in Lima, Mother Laura Rew, safeguarded her house by flying the British flag. French Vice Admiral Dupetit-Thouars, who was cruising nearby, also looked after the welfare of the Sacred Heart. At the time of the occupation of Lima, in January 1883, San Pedro served as a refuge for three hundred frightened civilians. By the Treaty of Ancón, in 1884, Chile took control of Tacna and Arica in the southern part of Peru.[94] Seventeen years later Mother Stuart reported that feelings were still running high. The Peruvians, who did not want to send their daughters to Santiago, Chile, where the novitiate had been transferred in 1888, begged for the reopening of a novitiate in Lima; they feared that their daughters would not return to Peru and that their dowries would be kept in Chile. "Haven't the Chileans taken enough from us?" was often heard. The war had reinforced

---

[93] *Lettres annuelles*, 1867-1868, p. 176.
[94] The region of Tacna did not revert to Peru until 1929.

a feeling of "superiority" among the Chileans, and Chilean religious did not "offer" to go to live in Peru or refused orders to go there.

After the Pacific war political life in Peru remained chaotic for a long time, and uprisings took place at the time of presidential elections, which set the leaders against one another. In 1885, one election opposed Generals Cacéres and Iglesias, who both had their daughters at the Sacred Heart.[95] Ten years later the Sacred Heart served as a refuge for the family of President Cacéres threatened by the revolution of Pierola and his *Montoneros*. The Religious of the Sacred Heart managed to avoid trouble. Mother de Lavigerie sheltered combatants of both parties under her roof, taking care to keep them from meeting each other. She had the guns that rioters had tossed over the walls buried in the garden, and she had lettuce planted to fool the agents searching for them.[96] During the street fighting between rival factions some soldiers took advantage of the fact that San Pedro appeared unoccupied: they went in and took refuge in the chapel of Our Lady: "Sister Jeanrot entering another chapel saw something moving near the altar: 'Who's there?' she said in a firm voice. '*Madrecita*, don't betray us,' a voice answered. A head appeared, then another, then a third....There were six of them. 'All right,' she said, 'but one does not barge into a convent in that fashion. Follow me.' The superior was in favor of their escape."[97]

After the independence of the Spanish colonies, Cuba was still governed by Madrid. Although Spain had made some liberal reforms in Cuba, they had been weakly applied and did not end the longing for independence so widespread among Cuban exiles as well as those who had remained at home. Southern planters in the United States, who hoped to expand their interests in the Caribbean, tried to persuade the federal government to buy the island.

Supported by the United States, which adhered to the Monroe Doctrine's "America for the Americans," a first war of independence was led at the end of 1869 by slaves demanding the abolition of slavery and by whites protesting a regime that inhibited equal recognition of European and American Hispanics. Slavery was abolished in 1870, but with no real reform, the rebels continued to call for independence. The war started again in 1875 and ended with the Peace of Zanjon; but twenty years later, the skirmish turned into a serious insurrection. Spanish troops rounded up the rural population in "reconcentration" camps. Sacred Heart alumnae attended to these internees, among whom were many women and children

---

[95] *Vie de la R.M. de Lavigerie*, p. 102. The house in Lima was then protected by Spain, as the superior was a Spanish national.
[96] *Vie...Lavigerie*, pp. 224-225.
[97] M. Recavarren, *Raices...*, p. 28. Excerpt from the house journal.

without resources. While a decree of independence was being drawn up, the United States intervened, offering at first to buy Cuba, then mounting an army against the atrocities committed by the troops of General Weyler. The situation degenerated into the Spanish-American War in April 1898, after the blowing up of the battleship *Maine* in Havana harbor.

The bombardment of Havana harmed no one in the house in the Cerro section where some lay people and the nuns of Tejadillo took refuge. The religious, who had proposed but failed to open a field hospital, did not have the supplies to help their neighbors:

> Our school children have touched us by their eagerness in coming to us, even though we no longer have a crust of bread to give them. The sacks of rice and beans brought by ladies for the poor seem to multiply. We have never been without the embrace of holy poverty or spiritual help.[98]

The religious had to be content with canned food and dried cod. American naval vessels also bombarded Puerto Rico. Between April and September 1898, Santurce sheltered local people. Faced with the growing conflict between the American navy and the island's Spanish troops, the religious ended up renting a house at Arecibo, which proved to be no safer than Santurce. With great hardship they returned to Santurce, spending two nights and a day crossing only about fifty kilometers of rutted roads.

By the Treaty of Paris, signed 10 December 1898, Spain ceded to the United States the Philippines, Guam and Puerto Rico for twenty million dollars and recognized the independence of Cuba. Soon, apostolic activities in Havana began again. However, Puerto Rico's becoming a protectorate of the United States meant that the Religious of the Sacred Heart had to give up their house, which they did not own, and which the Americans reclaimed, interrupting their work. They rented a property in San Juan for a community and a day school, and they established a boarding school at the beginning of the twentieth century. The aftermath of the Spanish-American War interrupted communications with Central America for a long time. In 1901, Mother Stuart had a great deal of trouble getting to Cuba from Puerto Rico. Her trip from Cuba to Panama was no easier: she had to return to New York in order to reach Colon![99] Puerto Rico was part of

---

[98] *Mémoires de la R.M. Tommasini*, p. 457.
[99] Maud Monahan, *Life and letters...*, Letter from Havana, 5 April 1901: "It seems simple enough looking at the map and sitting reflectively in the Old World to say, 'How absurd to go to New York! I should certainly not do so'– but when you have to work the matter in practice from the West Indies, and that since the war, it is a very different thing" (p. 131).

the vicariate of New York between 1904 and 1908 and thus entered a new cultural domain.[100]

In the history of Spain, 1898 marked a year of disaster. The humiliation of defeat, the loss of prestige from the demise of a colonial empire on which, since the reign of Charles V, the sun had never set, led to an anti-militarism that appeared when Spain tried to gain holdings in Africa. In 1909 at the news of incidents at Melilla, the government sent troops to Morocco. Supported by the Socialists calling for a demonstration, the soldiers mutinied. In Barcelona, the violent rioting that began 26 July was accompanied by a flare-up of anti-clericalism, for which churches, convents and schools run by religious paid the price. The Religious of the Sacred Heart had to seek shelter in the homes of friendly families and take refuge at Sarriá. The uprising was crushed by the army during the "tragic week."[101]

The history of the Society of the Sacred Heart mirrors history in general, because the congregation, already spread widely throughout the world, inevitably felt its repercussions. The religious experienced events that threatened their physical or mental health. But they were not simply spectators of conditions that sometimes went unrepresented in the house accounts. They had to carry out their apostolic mission in the real geopolitical environment where they lived. During earthquakes, during battles sometimes next door, they had to care for the children entrusted to them. They gave proof of a courage asked for in prayer and practiced with integrity when an emergency required. Fortunately, the upheavals, however many, were not the common currency, and many communities were able to live quietly and in peace.

---

[100] The United States granted American citizenship in 1917 to the inhabitants of the island. Puerto Rico was part of the vicariate of Havana from 1908 to 1961.

[101] The vicariate of the North of Spain aided in the reconstruction of the convents and the renovations of damaged churches (*Vie de la T.R.M. Vicente*, pp. 69-70).

Chapter IV

Passion for the Education of Youth

After 1865 the Society of the Sacred Heart gathered the fruits of its experience in educating girls. Its founder never planned to compete with congregations with the same mission; but education at the Sacred Heart had a character that drew a wide public. Did social standing have an effect? Without a doubt. Its attraction among the political and social elite had made convents of the Sacred Heart "convents *à la mode*." Caricaturists of the July Monarchy satirized the Rue de Varenne. In France, however, not all students were the daughters of aristocrats; the free schools educated two to five times as many children as the boarding schools. Even though education at the Sacred Heart was founded on tradition, it did not cultivate a ghetto mentality.

The Educational Principles of the Society of the Sacred Heart

The Sacred Heart owed its success to the practice of educational standards that Madeleine Sophie Barat had maintained against contemporary currents that had sometimes been adopted by other religious congregations. Her principles were all directed to one end: to win young people to the Heart of Jesus.

Uniform Teaching

From 1820 on Mother Barat had judged that uniformity was necessary. Therefore, she insisted that the Plan of Studies and the School Rule be followed in every house. In the original Plan each class was entrusted to a single teacher who dealt with the whole curriculum. This arrangement reflected a point of view quite common in France and in most Latin countries. Anglo-Saxon countries, on the other hand, preferred organization

Monique Luirard

by courses in the belief that specialization developed extended knowledge of general culture. No doubt this preference was one of the reasons the congregation developed slowly in England. Not only did the Convent of the Sacred Heart appear to be a French establishment, its pedagogy ran up against local customs. The continual monitoring of children seemed to run counter to free personal development. British nuns, who wanted to make changes in order to bring practice at the Sacred Heart closer to national traditions, ended up admitting, with Mother Henrietta Kerr, that "the devil is as busy in England as he was in the earthly paradise to bring to naught the work of God in souls."[1] Mother Barat had conceived her educational system not through pessimism, but rather through reality and a strong and watchful love for the child. The Religious of the Sacred Heart were to give to those confided to them the means of taking to heart the guidelines necessary to social life and to the best development of their gifts.

Education at the Sacred Heart did not vary: the students followed the same program worldwide. Catholics attended daily Mass. There was a procession every first Friday of the month. For liturgical celebrations, students sang in the choirs. The mistress general spoke to them frequently about the intellectual, moral or spiritual aspects of their life. Each week at an assembly presided over by the superior the students received the results of their class work as well as reports concerning their conduct. They were given various colored cards with a range of "notes:" from "*très bien*" (very good) to "*assez bien*" (pretty good), but only the "*très bien*" was really considered satisfactory! "*Bien*" represented some blemish on the record, and "*assez bien*" meant that the child had committed a deplorable misdemeanor. The presentation of the last named card was sometimes accompanied by the comment "She knows why!" Thus the fault did not have to be identified before the assembled student body.[2] Ribbons of Merit were distributed to the students two or three times a year: blue for the higher classes, green for the middle school and pink for the little ones. Blue ribbons were awarded by vote of the student body, "ratified by the votes of the religious." *Congés*, held at the discretion of the superior and the mistress general, provided for a whole day of recreation.[3] Festive celebrations took place on the feasts of the superior and the mistress general and on the eighth of December, when the lily procession was held. The month of Mary was especially honored. In Nova Scotia, on account of the first settlers or the later immigrant

[1] *Religieuses du Sacré-Cœur*, vol. 3, p. 87.
[2] "It was such a disgrace to have an *assez bien* that [in some houses] the card was not handed to the student! It was placed on a table and the one who received it had to pick it up. It was difficult grasp it gracefully, as the students were wearing gloves during the assembly" (Account of Joan Stephenson).
[3] The day the fiftieth or hundredth pupil enrolled was especially celebrated.

population, the birthdays of the sovereigns and the feast of Saint Patrick were celebrated. Even though all the schools operated by the same rules, the founder of the Sacred Heart allowed for the use of the language of the country in teaching. The practice of bilingualism or even multilingualism little by little became general in European and American boarding schools. Ultimately, the routine calendar of school life depended on the local climate.

Education Based on Solid Studies.

Mother Barat was an educated woman, and she was very much concerned about maintaining the level of the teaching offered at the Sacred Heart. Aware of the capriciousness of fashions, she wanted the studies to be strong and solid. At stake were the reputation of the Society's service in the Church and the very existence of the congregation, for it was not the only one educating young women of the upper classes. In France some pre-revolutionary congregations were being reestablished. New institutes were appearing, based on different premises but all equally attractive to the public. Courses and lessons given by lay teachers were many and flourishing.[4] Any deviation from the Plan of Studies had to be avoided, for the curriculum of the Sacred Heart was unique to it. "If we grow weak in the science of teaching, we will provide weapons to be used against us," Mother Barat admitted.[5]

Advice and counsel to the religious to become not only holy but learned,[6] creation of the position of mistress general of studies to supervise the teaching in schools of the Sacred Heart: these had been set in motion to maintain the level of instruction. Very early Mother Barat envisaged a reform of the studies brought about by the evolution of French politics. In 1851, at the time of the struggles that had set Catholics against liberals on the subject of freedom of teaching, Mother Gœtz followed the parliamentary debates in order to learn about the university requirements.

---

[4] It was only in 1867 that Victor Duruy, minister of public instruction, created the first public secondary schools for girls.

[5] *Circulaires de la T.R.M. Barat, 1ère partie*, 29 December 1845, p. 126.

[6] *Lettres choisies aux Mères en charge*, p. 68. Mother Barat had written, from Rome, 12 February 1833, to Aimée d'Avenas, the young mistress general at the Rue de Varenne: "If you knew how much the Society needs holy scholars (*saintes savantes*), you would hasten to become one. Here in the Roman novitiate we have a certain number of the first (*saintes*) but of the second (*savantes*) not one. It is good to lay down solid foundations; nevertheless the union of the two: virtue and instruction would give perfection to the work. Thus link the two and you will fulfill the whole extent of your vocation."

In 1864, Mother Anna du Rousier had confirmed Mother Gœtz in her hope for renewal by offering observations she had made in America. She showed her that if she wished to raise the level of the teachers, she had to raise that of the boarding schools, since they were the source of vocations. In one of her last circular letters, Mother Barat came back to this point, owing to the competition between religious and secular schools:

> Education is no longer what it was some years ago; the profusion of institutions that make major concessions to the mindset of our century makes us seem outdated. Please God that we do not wish to compromise our responsibilities and sacrifice our principal goals to these attitudes, but we must reexamine where we can adapt and review our plan of studies.[7]

After her election, Mother Gœtz saw that the teaching at the Sacred Heart was no longer following its initial objectives, and she blamed, as had Mother Barat before her, the weakness of elementary teaching, recalling that its goal was "to maintain in teaching the strength and high quality that matched current needs, by giving the young persons brought up in our schools, along with the valuable lessons of faith, duty, and solid virtue, all the knowledge that they have the right to expect of our diligence in order to receive a strong, full and quality education." But while the teaching needed improvement, its strengthening ought never to come from "personal initiative in one or another house, our activity must hold to a consistent uniformity; if some improvements are seen as necessary, they may be proposed and, after mature examination, may be adopted for all the schools, a measure which, marked by the very seal of authority, will receive a special blessing from God."[8]

Before undertaking a reform, Mother Gœtz took the advice of Father Olivaint, who had left the University for the Society of Jesus, and of Bishop Dupanloup, who was considered the most competent specialist in the field of women's education. Mother Gœtz wanted to introduce the teaching of philosophy in order to steady the students in their faith. In September 1866, she announced the nomination of a new mistress general of studies and a nine-member commission of studies, who would have the task of reviewing the Plan of Studies, dividing the material by year, reorganizing a six-year curriculum, choosing textbooks and eliminating those[9] hostile to religion or to the Society of the Sacred Heart. For the first time, the Society, while

---

[7] *Circulaires de la T.R.M. Barat, 1ère partie*, 10 March 1864, p. 198.
[8] *Circulaires de la T.R.M. Gœtz*, 19 April 1869, p. 95.
[9] The target was the manuals of Larousse.

keeping some older course manuals, adopted textbooks that had not been composed specially for it.

The goal of the new Plan of Studies was to add to the curriculum the rudiments of philosophy and logic in order to "strengthen the reason and character of young persons by basing their faith on solid principles derived from rigorous proofs from logic and a sound philosophy."[10] The plan was to introduce the students of the three higher classes to these subjects. Mother Gœtz decided also to introduce the teaching of natural science that had for its purpose to "arrive at solid, useful and practical applications, while avoiding whatever could lead to pedantry and inspire vain pretensions."[11] They had to instruct the girls without frightening the families! Finally, she recalled that the lessons in the *arts d'agrément* and in foreign languages would be entrusted to lay persons; some religious, without these aptitudes or the opportunity to acquire them, risked giving incomplete instruction or using outdated methods, thus penalizing the students.[12] Her decision flowed from her real respect for the children and for the quality of their entire education.

Mother Gœtz also revamped the training of the young religious. The "juniorate" that she created for them had as its aim to develop their talents, to bring them the "light of understanding, strength of will, and wise direction of their sensibilities by cultivating the beautiful."[13] While in the past in the Society, apprenticeship in teaching took place "on the job" by osmosis, thanks to the transmission of experience from the older teachers to the new ones, the juniorate was to be a center of professional formation and of initiation into active life.

The elementary juniorate was opened at Conflans on 29 September 1866, with eight participants, entrusted for six months to the mistress general of studies, Mother Anne-Marie Martin. Mother Gœtz sought to arrange for the "juniors" the best possible conditions for study, giving them separate quarters and a dormitory, seeing to the tables and chairs and windows of their study hall herself.[14] She wanted to develop their capacity for reflection. In 1874, oral lessons, delivered by the teachers rather

---

[10] *Circulaires de la T.R.M. Gœtz*, 19 April 1869, p. 101.
[11] *Circulaires de la T.R.M. Gœtz*, p. 102.
[12] *Circulaires de la T.R.M. Gœtz*, pp. 56-57.
[13] Gen. Arch. C I C 3, Box 9, General Congregation, 1874.
[14] *Vie de la Mère Fornier*, p. 103. The juniors formed "a little family," completely separate from the community. The superior gave them a commentary on the Rule twice a week. They edited a little magazine, *L'Echo de la vérité (The Echo of Truth)*, containing some of their papers, which they sent to the superior general.

than textbooks, came in for high praise, just as Mother Gœtz had always believed.

The war of 1870, then the death of the superior general, delayed the creation of the upper level juniorate, which was opened at the motherhouse in 1876. The juniorate followed the period of aspirantship and gave participants an opportunity to go back over the experiences of the preceding years. At the beginning the courses were held only in Paris. The juniors spent six months at the *Maison des Anges*, on the Boulevard des Invalides, where they received theoretical formation. They were initiated into educational theory through a series of lectures on pedagogy; they learned to prepare class plans and took elocution lessons. Then during an in-service period, they taught classes at the Rue de Varenne. The superior juniorate, which brought together French-speaking religious from different vicariates, allowed for intermingling, somewhat like that during probation. In 1884, the general congregation decided to create an upper level juniorate in the United States.[15] Following that, others were begun elsewhere.

To bear fruit, the superior juniorate required excellent educators and regular re-examination of their methods. In 1894, the vicars objected that the training was more theoretical than practical. They were aware that other congregations were more advanced in teacher training and that public normal schools offered two years of pedagogical preparation. Many young religious were skipping the juniorate because their superiors wanted to put them to work immediately or did not want to send them to study for fear of upsetting the running of the school. Mother von Sartorius carried out a reform in 1895; to standardize the formation, she decided to bring together both the elementary and superior juniorates at Conflans. However, it was Mother Digby who transformed the training; she organized the superior juniorate by semesters, following the pattern of the probations. The study of scholastic philosophy, given a place of honor by Leo XIII, had pride of place in the program. Mother Digby sought also to advance the juniors in teaching science by giving them good equipment: a telescope, the latest instruments for teaching physics, complete collections of minerals, as classified by a renowned geologist, Lapparent. His confrere at the *Institut catholique de Paris*, Abbé Debus, taught them algebra, physics and chemistry. Highly educated Religious of the Sacred Heart, like Mothers Durand and Nerincx, played an important role in running the juniorate.

In the juniorate, young religious received help in leading their apostolic life. Mother Fornier, who was responsible for it in the 1880's, used to say to them:

---

[15] Gen. Arch. C I C 3, Box 9.

> Don't imagine that you can make of your interior life and your employments two distinct things; No, the occupations that fill your day could never be an obstacle to your union with God; to think that way would be to understand nothing about the life of a Religious of the Sacred Heart. Never go to the children without having spoken to Jesus about them.[16]

Practical advice came from women who had spent a large part of their lives in schools:

> Don't flatter yourself too quickly that you know the children. Two months of vacation are enough to change them completely. But above all do not try to treat them all alike; that would result in failure. Do not favor the gifted ones on the pretext of maintaining a superior level of studies. On the contrary, help the weaker students, encourage them so they do not feel passed over but rather included as part of the family.... A teacher who is late answers to God, not only for making the children impatient, but for the loss of all positive effects of her being at her post.[17]

The program included common sense that the nuns adapted according to the country to which they were sent.

The community was itself an excellent means of formation. Young religious found there a place to apply the theory they learned to the real-life situations they met. The superiors and the mistresses general, who acted like tutors for the teachers, had the responsibility to integrate the youngest and to help them learn to teach. One anecdote about an American will suffice. Sarah Randall was sent to Eden Hall, where she had been a boarder, to give a course in the upper school: "Before long her worst fear was realized: a student asked a question about botany, which she could not answer." Cleverly, she postponed answering, but after class, she went to her superior, Mother Tucker, and admitted her shortcoming.

> She listened to a complete explanation of the material in question given in a motherly way by her superior who, afterwards, handed her a very rare flower with a complete description of its species and all of its parts. "Tomorrow at class," she said, "show this flower to the children, analyze it; then turn as if by chance to the child who asked the question today;

---

[16] *Vie de la Mère Fornier*, p. 103.
[17] *Vie de la Mère Fornier*, pp. 104-105.

give her the promised answer." The obedient religious carried out the plan so skillfully that her reputation for expertise was secure from then on.[18]

The superiors general who succeeded Mother Gœtz weighed educational practices. "We are giving too many medallions, ribbons, *très bien* and even admissions to the sodalities," wrote Mother Lehon. "These means, valuable for urging our children to work at correcting their faults, and which our first Mothers used with such wise reserve, are losing their worth in large part because they are so freely given; it lowers the level of good behavior in the boarding school."[19] Recognizing and encouraging merit had to balance the prestige of the rewards: "Do not overuse the superlative, which applies only to sustained regularity, politeness and hard work." Pedagogy was to have the highest priority.

> Let us try to establish faith, the fear of God, in souls, and let us minimize the number of surveillantes; let us not settle for external discipline, for our children will shake off its yoke unless they take it to heart, for only real fervor can make them love it. Devotion to the Sacred Heart of Jesus, cultivated by fervent mistresses, themselves filled with his love, will enter these young plants little by little and allow the sap of life to flow there.[20]

Another subject of concern was the length of vacations, about which "reasonable parents" were complaining.[21] In 1881, it was decided that vacation was to be limited to two months, and in 1884, that it could be shortened.[22] Finally, the development of further courses for students who had finished their education was foreseen,[23] a plan that took shape later. At the time, the Society of the Sacred Heart had to modify its course of study in order to comply with new state requirements.

Glorify the Heart of Jesus through Education

While revamping the Plan of Studies had been a necessary step, even more important was the preservation of its core: instruction at the Sacred Heart was at the service of education. Because their work aimed at glorifying the Heart of Jesus, the religious made a fourth vow of education of youth. Education of the whole person was primary; academic courses supported

---

[18] *Lettres annuelles,* 1906-1908, p. 77. The anecdote relates to the beginning of the 1870's.
[19] *Circulaires de la T.R.M. Lehon,* 12 October 1876, p. 45.
[20] *Circulaires de la T.R.M. Lehon,* 12 October 1876, p. 47.
[21] *Circulaires de la T.R.M. Lehon,* 25 May 1881, p. 89.
[22] *Circulaires de la T.R.M. Lehon,* 7 April 1884, p.115.
[23] *Circulaires de la T.R.M. Lehon,* p. 117.

it. For this reason Mother Barat had tried to keep her congregation independent of the state. For her it was a matter of conscience that she had to obey, because she believed that the Society of the Sacred Heart held its mandate to teach from God and the Church, then from the families who confided their children to it. To allow the state to inspect her schools would have forced the Sacred Heart to adopt methods and principles at odds with theirs. The Falloux Law of 15 March 1850 had reassured her, since it accorded religious congregations full liberty in their teaching; and the religious had only to produce a letter of obedience from their superior to be able to teach, without having to be examined on their qualifications.

Nonetheless, as educational practices evolved, Mother Barat allowed modifications to her policies in countries where she hoped to found schools. She went along with inspection in Galicia and in the Veneto, because in Austria the imperial power controlled the Church. In Prussian Poland and in the Netherlands the religious took state examinations. But when in 1855 Piedmont administrators proposed to inspect the school at Chambéry, Mother Barat closed the boarding school;[24] she certainly had no illusions about a government that had expelled the Society of the Sacred Heart from the North of Italy. At about the same time, urged to make a foundation in Madrid, she made dispensation from inspection a condition of the congregation's approval. Spain's recognition of the Sacred Heart, however, did not afford complete liberty for the institute; the royal decree of Isabella II authorized its establishment in overseas provinces provided that, although in Cuba the religious did not need diplomas, they were to teach literature, geography and history from Spanish texts and employ teachers who were Spanish, whether men or women.[25] Mother Barat's position was not intransigent. The founder knew how to adapt to circumstances, and her policy was in line with that of the Holy See as relayed by local bishops. In 1859, in France she had agreed to state inspection of the free schools.

In the second half of the nineteenth century, governments became more interested than formerly in the education of youth. Liberal regimes, anxious to fight against clerical influence, either created competing institutions or tried to exercise control over the schools of religious congregations by taking charge of curricula and the training of teachers.

In Rome, after 1870, the Sacred Heart had to conform to Italian legislation. Programs had to be uniform, and at the Trinità dei Monti they had to be in Italian, even though French continued to be taught there. The

---

[24] She had maintained the school for deaf mutes and financed it through the Society and its benefactors.
[25] *Bulletin des Archives*, 9 February 2002, N° 23, pp. 10 and 11.

religious had to pass qualifying examinations. The pope, who feared that Catholic schools would disappear, had recommended to religious orders "to make all the sacrifices necessary to preserve for children the benefit of Christian education."[26] Municipal schools established in Rome by the new authorities did not offer competition to the Trinità and Santa Rufina. These houses even had to add new classes. The increase of numbers in the day schools was due not only to new children from middle class families, but also to working class families who sent their children there.

> It is a source of consolation for our Mothers to hear working class parents and their children express with their southern vehemence their love for the pope and their indignation at all the harm done to the Church by its enemies. A poor laundress, wife of a doorman, brought her daughter to the school: "Listen, Mother," she said, "I am bringing you my child; I dare say I was curious enough to go to see one of those city schools: my God, what characters I saw there! So I said to myself: 'And I, shall I put my daughter in their care? Not even if the eternal Father came to tell me to do so!' So, here she is!"[27]

In Austria, the reform of 1867 gave a certain cultural autonomy to nationalities included in the empire and introduced the study of the national language into the schools. The Sacred Heart created a program for teaching Polish in Galicia, where its plan of studies was accepted.[28] The house in Prague, which had been opened to accommodate Polish boarders, offered teaching in German in response to government requirements. At the end of the century, its free school, which enrolled mostly children of Polish workmen, was closed because it was required to teach in both German and Czech.[29] Education in Czech was in any case difficult to carry out because there were very few religious able to teach in that language. No doubt that was one of the reasons that the house in Prague did not flourish with the local townspeople[30] and that it had hardly any children in its Sunday school

---

[26] *Lettres annuelles*, 1872-1873, p. 27.
[27] *Lettres annuelles*, 1870-1871, p. 41.
[28] Alina Merdas, *La Société du Sacré-Cœur en Pologne*, pp.12-13. Polish was systematically taught in the schools.
[29] Merdas, p. 16.
[30] Arch. Gén. C IV 1) Prague. On the occasion of the first regular visit of the vicar, Mother von Gagern, in 1889, it was noted that the government required German in the classes, while the families of the boarders wanted the classes in Polish, and the Czechs were astonished that the teaching of their language was not adequately provided for.

and its free school.[31] The Sacred Heart did not receive accreditation of its fee-paying day school, where teaching would have been in German; and it found it hard to prepare religious who could obtain the necessary Czech diplomas.

After 16 May 1877 and the consolidation of the Republic in France, school policy was rapidly secularized. In her circulars Mother Lehon did not allude to the Camille Sée law, which, in 1880, had created secondary instruction for girls of the middle classes, or to the laws of Jules Ferry which, in 1881 and 1882, made primary instruction free, secular and obligatory. She limited herself, on 25 May 1881, to noting the state's attacks on the teaching congregations, adding: "Let us not fear to hunt down all the points that need correction or improvement in our education."[32] Neither did she evoke the law of Paul Bert-Goblet, which in 1886 secularized the personnel of the public primary schools. It is true that the Sacred Heart had only one public school, the one in Beauvais. When the Society had to give it up, it opened a free school in the city, allowing it to educate the same group of children. The Society's status as an authorized congregation left it immune from the attacks of legislation aimed chiefly at unrecognized institutes. But in the face of the secularizing legislation being planned, Mother Lehon had the religious undergo the required inspections and agreed to prepare the students who so desired for public examinations.[33] The new legislation made the professional training diploma (*brevet de capacité*) obligatory for all teachers and suppressed the equivalent qualifications allowed by the Falloux law. The situation in France was getting close to that of other European countries where religious had been required for a long time to undergo tests of their expertise. On the other hand, the preparation of students for public examinations was not much encouraged, for families of the social class from which the boarders were recruited were not in favor of it, likening a "young lady with a diploma" to a school mistress or even a pedant. Therefore, the examination classes were not offered universally.[34]

The "war against religious education" in France can be tracked, thanks to the circular letters of Mother Lehon. In 1883, she denounced "the galling nitpicking that is always on the increase." She had to admit inspectors to the boarding schools: "Resistance is becoming impossible and would put us in danger of having to close our boarding schools. I believe, therefore, that yielding to the storm we must simply put up bravely with the dreaded inspection." But she wrote, "It is extremely important to introduce [to the inspectors] as class

---

[31] In 1916, the vicar, Mother von Waldstein, notes also that the poor school has little success because there are other religious schools in Prague.
[32] *Circulaires de la T.R.M. Lehon*, p. 88.
[33] *Circulaires de la T.R.M. Lehon*, p. 116, Advice for Superiors, 7 April 1884.
[34] *Circulaires de la T.R.M. Lehon*, p. 116.

mistresses only teachers with diplomas or those dispensed by the law of 16 June 1881, who have been named on earlier lists. To accomplish this, some houses will have to have several classes recite for the same mistress; each section will be considered a division of the one class. The children will be rehearsed in advance so that they do not appear surprised."[35] Most of the schools did not meet the norm, since the Society of the Sacred Heart employed religious who were not qualified and were thus subverting the law.

The problem of the textbooks required for preparation for examinations remained. Should the official works of doubtful content be used? Mother Lehon settled it in 1884:

> University requirements, preparation for public examinations, have adopted some books outside our plan, and foreign to our spirit; a detailed list of all the works that we believe appropriate will be sent along with their evaluations. Our Mothers will understand that for us it is a sacred obligation to determine just how far we may go in the way of concessions, and where it is appropriate to stop.[36]

She recalled three months later that "once the books needed for the examinations are no longer necessary, even the least harmful for teachers or students, must be removed. As to books on the Index, we will never use them without having asked express permission of ecclesiastical authority."[37]

The question of the manuals came up again in connection with the study of philosophy, which was being introduced in the novitiates because it was "recognized by the highest authorities as a serious preparation for the work of the spiritual life."[38] In 1884, it was expected that Father Jaffre's text would be abandoned as it contained "gaps and explanations possibly dangerous for the children," and it made a distinction between catechism and apologetics. The Vatican had condemned it. Because "light comes from Rome and it will always be our joy to follow it,"[39] Mother von Sartorius adopted the manual of Abbé Gouin, and the teaching of Thomism began at the Sacred Heart. Did this innovation have repercussions on the standing of the course of studies? It is hardly possible to evaluate that level in France. According to the witness provided by Mrs. Miller, a Protestant American whose daughter was placed at Marmoutier at the beginning of the twentieth century: "At the Sacred Heart, French grammar, history and

---

[35] *Circulaires de la T.R.M. Lehon*, pp. 96-98, 18 January 1883.
[36] *Circulaires de la T.R.M. Lehon*, pp. 106-107, 1 January 1884.
[37] *Circulaires de la T.R.M. Lehon*, p. 117, 7 April 1884.
[38] *Circulaire de la T.R.M. de Sartorius*, 19 August 1894.
[39] *Circulaire de la T.R.M. de Sartorius*, 29 January 1895.

geography of France, that of the Holy Land, and sewing were all well taught, but the children learned only a few ideas about the sciences. It is difficult to teach astronomy or geology when one believes literally the content of the first book of Genesis."[40] But she goes into rapture over the excellence of the education given to the pupils. Nothing suggests that the level of the studies in other French private schools for girls, whether religious or secular, was any better.

In North America, developments resulted from historical circumstances. In Nova Scotia the Halifax Free School Act, passed in 1864 under the influence of Sir Charles Tupper and Bishop Connolly, absorbed the free schools into the public system.[41] But the presence of religious, with their required teaching certificates, made the schools officially Catholic. In the United States, after the Civil War, the Society of the Sacred Heart benefitted from the closing of many religious or secular schools. Resentful of the Northern side in the war, English-speaking families had stopped sending their daughters north. The boarding schools then recruited more Protestants, who made up a third of the enrollment at St. Michael's in the 1870's.[42] It is true that the war they had waged in common had in the South drawn Protestants and Catholics together.

An important change was the implementation of racial equality in the schools. The bishops of Louisiana thought that only religious congregations were capable of taking charge of the religious and personal education of the African Americans. After the Council of Baltimore, in the course of which the American episcopate had decided to open schools for them, Archbishop Odin of New Orleans asked the Sacred Heart for its collaboration because he thought the reputation of the congregation was such that it could take charge of the schools without causing too much stir in Southern society.[43] A trial was prudently carried out at St. Michael's in 1867. "We have opened a school for little Negro girls, but to respect the sensibilities of our people of the South, we have judged it apropos to name as director a Mulatto woman well known for her irreproachable character and devotion."[44] In 1868, a choir nun, aided by coadjutrix sisters, took charge of the school, where the children learned catechism and reading. Other religious were sent to St. Michael's little by little, and a similar school was opened at Grand Coteau. The hostility of the white population toward these new schools was not overt, no doubt on account of

---

[40] Prov. Arch. France, signed by Emily A. Miller.
[41] The teachers were paid by the government, and the College Street building was rented to the religious.
[42] *Lettres annuelles*, 1867-1868, p. 169.
[43] L. Callan, *The Society of the Sacred Heart*, pp. 539-542.
[44] *Lettres annuelles*, 1867-1868. Before the war the nuns had instructed the children of their slaves.

Mother Shannon's tact. On the other hand, at Natchitoches, only religious instruction for black children was tolerated. When at the beginning of 1868, a mixed race child was admitted to the day school in New Orleans, it was deemed necessary, as a result of anonymous letters, to send the child away to put an end to the trouble. Her father, a state senator, sued the Society, but Mother Shannon won the case.[45] Schools open to persons of color developed gradually in later years. Schools of the Sacred Heart accepted children of Native American origin in the United States as well as in Canada and Chile.

Personalized Education

An education aimed at a socially privileged population was an advantage for which the Sacred Heart was known. As Mother Barat explained it at the beginning,

> The upper classes were completely neglected; it was for them that the Society was established. The first members of the Society had put aside their attraction for the contemplative life of Carmel in order to serve children who were destined for significant positions in life and needed solid Christian instruction and a firm faith to support them amid the dangers that awaited them.[46]

Because of the good results of this orientation towards the ruling classes, Mother Barat wanted the Society to excel in it.[47] It was for this very reason – to secure a polished education for the daughters of the nobility of the Papal States – that Pope Leo XII had called the Society of the Sacred Heart to Rome.[48]

We have little reliable information on the percentage of girls from the aristocracy in the boarding schools. In Toulouse, 38% of the pupils between 1864 and 1904 had names indicating nobility. It is hard to know whether

---

[45] *Vie de la Mère Shannon*, p. 170.

[46] *Journal de la maison d'Amiens*, 17 October 1843.

[47] *Lettres choisies*, p. 131, 12 February 1856: "Ordinarily we succeed with this upper class, and we must stay with it all the more as the education of the other classes finds a thousand resources in a number of religious congregations that have as their end precisely that kind of education."

[48] The boarding school at the Trinità dei Monti was not reserved for the local nobility. Its first pupil was a young English girl; it was international from the start, recruiting the children of diplomats accredited to Rome and foreigners residing there. The situation was the same in schools in other capital cities.

that proportion was unique to that city,[49] for if the Sacred Heart had recruited only among the nobility, it could hardly have continued its work. It drew from families faithful to the Church. The families of the boarders had to have good reputations as well as social position, as did the middle class families. However, even if the pupils came from a homogeneous social milieu, it did not follow that the families were of the same political persuasion. In the boarding schools children came from countries where civil war was raging; the religious had to be careful to avoid confrontations or hurtful words.

Education was understood as formation passing from one person to another; each of the pupils was to be cared for as if she were the only one. Application of this principle provided respect across the social divide. In Rome, after 1860, three daughters of the king of the Two Sicilies, who had taken refuge in the Papal States, entered the Trinità dei Monti. Although day students, they had an apartment to themselves; their meals were served in a separate dining room, and a young religious was assigned to them. The Spanish *infantas*, pupils at Montigny and in Paris, the children of royal families of Belgium and Central Europe boarding in Brussels, all received the same treatment. We can assume that the other boarders were encouraged "to treat them with the deference due to their rank."[50]

Regard for individualized education allowed admission to the "junior school" of children whose age and circumstances had to be given special consideration. At the Trinità dei Monti, in 1873, a little girl three years old grew so fond of Mother Lehon during one of her visits that she did not want to leave her; she spent most of her time playing in her room and ran to her arms as soon as she caught sight of her. At Marmoutier and at Roehampton, Mother Digby accepted very young orphans.[51] The Sacred Heart also accepted children whose mothers, awhirl in social life, did not pay attention to their education. Mother Barat complained of these women whom "Holy Scripture compares to ostriches who abandon their eggs on the sand to the sun's rays."[52]

---

[49] Germaine Bourgade, *Contribution à l'étude d'une histoire de l'éducation féminine*, p. 145.

[50] *Vie de la R.M. de Pichon*, p. 61.

[51] *Vie de la T.R.M. Digby*, pp. 189-190. At Marmoutier, some of the youngest used to play in her office while she worked or conferred with the religious. A four-year old had permission to call her "Aunt Digby." Once when the child was sick, Mother Digby placed her bed near her own room. At Roehampton, she accepted some children whose mother had just died in St. Petersburg. A maid took care of the youngest, who was nine months old.

[52] P. Perdrau, *Les loisirs...*, vol. 1, p. 292.

More widely, the application of this principle led to close monitoring of those students, "neither good nor bad," who were at risk of going unnoticed in the group. Because every child is unique in the mind of God, Religious of the Sacred Heart were to give each one the same attention, especially those of limited ability. Mother Barat had often asked the religious to look out for the most vulnerable children, for she wrote: "Good spirit is to put aside one's own talent in order not to crush those with less."[53] This same idea led Mother Asunción Olivella, mistress general at Bilbao, to say that it "would be a great injustice to treat all souls alike, instead – thanks to close study of each one's character – one should imitate God who adapts the care of his Providence to their infinite diversity."[54] Therefore, the Plan of Studies provided for supplementary classes for "young persons whose weak intelligence or simply poor memory render them incapable of following the course of study in its entirety; for others whose primary education has been neglected, whose delicate health or some other cause has resulted in their being behind the other students of the same age" or foreigners "who, though well instructed in other ways, do not know the language well enough to follow the class." "In all these cases the mistress should make the effort to have them study not much but well, and to prepare them to enter the right classes as soon as possible."[55]

To give each child the attention and care needed, the classes had to be small. The religious were to be guardians, as it were, of the children, to have a motherly love for them, to be devoted and hard-working. "Four things attract my attention when I visit a school," said Mother Digby, "the backs, the teeth, the nails and the shoes; if all those are cared for, I know the children are being properly followed up." But above all the religious were to be indulgent when necessary, and always show the children a deep respect that translated into the tact with which they kept their confidences, the attention they paid to their physical well-being, their patience in not trying to hurry a child's adjustment and their concern to develop their judgment. They were to give special care to the "difficult cases," to seek to understand the reasons for their strange behavior and to try gradually to help them grow.

A work of faith, education at the Sacred Heart had to demonstrate patience and understanding. It had to take into account new ways of looking at the child. Changes in family relationships and new means of communication in the second half of the nineteenth century altered customs. Not only did the pupils leave school for vacation, but the parents

---

53   *Lettres aux Mères en charge*, p. 77. To Mother d'Avenas, 10 July 1843.
54   *Religieuses du Sacré-Cœur*, vol. 3, p. 151.
55   Plan of Studies (1852), pp. 111-112.

wanted their daughters to take part in family events. When they traveled near the school, they wanted to be able to spend time with their children. These requirements called for new ways of managing the schools that took into account the good of the institution as well as that of the individuals.[56]

To respect the child could mean to accept that her family did not belong to the Church. The Society of the Sacred Heart evolved first in Catholic countries, and in its boarding schools it accepted Orthodox and non-Christians, but the greatest number of non-Catholics was Protestant. In Protestant countries or those of mixed religions, the number of non-Catholic children was rather significant. The general congregations of the Society were preoccupied by this, not questioning the principle of admitting them, but trying to settle on how to occupy them while their Catholic companions were at Mass or religious instruction. In 1890, it was decided that the Protestants were not to become the majority in the school, so that they could not "propagate their religious ideas." They were to follow the general school schedule, including Sunday's. At the time of their admission, they should be reminded that attendance at religious instruction and Friday abstinence were mandatory. Finally they were not to be taken to the Protestant church or encouraged to participate in "the exercises of their religion," which would have been "a tacit approval of error." Jews were to be treated like Protestants. But at the time of the Dreyfus affair, the general congregation thought that "in France their admission would shock Catholic parents," which was to say that they should not be admitted.

The way of educating non-Catholics, whether Christian or not, was surely more tolerant than these words would suggest. The Religious of the Sacred Heart counted on the power of the good example given by the Catholic students to attract those who were not of the "true faith." But if they did not put pressure on the pupils, they did rejoice in the many renunciations of heresy that took place in the schools or in the conversions they witnessed. At the same time, they did not call attention to these events in order to forestall prejudice against their institutions. The Vatican knew about this issue: during the process of beatification of Mother Barat, the Devil's Advocate objected that the founder of the Sacred Heart had accepted non-Catholics and non-Christians in her schools and had not set much store on obtaining their conversion.

Diversification of Educational Works

The houses of the Sacred Heart, the workplaces of the religious, were both the home where they lived and the setting of their apostolic activities.

---

[56] Gen. Arch. C I C 3, Box 11, General Congregation of 1895.

Monique Luirard

Although each house had its own cachet because of its pupils, the needs of their families and the religious in charge, all the houses had a unique spirit recognized by contemporaries, as well as by the pupils and the religious themselves.

Boarding Schools

Undeniably the boarding schools were the jewels of the Society. The Religious of the Sacred Heart had better prospects of inculcating their educational principles there because the pupils were under their care day and night; they spent several years there, and vacations were short.

A boarding school sometimes opened with very few students. Portici, on the Bay of Naples, started on 8 November 1873, with five children, one of whom was seven years old; and after a year there were only sixteen. Carlisle, in England, had only five pupils for several years. But it was not the number that mattered at first; Mother Barat is quoted as having said often that to save the soul of a single child she would have founded the Society of the Sacred Heart. Boarding schools located in vacation spots were open to children who stayed only a few months during their parents' sojourn. Others welcomed children whose families lived in their country houses during the summer. The boarding schools most often seemed to recruit regionally. Schools in capital cities took in more girls whose parents had to live abroad.

Some houses had difficult openings. Those who invited the congregation did not always keep their promises or students did not come. The nuns often began by giving private lessons. In Bohemia the Sacred Heart failed to attract the children of a local aristocracy considered very aloof,[57] who lived on their own estates and did not particularly want to have their daughters brought up away from home. At that time many upper class children were taught at home by tutors and governesses. If need be, parents thought it a good idea to send girls to a convent to prepare them for their First Communion. In that way the Sacred Heart gained pupils and won their allegiance.

Boarding was costly. The price scarcely changed during the nineteenth century because of the stable currency. In Toulouse, in 1876, the Sacred Heart was the most expensive boarding school in the city. The annual cost of boarding, 650 francs, payable by semester, was doubled by additional

---

[57] Gen. Arch. C I C 3, Box 12 and C IV 1 Prague. Regular visit, 1889. The situation did not improve later. In 1904, the vicar noted that one sixth of the boarding school was made up of children of the aristocracy, who formed "a separate clique."

fees;[58] it increased with the age of the student. The annual payment could be a burden for families who sent several of their daughters to school at the same time, even when they were given a reduction. The cost was considered too high in London, Ontario, where some children came more for the courses in music and religion than for other subjects. At the Sault-au-Récollet, the cost limited access to the higher classes to a few girls whose parents were well off.[59] The cost varied for each house.[60] Conflans gained some boarders because the fees asked at the Rue de Varenne seemed too high to many parents. Sacred Heart schools were aimed at a wealthy population, a fact that helped to limit their recruitment or at least to allow the religious to screen the candidates. On the other hand, parents knew that by paying high fees they were contributing to the functioning of the free school and to other works of the congregation.

Handicaps blocked the expansion of certain boarding schools. The location could be one: the house was situated either in an urban setting with no room for further building, or on the outskirts of a city making access difficult. Many schools have had to relocate in both Europe and America. In the decade following the death of Mother Barat, the boarding school in Dublin left Glasnevin for Mount Anville.[61] Eden Hall, in a suburb of Philadelphia, expanded and built healthier and more comfortable quarters; Rochester and London both changed location. The houses of Rosecroft and Selma, for which there had been great hopes, had to be closed because demographic changes limited their growth.[62]

Sometimes the properties, though prestigious, were not well suited to school life. In Algiers, the Sacred Heart occupied a former Moorish palace with rooms richly decorated in marble, and the former Hôtel Biron in Paris was an eighteenth century jewel. In Palermo, if one believes the memoirs of Prince Fulco di Verdura, the convent of the Sacred Heart seemed like both

---

[58] These fees could be for music and art lessons, lessons in deportment, but also for accessories and supplies, like uniforms, including the white and black veils worn for religious services, and the linen room. Those who were received into the sodalities had to have a white dress and veil (G. Bourgade, pp. 147-148).

[59] Luc Pelletier, *Histoire de l'école Sophie Barat*, Montréal 1997. The board in 1868 was $100, to which was added $48 for art lessons. In Halifax, the board was $194 and supplementary fees were $74.

[60] Pelletier and Prov. Arch. Canada, *Cor unum et anima una, Canada, 1842-1992*.

[61] *Lettres annuelles*, 1867-1868.

[62] Gen. Arch. C I C 3, Box 9, 1874. In Selma, Catholics were an infinitesimal minority. The place was a center of significant rail communications at the time; ten years later it ceased to be important when the frontier moved west. The population was so reduced that the Sacred Heart had only Protestant and Jewish girls in the school.

"a prison and a barracks;" it is not clear whether the memoirist referred to the architecture or the life style of the boarders![63] When the Society built, it employed local architects, who built according to the styles typical of the region. The bishop of Halifax recommended building a house that looked less like a traditional convent and more like lay people's homes in order to attract families. Nevertheless, there is a Sacred Heart style, recognizable for its long corridors and arched windows. Most of the chapels built in the second half of the century were in the much favored neo-Gothic style. The size of the properties varied. That of Lille, right in the center of the city, was quite small, considering the number of students and nuns who lived in the house.[64] On the other hand, the size of the properties of Chamartín, of Pressbaum and of so many of the boarding schools in the United States and Canada was impressive. To the size of the outbuildings and the beauty of the site, on which the prospectus elaborated extensively, was added the advantage of the healthfulness of the setting, which parents sought more and more. Many of these elegant properties had been the gifts of generous donors.[65]

Aristocrats frequently visited the boarding schools that were known to be welcoming. Members of the armed forces went there with pleasure. Because of the proximity of the château of Laeken, the queen and the princesses of Belgium used to go to Jette for repeated short visits.[66] The Spanish court went often to Chamartín. The Bourbons, exiled from France and Italy and settled in Switzerland and Austria, and other members of European royal families used to visit Riedenburg. All these illustrious visitors were received with the honors due to their rank. When they arrived, classes stopped; the children had to curtsey and reply unrehearsed and politely to the questions they were asked. These visits might have been

---

[63] Edmonde Charles-Roux, *Une enfance sicilienne d'après Fulco di Verdura*, p. 64.

[64] Mother Gœtz had ordered the purchase of the house next door, if it came up for sale, which happened 1881. Although enlarged, the house, which had to accommodate a hundred nuns, lacked adequate space.

[65] In Spain, the Duchess of Pastraña made a gift of thirty-two hectares to Chamartín and of a city house in Madrid. The Countess of Villanueva was a benefactor of Havana, Sarriá and Séville. She died in 1866 at Chamartín where she had retired. In Italy, Countess Aurore Boutourlin, a native of Poland who had become Russian by marriage, lived in Rome most of the time; she was considered by Pius IX a "lay saint." She financed the construction of several buildings in Rome and in Padua. Countess Clémentine de Briançon donated the house of San Tommaso in Avigliana.

[66] The boarders were charged with entertaining the Belgian princesses. The house at Ixelles was opened at the request of Queen Marie-Henriette, wife of Léopold II.

lessons in *savoir faire* and exercises in good behavior, but they disturbed the life of a school.[67] Such princely habits had annoyed Mother Barat, who did not wish the benefactors of the Sacred Heart to become burdens, but their visiting patterns changed very little after her death.

There were many occasions for lay people to be seen at the Sacred Heart. They could assist at liturgical services when they knew members of the royal families would be there, when there would be excellent singers or when the organ playing was exceptional, as at the Trinità dei Monti. The distribution of prizes was always an event of the "season," because of the songs and plays presented by the students and by the well-known people who took part. In New York ladies tried to obtains invitations months in advance, because at the Sacred Heart, the celebrations were "beautiful and distinguished." Troubled by the worldliness of these displays, Mother Barat had asked at the end of her life that invitations be given only to the pupils' parents. This decision was not always respected later. On the other hand, ecclesiastics were welcomed for the distribution of prizes; they very much wanted to be there. At Almagro in Argentina,

> The priests who assisted at the ceremony last year were so appreciative of it that they were vying for the honor of coming this year. The Jesuit fathers, knowing that we have just a few places, asked the rector for permission to come to the rehearsal so that others can be present on prize day. Besides the archbishop there were several canons, the rector of the seminary, three Jesuits, two fathers of the Sacred Heart, the parish priest of *Merced*, his brother and twenty-three other priests who honored us with their presence.[68]

The prizes were always distributed in the presence of a bishop, sometimes several. No doubt these prestigious audiences reinforced the reputation for

---

[67] In the century following, the members of royal families continued this tradition. Until the fall of the monarchy, King Alfonso XIII visited the Sacred Heart in Madrid, and the royal family gave various gifts to the charity bazaars. At San Sebastián, good relations with the royal family were facilitated by the fact that the convent was next door to the royal residence. During their sojourns in Ostend, members of the Belgian royal family visited the Sacred Heart. French princely families stopped by the Trinità dei Monti when they were in Rome. In Canada, the students went out to greet the royal couple in 1939, and after the Second World War, Queen Elizabeth and Prince Philip. In May 1960, Madame Pauline Vanier, alumna of Montréal and wife of the governor general of Canada, visited Vancouver and gave a *congé* to the school. The pupils of Winnipeg sent layettes to Queen Elizabeth II and to Princess Michiko.

[68] *Lettres annuelles*, 27 December 1885.

snobbery that the founder had deplored. But how could the superiors not have opened their doors to their alumnae, to the parents who had confided their children to the nuns and to princes of the Church?

The only way of fighting against affectation when it manifested itself too ostentatiously was to deal ruthlessly with it. In 1873, Mother Gœtz said to the older girls at the Rue de Varenne: "The closer we come to Christmas the more we must clothe ourselves with the spirit of the Infant Jesus." "Alas, Mother," exclaimed Mother de la Guibourgère, who was mistress general, "Some of them do not understand humility at all; there are even some who are not humiliated by their being proud." Mother Gœtz could not keep from smiling: "Not possible! No, it is not possible, Mother Blanche. If some seem to think that way, it is only on the surface; there cannot be 'free thinkers' among your children. That would be to accept the spirit of the world, quite opposed to that of Our Lord who said 'Learn of me that I am meek and humble of heart.' We must make pride disappear, even its appearance; we must have a horror of it!"

On her death bed a few days later, when Mother de la Guibourgère asked a last word for her students, Mother Gœtz responded: "You have to tell them to be humble."[69] The lesson bore fruit, at least for the moment! The image of haughtiness attached to the Sacred Heart was suggested by the vanity of the students, fueled by the envy of those who had been refused acceptance or by that of competitors, whether directors of private schools or of rival congregations.

The kind of education Mother Barat wanted called upon the religious to pay close attention and to be creative so that the children would feel at home in their new setting. The boarding school meant separation from family and familiar surroundings. Therefore, the teachers were careful when first meeting their pupils, especially the youngest; but they had to maintain the same level of receptivity and listening all year long. At Roehampton, Mother Henrietta Kerr had transformed one window of her office into a bird cage, convinced of "the value of a slight joy in a boarder's day and of the lesson from a bird's song or the beating of wings." There she sheltered some birds, a gift to a young pupil.[70] The mistresses general also knew how to lighten the days when they had to; they let the children play in the garden and organized games of *cache-cache*. The goal was to make the boarders happy.

---

[69] *Religieuses du Sacré-Cœur*, vol. 3, pp. 19-20.
[70] *Religieuses du Sacré-Cœur*, vol. 3, p. 88. Mother Mary Gilmore went further in allowing a boarder whose family lived in the Philippines during the Second World War to keep a bird in her room (*Lettres annuelles,* 1958-1961, p. 29). She rightly believed that an unhappy pupil could spoil the spirit of the whole school.

The educators sought also to find innovative ways to develop the children's intellectual capacities. At the Sacred Heart, as in Jesuit pedagogy, entertainment held an important place. The students played roles in theatricals, composed by the nuns on religious or allegorical subjects, in costumes from "the play closet." These "dialogues" were presented on the occasion of the feasts of the superior and the mistress general, of the visits of religious or civil authorities and at the distribution of prizes. At the end of the century the general congregations opined that theater occupied too important a place in Mexico and in Florence. It was not the subject of the scenes that was worrisome, but rather the behavior that surrounded them, the length of the pieces, the fact that the girls played masculine roles, that they wore costumes ordered by their parents from theatrical suppliers and that the plays drew a large audience beyond that of the parents of the young actors.[71]

To instill their standards through sayings and maxims, easily remembered and expressive of values that would last a lifetime, the religious created literary sessions on the model that had existed at Jette and that had been appreciated by the future Leo XIII. In 1879, Mother de Pichon began at Pau a literary session that she called "the Game of Roses." Created after the model of the Floral Games of Toulouse, it allowed students to practice writing compositions in various genres, epistolary, historical, philosophical or poetic or in a work dedicated to the Blessed Virgin. The pieces were presented on an evening in May in the garden, illuminated for the occasion, before the pupils, the superior and mistress general, who offered suggestions and incisive critiques, and the teachers of the higher classes. The "captains of the games" tried to spot the pious platitudes and to reward simplicity and good taste. The prizes consisted of rosary beads wrapped in an artificial rose in honor of the "Mystical Rose."[72]

Other houses took up the idea. At the Trinità dei Monti, the sessions allowed the students to display their mastery of French, their ability to argue and their sense of humor. In 1895, each one chose a flower, which she had to praise. One of them chose the mignonette and gave it the motto "to be rather than to appear," and said:

> This little flower is the image of a true child of the Sacred Heart. By her kindness she refreshes her family quietly, lovingly, without fuss. She always thinks of the good of others, is ready to sacrifice herself to make her family happy. "How shall I make them happy?" she asks every day, and

---

[71] Gen. Arch. C I C 3, Box 11.
[72] *Vie de la R.M. de Pichon*, pp. 96-97, and M. O'Leary, *Education with a Tradition*, London 1936, pp. 189-193.

> beginning in the morning she sets herself the task of giving herself to others. Faced with a duty, she does not say to herself, "How can I do it the easiest way?" but "How can it best be done?" Then she does not think of her own enjoyment and happily sacrifices an outdoor game, an evening party in order to care for one of her family.... Be a humble mignonette in a corner who wishes to be rather than to appear, to act rather than to speak, to be devoted rather than to be seen. To be rather than to appear, that is my byword so that one day I shall appear in glory in the palace of the elect.[73]

Clearly this education aimed at conveying a sense of duty.

In the boarding schools the pupils ought to feel at home. Mother Barat was ever attentive to that. The number of boarders was kept low so that the children could relate to one another as a family. The youngest lived separately in the "junior school," directed by a special mistress general, with a schedule and quarters suited to their age. The pupils were to think of their companions "as sisters who form a large family," to welcome "their new companions affectionately, remembering that they also experienced uncomfortable moments and little problems when they first arrived at the boarding school." The Rule provided that they "make it a duty to love all their companions, to show their affection by a loving readiness to help and above all by gently putting up with their defects, remembering that they, too, have some for others to tolerate."[74] These affectionate relationships were perhaps fostered by the fact that many pupils found their sisters, cousins and other relations in the school. In France, in the provinces at least, the milieu from which the Sacred Heart recruited was narrow enough for most of the pupils to be acquainted with one another.

Daily life sought to preserve this familial character. In good weather lessons took place in the garden. The mistress general, during meals, before and after the reading, talked with the students and shared news that would interest them. In the evening before prayer and going to bed, she commented on the events of the day and tried to calm things down if there had been some unfortunate incident. On Sunday the boarders met with her "as a family," and she varied the activities, told a story, began a general conversation, organized games or invited those who played a musical instrument to perform. Most likely it was this aspect of the education, the strong relations between children and adults, that caused boarders in Halifax not to want to go home for vacation.[75]

---

[73] Arch. Trinità dei Monti. *Cahier d'Antonia Gaetani*.
[74] Rule of the Boarding School (1852), pp. 32-33.
[75] *Lettres annuelles*, 1867-1868, p. 8.

The education should enable the girls afterwards to take on their social obligations.[76] It aimed at forming in each one a sense of responsibility, and it was austere. The young Spaniards found it so in any case and thought that the constant silence required was excessive. They had to get used to it! Uniforms seemed off-putting to the adolescents of Louisiana, who were shocked at having to wear a cotton apron. The reason explained, they considered "the uniform a mark of distinction that placed them in the ranks of the Sacred Heart and enrolled them in a life style that called them to all that was greatest and noblest in Christian life."[77] In France during the Second Empire, the older girls were allowed to wear crinolines, at least before Pius IX registered his distaste for that type of clothing![78]

At the Sacred Heart, the goal was ongoing personal and spiritual progress attained through a pedagogy based on emulation.[79] By being charged with small responsibilities, the children learned self-control. The boarders received "honorary" charges: *adjutrice*, that is, mistress of orderliness, librarian, sacristan, song leader, almsgiver, games leader and organist. Each charge was held by two persons who took it in turn. These responsibilities were usually given to the best behaved and the most reliable, to those with both intelligence and faithfulness; but they were also given to those from whom some effort was expected. As it was not particularly pleasant to be an *adjutrice* of a classroom, erasing the boards and tidying the room, this task was sometimes given to a pupil who did not shine where humility was concerned or who was noteworthy for her disorder. In the refectory, the table president had an important role because children of different ages sat at each table:

> The table presidents, chosen from among the eldest and most sensible, learn to do the honors by carving the meat and serving their companions. They look after the silence and good manners of their table fellows, holding firmly to politeness, cleanliness and a pleasant manner. The vice-president pours the water, usually serves dessert and learns little by little to fulfill the functions of president.[80]

The reason for this rubric was to serve everyone and at the same time prepare the pupils for their role as mistress of a household and, by teaching them *savoir-vivre* and tact, to ready them for their mission as mothers of

---

[76] "We had to be able to walk correctly, and if we did not, someone took us aside and corrected our way of doing so" (Testimony of Joan Stephenson).
[77] L. Callan, *The Society of the Sacred Heart...*, p. 547.
[78] M. O'Leary, p. 187.
[79] Habitual rewards were permission to visit the poor and to assist at Holy Hour.
[80] *Règlement du pensionnat*, p. 73.

families. The table president must have had to eat everything to make sure that her companions did the same. Some educational practices were in use for a long time. We will mention only one: the "potato novena," which alumnae on all continents remember.[81] It was part of the Advent "practice," that is, a spiritual exercise that consisted of keeping silence each day in order to earn a potato to give to the poor. This effort prepared each student for Christmas by drawing her attention to the suffering of the poor. It appealed to the individual conscience, because each pupil placed her potato in a basket in public, if she thought she had earned it. "This had as its purpose to make us examine our conscience. It created a cruel dilemma: either I am good, and I have the right to the potato, so I have aided the poor; or in spite of my not quite clear conscience, I take the potato; or I do not take it and thus deprive a poor person."[82] "Better to be humiliated than to lie," the children were reminded.[83] "Death to lies," was one of the favorite mottoes of Mother de la Guibourgère, Rue de Varenne. "Dare to be true" was the version in Canada [and at Eden Hall].

What values were passed on? Mother Kerr enumerated the obstacles that boarders at Roehampton had to overcome:

> human respect, the desire to be noticed, fear of risking one's reputation, gossip. A child educated at the Sacred Heart ought to have the "desire *to do something for God*: Can we spend our life on little nothings? Will it be said that one of you has no goal, no object in life, thinking only of killing time, of dress and make-up, of running after worldly amusements? *Always desire to become better*. We may discover new faults in ourselves, and even more old faults, but if we desire to become better, if the will to do better persists, all will be well. *Desire to help others*. That is a holy ambition to embrace. Saint Francis Xavier complained to God that merchants had entered Japan before he did. Are we going to reject this appeal, plunged in ourselves, in our egoism, our vanity, our worldliness, not doing all we can to correspond to the invitation, to the choice of the Sacred Heart? God asks our cooperation…God, jealous of our hearts…How amazing!"[84]

Mother de Neuville, at Marmoutier and Rue de Varenne, had defined her objectives by "three D's:" "First serve God [*Dieu*]; make Duty your prime pleasure; Give [*Donner*] happiness to others in order to be able to do them

---

[81] Mona Latif-Ghattas, *Les filles de Sophie Barat*, pp. 62-65.
[82] Marie Madeleine Genevois-Le Deuff, *Institution la Perverie*, p.37.
[83] M. Latif-Ghattas, p. 65.
[84] *Religieuses du Sacré-Cœur*, vol. 3, pp. 90-91.

good." She also had identified three things to avoid: "Everything creeping, everything clinging, everything crooked."[85]

Bad habits and mischief had to be corrected, but judiciously, without harshness. On a *"congé sans cloche,"* that is, a day of games and get-togethers, days without reprimands or punishments, the children could do what they wished, within bounds. In Amiens, some pupils decided to go on an expedition on the Somme, a forbidden adventure. They were getting into the boat when they heard Mother Antonia Frey, who was not their class mistress, ask them if there was room in the boat for her.

> There was not a trace of disapproval on her face, so in a minute they had made room for her, and soon the whole party was floating down to the edge of the convent property. There Mother Frey suggested calmly that by rowing hard they would be just back in time for *goûter*, and so they were; and the adventure ended happily without any further mention, but with new gratitude and respect in the hearts of all the girls.[86]

A second anecdote comes from the boarding school at Sault-au-Récollet. In the middle 1880's, some young Canadians decided to snatch some apples kept in the cellar, threading a long stick through a transom; it missed its mark often, scattering the fruit on the floor. That caught the attention of the *"dépensière,"*[87] who reported the offense to the mistress general. The marauders had to appear before the superior. "Dear children," she said kindly, "I have heard that you like apples, so I have ordered that they are to be served to you at all your meals for a while: breakfast, lunch, *goûter* and dinner."[88] Apples lost all their appeal. The mistresses never referred to the incident again. Besides, it was a tradition at the Sacred Heart: a misdeed forgiven was never mentioned again.

In 1886, Alessandra di Rudini was enrolled at the Trinità dei Monti. She was ten years old and had always done as she pleased at home. She quickly terrorized the nuns and scandalized the good children; for even though she was a great companion, she showed a chronic lack of discipline and drew attention to herself by weird tricks: she pretended to be a ghost in the dormitory and poured ink into the holy water fonts. "The superior always recommended that we win her by gentleness and kindness. So when we went to complain of the child's frequent pranks, she only recommended patience, indulgence and prayer for this child who seemed

---

[85] *Lettres annuelles*, 1947-1952, p. 233.
[86] M. O'Leary, p. 187.
[87] The religious in charge of the storeroom.
[88] *Reverend Mother Hughes*, pp. 6-7.

so difficult to us." At the end of the year she was sent home. "From a distance, the Mothers continued to follow her and, learning of her troubled life, surrounded her with a web of prayers. Mother de Loë always prayed to our miraculous Madonna, *Mater admirabilis*, for her, when she became the worldly Marchioness Carlotti."[89] Alessandra di Rudini Carlotti, after a stormy love life, entered Carmel. She wrote one day to one of her cousins who had placed her daughter at the Sacred Heart that it was "a cage that does not clip one's wings." She had no doubt experienced that herself.

The ultimate aim of education at the Sacred Heart was not to produce pious women: "Make them Christians before making them pious," Mother de Kérouartz used to say to her daughters.[90] At Roehampton, Mother Kerr presented devotion as "ardent, personal, practical love for Our Lord, consisting in generous accomplishment of one's duty."[91] Everywhere she went, Mother de Neuville pointed out to the students that their lives had a profoundly religious meaning: "Not bigotry, not love of rose water devotion — one of her expressions — but she taught us to consider everything from a point of view from on high. Everything, even our least actions was to be done for God with heaven in view. And that, with enthusiasm, cheerfulness and breadth of mind."[92] The students had choices to make. They were to "avoid making a fuss, noise, showing off in devotedness," do a great deal but invisibly, except in the eyes of God. To the Infanta Paz, age fourteen, Mother de la Guibourgère wrote in 1876: "Ignore the adulation of the court; see yourself as God sees you: with all your weaknesses and miseries, your cowardliness, perhaps, and with humility take yourself in hand, by giving the first place to Jesus, today your friend, tomorrow your judge. Like little Mary, learn to offer your morning sacrifice, that is, the choice you made as a young girl to serve God."[93] This sense of personal responsibility helped young Catholics have a sense of their own worth in countries where Protestants outnumbered them.

Spiritual exercises for pupils of every age group developed their spirit of faith. Preparation for First Communion was a time to help them really meet Christ. In the houses where she lived, Mother Barat had a visit with the first communicants before or after the great day. The motherhouse continued this ritual after her death. The first communicants of the Rue de Varenne were welcomed there: Mystified, they went into the community room to see the Mother General. Through half-open doors they glimpsed

---

[89] *Alessandra di Rudini, carmélite*, p. 34.
[90] *Vie de la R.M. Zaepffel*, p. 118.
[91] *Religieuses du Sacré-Cœur*, vol. 3, p. 92.
[92] *Lettres annuelles*, 1947-1952, p. 233.
[93] *Religieuses du Sacré-Cœur*, vol. 3, p. 25.

the Mothers who worked steadily, not even looking up to see them. Impressed with this silence, some walked on tiptoes, saying to themselves, "Everyone is dead in this house."[94] The evening before the day itself the first communicants were invited into the community room; they knelt to ask pardon for their faults. The superior granted it in the name of the community; then she had them get up and embraced them.[95] Alumnae remembered with emotion the attention and the respect with which the religious surrounded them at the time of their First Communion.

The students who wished to join one of the sodalities suited to their age group received special attention. Those admitted to the Children of Mary, sometimes after a rather long probation, formed a kind of elite at the heart of the school. They wore a medal.[96] They had meetings that helped them grow in their life of faith, initiated them into personal prayer and helped them to carry out their duties with vigilance and responsibility.[97] The sodalities prepared both remarkable mothers of families and good religious. For Mother Barat, the moral and spiritual formation given at the Sacred Heart aimed at laying in souls the foundation of faith and charity. At her school the religious sought to be "instruments who draw souls not to oneself, but to Jesus Christ."[98] By their united and harmonious lives they had to touch the souls of their pupils, who would be able to say assuredly, "See how they love one another." "These examples of the earliest faithful made Christians of others," Mother Barat had written to Mother Mayer, then mistress general at Riedenburg, "and with you, daughter, it will be adorers of the Sacred Heart of Jesus and probably a few vocations."[99] That pattern of behavior continued from then on.

Day Schools

Developments in French society under the July Monarchy pushed Mother Barat to wish to extend recruitment in her schools to girls of the middle class, in spite of the reluctance of some of her assistants general. She knew that each stratum of society could identify an élite who could influence their surroundings. Not all middle class families wanted to send their children to boarding schools, so from the middle of the 1840's day schools were opened in France. The pupils received the same instruction

---

[94] *Religieuses du Sacré-Cœur*, vol. 3, p. 4.
[95] It seems that this ritual lasted until the First World War.
[96] They could have a motto of their choice engraved on their medal.
[97] They got up ten minutes before the others in order to pray privately.
[98] M. S. Barat, *Lettres aux Religieuses*, vol. 1, p. 309, 9 March 1819.
[99] M. S. Barat, *Lettres aux Mères en charge*, 6 October 1856, p. 148, and 3 March 1859, p. 150.

as the boarders without mixing with them, except during class.[100] This arrangement became common during the second half of the nineteenth century. Such a division sometimes took place between houses in the same city. In Lyons, the house on Rue Boissac took day pupils from the age of seven, while *Les Anglais* took the boarders.

The day schools did not receive full acceptance in the congregation. Mother Lehon believed that they made the boarding schools slack off or see reduced enrollment, and that the education given to the day pupils did not have the same solidity as that provided for the boarders. But from then on many families opted for that arrangement for financial reasons and suitability. Other religious congregations proposed the same idea. The Society of Jesus offered boarding schools and day schools; it was not clear why boys could be brought up in day schools while girls had to be boarders. Finally, some parents wanted to be with their children every day and prepare them for the social setting in which they would later find themselves.

In 1890, the general congregation decided to open day schools in all the houses where the boarding school had fewer than a hundred pupils. At the same time the day schools were given a uniform rule, but with the understanding that American schools did not have to be like those in Europe, because of their different life styles.[101] Their number increased. There was additional urgency because, in the United States if the Sacred Heart had not allowed day schools, many children would have been placed in Protestant or public schools. Sometimes boys were accepted. Mother Stuart, who accompanied Mother Digby in visiting the day school in Chicago in 1898, recalled that this situation was almost unique and that the boys were in a separate section of the school.[102]

Opinions on the day schools remained mixed all the same. The religious thought that the day scholars missed out on the inspiration that the mistresses general gave the boarders, by means of short instructions followed by a time of prayer at the beginning and end of the day, and that outside the boarding school there was no chance to work on character, punctuality and order. They observed that teachers had to exercise great prudence when the children came from families hostile to religion, for their comments were quickly spread around outside. Therefore, they did "the possible good rather than the most desirable."[103] At the same time, it was

---

[100] There were different refectories or separate tables for boarders and day pupils.
[101] Gen. Arch. C I C 3, Box 11. The principle was to keep the day pupils in school as late as possible and to have them come back on Sunday to give them devotional habits and to place them "under the sisterly influence of the boarding school."
[102] M. Monahan, *Life and Letters...*, p. 115.
[103] Gen. Arch. C I C 3, Box 11, Report from Nantes.

recognized that there were certain advantages to this kind of education. Day pupils learned early to be devoted. Their sense of responsibility grew, because they had to overcome obstacles to the performance of their spiritual exercises. As a religious in Nantes remarked sensibly, "If we succeed in strengthening them [day pupils], there is nothing to fear for them from the transition that the boarders have to undergo when they leave us." As the day pupils were already living in the world, they would not experience the same transition.

Education among the Working Class

From its foundation, the Society of the Sacred Heart was concerned with the education of the poor. According to a felicitous formula of Jeanne de Charry, if "the boarding school is in the order of apostolic effectiveness, the first and most important means, the first end the Society proposes for the glory of the Sacred Heart of Jesus, the poor school is first in the order of affective preference because it is, par excellence, the work dearest to the Heart of Jesus, the one to which each religious must desire to be called."[104] Besides, a religious could express a preference only if she wanted to work in the poor school. Mother Barat had written to the nuns in Rome that they ought to be impartial as to working with different classes, "some by instilling virtue in the young Roman nobility and others by lavishing their care on the children of the Trastevere. In that way, everyone will accomplish her mission. Those who work among the nobility will always be ready to throw themselves into the service of the poor; those who work in the service of the poor will never refuse to care for the rich, since in the end all souls are dear to Jesus Christ."[105]

The Society of the Sacred Heart had been engaged enough in popular education to have gained some competence. In Beauvais a primary school and a public orphanage cared for children from eighteen months to seven years; the school became a center of experimentation in pedagogy and teacher training for the religious. Mother Marguerite Duquez, who was mistress general of the poor school for thirty-five years, developed such competence that the city awarded her a medal in 1852. Sister Augustine Leguillon received the same decoration by order of Emperor Napoleon III in 1867. At Montigny, the Sacred Heart taught children of the town in its free school. Because of this school, the town did not have to open the

---

[104] Jeanne de Charry, *Histoire des Constitutions de la Société du Sacré Cœur*, Rome, 1979, p. 153.

[105] *Conférences*, vol. 1, pp. 214-216, 5 May 1833.

public school required by law; the congregation was thus able to obtain authorization for the whole establishment.[106]

Popular education took different forms at the Sacred Heart, some permanent, some temporary. Although the establishment of a school for the poor was second, though not secondary, it was sometimes delayed by reason of circumstances. Some houses did not have one because there were already enough teaching religious in the city, because the extent of the property did not permit it or because the house was located too far from the places where likely pupils lived. Sometimes the Sacred Heart had to give up one of these schools at the request of ecclesiastical authorities who wished to foster the work of congregations that specialized in the apostolate among the working class. But it benefited also from transfers in its favor; in Calais and Bourges, for example, it replaced congregations from which the authorities had withdrawn their approval. The school policy of the Third Republic also pushed bishops to encourage initiatives that they had approved of earlier.

Sometimes the poor school preceded the boarding school. Though the case was rare in France, many *externats* [day schools for middle and working class children] were established in Europe or in America. The Society of the Sacred Heart had difficulty in getting started in London, where it was not appreciated by Cardinal Manning. In the end it settled in Hammersmith, a section that was then the most Catholic but the least affluent in the capital. They could not open a *demi-pensionnat* [day school for the upper class], for there were not enough families who were well enough off; but the nuns began various educational projects, then a successful free school for girls and boys.[107] In 1889, a free school, first opened in Carlisle for the children of Irish immigrants, moved to Fenham, near Newcastle, when it became evident that that city was growing. In Canada, the schools for the poor were parochial schools. In the United States they became parochial in the last twenty years of the century.

Besides free schools, *externats* where students paid were opened for families of some means. Some of these were created to accept children of exiled families. After the fall of the Kingdom of the Two Sicilies, the one at the Trinità dei Monti had been opened for the Neapolitans. The one in Pau received Spaniards whose parents had fled their country during the Carlist wars and who sometimes arrived in France completely destitute. In addition, the Sacred Heart directed workrooms, classes in which one

---

[106] In the 1880's, in France, the religious gave public school children catechetical instruction in the evening.

[107] *Vie de la R.M. Rumbold*, pp. 102-104. See also M. Quinlan, *Digby Stuart...*, pp. 12-25.

learned a trade and which were extensions of the poor schools. These workrooms offered various types of training according to local needs, but most often they trained seamstresses and laundresses, to be placed afterwards "in good houses," no doubt those of alumnae of the boarding schools.

The congregation also maintained orphanages necessitated by the recurring epidemics of the nineteenth century. But orphanages were intended also to help parents whose poverty required placement of their children, for a while or permanently. They sometimes charged a fee. Mother Gœtz took care not to open too many of them, for "orphanages are not named in our rules as a central work of our vocation; they must be established in our houses only with great circumspection and never to the detriment of the free school."[108] Therefore, she asked that the orphanages not compete with those of other congregations and not be in a house with a free school. Mother Gœtz specified that the orphans' food must be healthy and strengthening and their work geared to their strength and abilities. They could be allowed "with prudence some outings that would teach them about the conditions of life and to arm them against pitfalls of ignorance."

The education of handicapped children was not a priority in the nineteenth century. The Society of the Sacred Heart, however, supported it through the school for deaf-mutes in Chambéry, which took children of all social classes and had to provide more than custodial care. At the end of the 1860's this school fell from grace with the Savoy authorities because the training given did not include pedagogical innovations practiced elsewhere. A change took place from 1872 on, when Religious of the Sacred Heart, who had been trained in Milan with the Canossian Sisters and in Bordeaux with the Sisters of Nevers, began to practice *mimique* [lip-reading] for which they substituted, in 1879, the oral method, which consisted in having the pupils become "deaf speakers," later adapted for the boarding school or the free school, depending on their social status. Mothers Marie de Morand and Elvira Tonti, who showed an interest in this apostolate, became specialists in this kind of education.[109]

To knit together the scholastic strands of the congregation, the Society of the Sacred Heart began to take an interest in a work not contemplated at the beginning, the education of boys. In the United States and in Canada, it was more widespread than in Europe; and in St. Charles, Omaha, New Orleans and Halifax boys and girls went to the same schools. The presence of boys in girls' schools did not meet with approval in Rome. The

---

[108] Gen. Arch. C I C 3, Box 9, General Congregation of 1865.
[109] *Religieuses du Sacré-Cœur*, vol. 3, and *Lettres annuelles*, 1905-1907, p. 552.

Vatican, however, withdrew its opposition after the intervention of many bishops, including the bishop of Chicago. In 1884, nonetheless, the general congregation decreed that boys younger than twelve could take classes in catechism and Bible history, particularly on Sunday, but this work was to be an exception.[110]

Quite early, the Society of the Sacred Heart was asked to open normal schools aimed at forming school teachers. Mother du Rousier conducted a first experiment in Piedmont, but it was in Latin America that this type of training, which was not part of the initial educational project of the Society, reached its fullest development.[111] Mother Barat was not opposed to it, since it involved forming educators who would work in Catholic countries, and the Society would thereby participate indirectly in the education of the poor. In Chile and in Peru, the governments agreed to pay for the voyages of the religious who were to be in charge of teacher training.

The first normal school that opened in Chile was sometimes described as a "second boarding school."[112] The Religious of the Sacred Heart had charge of adolescents from twelve to fourteen years of age whose early education they had not provided.[113] There were between ten and twenty students in each class. During about thirty years the Society of the Sacred Heart in Santiago trained nearly four hundred teacher candidates from throughout the country. The normal school was handed over to German teachers in January 1885. Between 1874 and 1878, the Society was in charge of one in Chillán. In 1903, Mother Elisabeth Windhorff and Father Bartolomé Mas, S.J., founded an institute for teachers in Chile in order to bring them together for Christian formation in support of their mission.

In Peru a normal school opened in 1877 for a dozen students. The school was difficult to promote, because the graduates were not always hired upon leaving school. The Religious of the Sacred Heart believed that the government did not have much interest in this training and that the examinations at the end of the course were not held under the conditions provided in the original contract. The troubled atmosphere after the war in the Pacific made conditions unfavorable for running the normal school.

---

[110] Gen. Arch. C I C 3, Box 10. Mother Digby tried without success to limit the number of boys in the school in Halifax; the government of Nova Scotia believed that there should be no discrimination in a public school.

[111] The first normal school had been founded 2 February 1854, in Santiago. The president of the Republic, Manuel Montt, had asked the Sacred Heart to train teachers to whom "the government wished to entrust the education and civilization of girls in the public schools...." The Sacred Heart was given a fully equipped building, including the chapel necessary for worship.

[112] *Lettres annuelles*, Santiago du Chili, 1865.

[113] *Vie de la R.M. de Lavigerie*, p. 122.

Change came at the end of the 1880's, when calm returned and when student recruitment was partially guaranteed by normal school alumnae who sent their own students to Lima. The Peruvian government began to face up to its obligations, increased the number of scholarships[114] and contributed appropriate equipment to the normal school by providing physics and experimental psychology laboratories.

The Society of the Sacred Heart did not offer teacher training in Europe, except in Great Britain, where there was some interest. The government decided, in 1870, that all children should receive elementary education. This measure pushed Catholics to organize committees to develop education among the underprivileged, and they had to train teachers for the schools that would be set up. In that era, the only training centers were the ones opened midcentury in Liverpool for women teachers and in Hammersmith for men. Classes of twenty students per year could not meet the needs. Cardinal Manning asked the Society of the Holy Child Jesus, in 1872, to open a normal school for women; but as this congregation lacked the necessary personnel, the project was handed over to the committee of Catholic schools. Mother Digby heard about it and sought to have the British hierarchy agree that the Religious of the Sacred Heart could have a place among the founding staff of such a school.

Even though the plan to engage the Society was agreed upon, Mother Digby could not overcome the opposition of Cardinal Manning, who thought that the Religious of the Sacred Heart were not made for the education of the poor. She had to find a site in the diocese of Southwark. In May 1874, a house was acquired in West Hill. The first normal school students stayed for the time being at Roehampton until the house at Wandsworth was ready to welcome them.[115] Another normal school was established in 1903 near Newcastle, first at Gosforth, then at Fenham. Afterwards, the experience gained in Great Britain was shared by Peru. The internationality of the Society allowed this exchange of knowledge and expertise.

In the training of young adults, the Society of the Sacred Heart most often answered to specific appeals from civil and religious authorities. At the end of the 1860's, in Beauvais, a Sunday class brought together girls from fifteen to eighteen, factory workers, to offer them the curriculum of the free schools, without the sewing course. They were "numbed by misery and the endless labor of their long days."[116] In Armagh, in Ireland,

---

[114] The school reached one hundred, then one hundred thirty students in the 1890's.

[115] In 1904, the normal school was moved to Saint Charles Square.

[116] *Lettres annuelles*, 1868-1869, pp. 11-12.

young factory workers went to the Sacred Heart on summer evenings for minimal instruction. Evening classes were started in Canada. In England, in 1903, Mother Thunder organized evening classes for the poorest girls of the Hammersmith section; then she expanded them to include the former students of the elementary school.[117] Another form of adult education was provided by means of people's libraries, youth clubs and in Chile "*l'œuvre des faubourgs*" [work among the working class living in the outskirts of the city]. In the final analysis, the educational programs of the Society directed to the least privileged populations were the most varied. When a free school could not be opened, creativity came to the rescue; Mother Barat had insisted that a work for the poor be associated with each boarding school, and Mother Gœtz saw to it that this principle was respected.

There is little information about the sites where these works were set up. At the beginning, former studios or abandoned factories had provided space for the students to assemble. In Halifax the College Street School was opened in a barn; and Catherine Hartigan, who was in charge, taught with a plank across her lap to serve as a desk. She shared the space with the cow![118] Renovations were made during the generalate of Mother Gœtz, who paid great attention to the quality of the spaces where the students gathered. Under the Third Republic, the French government became more concerned about healthful conditions. The Society of the Sacred Heart then built new buildings for its schools: their spaciousness attracted students. Some installations, however, were makeshift. In October 1882, in the hall of the orphanage at Marmoutier, crates covered with hay were set up for the children's siesta. But comfort was in short supply in public as well as private schools.

While the boarding schools deliberately limited the number of pupils, the free schools enrolled an impressive number. In Posen the school was as full as the premises allowed.[119] In order to accept more children a new school was built at Wilda. In Chicago, as the four hundred and fifty children of the school were crowded into two rooms in a small wooden building that could not be protected from either cold or heat, Mother Barat decided to have a new building constructed.[120] She was responsible also for the free school at the Sault-au-Récollet.

There is little data to evaluate the quality of the instruction in these schools. It was based on principles of which Fénelon would not have disapproved: he affirmed that "knowledge for women as for men must be

---

[117] *Life of the R.M. Rose Thunder*, p. 72.
[118] The motherhouse paid for a new building in 1870.
[119] *Lettres annuelles*, 1863-1866, p. 106.
[120] *Lettres annuelles*, pp. 150-151.

limited to instruction that supports their functions in life. The differences in their activities must determine the differences in their studies."[121] The pupils of the schools were to acquire a strong religious education as well as good primary instruction, that is, mastery of reading, writing and arithmetic and professional training that enabled them to earn a living.[122] For Mother Barat, the objective was to help them to be self-sufficient and thus escape having to live by begging. The instruction provided to the orphans brought up at the Villa Lante enabled them to become school teachers in the villages of the Roman *campagna*.

Sometimes the authorities required inspection of teaching in the schools. In Greater Poland, the demands of the Prussian government led to strengthening the education or at least prolonging it. "We are keeping our dear children longer," observed the religious, without specifying whether it meant an increase in the duration of the program or the length of the school day.[123] At Montigny, in 1865, where the children were divided into three groups in three different classrooms, discipline left nothing to be desired, but the teaching was inadequate and the families complained.[124] Three years later the inspector noted that the teachers appealed too little to the intelligence and too much to the memory, that the teaching of arithmetic and spelling was weak, and there was almost no teaching of the metric system. He remarked also that the teachers, "sub-mistresses," as he called them, had a less distinguished costume than that of the other religious of the house; and that they were very inferior to the others as to education and instruction.[125]

The change in policy on instruction under the Third Republic led to an improvement in the level of the studies offered in the free schools. The schools had to prepare the pupils to pass a certificate of study or lose them. In Beauvais and at the school in the Rue de Babylone in Paris, the pupils succeeded. But "everywhere that we can still hold to what is essential, we must hold to it," noted the general congregation in 1884. All the same it had "to accept changes needed to keep the children from going to the public school."[126] The vicar of Canada, Mother de Sarens, understanding that the poor school was unacceptable there, improved the programs. Clearly the

---

[121] Cited by Msgr. Baunard at the *Congrès des Œuvres*, in Paris in 1900, p. 11. Gen. Arch. C I A 5 d, Box 6.
[122] *Constitutions*, § 205 and 206. The program was approximately the same in the orphanages.
[123] *Lettres annuelles*, 1867-1868, p. 32.
[124] The superior made sure that the teaching staff was reinforced by a choir nun.
[125] Apparently coadjutrix sisters continued to be employed (Reports of inspection quoted in François Reitel and Lucien Arz, *Montigny lès Metz*, p. 205).
[126] Gen. Arch. C I C 3, Box 10, session of 5 March 1884, p. 23.

religious continued to feel this kind of pressure. In 1910, the account of a session of the general congregation summarizes Mother Digby's viewpoint on the question of the schools: "In certain countries, we ought to do more to modernize in the good sense of the word. It is not a question, says our Mother, to teach the children things that will be of no use, but the premises must be suitable, well maintained and the teaching adequate...."[127]

Life in the schools and orphanages was not always easy because the children were sometimes confused by a pedagogy that forbade corporal punishment. Attendance fluctuated according to the seasons or the days of the week, or the family's needs; children's work added to the family resources, but sometimes interfered with attention to their studies or religious formation. At First Communion time, punctual attendance at the instructions or the retreat cost many children a real expenditure of energy.[128] The schools attracted children of families that had lost standing or those destitute culturally as well as economically. This was particularly the case in cities, where the living conditions differed greatly with social class. In Seville, the school had children whose families, though impoverished by the change in the political regime, were educated, as well as those who lived in the *corrales*, houses "in which up to one hundred families lived, heaped on top of one another hardly having enough air to breathe."[129]

This apostolate, although unrewarding, also schooled the religious in reality. Through contact with their pupils they learned of acute poverty, of the extent of anti-clericalism or the level to which the working class was not Christianized. Many mothers whom the nuns instructed in catechism had not made their First Communion or been married in the Church, without breaking all ties with "religion." In Calais,

> ...these poor folk would be embarrassed if they had to explain what they understood by the word religion. "Madame," said the mother of one little girl, as she brought her to school, "I am bringing Catherine to you so that you can bring her up piously; for you see, in my family, piety passes from mother to daughter; so, pay attention that my daughter has all she needs on that side." Now piety in that family consists in going to Mass when the housework is finished on time, in sending the children to catechism for First Communion

---

[127] Gen. Arch. C I C 3, Box 12.

[128] *Lettres annuelles*, 1886-1887, Calais: "The eve of First Communion, a child in the catechism class was weeping hot tears on leaving school: 'What's wrong?' she was asked. 'Ah!' she said, 'How I am going to be beaten on going back home! Mama is so angry that I am coming to the retreat instead of working, and she told me she would kill me if I came home without money.'" Happily a kind person came to the aid of the poor child.

[129] *Lettres annuelles*, 1869-1871, p. 175.

and in lighting candles in the cemetery. As to Sunday observance, abstinence, reception of the Sacraments, there is no question of any of it.

Many of the children had received no religious education whatever. Sometimes even their parents limited their religious practice, opposed it or fought against wearing religious insignia, even forbade their children to pray.[130] It was sometimes with great difficulty that the little ones were taught to do what their parents were not doing: "Papa and Mama never pray, I want to be like them," said one of them.[131] In "the horrible London suburb of Blackheath," the Sacred Heart had pupils who had not been baptized.[132]

Religious who worked among the working class admired their pupils who seemed receptive. In Calais, "the smallest children in the school show good dispositions, of which we could take advantage if it were not for the bad influences that often paralyze our action; they have tendencies to piety, to charity, in which we discover the grace of baptism still acting without obstacle in these souls." The class mistresses witnessed the charity and the sense of sharing that enlivened their pupils, their generosity in living their faith. As one of them wrote about the pupils in Beauvais, they were dealing with "souls of good will."

That apostolate also put the Religious of the Sacred Heart in contact with people of different ethnic origins. The house in Algiers had been requested for children of French families, orphans and young Muslims who had converted. The boarding school had few recruits. As for the poor school, it had children of French, Italian and Maltese families and also Algerian pupils, more often Jewish than Muslim. In the United States the religious worked for decades among the Native Americans. Thanks to their extended stay among the Potawatomi, they discovered the qualities of this people who were confronting "civilization" little by little, as the railroad passed close to their school.

> Our dear Indian girls give us ample compensation for our efforts and our care by their good spirit, their simplicity and above all by the innocence that we see in them. Our good Indian men are committed to approaching the Sacraments; every Sunday there are more than a hundred at the holy table and on Easter, since they live five or six miles away, they come Saturday and pitch their tents near the church returning home only the next day after the high Mass.[133]

---

[130] *Lettres annuelles*, Beauvais, 1887-1888, p. 53.
[131] *Lettres annuelles*, 1859-1862, p. XXXVII.
[132] *Life of Mother Gertrude Bodkin*, pp. 28-29.
[133] *Lettres annuelles*, 1867-1868.

Monique Luirard

In Canada, the Sacred Heart took charge of some Iroquois.[134] In Chile and in Mexico the religious worked with indigenous children and adults. The normal school in Chillán accepted Araucanians. We have a delightful anecdote about them. Because the daughter of a chief stubbornly refused to obey every order, her father, when told about it, used an argument to which there was no possible reply: "Listen, Victoria," he said, "if you do not obey the mothers, I will bring you home and give you in marriage to the ugliest man in the tribe." Victoria gave in![135]

European schools also could draw students with unfamiliar customs. In Andalusia, the religious met Gypsies:

> A quite separate race exists here, the Gypsies. They are a type of Arab, recognizable out of a thousand: their lack of cleanliness, their carelessness, their language and their ease in lying, everything about them is unusual; their dress is light, winter and summer; they are all dark-skinned, with curly hair floating on their shoulders, full lips. They are such a separate group that they have their own king in whose neighborhood we have the honor of living. We have a certain number of these Gypsies in our school, and when their mothers come to speak to the teachers, they use quite saccharine language: *Madrecita de mi alma, Ves mas bonita que la estrella de la mañana* (Little Mother of my heart, you are more beautiful than the morning star). At the end of the conference, the teacher has to be on her guard, lest with a kiss she receive a touch of the oil from the woman's hair. Let no one be put off, however, by this picture: the Gypsies can be civilized, and we have proof of it; already several of these little savages are becoming apostles, bringing us others, and in order to be sure they are accepted they get a recommendation from the parish priests, who actually do not need to be encouraged, for they are sending them to us from all parts of the city. The name of the mistress general is really well known in this country. Among other successes, we can note cleanliness – something astonishing; there is no odor in the classrooms, and these little girls, poor as they are, faithful to our recommendations, arrive quite clean every day; their mothers make them go to bed early on Saturday in order to wash and iron the one dress they own, most often because they have received it from us.[136]

---

[134] M. Monahan, *Life and Letters*, p. 451. In 1914, at Caugnawauga, Mother Stuart met some converted Iroquois, whose babies she kissed as they were presented to her.

[135] M. d'Ernemont, pp. 187-188.

[136] *Lettres annuelles*, 1867-1868, Seville, pp. 95-96.

It is not easy to warm to people who seem rough and uncouth, with vexing habits. To the religious in Great Britain the children of very poor families looked dirty and wild; but these children learned to love those who took them in and knew how to show them affection. For them too the Religious of the Sacred Heart learned how to be mothers, keen to nourish their best qualities. When Mother Swart, who had charge of the poor school and the orphanage at Blumenthal, died in 1872, the young women whom she had educated all asked for a portrait of her.

Cultural and Educative Identity in the School of Charity

Semi-cloistered, the Religious of the Sacred Heart could carry on an apostolate outside their houses only through their students. They were fully mindful of this fact, as we see in an account from Beauvais that describes this principle:

> The child who receives the seeds of the faith and develops them through grace, from the seats of the primary classroom up to the benches of the highest class, is going to take them home with her and share them with her poor family. To her father she preaches by example and sometimes by a few words, and the mother as well, touched by the piety of her daughter and some instructions she hears at the St. Anne meetings, ends up kneeling alongside her daughter at the holy table.

Through the youngest children the teachers could lead the adults to respect the laws of the Church and to the catechism. In Padua a child taught her parents to make the sign of the Cross. Thanks to the example given by his daughter, a husband stopped mistreating his wife and gave her his wages. A little citizen of Calais tried to instruct her illiterate mother: "Every evening," she said, "instead of having fun, I show her how to read and I teach her her prayers. She already knows the Our Father and the Hail Mary, but she doesn't yet make the sign of the Cross very well."[137] Mother Barat had wished to form the *formatrices*. These little girls were the proof that the project could flourish at any age.

The pupils of the boarding school were separated from those of the free school. But the education in each school flowed from the same principles and applied to all, no matter what social class. The free schools were organized in the same way as the boarding schools. The pupils were divided according to their age and capacities into classes, with a teacher in charge under the direction of a mistress general. She was in touch with

---

[137] *Lettres annuelles*, 1856-1858, p. 46.

parish priests concerning the religious practice of the children. Like the mistress general of the boarding school, the mistress general of the poor tried to help the parents in teaching their children and to influence them discreetly, as much as they could, to pay attention to their salvation.[138] Rewards were provided periodically in the schools and in the orphanages. The orphans were held to the same standards as the boarders: discretion, mutual respect, use of *vous* [formal manner of address], watchfulness concerning friendships. Spiritual offerings, like forms of personal prayer, adoration of the Blessed Sacrament, participation in the Mass, frequent communion, were the same everywhere. "It is above all by their willingness to work that [the orphans] show the strength of their earliest piety. Everyone, even the littlest, goes whole-heartedly to her tasks, even the difficult ones. They have asked as a favor to do the boarding school laundry themselves, and it is with the same eagerness that they help our sisters serve the boarders."[139] Using the orphans in service this way did not seem to trouble the religious. Before 1865 some superiors had thought about opening an orphanage because of "the difficulty of procuring a sufficient number of coadjutrix sisters for the housework." Mother Gœtz had written, "This reason seems illusory to me."[140]

There were contacts between the boarders and the pupils of the school. The boarders were urged to be generous towards the poor, and the pupils in the school and the orphans offered them an ample opportunity. They prepared them for their First Communion and gave them clothes. They served their meal on Holy Thursday after washing their hands and faces. In general it was suggested to the boarders that they make small sacrifices, in money or in kind, for the poor.[141] Often the little treats and the gifts provided for the distribution of prizes were turned into meat, bread, rice and potatoes for the school children who came dressed in rags. At Chamartín, the boarders made hats and skirts for the children of the school, using remnants of wool and silk cloth. This charitable practice grew out of the sewing lessons. The boarders worked hard on these tasks during Lent or on the eve of great feasts. They sometimes used their few minutes of relaxation, the "five minutes" and recreation time. At Besançon, permission to visit the orphans of Saint-Ferréol was a reward. At Chambéry, they were taught sign language so that they could communicate with the deaf-mute students of the school. In the same spirit, the children

[138] *Constitutions,* § 213 and 214.
[139] *Lettres annuelles,* 1868-1869, IV, p. 14.
[140] Gen. Arch. C I C 3, Box 9, General Congregation of 1865.
[141] The description of these charitable gestures takes up most of the space in the *Lettres annuelles.* In Montréal, the boarders were obliged to donate clothing to poor pupils.

of the free school learned to take an interest in those who were poorer than they and, by going without, to aid impoverished families in their neighborhood.

The aim was to turn their gaze toward Christ, the poor man, par excellence. At the Sacred Heart to inculcate charity was just as important as to develop habits of work and discipline. The boarders from affluent milieus learned that those born with means must exercise their birthright while doing no harm to others and that they must manage their resources justly. Poor children, who learned that true happiness resides neither in wealth nor in well-being, were urged to make ethical choices. They all were to practice Christian virtues. For them to be kind was to learn to pay attention to others. One religious said of the spirit she saw in the school in Roscrea: "Blessed are the poor, for the kingdom of heaven is theirs. Here, truly, that word of Our Lord is fulfilled. When entering the poor school for the first time, one is struck by the atmosphere of happiness on these little faces. Nothing equals the confidence in God, the peace, even the cheerfulness of our poor Catholics in their need and their cruel sufferings."[142]

The Sacred Heart supported the principle of legitimacy as it applied both to politics and to society. This concept rested on the assertion of a natural order in societies: Men were equal, not under the law, but in dignity before God. Social harmony was born of respect for differences and came from individual fulfillment. It appeared also in fidelity to the Church. The Society of the Sacred Heart took part in a system that was not egalitarian and that yielded both gratitude and rancor. The case of an orphan at Conflans who was very attached to Mother Gœtz gives a somewhat ambiguous example. She was offered a position far above her station. She refused it, for "Madame Gœtz told us that she would no longer recognize us as her orphans if we were to rise above our place."[143] We satisfy ourselves with praising the good spirit of this girl!

Mother Gœtz, who had vowed during the war of 1870 to develop the schools that undertook works among the working class, seems to have been preoccupied with the consequences, foreseeable or not, that the diminishing barriers between social classes could bring about. As Mother Digby recalled in 1895, "Our venerated Mother Gœtz regretted in some way the work with the orphans in the boarding schools. When the orphans, meeting the boarding pupils, forget the poverty they came from and to which they will return, and that they belong to the lower class, is this really charity? So one wonders, especially when they are not really orphans and they bring

---

[142] *Lettres annuelles*, 1863-1866, p. 67.
[143] *Lettres annuelles*, 1866-1867, p. 48.

Monique Luirard

in a small fee."[144] In the rule for the orphanages and workrooms that she composed in 1865, Mother Gœtz wrote that the orphans had to occupy "in our houses quarters separate from those of the [boarding] pupils, for fear that contact with them will give the orphans tastes beyond their status."[145] For the same reason Mother Digby found "excessive" the "alms" of certain houses extended to non-paying students in the boarding schools. "It is to render them no service. Our boarding schools do not prepare them to earn a living, if they had to."[146] In that era, one did not question the social structure. By its attitude and its works the Society of the Sacred Heart strongly underlined the eminent dignity of the poor, including that dignity in its spirituality and its world view. It was not just a matter of support. If to be charitable was a sign of God's love for each person, it followed that one must love the other as a sister, no matter what her status. The Society always tried to foster interpersonal relations among members of different social classes. It would be anachronistic to be surprised that the Society was neither involved in nor a center of social protest. It sought, sometimes with difficulty, to work in a changing world, where poverty was not necessarily synonymous with destitution and could function in different ways depending on the person involved. The standard and the intent of personalized education sometimes led to finding means of coping with it.

In approaching working class milieus the Religious of the Sacred Heart responded to appeals made to them. In Aberdeen, they gave religious instruction to boys in a correctional school. In Lille they gave religious instruction and prepared for First Communion children and adolescents who were working in a traveling circus during their brief stay in the city. They also answered distress calls from beggars, vagabonds or "bohemians." The religious had difficulty sometimes in getting these children and adolescents to understand respect for others and were occasionally surprised. In the Southwest of France, to the question: "What must one do to be saved?" a nun received an unexpected answer but at least one drawn from real life: "You have to pull your knees up to your neck when you see the police coming!" Political upsets, climatic variations, economic crises, accidents at work, all contributed to poverty. In this case, the nuns gave food to those who sometimes came for it from quite far away, and often it was their only meal of the day. They took the occasion to encourage them to bear their suffering and sometimes were able to give them spiritual encouragement. "Drawn at first by necessity they also benefited from

---

[144] Gen. Arch. C I C 3, Box 11.
[145] Gen. Arch. C I C 3, Box 9.
[146] Gen. Arch. C I C 3, Box 11.

spiritual alms and material help."[147] Many were encouraged to return to the sacraments.

The vicars and superiors tried to help their neighbors. In Belgium as well as in Spain Mother de Cléry "was ingenious in giving work to laborers, and her gift for organization and improvement, always sharp, marvelously affirmed her generosity."[148] She acted like those abbesses of the Middle Ages, who had managed their monasteries and the people who lived on their lands. In Besançon, the religious held a weekly meeting for the "autumn flowers,"[149] women over sixty, alcoholics and often beggars. In Santiago de Chile, Mother du Rousier took in hand the women who lived just outside the city. "These unfortunate women," she wrote, "would pull at your heart with their depravity and their ignorance. They are terribly indifferent, not only to their spiritual state, but even more their material well-being; they do not even think of their children." The rules of the sodality she organized for them included "the obligation to wash and comb their hair daily, to clean the house, to make sure the children do not sleep on the damp floor, to care for them, to take care of their husbands and bear with their moods." A sense of dignity had to be built and rebuilt: in Chile as elsewhere the religious tried to help. But they had to stand with the women in their well-understood plight. In Santiago,

> One of the sodalists asked one day: "Mother, may I beat my husband when he is drunk? He mistreats the children, breaks everything, and even blasphemes; it's horrible. Three or four times, I took a big stick and gave him a good blow! He kept quiet right away and went off and hid. Since then it has happened less often."

This question of conscience, maybe not so rare as one would suppose, was given to a Jesuit. He "did not hesitate to respond that, in this case, the woman was acting prudently by using the stick and she did well to use it as hard as she did!"[150]

Follow-up Projects

Alumnae Associations of the Sacred Heart

The education aimed at preparing girls to take on a role in society enlightened by their faith. The religious thought they should maintain

---

[147] *Lettres annuelles*, 1867-1868, Chamartín.
[148] *Religieuses du Sacré-Cœur*, vol. 3, p. 119.
[149] The theme of it was "Flowers need water."
[150] M. d'Ernemont, p. 180.

relationships with their former students in order to support them in their everyday life and, according to a saying of Mother Barat, "to be a link between souls and God."[151] Alumnae associations were formed in every city where there was a house of the Sacred Heart, and a sodality of the Children of Mary brought together former students of the boarding school. The purpose was "to aid young girls and women of the world to persevere in the faith, in devotion, in modesty and charity, to provide spiritual help in the midst of their difficulties and consolations in the troubles of life, to unite them by bonds of Christian friendship, in a holy, concerted effort in works of zeal and mercy, to procure for them the means of final perseverance through spiritual exercises, faithful listening to the Word of God, regular reception of the sacraments, devotion to Mary." The members had an obligation to give good example, to work at their personal salvation and to make the Sacred Hearts of Jesus and Mary known and loved. The alumnae of the free schools, married or single, could join the sodality of the Consolers of the Sacred Heart and either an association of Christian mothers or the sodality of Saint Anne. There were also sodalities of Friends of the Sacred Heart [girls] or Little Friends of the Sacred Heart of Jesus [boys], established for those who had come to catechism classes at the Sacred Heart without having gone to school there. In order to allow alumnae to return to the Sacred Heart more easily, during the last ten years of her generalate Mother Barat had wanted houses to be opened in urban centers.[152]

At the beginning there was confusion between alumnae associations and the sodalities of the Children of Mary, but they did not have the same purpose. The sodalities accepted people who had not been educated at the Sacred Heart. Sometimes religious congregations competed for members, or religious order priests and diocesan clergy vied with each other to direct them.[153] It was to avoid confusion with the sodalities that associations of alumnae were formed at the end of the nineteenth century.[154]

The public that joined either of these groups differed according to region, country and ethnicity. In Vienna, Mother de Montalembert found the association of alumnae particularly "posh:" it is true that with the archduchesses among its members, women not associated with the Court

---

[151] Arch. Gén. C I A 5 d, Box 6, quoted by Msgr. Baunard at the *Congrès des Œuvres*, p.17.

[152] Hammersmith in London was opened so that the adult Children of Mary did not have to go out to Roehampton. The popular education projects were only secondary objectives of this foundation.

[153] *Vie de la R.M. de Pichon*, pp. 236-237.

[154] A. Merdas, p. 13. The association was founded in Poland in 1913.

were unlikely to be at home there.[155] In the United States, in Mexico and in South America, sodalities were organized for persons of color. Sometimes sodalities were provided for a particular trade or profession. In Perpignan, one of them brought together gardeners and farm workers; the Religious of the Sacred Heart also founded sodalities for men, like the Honor Guard of the Blessed Sacrament at Jette and the one for miners at Bois-l'Évêque. At the Sault-au-Récollet, the woodsmen who manned the barges carrying the wood down the rivers, the *cageurs*, were first organized by the nuns, who subsequently turned the work over to the bishop of Montréal.[156]

On several occasions, the Religious of the Sacred Heart questioned the criteria for recruitment for the sodality of the Children of Mary. They wanted membership to result from a true commitment and not one just inspired by a desire to keep in contact with former schoolmates. Demands of the sodalists were extensive, even addressing social life. In 1890, the members were not only to stay away from the theater, but "at balls and evening parties, every Child of Mary will avoid staying until the end when people more freely dance unsuitable dances, like the cotillion. If they give these parties at their homes, they must eliminate these last dances." That being the case, it would be better not to give a ball at all. Neither should they hold receptions during Lent, and they should distinguish themselves by modest bearing.[157] With good sense Mother Lehon concluded the discussion: "Let us try at least to show our pupils the vanity of all this by developing their piety!"

Sodality exercises were about the same everywhere. Sodalists met each month to listen to spiritual reading and to hear a talk, during which they would sew vestments for poor churches. In 1900, if we can believe the figure given by Msgr. Baunard, they had completed throughout the world in a single year 600 copes, 2600 chasubles, 340 humeral veils for Benediction of the Blessed Sacrament, 160 banners, 400 albs, 500 or 600 altar cloths, 2600 amices, 4400 purificators, 2600 corporals, 1560 palls, 2800 finger towels. They had also donated 200 sacred vessels. The author omitted the number of rosaries that had accompanied these labors. For the working class sodalists the meetings, which took place every Sunday, mixed relaxation, short talks, time for prayer and participation in Vespers. Assisted by some religious and young workers, the mistress of the poor school directed them. Sometimes a hundred, even several hundred, girls and young

---

[155] *Vie de la R.M. de Montalembert*, p. 295.
[156] *Religieuses du Sacré-Cœur*, vol. 3, pp. 329-330.
[157] Gen. Arch. C I C 3, Box 12. This sketch of the rule ends with this consideration: "Before making these decisions, it would be good to sound out prudently some holy and experienced priests, for example, the provincials of the Jesuits and some others on whom we can count."

women flocked to them, the sodalists bringing with them their friends and relatives.

Sometimes sodalities tried gathering alumnae of both boarding school and free school in one group. But this plan, however good an idea, did not leave much liberty to the members from the free school, who could find themselves taking a back seat out of gratitude to those seen as their "protectors." When the sodality of *Marie Affligée* [Consolers of Mary] for the alumnae of Santa Rufina [a free school] in Rome was received at the Vatican in 1870, the address to the pope was read by Countess Cocacicchi, president of the Children of Mary.

Alumnae associations and sodalities were extremely active in some areas. In Rome, the Children of Mary worked to promote religious instruction, to learn about "good schools," which "in spite of the wrath of hell were quietly continuing the work of Christian instruction."[158] The sodalities were sometimes a seed bed for parish works. The members were generous with their time and money. In Brussels, after learning that the vicar was not able to pay twenty-five girls in a workshop a wage intended to keep them from choosing secular professional schools, the Children of Mary offered to sponsor them.[159] Alumnae everywhere devoted themselves to serving the sick, visiting hospitals and prisons. In New York, they took care of abandoned children and prepared those in their parishes for First Communion by providing catechism class every Sunday. In Chicago, in response to an influx of Italian immigrants, they organized church, school, and catechism classes for them as well as clubs where young people and adults could learn English.[160] In France, where regional languages remained largely in use in the outlying provinces, some alumnae carried on an apostolate in the regional language.[161] Many sought to bring back the people with whom they worked to the practice of religion. "Thanks to them, baptisms were performed, marriages were rectified, latecomers approached the sacraments of penance and the Eucharist."[162] These remarks concerning the sodalists from the school at the Trinità dei Monti could apply to them all. Without a doubt the education received at the Sacred Heart urged the alumnae to give open witness to their faith. As the religious in Halifax

---

[158] *Lettres annuelles*, 1870-1871.
[159] *Lettres annuelles*, 1872-1873.
[160] *Enfants de Marie*, vol. 2, p. 29.
[161] *Lettres annuelles*. In 1866, after nine months of novitiate, Henriette Kernafflen de Kergos died. Before entering religious life, she had prepared children of her parish for First Communion in the Breton language, and every day she read and commented on extracts from the lives of the saints for her domestic help.
[162] *Lettres annuelles*, 1890-1891, p. 17.

noted, "The good done outside by the sodalities is remarkable."[163] In the course of visits to the sick the members did housework and offered "good reading." They had learned to combine visiting the poor with offering the witness of their own lives and basic, fruitful catechizing.

The Society of the Sacred Heart, like the Society of Jesus, had put in place a self-governing system that worked both within their schools and outside them. But sodalists of the Sacred Heart also encouraged new endeavors and did not just support those who had educated them. In England, they assisted the Sisters of Charity and the Helpers of the Holy Souls to get established in London. It is true that the founder of the Helpers was an alumna of Lille. The alumnae of the Sacred Heart knew they could count on the assistance of other alumnae in developing their good works. A real network of mutual aid developed among women who did not know one another but who could say: "I recognize her Child of Mary medal...that is enough!"[164]

For Mother Barat, the spirituality of the Sacred Heart urged putting oneself at the service of others, showing the love of God that she had discovered because she herself was loved. Madeleine Sophie had wanted the education provided in her schools to contribute to the formation of "strong, virtuous women through faith."[165] The alumnae showed that this project was not utopian. They were particularly effective when the Sacred Heart experienced difficulties with political authorities, offering a refuge to the nuns and striving to safeguard their pursuits.

Their sense of duty and responsibility and their devotion were nourished by the contacts they maintained with their former teachers. Besides, the superiors made the contacts a priority, keeping in touch through visits, correspondence and, of course, prayer. Everyone carried out this task in one way or another. In Perpignan, Mother Guiraudet:

> ...wanted the members of the sodality, placed by their title and its privileges at the center of devotion to the Sacred Heart, to spread it all around them by their influence and example. She said, "If the Heart of Jesus is, so to speak, your special property, you must in turn see yourselves as the born promoters of a devotion called upon to regenerate the whole of society and each individual soul. Could one imagine the heart of a Child of Mary without this zeal that is simply the flame of love, and could you allow anyone to surpass you in ardor in spreading a devotion that is so dear to you?"

---

[163] *Lettres annuelles*, 1863-1866, p. 141.
[164] *Enfants de Marie*, vol. 1, p. 125.
[165] *Lettres choisies*, p. 104.

She suggested regular "practices" and made suggestions "that were not merely formulas but ideas to be meditated on and weighed and applied to specific needs."

> Increase before Our Lord souls of adoration and reparation and be sure that he will be divinely grateful for your efforts. If you are concerned with him, he will think of you; if you take in hand the cause of his glory, he will not forget your interests; and what graces flow for you from this precious and divine exchange! If Our Lord can count on the generosity of your devotedness, you will be able to rest securely on his sovereignly faithful heart.[166]

At Montpellier, Mother Marie de Cabanous could find just the right words when speaking to the working class sodalists so that they were on the point of tears as she began: "We fell to weeping!" They even accepted her criticism: "*Saccagez-nous [sic], Madame Marie, saccagez-nous,*" [Shake us up…] they used to say to her.[167] The spiritual side of the life of the alumnae was firmly linked to charity. Their teachers nourished it by directing the most diligent ones along the best paths to spiritual renewal.

Retreat Work

From the beginning the Religious of the Sacred Heart knew that education had to go beyond the classroom. To make sure the pupils were followed up, the Constitutions had called for the organization of retreats for "women living in the world." This apostolic activity was seen as

> the continuation and consolidation of the good they have done by educating young girls and giving them an opportunity, after their entrance into the world, of coming back, from time to time, to refresh and strengthen those good principles and values that they had acquired in the course of their education and that the dangers of the world have weakened.[168]

Until the end of her life, Mother Barat tried to enhance the work of retreats. In Rome and in Paris, she encouraged setting aside spaces for this mission. She had even thought about founding a "spiritual center"

---

[166] *Vie de la R.M. Guiraudet*, pp. 30-31.
[167] *Religieuses du Sacré-Cœur*, vol. 3, pp. 332-333.
[168] *Constitutions* of 1815, § 217.

where the religious would have been freed from teaching, but it did not materialize.

Nothing indicates that the retreats foreseen by the Constitutions were destined only for alumnae, although the vocabulary suggests it. In fact women who were not alumnae came to these retreats, "closed" or not. The retreatants stayed in separate quarters where rooms were prepared for them. They could use the chapel of the day school or the boarding school and the community garden.[169] There were also day-time retreats. The retreats were held during school vacations, which meant that the nuns were free and space was available and quiet, above all on the eve of Lent, a way to keep the young women away from taking part in the alarming excesses of Mardi Gras festivities. Individual retreats were also offered to women who came whenever they could. Some were sent to the Sacred Heart by Jesuits who continued to direct them during or after this time of renewal.[170] It was not only women who were considering possible entry into religious life who came. From the middle of the 1840's, retreats had been offered to those who had been pupils in the free schools. The proposal was broadened to include other women of the parishes. Those who came to these retreats varied with the social structure of the region. Depending on the locale, working women, country women, school teachers, laundresses were all welcomed. The retreats were silent, and they were publicized in the local press.

For working women, to make a five-day retreat was all the more laudable because they had to give up their wages during it. They worked longer days or worked at night so that their families did not suffer. To minimize expenses they returned home to sleep and brought their own lunch. Often the religious accepted gratis those without the means to pay. For young mothers child care was an issue. In Calais, at the end of the century, the nuns arranged that during the retreat the boarders would baby sit the children. In many cities husbands no longer objected to their wives' retreats, when they saw the good results. Some even urged them to go, even if they had to take care of the children in their wives' absence. Sometimes they asked to take part themselves, and so as not to disturb the women, they were happy to listen to the instructions through a window onto the courtyard, or they were seated in a separate chapel. At Conflans, the novices were in charge of welcoming the retreatants, the singing and the rosary.[171]

Individual and group retreats were a source of uplift and thanksgiving for the Religious of the Sacred Heart. At the Trinità dei Monti,

---

[169] In May 1937, the pupils at Winnipeg were sent home, armed with class work, to make room for a ladies' retreat!

[170] It was one of the special activities of the Trinità dei Monti.

[171] *Vie de la Mère Fornier*, p. 112.

Retreatants established in the world have given us an example of humility and self-denial. We could mention a Russian princess who worked hard not to stand out and a young marchioness who, having fasted on bread and water, asked as a favor to wait on the pupils, and when told she could not, was only too happy to wash the dishes; she thought of the humiliation it was for the Mother of God to have to do such work and found it neither trouble nor disgrace.[172]

But all the retreatants were admirable, particularly those who walked thirty kilometers to the Sacred Heart or who, after spending the whole night in expectation of their mistress's wake-up call, slept only two hours so as not to miss the morning meditation.

The data we have show that hundreds of women followed these spiritual exercises every year. Between 1863 and 1866, the Villa Lante welcomed 891. Riedenburg had 550 retreatants in 1867, plus 700 the following year. The same year, Poitiers hosted 400. In three years, Detroit welcomed 1362. The religious looked for the best preachers to give the "exercises." They offered spiritual enhancements. They clearly had found an apostolate that proved to be both effective and successful.

To be adorers of the Heart of Jesus and to form adorers: the aim the young Sophie Barat had envisaged for the women who joined her was carried out wherever the Society of the Sacred Heart was established and by every means the religious had at their disposal. It is thanks to the alumnae that the devotion to the Sacred Heart was spread in countries where the Catholic Church was represented by only a handful of the faithful and where there was no church structure to promote it. The religious of Roscrea, shortly after the death of Mother Barat, were fully aware of this. Through their alumnae, daughters and wives of diplomats or British army officers, the Heart of Jesus became known to the ends of the earth.

> The devotion to the Sacred Heart consoles them in the distant countries to which many are sent. At this moment our children are invoking this divine Heart on the burning coasts of Hindustan and the Cape of Good Hope, on the heights of the Himalayas, in the most remote corners of Australia, in the various states of America as far as California.[173]

Coming from countries where the state supported religion, the Religious of the Sacred Heart saw that elsewhere Christian presence could be assured even without state support. In Catholic countries, in countries where

---

[172] *Lettres annuelles*, 1852-1853, p. 141.
[173] *Lettres annuelles*, N° 19, pp. 65-66.

Catholics were a minority and in non-Christian countries, wherever the Society of the Sacred Heart had not been able to make foundations, lay persons played a major role in the spread of devotion to the Sacred Heart. The religious had helped them to develop a solid, human and spiritual presence: their work had borne fruit.

Chapter V

CONSOLIDATION OF THE SOCIETY OF THE SACRED HEART

When Bishop Pie of Poitiers sent his condolences after the death of Mother Barat, he wrote: "The loss of a founder and first superior is always a serious event for a congregation."[1] The event had been dreaded for a long time. To mitigate its effects Mother Barat had sought to avoid a struggle for succession by naming a vicar general, who, she thought, would be elected superior general. The assistants general gave their support to Mother Gœtz. On 26 May Mother Prévost assured her of her support[2] and on 29 May, after the burial of Mother Barat, Mother Lehon had the assistants general make "an act of submission to the vicar general until the election of a superior general,"[3] evidence that the allegiance to the vicar general was not permanent. Mother Gœtz was elected unanimously. The quick trip she made to Rome gave her the assurance of being confirmed in her office by Pope Pius IX.

The succession was settled; it did not follow, however, that the Society of the Sacred Heart would avoid some instability in its direction and governance. In 1874, Mother Lehon recalled that Mother Gœtz "had continued and consolidated the work of the founder with devotedness and abnegation."[4] Mother Desoudin agreed, judging that "she had found the Society on an admirable path of obedience and religious spirit, but it needed consolidation; some of the intentions of our venerated Mother that her age had not allowed her to carry out called for implementation."[5]

---

[1] *Lettres annuelles*, 1863-1865, p. 188.
[2] *Lettres annuelles*, 1870-1872, p. LI.
[3] P. Perdrau, *Les Loisirs...*, vol. 1. p. 334.
[4] *Circulaires de la T.R.M. Lehon*, 10 January 1874, p. 9.
[5] *Vie de la R.M. Desoudin*, p. 171.

The Society of the Sacred Heart commonly regards with understanding Mother Gœtz's concern to govern exactly as had her predecessor and explains it by her rigid education. Certainly her formation and her humility could have steered her in that direction. However, Mother Gœtz was a woman of sufficient intelligence to grasp that after the death of the revered founder, "so providentially preserved for her large family,"[6] the congregation had need of being confirmed in its principles and of being urged to be faithful to them against all odds. That was also the opinion of the Vatican. When she met Cardinal Antonelli, secretary of state, Mother Gœtz heard him speak with great esteem of the Society of the Sacred Heart: "It does much good," he said. "In order to conserve it and make it grow, take great care to preserve your primitive spirit; avoid innovations; your experience of living your rules ought to give you every confidence in the future; your Society is strongly constituted; maintain faithfully the spirit your Mother Foundress has established for it."[7] The superior general concluded: "These precious remarks of benevolence of the head of the Church and of the venerable prelates associated with him must be for us a new stimulus to fervor and to the desire to preserve intact the religious spirit our venerated Mother Foundress strove to inculcate in our souls."[8] This critical time called on Mother Gœtz for prudent management that would reassure both members of the Society of the Sacred Heart and its public.

The Work of Consolidation

Putting in Order and Taking Hold

Mother Barat no longer traveled at the end of her life, and her assistants general, on account of their age, had been in no state to do so either. In governing a congregation, visiting the houses is indispensable so that its common spirit can support its mission everywhere.[9] Visits enabled Mother Gœtz to get to know the reality of the Society of the Sacred

---

[6] *Lettres annuelles*, 1863-1865, testimony of the Jesuit provincial, Père de Ponlevoy, p. LXI.
[7] *Circulaires de la T.R.M. Gœtz*, 9 December 1865, p. 32.
[8] Gœtz, *Circulaires*, p. 33.
[9] Mother Digby took the risk of going to North America in 1898-1899, even though at the time she had a heart condition that caused people to wonder if she could stand the journey, because she thought her visit would strengthen the bonds between the houses of the new world and Europe (*Life of Mother Gertrude Bodkin*, pp. 22-23).

Heart, an important step for her, as she had not participated in the central government before 1864.

Between 1865 and 1870, accompanied by Mother Lehon, Mother Gœtz systematically visited of most of the European houses. Some of those most recently opened had never received a visit from Mother Barat. Visiting these sixty houses allowed Mother Gœtz to make contact with the religious, to become familiar with the places and to get an idea of the work. She inspected each school, examining the exercise books of each class and the class preparation of the teachers.[10] What she had done herself the superior general could ask of others. She recommended that the vicars undertake formal visits of the houses in their charge and that they take an interest in all the religious, including the sisters.[11] She determined to put an end to carelessness, to a tendency to independence and to some of the departures from the rule that could result in lack of fervor. She reminded superiors that the management of temporal affairs, acquisitions and sales, depends on the superior general, who alone has the right of administering, acquiring and selling and of accepting legacies.[12] These reminders suggest that these principles were not being followed everywhere.

Like the founder, the new superior general was particularly concerned about the practice of poverty. Relying on advice asked earlier of Father Rozaven, she arranged that in the boarding schools there were to be no "additional fees" asked of the pupils that did not represent an actual service. Those in charge were not to try to make a profit. She raised the delicate matter of the remuneration for their work received by pupils in the free schools and the orphanages. She said that Father Rozaven had suggested that this money be used for the relief of the poor. She emphasized that pressure was not to be put on students of means by demanding too much generosity of them.

> The use of the pupils' money must be handled with great delicacy. While it is admirable to inspire them with good will and the spirit of almsgiving and to lead them to practice this duty, we must not ask too much, still less spend their small allowances without their knowledge, or tax arbitrarily this or that expense weekly or monthly. Justice can suffer in this way.[13]

There were also decrees to be carried out. Mother Barat had not always followed the one that regulated the term of office of superiors; this

---

[10] P. Perdrau, *Les Loisirs…*, vol. 1, p. 415.
[11] *Circulaires de la T.R.M. Goetz*, 22 September 1866, p. 49.
[12] *Circulaires*, 24 October 1865, p. 27.
[13] *Circulaires*, p. 55.

question had come up in 1864 and 1865. In 1869, Mother Gœtz made an example of the Rue de Varenne, which had always enjoyed a separate status,[14] by sending to Rome the mistress general who had occupied that post for eighteen years. Mother Prévost, who had been superior at Moulins for fifteen years, retired there voluntarily, but this loss of authority pained her. That was not the only "exceptional" case. In effect, the trend was to keep superiors in office for a long time, even to choose them from among the other officers of the house, which was a rather monastic way of governing.

On several occasions Mother Gœtz asked religious in positions of responsibility to fulfill the obligation to send in from time to time their organizational plans and the consultations required of them.[15] Superiors were to have the aspirants arrive on time for the opening of probation; the treasurers should provide an accurate picture of the finances of their house and pay the *dixième*, the tenth of their revenues, when they could.[16] Mother Gœtz required each one, conscience bound, to reread the decrees concerning her charge and to weigh before God the duties it imposed on her.

One of the ways of maintaining and reinforcing unity was periodically to gather the religious with the superior general. The founder had wished to have superiors join her for a retreat. In August 1869, Mother Gœtz invited some of them to the motherhouse for a meeting so that she could get to know them personally and share with them her ideas about the reform of the studies she had in mind. This meeting was simultaneously a retreat and a learning session aimed especially at those who had recently been named superior.[17]

Little by little the Society developed policies in areas that earlier had been left to improvisation. Mother Desoudin was given charge of the reform of the probation. She began the practice of forming groups of probanists who began on a fixed date. She took charge also of the long retreat that preceded final commitment.[18]

Government and Fidelity to the "Primitive" Spirit

In 1865 everyone had hoped that a long generalate would consolidate a congregation that was already vital; however, Mother Gœtz died on 4 January 1874. From then on the question arose: how to know what

---

[14] It had never had a regular visit.
[15] *Circulaires de la T.R.M. Goetz*, 30 July 1866, p. 44.
[16] *Circulaires*, 28 December 1869, p. 107.
[17] Invitations to Paris of superiors outside of Europe were an exception. For them a retreat was added to a meeting of superiors, or a meeting and retreat were planned in conjunction with the visit of the superior general.
[18] *Vie de la Mère Desoudin*, p. 144.

fidelity to the original spirit should mean. In order to consolidate what they had inherited, the superiors general chose to govern in the same manner as the founder and her successor. Announcing her nomination, Mother Lehon wrote to the Society, 4 June 1874: "Let me repeat to you that you will find that as far as is possible my governing will be the same: we will follow step by step in the footsteps of those who have preceded us."[19] During the general congregation, Bishop Pie had "augured for the strength and the duration [of the Society of the Sacred Heart] in the future by its close conformity to the primitive spirit," with which its first mothers had inspired it. It must demonstrate the same virtues, "and then the divine Heart will watch over his little Society, no matter its governing instrument."[20] One could imagine many means of achieving this objective. On 12 May 1882, Mother Lehon presented the one she considered the best: "Read and reread the circulars of our first Mothers and the decrees; they complement the rule, and I know of nothing more useful for guiding us in the true spirit of our vocation. How many problems would be avoided if each one were guided by them."[21] In 1884, she specified that the goal of a general congregation was "not to invent, our venerable Mother having foreseen everything, but to reinvigorate what might have grown weak and to maintain the law of our Society."[22] This observation was repeated at the election of superiors general until the middle of the next century.

There are many possible reasons for this governmental direction, among them Mother Lehon's age at the time of her election – she was sixty-eight years old – and the fact that her generalate lasted twenty years. For almost fifty years the superiors general were chosen not only because they were excellent religious with varied experience and genuine gifts, but also because they had governed with the founder or because she had known them.[23] Mother Lehon had spent most of her religious life in Italy, where she had held the offices of vicar, superior and mistress of novices. She spoke Italian perfectly and was at home in Roman society,

---

[19] *Circulaires de la T.R.M. Lehon*, p. 24.
[20] Lehon, *Circulaires*, pp. 28-29.
[21] Lehon, *Circulaires*, p. 93.
[22] Gen. Arch. C I C 3, Box 10, 29 February 1884.
[23] *Vie de la R.M. de Lavigerie*, pp. 127-128. Mother Desoudin wrote to her [R.M. de Lavigerie] on the eve of the general congregation of 1894: "Pray with us for this solemn and important meeting. All the first mothers have disappeared; a new generation is called to decide the fate of the Society, the preservation or the weakening of its spirit. The congregation will include twenty-two, of whom only three or four met the Mother foundress when they were novices. I am actually the only one who knew her as I was superior myself. You understand...."

both lay and ecclesiastical; she was respected by Pius IX and the members of the Curia. Her education put her at ease in personal relations, and she had skill at repartee.[24] Named assistant general in 1864 by Mother Barat, who appreciated her generosity, courage, daring and firmness, she had demonstrated these qualities during the siege of Paris and the Commune. Mother von Sartorius, who was German, had governed houses in Germany, Netherlands, France and Belgium. Vicar of Louisiana between 1884 and 1886, she had direct knowledge of the United States, unlike those who had preceded her. The circumstances of Mabel Digby's conversion and her desire to enter religious life had interested Mother Barat, who herself took charge of her preparation for final profession.[25] Mother Digby had been among the last probanists to receive the cross and ring from the hands of Mother Barat. She had enjoyed the confidence of Mother Gœtz, who had named her mistress of novices and vicar of England.

There were, however, other internal reasons. In the Society of the Sacred Heart, as in the rest of western society, education encouraged respect for authority and tradition, to the point that "all innovation [was viewed as] threatening danger."[26] Besides, why innovate when the balance sheet was in the black? The Constitutions of 1815 had proven their worth. After the shock experienced during the long crisis of 1839, no one had thought to call into question the kinds of authority that had fostered the growth of the Society. The very extent of that crisis had created the fear that any change might undermine or even destroy the edifice.

Even so, was it necessary to keep all the same governmental procedures? Not all the religious at the heart of the congregation thought so. On the eve of the centenary of the Society, Mother Digby wrote: "Our traditions are venerable now after a century of trial, but the spirit that animates them must never lose the vigor proper to youth, for it is only in the Kingdom of God that the maturity of age and the ardor of youth are united."[27] However, like her predecessors, she herself sought to reinforce submission to the decisions of the "center." She wrote one day in exasperation: "It is too elementary to add that whenever advice or a decision is requested, we must wait for the answer before acting. We are a long way from the era when the slowness of the mail delayed the expedition of business, and for all that nothing is lost. A statesman said: 'Difficult

---

[24] P. Perdrau, *Les Loisirs...*, vol. 1, pp. 373 and 414.
[25] Mother Digby recounted during her visit to the United States that Mother Prévost had refused her first attempts to enter. It was Mother Barat who accepted her into the novitiate.
[26] Gen. Arch. C I C 3, Box 9, 1874.
[27] *Circulaires de la T.R.M. Digby*, 18 November 1899, p. 90.

matters settle themselves provided one knows how to wait,' and we have experienced this truth very often."[28]

Originality of Several Governmental Practices

After Mother Barat's death, Mother Gœtz reflected on government in the Society of the Sacred Heart. She did not have a chance to share the results, but those who succeeded her made use of her notes. Her attention had been drawn especially to the naming of the assistants general and the role of the general congregation.

The Society of the Sacred Heart was a congregation with a central government, with its power strongly concentrated in the hands of the "first authority," the superior general. She stood at the hub, and final decisions were her responsibility. Because of the spread of the Society and general developments of political life in the countries where the Society was established, the question arose as to who could help the superior general succeed at her task without, however, challenging the centralization of government. Beyond prayer, devoted cooperation, deepened knowledge of the Constitutions, the teachings of the founder and the traditions of the Institute, was there not possible a division of labor among the superior general and her assistants in the administration of the Society? The assistants general, named every six years by the general congregation, were aides, advisors and supports for the superior general, but what powers did they hold?

In the middle of the 1830's, Mother Barat had tried to learn more about the workings of government in the Society of Jesus. Father Rozaven had given her information on the powers and the role of the assistants general and the provincials, and he had also offered tactical advice on the choices to make at the time of the nominations. The founder had said how, by whom, with what limits her authority could be supported:

> We will give our Mothers assistant general, when we judge it apropos, charge of details of some houses, without, however, abandoning any portion of the dear flock confided to us; likewise, our Mothers assistant will act only in agreement with us and according to our advice, communicating carefully with us what is addressed to them or to ourselves during our absence, always aware of when we are in Paris. Local superiors will never let a month go by without writing to us directly about the houses in their charge, and we will always decide ourselves whatever concerns poverty and changes in the employments that are

[28] Digby, *Circulaires*, 17 June 1898, pp. 77-78.

ours to appoint. Although our plan in general is to delegate the visit of the houses to our assistants general, we will not, however, entirely give up this important provision; we will dedicate three or four months every year to seeing some of them, then return the rest of the time to the motherhouse, our place of residence.[29]

It was concluded that the assistants general in the Society of the Sacred Heart were to live near the superior general to aid her with their advice and their zeal without having any authority on their own except in the rare cases provided by the Constitutions. They formed the council of the superior general, who could appeal to their devotedness in the service of the Society.

The founder had governed the Society of the Sacred Heart with the cooperation of religious who were her friends. To be so surrounded met her needs and reassured her, but it was also a governmental process that had allowed her to channel the dynamism of certain of her contemporaries and to neutralize some strong personalities. In consequence, she had rarely changed her assistants general, limiting herself to replacing the ones who died, those whose health was too precarious or, at the end of the 1839 crisis, those who did not believe they ought to continue and whom she would have been obliged to replace in any case.

After Mother Barat's death, maintaining the assistants general in office became the norm. If we consider the cases of those named between 1865 and the end of the century, we observe that with two exceptions, Mothers Nathalie de Serres and Clémence Fornier who died after two or three years in office, all had long, even very long terms. Mother Hardey was assistant general for fourteen years. Mother Cahier held the office for twenty years; and as she had been secretary general for a large part of Mother Barat's generalate, she had known the business of the government for a very long time. The extreme cases, however, are those of Mother Desoudin and Mother Césarine Borget. A victim of pulmonary congestion at the beginning of 1896, the former decided to resign as mistress of probation the following 2 June. Mother Digby commented thus about her decision: "She is the only one who is happy about it. If Our Lord had deigned to preserve her for us, we would always have considered her as our devoted assistant, our support, our advisor."[30] Mother Desoudin died a few days later at eighty-five, having been assistant general for thirty-one years. As for

---

[29] *Circulaires de la T.R.M. Barat*, 4 June 1835.
[30] *Circulaires de la T.R.M. Digby*, pp. 33-34. In the United States, Mother Digby said of Mother Desoudin: "I miss her so much. I valued her advice, for she paid me no compliments but told me straight out what was not working so that I could remedy the situation" (Gen. Arch. C I A 5, Box 6, p. 29).

Mother Borget, she died in 1917 at the age of ninety, still treasurer general! She had held this office for forty-five years, combining it for forty years with that of assistant general. She had beaten the records established in Mother Barat's time by Mothers Desmarquest and de Charbonnel, assistants general respectively for thirty-eight and forty-one years.

At the general congregations, on an average half the assistants general were renewed in office[31] or interim appointments were ratified. Long terms of the assistants general allowed continuity in the management of the Society at the time of the death of the founder and later, after generalates of short duration. But they impeded the renewal of the councils. Since the assistants general left office often very advanced in age, even handicapped, the superior general out of courtesy did not dare to ask for their resignation. The system had evolved towards assistantship for life, comparable to the life term of the superior general.

In practice this system risked complex, even ambiguous, consequences. When she took charge, the superior general inherited those who had been appointed by her predecessor, with whom she had sometimes worked, but who were often older than she and whose ideas and ways of acting she did not necessarily share. She could adapt to the situation; but if it did not suit her, she could also look for ways around it by setting up debatable governmental practices not based on the provisions of the Constitutions. Mother Digby was the first to make use of this expedient. This very intelligent woman endowed with a strong personality did not have the gift of working with a team. She frequently administered the congregation without referring to her assistants general, confiding important missions to a vicar, remarkable herself for her gifts, but not a member of her council, Mother Janet Stuart.[32] Mother Digby did not hold council meetings regularly; she did not pass on necessary documents to her assistants and limited herself to asking them to answer a written question on a matter of extreme importance simply with "yes" or "no." This manner of governing was the basis of the crisis that broke out in 1904, in the course of which the superior general was accused of authoritarianism.

The "affair of 1904" was not fully known in the Society, even by the superior general herself. Mother Digby afterward had Mother de Lavigerie and Mother von Loë, the vicar of Italy, inquire at the Vatican in order to

---

[31] Except in 1895, since new nominations had taken place the preceding year.
[32] People reproached Mother Digby for having chosen Mother Stuart as her companion in North America but above all for having sent her to South America as visitatrix when she did not speak Spanish. She should have included Mother de Lavigerie. During this journey Mother Stuart kept a double correspondence, one in English with Mother Digby and the other in French to be communicated to the assistants general.

find out exactly what had happened. Mother von Loë prepared a report, to which she added notes that allowed for further discussion of the question so as to avoid similar difficulties in the future.[33] She saw in the affair an attack of "the enemy of all good," who sought "to sow discord in the field of the father of the family and who worked with only too much success, alas, to divide the members of the private council."

Two assistants general were at the heart of the storm: Mother Juliette Depret, superior of the *Maison des Anges* in Paris, and Mother Sophie du Chélas, in charge of the probation; they had both been appointed assistants general in 1894: "They found fault with the government [of Mother Digby] and ended up believing that the Society was going to lose its primitive spirit, to be led in ways that were foreign to our principles and practices."[34] In such a case, the Constitutions provided that the *admonitrice* general should be informed of the dispute and herself inform the superior general. Otherwise, it was up to the cardinal protector to intervene. It is quite possible that Mother de Pichon, the *admonitrice*, did not exactly play her proper role in this situation.[35] However that may be, Mother Depret, who had written to the cardinal protector, must have mentioned her difficulties to her confessor. He was a diocesan priest who, no doubt frightened by what he had heard, informed Cardinal Richard [archbishop of Paris]. About the same time the priest was sent to Paray-le-Monial. Under unknown circumstances and probably in the context of spiritual direction, he shared his concerns about his former penitents with some Jesuits. They advised him to send the report he had written to Rome, and they made sure it got to the Congregation for Religious. Pius X knew about it.[36] Other interventions also informed the Vatican of the perils threatening the Society

---

[33] Gen. Arch. C III C 13, 1904, XV.

[34] Gen. Arch. C III C 13, 1904, XV. Report of von Loë, p. 1.

[35] In January 1905, before making her annual retreat, Mother Digby had written to her [Mother de Pichon] asking her to point out the faults that she had noticed. Mother de Pichon answered in the name of the assistants general: "We have received with deep feeling the kind words you have written as you went into retreat in which you give free rein to your humility. That has encouraged us to demonstrate humility also, with greater justification. Very Reverend Mother, allow me to ask you to pardon me for all you have had to suffer from me because of my many faults and self-centeredness" (M. Quinlan, *Digby Stuart...*, pp. 195 and 282-284). [It was the duty of the *admonitrice* to admonish the superior general, to advise her of any faults or lacks in her manner of governing. The *admonitrice* was usually the eldest assistant general. Translator's note.]

[36] Report of von Loë, p. 2.

of the Sacred Heart.[37] According to Mother von Loë's investigations, Cardinal Richard was the first to tell the Holy See of the division within the general council, and he asked to be in charge of monitoring the general congregation that was about to take place. Instead of probing the details about who was responsible for these inopportune communications, it might be interesting to consider certain complaints against Mother Digby. She was reproached with authoritarianism, with government in the English fashion [*à l'anglaise* (sic)] and with not conferring with her assistants general on matters of government.

Cardinal Richard received a rescript from Rome naming him apostolic delegate to the General Congregation of 1904. He was charged with presiding at the assembly and the elections and with questioning the vicars. Mother Digby, on her part, was ordered to invite the two French vicars whose houses had already been closed to take part in the general congregation. The general congregation opened amid deep uneasiness. Its deliberations did not conclude that Mother Digby had contravened the primitive spirit. Finally, one of the eldest of the vicars "stood up to protest in the name of all her fidelity to the superior general and her complete confidence in her about the decisions to be made for the communities in France."[38] This statement suggests that the dispute had to do, at least in part, with the question of leaving France. It is clear that the role of the archbishop of Paris in the proceedings of the general congregation recalled the unfortunate precedent of the crisis of 1839. Cardinal Richard personally met with each member of the general congregation. As may be imagined, the terms of the two assistants general who had brought about the scandal were not renewed.

The "affair of 1904" provided an opportunity to reflect on authority and on the division of powers within the general council. In a document in her own hand, Mother Digby placed in parallel columns the questions posed and her own answers. Ordinarily it was considered normal that a religious speak with her confessor when in a dilemma. For Mother Digby, that was wrong. She believed it reasonable to reproach a religious for speaking to her confessor concerning the government of the institute: it is an even more serious indiscretion for a member of the council who is pledged to hold such matters in confidence. A religious ought not to address a bishop who is not the superior of the institute – the reference was to the archbishop

---

[37] M. Quinlan.

[38] Report of von Loë, p. 3. It must have been Mother de Cléry. Mother Deidier, the oldest of the vicars, noted her regret that none of the vicars had been informed in advance of the pontifical decree appointing Cardinal Richard apostolic delegate, "which was a change with regard to our tradition and our customs."

of Paris – but only the cardinal protector.[39] Mothers Depret and du Chélas were evidently accused of having "sold out" their superior general, since the expression appears twice in the notes. Mother Digby evaded this point, but in the following paragraph, which objected that the superior general should "show herself open to a filial representation," she stated that "a superior general is in no way obliged to bow to the opinion of an assistant general and that the latter is in no way authorized by this fact to turn to someone outside to put her opinion forward." Moreover, she underlined that the action of Mothers Depret et du Chélas had gone against "the spirit of our Constitutions, which give great authority to the superior general and to the means chosen for preserving the unity of the congregation, that is, to have a cardinal protector, and in this case, to limit the delegated bishops or prelates to presiding at the elections." And she concluded her remarks by showing that in 1904,

> ...under the pretext of abuse of power, there was a movement to destroy the specific characteristics of the institute, those of authority, hierarchy and obedience, characteristics absolutely essential to those others, union and charity. For it is in vain that we can hope to be united among ourselves unless we are united with authority. Obedience is a bond as charity is a bond. "Mine are obedience and love," and for authority to be exercised to the fullest it must be understood and supported. In 1904 there was a deviation from the Constitutions that shook the principle of authority.

In these notes Mother Digby did not distinguish what related to the principle of authority, which she defended energetically, from what related to its exercise; and she did not try to distinguish either between authority and authoritarianism, of which the two assistants general had accused her and of which other religious had complained.

Mother von Loë for her part wrote "*Notes sur les R.M. Assistantes générales*." She recalled that the assistants general "should never lose sight of the fact that they are only deputies and channels and that authority comes to them only from the head of the Society."[40] She noted also that "the more the assistants general can be kept *au courant* of the affairs of the Society the better it will be, but the final decision concerning these affairs belongs always to the superior general." She recognized that there could have been some failures in that regard in the time of Mother Digby. Further, it seems that Mother Digby's method of governing did not change after the crisis

---

[39] Mother Depret had actually written to Cardinal di Pietro.
[40] Notes on our R.M. Assistants General, §8.

of 1904. Division resurfaced and at least one assistant general, Mother de Lavigerie, complained that Mother Digby chose her councilors from outside the council.[41]

Besides the members of the general council, the general congregation included the vicars. In 1851, Mother Barat had obtained from the Holy See the possibility of being seconded by some local superiors, vicars, to whom she delegated some of her authority. According to Mother Gœtz, their role was to instruct superiors placed under their authority in the art of governing according to the spirit of the Society. An anonymous report specifies:

> The vicar is their [superiors'] primary support, their advisor, their recourse in trouble; therefore, it is desirable that, not content merely with the regular visits, she could devote more time to them according to need and circumstances. It may be to establish a young superior in her charge, to guide an officer, to comfort a house in trouble.... Let the vicar give of herself entirely; that is the great point of her mission; if she imparts wise and strong impetus to the hand that governs, the whole community will be led with strength and wisdom in the way of zeal and perfection.

The vicar should know her personnel very well, the abilities, talents, characteristics and attractions of each one so as to use them to best advantage. After 1874, she was in charge of placing the religious and appointing the officers.

Although the assistants general were usually elderly on the average, it was not true that the government of the Society was a gerontocracy. The vicars had to be in the prime of life. In 1895, they had on average thirty-eight years of religious life; but ten years later the group had aged a great deal. The average length of the term of vicars was then eight and a half years. It is likely that from then on their terms of office would not be so long.

The general congregation elected the superior general and every six years examined the workings of the congregation; this organizational pattern troubled Mother Gœtz. In effect, the Society of the Sacred Heart did not offer the classic scheme in the world of religious life of a government formed of two powers, a superior general and an assembly composed of delegates elected by the professed and, under certain conditions, independent of the superior general. As Mother Nathalie de Serres established in a remarkable report, the general congregation did not have to represent the Society, for it was not sent by the membership.

---

[41] M. Quinlan, *Digby Stuart*, pp. 118-119.

It was, in fact, constituted by religious all named by the superior general and subject to recall at will. The assistants, the treasurer and secretary general were chosen from the body of the vicars. While these last named were designated by the general congregation, "the independence of these appointments was illusory since the general congregation itself was formed by the superior general. It followed that everything emanated from her and that no power in the Society went against her authority." In the Society of the Sacred Heart there had never been an instance of real autonomy, because the Council of Twelve, which had been in place for a while, had been a "kind of oligarchy, no example of which is found in any other order." For Mother de Serres, the situation that ensued henceforward was the consequence of the scale of the crisis of 1839 in the Society: "Before guaranteeing the future, it was necessary to deal with certain dangers of a stormy present. Probably the best means appeared to be to concentrate all the power in the hands of the superior general," a system that was "in opposition to what Rome had always required of all religious orders." Therefore, Mother de Serres was proposing that the general congregation be composed of vicars and a deputy from each vicariate. She thought that the time had come to undertake this reform, for she wrote,

> I do not know if there has ever been more unity in the Society, more respect, more submission to the first authority. Union of minds, of hearts, that is the meaning of *Cor unum* in its truest sense. Does not the time seem favorable to organize the Society as our venerated Mother Foundress had desired and had asked [in 1852] and as our Very Reverend Mother Gœtz so strongly wished?[42]

When the general congregation debated the question in 1874, this proposition was included in a broader series that included the extension of the vicariates and the expansion of the powers of the vicars, to whom it was proposed to give "more of a role." These plans could have led the Society of the Sacred Heart toward less centralization, but they were much less fundamental that the ones envisaged by Mother de Serres. In any case, although the reforms she proposed were recognized as "good in principle," they were not adopted, for "the times through which we are passing are not favorable to change, all innovation being fraught with danger," one reads in the verbatim of the deliberations. The result was that the "defect" that existed in the Constitutions, the potential danger that consisted in "having everything dependent on one head," to use Mother de Serres' terminology, remained. Considering what was imposed upon religious orders in general,

---

[42] Gen. Arch. C I C 3, Box 9, 1874.

the Society of the Sacred Heart remained outside the law, until the changes adopted by the Special Chapter of 1967 and confirmed by the new Constitutions of 1982.

A recurring measure that went back to Mother Barat introduced certain practices at the time of the nomination of the superior general. In the Society of the Sacred Heart, as in the Society of Jesus, the superior general held office for life. This provision did not pose any problem when the superiors general were in possession of all their faculties and enjoyed good health. On the other hand, it created a delicate situation when they were ill or very old. The Constitutions provided for a new election in these cases. In 1864, Mother Barat had thought of resigning, but her assistants general had dissuaded her. Building on that event, they no longer had recourse to resignation when a superior general was not fit to govern or could do so only at the price of awkwardness and suffering. On 23 May 1851, Mother Barat had obtained from the Holy See, the right to designate a vicar general by a "secret note."[43] In July 1864, she asked the Vatican for this designation while she was still alive. The general congregation that met soon after ratified her choice of Mother Gœtz. Mother Barat had thus introduced a recourse that did not figure in the Constitutions as such.[44]

This measure, which set a precedent thereafter, avoided the resignation of the superior general when she was no longer equal to her charge as well as the upset occasioned by an election. Several times in 1873, Mother Gœtz thought about resigning on account of her health, but her assistants general did not agree. She solved the problem by appointing Mother Lehon vicar general. Mother Lehon also thought to terminate her charge in the 1880's, but her council suggested that she be assisted by a vicar general,[45] a suggestion she followed by designating Mother von Sartorius. At the end of her life Mother Lehon once again had recourse to the secret note, re-naming Mother von Sartorius, who had resigned earlier from her office of vicar general. Mother von Sartorius named Mother Digby by secret note. She herself proposed resigning in 1910 and named Mother Stuart vicar general by the same procedure.[46]

---

[43] *Annales de la Société du Sacré-Cœur*, 8 September 1865.

[44] Article 1, chapter 2, of the fourth part on the government of the Society, "Of the persons given to the superior general to help her in the duties of her charge," provides for aides who must be faithful and zealous, but the text is ambiguous as to the manner of their appointment.

[45] In 1884 and in 1890, Mother Lehon proposed her resignation at the time of the general congregation. She asked for a vote in both cases.

[46] On 8 September 1913, before setting out on her journey round the world Mother Stuart named Mother von Loë vicar general.

The superior general could freely choose her vicar general. Sometimes she named her a short time before her death without informing the nominee of her choice. After the death of the superior general, the assistants went to the chapel to open the note deposited in a small box and learn the name it contained. Mother Stuart learned that she had been named vicar general when, after praying by the body of Mother Digby, she asked where she should take her place in the chapel. The eldest of the assistants general, Mother de Pichon, pointed to the empty stall of the vicar general! It was a shock to her: "After a little while I shall be able to laugh at the way in which it was broken to me, but it is still too bad to be thought of…" she wrote.[47] The vicar general was or was not chosen from the assistants general. In 1911 and in 1913, the choice fell on Mothers Stuart and von Loë, vicars respectively of England and of central Italy. Was this procedure approved of in the Society of the Sacred Heart? There is no known answer. However, at the time of the "affair of 1904" one of the grievances put forth by Mothers Depret and du Chélas concerned the relationship Mother Digby had maintained with Mother Stuart: they feared already that Mother Digby wished to make Mother Stuart her successor.

It is clear that in this context the election of the superior general became a formality, the council members being content to simply ratify the choice of the deceased. The process took a very short time: the election ended on the first ballot with an absolute majority or, in the case of Mothers Gœtz and Digby unanimously. Mother Digby's election lasted twelve minutes![48] It is true that the number of electors was limited then to twenty persons. This system flew in the face of contemporary politics. As modern democracies, with the spread of parliamentary government, were evolving towards a multi-party system with multiple candidates, it could seem incredible. In order to protect itself from adversity, the Society of the Sacred Heart had perfected a kind of "dynastic" system in use in the religious world, a form of nepotism that would last until 1967. One might question a mode of replacing that risked, more or less long term, emptying the Constitutions of their reality and checking transformation within the congregation.

Renewed Relationship to the Founder

There is no doubt that the religious in charge of the Society of the Sacred Heart insisted so much on the their fidelity to what Mother Barat wanted because of the strength of the bonds that existed between the founder and

---

[47] M. Monahan, *Life and Letters…*, p. 311, letter of 22 May 1911.
[48] Monahan, p. 105.

her daughters. The personality of Sophie Barat had been radiant enough to command respect and even an affectionate love among religious of every generation. She drew nuns of all ages to herself through the friendship she both gave and received from them. The charism of the Sacred Heart was oriented towards strong and vibrant interpersonal relationships. The Constitutions provided that the love the religious were to have for the Heart of Jesus would be the surest means for all and each to love one another, and by living thus closely united to make real the motto of the Society, *Cor unum et anima una in Corde Jesu*.[49] Mutual love was not friendship, but it presupposed warm and cordial bonds.

The relationship that existed between the religious and their founder ought to have weakened as time passed. That did not happen because a sort of cult of Mother Barat developed quickly in convents of the Sacred Heart and among the public, even before it was authorized by the Church. The spiritual reputation of Mother Barat was such that at her funeral, both lay people and ecclesiastics, who entered the parlor where her body lay in state "wanted to touch medals, rosaries and other religious objects to her blessed remains."[50] Mother Gœtz discreetly encouraged this veneration; she had published for the use of the religious the very hagiographical letter written by Father Gamard, a Jesuit from Amiens, who was Mother Barat's confessor and had assisted her at the moment of her death.[51] The religious had often been respectful, astonished witnesses of the intensity of the spiritual life of their founder, for obvious manifestations of her relationship with God could hardly be invented. As Pauline Perdrau noted, when Mother Barat had breathed her last, "This soul was, we hoped, already blessed, united to Jesus Christ eternally and enjoyed having been the humble instrument of his mercies to young people, who surrounded her inanimate body with such veneration and love."[52] Contacts between the founder and the pupils of the Sacred Heart had always been warmly affectionate. Therefore, the devotion the pupils showed after the death of Mother Barat was notable, though not unexpected. Her deathbed photograph was placed in all the classrooms. The boarders made novenas and announced the blessings they had obtained through her intercession.

---

[49] *Constitutions*, Chap. V, "Of the Means of Preserving the Society in the Spirit of the Institute," § 20 and 31.

[50] *Circulaires de la T.R.M. Gœtz*, p. 9, 2 June 1865. Mother Prévost had proceeded in the same way in the presence of Mother Gœtz. She had taken a religious article belonging to Mother Desmarquest, who was blind, to touch it to the remains of the founder.

[51] Gœtz, *Circulaires...*, 4 June 1865, p. 17.

[52] P. Perdrau, *Les Loisirs...*, vol. 1, p. 494.

Cures of all kinds were attributed to Mother Barat. The first seems to have been that of an aspirant at Blumenthal, Baldwine von Schütz, who had been suffering for several months from an ailment of the knee joint that meant that she could no longer kneel or walk without crutches. On the feast of the Sacred Heart in June 1865, her superior proposed asking for relief from her pain through the intercession of Mother Barat. At the end of the novena, fluid drained from her knee and she was completely cured. Doctors authenticated her cure and considered it inexplicable.[53] Afterwards, there were rumors of the cure of nuns, of pupils, of an orphan at Conflans. The mother of an "orphan" was also cured. Incapable of working because of her poor health, this woman wanted to take her daughter out of school so that she could earn the family's livelihood. Cured, she could find work, and she left her daughter in the orphanage as the daughter wished. A boarder in Toulouse and two coadjutrix sisters in Lyons and Angoulême were able to receive the last sacraments before their deaths.

The cult of the founder spread rapidly. From Roehampton, Dublin, Sarriá, Detroit, Saint Louis, Saint Marys in Kansas, in Chicago and Saint Michael's, people asked the motherhouse for pictures of Mother Barat and linen that had belonged to her; the nuns were distributing bits of fabric that she had touched. The sick of all ages, men and women, afflicted with paralysis, leg pains, skin cancers, poor eyesight, deafness and seizures were cured through her intercession. In Chicago, "the veneration of our holy Mother Foundress increases daily. We can hardly provide enough relics for all those asking for them." In Saint Louis, "the blind, deaf-mutes, the lame, all are running to the Sacred Heart to obtain relics, they said, of Madame Barat." At the beginning of October 1867, the cure of Nancy Bakewell of a hip ailment was authenticated by two doctors and an account sent from the convent in Saint Louis.[54] Nancy Bakewell was the granddaughter of an alumna of the Rue de Varenne, the recipient of the first medal of the Children of Mary.[55] Her cure was one of the miracles accepted for the beatification of Mother Barat. The miraculous power of the founder of the Sacred Heart was celebrated from the pulpit. In May 1868, Mother Gœtz wrote to the Society that "several of ours have obtained favors, whose accounts will appeal to the filial devotion of all. Already ecclesiastical authority has deigned to note these events in which supernatural

---

[53] *Lettres annuelles*, 1863-1866, p. 44.
[54] *Lettres annuelles*, III, pp. 2-3.
[55] When in 1898, Mother Digby asked her to give that medal to the Sacred Heart, which had no copy of the 1824 medal, Mme de Lauréal refused. The superior of Maryville brought up the matter again in 1903, without success. But Mme de Lauréal asked that it be handed over to the Sacred Heart upon her death; that was done in 1904.

intervention is unmistakable."⁵⁶ In the following years there were regular announcements of cures, among the religious as well as the pupils, in almost all the houses of the Sacred Heart.

Mother Gœtz and her assistants general were sure that Mother Barat would one day "achieve the honors of the altar;" bishops and priests who were their friends led them to believe it. Foreseeing that the process would take place, immediately after her election, Mother Gœtz charged Mother Cahier, secretary general, with collecting testimonials concerning the founder. Officially she had charge of collecting the papers of the deceased and of writing the usual circular letter, the "notice." She composed a preliminary work, *Les pensées et maximes*, "Thoughts and Sayings," culled from the letters of Mother Barat.[57] She had responsibility also for collecting the founder's circular letters. Mother Gœtz wanted all the houses of the Sacred Heart to have a complete set,[58] for "there is found the original thought of our Society."

Mother Gœtz' desire to see the beatification of Mother Barat coincided with the concern of the Church to recognize the merits of the founders of religious orders, in which it had found a support. It is not known who took the initiative of the process directly, but on one of his visits to the Trinità dei Monti, Pius IX himself suggested beginning to collect memories of Mother Barat. The new cardinal protector, Monaco la Valletta, in January 1870, made similar remarks to Mother de Bouchaud, the superior of the Trinità, who sent them on to Paris.

Mother Gœtz played an indisputable role in the postulation of the cause of Mother Barat by immediately taking up the suggestion. In fact she considered it an important step for the prosperity and extension of the Society of the Sacred Heart,[59] which itself was evidence. Therefore, she acted quickly, as she herself recognized.[60] Her visit to Rome in the spring of 1870 was linked to the introduction of the cause of Mother Barat. She made contact at that time with Msgr. Borghi, who had directed the process of beatification of Margaret Mary Alacoque. A lawyer was chosen, and the questions to be posed to the witnesses were drawn up.[61] The preliminary process began in Rome in 1873; Mother Lehon had to take charge of it, as Mother Gœtz' health no longer permitted her to travel.

---

[56] *Circulaires de la T.R.M. Goetz*, p. 86.
[57] *Circulaires de la T.R.M. Goetz*, 12 February 1866, p. 37.
[58] Gœtz, *Circulaires*, p. 35. It was only in 1875 that this edition could be produced, hand written.
[59] Gœtz, *Circulaires*, 12 February 1870, p. 110.
[60] Gœtz, *Circulaires*, 4 July 1870, p. 128.
[61] *Vie de la T.R.M. Goetz*, pp. 363-364.

The question of the biography of the founder remained to be settled. Mother Cahier, who had been given that mission, took the task to heart, made use of the immense amount of documentation she had collected during her years as secretary general and, most importantly, set about creating oral archives by interviewing witnesses. She used to read pages of the work she was composing to communities she visited. Mother Gœtz familiarized herself with the first chapters and communicated them to the superiors gathered at the motherhouse for a retreat. This reading revealed to them details new to them, as well as the "treasures of hidden heroic virtue" in their founder. "It also posed questions: 'Should it be published?' 'Should one of us be charged with it?'" Would this publication feed, in opposition to the Society of the Sacred Heart, "prejudices that it had an advantage over other religious orders, less well known and more modest?" Mother Gœtz was struck by this judicious advice, which she had expected. It worried her to hear Mother Cahier announce that the biography she was writing would be printed: "What a huge affair, what a storm is gathering on the horizon of my authority," repeated Mother Gœtz, trembling; "let us get rid of this business." In order to compose the official biography of Mother Barat, she thought that the best solution was to choose a churchman but not a Jesuit.[62]

The point was to advance the cause of the founder of the Sacred Heart and to interest the public in it without, however, provoking suspicion, even mistrust of the Society. The Abbé Baunard was chosen to write the biography. Mother Cahier had to give him all her research, and it pained her to give up this mission. The first edition of Abbé Baunard's biography appeared in 1876; it had neither the same rigor nor the same historical quality as Mother Cahier's, which was disseminated for use within the communities from 1884 on. Neither did Baunard's meet with unanimous approval outside the congregation. Even so, the dossiers being prepared for the beatification, the collection of testimonials, the works of Abbé Baunard and of Mother Cahier meant that the Religious of the Sacred Heart could keep alive the memory of their founder and study her life and her writings more completely, at least those available to them. Each stage of the postulation of the cause of Mother Barat was carefully announced; on each occasion prayers were asked. In 1879, the centenary of the birth of Sophie Barat,[63] her cause was officially introduced, permitting her henceforward to be given the title of "Venerable."[64]

---

[62] P. Perdrau, *Les Loisirs…*, p. 496.
[63] *Circulaires de la T.R.M. Lehon*, 20 November 1879, pp. 81-82.
[64] Lehon, *Circulaires*, 21 July 1879, p. 79.

In her native city people began to honor this child of their region, who had contributed to drawing public attention to Joigny. In 1876 and 1877 stained glass windows were placed in the Church of Saint Thibaut, where Sophie Barat had been baptized. In a chapel adorned with a statue of the Sacred Heart, a somewhat erroneous dedication recalled her work. Madame Cousin, Mother Barat's last living niece, donated the window in the chapel. Its purpose was to associate with Mother Barat the memory of her nephews, Louis and Stanislas Dusaussoy, brothers of the donor, who had recently died.[65] In 1886, the Society of the Sacred Heart began to acquire the houses on either side of the birthplace. The owner, a relative of Mother Barat, agreed to allow visits and renovations in case the beatification took place. From 1888 on, the house at 7 Rue Davier was purchased and raised two stories; a chapel was installed. One of the walls was ornamented with stained glass windows in 1895. The two lateral panels reproduced the seal of the Society of the Sacred Heart. The central panel, the widest, represented the presentation of Mary in the Temple. In the picture the carpet on which the high priest stood was decorated with graphics in which the two initials "S" and "C" made reference to the society founded by Joigny's young citizen.[66]

The process of beatification of Mother Barat offered the religious the means to renew themselves in the spirit of the origins of the institute, all the more as the cause passed successfully through the traditional stages. In 1889, the session entitled *fama sanctitatis* reinforced the homage paid to Mother Barat for a long time. Every effort was made to bring about the much desired beatification. In 1890, the Society decided to launch the process leading to that of Philippine Duchesne. While the virtues of the United States founder were undeniable, Mother Lehon linked this possible beatification to the cause of Mother Barat, which, of course, had priority. She explained to the members of the general congregation that "the cardinal protector believed it useful for the cause of Mother Barat that we are working on a second cause in the Society."[67] The collection of testimonials concerning Mother Duchesne was entrusted to vicariates in the United States.[68]

---

[65] In the lancet on the left of the window, Mother Barat is on her knees before a statue of the Sacred Heart; in the one on the right appear Saints Stanislaus Kostka and Aloysius Gonzaga, the patron saints of her nephews.

[66] One can also read the initials as "J" and "C."

[67] Gen. Arch. C I C 3, Box II.

[68] The beatification process of Mother Duchesne, halted for a time, was restarted at the end of the century. Mother Digby's journey to the United States in 1898 also had as an aim to choose the witnesses for the beatification process; for the Holy See had authorized the Society of the Sacred Heart to reopen the cause,

The important moment on this path towards Mother Barat's beatification was the opening of her coffin deposited in the crypt at Conflans. On 2 October 1893, the body was found intact, a fact that the Church does not consider a proof of holiness; but this discovery confirmed the Religious of the Sacred Heart in their conviction that their founder was among the blessed. It was also a moment of real emotion for both Mothers von Sartorius and Lehon. Mother von Sartorius, seeing that Mother Barat was not wearing her profession ring, slipped her own ring on her finger. Mother Lehon held Mother Barat's hand in her own for a moment. She wrote, "With what ardor I promised that we were going to redouble our generous efforts to show ourselves her true daughters. How could I not have thought to ask her that this little Society that she founded remain strong, unchangeable in its principles and in its structure?"[69] On 8 May 1894, Mother Borget installed a community in Joigny; she had had the additions that disfigured the birthplace taken down.

The consecration of the human race to the Sacred Heart by Pope Leo XIII, 11 June 1899, preceded by a few months the celebration of the first centenary of the Society of the Sacred Heart. Implicitly, this pontifical act confirmed Sophie Barat's founding intuition and, as an after effect, strengthened the Society of the Sacred Heart in its charism and in its service in the Church. However, the fact remained that Mother Digby had to work hard to supply answers to the 120 objections of the Devil's Advocate in the cause. The discussion concerned Mother Barat's attitude during the crisis of 1839 and particularly her difficult relations with the archbishop of Paris.

Portrait of the Model Religious of the Sacred Heart

After the death of Mother Barat, the Society of the Sacred Heart had to conserve religious virtues in all their purity. This mission fell, first of all, to the superiors general, whose primary task was

> to govern the whole Society according to the rules and spirit of the Institute, that is to say, to watch without ceasing over the interests, the well-being, and the advancement of a work the aim of which is to glorify the Sacred Heart of Jesus by labouring for the perfection of those whom

---

but in Rome (M. Monahan, *Life and Letters...*, p. 116). The cause of Philippine Duchesne was introduced on 10 December 1909, and the process opened in April 1910.

[69] *Vie de notre T.R.M. Lehon*, p. 403.

He chooses as His spouses, and for the salvation of a great number of souls called to sanctify themselves in the world.[70]

All those who succeeded Mother Barat have done so, each in her own way, according to her spiritual orientation. The fact remains, however, that convergences are discernible in their manner of defining the qualities that were to characterize a Religious of the Sacred Heart.

From the time she took charge, Mother Gœtz spoke to the virtues that a member of the institute must practice. The very insistence with which she followed this point so closely shows even that if she had not perceived gaps between the model proposed and the reality, at least she must have feared a weakening of the tradition. Since the publication of the *Syllabus of Errors*, Vatican policy had been tracking down developments considered pernicious in comparison with what was thought of as the norm. This trend certainly moved Mother Gœtz to action. Everyone had to be of one mind.

On the spiritual level Mother Gœtz limited herself to repeating in her own words what Mother Barat had already expressed and what was found in the Constitutions. She underlined the link between the institute and the Heart of Jesus. The context was a powerful one, since the Sacred Heart was the object of a more and more widespread devotion:

> If in the midst of the universal shipwreck that is threatening us, simple Christians hasten towards the port of salvation, what have we not to hope for, we who dwell in this place of refuge and who possess the key to the treasures enclosed therein (…). Let us not forget that the essential and constitutive foundation of our religious spirit rests on real, practical devotion to the Sacred Heart of Jesus (…). The Rule traces the itinerary of the route we must follow in order to arrive at the end God proposed in calling us to religious life. Jesus Christ studied and reproduced in the dispositions, the affections and actions of his adorable Heart: such is for us the way, the truth, the life and the realization of the sacred promise made on the day of our consecration "to live in union and conformity with the divine Heart." Ah! If we were faithful to this admirable precept that our religious law develops for us, our souls would be constantly consoled and strengthened; the practice of virtue would flow from the source into all our exterior actions; gentleness and humility, those distinct characteristics of the Heart of Jesus, would become our most efficacious means of action with regard to our neighbor. It is not rare to meet religious who walk in a way that is anxious, painful, complicated, who believe themselves incapable of spiritual development, have little

---

[70] *Constitutions*, Of the Superior General, II.

attraction for prayer, the holy Eucharist, little zeal for the advancement of the neighbor, are deprived in a word, of the sacred fire that enlarges the heart, makes one run in the way of the precepts and attracts others. Often this defective development, this spiritual sterility have their cause in a false impulse that these religious themselves give to their interior life; they do not base it at all on the knowledge, the love and the imitation of our Lord Jesus Christ; his divine Heart remains, alas! a closed book, while it ought to be constantly open under the eyes of the soul, in order to communicate the light and strength that would lead her to detachment from things of the senses, to divine union and the practice of solid virtue.[71]

The Religious of the Sacred Heart was called to a heart-to-heart relationship with Christ always and forever. Like him, she had to give evidence of self-denial, of gentleness and of humility.[72]

Succeeding superiors general commented on other elements of the charism. Mother Lehon emphasized the union and charity that should distinguish the Society of the Sacred Heart, since they were expressed in its motto: She wrote

> I know that its constant practice requires humility and self-denial, that daily contact with different characters gives the opportunity for many obscure but meritorious acts; let us embrace them generously for the love of the divine Master who bears with us with such kindness, and let us try to preserve in our relationships the politeness, the mutual regard that distinguished our first Mothers and that are at the same time the ornament and the safeguard of charity.[73]

Mother von Sartorius recalled that interior spirit should be supported by the life of prayer:

> It must be the foundation of our spirituality, for it is the aim of our vocation and the basis on which the Society rests. Union with the divine Heart to which we are called and must unceasingly move toward will be the measure of our perfection, as our Constitutions point out. May we jealously safeguard this intimate union of our soul with God, source of all holiness, never allowing our absorption in works of zeal to lessen it in any way. I have the consolation of finding in your souls the germ of that spirit

---

[71] *Circulaires de la T.R.M. Goetz*, 9 May 1872, pp. 132-134.
[72] Gœtz, *Circulaires*, 6 May 1868, p. 86.
[73] *Circulaires de la T.R.M. Lehon*, 30 August 1883, pp. 102-103. This insistence on charity was Mother Lehon's legacy to the Society, according to her successor.

that characterized the beginnings of our little Society, but we must not be satisfied with stating the mere principle, but must develop and perfect it more and more by mortification of the senses and the constantly remembered presence of God for whom we act.[74]

Mother Digby, on several occasions forcefully stressed the spirit of contemplation that was fundamental to religious life at the Sacred Heart.

Mother Barat had shown how the fate of the Society of the Sacred Heart was in the hands of the religious: "It may perish through their fault, while at the same time it will receive through their fidelity fresh increase for the glory of the Heart of Jesus and for the salvation of souls."[75] To have the sense of the whole body meant "to know how to suffer for the Society, to love it even that much, for itself, not for such and such a person. There can come a time when it is presented to us under appearances that we like less, in disguise, so to speak; always know how to recognize it, itself, despite everything, and love it."[76]

> To love the Society is not to be attached to a superior, to a house, to certain children rather than others; it is to be broadly, universally ready to serve, to work, to sacrifice oneself for the Society; it is to seek its interests and its greater good in everything; it is to enter into its views, to be penetrated with its spirit, to aim at conforming ourselves to the divine Heart, whose glory is its end.[77]

If there was unanimity on the fundamentals, there were, however, many possible ways of expressing them. Mother Gœtz gave as a model to the religious the first companions of Mother Barat, one of whom, Mother Félicité Desmarquest, died in April 1869. Mother Gœtz noted her behavior on her deathbed: "Her gentleness, her fervent piety, her perfect obedience [edified] all those who had the joy of going to see her. No cloud [altered] the admirable serenity that we had witnessed for so many years." Mother Desmarquest was

> a living memory of our venerated Mother Foundress.[78] Tranquility of soul and absolute self-mastery were outstanding characteristics of her sanctity. Her evenness, firmness and discretion joined to a gentleness

---

[74] *Circulaires de la T.R.M. de Sartorius*, 14 January 1895, pp. 269-270.
[75] Summary of the Constitutions, § XXVI.
[76] *Vie de la R.M. Dupont*, p. 126. Commentary to the novices on the Rule.
[77] *Vie de la R.M. de Pichon*, p. 205.
[78] *Circulaires de la T.R.M. Gœtz*, 10 March 1869, p. 90.

full of courtesy won all hearts. Her complete self-possession was visible in her whole mode of acting on all occasions according to Rule, order and duty. Her sense of justice brought great wisdom and maturity to her judgments, in which there was never anything arbitrary or impulsive.... Are not such touching memories destined by Providence to be for us a safeguard against flightiness and inconstancy, the cachet of our unhappy era in which the wind of revolution blows with its property of destroying, overturning, changing, innovating?[79]

The Society of the Sacred Heart had to go to school to those women who had created it. With respect to authority first of all, since they had exercised it and incarnated it:

God granted to the Mothers we venerate, as once to Moses, the spirit of wisdom, knowledge and counsel, by which they formulated and established our religious law. We cannot but be convinced that this was a divine mission when we consider the wisdom of the rules in which they outlined the code of our religious life and laid down directions for all our works. It is our duty to acquire their spirit, to meditate on their instructions, and above all to practice what they taught, with persevering fidelity. This is the only way in which we can intelligently and wisely steer our course. Far from us be the inconstancy of a spirit that is swayed by passing impressions, and whose decisions are changeable because hastily and rashly made; works of zeal, hurriedly undertaken if unaided by prayer, are bound to be unfruitful, for God's blessing is not on them. "Patience hath a perfect work," says St. Paul. All manner of complications arise from precipitate action, both in ways and means and in material arrangements, often at the expense of holy poverty. The same changeable spirit is responsible for the habit of questioning and reiterated demands for new decisions, soon in their turn forgotten, whereas light is to be found in the Rule and in oft-repeated recommendations, did we but seek it there. Lastly, it makes us ready to adopt innovations and even new devotions, forgetting all the prayers, thought and perhaps suffering that these decisions may have cost our Venerated Mothers! But the saddest effect of the changeableness I have allowed myself to describe at length, chiefly to our young religious to whom I give a solemn warning to avoid it, is that it makes true virtue an impossibility, through the instability of the will, since the noble and unerring motives that should move it, are replaced by the flightiness of impressions.[80]

---

[79] Gœtz, *Circulaires*, 19 April 1869, p. 92.
[80] Gœtz, *Circulaires*, p. 93-94.

Therefore, in this spirit, those in charge of formation sought to instill in young religious a way of acting, of practicing religious "modesty," of speaking and of behaving. It was said that Mother Barat had a way of walking that gave the impression that she was gliding across the floor. Consequently, the assistants general made themselves pace up and down the corridors of the motherhouse with the probanists whose steps they found too lively! The biographical notices marveled that Religious of the Sacred Heart had a certain manner of greeting with a discreet smile. A century later a young student in Cairo would be equally impressed and would try to transcribe such codes.[81] In the Society of the Sacred Heart, the aim was dignity and good form; sometimes it was difficult to tell the difference among politeness, secular conventions, religious spirit and the practice of interiority.

The points on which the biographers insisted reveal a mindset and behavior that were not only to be admired but imitated and that are often expressed by pairs of terms. Because they were to be animated by interior spirit, the religious were to manifest evenness of character in every circumstance, to be both calm and active,[82] to express closeness both to their sisters and to the children of whom they had charge without over-familiarity either in words or gestures. Religious gravity was to be combined with gracious courtesy.[83]

The training led to setting a high value on *disponibilité*, availability. The young religious were to be "supernatural" and "impersonal." What was understood by that? Was it that their conduct was no longer explained

---

[81] M. Latif-Ghattas, pp. 152-153: "When one of the Mothers lightly waved her finger towards her nose while looking fixedly at one of us, that meant, 'Come here, my child.' When she stopped suddenly in front of one of us, that meant, 'My child, I have something to say to you.' When she raised her chin towards heaven, we understood, 'No reply.' When she looked us straight in the eye, that meant, 'Lower your eyes.' A Mother who took us by the hand in silence and led us into her office wished to indicate, 'You have done something stupid, and you know it, then admit the stupidity.' Her silence in the face of all justifications meant, 'You have not yet told the truth.' When she led us to the chapel of *Mater* and put her hand on our shoulder, that meant, 'Kneel down.' When she knelt next to us, she meant, 'Reflect, my child.' When finally she touched our elbow, that meant that it was time to get up."

[82] *Vie de la R.M. Dupont*, pp. 122-123: "Act tranquilly and without precipitation, without that multiplicity that depletes strength instead of regulating intensity; finally, possess yourself to be able to sustain effort and advance at an even pace. This deliberate moderation is a continual renunciation, the meeting with the good *par excellence*, the cross, an incalculable, expansive and vivifying force."

[83] *Vie de la R.M. de Pichon*, p. 130.

by nature or that their conversation, no matter with whom, had no other aim than "to contribute to the salvation of souls by their words and example and by the good odor of virtue" that should always accompany them?[84] That their behavior should willingly lack individuality and be "depersonalized?" Undoubtedly it meant to get rid of a false self so that the true self could emerge. Impersonality was a synonym for self-forgetfulness and the absence of one's own will.[85] Without ignoring reason and common sense, one had to "let things drop" or "rise above them." As Mother Thunder said, "Believe me, nothing can compensate for a life that is strong and supernatural *'une vie forte et surnaturelle,'* but that can only be obtained at the price of death to self. It is worth the price, whatever it costs. God bless your efforts and your determination to accept the ways and means He gives you."[86] For Mother de Gibergue, to give proof of impersonality meant to make a gift of one's best and to show deference to authority: it involved submitting one's judgment, anticipating the opinion, the tastes and desires of one's superior.[87]

By their modest behavior, Religious of the Sacred Heart were to be gentle and attractive: they were to love and desire simplicity that proceeded from "the calmness of a soul that seeks and longs for nothing but her God, and who without of any thought of self or of her own interests, looks only to God Whom alone she wishes to love and please in all things."[88] These "little virtues" Mother Barat had lived intensely: the task was to apply them and pass them on.

To choose to take the founder and her first companions for models meant to act as they did and to share their desires and their repugnances. Mother Lehon, who had very bad teeth and suffered from them, for others as much as for herself, "constantly refused to have her mouth attended to, alleging the example of our Mother Foundress and of Reverend Mother Desmarquest, who never wanted false teeth."[89] One wonders whether admiration had to lead to such imitation! If one wished to imitate Mother Barat and her first companions, it was in order to maintain the level of

---

[84] *Constitutions*, 3rd Part, § XIV.
[85] Mother de Lavigerie said to probanists on the eve of their final profession: "Be truly supernatural religious, religious of faith, who can be sent to any country whatsoever, to do any employment on the right or the left, without seeking felt consolation or success, but only God's good pleasure and success in your souls" (*Vie de la R.M. de Lavigerie*, p. 274).
[86] *Life of R.M. Rose Thunder*, pp. 46-47. The words in quotation marks are in French in the text.
[87] *Lettres annuelles*, p. 229. She died in 1941.
[88] Summary of the Constitutions, XIX.
[89] *Vie de la T.R.M. Lehon*, p. 238.

the reputation that the congregation had attained, thanks to them. Mother Lehon expressed it to one of her correspondents:

> When I read the letters of our Mothers, or when I recall their example, I find myself so far, so far from these models, that I fear seeing the Society tumble down in the measure that these supports are lacking. Let us try to imitate them, by forgetting ourselves and refusing Our Lord nothing. Our venerable Mother used to say: "In order to be an acceptable superior, we must carry fidelity to the extreme and not allow voluntary infidelity to be ignored."[90]

Therefore, as Mother Barat had done, all those who succeeded her placed a heavy emphasis on obedience. During the Vatican Council of 1870, Pius IX had granted Mother Gœtz an audience, during which he returned to the subject of obedience, all the more as papal infallibility was under discussion and the temporal power of the Holy See was being disputed in the name of modernity. Upon her return from Rome, Mother Gœtz took up this theme by relying, as was the custom, on the letter of Saint Ignatius:

> I insist, Reverend Mothers and dear Sisters, on this fundamental habit of religious obedience. When it is seriously established and maintained in the soul, it avoids many troubles, difficulties and faults; it singularly fosters action of the whole; it preserves above all from a defect to which I cannot call sufficient attention to each one, that of imprudent and imperfect communications, which are the ruin of submissiveness as also of charity and religious spirit.[91]

The message had been so firmly expressed that it needed no further development. Nevertheless in May 1882, Mother Lehon returned to the need for obedience:

> Far from us the detestable mania, too widespread in the world today, to blame the actions of authority without respect even for the highest. Even though there is no attack on the faith, the consequence of free examination and of false liberty, fruit of pride, is to submit everything to its own judgment. We must guard ourselves and our pupils against this bent, into which it would be easy to let oneself be drawn.[92]

---

[90] *Vie...Lehon*, p. 321, no date.
[91] *Circulaires de la T.R.M. Gœtz*, 4 July 1870, p. 123.
[92] *Circulaires de la T.R.M. Lehon*, 12 May 1892, p. 92.

The biographical notices all developed at length the obedience practiced, of course, in an exemplary manner by the deceased. It may be interesting, however, to consider how obedience was presented in the novitiates and communities. At Kientzheim, Mother Voitot was only commenting on the Constitutions when she said to her novices:

> See God in superiors; everything is there. If the noviceship does not give you this second sight, we have done nothing. Believe firmly in the merit of obedience, believe in its power, believe in its promises and you will not know discouragement. Believe that, as the Rule says, you can only procure the glory of God there where holy obedience will place you; but believe also that wherever you are in his name, infallibly you will glorify the Heart of Jesus. Believe, finally, that obedience alone will give you the most precious good for your hearts: union with that of Jesus.

Strongly impressed by this teaching, "the novices composed an act of faith in obedience that they wanted to keep as the testament of their holy mistress."[93]

Mother Guiraudet thus described religious life at the Sacred Heart:

> A religious must be under divine government. It is God who, through the instrumentality of our superiors, manifests his will in the slightest details; therefore, let us allow him to act. What difference does one thing or another make? There is only God's will to consider; it is an infallible compass that never deviates. Be supple under the hand of Jesus, desiring, seeking him alone in everything. Let Jesus be everything to you and the rest will affect you less and less. In other words, may he alone live in you according to his desire (....) provided we are pleasing Jesus, living for him, in him and with him, what does all the rest matter![94]

Union with Jesus Christ, the gift of self through love, explained a strict practice of obedience. There is hardly any information on the reactions of religious when they had to obey. We will single out only the behavior of an Irishwoman and a Scot, both gifted with a forceful personality. Gertrude Bodkin, who had been raised in a family with strong principles, had kept her inner independence. In the novitiate she realized all that she was called

---

[93] *Vie de la R.M. Voitot*, pp. 54-55. Undoubtedly in 1871-1872.
[94] *Vie de la R.M. Guiraudet*, p. 65. It is the same teaching that Mother Drujon passed on to the novices of France after the Second World War: "Do not put a hand on your own destiny. It is better to be a little wheel in a great whole than head of an enterprise" (Testimony of Geneviève Bovagnet).

upon to give up when she saw her name on an employment list, about which she had not been consulted. She said later:

> Do you mind being on a list, just disposed of? It rather hurts until we think it out and accept it. It hurt me so the first time I was disposed of – I didn't know until long afterward what was the matter. But when you just form a tiny part of a great whole, it is inevitable that you will be sent around here and there. If you think it out, it is a wonderful and glorious thing to be wholly at Our Lord's disposal.[95]

Alice Forbes wrote in her notes: "In every act of obedience, of renunciation both of will and judgment, we offer to Our Lord a perfect sacrifice of love and praise.... [He says:] 'Be there until I tell thee, in the place I choose, in the circumstances I choose, in the employment I choose, with the people I choose.' It is all in His power and according to His Wisdom."[96]

In a religious congregation, one cannot insist on obedience without recalling that each religious is called to live it, no matter what her status or seniority in the consecrated life. So that a religious may live the vow of obedience fully, it was crucial that her relationship to her superior should be clear and that the duties of the latter be precisely defined. The question of the exercise of authority was quite as important as that of obedience, even though there were few allusions to it. While she was vicar general, Mother Gœtz wrote a note on government, which shows that this question interested her. In this document, she describes several types of weakness.

> Superiors might allow imperfect habits and relaxed customs, and tolerate infractions of poverty, obedience, charity, silence, exactitude, common life, care of little things without calling attention or exacting reparation and amendment. They dispense from the rule without a legitimate reason, – neglecting supervision and inspection of the employments.

A second type of weakness is manifested when, afraid of the opposition they may

> encounter in the correction of difficult subjects, superiors hesitate, recoil, close their eyes to the troubles that are sometimes a cause of distress and almost a scandal to the entire house, whereas by putting a stop to the evil

---

[95] *Life of Mother Gertrude Bodkin*, p. 19. She made her noviceship at Roehampton between 1894 and 1896.
[96] *Mother F.A. Forbes*, p. 19. She entered the novitiate in 1900.

from the beginning by firm control, one would have achieved reform, whereas impunity and habit render it impossible after a certain time.

A third form of weakness was manifested when superiors lacked energy in cultivating and developing the skills of their religious.

> For these superiors, persons and things have to be already perfect. In addition to the serious detriment that affects the whole work, it happens that natures rich in valuable resources for the works of our vocation, persons who would have been able to do more and better with the help of a little intelligent care, are not cultivated in proportion to their value; people spend the best years of their life in occupations where others would have been able to replace them easily.

Justice was at stake for those neglected religious and for the congregation that would have profited from their education. Too great a severity was just as harmful:

> It irritates, closes hearts, and thereby destroys the most effective motivation of religious government. When in commanding and above all in correcting, superiors express passion and distress rather than sincere affection, use harsh, haughty or offensive words, employ violent means, ill proportioned to the wrongs they are reproving or to the moral state of the persons they are correcting, instead of applying a salutary remedy to the evil, they aggravate it and sometimes render it irreparable.

Sometimes timid superiors faced with those who could resist them "showed themselves despotic and absolute toward those from whom they have nothing to fear – or by uneven conduct, the result of moods or capriciousness, [let everything go by] on some days and [tolerate nothing] on others." Superiors ought to envision their mission with peaceful energy.

> The more they are filled with the spirit of a society wholly consecrated to the divine Heart, center of love and charity, the better they will understand that the means for attaining the end of this Society can have only one cachet – the one that Jesus invites us to study in his divine Heart: humility, gentleness, love. Now Scripture says, *love is strong as death*, nothing can resist it.

In consequence "without ever sacrificing anything to weakness, to human fears, to the spirit of the world," they have to clothe all their actions with "those forms of benevolent, humble, calm, patient charity, in a word, with the gentleness and good will that wholly governed Jesus." The good will of a superior was to manifest itself above all "in the exercise of support and correction of defects. In imitation of the divine Master, who did not come for the healthy but for the sick, let her not tire of enlightening, warning, reproving, encouraging, bettering the souls confided to her care." It is a matter of joining effectiveness, firmness and gentleness, for "the best government is, according to St. Ignatius: *that which is gently efficacious and efficaciously gentle*. According to St. Francis de Sales, it is *that which is characterized by firm gentleness and gentle firmness*."[97]

This text has the merit of introducing shrewd remarks at the psychological level into the practice of government. General congregations have also tried to limit the forms of authoritarianism that could appear here and there and were shocking or seemed excessive, even at the time. Alerted by observations of the Sacred Congregation of Religious, they specified what concerned "opening of the heart," recalled the necessity of respecting everything concerning the conscience, attempted to define the relationships among superiors and confessors. Taking as a starting point the case of a superior who had deprived a religious of communion for several days because she refused to accuse herself of a fault she said she had not committed, the writer reminded superiors that they must not allow that punishment. However, this practice was followed for a long time.

How did superiors see the mission confided to them? Elements drawn from biographies are telling. Mother Franquet defined the way she wished to exercise her charge: "To work to make my government gentle and strong, permeated with the love of God and of his spirit. To have the rule observed with jealous care, to fulfill it myself with the greatest possible perfection. To have recourse to God in everything, never to make a decision without having prayed, to efface myself, to live under the action of God in a total, confident sense of mission."[98] She was fully aware that all the religious, whether they had an office or not, were to submit to the will of God. Mother Voitot said one day: "The superior must have others carry the Lord's yoke, not hers; there is grace in religious life to carry the Lord's yoke, that is, the Rule; the superior must carry it with each one of the souls confided to her; she is superior only for that."[99] In day-to-day living, these principles could be translated into confidence in the officers and support of their authority. As Mother Barat recommended, a superior had to allow each one the liberty and responsibility of her action, to be attentive to

---

[97] Gen. Arch. C I C 3, Box 9, 1865.
[98] *Vie de la R.M. Franquet*, p. 17.
[99] *Vie de la R.M. Voitot*, p. 66.

accommodating all interests and always to place the general good above the individual. But Mother Voitot

> was careful at the same time to lead her daughters to perfect obedience, giving them the example by her profound veneration and entire dependence towards our first Mothers. She did not understand even having the thought of criticizing their decisions; and when the sacrifice of some officers was asked of her in favor of another house, she did not permit the slightest reflection on the subject; she said: "Are we not too happy to be able to come to the aid of our Mother General who carries all the difficulties of all the houses?"[100]

All the religious had the same attitude towards authority. Mother de Cléry, a Belgian who was vicar of Belgium, then of Spain, exclaimed one day: "If I learned that our Mother General asked me to go [from Jette] to Paris on all fours, I would simply make sure I had understood and I would not hesitate. It is the will of my superiors; therefore, I have the grace."[101] In the United States, Mother Hardey preached unlimited submission to her daughters; she used to say:

> You know the Constitutions of the Society; you have promised obedience to our venerated Mother General; but as she cannot personally direct all the houses, she has confided some of her authority to others; in disobeying them or in criticizing their orders, it is she to whom you are disobedient, it is her orders that you are criticizing. And not only are you disobeying her, but God himself since he said in Scripture: "Who hears you hears me." Obedience is the characteristic mark of our Society; our Holy Father the Pope gives us a magnificent testimony. A Carmelite once asked him to be dispensed from her vows so that she could enter the Sacred Heart. He answered that he would do so willingly because, if at the Sacred Heart there were fewer corporal austerities, he, nevertheless, considered this order more perfect because of the high degree to which the vow of obedience is practiced.[102]

From the beginning, Mother Barat had formed her daughters to be fully obedient, which she supported by introducing governance attentive to persons, firm but gentle. She had admitted: "I am always astonished to find such submission and obedience among all my daughters, and I feel

---

[100] *Vie...Voitot*, p. 67.
[101] *Religieuses du Sacré-Cœur*, vol. 3, p. 114.
[102] *Vie de la R.M. Hardey*, p. 246.

quite sure that a wiser hand than mine is leading them."[103] Mother Lehon expressed the same feeling more imaginatively in saying to Mother Brocard, whom she was sending to Pau to be superior: "Be afraid of nothing. Obedience is such in the Society that if I sent a broomstick, they would obey it."[104] One took pride in that. Inviting the probanists to reflect on the way authority was transmitted to a vicar general upon the death of the superior general, Mother Desoudin used to say to them: "Admire the strength of the Society to which you belong; without turmoil, without hesitation, authority passes immediately into other hands; the vicar general takes over the government and everything rests on her."[105] She could have extended her remarks to all the other situations in which obedience was involved. Obedience could demand sacrifices and prove painful; it was not less practiced for that. Its exercise was manifested, of course, on the occasion of a change of assignment, employment or house. Obedience was always presented then as involving a sacrifice; that was not necessarily the case, especially if the new appointment allowed for the settling of a conflict or offered a person the possibility of making better use of her talents.

At the beginning of their training, young religious were exercised in obedience by means that have since fallen into disuse. After her first vows, in August 1867, Marthe de Pichon was placed in the boarding school at Quadrille, near Bordeaux.

> After a few months, she was sent to Layrac; and this first change was carried out in the primitive, vigorous form then still in use: the aspirant left her morning class, loaded down with notebooks. The portress approached her, took hold of her bag, and said without preamble: "Little sister, go quickly, quickly; Mother is asking for you at the front door and the carriage is waiting for you to leave. – I'm on my way, answered the poor person addressed, trembling a little, but I have to get my things from my desk. – Unnecessary! Mother said we will send them to you…the coachman is impatient because it is late." And the inexorable portress dragged the departing one, hardly giving her time to say a quick, emotional good-bye to her mothers and sisters whom she met on the way.[106]

One may suppose that superiors acted this way only with those known to be particularly generous! Testimonies show that sometimes a kind of

---

[103] *Lettres aux Supérieures*, vol. 1, p. 5, 6 July 1826.
[104] *Vie de la R.M. Brocard*, p. 33.
[105] *Vie de la R.M. Desoudin*, p. 171.
[106] *Vie de la R.M. de Pichon*, pp. 35-36.

agreement was made between vicars and the families of the nuns, providing that the religious stay in a house near her family home.[107] This kind of arrangement doubtless allowed young women to overcome the opposition of their parents to their entrance into the novitiate. Superiors always had the option of adjusting the employments according to the an individual's characteristics; but they always sought to have them try something out, free if necessary not to pursue the experience if it was not productive.[108]

Obedience has been associated with cloister, to the point that in the end obedience and cloister have given the impression of being two sides of the same reality. In September 1866, Mother Gœtz wrote:

> During the year I have spent with [Mother Barat] I have often heard her express regret about too frequent movement of some of our Mothers vicar and superiors. Her formal intention was to reserve to herself alone authorization for travel….In what concerns journeys, I believe myself to be obliged in conscience to recall the recommendations of our venerated Mother Foundress and to hold to carrying them out. Here is what I find in notes written in her own hand a few months before her death: "To return seriously to our cloister, to stabilize it as far as possible, to be stricter with regard to dealings with domestics, surveillance of the parlors, too frequent traveling of ours."[109]

Therefore, Mother Gœtz wished the vicars to go out only for the visits of the houses in their jurisdiction, once a year or every two years. She connected this practice with poverty and respect for the interior life. Therefore, certainly to give good example, when she visited Spain, she did not allow herself a visit to Loyola, when she was passing close by; she did not make many visits to places of interest during her sojourns in Rome. Did Mothers Barat and Gœtz fear excesses? The fact remains that the founder had wished to create a congregation in which cloister was allied to apostolic activity and did not inhibit it. The notes to which Mother Gœtz alludes had been written when Mother Barat was almost eighty-five and no longer able to travel, but Mother Gœtz' letter of 1866 set a precedent for a century and

---

[107] Benjamin Chomel, *Vie de Madame Louise Chomel*, p. 55.

[108] *Vie de la R.M. Dupont*, p. 106: "Though very kind and compassionate, Reverend Mother did not allow concessions to nature. To a religious who, because of her health, was frightened of an employment that seemed to her to be too tiring: 'Try it,' she said, 'We can always try. If the work is beyond your strength, I will free you of it. But you will have the merit of having obeyed and maybe of having succeeded.'"

[109] *Circulaires de la T.R.M. Gœtz*, 29 September 1866, pp. 49-50.

thereby blocked developments that would have furthered the success of the works.

Frequent recall of the obligations of cloister could provoke scruples in the most faithful religious, especially when their charge put them in contact with civil or religious authorities. A good example is that of Mother von Sartorius. When she was vicar in Louisiana, she had to do some business with the bishop. He summoned her to the chancery. She had to go without being able to ask permission of Mother Lehon. She acknowledged this failure most humbly afterward.[110] Cloister was to be respected in all circumstances, even aboard ship. When Mother Barat sent religious to the United States in 1848, she had specified that it was forbidden for anyone to be on deck alone and that no one was to be there after eight o'clock in the evening. "Our cabin was to be our cloister." Mother Tommasini adds in her memoirs:

> I mention in detail all our Mother Foundress' recommendations to show with what care she safeguarded our religious life and also to make it clear that the customs of the first days of the Society are still in use. When after my visit to the motherhouse in 1875, I was coming back to America, I asked our very reverend and venerated Mother Lehon what her desires were for the crossing; great was my satisfaction in seeing that she made the same recommendations as our first Mother. A joyous smile lighted up her face when I commented on that. "You please me very much," she exclaimed, "for I would like none of our traditions to be lost."[111]

The repetition of recommendations concerning cloister shows that it was not always respected as well as it should have been and above all that it was not observed in the same way everywhere. Regular visits and the comments sent to general congregations seem to indicate that it was less strict in America than in Europe. In Louisiana, religious traveled alone without being accompanied, even when they had to spend several days on a train. It happened that some of them were accompanied by a domestic, even by a "gentleman who was a friend." No one hesitated to send novices alone from New Orleans to Grand Coteau, or even at Grand Coteau to send them unaccompanied to take classes with the Jesuits.[112] To be sure, the two properties were adjacent.

It could be that in vicariates far from the "center" people had a rather lax interpretation of cloister. Ultimately, everything regarding cloister was

---

[110] *Vie de la T.R.M. de Sartorius*, p. 163.
[111] *Mémoires de la R.M. Tommasini*, pp. 87-88.
[112] Gen. Arch. C I C 3, Box 11.

evaluated. At the end of the century a general congregation spent a long time reflecting on whether it was possible or not to use trams on account of the lack of privacy they entailed. With good sense they ended up comparing *"chars électriques"* [*sic*] to railroad trains, whose use was approved, and where one was also in contact with travelers, both men and women, not of one's own choosing.

In requiring such respect for religious customs, tied to cloister or not, one risked an attachment to the Rule, "for the Rule's sake." One may wonder if the example of certain superiors general did not encourage that. When she was to arrive at Sarriá on 23 May 1866, towards nine o'clock in the evening, Mother Gœtz refused permission for the nuns to stay up late. She was welcomed, therefore, by women of the village and the children of the free school. Her humility and her respect for custom were certain, but was it not forgotten that Mother Barat, a young superior general, had put off the time of going to bed at Poitiers so that her novices could greet her upon her return from a journey? Mother Lehon always wanted to be seen as guardian of the Rule. She was particularly concerned about this when she was named local superior of the motherhouse. She refused to give dispensations that some religious needed in order to do their employments. It seems that there was some conflict on this point with Mother Gœtz, who believed that the secretaries should have special treatment.[113] At the end of her life, Mother Lehon had become a "living rule."

> A superior visiting at the motherhouse could not understand how with so many occupations, she could assist at all the offices and all the reunions: "The thing is very simple," answered Mother Lehon. "When I was named superior general, I said to myself, I have neither the virtue nor the capacity of our first two Mothers, but I am going to apply myself to observe the Rule and have it observed; I will thus be able to render service to the Society."[114]

The comments and the anecdotes in the biographies of the assistants general or vicars illustrate that orientation perfectly; it became the norm in the following years. We will cite merely a remark of Mother Fournier: "Study the Rule; to study it is to know it; to know it is to esteem it, and study and esteem, that is love. We seek perfection; we ask for the means of perfection, but it is all in the Rule. I never hear it without discovering something new, something I had not yet understood well until now."[115]

---

[113] *Vie de la T.R.M. Lehon*, p. 236.
[114] *Vie...Lehon*, p. 238.
[115] *Vie de la R.M. Fornier*, p. 136.

Was it always possible to observe the decrees when one was in a "mission country" or very far from the "center" of the congregation? The question was not addressed; but in 1869, Mother Gœtz sent the religious of North America a letter in which she tried to define the original characteristics of their national mentality and to indicate the way to refer to obedience in their cultural context:

> I seem to have discovered in the characteristics proper to your noble country natural qualities destined in the designs of divine providence to serve as the basis for the most sublime virtues; here I do not indicate only that straight good sense, that persevering energy, attached to the American genius, which must powerfully second the élan towards great things; but I wish to speak of that native pride, the spirit of independence, so opposed on first thought to religious abnegation, but in which I like to see, on the contrary, a powerful help to perfect obedience and charity.

Consequently, to her obedience seemed more meritorious in North America than elsewhere, and she defined it as "a holocaust offered to God alone." The rest of the letter shows that for Mother Gœtz, charity depends on obedience and that it is indeed obedience that is at the basis of the *Cor unum*:

> And as obedience enlivened by these insights of faith unites all the members among themselves and with their head, charity necessarily flows from the faithful practice of this virtue. In seeing Jesus Christ in our mothers and in our sisters, we esteem them and we love them in him. Our mutual relations will become holy and easy, and we will reject energetically all that could tarnish that charity that Jesus Christ shows us as the distinctive characteristic, with humility, of his divine Heart. He traced for us the supreme law in these words: "What you do to the least of my brothers, that you do unto me."[116]

The concern for a demanding obedience was a constant in the nineteenth century, when education was based on authority, that of parents and that of teachers, lay or religious. However, this form of respect for the Rule could bring with it a rigidity that was not in accord with the importance the Society of the Sacred Heart gave to the rhythm of development of the person. The religious who wanted to follow Mother Barat in every particular had perhaps forgotten that their founder, who had preached obedience forcefully, was also capable of bending a rule when the clear

---

[116] *Vie de la T.R.M. Lehon*, Letter, 22 August 1869, pp. 104-105.

interest of a person was at stake. An alumna of the Paris boarding school, mother of a Religious of the Sacred Heart, gave this testimony after the death of Mother Barat:

> Never have I seen such maternal tenderness, such gracious and loving charity as that of my dear Mother Barat. When I was a rather naughty little girl at the convent of the Sacred Heart, Rue des Postes, when they came to fetch me to punish me, moved by my supplications, she used to hide me behind her chair.... My heart is eternally grateful to her, and I said to myself that love is permitted to win out over the rule.[117]

The challenge remains in a closed world to know how to discern the time when love may prevail over the rule.

When examining the formation given the religious, we must to avoid anachronism. The historian no longer has the means to study the way in which religious formation was presented and received, as the sources tend to insist on a certain uniformity in behavior and to show the efforts of the religious to melt into the mold, into the group. The goal was the reason: to enter into a religious body would allow one to realize her vocation and to follow Jesus Christ in a form of spirituality that attracted her. But a formation both human and spiritual manifests its quality in the crises that the persons who have received it are called upon to endure. In the difficulties of apostolic life, the Religious of the Sacred Heart had already demonstrated its effectiveness during the second half of the nineteenth century. At the beginning of the twentieth, the effects of anti-clericalism in French politics provided an exceptional test of the vow of obedience and of the religious indifference taught and lived in the Society of the Sacred Heart.

---

[117] *Lettres annuelles*, 1863-1865, p. LXII.

Chapter VI

THE SHOCK OF THE EXPULSIONS

The Society of the Sacred Heart in France was recognized by the government, but the legal situation of its individual houses varied from one to the other, and the reason for the difference was not clear. Twenty-eight houses were authorized; two were authorized for a part of the establishment; five belonged to a foreign religious; one was held jointly by several religious; two were in the hands of a private corporation.[1] Avignon, in 1869, was the last house authorized. Afterwards, the superiors general no longer asked for the approbation of the state for their foundations, and they diversified the legal framework of their holdings. Was that because after 1870 "one felt the storm coming?"[2] Or because the Republic was a regime that did not inspire confidence? Or because the state no longer wished to authorize new foundations and had made that fact known? Whatever the cause, fifteen French houses were not authorized; among them were the seven opened between 1873 and 1895.

Faced with Legislation for "the Defense of the Republic"

The first attacks on religious orders were fiscal. Undeniably the Society of the Sacred Heart was one of the best financed. Its assets came from gifts but also from the dowries and legacies of the religious.[3] It is impossible

---

[1] Some houses were managed by tontine, that is, they reverted to the survivors of the initial group, which was regularly renewed.

[2] Gen. Arch. C I A 5 d, Box 9, note of 1916.

[3] In 1874, the general congregation had abolished an earlier decree, which had put the goods, the movable assets and property of each religious at the disposition of the superior general; the decree was contrary to the *Constitutions*. In 1895, the general congregation recognized that the religious could dispose of a significant part of their fortune in favor of their family or for good works, with permission.

to assess the amount, for there is no document that allows us to estimate movable wealth constituted by investments, liquid assets, works of art and gold articles used in the chapels. The only traces are in grants from the state or individuals to pupils, but these are relatively rare. As to the worth of the real estate owned by the congregation, it was evaluated in 1880 at twenty million francs. The Society of the Sacred Heart held property valued as highly as that of the wealthiest congregations, although it did not figure among the twenty-five congregations having the most members.[4] Large properties were necessary for cloistered religious and the buildings that housed their works, properties both purchased and donated. These properties were not inconspicuous: their combined land equaled two hundred forty-two *hectares,* [about 598 acres] forty-nine of which were held by unauthorized houses. At the beginning of the twentieth century, the whole was evaluated at twenty-six and a half million francs. This capital supported the foundations outside of France. Mother Barat had made sure that goods the religious brought in were held in common at the central level of the Society; allowing them to be held by local communities could have had consequences for the mobility of personnel, for indifference as to assignments and for the reality of the *Cor unum*.[5] Even so, some houses were richer than others, either because their apostolic activities were flourishing or because certain members received an income from their families.[6]

In 1880, the houses in France were taxed for 46,000 F. Mother Lehon [superior general] drew a spiritual meaning from this burden:

> Let us draw real profit from it by becoming more attached to holy poverty, and let us not fear the effects too much. We can get accustomed easily to lacking nothing: in offices, in material arrangements, we would like the

---

[4] C. Langlois, pp. 380-384.

[5] *Circulaires*, I, pp. 98-100, 16 June 1841: "Several of ours, not to say the majority, who receive dowries, inheritances, gifts from their relatives ask if these may be given to the house in which they reside. Doubtless it is for a good reason, but they do not consider that this request is contrary to indifference and to absolute renunciation of goods. Each one sees only the needs of the house where she lives; she loses sight then of those of the whole Society, the mother of all, which has only this one resource to support foundations, especially those in Protestant countries.... How then support the new foundations? Deprived of resources, would we be forced to abandon them? Are we not all one?"

[6] In 1874, the general congregation decided that these would be assigned to a house permanently, so as to avoid the difficulties at the moment of an "obedience" that had occurred in the past.

most convenient, the best, and we want our least imposing houses to be on the same level as those in large cities. I am afraid that the spirit of the world enters by this door and that some of us forget to impress deeply upon their hearts the love of abjection, of humiliation and of poverty.[7]

The state would have liked to impose a tax on each house. Through a lawsuit of 1883, the Sacred Heart won the judgment that the tax would be paid by the Society as a whole, a less costly arrangement. Even though Mother Lehon thought this law ruinous,[8] she wrote:

> I find your hearts all preoccupied by the unjust demands by means of which, in our poor France, some would like to ruin religious congregations. However, I must add with our venerable Mother: I do not believe that these dangers are of a kind that fills me with painful solicitude. Oh, no! My heart would feel it much more if one single point of our rule were neglected, an infraction of charity tolerated; that I would bemoan before God. Before a law that intends to devastate us, let us become poorer in affection and in practice. Before calumnies, let us try to be more humble; if they criticize our teaching, let us work to make it more solid.[9]

During the generalate of Mother von Sartorius the situation worsened. In 1894, a law "of growth" required congregations to pay an inheritance tax on the property of deceased religious. From February 1849, there had already been a tax on property held as mortmain, meant to replace the capital gains taxes required at the time of gifts among living persons or of transfer of goods after death; but it was much lighter than this new measure. The Church in France mobilized against the new tax and the Society of the Sacred Heart refused to submit to it. On 16 April 1895, the law of "subscription" modified it, while maintaining the principle of a tax on all categories of the goods of religious congregations. The treasurer general, Mother Borget, thought that it would be necessary to take funds out of capital each year to pay the 121,300 F demanded.[10] If the Society did not pay the required taxes, it ran the risk of seeing its right to exist withdrawn, its property confiscated and its authorization to teach annulled.

---

[7] *Lettres circulaires de la T.R.M. Lehon*, p. 88, 25 May 1881.
[8] Lehon, *Circulaires*, p. 157, 22 December 1889.
[9] Lehon, *Circulaires*, pp. 162-163, 30 December 1890.
[10] As she had not paid the *droit d'accroissement*, she had to fear a penalty of 578,546 F.

In the spiritual notes she wrote during Holy Week Mother Borget evaluated the issue thus:

> One might believe that this year one could assist more intimately at the passion of Our Lord, so much has it become real now: Jesus sold for thirty denarii; his religious, his members in discussion before the Chamber and the Senate to extract from them thirty centimes, endlessly repeated, in a manner quite unjust: "They have persecuted me, they will persecute you also." Oh, yes! Like the Master and with him, we wish to be persecuted and to keep united to him, more dependent on his grace, more faithful in details, poorer above all in all that the world covets. We will live more detached, spending for only what strictly useful, for him and for the real interest of souls. There is the beautiful side of this iniquitous law; it will make us more humble, holier, more conformed to our unique Jesus.[11]

But she led the fight. The Society of the Sacred Heart participated in the anti-fiscal rebellion under the auspices of the archbishop of Paris, and it practiced passive resistance. Threatened with confiscation, it appealed to the courts; but it lost the suit on appeal and in the high court. In 1901, as the furnishings of the house of *Les Anglais* in Lyons were at the point of being seized, the Society submitted. The legal advisers of the congregation succeeded in having the sum of money owed to the State reduced by one third – it reached 1,422,722 F – and in having the payments spread over ten years. To obtain the money Mother Borget borrowed and mortgaged the motherhouse. She wondered if the government was not making use of this fiscal pressure as a means of blackmail in order to force the Society of the Sacred Heart to have all its houses recognized officially.[12] Whether that was true or not, the sum of the taxes in 1902 had doubled compared to that of the year before!

It was in this context that the Society learned of the law of 1 July 1901. Three years earlier, the Dreyfus affair had fed an atmosphere of nationalist and anti-Semitic agitation. The values of the Republic seemed endangered, and the elections had sent a majority of *"Défense républicaine"* to the Chamber of Deputies. Pierre Waldeck-Rousseau, president of the Council and minister of the interior and of worship, had begun by dealing ruthlessly with the unauthorized congregation of the Assumptionists, who had made an anti-Semitic platform of their newspaper, *La Croix*. In 1899, he had decided to introduce a law against "associations," a part of which would deal with religious congregations. Debated beginning in January 1901

---

[11] *Vie de la R.M. Césarine Borget*, p. 174.
[12] Gen. Arch. C I A, Box 10.

in the Chamber, the law was passed by the deputies two months later. While Waldeck-Rousseau had wished to make it just an instrument of control, the deputies made it stronger by forbidding teaching by unauthorized congregations. After its passage in the Senate, the law was promulgated in July 1901.

The law of 1901 awakened anxieties in religious. In a letter to vicars and superiors only, on 17 September 1901, Mother Digby, echoed these anxieties:

> Some regrettable indiscretions on the part of several young religious have been reported to me from outside. Let me beg you to exercise the greatest vigilance over letters written by ours. We must not make any allusion to the law, or to what might result from it for us; and in case questions are addressed to you in community or in the parlor, I ask you, Reverend Mother, to give no information yourself or to permit no information to be given, confining yourself to answering briefly and referring the question to Paris for further details. If you are interrogated officially, you must say that your establishment belongs to a recognized and approved congregation with its seat of government at the motherhouse, 33, Boulevard des Invalides; that you are ignorant of what has been decided and arranged with regard to your house; but if there is some action to be taken, the motherhouse is taking care of it or has already done so.

On the same occasion Mother Digby asked superiors to make a list of the religious with their ages and places of birth, indicating those who were directors or teachers in the boarding schools or free schools. At the very least she wanted to have the material necessary to create files. In 1904, she noted that, as the law of 1901 did not mention unauthorized establishments belonging to recognized congregations, the Society of the Sacred Heart did not have to request authorization for houses opened with only academic authorization. At the end of 1901, she noted, "a few large congregations gave in," but not the Society of the Sacred Heart, which maintained its position. In fact, on 19 December 1901, the Prefecture of the Seine had reminded it "that the authorization granted did not cover at all dependent houses irregularly created and that a request for authorization was to be introduced for each one of them," but it had given a delay until 25 January 1902, under threat of closing. At the very last minute, on 13 January 1902, the motherhouse filed a request for regularization for thirteen of the non-authorized houses but not for Joigny or for the day school in Marseilles, which was to close.

The day school in Marseilles was reopened in a house previously authorized but which the school had left for want of sufficient space. In Joigny, the religious evacuated the birthplace of the founder on 10 January 1902 because "to leave the blessed house of our venerated Mother was the only way of preserving it for the Society."[13] It was put in the name of a relative of Mother Digby; but the affair took an unexpected turn, for a liquidator was named in March 1902. The tenant, Colonel de Guilhermy, and his butler objected to the taking of an inventory of the house, carried out under the supervision of the police. They were both fined fifty francs and condemned to three days in prison for insult and assault on authority; and the judgment was confirmed on appeal. The Society of the Sacred Heart then filed a suit against the state, which it won in June 1902. The reasons adduced specified that an authorized congregation had the right not to ask for authorization for a house that it did not desire to keep, while the state had neither the right nor the power to name a liquidator for a congregation that was a legal entity. This decision set a precedent.

During the summer of 1902, other warnings were noted. The Sacred Heart was ordered to close Angoulême and Saint-Ferréol, houses believed to have been authorized and for which authorization had been requested.[14] When an injunction came to close the poor school in Paris, the general council was worried because that school was located on the property of the motherhouse. After the complaint, the Prefecture of the Seine declared its injunction null, as the school did not constitute a private establishment. The state thus admitted that the motherhouse, which was authorized, formed a single establishment including its various works.[15]

The elections of 1902 were bitterly contested between partisans and adversaries of anti-clerical policy. But the ballot boxes returned a Chamber of Deputies more leftist than the preceding one. Waldeck-Rousseau was replaced by the radical senator Émile Combes, whose name gave birth to the term "*combisme*," synonym for the fierce struggle against the Church and freedom of conscience. It was predictable that Combes would try to suppress the religious congregations. His "secular campaign" took shape at first by the promulgation of decrees concerning the establishments of the teaching congregations opened after 1 July 1901. The Society of the Sacred Heart was not affected by this measure. Then aim was taken at the non-authorized establishments founded before 1901. The law of 1901 had

---

[13] *Lettres annuelles*, 1901-1903, p. 220.

[14] *Lettres annuelles*, 1901-1903, p. 366. In Angoulême, the originals of the acts of authorization had disappeared from the prefecture, which refused to recognize the value of the copies that were produced.

[15] Report of Mother Digby to the General Congregation of 1904.

provided that the authorized congregations would have the possibility of having the situation of their non-recognized establishments regularized. But Combes refused to transmit the requests for authorization to the council of state. The closing of non-authorized houses of the Sacred Heart began, on 25 March 1903, with Moulins and Orleans. By October, eleven other houses succumbed to the same fate. Angoulême was closed in March 1904. The Society went to court about Saint-Ferréol, where it had not re-opened the boarding school in October 1903. It had refused to ask for authorization for the orphanage alone, as the prefect of Doubs had suggested. As for the authorized houses, they were not touched until 28 March 1904, the date of the dissolution of the Society.

The Society of the Sacred Heart closed its non-authorized establishments without resistance. Mother Digby justified her decision afterwards by explaining that it was impossible to continue the works with the prospect of trials, searches and expulsions. In fact, the fear was that resistance would compromise the fate of the authorized houses, above all the motherhouse, and risk loss of the properties of the closed houses. But the reaction differed from place to place: the religious waited until the last minute to depart, or moved before they had to, or closed only a part of the establishment. At Aix-en-Provence, the orphanage was suppressed in order to preserve the rest of the house. Bordeaux was evacuated, for the day scholars could go to the boarding school at Quadrille.

Life went on calmly everywhere while awaiting closing. It proved difficult because as establishments of religious congregations were closed, those that remained open took in the pupils of others, and expelled religious found refuge in houses still open. In Nantes, "it was necessary to make prodigious combinations, even a sort of compression. We saw the corridors transformed into dormitories, the alcoves bearing the names of *marquises*. The classes were no sooner over than they gave way to piano lessons all at the same time."[16] The Sacred Heart momentarily sheltered religious of other orders who were going abroad, or it offered the hospitality of its chapels to religious, secularized or not, who were having difficulty in carrying out their spiritual exercises outside of their convents. Communities discreetly received dispersed Jesuits in friendly houses and who, depending on the location, were more or less under surveillance. The communities gave them the use of a confessional and sometimes a safe place to meet, and they housed their apostolic works.

It was necessary, however, to prepare for departures and moves and to go through real mourning, for to depart meant leaving an area where one had lived often for a long time and abandoning flourishing works. When

---

[16] *Lettres annuelles*, 1917-1919, p. 834.

the closing of a house was announced, the superior would refuse to sign the inventory, making herself the guardian of the objects inventoried, since the Society was their owner, and to take an oath affirming that nothing had been forgotten on the list of furnishings. The motherhouse had asked that the religious leave quickly in order to avoid prosecution and sealing off the houses. After the closing only a few caretakers remained, choir nuns and coadjutrix sisters, who came to support the superiors of houses already closed. The length of this custody was variable, but it lasted two or three years in Amiens, Besançon, Perpignan, Toulouse, Algiers and Bourges. In Brittany, the people mobilized to retain the religious, both men and women, repeating petitions and demanding a stay of the orders to close. Therefore, at Quimper, during the summer of 1906, the vicar decided to resist "until the end," setting the date of the *rentrée* [opening of school], organizing appeals to the prefect. It was only a year later that the house was closed.

Here we will recount the visit of the liquidator to just one house, Amiens, as Mother de Rudeval remembered it. Everything imaginable, furniture, dishes, all kinds of utensils and objects from the sacristy, including the holy oils, were collected in the wine cellar in order to "save them from the rapine of the wolf that was preparing to descend upon the sheepfold." The government agent who was very ill at ease heard the "beautiful protest" of the superior with "a gloomy look and his tail between his legs." Mother de Rudeval recounts how the snuff-taking commissioner walked sheepishly behind the nun charged with showing him the house. She had him making so many turns and detours that he would not know exactly where he was and, therefore, not realize that some rooms were not open to his investigation! It was an "ungrateful task" clearly one not much appreciated by the administrators who were obliged to undertake it, but Mother de Rudeval thought that the snuff-taking commissioner left the Sacred Heart with "painful remorse and his honor besmirched."[17]

The fate of the motherhouse was problematic. Should it be closed before the last establishment had been closed? It was agreed to "preserve the registered office of the Sacred Heart, for the closings were legal only if notice was given to the superior general. And where could notice be given if the legal domicile were suppressed?"[18] But the departure that finally had to take place was the occasion of a heart-wrenching sacrifice felt by the whole Society. To leave the Boulevard des Invalides was to abandon a place where the founder had lived and died, as had those who had succeeded her and most of the assistants general;[19] many of the

---

[17] Prov. Arch. France. Letter of 4 September 1904 to an assistant general.
[18] Gen. Arch. C I A 5 d, Box 9 bis.
[19] *Lettres circulaires de notre T.R.M. Digby*, p. 200, 24 July 1907.

professed had made their probation there. Mother Digby nailed a protest to the door of the motherhouse reminding the despoilers that they were incurring excommunication. She then left Paris for Conflans on 10 August 1907. It was only on 30 July 1909 that she left for Belgium with the general council. A month later, the caretakers of Nantes reached England. "All was consummated." There were no longer any Religious of the Sacred Heart in France.

Modalities of Withdrawal

There is no doubt that Mother Digby had decided in 1901 to leave France, but that she announced it indirectly to the religious only in 1902 by writing in a circular:

> If God our Lord, addressing each one of us, says, "Go and teach in other lands," we will answer with the same enthusiasm with which at his first invitation, "Come, follow me," we left everything; for if Our Lord sows his chosen grain far and wide, will we not be happy to know that we are vowed to his service, that we belong to the Society of his Heart and are consecrated to him for time and for eternity? Will we not say to him, like Ruth to Noemi: "Wherever you go, I will go, and where you live, I will live also?"[20]

She had found fallback positions and had had the archives of the general secretariat moved.[21]

The Society of the Sacred Heart had two advantages that not all the French congregations enjoyed. The first was its internationality. It was possible to send the nuns to houses located outside of France. As Mother Digby said to the Trinità dei Monti on 30 December 1902, "It is not an easy thing to place three thousand persons, but in this case the walls of our houses will expand, will they not?"[22] Most of the religious went individually or in twos and threes to existing communities. The youngest were sent to the most distant countries and to the "missions." Religious could not be sent to Alsace or Moselle, for a decree of the German authorities had forbidden receiving the French.[23] The second advantage was financial. The

---

[20] Digby, *Circulaires*, 18 December 1902, pp. 125-126.
[21] *Vie de la R.M. Le Baïl*, p. 90.
[22] *Journal de la Trinité des Monts*, Rome.
[23] Gen. Arch. C III, Egypt. Letter of Mother Digby to the Cardinal Protector, 26 October 1903. The bishop of Metz succeeded however in avoiding a new expulsion of some religious who had been sent there. Four nuns from Nantes were sent to Kientzheim in 1909.

scope of the Society of the Sacred Heart gave it the means to reestablish itself outside of France. To pay for the journeys, buy or rent buildings abroad, without having liquidated possessions in France or even being able to sell them for what they were worth, required assets not available to all congregations. In this regard there was a considerable distance between international institutes and diocesan congregations, whose members did not always have the economic and cultural means of defending their rights or their concept of religious life. In the spring of 1902, the Society bought the château of Flône, in Belgium, and in 1903, it opened twenty-one houses in Belgium, Italy, Austria and Spain. Foundations continued in Europe until the final departure from France in 1909.[24]

It was possible to relocate the youngest nuns rather rapidly, but the priority was to consider the oldest. "Refuges" at the borders gathered the sick and elderly mothers and sisters who lived there in French language communities and carried on a light apostolate. The shock of the event caused some deaths even before the departure or upon arrival. Four of these refuges were opened, thanks to gifts, loans and purchases, in the North of Italy at Cioché, Cassinetta, Lubliano and Trinità; three in Belgium, at La Ramée, Fontaine-l'Évêque and Wetteren. Others were established in England, in Austria and at San Sebastián in Spain. Foundations at Nijmegen, Ostend and Antwerp likewise became refuges. In 1904, the issue was sending the youngest away. During Holy Week the juniors and the choir aspirants left for Cioché. During the summer the novices from Conflans arrived at

---

[24] Mother Alix Noély summarized in a notebook the destinations of the religious of Laval, Saint-Brieuc, Quimper and Nantes where she was sent successively before leaving for Ireland:

	Laval (1904)	Saint-Brieuc (1905)	Quimper (1907)	Nantes (1909)
Belgium	12	8	25	13
Spain	8	20	2	16
Italy	2	1	1	2
Ireland	3	1	1	1
England	2	10	5	29
Netherlands				3
Poland (Austria)		1	1	1
United States	1	2	1	1
Canada	1			
Mexico		1		1
Brazil		1		
Uruguay				1
Japan				1

Jette, and those of La Ferrandière went to Rivoli. The last *prise d'habit* took place at Conflans on 11 July 1904. The French probanists were dispersed, but a last probation of sixteen Italians, Austrians, English and Americans discreetly opened at Conflans on the first of September, 1906. We have seen that Mother Digby had decided to send away the coadjutrix aspirants. She committed herself, however, to take them back if in the future the Society could return to France and if they had persevered in their vocation. Perhaps fearing profanations, she decided to ensure the safety of the body of Mother Barat, which was sent clandestinely to Jette on 29 April 1904.[25]

The religious had to settle close to France if they wished to continue to accept children whose families wanted them to remain at the Sacred Heart for their education. Boarding schools were opened at San Sebastián to welcome pupils from the Southwest, at San Remo for those from Aix-en-Provence, at Avigliana, for those from Lyons, in England for those from the West. From the moment of the announcement of the probable closing of Lille, parents of the pupils asked for the opening of a school in Belgium. In May 1905, they searched out available properties. Rejected at Tournai, they purchased the château of Lindthout, near Brussels.[26]

The departure of more than 2600 persons required careful organization. The Mother General had asked superiors for precise information on the state of health and the qualifications of their religious, in particular their knowledge of foreign languages. The superiors added their advice on the adaptability of one or another. Assisted by the vicars and by her personal notes, Mother Digby undertook to establish the "obediences" (the destinations). That lengthy task was not easy. The lists that have been saved show the traces of her reworking and of the resulting changes of assignment, sometimes at the last minute. It is said that she tried to lighten the conditions for certain departures, based on what she knew of

---

[25] The Jesuits had proceeded in the same way in 1877 when they had been threatened with expulsion. They had then asked the Society of the Sacred Heart if it would take charge of the remains of Father Varin. Mother Lehon had his body interred at Conflans. The novices often went to pray at his tomb to ask to acquire the spirit of the Society through his intercession (*Vie de la R.M. Fornier*, p.111). Mother Digby sent his coffin to Roehampton, as well as that of Marie Lataste. Mother Hardey's body was sent to Kenwood in January 1905. It would seem that it was the Vatican that pushed for the transfer of the body of Mother Barat, whose beatification process was ongoing.

[26] The Religious of the Sacred Heart were received reluctantly at Ostend by the bishop, who already had a congregation dedicated to the Sacred Heart in his diocese. Also founding a house in a country resort was questionable. It is true that the house was near the one where the Shah of Persia used to stay, and that did not make it a neighborhood of complete repose!

the feelings of the religious; for example, she sent one who she knew had a passion for flowers to a house with a beautiful garden.[27]

The Religious of the Sacred Heart demonstrated, as usual, the quality of the formation they had received and the intensity of their religious life. They knew that they could be called to leave their country without hope of returning, and they were conscious that the apostolate took precedence over every other consideration. The facts were impressive. A young sister, whom Mother Le Baïl asked about her destination, answered simply: "I am not sure; the Mother Assistant told me but I have forgotten. But if you wish to know, it is written on my trunk!" Another, asked about her ability to get used to extreme climates, answered, "Mother, to obey I fear neither cold nor heat nor beasts nor people."[28] The nuns learned of their obedience upon going to their chapel stall. As Mother Baillot d'Estiveau wrote at the moment of leaving Quimper, "All our furniture has its obedience, but the persons are still ignorant of their destination.... It is always 'with him' that the Master waits for us, it is always the same invitation: 'Remain in my love.'" Destined for Tijuca in Brazil, she ended up in Poland!

The departures were painful and the trial repeated itself, as most of the nuns had to leave one house after another.[29] Some feared the conditions they would have to adapt to, or difficulty in mastering the language of the country of welcome. "Don't say that," replied Mother Borget to one religious who had expressed these fears, "there are potatoes to be peeled everywhere," and she added, "Let us be grateful to the Society that we always have work to do, and let us consider ourselves honored; so many people in the world suffer and complain because they cannot find work! Our way of thanking our mothers and sisters for all they do for us is to perform our work well."[30] Not one Religious of the Sacred Heart used the pretext of the situation to ask for a dispensation from her vows. The phenomenon was rare enough to call attention to it, for in many congregations of both men and women, some religious did not have the courage to leave their country.

While there was still time, the Society had to save its possessions. The superior general had taken the precaution of keeping two irons in the fire. To preserve the Society's properties as far as possible, in January 1903 she asked the Vatican to dispense the professed from the vow of poverty so

---

[27] M. Quinlan, *Mabel Digby...*, p. 94.
[28] *Vie de la R.M. Le Baïl*, p. 95.
[29] Notice of Mother Baillot, p. 8: "In August 1907, I tasted the bitterness of the last good-byes for the second time."
[30] *Vie de la R.M. Borget*, pp. 183-184 and 201-202.

as to be able to put the properties in their names.[31] But the basic policy consisted of making the most of the movable assets and the real estate. Mother Borget, in spite of her age – she was seventy-seven years old – was the exceptional architect of an operation that demonstrated her lively intelligence and her business sense. From 1901 on, she liquidated the outbuildings, the chaplains' quarters, the non-recognized buildings of the authorized houses, as well as the properties that had been put in the names of religious. She sold on the spot items that could not be transported or that were worth less than the cost of shipping. An alumna of Quimper described the state of the house before the closing: "Permission was given to go into the whole boarding school and take whatever we wanted. It was distressing. In Saint Michael, the dormitory upstairs, windows, shutters, everything had disappeared. In the junior school, a beautiful room with a parquet floor, there was only an immense hole, no floor. Outside, free entry. Poor people were coming with hand carts to cut and carry away wood. In the cloisters two workmen were making a deafening noise by taking up the pavement."[32]

As it had been decided to leave nothing, an inventory of furniture was prepared and sent to all the houses so that they could ask for what they needed. In a little notebook[33] everything that had been sent away was listed with the place of origin and the destination of each object or category of objects. Everything went: clocks, organs, altars, communion rails, pulpits, benches, *prie-dieu*, confessionals, tabernacles, holy water fonts, lamps, sacred vessels, bells, candelabra, processional banners, statues, liturgical vestments, relics. Everything that was useful to schools and communities, – libraries, furniture, linen, physics and natural science cabinets, greenhouses – all left France. The cedar that Mother Barat had loved was sawed into planks. Parquet floors were taken out, sometimes even the shutters, the stained glass windows and the window sills. At the Boulevard des Invalides, in expectation of the "expulsion," some furnishings had been removed. Mother Digby could no longer house visitors, for they had kept only one bed for each person. In her quarters she had a few old straw chairs, and some boxes served as book shelves. The nuns were "camping out."[34]

Most numerous were the objects sent to Belgium, because it was the vicariate that had the most foundations and because it was advantageous to send things there, since less valuable objects could go by wagons directly,

---

[31] Jean-Dominique Durand, "*Rome, les congrégations et la France*," *Le Grand exil des congrégations religieuses françaises, 1901-1904*, Paris, 2005, p. 104.

[32] Letter of Elisabeth de Kerautem, communicated by Marie-Guyonne du Penhoat.

[33] Gen. Arch. C I A 5 d, Box 5.

[34] *Vie de la R.M. Le Bail*, p. 96.

thus saving the cost of packing. The vicar, Mother Betzy Nieuwland, had in fact obtained an exemption from customs duties. These duties, varying according to countries, guided the strategy of expedition. England received only valuable objects because, even though there were no taxes, the cost of overseas transport was expensive. The duties charged by Austria and Italy were high and those of Spain almost prohibitive, so arrangements were made with "clever shippers" to send the sacristy items clandestinely. Only objects that could not be obtained locally were sent outside of Europe. Not everything arrived intact at the destination. The statues of Saint Joseph and of Saint Philomena coming from Montpellier were broken when they were unpacked in Cairo. The plaque from the altar of the chapel of *Mater admirabilis* could be repaired, but it retained a trace of the break on account of inadequate packing. The material labor needed to prepare all these parcels was considerable.[35]

This "scorched earth" tactic bore fruit. In 1910, Mother Borget thought that the closings had been a disaster and that she had been able to save only "pieces of wreckage."[36] Even so the sale of real estate, completed before the appointment of the liquidator, allowed for payment of the costs of liquidation. As the surplus of receipts from the liquidation of a congregation had to go to similar works, in the case of a teaching congregation, to public schools, the Society of the Sacred Heart had decided not to leave anything remaining. It transferred, exchanged and sold securities outside of France only abandoning to liquidation two registered bonds of little worth. The sheltering of the movable assets avoided the heavy cost of foundations outside of France.

Nevertheless, the most fruitful operation concerned the recovery of the dowries and gifts of religious living and deceased, allowed by the law that protected the rights of individuals. Mother Digby did not wish to undertake this effort, either because she thought it would lead to nothing, or because she did not wish to have it known how large were the amounts received. Mother Borget and the Society's lawyers did not share this opinion, and they ended by winning the day. Only the professed were asked to make claims, and no one was forced to do so, in order to avoid family difficulties.[37] The magistrates showed themselves sympathetic, except for property that could have served to reestablish the congregation. They did not require proof of the donation; it was necessary only to offer assurance that the fortune of the family was or had been sufficient to have made such a gift and, in the case of the deceased religious, that the sum had really been paid out.

---

[35] Nantes sent more than 1200 packages of different sizes.
[36] Gen. Arch. C I C 3, 1910, Box 16.
[37] One professed, who had a deputy in her family, refused to make a claim.

Almost all the claims were granted by the tribunals. The largest number of the sums recovered varied from ten to twenty thousand francs. There were, however, many much larger. The Society of the Sacred Heart, which seemed to be the congregation making the most claims, recovered about 85% of what it claimed. Payment was completed only after the First World War. Mother Stuart decided to reserve that sum and the income attached to buy back houses in France when it would be possible to return.

The sale of the real estate of a congregation afforded the state the necessary funds to restore the dowries and gifts. The properties of the Sacred Heart were as difficult to sell as to rent because of their size. They were acquired by companies, by dioceses, transformed into schools, hospitals or barracks. The people who acquired the properties of Lille,[38] Amiens, Joigny, Marmoutier, Bordeaux and Marseilles committed themselves to returning them, if the congregation was reestablished in France. But some acquisitions were suspect in the eyes of canon law; properties were divided up and buildings destroyed. The most complex case was that of the Hôtel Biron. The descendants of the former owner, the Duchesse de Charost, went to court, for they claimed that the Sacred Heart had not bought the property of the Rue de Varenne but had received it as a donation. It was not until April 1909 that the soundness of the Society's position was recognized and that the liquidator could put the property up for auction. Several possible buyers were in line, but the intervention of Catholic deputies in the Chamber, which the Sacred Heart considered "unfortunate," drew the attention of the government to this property of five hectares, situated in the heart of Paris. The president of the Council, Aristide Briand, came to visit it and had the government buy it for six and a half million francs.

An Intransigent Attitude: Causes and Consequence

The Society of the Sacred Heart, well advised by its lawyers, was able to drag out matters; and by different legal proceedings against the liquidators for flawed language, it could remain in place longer than had been foreseen. But while using all the expedients the law offered, it avoided outright confrontation. The dispersion of the religious was sometimes hurried up in order to avoid a police raid.[39] When the superior general and her assistants

---

[38] Except for the building of the former prefecture that Mother Digby had given over to the bishop of Lille for his headquarters.

[39] In Quimper, the nuns were to leave on 25 September 1907. But on the 16th, the prefect gave the order to the army to surround the house. After a last Mass celebrated by their chaplain on 17 September at four o'clock in the morning,

left Paris, they did so discreetly without letting anyone know. It was the "friends" of the Sacred Heart, in fact the relatives of the nuns and of the boarders, who took steps to delay the closings. In Lille, Mother Catherine de Montalembert was warned six months in advance of the closing of her house, no doubt by her cousin, Count Emmanuel de Montalembert, deputy from the North, who accompanied her in a carriage as far as the train station when she was leaving for Belgium. It was thanks to another Catholic deputy, Plichon, whose three daughters were boarders at Conflans, that the house received two years of respite and could thus serve as a refuge for the general council. The children got together and said novenas so that "the Mothers" could stay in France. In the boarding schools, every fifteen minutes the bell rang in the study hall, and at the invocation, "Sacred Heart of Jesus," all the pupils answered, "Keep our Mothers for us and save France."[40] Before leaving Paris, Mother Digby gave each of the pupils of the Rue de Varenne a medal with the inscription, "Who shall separate us?"[41] To save Conflans, the children of the free school divided up the sections of Charenton and one by one collected signatures on a petition.[42] The religious did not seek out the publicity or the expressions of sympathy they received at the time of their departure; but everywhere they were escorted by their pupils and their parents in processions in which rich and poor mingled.

Questions remain about the reasons for an intransigence that some other French congregations emulated. As Mother Digby said at the time of the general congregation in 1904, she did not wish to negotiate: "It seemed at the same time worthy and useful not to be expelled violently and not to ask for the shadow of favor from a government already prepared to forbid all religious congregations to teach."[43] It is clear that she did not wish to provoke by excessive resistance a scandal that doubtless seemed to her to be incompatible with her concept of religious life. But everything indicates that neither did she wish to deal with the state. Her decision was not necessarily the result of pressures from the Vatican. The account of the audience the pope gave her on 24 December 1904 indicates that Pius X did not connect the closing of establishments with the departure from France, since he asked Mother Digby if it was not possible for the Society of the Sacred Heart to remain.[44] She answered: "Most Holy Father, one law granted us authorization; another law has lifted it; there is nothing to be

---

the religious left their convent, the doors of which were forced open at five o'clock (Letter of E. de Kerautem).
[40] *Lettres annuelles*, supp. 1958-1961, p. 176.
[41] *Vie de la R.M. de Neuville*, p. 8.
[42] *Religieuses du Sacré-Cœur*, vol. 3, p. 259.
[43] Gen. Arch. C I C 3, 1904.
[44] *Circulaires de la T.R.M. Digby*, pp. 166-167.

done!" The statement shows that she confused, or wished to confuse, the authorization granted to a congregation in recognition of its legal existence and one which concerned its activities.

The decision to leave France did not meet with unanimous approval either outside or within the congregation. Parents of the pupils believed that in leaving, the Society of the Sacred Heart left those in its charge without support and that it abandoned its works to the competition, whether that of the state or of the congregations that remained. Other reasons were more petty. Were lay teachers going to demand higher wages than the religious had asked?[45] Worried about the fate of private instruction in France, the bishops were not of one mind concerning the departure of the religious.[46] From 1908 on, Mother Digby became aware that some congregations that were staying, including some Ignatian congregations, were preparing to replace the Sacred Heart, looking to appropriate its prestige and its symbols. To that end, she ordered the destruction of the dies of the Child of Mary medals. So that the alumnae associations would not be without support, Mother Digby authorized a few religious to return in secular dress and spend a few days in France in the cities nearest to the borders to follow up on the spiritual accompaniment of the alumnae. Undeniably some alumnae were displeased by the departure of the nuns. Even though the *Entente cordiale* had been signed in 1904, part of the French population manifested latent mistrust of the British, revived by the conflict in the Sudan in 1898, in which Generals Marchand and Kitchener fought for the possession of Fachoda. Some alumnae wondered whether the nationality of the superior general had not carried weight in the decision to leave France and whether the religious had had anything to say about it.[47]

Although there were no murmurings in the body of the congregation at the announcement of the departure, before 1904, the general council had not been unanimous as to the strategy to adopt. The conflict, in which the superior general was opposed by two of her assistants, was broader and concerned Mother Digby's governance, which differed from that of the Mothers General who had preceded her. Even so one of the causes had a bearing on the way she handled the fate of the Society in France. Her health

---

[45] Gen. Arch. C I A 5 d, Box 10.

[46] Cardinal Sevin entered into conflict later with those who had opposed Mother Digby on this point.

[47] Elisabeth de Kerautem, who was present at the departure of the nuns from Quimper on 16 August 1907, wrote to her cousin, Mlle de Kermenguy, an alumna of Vannes: "Mother General Digby was English! Let's not make rash judgments. But you understand, with a Mother General and a Mother Provincial, the superior of Quimper was only half free. Perhaps that is why they left?"

required that she spend part of the year in Rome, and her office demanded travel in Europe. However, given the gravity of the situation, it is astonishing that she did not give priority to sojourns in Paris or that she did not bring some of her assistants general to Rome, for she could not discuss matters with her council except by mail. The general archives has kept little notes with the question, "Must we try to stay in France?" It seems clear that there was no real discussion within the council on this fundamental question and that Mother Digby asked the opinions of her assistants general only as a matter of form. The future of the Society in France was, in fact, one of the issues in dispute. Mother Juliette Depret was the superior of the *Maison des Anges* in Paris. In contact with people of different backgrounds, including politics, she thought that at least a few houses should be kept open in France to wait until the tumult died down so as to be ready to return. Tradition has it that she suggested keeping open those houses that had developed promising apostolates among the working classes.[48]

Because she did not wish to negotiate, Mother Digby did not allow herself to take advantage of certain provisions of the law of 1901. She did not take issue concerning the house in Algiers, one of the oldest institutions of Catholic education in Africa, dating from the year 1842. Since the government made a particular case of congregations having bases in the Empire and usually did not export its anti-clerical policies outside of metropolitan France,[49] Mother Digby could have argued from the fact that Sacred Heart boarding schools abroad accepted children of the upper classes and that they contributed to the renown of France by working for the spread of French culture. Finally, an excellent argument for maintaining the congregation would have consisted in recalling that the general novitiate was established to provide nuns for houses abroad. The Leygues amendment, adopted 21 March 1904, stipulated that novitiates that formed personnel for the teaching of French in foreign countries and the colonies could remain open.

Mother Digby's strategy was developed rapidly, maybe too rapidly, but it must be noted in her favor that the legal situation of the French houses was one cause of the imbroglio. In spite of excellent records, those responsible for the Society did not always have a clear understanding of the real status

---

[48] Testimony of Vincenette d'Uzer concerning Layrac.

[49] In the verbatim of the General Council of 1904, we read that the superior general knew of this provision of the Leygues amendment: "The application of the law does not seem to be of obligation in the colonies; perhaps the house of Algiers will be preserved." Still the possibility should have been explored; this step was not taken. It is true that the boarding school in Algiers had never flourished and that on several occasions Mother Barat had wondered if the Society ought not to leave Algeria.

of its establishments. Moreover, the Religious of the Sacred Heart did not have confidence in the republican regime.[50] Therefore, the motherhouse anticipated events; the abandonment of the house in Joigny is the proof of that, and the justifications supplied *a posteriori* by Mother Digby are totally anachronistic. How are we to know what discernment she engaged in? She gave proof of intransigence, "like the Jesuits," people said. But the refusal to bend did not have the same consequences for semi-cloistered nuns as for male religious who could blend into the population while pursuing their ministry and even ask to be integrated into the diocesan clergy.

A letter of August 1904 demonstrates that the general council thought about secularization and giving up the habit: "Our Very Reverend Mother says that from outside come numerous demands for secularization for us, to which she responds that we will never give up our habit or our vows or our religious life. As long as the Holy See exists, the Religious of the Sacred Heart will remain what they are."[51] Perhaps a distinction ought to have been made between wearing the habit and the practice of the vows; but it is difficult to see how Religious of the Sacred Heart could have renounced community life. To live in two's and three's could constitute an "offense against the congregation."[52] A tradition within the Society has it that Mother Digby, influenced by memories of the Revolution, feared that a persecution would put the lives of the religious in danger.[53]

If the law of 1904 did not imply the dispersal of a congregation, it impeded its teaching activities, which certainly had to prevail. To glorify the Heart of Jesus, the Society of the Sacred Heart made available besides formal education spiritual accompaniment. It does not seem that Mother Digby thought about counting on this form of education in order to remain in France. On the other hand, after 1909, she re-inaugurated the work of retreats and spiritual accompaniment in all its forms. Mother Stuart, in her turn, let it be understood that the "third" and "fourth" means of apostolic action provided by the Constitutions were to substitute for formal education, when the latter was no longer possible. It must not be forgotten

---

[50] Prov. Arch. France. Emily A. Miller indicates that the religious were "strongly royalist" and that at Marmoutier the 14th of July was not celebrated: "Classes took place as usual, whereas on the 4th of July there was a holiday for the whole school," because of the presence of two students from the United States!

[51] Prov. Arch. Egypt, Correspondence I. Letter received in Cairo.

[52] The political and judicial authorities did not pursue secularized religious who continued openly to live together, even to carry on teaching activities.

[53] Was she referring to the Revolution of 1789, or to the English Revolution? A member of her family had been condemned to death and executed under atrocious conditions at the time of the Gunpowder Plot.

Monique Luirard

that the boarding school supported the community and other educational activities. How could the nuns manage financially without the support of the fees paid by the pupils? There was no thought either of transferring the direction of the boarding and free schools to lay persons.

Doubtless Mother Digby's spiritual vision of the situation can explain her conduct. From 1902 on, she always presented the policy of the French government as an effect of the clash of good and evil. It is "a war that we see as declared on God," wrote the secretary of the house in Algiers, summarizing the common opinion.[54] A "warrior" spirit was felt at the motherhouse as well. In 1903, the fear of espionage there was such that the superior general used the British diplomatic pouch for correspondence with countries abroad.[55] Letters were in code, including the one that announced the transfer of the body of Mother Barat to Belgium.[56] A demonstration of this state of mind comes from a delightful anecdote. Mother Borget kept on her mantelpiece a little bottle in which a white paper was swimming. "These are the ministers soaking in holy water," she explained to her astonished visitors.[57] She had copied their names onto a piece of paper, which when plunged into holy water had lost color! The rupture of diplomatic relations between France and the Vatican, then the separation of church and state formed a "tragic" background to an "extraordinary" period. Mother Digby described the law of 9 December 1905, as a "crime that, though long in preparation, does not cause less bewilderment and demands atonement."[58]

Mother Digby's desire to follow Jesus Christ implied for her facing all sorts of persecution. One had to fight, to give proof of generosity and of courage, to manifest a radical love of Christ, "by reliving the mysteries of the sorrowful passion of Jesus meek and humble of heart."[59] The sacrifice was burdensome, but it was not to be made "for anything but love."[60] Mother Digby had always wished for herself and for her daughters that they be worthy of their founder, who had given her first companions generosity as a motto.[61] At the time of the centenary of the foundation of the Society

---

[54] *Lettres annuelles,* 1901-1903, p. 286.

[55] Gen. Arch. C I A 5 d. Thanks to George Attlee, the nephew of one of the nuns, who was assigned to the British Consulate in Paris.

[56] Prov. Arch. Belgium. Jacqueline Parmentier, *Sainte Madeleine-Sophie à Jette*.

[57] *Vie de la R.M. Borget*, p. 176.

[58] *Circulaires de la T.R.M. Digby*, 6 January 1906, p. 180.

[59] Digby, *Circulaires* p. 206, 1 January 1908. On the eve of the departure from Quimper, the superior gave the alumnae a copy of a book by Msgr. Laty, *Gethsémani* (Letter from E. de Kerautem).

[60] Digby, *Circulaires*, pp. 148-149, 19 June 1903.

[61] Digby, *Circulaires*, p. 130, 18 December 1902.

of the Sacred Heart, she had written to them: "It is not right that we live on the former prestige of the Society, the name of which exercises a magic power over those whose memory goes back to those first years."[62] Therefore, she demanded that they reinforce the religious virtues, obedience and union, and manifest courage and fervor.[63] In 1904, the Society learned that "the superior general and her council [would try] to resist to the end: we are in our domicile, it is our right to remain there! We will perhaps undergo difficult moments, but as long as we are alive, we will have to struggle and not surrender our arms."[64] The proclamation of the heroicity of virtues of Mother Barat, 12 February 1905, and her beatification, 25 May 1908, doubtless strengthened Mother Digby in her firm position. We will never know, of course, whether for her a return to France was conceivable. In any case, by making the decision to leave, she burned bridges to the country that had seen the birth of the Society of the Sacred Heart and that had supplied it with resources and vocations. Some male religious had wondered if women were capable of resisting hostile political measures.[65] Undeniably the Religious of the Sacred Heart had been called to give proof of their "virile" virtues, of their devotedness and their firmness, and they obeyed. When Mother Digby had converted from Protestantism to Catholicism, against the advice of her father and some of her relatives, she had made a costly choice, renewed at the time of her rapid entrance into religious life. The decision she made to leave France was equally radical. It was also what obedience exacted of her daughters. But for her and for the others that resolution was not without pain.

A decision can, in fact, be made in suffering without necessarily expressing the suffering in a text or speech, especially in an era when education trained people not to let their feelings show. Neither courage nor generosity is synonymous with hardness. They can appear also in weakness and fragility. Some cues are subtly revealing. A letter of 1904, received by a religious in Cairo, shows the state of feelings in Paris: "The wish of our Very Reverend Mother for her daughters is that each one be ready to go anywhere.... Our Mothers are calling the present probation 'the miraculous one;' the probanists aspire to the name of 'probation of nothing.' They wrote to us that on the feast of the Immaculate Conception Reverend Mother Borget, reading the act of consecration, burst into tears at these words, 'Bless those who carry the whole burden of the Society,'

---

[62] Digby, *Circulaires*.
[63] Digby, *Circulaires*, pp. 182-183.
[64] Gen. Arch. C I C 3. Report of the Superior General.
[65] Guy Laperrière, *Les congrégations religieuses. De la France au Québec, 1880-1914*. Vol. 2, *Au plus fort de la tourmente, 1901-1904*, Québec, 1999, p. 173. The Eudist fathers posed the question.

and could not finish."⁶⁶ At the motherhouse it had been "agreed that no one would be weighed down by the difficulties of the times,"⁶⁷ which was a way of keeping up their morale. The sadness was general: the religious who received things sent from France were pained to see "relics of houses destined to die. What emotion for those who had been at Montpellier to see all its wealth again! What heartbreak for our Mothers who have seen these things leave and for the Children of Mary who had given them."⁶⁸ Those in Cairo consoled themselves saying that "thanks to this flight into Egypt, these things were sheltered from danger and would not [fall] into the hands of modern Herods."⁶⁹ But Mother Borget wrote to a correspondent: "If you only knew how sad it is to see everything thus taken away."⁷⁰

The expulsions were for the religious congregations that underwent them a proof that the solidity of the Society of the Sacred Heart could continue, but they transformed it and caused it to enter a new stage of its history. Until then the congregation had always been directed from Paris where the superiors general resided. There is nothing to indicate that a transfer to Rome was considered; but for Mother Digby, an installation in Belgium was necessary because it was important to stay as close to France as possible in order to prevent "grave detriment to the goods of the Society."⁷¹ Belgium was also a neutral country whose tranquility was valued. To insist on the transitory character of the transfer of the motherhouse was also a way of calming the fears of the French religious singularly touched by the situation. The abandonment of France, however, could not remain without administrative and human consequences. Beyond the multiplication of vicariates that took place in European countries, it was a "new" Society of the Sacred Heart that was to be constructed or reconstructed, more international and, henceforward, present on five continents.

---

66 Prov. Arch. Egypt, Correspondence I.
67 *Vie de la R.M. Le Baïl*, p. 93.
68 Prov. Arch. Egypt, Journal of Cairo, 12 March 1904.
69 Journal of Cairo, 25 July 1904.
70 *Vie de la R.M. Borget*, p. 219.
71 *Lettres de la T.R.M. Digby*, 26 June 1909, p. 278.

Second Part

INTERNATIONALIZATION OF THE SOCIETY OF THE SACRED HEART
1909-1957

Chapter I

A New Departure

After abandoning France and closing its seven vicariates and fifty houses, the Society of the Sacred Heart reorganized its administration. After 1906, the number of vicariates was increased in Great Britain, Italy and Spain. The situation offered an opportunity to rethink the position of the congregation throughout the world. The availability of the French religious allowed for a redistribution of personnel and the establishment of new houses. These tasks were accomplished during the last years of Mother Digby's generalate and over the course of that of Mother Janet Stuart.

A Generalate Full of Promise

The death of Mother Digby in 1911, shortly after the expulsions, marked the end of an era. The one called to replace her was born in 1857 in England, the daughter of an Anglican rector. Janet Erskine Stuart was converted to Catholicism in 1879; while seeking her life's direction she led a life in the world in which hunting played a great part. In 1882, she entered the novitiate at Roehampton without having had any earlier contact with the Society of the Sacred Heart. Therefore, she had not been influenced by the traditions handed down directly or indirectly in the boarding schools. She was the first superior general who had not known Mother Barat. As she noted at the time of her election, "Up to this time our Mothers General have all personally and even intimately known our Blessed Mother. This direct contact with the Foundress, prolonged far beyond what could have been expected, has strengthened the foundations of our religious life."[1] The generation that had to maintain and propagate the tradition and the primitive spirit drew new strength from the beatification of Mother Barat: "…at that precise moment the loving Heart of Jesus has designed to

---

[1] *Circulaires de la T.R.M. Stuart*, p. 15, 21 September 1911.

give us our blessed Mother as model and guide through the hands of the Church...."[2]

When the new superior general completed the choice of her council in August 1913, she named as assistant general Mother Catherine de Montalembert, who had been accepted at the Sacred Heart by Mother Barat. Mother Stuart wrote:

> She has knowledge of the spirit of the Society and of its traditions that goes back to the last years of our blessed Mother and in active life to the generalate of our venerated Mother Gœtz. You will easily understand the importance for us of prolonging this traditional heritage, which must link our present time with our origins, and with what care we wish to conserve this living chain, as long as God leaves us the links."[3]

It was a matter of smoothly ending a tradition, for from then on there were few religious of that generation capable of exercising an office in the central government.

In 1911, the succession could have been a delicate matter, for Mother Digby had made her mark strongly on the Society. Her personality, her manner of governing and some of her decisions had not been unanimously appreciated. Mother Stuart had been chosen by Mother Digby, but she was aware that the Society had to adapt to the times while remaining faithful to itself. She wanted to dedicate the first years of her generalate to understanding the reality in which the religious had to live. The intercontinental visit she undertook was also her means of getting to know the members of the Society. After her death, many said that they were stimulated by her visit and by the hope and optimism that emanated from her conferences and letters.

Mother Stuart was able to create an atmosphere of cordiality at the motherhouse that was quite close to what the founder had wanted and that contrasted sharply with the previous one. The cardinal protector had written to her after her election:

> Perfect union and mutual affection between you and the Mothers assistants general is very salutary for the Society in which — we have entire confidence — Our Lord will always watch over that union, so advantageous and so cherished, which is expressed in the words: *Cor unum et anima una in Corde Jesu*. You will have in the Constitutions and in the

---

[2] *Circulaires...Stuart*, 18 January 1909, pp. 313-314.
[3] *Circulaires...Stuart*, p. 366.

luminous example left by the Blessed Founder…a judicious rule of good and wise government.[4]

Mother Stuart did not need this discreet advice. For a long time she had created close relationships with the religious of her vicariate. In the conferences she gave to the superiors of the United States at Manhattanville in 1914, she reminded them that "the only way to govern is to love."[5] The religious who held offices were to have "real, deep, personal affection" for each one whom they served: "If we love the members of our community, no one will resist us." Like the founder, Mother Stuart believed that the congregation could only be governed by love. The Society of the Sacred Heart, she said, is

> an order of women, and it must be governed in a woman's way, by the heart and not by the logical mind. The heart is the principal source from which women's government must emanate. Still more, what brings us close to the heart of people gives us great power. Selflessness and love are our levers. Through these we will do something for our community and for God.

She pleaded for balanced relationships between the religious and those in authority, and she reminded superiors that the Society of the Sacred Heart was not composed of nuns who had to be treated like novices, but it wanted "perfect, full-grown, responsible professed."[6] Neither were the religious to be interchangeable:

> We must never try to be copies one of the other. No matter how excellent the model, copies are always deplorable. God never meant us to be copies. If we imitate too closely the actions of another, we are not truly ourselves and we cannot give the true, real note that we should give if speaking with our own voice, and the result is necessarily disappointing.[7]

It was a matter, perhaps, of admiring those in authority, but no longer of imitating them as had often been the case in the preceding generation.

The new superior general was aware that the Society of the Sacred Heart had to adapt to its surroundings intelligently. Her own characteristics, the offices she had held, what she had already discovered on her journeys in

---

[4] M. Quinlan, *Digby Stuart*, p. 193.
[5] Quinlan, p. 189.
[6] Quinlan, p. 182.
[7] Quinlan, p. 179.

North and South America, all had helped to mature her thought. Spiritually solid and intellectually brilliant, she had written works on the spirituality of the Sacred Heart and on the education of girls. These were still not known in Latin countries, perhaps because they had not been translated into French, but they were considered authoritative in Anglo-Saxon countries. Through her office of mistress of novices in England, she had formed religious mostly from Anglo-Saxon countries who spread the teaching they had received.

Janet Stuart had lived "in the shadow of Mother Digby"[8] who had formed her and to whom she had become extremely close. Mother Digby's support had helped her to find her place in the Society of the Sacred Heart, but her own human and spiritual qualities would have led her to the same end. She had an original way of expressing how fidelity to the spirit of the Society's origins had to be combined with progress and modernity. At Manhattanville, referring to the thought of Montalembert, she explained that it was necessary to distinguish fidelity from attachment to traditions, venerable certainly, but no longer responding to the needs of the time: "We must not do what our fathers did, but what they would do, were they here today. Not what our holy Mother did in her time, but what she would do here today."

Undeniably another kind of governance was on the drawing board. Mother Stuart did not live long enough to put into effect and to give impetus to all she was thinking, but she wanted to proceed slowly so as not to create ripples. During the three years of her generalate, she demonstrated an art of governing that was lovable and winning. The Religious of the Sacred Heart experienced great sadness in learning of her death. It put a momentary stop to a thorough renewal in the mission and the manner of living religious life that could have been accomplished, given the upheaval that the congregation had just been through.

"Continuing Blessed Mother Barat's Work on Other Shores"[9]

In the second half of the nineteenth century, the human resources in the Society of the Sacred Heart, although on the increase, had not permitted the establishment of houses everywhere that needs were felt. The religious evacuated from France were an undeniable support to expansion, either because they were sent on foundations or they allowed others to go without adverse effects on the life of the houses they left. Their presence contributed to reinforcing the quality of the teaching of French in the

---

[8] Title of a chapter in the biography by Mary Quinlan.
[9] *Lettres de la T.R.M. Digby*, 26 June 1909, p. 279.

houses where they lived. Thanks to them, students learned to converse easily and to speak with a correct accent. In Canada, with classes in English in the morning and in French in the afternoon, the students quickly became bilingual. The reputation of the French boarding schools was sufficiently well known throughout the world that the Sacred Heart elsewhere profited from their fame and the contribution of the "Mothers" who had directed them.

The expulsions gave an impetus to the extension of the Society of the Sacred Heart. It was a tradition in the congregation to open a new "tabernacle" for every one closed, which meant it was necessary to make as many foundations as closed houses.[10] In this regard the expulsions were quite a providential event allowing the Heart of Jesus to become known under other skies, as Mother Digby said during the General Congregation of 1910. She had written to the cardinal protector: "The Society is at a new point of departure with so many recent foundations in different countries. We are continually asked for others, more than we can make; as the last ones are not yet complete in personnel, we have had to refuse new ones, above all in pagan countries."[11] Until the First World War, expansion continued in countries where the Society was already established, but the institute was also introduced in new places.

In Europe, the network of houses became more closely intertwined. The vicars were obliged to find new locations, by means of generous gifts[12] or by making purchases. Attempts were made to introduce the Society where it had never been able to go before for politico-religious reasons. Mother Digby wanted to make a foundation in Russia, actually in Poland annexed by Russia, "the key to Russia," she thought.[13] Profiting from the freedom of worship that Tsar Nicolas II had granted following the agitation of foreigners and of the Revolution of 1905, Mothers de Montalembert and Nieuwland went to Warsaw. Even though they were warmly received by prominent Polish people whose daughters had been educated at the Sacred Heart or who had known the Count de Montalembert, they did not succeed in their mission. A new attempt in 1909, as clandestine as the preceding one, yielded no better results. Mother de Montalembert did not find an available property. The Russian authorities were hostile to the establishment of a religious congregation consecrated to the Sacred Heart, as the devotion was forbidden in Russia. On the other hand, in 1913, a foundation was

---

[10] The Holy See authorized the selling of a house only if another was to be opened.
[11] Gen. Arch. C I A 5 d, Box 6, Letter of 12 May 1909.
[12] Placeres in Galicia was founded, thanks to the gift of a property with the condition that the Society of the Sacred Heart would open a school for poor children.
[13] *Vie de la R.M. de Montalembert*, p. 371.

made at the extreme boundary of the Austrian empire on the shores of the Adriatic at Lovrana, a resort town in Istria. This territory, populated largely by Italians, formed a part of the lands claimed by Italy. The founders were immediately recalled to Vienna after the assassination at Sarajevo.

In Latin America, new foundations were unquestionably linked to the redistribution of personnel. The opening of the Chalet of Chorrillos in Peru — which at the beginning served as a country house for the nuns of Lima — dated from 1903; the one in León de Andrade, also in the capital, made it possible to separate the boarding school from the normal school in 1908. The community included several French religious. In Mexico, the foundation in Monterrey in October 1908 was explained both by the success of the Sacred Heart in the eyes of the bishops and of local society, since it took place at the request of Bishop Leopoldo Ruiz y Flores and prominent persons of the city, and by the arrival of French religious.[14] New Latin American countries opened their doors to the Society for the same reasons.

In 1852, at the request of the papal nuncio and some Brazilian alumnae who had been educated in Europe, Mother Barat had encouraged Mother du Rousier to make a foundation in the sole Portuguese-speaking country in Latin America. It was only at the moment of the expulsions that Mother Digby decided to sound out Bishop Arcoverde of Rio de Janeiro to determine whether he was favorable to a Sacred Heart establishment in his diocese. Prepared by the vicariate of Chile, the foundation was made at Tijuca near Rio shortly after the General Congregation of 1904. For fifty years all the superiors and mistresses general were French. The Sacred Heart educated the elite of the country.[15] In 1909, a day school was opened in Rio. In Montevideo in 1908 the vicar of Chile, Mother Jackson, opened a boarding school, although it was threatened by an anti-clerical government. This foundation in Uruguay brought about a change in administration in South America: Argentina and Uruguay formed one vicariate under Mother Jackson; Chile, and Peru remained united as one vicariate with Mother Isabel Battista, a Cuban, in charge.

The entry of the Society of the Sacred Heart into Colombia took place in November 1907. The availability of French religious, who constituted three quarters of the community in Bogotá, made the foundation possible; but it is clear that the extremely favorable conditions the government offered contributed to the decision of the motherhouse. The head of state, General Rafael Reyes, did not want young Colombians to be educated abroad, for he feared they would not maintain the traditional values of

---

[14] Mothers de Montcheuil, Gurdon and de la Randière formed part of the founding community.

[15] Testimony of Maria Luiza Saade.

their country, their faith, their love of family and fatherland. Therefore, he was ready to favor foundations by teaching congregations, even to paying the expenses of the journeys and of the first buildings. The founders embarked at Cherbourg. The superior, Mother Guadalupe de Bofarull, had been chosen because of her experience and her strength of character and because she could be counted on in all circumstances. The choice of a Spanish-speaking religious could only further the success of the foundation.

The arrival of the Religious of the Sacred Heart in Egypt and in Japan was unquestionably the most original feature of the period. Except in Algiers, the Society of the Sacred Heart had never been in direct contact with non-Christian populations. From this moment they were going to carry on their work in an Islamic land and in a country whose population was principally Shinto or Buddhist.

The approach to the "East" was made first by a foundation on the island of Malta. Mothers Stuart and von Loë, the vicars of England and Italy, and Mother Helen Rumbold, superior at Hammersmith, went to Malta in January 1903 to explore the possibility of a foundation to be part of the vicariate of England, for Malta had been an English colony since 1810. The founders arrived there on 12 August 1903. The group included one English and one Irish nun, a Swiss, a German and two Italians. They found themselves in a picturesque Christian world, and they were delighted by the patriarchal character of the Maltese people: "They lived on the door step and the goats formed part of the family. In the evening the men returned from work saying the Rosary; they greeted the nuns respectfully, while the children ran to them at all hours to kiss their crosses and receive holy cards .... Theft was unknown."[16]

Activity began at Villa Portelli, close to the Blue Sisters who lent considerable aid to the founders; they also received support from the English Jesuits who had a boys' school at Saint Julian's. In October 1903 a small school for boarders and day pupils was opened with eight students; the number soon grew to eighteen. A year later the school of the Rosary opened with forty students. In January 1904 the purchase of a property close to Saint Julian allowed for the installation of the community, the boarding school and the day school after three years of work. Malta was original not only in accepting boys in the primary school in 1910, but above all in gradually mixing them in with the girls. The house was equipped, thanks to the spoils from the closing of Algiers, Marseille and Avignon. Not only did the foundation develop with its own characteristics, but it was a step towards the establishment of the Society of the Sacred Heart in an Islamic country.

---

[16] *Vie de la R.M. Helen Rumbold*, pp. 119 and 122.

In order to compensate for the abandonment of Algiers, the motherhouse thought about Egypt, then theoretically a province of the Turkish Empire, where a large European colony was living. Egypt had been occupied by Great Britain since 1882, but, since the expedition of Bonaparte, the cultural influence of France was strongly felt there. In May 1903, Mother Digby sent Mother Rumbold, superior in Malta, and Mother d'Oneto, superior of Santa Rufina in Rome, to Alexandria.[17] Their trip was somewhat impromptu; they were obliged to stay at the Hôtel Khedivial, but "they soon realized that it was not a hotel for poor religious for its luxurious furnishings were altogether Turkish!"[18] They were to ask for authorization from the apostolic delegate to Egypt to open a house in Alexandria. The religious met with a refusal because in order not to undermine religious congregations already established in the Nile delta, Bishop Bonfigli had decided not to accept any of the orders expelled from France. He suggested that they go to Cairo in the part of the country that depended on the apostolic prefect of the African Missions, Father Duret. He knew the houses of the Society in Lyons and gave his consent for the region of Abbasieh, located close to the desert. The two emissaries sent a telegram to Paris with just a single word, "hope," and they went home.[19]

Mother Digby negotiated with the cardinal protector to obtain a pontifical brief of authorization, for the Curia was not favorable to an influx of "French" congregations in Egypt. On 26 October 1903, she wrote to him:

> The precious rescript authorizing us to found in Egypt, in Cairo, has just arrived; allow me, Your Eminence, to express our deep gratitude. I always had confidence in my heart that the intercession of our venerated protector would obtain this grace for our Society in its present difficulty, and without delay we will set about finding a house and learning Arabic in order to establish a house in Cairo and open a school there for poor children. It will compensate us for the continuing suppression of our houses in France.[20]

---

[17] The choice of Mother d'Oneto is doubtless explained by the fact that the apostolic delegation in Egypt had been entrusted to an Italian and that Alexandria had a large Italian colony.

[18] Prov. Arch. Egypt, *Journal du Caire*, p. 2.

[19] They returned to Egypt upon the arrival of the founders to take charge of all the official proceedings for the acquisition of land necessary for construction. Mother Angelica della Chiesa, superior in Naples, who spoke English was an additional member.

[20] Gen. Arch. C III, Egypt.

A place was found northeast of Cairo near the military zone. It was located in the most pleasant and healthful part of the city in a growing area for which there was a great deal of hope.

The first Religious of the Sacred Heart arrived in Cairo in November 1903 and lodged with the Missionary Sisters of Africa.[21] Two were French and came from Algiers and two were Irish. They were joined by Mother von Zaufal, an Austrian who arrived from Pressbaum; she had been named superior of the foundation. The founders stayed in the house of Pasha Zakakini. They undertook to have a house built, which was ready on 26 August 1906. In the meantime, their life was not easy, for they had to get used to mosquitoes and to the Turkish coffee always served at meetings with Egyptian and European authorities. Obliged to do errands in the teeming streets of Cairo, they were surprised at some sights they met in this highly colorful city:

> It seemed very strange at first to find ourselves, Religious of the Sacred Heart, in the midst of this crowd full of curious contrasts: Arabs in their national costume, the *galabeyah*, Europeans, Bedouins, Blacks, camels, donkeys that are very handsome here, cars. There is such variety in civilian and military costumes that ours hardly attracts any attention. The effect of the whole is to make one think of the prelude of Saint Ignatius describing the state of the world before the Incarnation. On all sides feverish haste and the constant struggle to acquire a fortune, joined to the oriental appearance of the buildings, remind one of Babylon. What makes the strangest impression is the astonishing contrast of ancient and modern life going along side by side without blending. Going to the Pyramids in a streetcar and seeing camels with their measured steps and disdainful bearing sharing the streets with bicycles, automobiles and electric streetcars, all has the effect of a dream.... In the streets there are wandering herds of goats, tolerated by the administration as auxiliary help in maintaining a relative state of cleanliness along the routes. Wherever there is a little grass, a few vegetable scraps or orange skins, the goatherd sits down by the side of the road and the goats graze; then when they have finished they go elsewhere in search of another meager pasture. The other day three little pigs looking for adventure came into our garden where sweet alyssum had been newly planted and would have settled in as if at home had someone not dislodged them.[22]

The Jesuits helped the nuns when they were moving in to open the innumerable boxes that had arrived mainly from France, and then again

---

[21] Later they took the name of Our Lady of Africa.
[22] Prov. Arch. Egypt, *Journal de la maison du Caire*, 13 and 18 January 1904.

with the move itself. Apostolic work began slowly; it could not have been otherwise, for Cairo already had Catholic schools maintained for a long time by other congregations. Some of them were very hostile to the establishment of the Sacred Heart for fear that it would take away their pupils.[23] The first pupil, age eight, whose father was an employee of the Egyptian government, hardly knew how to read when she arrived on 1 March 1904. Each month the nuns accepted one boarder. In October 1904, with ten recruits, they established the boarding school. Only in 1909 could they open a day school, in which the teaching was in both French and Arabic.

The boarding school in Cairo rapidly became international, and it brought together Copts, Catholics, Orthodox, Syrians, Armenians and Turks, all more or less Europeanized, as well as a few children of English, French, Italian and Austrian families.[24] At the beginning it accepted only Christians. This restriction had permitted the Holy See to authorize its establishment in Cairo without prejudice to the congregations already present in the Egyptian capital, which had succeeded in attracting Jewish children and above all Muslims, daughters of officials in the khedival administration and in the court. Even so in 1911 Mother Rumbold learned that a member of the Egyptian government was astonished that "the Religious of the Sacred Heart are established [in Egypt] without authorization and that they refuse to accept our daughters." The vicar, who lived in Cairo, obtained a decree from the Propagation of the Faith permitting the Society of the Sacred Heart to accept Muslims and Jews. She decided then to found a house in Heliopolis at the explicit request of the prominent Egyptian, Sedki Pacha. He had come from Alexandria and was looking for a school for his daughters who had begun their studies at Notre-Dame de Sion. The new city of Heliopolis begun by Baron Empain was a fashionable place under construction and was welcoming families of Egyptian authorities, but Muslims were still few in number. The Sacred Heart wished to open a day school [*demi-pensionnat*] but accepted some boarders from the beginning. It was the first Catholic educational establishment in Heliopolis, thanks to the support of Bishop Duret, the first bishop of Heliopolis. From 1912 on the house included a boarding school and a fee-paying day school, since from the beginning it served an affluent population. It accepted Muslims and a few Jewish girls. The

---

[23] Prov. Arch. Egypt, *Rapport de la Mère du Chamerlat*, June 1924. In July 1904, Mother von Zaufal decided that her community would make a novena for the prosperity of their boarding schools, in particular for the one run by the Religious of the Mother of God who were the most unfavorable to the establishment of the Sacred Heart!

[24] *Vie de la R.M. Lamb*, p. 58.

Muslims arrived at school veiled and at the end of the day put their veils back on before crossing the threshold of the front door.[25] The convent chapel was surmounted by the first cross ever seen in Heliopolis. The establishment succeeded rapidly and already had forty-eight students by January 1913.

The Sacred Heart still wanted to have a house in Alexandria, where Notre-Dame de Sion had prevented its opening a boarding school. At least it wanted a permanent place where the nuns could spend vacations at the seashore. Mother Rumbold succeeded in acquiring a villa at Ramlah, where the religious who had left Conflans a little earlier settled in March 1908. The villa had a large, beautiful garden looking out on the Mediterranean and a forbidding appearance, decorated as it was with marble lions.[26] It was enlarged after the opening of Heliopolis and during the summer welcomed the nuns in groups of twelve. A small community had charge of it; they gave private lessons, conducted a sewing room [to make vestments] for poor churches and took care of some Bedouins: these were the only activities authorized by the apostolic delegate. After 1922, the villa was no longer occupied except during vacations. Before the First World War, foundations were asked for in Damascus and Istanbul; but as they were never made, for more than half a century Egypt was the only country in the Middle East where the Society was present.

The establishment in Japan took place in a different context. During the Meiji Era there was a favorable development in the attitude to a Christian presence. Persecution of hidden Christians and new converts ceased in 1873. In February 1889 a constitution granted religious liberty to the Japanese, and in June Leo XIII established the episcopal hierarchy in Japan. From 1886 on, the Propagation of the Faith had asked the Society of the Sacred Heart to go to Japan to open free schools and a boarding school for the daughters of the aristocracy; but neither Mother Lehon nor Mother Digby followed up on the appeal and those that came later. Therefore, other teaching congregations preceded the Society in Japan. After the Russo-Japanese War rapid change took place. In 1906 Pius X sent a delegation to Tokyo to thank the emperor for the protection he had provided for Christians in Manchuria. His messengers were received by the imperial family and by several people who made known the fact that Japan needed outside assistance in order to provide higher education for the country. Pius X immediately appealed to the Society of Jesus and to the Sacred Heart to respond. In consequence, Mother Digby decided to make a foundation in Japan with religious from Australia.

---

[25] Prov. Arch. Eygpt, "Notes," 1950.
[26] Prov. Arch. Egypt, Description of Simone de la Hitte.

The first four founders[27] were from Ireland, New Zealand and Australia, and one was a coadjutrix novice. After a crossing of a month, they disembarked at Yokohama on 1 January 1908. Welcomed by the Dames de Saint-Maur, they settled in a tiny house that was completely empty of furniture, and they experienced an earthquake on the first day. A second group of eight, Irish, French, Belgian and English, arrived in February 1908, necessitating another lodging. Finally the community was reinforced in September by a Belgian and three Germans, one of whom was Mother Hermanna Mayer. She was destined to remain in Japan until her death and left an exceptional record of her talents, her manner and the relationships she established with the local population. The presence of German religious had to be appreciated in Japan where the imperial regime, inspired by the institutions of the Reich, admired its aristocratic, military and bureaucratic character. Other Europeans, Australians and New Zealanders were sent to Japan in the following years.

The Religious of the Sacred Heart knew nothing of local customs. They related how at the beginning of their stay they had no idea that they had to take off their shoes to walk on the *tatami*, which they took to be ordinary floor mats:

> Every day a few missionaries came to visit us, and they left their shoes at the door, teaching us a lesson that we were so slow to learn. Lovely people, perfect strangers, brought us presents wrapped in *furoshiki*. We accepted the presents with much gratitude, and we were greatly lacking in etiquette in keeping the *furoshiki* also.

But the bewilderment was reciprocal for Japanese suppliers who came to the house stayed to watch how the sisters prepared the meals and did the ironing. The ironing of the nuns' caps intrigued them especially.[28] The founders recounted also how disconcerted they were by traditional Japanese forms of politeness and by the absence of children's smiles when adults were present.[29]

On 29 June 1908, the community settled in the suburbs of Tokyo on the Sankocho hill, where the Society of the Sacred Heart had acquired the former hunting lodge of a Christian *daimyo*, Prince Satsuma. When the chapel was built, it was furnished with the choir stalls from Conflans. In

---

[27] They were Bridget Heydon, Mary Scroope, Elizabeth Sproule and Mary Casey.

[28] Margaret Williams, *The Society of the Sacred Heart in the Far East*, Tokyo, 1982, pp. 27-29.

[29] Prov. Arch. Japan, Biography of R.M. Sheldon. She recounted that at her arrival in the boarding school the westerners made a curtsey and the Japanese bowed deeply before her.

order to modernize, the Japanese needed to understand western cultural models. The British and the Americans had become their principal consultants in economic, diplomatic and military matters. Therefore, the Religious of the Sacred Heart had been asked to open an English-speaking "foreign school". In April 1908, they still had only a few pupils, two of whom were Japanese; but they quickly accepted the daughters of diplomats and, thanks to the relationships with them, the nuns came into contact with the political and social elite of Japan. The superior, Mother Bridget Heydon, received help from them but strove to preserve her independence. This support was effective on several occasions.

While the Religious of the Sacred Heart were able to establish their regular educational system in Japan, they had to obey the imperial rescript of 1890 that had prescribed that education must be based on sacred tradition and the teaching of the ancestors. They understood that they must not look on Japan with western eyes. They visited contemporary Japanese schools for girls, and they were assisted by accomplished Japanese teachers. In December 1909, they obtained permission to open a kindergarten and a primary school besides the "foreign school," then in February 1910, a secondary school. From November 1909 on, the *Seishin Gakuin* was directed by a Japanese lay Christian, Madame Hirata. At the time of her visit to Japan, Mother Stuart gave orders to respect and obey her as if she were "one of ours."

This director made it possible for the religious to avoid blunders and *faux pas* and little by little to get to know the local customs, for they had to adapt the educational principles to the customs of the country. This adaptation included everything from the juxtaposition of uniforms and kimonos, even to the adoption of a long pleated skirt down to the ankles to cover the multi-colored kimonos of the students, to the more serious question of how to apply the plan of studies. In the "foreign school" there was no difficulty in using it, but in the Japanese school it was necessary to integrate Confucian principles into the curriculum. The pupils of the two schools shared the same dormitories and refectories, but they went to class in separate buildings. The religious taught the students in the "foreign school," but those in the Japanese school had Japanese teachers. It became clear that the rewards traditional in the Sacred Heart boarding schools, like the ribbons of merit, could not be used because they did not suit the Japanese mentality. No free school for the poor was started, for in Japan, public primary schooling had been free and obligatory since 1872.

As the Meiji Era came to an end in 1912, the Society of the Sacred Heart was well established in Tokyo. The twenty-eight religious living there felt that they could expand their activity, including the teaching of the Catholic religion; but they knew that in that regard they had to be very prudent. In their correspondence, therefore, they took care not to use certain expressions. During the First World War, under censorship, they used metaphors to refer to conversions and baptisms. In 1917 one of them wrote: "We rejoice when we deliver a soul of Adam's descent, especially if the crossing of the Styx follows soon after and the eternal shore is reached in complete safety." They had to be content with "following a middle course and sowing good seed on the roadside."[30] Even so in the boarding school, the nuns who spoke Japanese held an "honorable conversation" each week, during which they brought up moral questions that touched on religion.

Acceptance in Japanese civilization required knowing the language. Mother Heydon wrote that all the new arrivals were "studying Japanese seriously, as seriously as they could. Not only is the language difficult, but the mindset is so different that grammatical constructions are reversed. But as the glory of the Sacred Heart depends on our use of the language, we must speak it!"[31] From 1917 on, during summer vacation the nuns tried also to master reading and writing *kanji*, Chinese characters used in Japan.

Japan could have been a departure point for other Asiatic countries. The Japanese authorities who had colonized Korea made an offer for a foundation in 1910; the motherhouse did not follow up on it. The Religious of the Sacred Heart, who had been invited to China in Mother Barat's time, only went there in the 1920's. During her journey around the world, Mother Stuart stopped in Manila. In the company of an alumna who served as intermediary, she visited a property close to the capital that could have served for a foundation. That project was not carried out. It was only in the second half of the twentieth century that the Society of the Sacred Heart was established in Korea and the Philippines.

Living Religious Life Elsewhere

At the time of the departure from France communities had been broken up, even though there was an effort to keep a nucleus of the former community when the nuns were sent to one of the refuges or to a house that received French boarding pupils. Therefore, it was in new groupings that the religious had to undertake the adventure of what was really a "foundation." The advice the motherhouse gave to the religious was to be open to living the mission in a new framework.[32]

---

[30] Prov. Arch. Japan, Biography of R.M. Sheldon.
[31] M. Williams, *The Society...Far East*, p. 53.
[32] In announcing the first departures abroad, Mother Digby had repeated the remarks of Mother Lehon to Mother Jeanne de Lavigerie who was leaving for

Mother Digby had forbidden speaking about "expulsions" and "exile" and referring to those "expelled" as "exiles."[33] For this reason no doubt the journals of the houses that received them did not mention the fact. The uprooted religious who had lost their familiar environment were not able to talk about what they had lived through.[34] Their silence was proof of heroic conduct; but, paradoxically, thanks to the trauma of the expulsions, many of them better understood the richness of their charism and deepened their understanding of the idea of their founder to glorify the Heart of Jesus even to the ends of the earth. That concern, until then confided to "missionaries," became the concern of everyone. Mother Charlotte de Kerguiffinec, who had left Angoulême to be superior in Chillan, wrote on 5 March 1904, during the crossing that was taking her to Chile: "The cord is broken on the side of created things…but with what strength Jesus is attaching me to Himself."[35] As another would say later: "Here or there in my own country I had still been somewhat at home. Jesus wanted me elsewhere to be at home entirely with Him."[36]

The biographies of the dead included only the part of the life story that the writer wished to leave to posterity. This concern "to save face" could have contributed to reinforcing the image of dignity, of tranquil courage, of the sense of duty, of respect for the order given, of submission to the Church, of self-control, an image that characterized the Society of the Sacred Heart and that conformed to the values handed on in its schools. However, the biographies also indicate the suffering of the religious sent out of France and the efforts of superiors to support and maintain them – according to the hallowed formula – "in the supernatural." The spiritual formation received showed its worth on this occasion, and most of the religious were able to profit from their trial. As Mother Adrienne Poncelet resolved in her notes: "To envisage the consequences of persecution for my soul as a choice grace from the Heart of Jesus, a call to greater holiness, a means of effectively procuring its greater glory by absolute detachment from the work I loved."[37]

Vicars and superiors everywhere did what they could to lighten the load for the uprooted French religious. Every means was set in motion: a

---

Latin America: "Forget your own country so as never to weaken your sacrifice by repinings, sadness, or day-dreams that carry you away to other climes than the one that has become your home…" (*Circulaires…Digby*, 19 June 1903, pp. 148-149).

[33] *Circulaires…Digby*, p. 163, 11 September 1904.
[34] Often at the time of a jubilee before or after the Second World War they related what they had lived through then. Statement of Margaret Phelan, about the United States.
[35] *Lettres annuelles*, 1940-1945. She was sent to Peru in 1911.
[36] *Vie de la R.M. Le Baïl*, p. 96.
[37] *Lettres annuelles*, 1958-1961, p. 176.

welcome at the train station by some religious or alumnae, even by a doctor when it was known that there were sick or elderly among those arriving,[38] a word of welcome in French at arrival, a daily visit with those who seemed lost.[39] But even though they were helped by the commonality of religious customs, the French nuns sometimes found it difficult to adapt to a new culture, learn the customs of the country and live in communities that had been together for a long time.

The first obstacle was that of language. "Without knowing the language of the country where one lives, one is only half a person," said Mother Amélie Schulten, from Westphalia. She had been vicar of Canada, then was sent to Mexico and Peru. Those who had learned the language of the country earlier set about reviewing it. Mother de Montalembert, who governed the vicariate of Austria from 1905 to 1913, wrote à propos of German, which she had to use from then on: "I am beginning to relearn my present language, learned forty-five years ago, then buried in oblivion. You can imagine that the resurrection is not instantaneous! But everyone is very kind and indulgent; so all is going well." She tested memory and creativity by asking her neighbor for the missing word or by inventing it. After a month, aided by her assistant, she could give a conference in German, but as one can imagine, she did not have perfect pronunciation.[40]

Most often the superiors had the newcomers take language courses. As Mother Joséphine Roussin, who was sent to Malta from Algiers, told it later:

> I knew only a few words of English, so it was impossible to understand or speak. An English Mother, who was as patient as she was devoted, became my professor. Thanks to her excellent lessons, coupled with a great deal of encouragement, I succeeded little by little in becoming less isolated. When one is in a country whose language one does not know, that creates a wall of separation. That wall never existed in Malta: there was rather "a clear passage:" everyone was so kind and repeated in French what we had not understood.[41]

That must have been echoed in many other places.

Not all the French could master the language of their new country; some spoke it with a poor accent or used incorrect vocabulary.[42] In many

---

[38] That is what Mother Vicente did at San Sebastián.
[39] *Life of R.M. Thunder*, p. 36.
[40] *Vie de la R.M. de Montalembert*, pp. 360-361.
[41] *Lettres annuelles*, 1955-1957, p. 498.
[42] In 1912, Mother Stuart required lessons in Polish to be given to the nuns during vacations (A. Merdas, *Histoire…en Pologne*, p. 12). It is clear that Mother de Montalembert did not speak Polish during her visits in Galicia.

communities meetings had to be held in French, a practice that had been given up long ago, placing a burden on the religious of the welcoming community. Some tried a procedure often used in foundations: superiors proposed using different languages during different weeks; everyone then had to make the effort to learn the language she did not know, and each had a chance to relax on the days when her mother tongue was spoken. Bilingualism did not take effect from the outset, however, and there were some comical incidents. At Brighton, a young English nun received a correction during reading from her French superior.

> If it had been an "English day," she would have answered spontaneously: "I will keep it in mind," but it was a French day. She remained mute for a second, thinking what she could say and the whole community in religious silence heard her answer, "Thank you, Reverend Mother, I will keep that in my coffin [*dans mon cercueil*]." It was hard to keep from laughing, but the superior's own unsuppressed laugh gave them all permission to explode.[43]

Vicars and superiors looked for preachers who could give the newcomers their annual retreat in French.[44] In Malta that practice lasted for several years, superiors even bringing in preachers from France.[45]

The nuns in contact with the students did not always know the language well enough to speak with them. The difficulty was even greater in the case of a mistress general. Religious who were the most competent in language had to help her or replace her. It was not normal for a vicar not to be able to speak the language of the country, to communicate with the religious and persons outside or for a mistress of novices who did not speak the local language to be named.[46] The superior general sometimes had to give a new obedience to religious who could not fulfill their mission for the simple reason that they did not have sufficient grasp of the language of the country to which they had been sent.[47]

---

[43] *Vie de la R.M. de Neuville*, p. 216. [The confusion is between *cercueil*, coffin, and *cerveau*, brain. Tr. note.]

[44] *Vie de la T.R.M. Vicente*, p. 76.

[45] *Lettres annuelles*, 1955-1957, p. 498.

[46] Mother Marie Deydier caused ill-timed giggles from her novices at Riedenburg when she tried to speak German. She was finally sent to Prague (*Lettres annuelles*, 1940-1945, p. 40).

[47] Maintaining, even enforcing, the use of French in the Society was necessitated by circumstances after 1915. Mother von Loë, who spoke French perfectly, could read English but did not speak it, and she neither understood nor spoke Spanish. She had the General Congregation of 1915 decide that not only would the novices study French seriously, but that the custom was to be

Monique Luirard

The establishment of boarding schools for the French students who had followed "their Mothers" also created difficulties. At San Sebastián, only forty Spaniards were accepted so as to leave as much room as possible for the French. At Sarriá, a day school was closed in order to give the building to the newcomers, and the original boarding school allocated some classrooms to them. Combining boarding school students coming from schools that were organized differently proved to be delicate. When Mother de Neuville took charge in Brighton in September 1904, the house was twenty years old. The boarding school was rather small, but its numbers were doubled by the arrival of about fifty French girls, most of whom came from the Rue de Varenne. They arrived with the higher classes, the "blue ribbons," the Children of Mary, a complete, well-organized "general staff." The English boarding school, which went up only through the second class, had neither "ribbons" nor Children of Mary. The French certainly showed some disdain towards their comrades whose school did not have the same reputation. For three years in spite of the efforts of both the French and the English nuns who helped one another to solve the problems of language and manners, life together was complicated, and it took a great deal of effort to achieve harmony between the two groups. They continued to remain at odds and ready to come into conflict.

In the schools located not too far from the regions from which the students came, the situation was less problematic. Excursions into France were organized periodically for the students of Lindthout. After November 1904, a journey by streetcar and train allowed seventy-eight of them, accompanied and supervised by their fathers, to spend three days in Lille and its surroundings. For Christmas, they were given five days of vacation so that they could be with their families. That allowed them to remain in contact. When the boarding schools were farther away, the pupils went home only once a year during the summer vacation.[48] Some parents, after a few months or a few years of this arrangement, ended by withdrawing their daughters from these schools across the borders.[49]

---

revived of reading the Decrees alternately in French and in the language of the country and that during recreation French was to be spoken alternately with the local language. She explained to the vicars that it was good to speak a second language, as was evident, but it did not necessarily make for easy integration of the communities (Gen. Arch. C 1 C 3, Box 13). And, of course, she asked that they write to her in French.

[48] Testimony of Simone de la Hitte who went from Toulouse to San Sebastián.
[49] The "French" boarding school at Sarriá was given up after the "Tragic Week" in Barcelona. In general the French boarding schools outside of France disappeared after the First World War and the reestablishment of the Society in France.

Another problem was linked to the many changes of superiors that affected communities already established. The motherhouse tried to give an office to those French who had had one before. The seven closed vicariates included many religious who had been superior, assistant or mistress general. The effort was made to use their competence and experience in another place. When they were sent to a refuge or a new community composed mostly of French nuns, there was hardly any risk of their not being able to fulfill their mission. On the other hand, putting them in charge of a community including members of different nationalities did not always have the expected results. Certainly, as Mother Digby wrote, to each religious,

> ...the Society our Mother secures hearth, home and work. As all our houses belong to her, we are at home everywhere (especially the Professed). National spirit will have no chance of asserting itself as long as there is a free exchange of subjects among all countries.[50]

Still it all must have seemed like occupied territory, and the widespread installation of French nuns as superiors could have appeared to be an invasion. It left mixed memories. Most of the new superiors were convinced that they had to act with tact. They quickly tried to express themselves in the national language, even if they had only limited fluency, and the native religious were touched by this courtesy.

Some of the difficulties seemed to have been due to the composition of the communities and to new conditions of apostolic life. In Belgium the first foundation destined to receive those expelled was that of Flône, a former abbey of the Canons of Saint Augustine. The first arrivals came from Moulins in 1903. They were joined by religious from two other houses. The combination of people from disparate backgrounds and unprepared beginnings made community life unpleasant during the first months. It took two years for the community to become united. Friction occurred by chance or from the unexpected clash of difficult temperaments, no doubt aggravated by the trial of departure from France. Even though the French had accepted leaving with obedience and faith, there was nothing to say that the abandonment of their country, which everyone believed to be final, did not involve deep interior resistance. It took time for everyone to see the spiritual aspect of the uprooting and to find herself at ease in new places, all the more so because at least in the beginning apostolic activities were not yet organized or were different from what the nuns were used to. In many places they could not open boarding schools. The local bishops accepted an

---

[50] *Circulaires...Digby*, 11 September 1904, p. 163.

expelled congregation if need be but did not wish to endanger the smooth running of institutions already established. On the Belgian side, for example, only foundations for convalescent children or for young women who had finished their schooling were allowed. Therefore, the Religious of the Sacred Heart had to use all their ingenuity to open workrooms, to organize catechetical programs, and to create every possible opportunity to establish contacts with adults and children.

The difficulties of the new communities were explained also by slow adaptation to buildings suitable neither for a conventual life style nor for the works of the Sacred Heart. In Belgium the châteaux of Wetteren, Lindthout and Fontaine-l'Évêque had been partially transformed before receiving religious and students; but at Wetteren, the refectories, kitchen and storeroom were set up in cellars that were hard to reach and not large enough. Further adaptation failed because of the urgency of the move, and it was decided not to enlarge the house until it was clear whether it would be kept or given up.

Material conditions sometimes proved singularly complicated in houses with insufficient resources. Although the Society of the Sacred Heart had foreseen "regional" boarding schools outside of France, not all the families were ready to send their daughters to be educated far from home; some may have been unwilling because the distance increased the costs. Families in Saint-Brieuc and Quimper refused to send their children to Goodrington, a house located on the Bay of Torquay, because of the distance and the danger of crossing the English Channel.[51] The community took in mending and kept up the linen room of the English boarding school.[52] In an area where the population was mainly Protestant, this house, which could accept only a few *grandes pensionnaires* and very few boarders, could not manage financially.[53] At Leamington, the nuns had so much difficulty in securing a livelihood that the vicar, Mother Stuart, sought to help them by providing lace making.[54] Poverty was the rule in foundations, but it ought not to be excessive or last too long, if the religious were to be able to pursue their apostolic life. The motherhouse had to give financial support to some houses that were far from self-sufficient and had little opportunity to develop works that would bring in funds.[55]

In the new European foundations, the first months and years were overshadowed by the number of deaths among the French religious. This

---

[51] *Lettres annuelles*, 1917-1919, p. 835.
[52] *Lettres annuelles*, 1917-1919, p. 836.
[53] It was closed in 1913.
[54] *Journal de la maison du Caire*, 8 and 12 March 1904.
[55] *Vie de la R.M. Borget*, p. 247.

increase in mortality could appear normal for aged religious or for those who arrived sick in the countries that welcomed them and who often were traumatized by the forced departure from France and by dangerous voyages. But deaths resulted also among those who had difficulty in adapting to a new climate or a new way of life. Some superiors who had had to close houses in France and who had not necessarily accepted abandoning them were ill for a long time in the houses that received them, a proof that the uprooting was a heavy trial. Certainly this increased mortality, as Mother Nieuwland, vicar of Belgium, noted, humorously or not, simplified the work of the infirmary,[56] but the increase of deaths among the French religious was an additional trial for everyone.

In the "missions," adaptation had never been easy, but one can believe that those who aspired to missionary life lived through the first stages with greater ease. It is possible that at the time of the expulsions more religious who did not desire it had been sent to the missions than formerly. In this case superiors needed a great deal of tact in helping those whose efforts they saw and whose suffering they understood. In Malta Mother Rumbold acted that way towards the French. Her biographer writes:

> She knew very well how to help people value the happiness of being chosen for a mission land…she said, "See what confidence our Mothers have in us in sending us so far away to an unknown land! And how necessary it is that we keep the rule in its integrity since it is we who are establishing the Society in the Orient where we are responsible for its reputation."[57]

She knew how to join psychology and spiritual advice to render each one capable of giving the best that was in her and of maintaining fidelity to her vocation.

Reaffirmation of Unity

Relations among Religious of the Sacred Heart had always been based on the principle: *Cor unum et anima una*. "Union of hearts and souls" was the third means proposed "for preserving the Society in the spirit of its Institute." This "close union" was "the infallible sign" which will "impress on their Society the character of God's work." A source of peace and of consolation for the religious, it would be a subject of edification and thanksgiving for others, and for "young people" a motive for committing themselves to following Christ in the Society of the Sacred Heart and finally

---

[56] Prov. Arch. Belgium-Netherlands. Account of regular visits.
[57] *Vie de la R.M. Rumbold*, p. 171.

a sight that Heaven will look down upon with delight. The Heavenly Father will recognize in [the religious] His children; Jesus Christ, His spouses; the Holy Ghost, His living temples; the Blessed Virgin Mary, so closely united to the Three Divine Persons, will look on them with tender affection and will declare herself their protectress and their Mother.[58]

In peaceful times, application of the motto was easy, even though it had to be renewed when the congregation branched out geographically. As Mother Digby wrote on the occasion of the centenary of the birth of the institute,

> One heart beats in six thousand other hearts, one soul in as many minds and wills – what a glorious reality – and difficult as we know it to be to maintain harmony, it can be done by the grace of our vocation, notwithstanding differences of language, race, circumstances and environment, for nothing is impossible to God, and our Mother Foundress realized that in this union lay God's Will for her daughters. She saw that the Heart of Jesus would Himself mold all these separate elements into *unity*, and that the very diversity of the parts would strengthen the whole.[59]

However, in a time of crisis, of which the beginning of the twentieth century was an example, it became a pointed question. They had to find an unpretentious way of living. As Mother Vicente expressed it one day, a house of the Sacred Heart, even at the other end of the world, was "one of our dear houses that I love without knowing it, a family composed of Mothers and Sisters who have the same rule as I, who lead the same life, are dressed like me, have the same desire, the same aspiration to glorify the Sacred Heart of Jesus."[60]

After the dissolution of the congregation in France, Mother Digby wrote:

> The Society is composed of many different members and communities, yet all are one body; a body must be animated by one soul, in spite of the great diversity of its members in race, language, and character. We are gainers by this diversity, for it adds richness to our religious life and a breadth that we ought greatly to appreciate. The strong life-blood of the Society is too vigorous and abundant to be confined by frontiers of any kind. It springs from one source and center and passes through manifold channels, bringing life to thriving offshoots, in the many lands where God

---

[58] *Constitutions*, Fourth Part: Of the Government of the Society, § XX to XXIV.
[59] *Circulaires…Digby*, 14 September 1900, p. 110.
[60] *Vie de la T.R.M. Vicente*, pp. 80-81.

has called us. It is our very dear duty to maintain this broad and eminently catholic spirit, and it admits no other distinction than that "of having a special love in Our Lord, for the nations that are not our own...."

Let us learn, for the glory of the Heart of Jesus to whom we are wholly consecrated, to value what is good in deed and thought, beyond our immediate surroundings, to appreciate the beautiful we shall meet abroad whether spiritual or moral – God's creation is too universal for one race or continent to have appropriated all His gifts...all these gifts are for us – beauties of nature so lavishly bestowed, the faculties of the mind, gifts of intellect, richness of idioms, stamped with His genius, historic treasures in which divine Providence is manifest...all these are ours, for instruction and full development of our powers.[61]

The scattering of the French and the extension of the congregation required still more prudence in order to maintain unity:

The expansion of the Society in different directions requires, nay, absolutely demands, the most intimate union of minds and hearts, otherwise we risk losing the most precious thing we possess: the primitive spirit of the Society. Let us then labour to cement this union and all that maintains and strengthens it.

Mother Stuart corroborated this analysis of the situation set forth by Mother Digby [62] when she wrote during her world tour:

The narrow, troubling, icy influence of [a national spirit] would be particularly misplaced in an institute where the end and the object are one, the countries represented many, changes frequent.... The ability to blend easily with persons of different nationalities gives a certain finish to religious formation.... The mix of nationalities tends to highlight the best in each one; it contributes to mutual understanding, calls forth what is good in everyone, at the same time that it imposes tact and proper reserve.[63]

These remarks made sense in an international congregation, but the context showed that internationality, if it was an opportunity, could be a challenge

---

[61] *Circulaires...Digby*, pp. 163-166, 11 September 1904, on the XXVIIth Common Rule.
[62] *Circulaires...Digby*, 30 April 1907, p. 210.
[63] Stuart, *The Society of the Sacred Heart*, p. 49.

to live in daily life. One had to revive every means of maintaining and increasing unity in the body of the congregation. Besides prayer and the love of each religious for the Heart of Jesus,[64] the Constitutions provided ways to sustain union, some of which were institutional or formed part of the tradition of the Society: the same formation to generosity given to the novices,[65] a superior general who was "like the one mother to a single family," the possibility for local superiors to have frequent exchanges among themselves and with the superior general, circular letters intended to give news of what was happening in the Society.[66] We have seen how Mother Stuart had decided to extend the travels of the superiors general to the whole world. These travels had been conceived in the Society as a means of government and of making the religious of one mind. The long journey she made allowed her to know and be known; it gave the religious the opportunity to renew their bonds with the rest of the Society.

Sending the French around the world helped the Society of the Sacred Heart to preserve the memory of its foundation years, of customs that Mother Barat had wanted, of the importance of France in the birth and expansion of the Society. It was likely for this reason that Mother Digby and her assistants general had decided that at Ixelles life would go on according to the customs of the motherhouse in Paris, then at Conflans.[67] Not always understood by the religious of later years who saw it as evidence of conservatism, this policy was indispensable at the moment in order to keep the Society united by fidelity in "little things."[68] Mother von Loë followed it, but based it on other assumptions. She spoke about these to the vicars in closing the General Congregation of 1915, giving examples that may be surprising:

> Our blessed Mother said rightly that the Society would be able to adapt to any country by taking into consideration in practice the requirements of the climate; but if there is nothing to be lost, let us hold to what our first Mothers did. Uniformity maintains union; when the probanists arrive and find at the motherhouse the same practices as those of their own country, they are so happy; on the contrary if there are differences, there is uneasiness, a painful note to hear. We have been trained to that end; we must preserve it. This fidelity is constant mortification; it is easier not to fold one's habit on Sunday than to do it; letting things go is more

---

[64] *Constitutions*, § XXIX and XXXI.
[65] *Constitutions*, § XXX.
[66] *Constitutions*, § XXVI to XXVIII.
[67] *Vie de la R.M. Borget*, p. 243.
[68] *Constitutions*, § XXXI. To wish to do "what was done at Conflans" meant to wish, by means of a common novitiate, to keep the original spirit exactly as it had been passed on.

convenient; it is a huge penance to practice all these little things! Our venerated Mother Stuart was a model of the perfection of common life, the first at everything! It was impossible to find the slightest fault in her; this perfection is within our reach; it is like a mosaic of little things.[69]

Unity maintained or consolidated, confused or not with uniformity, but essentially drawn from and maintained in prayer, was going to prove particularly necessary during the First World War.

---

[69] Gen. Arch. C I C 3, Box 13.

Chapter II

The Great War and the Religious of the Sacred Heart

Europe had not known a continental war since 1815, and the conflicts that had bloodied it since then had been contained in time and space. Austria and Russia had recognized the influence of Germany established in 1870, but it took the genius of Bismarck to "make the impetuous Russian elephant walk between the tame elephants, the German and the Austrian." The pact of "three emperors," designed to isolate France, did not take into account the interests or the ambitions of Austria and Russia in the Balkans. In the decades following, Austria's gains in the southern Balkans had pushed Russia to accept France's diplomatic overtures.[1] With William II's accession to power, Germany initiated a worldwide policy threatening enough to commit European countries to neutrality or to incite France, Great Britain and Russia to constitute the Triple Entente in the face of the Triple Alliance, which from then on included Germany, Austria and Italy.

Harbingers of Confrontation in the Dark Days of Summer 1914

More than ever rival ambitions engendered crises. In 1912, after the creation of the Balkan League, Mother de Montalembert, fearing a confrontation between Russians and Austrians in Galicia, sent the boarders away from Zbylitowska Gora. She sent the nuns and those boarders who could not go home to Prague and Pressbaum where they stayed until January 1913. The thrust of nationalism in the Balkans was creating a powder keg that could explode at any moment. The assassination of the heir to the Austrian throne, Archduke Francis Ferdinand, at Sarajevo, on 28 June 1914, unleashed a process that would lead to war. At the same time it was seen as a means of consolidating the Austro-Hungarian Empire threatened

---

[1] The Franco-Russian Alliance was signed in 1893.

by break up under the pressure of nationalization and as an occasion to reduce the influence of Russia by settling the lot of Serbia. Whereas before, pressure by Germany and Great Britain had kept conflicts within local bounds, in 1914, the European powers accepted the risk of a general war that would result in millions of deaths and that completely overturned the relationships of European states.

On 28 July 1914, Austria-Hungary's declaration of war on Serbia provoked partial, then general mobilization in Russia, Austria-Hungary and Germany. Italy decided to remain neutral. After Germany declared war on France on 3 August and Belgium refused to allow German troops to pass through its territory, Belgian neutrality was violated, and Great Britain in turn entered the conflict. From Ixelles Mother Stuart wrote: "What comfort to know that the whole Empire is fighting in unison for a noble cause! Reality is needed to awaken the British lion, but what a courageous young lion is the Belgium for which we are fighting!"[2] Fighting was going to break out simultaneously in Eastern and Western Europe.

Galicia was one of the pivots of military operations on the eastern front. After pushing back the Austro-Hungarian armies, the Russians occupied the eastern part of the empire. In the spring of 1915 Lemberg was taken by the troops of the Central Powers, then in 1918 by the Polish. The Convent of the Sacred Heart became a military hospital, occupied successively by first one army and then another. The nuns cared for Hungarian, Russian, Cossack, Tartar and Persian wounded. As the months went by, the religious were able to organize retreats for the alumnae, to prepare children for First Communion and to give hospitality to the families of the wounded. They reopened the day school, then the boarding school. The convent in Zbylitowska Gora, occupied by the Russians on 13 November 1914, was damaged by Austrian cannon fire. Its nuns were dispersed and sent to Vienna and Pleszow, a little château located near Krakow. After the Austrians retook Galicia, the boarding school and the free school were reestablished, as in Lemberg, and functioned until the end of the war. In Styria Graz opened its doors to a field hospital and its classrooms to the public schools.[3]

In Lorraine the military governor of Metz asked the nuns to serve as nurse's aides.[4] Mother Fromherz, the superior of Montigny, refused because "being cloistered the members of the community could not fulfill the functions of nurses outside the house,"[5] but she accepted the installation

---

[2] M. Monahan, *Life and Letters...*, p. 482.
[3] Gen. Arch. C IV 2. The field hospital seems to have been closed in the summer of 1916. The "other school" was operating there in March 1917.
[4] Arch. Dép. Moselle, 29 J 599, *Gouvernement der Festung Metz Sekt Ivb Nr 25 M Metz den 2 August 1914*. Information from M.T. Houdoy.
[5] Letter of 2 August 1914.

of a field hospital run by the Sisters of Charity. German nuns worked in it until November 1916 when they left Montigny. In August 1914, the French were expelled from Montigny. The oldest nuns and the sick went to Riedenburg; the others who could not find space in the overfilled Austrian vicariate were sent to Holland and the North of Italy, as were the nuns from Kientzheim.[6]

The German high command, who wished to make a quick end of the French army, had decided to surprise it by passing through the North. Fierce combat took place in Belgium. Liège fell on 15 August 1914, and Brussels was occupied on 20 August. Because of the speed of the march to the sea, all of Belgium became a combat zone. Recourse to reconnaissance and combat aircraft terrified the population. The Belgian houses were requisitioned. At La Ramée, "a German general refused to lodge at Bouloy, finding it below his rank, but the officers were happy with it."[7] Flône was declared a "house for the sick" and thus avoided lodging troops. The move afforded its inhabitants relative peace. The hill of Bois-l'Évêque, exposed to the fire of German artillery, became untenable. From the beginning of the combat the oldest, the sick and the youngest nuns were sent away. After the fall of the city the rest of the community, with the exception of the superior and a few caretakers, took refuge with private citizens, then reached Ixelles. Tournai was also a victim of the confrontations between German and French troops. Mothers Adrienne Buhet[8] and Madeleine de Brolac were killed by cannon fire when they went to the upper story of the house to see where the danger was coming from. Wetteren on the Escaut interested both camps. The Religious of the Sacred Heart took in Belgian and French soldiers. The "Prussians" entered the city on 4 September, preceded by hostages taken in the neighboring towns. After the bombardment and fire in part of the city, the nuns left in small groups under a rain of artillery fire for Ostend,[9] which appeared to be a possible place of refuge as King Albert I of Belgium had succeeded in holding the region of Ypres. The religious of the Belgian vicariate converged gradually towards this house. Ostend was taken in turn.

Antwerp was a strategic spot since the port controlled shipping in the North Sea. The Sacred Heart convent, occupied by about thirty religious, took in a field hospital. At the announcement of a possible bombardment of the port by the Germans, the hospital was evacuated. The nuns

---

[6] Gen. Arch.C I 7 d, Box 4.
[7] Prov. Arch. Belgium-Netherlands. *Notes sur les maisons du Sacré-Cœur.*
[8] She had been vicar of Lyons and Brittany.
[9] Gen. Arch. C I 7 d, Box 4, and Prov. Arch. Belgium-Netherlands. *Notes sur les maisons du Sacré-Cœur.*

delayed putting the place in order without really expecting the worst. The bombardment began on 6 September, and after a night of anguish they left the house, famished, without provisions, armed with only a suitcase or a bundle, only to discover that there were no more trains and that they had to get to Holland on foot: "We were in a state of suffering that only God knew. We tried to be cheerful to support one another," they wrote afterwards. After several missteps they arrived at the border and reached The Hague in cattle wagons. Others used a barge that made progress only with the outgoing tide, but they did not pay for their transportation, as the boatmen were taking aboard everyone who came along. These journeys took place in an indescribable melee and in a Dantesque atmosphere for "petrol deposits had been emptied to avoid an explosion and their contents poured into the Escaut. A thick layer of petrol covered the water making it unusable even for cleaning. Bombs were flying over our boats."[10]

There was apprehension about the fate of the motherhouse because of the nationality of the superior and assistants general and the presence of twenty-four probanists from all parts of the globe. Mother Stuart, who had returned from her world tour on 9 July 1914, had the English and American new professed leave before the route to Ostend was cut off. The others returned to their countries afterwards[11] and informed the communities that the motherhouse was totally isolated, even from the rest of Belgium.[12] Ixelles was not occupied, but as Mother Stuart wrote: "We know nothing, except that God is directing events and decides how they will go, 'so far and no farther' as he pleases. No lesson can teach us better detachment and confidence in God."[13] She tried to obtain the assistance of the legations of the United States and Spain, which were neutral, to send messages but without success. On 24 August, thanks to the German military government

---

[10] Notes....

[11] *Vie de la T.R.M. de Loë*, p. 333. The journey of the Italians took place in trains packed with soldiers or wounded. The motherhouse had not been able to inform those concerned that the superiors' retreat had been cancelled and that the following probation had been postponed. A small probation of a dozen aspirants from the houses in Belgium was opened in the fall of 1914. Mother Borget took charge of giving the instructions and received the professions in February 1915.

[12] In her circular of 10 August 1914, Mother Stuart had written: "For us at the motherhouse, the hardest thing is to have no news of the houses that are suffering the most, but the consolation is the intimate assurance that God will watch over everything that is his and that in the Society the tradition of courage and confidence that it has kept from the beginning will not be forgotten"(*Circulaires de la T.R.M. Stuart*, p. 386).

[13] M. Monahan, *Life and Letters*..., pp. 483 and 485.

in Brussels, she was able to let Vienna know that the houses in Belgium were unharmed.[14] She had some knowledge of troop movements, thanks to some friends who gave her information they were able to glean and to the family of Mother Nerincx, whose brother was vice-president of the Chamber of Deputies.

This isolation could damage the Society. Arguing from the precedent of 1870, her advisers proposed having Mother Stuart leave. Through arrangements made by of the superior of Ostend, the nephew of a deputy mayor there arrived at Ixelles on 3 September with letters from London urging Mother Stuart to go to England with her office staff while there was still time. After deliberating with her assistants, the superior general, accompanied by the secretary general and a sister, left the motherhouse with him the next day, without baggage so as not to attract attention. "It was for God and the Society," she wrote later. She left without a passport, expecting that her nationality would allow her to embark. Mother Stuart reached Roehampton on 5 September. There she found the superiors of Egypt, Australia, Japan, the United States and Canada, who were all held up in England. Her state of health deteriorated rapidly, and after two unsuccessful operations she died on 21 October 1914. Mother Stuart's generalate, from which so much had been expected, came to an abrupt end.

The assistants general, who had remained at Ixelles, had news of Mother Stuart only through messengers; they learned of the decline of her health on 20 October by telegram from Blumenthal. Two days later a wire from The Hague, transmitted through Cologne, announced her death. The superior of Blumenthal, Mother Becker, advised Mother von Loë that she had been named vicar general. Doubtless the choice had been made because Marie von Loë, who was vicar in Italy and had resided in Rome for a quarter of a century, was undeniably a significant personage in the Society of the Sacred Heart.[15] Under the circumstances her nationality proved useful. Her journey from Venice on was arduous, for in Austria and Germany trains were reserved for the troops; she had to undergo long and frequent stops. Mother von Loë, who was German, was able to reach Holland without coming up against too great obstacles. Mother de Montalembert, however, had difficulty in obtaining a passport to go with

---

[14] Monahan, p. 486.

[15] She had taken an active part in the meetings that resulted in the beatification of Mother Barat. She had frequent contacts with the Sacred College and had often served as intermediary between the motherhouse and the Vatican. During an audience Pius X had said to Mother Stuart: "Mother General, do you know that you have here in Rome at the Villa Lante a head that would be capable of governing, not just one, but three Societies of the Sacred Heart?" (*Vie de la T.R.M. de Loë*, p. 347).

her. They left for Belgium in the company of Mother Le Baïl, secretary general, who had returned from England.

At Ixelles life was untenable. Telephone service was cut off and censorship made correspondence problematic. Quickly the vicar general decided to return to Blumenthal in neutral country. She left with two of the assistants general, Mothers de Lavigerie and de Montalembert, and the secretary general. Mother Borget stayed in Belgium with Mother Nerincx, whose state of health did not allow her to travel. This decision was hard to bear, as Mother Borget wrote; she proposed to remain at Ixelles with Mother Nerincx: "Impossible to leave her alone! My age is a reason for staying at Ixelles; but it is a sacrifice for we need to be together."[16]

Again a decision had to be made as to where to hold the general congregation. It was impossible to have a meeting in a country at war or in Holland, which was too near the combat zones. Mother von Loë decided therefore to convoke it in Rome, 18 February 1915. She left for Italy herself on 5 February with one other choir nun and a German sister; they reached Rome unhindered by going through Germany and Switzerland. The assistants general and the vicars from belligerent countries had a different fate; they had to travel by sea just when submarine warfare was beginning. After several adventures and going by way of England, Mothers de Lavigerie, de Montalambert and Le Baïl ended by crossing France and Italy "at the cost of fatigue and numberless privations."[17] Mother Borget had a more peaceful journey through Germany and Switzerland, but it lasted more than four days.[18]

On 22 February 1915, Mother von Loë was elected superior general on the first ballot, though by a slim majority.[19] As Mother Borget, dean of the assistants general, wrote to the Society: "For the first time the election could not take place at the motherhouse, as until now events do not allow us to meet there, but it is in the shadow of St. Peter, under the eyes of our most

---

[16] *Vie de la R.M. Borget*, p. 276.
[17] *Vie de la R.M. de Montalembert*, pp. 427-428.
[18] Mother Nerincx, who had not been able to leave Ixelles for reasons of health, was relieved of her office of assistant general and was replaced by Mother Rumbold.
[19] Mother Marguerite Benziger wrote in her memoir (*Austria Nazified, 1938-1946*) that in France many alumnae were shocked at the election of a "Boche" and that some of them resigned from the Children of Mary. It is not known if Mother von Loë's nationality played a role in her election, but the results show that the vicars who did not vote for her did not scatter their votes but cast them for Mother Amélie Salmon, who was French and vicar of Australia, one of the countries of the Commonwealth at war with the Central Powers.

Holy Father, that the choice was made."[20] Because she could not return to Belgium, the new superior general decided to settle in Rome where she could at least bring together the probanists from neutral countries.[21] Until the end of the war, she made use of the diplomatic channels of the Vatican and was able to obtain information on the state of Sacred Heart houses through the intermediary of the nunciatures.[22]

The general congregation broached the question of the transfer of the motherhouse to Rome.[23] Some of the objections having to do with the difficulty of bringing the probation, the general novitiate and the superior juniorate to Rome were quickly swept away, for Rome was no more difficult to reach than other European cities, and the city offered the possibility of spiritual guidance in all languages. The weather was certainly hot in summer, but malaria had been eradicated and "What climate does not offer something to suffer from?" On the other hand, other more important disadvantages were brought forward. First of all, people wondered if placed so near "the primary authority of the Church," the superior general would or would not be free to exercise her government. This concern did not seem a serious one to Mother von Loë, whose retort was that "Rome respects more than any bishop in the world constitutions approved by the Holy See and the Mother General governs only in conformity to the Constitutions." Above all, "Should she not, more than anyone else, seek to enter into the views of the Sovereign Pontiff and look for light and strength from contact with the Vicar of Jesus Christ?" Another objection concerned the role of France in the congregation up to that time: "To the extent that vocations and financial resources had come principally from France until the expulsions, was there not a risk in establishing the motherhouse in Rome?" Mother von Loë dissociated these two elements and, while believing that "no nation had surpassed France in generosity," she asked whether "a religious order ought to fear poverty or well-being." The last objection concerned the guarantee of safety that Italy could offer. Mother von Loë recognized that there was none. "But what country in Europe could offer any? What country seemed safer than Belgium? The stability of Rome does not come from the government but from the

---

[20] *Lettres circulaires de la T.R.M. de Loë*, p. 14.
[21] After Italy declared war on Austria in May 1915, it was not possible for Austrian probanists to go to Rome. For those of the United States, Mother von Loë asked the parents to authorize their daughters to cross the Atlantic (Helen Tichenor, *Mother Eleanor Regan*, p. 25). After their departure from Italy, the American new professed were detained for several months in Spain; they returned to the United States through Cuba.
[22] *Lettres circulaires de la T.R.M. de Loë*, p. 67, 12 December 1918.
[23] Gen. Arch. C I C 3, Box 13.

presence of the Holy See," she concluded with political boldness. It was clear that she had made her decision. However, it was not until the end of the war that she began the search for a suitable property for a motherhouse. In July 1919, she announced the purchase of a building on the Via Nomentana,[24] where the motherhouse was established for more than half a century. It seems that the news of the transfer to Rome was welcomed throughout the Society.

Aspects of a Four-year War

Life had to be organized in relation to military operations and the extension of combat zones. Because of its strategic position in the Mediterranean, Malta received allied ground and naval troops, both English and French, and wounded: "The convent became a refuge for those looking for friendship and spiritual help, willingly given by French and English religious. The pupils provided entertainments in the form of concerts. Many soldiers and sailors asked for religious instruction or returned to the faith. There were baptisms, First Communions and confirmations in the chapel."[25] In Egypt, where Great Britain established its protectorate on 18 December 1914, confrontations were feared between troops of the Entente and the Ottoman Empire. The latter had allied itself with Germany and declared itself in a state of armed neutrality. In 1916, the Turks failed in their attack on the Suez Canal, the east bank of which was occupied by the English. Four German sisters had to leave Egypt then, but the apostolate was not interfered with and the number of pupils increased. Although crossing the Mediterranean became chancy, fifteen nuns arrived from Europe, after many detours and delays. The house in Alexandria lodged the Dames de Nazareth of Khaifa for several months. In Cairo and Heliopolis, the Religious of the Sacred Heart welcomed British soldiers who came for a sermon and Benediction and gave them tea and "some sweets."[26] In Japan, allied with the Entente, the German nuns gave up their charges and avoided speaking with the children. The nuns felt the effects of censorship and had difficulty in communicating with Rome.[27]

---

[24] *Lettres circulaires de la T.R.M. de Loë*, 16 July 1919, pp. 74-75.
[25] Pauline Curmi, *Malte, notre histoire*.
[26] Prov. Arch. Egypt. *Petite histoire de nos maisons entre 1914 et 1950*.
[27] M. Williams, *The Society...Far East*, p. 51. In 1916, they were not able to let Rome know of the almost simultaneous deaths of the superior and assistant in Tokyo. The vicariate of Australia had difficulty also in informing Britain of the news. After the war, Mother Sheldon wrote to the superior general: "Neither the censors nor the fish will any longer enjoy our secrets."

Houses of the Sacred Heart were requisitioned in Great Britain.[28] Ireland welcomed the English-speaking probanists who could no longer go to Rome. One hundred and thirty-five Belgian religious who had taken refuge in Holland were sent to England and Ireland in October 1914.[29] After the German troops had moved towards Paris, less pressure was exerted on Belgium, and some religious were able to return to Antwerp, Wetteren and Strée, but not to Ostend.[30] It was too close to France where the fighting was fierce and indecisive in 1915 and 1916. Fontaine-l'Évêque, Strée and Tournai were closed in 1916 and 1917.[31] In 1917 and 1918, air raids gradually became daily in London and were a source of anxiety in England.[32] In 1918, Bois-l'Évêque became a military hospital, and the religious had to give up part of a wing of the house.[33]

Italy's entry into the war in May 1915 had immediate consequences in the Veneto. Bombardments caused damage in Venice but no loss of life. The vestibule of the house was converted by local authorities into a shelter where the neighbors came to take refuge in the evening. Padua had to send its boarders and students away. The Austro-German offensive, which broke through the Italian front on the banks of the Tagliamento, resulted in the rout at Caporetto, 28 October 1917. The question arose whether it would be necessary to evacuate the Veneto. Pope Benedict XV advised "resting firm at one's post unless a formal order obliged departure."[34] When the Italians succeeded in stabilizing the front at Piave at the end of November 1917, the motherhouse decided to send the nuns from Venice to Florence and those from Padua to Montecchio in the province of Arezzo. San Remo and Florence took in field hospitals and Rivoli, refugees.

The diplomatic reversal of Italy risked impeding the action of the superior general. Mother von Loë feared it: "May our Lord deign to allow us to remain in Rome," she wrote. "From so many points of view, a departure would be regrettable!"[35] It was above all unimaginable, and doubtless she did not know where she would go. Her nationality had become worrisome. From 1915 the *Questura* had been taking a census of

---

[28] The house at Brighton sheltered nurses, not without difficulty for the observance of the Rule! (*Lettres annuelles*, 1947-1952, p. 28).

[29] *Life of R.M. Thunder*, p. 79.

[30] Gen. Arch. C I C 3, Box 13. *Rapport de la vicaire générale, 1915.*

[31] Gen. Arch. C I 7 d, Box 1.

[32] *Life of R.M. Thunder*, p. 78.

[33] *Vie de la R.M. Symon*, p. 100: "It was agreed that there would be neither complaints nor recriminations. '*Dominus est.*' Partitions separate us from the importunate guests, but even more our silence and our perfect dignity."

[34] *Vie de la T.R.M. de Loë*, p. 372.

[35] *Vie…de Loë*, p. 367.

persons from the countries of the Alliance residing on the peninsula. In 1917, Italy decided to intern the Germans and Austrians of Piedmont, Liguria and Rome. A first exemption for the superior general was obtained through the intermediary of an Italian councilor of state, but in 1918 only the personal intervention of the pope allowed her to circumvent a new edict. Although Mother von Loë avoided internment, about fifty Religious of the Sacred Heart were interned at Montecchio and at Arpino, near Caserta. These sojourns in a religious community of hospital sisters or with the refugees in Padua did not impose great hardship.

Restrictions and privations were evident throughout the countries at war. The spread of the conflict and the dangers on land and sea prevented "obediences" for a long time. Families came forward to ask that their daughters be kept nearby to make up for the absence or loss of their sons. Superiors had also to deal with the requests of religious who "believed it their duty in turn to explain their reasons for a change of house or employment."[36] For some of them, to live in a country at war with their own was a bitter trial to endure.[37] Their families who had no news of their daughters asked the motherhouse what had become of them.[38] As "spy mania" became general, even nuns in neutral countries had difficulty in reaching a country at war. Mother Vicente, whose name had been taken by a spy, had to go to Paris in order to obtain a passport from the Spanish Embassy to go into Italy when she was named assistant general. Her companions, the vicar of Sarriá and the superior of Barcelona, were stopped at the Italian frontier and had to return to Lyons to obtain safe-conducts. Doubtless they were not the only ones to experience such misadventures. It was a new situation for Religious of the Sacred Heart to have to leave their convent to carry out administrative procedures. As the superior general recognized later,

> The requirements of the time often obliged us to set aside our customs. We had to obtain passports, visit consulates, provide for urgent needs, go to the bank and secure provisions. Religious of the Sacred Heart were seen circulating in the streets and mingling with the crowds.[39]

---

[36] *Circulaires de la T.R.M. de Loë*, p. 64, 12 December 1918.
[37] Mother Marie-Antoinette Kammerer, who had spent the war in the Austro-Hungarian Empire, wrote: "Effectively, I left my country and I would not like in any way go back on that offering; I made it with my whole heart, but these war years make the sacrifice more painful."
[38] Gen. Arch. C I 7 d.
[39] *Circulaires de la T.R.M. de Loë*, p. 64, 12 December 1918.

Far and wide morale had to be sustained. On 10 August 1914, Mother Stuart had written:

> Let me say to all who have family members fighting under the flags – and that is most of us – how much we are recommending them to God so that he will protect them in the accomplishment of their duties, or if they must give their life that he will sustain them by his grace and receive them in his divine mercy.[40]

In multi-national communities one had as always to avoid altercations, "to hold on and serve." In the same circular, Mother Stuart wrote:

> In every country the Society has its share in the sufferings of the present time; that must be, our name causes us to believe that. It is God's hour; the greatness of events so surpasses the ordinary measure of human affairs that we may give ourselves over to God with all the more confidence for the present and for the future. Our part is to draw down on the whole world by prayer and renunciation the grace and light that will conduct all these things to deliberate faith in Him. Each one will throw into the balance everything that the present moment offers: suffering, worries, privations, penances, sure that love will give it weight beyond what we can measure.[41]

Superiors took care to develop the life of prayer and study. Some priests from religious orders supported them by coming to give lectures. It was a question of "remaining at the front of the conquest of the world in order to assist Redeemer in his work," as Father Pierre Charles, a Jesuit, suggested at Bois-l'Évêque.[42]

In one of her first circulars, Mother von Loë reminded the religious that events ought to lead them to develop their interior life:

> It may be that natural activity is sometimes mingled too much with our zeal. The need to keep informed of all the news, to multiply verbal and written communications interferes with a serious tendency to recollection and interior life in some people. Conjectures, indiscretions, comments, often inexact, follow easily from this thirst for news. Through the serious events that surround us our Lord has limited us and with his powerful hand has been pleased for several months to impede the communications

---

[40] *Circulaires de la T.R.M. Stuart*, p. 387.
[41] *Circulaires…Stuart*, p. 385.
[42] *Vie de la R.M. Symon*, pp. 99-100.

that seem most legitimate, projects that aim however only at his glory, satisfactions of the heart that in normal times are within our reach. Happy the religious soul who can enter fully into the crucifying views of the divine Master, who centers all her aspirations on the one thing necessary with the firm resolution to advance greatly the work of her sanctification. Happy is she who believes firmly in the love of her God and sees his Heart through the veil of sorrow, uncertainty, restraint…. To have patience; to abandon ourselves blindly with all that is dear to us; to count on the Sacred Heart with unshakable confidence: are these not the great lessons of the present time?[43]

In combat zones the boarding schools were temporarily closed. On the other hand, all the free schools were kept open. In Galicia and Belgium alumnae were brought together for retreats. The apostolate diversified. In Venice the nuns took care of the people who came to their house for shelter at night; they led prayer and reading while the bombs were exploding around them. In the spring of 1915 Bois-l'Évêque opened a boarding school for thirty war orphans or victims of destruction, but in 1917, it had to be closed because of the dearth of food. The nuns tried to lighten the situation of prisoners of war, of their families and of the neighborhood. In May 1917 the German offensive pushed into Belgium refugees from the North and East of France whose villages had been devastated; they were welcomed at Strée. Peasants whose thatched houses had been burnt came to take refuge with their families and their animals at Lemberg.

Many religious gave proof of undeniable bravery. We give the example of Mother de la Sauzaie, assistant at Lemberg:

> When bombs were raining down on the house, causing fire to break out, it was she who brought help at the risk of her life. As if by right, she went everywhere even where others could not or ought not to go. By her prompt decisiveness, her perfect calm, her spontaneous and ingenious interventions she was able to get out of the most difficult situations. And there were many of those with the continual changes of the directors of the field hospital. These, whether Russians, Austrians or others, became providers, even protectors in times of danger.[44]

Other activities, which combined charity and patriotism, could have had heavy consequences for those who undertook them. The Polish *"Aiglons,"* child-soldiers aged ten to nineteen, found a hearty welcome at Lemberg:

---

[43] *Circulaires de la T.R.M. de Loë*, pp. 25-26, 12 December 1915.
[44] *Lettres circulaires*, 1932-1937.

Worn out by fatigue, from watches and fighting, bent under the weight of heavy firearms, they came unafraid. Mother de Sauzaie welcomed them with open arms and gave a hearth, clothing, food, even a hiding place, to these children who were as intrepid in courting danger as war veterans. She was always deeply moved at the sound of their song, which had become so popular in Poland.

After the war she received the *Légion d'Honneur*, a decoration that at that epoch was hardly ever given to a woman unless she had given proof of heroic courage. Bois-l'Évêque was a nerve center for those who needed passports to go into Holland, and Antwerp took in patriots who sought passage into England.

In 1917 the Germans were liberated on their eastern front by the Russian revolution then by the defection of Rumania and galvanized by the failure of a French breakthrough in Artois and Picardy. The authorities then decided to push their advantage in the West. They dealt ruthlessly with those who obstructed their movement. Mother Adèle Symon had helped young Belgians and French and English officers to rejoin the front. She was arrested on 1 September 1917and freed after forty-seven days in detention.[45] As a result of a betrayal the German police learned that the house in Antwerp had sheltered fugitives. Mother Hélène de Burlet was arrested on 10 September 1917 and kept in solitary confinement. In the course of questioning she learned that she was accused of having acted in concert with the Jesuits, of being an undercover agent of Cardinal Mercier and of using her influence on the "young ladies" to make of the house in Antwerp a center of patriotism and of resistance to the occupation. She went before the war council on 6 April 1918 and was condemned to two and a half years of forced labor for treason. When Lüdendorf launched the indecisive "great battle of France," her penalty was commuted to imprisonment. She thus avoided transfer to Germany. The military situation was reversed after the offensive by the troops of the Entente under the command of General Foch, reinforced by those of the United States. In September 1918, foreseeing the outcome of the war, the Germans ameliorated the detention conditions of political prisoners. Mother de Burlet was transferred to a military hospital on 10 October and liberated on 23 October 1918. Her long detention left its mark on her health. Cardinal Gasparri and the Belgian nuncio had intervened in favor of the two religious.[46] After the victory

---

[45] *Vie de la R.M. Symon*, pp. 102-105.
[46] *Vie...Symon*, p. 105, and Odile Biolley, *Une âme d'élite, Mère Hélène de Burlet*, p. 63. A Sacred Heart postulant was also interned in the prison in Antwerp. She entered religious life afterwards, Mother Siret.

Belgium recognized the services that the Religious of the Sacred Heart had rendered during the war: thirty-six were cited or decorated.[47]

Material conditions were a universal cause for anxiety. From the beginning of the war the general treasury, which did not have the means to assist communities in trouble, had asked for the greatest possible reduction in expenses, even when many houses had to shelter refugees. As the war was prolonged, all the houses suffered from the lack of basic necessities.[48] In Belgium the situation deteriorated seriously in the last years of the war. At Strée,

> Rationing, though well organized, functioned badly and did not provide very much: the bread ration was insufficient; the greatest difficulty came from the fact the German authority forbade goods to be taken from one commune to another or even to sell them on the spot. Extreme misery surrounded us, and the time came when we could no longer continue to give soup and a bit of bread to the poor unfortunates who came begging on their knees. Their hunger was so great that they refused the coin that was offered them because they could no longer find anything to buy.
> In this land of coal, there was no coal, for want of trains and horses to transport it. As always misery and lack of work excited evil passions. Bands of thieves pillaged the country for three months looking for food; our vegetable garden was devastated before we could bring in the winter vegetables, while at the edge of our property these bold troops came to cut the farmers' stalks of grain.[49]

In Antwerp to keep the rolls destined for the children from becoming a black market commodity, the Catholic Schools Committee required the children to eat them right away. In the communities portions were counted: "From time to time a notice or a sign appeared in the refectory asking each one to take only two potatoes, a large one and a small; the large ones were hardly that and the small ones very small." The rations of the most essential goods were reduced. "We are rejoicing in living like truly poor persons and the little privations make us say, 'Thank you, God!' But the solicitude of our mother and sisters who provide for us grows day by day." Communities less badly off shared with the others and gifts in kind became highly prized. The treasurers sometimes managed to make an arrangement with farmers

---

[47] Gen. Arch. C I 7 d, Box 4. Mother de Burlet received the *Croix de Chevalier de l'Ordre de Léopold*.

[48] Prov. Arch. Egypt. In Egypt, "Getting supplies became extremely difficult; some things were completely unobtainable, like coal, shoes, fabric, soap."

[49] *Lettres annuelles*, 1917-1919, *1ère partie*.

or with religious congregations that had farms. Clothing became even more problematic; fabric could not be found. In the winter of 1917-1918, mattress ticking, then the mattresses themselves were requisitioned.

> We are sleeping on "war time mattresses" thin as wafers that turn over as easily as an omelet; some are horsehair, some straw or hay. There was even a notice in the city ordering us to stop using these materials as they had become too scarce but to make the mattresses out of cut up paper! But that also is the rarest of things.[50]

As they were gradually liberated, the Belgians were able to make use of provisions from North and South America. The Sacred Heart also had help from the houses in America and could share with those with whom they were connected.[51]

Life was equally painful in Central Europe. At the end of 1914 the countries of the Entente, failing to conquer the Central Powers on the ground, decided to stifle them economically and to prevent the neutral countries from giving them fresh supplies. In Prague famine raged from 1915 on. At Riedenburg the novices went to gather herbs to nourish the community and the boarders. They had to be content with field beets [cattle fodder] and oats that could be ground in a coffee grinder.[52] In 1916, rationing became very strict. In Prague, wrote Mother Deydier, "Our poor sisters have enormous work to do to hide our provisions from the eyes of the inspectors by changing their storage places, and this without enough nourishment to keep up their strength." Misery aggravated by the failure of the military offensives fueled agitation in the cities. The collapse of Russia in 1917 and the Peace of Brest-Litovsk allowed the Central Powers to occupy Ukraine, whose basic materials, animals and grain, were indispensable for the revitalization of their economies and of their population. In February 1918, the Ukrainians of Eastern Galicia received their autonomy in return for deliveries of grain products.

Tuberculosis ravaged the communities of Austria and Hungary. In Prague seventeen nuns died, some of hunger.[53] As the famished urban population began to resort to pillage, the superior at Riedenburg had the sacred vessels buried in a cave. The situation did not improve after the armistice. At Pressbaum, in 1919, the religious went into the forest to look

---

[50] Gen. Arch. C I A 7 d, Box 4.
[51] *Vie de la R.M. Symon*, p. 101. Mother Symon made use of the aid in favor of prisoners of war and organized the work of the war godmothers.
[52] *Souvenir de la Mère Maria von Jordis*, Gen. Arch. C IV OSU, Budapest, *Mémoires*.
[53] *Lettres annuelles*, 1940-1945, p. 41.

for logs and sawed them in the courtyard. Only a few rooms in the boarding school were heated for a few hours and those used by the community not at all. During the summer of 1920, "one day the *dépensière* came in tears to tell the Mother assistant that she had absolutely nothing for dinner. The assistant sent the sisters to gather mushrooms in the woods."[54] Graz had to be closed when the famine was such that the nuns were falling ill and could not maintain a boarding school.[55] As a consequence of dangerous sanitary conditions, Spanish influenza wreaked its havoc. In Rome, in the fall of 1919, there was an epidemic thought to have been caused by contamination brought by a probanist who had had to cross battle fields; it lasted three months and caused two deaths among the young nuns. It provoked understandable anxiety at the motherhouse.[56]

The Return to France

The war brought about an unexpected change inasmuch as it permitted the return to France. With a view to fostering national consensus, the Interior Minister, Louis Malvy, had given the order, on 1 August 1914, not to arrest militants on the extreme Left considered possible defeatists. The next day he suspended the measures opposed to religious congregations. The president of the Republic, Raymond Poincaré, put forth the famous formula "the sacred union." He wrote to the members of Parliament,

> The country will be heroically defended by all her sons; nothing will shatter their sacred union in the face of the enemy; they are fraternally assembled today with the same indignation against the aggressor and with the same patriotic faith.

The sacred union was welcomed with surprise abroad. Without annulling the law of 1901, France put in place a measure of appeasement that had immediate effects, since exiled male religious of an age to bear arms had asked at the consulates to be mobilized. Their behavior showed that one could be both a religious and a patriot.

From the fall of 1914, the "true friends" of the Society began suggesting that the Society take advantage of the circumstances to return to France, as had other women's congregations. In September 1914 the father of two Religious of the Sacred Heart informed Mother Stuart that the Sisters of Charity, who had not been secularized, had been able to register

---

[54] Testimony of M. von Jordis.
[55] *Lettres annuelles*, supp. 1961-1963, pp. 135-136.
[56] *Vie de la T.R.M. Vicente*, pp. 125 and following.

their orphanage with the prefecture of the North and that some Ursulines had returned to Amiens. In October, the archbishop of Paris, Cardinal Amette, wrote that there would be no risk if women religious came in small groups to settle in private houses. He suggested that they care for the wounded, "an additional safeguard." But there was no question of teaching unless they relinquished the habit. Cardinal Sevin, the archbishop of Lyons, had already said to the religious at the Trinità dei Monti on 7 June 1914:

> You too, daughters, make an opening in this little corner of France; lend your ear and you will hear the children of France crying "Come back!" In Lyons your three houses await you; the generations you have educated have not forgotten you. Soon, I hope! The first time I met your Very Reverend Mother,[57] I was almost angry with her. I said to her: "You will come back to us; but at first it must be without the habit." And that is my deepest conviction. I pleaded my cause with the Holy Father, and I won. He said to me: "The issue of the habit must not stop them. Those who were born in France must fight[58] on their native soil, struggle where you struggle." You see that I have gained a powerful defender.[59]

The Jesuits pushed in the same direction. In September 1914 Mother Stuart sent for a French religious to return from North America, telling her that she was destined for France as soon as a return would be possible.[60]

Lawyers consulted thought it better to hasten to take up residence in France without waiting until they were recalled, an event that had little chance of happening. A reestablishment would allow taking charge at first of some of the secondary works of the Society, spiritual accompaniment of the Children of Mary and of sodalities for working class women, reopening youth centers and providing First Communion preparation. The ultimate objective, however, was surely to reopen the institutions, even if it meant preparing the young nuns to pass the necessary examinations. For the moment prudence consisted in having Belgian religious among the personnel and giving them charge of relations with the outside, for "Lawyers think that the government would not dare to take action against refugees if ever it paid attention to our return to France." Lyons was chosen for the first attempt, since Cardinal Sevin wished the Society to return to his city,[61] but there was no question of giving up cloister and the religious

---

[57] It was Mother Digby.
[58] The pope evidently alluded to the "fight" to maintain freedom of teaching in France.
[59] Gen. Arch. C I C 3, Box 8.
[60] *Lettres annuelles*, Supp. 1940-1945, p. 102.
[61] Gen. Arch. C I C 3, Box 13.

habit. The decision to return to France was officially made at the General Congregation of 1915, at which it was approved by twelve votes to eight; three others were of the opinion that it was premature.

After 1915 the Society of the Sacred Heart was reestablished in France. Mother Marie Joyaut de Couesnongle, former mistress general at Rennes, had as her mission to find a place to settle in Brittany. She arrived in the spring of 1915 at Paramé with four other religious, unsure whether to make a foundation at Rennes, Le Mans or Nantes. The alumnae quickly found a location in Nantes. The Society had to leave this first site in 1919 and finally it bought *La Perverie*. Foundations were often temporary, as in Lyons where the nuns took over a Jesuit house on the hill of Fourvière. In any case the Society gradually got back the properties that had belonged to it. The first activities were modest. At Paramé, then in Nantes, the nuns gave religious instruction and classes in needlework. As soon as they were sure of recruiting pupils, they opened a boarding school, officially under the direction of a laywoman. In September 1917, the twenty-four French novices left Rivoli for Rougemont, while waiting until Marmoutier was free, as it was occupied by a Jesuit college.[62]

By January 1920 eleven houses had been reopened. It had been possible also, as Mother von Loë informed Pope Benedict XV,[63] "to resurrect" the three houses in Alsace-Lorraine, since France had recovered its lost provinces. In April 1919, French religious had reestablished a boarding school at Montigny.[64] Reopening houses in France meant closing the refuges or transforming the houses that had been dedicated partially or totally to receiving French nuns and boarders. Some of these, like Fontaine-l'Évêque and Strée, had already been given up during the war. Flône, Trinità, Rivoli, Leamington and Sartario were sold in 1919 and 1920.[65] San Sebastián became a Spanish boarding school. In 1927, the houses in France were reorganized into three vicariates, Paris, the East and the South.

The Days Following the Armistice

On 24 October 1918, the Italians and the troops of the Entente gave the *coup de grâce* to the Austro-Hungarian Empire by unleashing the allied offensive on the Piave. The losses were heavy in the ranks of the imperial

---

[62] *Lettres annuelles,* 1954-1958, pp. 41-42.

[63] *Circulaires de la T.R.M. de Loë,* p. 89, audience of 8 January 1920.

[64] At Metz, the military governor decided that the daughters of officers would go to the Sacred Heart. The house thus gained about a hundred pupils, and it was necessary to build in order to accommodate them. (*Lettres annuelles,* 1940-1945, p. 41).

[65] Gen. Arch. C I C 3, Box 13.

and royal troops, and signs of disintegration appeared in the army. When on 4 November the armistice took complete effect, there was no longer a state. Without abdicating, Emperor Charles I, who earlier had not been able to have his peace proposals admitted, ceased to exercise power. Without combat, on 28 October, a "velvet revolution" set up a national assembly in Prague aimed at giving shape to a Czech state. In Vienna, the monarchy was dissolved and the Republic of Austria founded on 12 November 1918. In Budapest, demonstrations and street fighting ended in the splitting off of Hungary from Austria and the proclamation of the Republic on 16 November. The government of Count Mihaly Karoly adopted universal suffrage, freedom of the press and of assembly and promised agrarian reform.

The armistice signed by the Germans at Rethondes at dawn on 11 November 1918 was not peace. The conference of conquerors drew a new map of Europe. The Treaty of the Trianon, signed with Hungary on 4 June 1920, placed that country, which had obtained territorial restitution in 1867, once more in the ranks of small nations. That of Saint-Germain en Laye, signed with Austria on 10 September 1920, recognized the independence of different Slavic countries that had been under the domination of the empire before. From the ruins rose up states issued from nations formerly in subjection. The territorial losses of Austria and Hungary separated hundreds of thousands of families by almost impermeable frontiers. Routes were cut off; economic markets broke up among several states. The political transformation of Central Europe modified choices of families regarding the placement of their children in Sacred Heart boarding schools. Graz, reopened in 1921, accepted those pupils from Yugoslavia, Hungary and Bulgaria[66] who before had frequented Slavic, German and Italian schools. This situation did not make for unity and posed the problem of which language to teach.

Poland was reconstituted and a French military mission mapped out its borders. In April Pilsudski, to whom power had been assigned, engaged in hostilities with Bolshevik Russia in the direction of Ukraine; in May he occupied Kiev. Foreseeing that the Soviets would not remain inactive, the officers of the French mission established at Lwow, formerly Lemberg – it had resumed its Polish name – urged the Religious of the Sacred Heart to leave the city. They took refuge at Zbylitowska Gora. The Red Army marched on Warsaw in the course of the summer of 1920. The Poles, supported by a French expeditionary force, stopped its breakthrough on the Vistula. The Peace of Riga, in March 1921, allowed the religious to go back to their houses. The Sacred Heart in Poznan was reopened. As it was not

---

[66] Gen. Arch. C IV 2, Graz, regular visits of January 1922 and May 1924.

possible to reoccupy the property of Wilda, they began by renting a house that soon proved to be cramped and badly situated. Very soon the general treasury bought a vast property at Polska Wies not far from Poznan. In 1933, thanks to a donation, a house was opened in the heart of the city of Poznan.

The Society of the Sacred Heart could not maintain its presence in Czechoslovakia. The house in Prague, which had been a refuge for the religious of Poznan after the Kulturkampf, had developed works among Polish exiles or emigrants. At the end of the nineteenth century the boarding school was populated by one third each Poles, Czechs and Germans; but it had never known real success among the local aristocracy or the bourgeoisie. The Sacred Heart was accused of wanting to Germanize the pupils. It is true that few religious were capable of speaking the "Bohemian" language, as it was then known, and therefore of having productive relations with the outside. In any case the fusion of nationalities in the boarding school had never been easy. The vicar had foreseen that in the event of victory by the Czechs, the house in Prague would not be viable. It was sold in 1919 to the state, which intended to set up the postal service there. The government moved the furnishings to the border without charge.[67]

The Revolution of October 1917 stretched on in Central Europe. The Spartacist revolt was unleashed in Berlin by the German extreme Left and suffered a bloody repression in January 1919. A republic took power in Hungary on 21 March 1919. It lasted until 1 August 1919, and was thus the longest of the revolutionary attempts that took place then. Bela Kun, who had founded the Hungarian Communist party in 1918, established a dictatorship of the proletariat. He then negotiated an agreement with the social democrats. He took as a model the Commune of Paris and gave evidence of aggressive anti-clericalism. The collectivization that he pushed forward was too hasty not to cause him to lose the support of a large part of the population. They were unhappy with the confiscations and the extreme policies that were enacted as well as the summary executions that took place. With the support of the countries of the Entente and of representatives of the former Alliance, Rumanian units joined with Hungarian troops who had defected or who had never enlisted and took Budapest at the beginning of August. Admiral Horthy, proclaimed regent on 1 March 1920, launched a "white terror" and directed the country until the end of the Second World War.

The Society of the Sacred Heart had two houses in Budapest. The older one, which had a boarding school, had been founded in 1893. Located

---

[67] Gen. Arch. C IV 1, Prague.

in the suburbs at Durer sor, after the beatification of Mother Duchesne, it was given the name of the *Philippineum*. The more recent, founded in 1914 in the heart of the city, was called the *Sophianum*; it consisted of a secondary school and space for meetings of the alumnae. The house journals of the two houses and several pieces of correspondence[68] reveal the shock people experienced at the establishment of the brutal dictatorship of the proletariat by Bela Kun. Lenin himself thought that Kun lacked a "sense of the masses." Mother Marie-Anne von Schaffgotsch, superior at Durer sor, wrote a fourteen page letter begun 16 May, when she did not know whether she would be able to get it to Rome. She sought to enlighten the motherhouse about the nature of a regime hitherto unheard of and gave a remarkable description with supporting examples of a country and a society placed under a Communist-style totalitarian system. This document describes the workings of censorship and daily surveillance set in motion to control the population, as well as the different modes of reorganization on the economic, social and religious levels of Hungary in a "communized" country, to use her habitual expression. The letter shows that the Religious of the Sacred Heart were remarkably well informed. Mother von Schaffgotsch, a German who had been vicar of Austria, had been sent to Budapest at the beginning of the foundation. She had been able to enter into the ways of thinking, judging and acting of a country that she knew well and loved.

The Hungarians, weakened by defeat and reined in by the police, reacted little in the face of the progress of totalitarianism; Mother von Schaffgotsch explained:

> It is a time of great suffering, of beautiful devotedness...but also of numerous betrayals and vile cowardice, of fatal illusions also, for communism is a utopia that easily deceives certain minds. Most people, tired out by the war, disappointed in its outcome, have fallen into a deadly lethargy; espionage is the order of the day, justice is terrifying; therefore, there is no reaction so to speak, or it is immediately suppressed. No one is happy not even the workers. We are at the mercy of a few hundred Bolshevik fanatics and...Jews[69] who have power and maintain it through

---

[68] Gen. Arch. C IV D 1, Box 2, 8 P. "Communism" contains extracts of the *Journal du Philippineum* (in French) for the period of 28 March to 17 July 1919, and of journals composed by groups of religious at the Austrian frontier (in French and in German).

[69] Bela Kun was the son of a Jewish employee. The fact that he was the founder of the Hungarian Communist Party and that he directed the Hungarian Soviet Republic contributed to maintaining or developing anti-Semitism in Hungary and had tragic consequences afterwards.

the Red Guard who alone have munitions. Deliverance will never come from inside where no one can organize any opposition. It is said that the Entente, interested in seeing that Communism does not extend further, is going to come to occupy the country and place us under a foreign dictatorship. Is that true? And when is that going to happen? It would be the only means of saving the situation. But from here every day is marked by ruin.... I am saddened especially by the harm done to the souls of children who are being perverted on purpose. That is irreparable.

The house journal of Durer sor itself evokes the "reign of terror" that had fallen on Hungary: "No one is sure of his fellow. No one knows whether in the next minute he will be denounced and imprisoned; consequently everyone is distrustful of his neighbor."[70]

The liquidation of religious establishments secularized by one of the first ordinances of the regime was assigned to defrocked priests or male religious. In the first place they sought to obtain the secularization of all religious women. At the request of the parents, the Sacred Heart closed the boarding school. The superior of the *Sophianum*, Mother Leonilda von Zaufal, partially dispersed her community. The nuns who were not Hungarian were sent to Vienna. In mid-March 1919, the superior and the assistant left with several Hungarian sisters for Kàm, a rural area near the Austrian frontier, in a less inflexible *comitat* [department.] They formed two groups; one settled in a mill belonging to the brother of one of sisters and the other, in a house someone had lent them. They had periodic contacts with each other. Through a mistaken decision the German and Austrian choir religious were sent there, while the Hungarians, who had no chance of getting a passport, were left in Budapest. There they were in greater danger than in the countryside, where they could have crossed the frontier clandestinely if necessary.

At the *Sophianum*, where the director and administrators were lay people, it was possible to continue teaching longer than at Durer sor. However, the ministry assigned a Jewish teacher there and began to implement the system devised for schools. A "directorate" composed of faculty monitored the director. One or two trusted students in each class formed a "students' directorate" in charge of monitoring the teachers and representing the rights and interests of the students. A Protestant woman director was placed at the head of the *Sophianum* and the teaching personnel were purged. Fearing pillage of the house, Mother von Schaffgotsch decided to withdraw the nuns, leaving only the treasurer, Mother Bisch who was French, a sister and some loyal domestics. To avoid attracting attention

---

[70] Gen. Arch. C IV 1, Budapest, Box 8 P.

to groups that were too numerous, the nuns were lodged with their families or with friends of the Society. Mother von Schaffgotsch herself went to Durer sor, where the authorities had placed about fifteen children from proletarian families and a treasurer who appeared to have as her chief mission to drain the house systematically.

The officer who presided over the American Mission put a provisional end to a situation that was becoming more and more dangerous. He persuaded the authorities that the Sacred Heart was a French order – an obsolete argument for the past ten years – that its houses should remain unharmed and its personnel entitled to the protection due to foreigners. He obtained it on condition that teaching stop in the establishments[71] and the nuns leave the properties. The last Hungarian sisters were then sent to families who took them in; the two houses remained in the hands of three strangers. Finally Mother von Schaffgotsch who was obliged, as she recognized, to live in "semi-secularization" settled in a suburb at Pest Ujhely, in a small house intended for a workman, where she was free to welcome her sisters. She saw that her mission was above all to keep up the morale of her daughters scattered throughout the city.[72]

Salvation seemed to have to come from without; but in case foreign troops entered, it was feared that there would be pillage or a massacre, of which foreigners would be the first victims. "But what shall we do?" wrote Mother von Schaffgotsch, "inasmuch as I have fourteen daughters who are not sheltered from the torment, I think I have the grace of office to stay with them and that it is my duty not to leave them." The future was somber. Either Communism would be maintained, and the only solution would be to have the religious leave for other houses of the Society with the hope of avoiding confiscation of the properties in Budapest or obtaining compensation from the state; or a new regime would be put in place, and it

---

[71] Gen. Arch. C IV D 1. *Journal de Durer sor*. On 3 May 1919, the measure was applied to the *Sophianum* (p. 69): "We must undergo this so as to avoid a worse evil. Besides, perhaps it is a grace from divine Providence that it will prevent communist lectures from being held and perverting our children."

[72] *Journal de Durer sor*. Month of April, pp. 59-60: "We left in a completely closed vehicle taking with us a few precious objects that we were determined to save from disaster. What a painful departure! Leaving this house in such a state in the hands of such people; it was one of those things mysteriously permitted by the Will of God, so impenetrable that we can only kneel and adore, knowing that God's designs are above our poor human comprehension. While thinking that this house of the Society was apparently soon going to be lost to us, we thought of the sorrow our V.R.M. General seeing such a prosperous apostolate among souls suddenly stopped, her daughters dispersed like sheep outside their sheepfold."

would remain to be seen whether the congregation could participate in its educational system.[73] Finally at the beginning of June 1919, the Religious of the Sacred Heart decided to ask the intervention of the ambassador of Germany, Count von Fürstenberg, a relative of Mother von Schaffgotsch. All the western diplomats wanted to delay the liquidation of the goods of foreign orders, hoping that the situation was going to turn against Bela Kun's government. The day of the feast of the Sacred Heart, 27 June 1919, the expected putsch was launched. The intervention of foreign countries ended the affair. On 3 August 1919, the Rumanians entered Budapest. While the domestics were putting back the furniture and pictures that had been hidden with friends out of precaution, Rumanian soldiers sought to set up a barracks at Durer sor. Finally they abandoned the place, leaving for the nuns some cans of food, which proved very useful.[74] The Society of the Sacred Heart was able to reopen its houses in September 1919.[75]

Although during the regime of Bela Kun the superiors living in Hungary had hardly any contact with Vienna and Rome, they had been able to receive a few rare messages that always gave them the same advice: to be prudent and not to expose themselves to danger, buildings being nothing in comparison with people's lives. The vicar of Austria, Mother von Waldstein, wrote to the superior at Durer sor: "Tell Aunt Marianne, dear friend, that she must not endanger health or lives for any less precious advantage: that is what the aunt wants said to her niece."[76] The two superiors of Budapest, who had not made the same choices, had at least acted for the best by making use of the influence of their relatives. As Mother von Schaffgotsch had written on 16 May to Mother von Loë: "Pray that your unworthy but faithful daughter by the grace of God will not make too many stupid mistakes. One never knows if what one does is really good and prudent."[77]

To put an end to the war, for which his general staff did not wish to take the responsibility, Kaiser William II had abdicated on 9 November 1918. A new regime, the Weimar Republic, appeared in Germany and would last until Hitler took power on 30 January 1933. Although the *Kulturkampf* was no longer having any effect even before the resignation of Bismarck, the Second Reich had been mistrustful of Catholics and of religious congregations inspired by the Society of Jesus. In 1898, feeling a change in the air, about fifty alumnae of Blumenthal decided to address a petition to the emperor to obtain the return of the Sacred Heart to Germany. William II put it in

---

[73] Gen. Arch. Budapest. Letter of May 1919.
[74] Budapest also received food supplies from the United States.
[75] The religious who had taken refuge in Austria returned on 28 August 1919.
[76] Gen. Arch. Budapest. *Journal du Philippineum*, p. 60.
[77] She left the *Sophianum* on 26 October 1919, exhausted, and was sent to Germany in March 1921.

the waste paper basket, displeased by the fact that the signatories, who had composed the text in German, had been so tactless as to put their aristocratic titles in French after their names! He shouted: *"Baronne de…, Comtesse de…"* then went on: "For religious who pray in French!" The alumnae then tried to have their relatives use their influence to win over to their cause the deputies of the Center Party[78] and the German episcopate before the annual meetings at Fulda, but without success. In 1903, the Reichstag finally abolished the law that had expelled the Jesuits. Both men and women religious could henceforth live in Germany, but they did not have the right to have communities there or to open schools. Even so, Mother Digby persisted in going back to Germany to the point of being willing to sacrifice Metz and Kientzheim because she believed that the existence of these houses was "a cause of annoyance for the German state [*sic*]."[79] She decided to have religious prepared to obtain the diplomas required for teachers.

The situation evolved subsequently. In June 1912 it was suggested to Mother Stuart then visiting Austria to send religious to Berlin to meet with Matthias Erzberger, one of the leaders of the Center Party. She was even advised to compose a memorial to prove that the Sacred Heart was not affiliated with the Jesuits, that the confidence of German families who sent their daughters to the Sacred Heart was legitimate because the congregation conformed to the requirements of the German educational system and offered a German education "along with a second language,"[80] and that if the Society were to open schools in Germany the majority of the religious would be of German nationality.[81] Mother Stuart did not pursue the affair, conscious that no one in Germany was favorable to the Society of the Sacred Heart, neither in the government, nor among the religious orders nor even among Catholics.[82] Besides, in May 1913 the Bundesrat refused to contemplate the establishment of the Sacred Heart in Germany.

---

[78] Gen. Arch. C III 3, Germany. In 1902, Mother Catherine de Montalembert contacted her son cousin, Prince von Arenberg, a deputy of the Center, to find out how to proceed in case the law that had expelled religious was abolished.

[79] Gen. Arch. C III 3. She asked Mother Nieuwland, the vicar of Belgium, her opinion on the question. The latter replied on 10 December 1903: "I was quite astonished at reading that you asked my opinion! First of all my opinion is always your opinion!" At least we can conclude that Mother Digby, who after all was in France during the 1870 war, was not aware of what Alsace and Lorraine represented for France and for the religious of that country!

[80] The reference is to French.

[81] The arguments had been provided by Count von Savigny with whom the assistants general had exchanged a sustained correspondence.

[82] Gen. Arch. C III 3, Germany. Unsigned report. Mother Stuart was loath – to her credit – to deny the service rendered by the Jesuits "from the foundation

During the war of 1914-1918 German Catholics had been integrated into the nation. As in other European countries at war, they had participated in the defense of their country and had shown their patriotism. It was, however, owing to the change of regime that the Sacred Heart was able to reenter Germany. There was no longer a state church, and the Weimar Republic renounced rigorous supervision of ecclesiastical activity. In February 1920 the Sacred Heart bought the property of Saint Adelheid near Bonn. Obviously it was from Blumenthal[83] in the Netherlands, the seat of the vicariate after 1921, that the foundation was provided for. Saint Adelheid vegetated because of its proximity to Blumenthal, which continued to attract German students. Construction continued over the next ten years. In 1930, the Society of the Sacred Heart went to Munich and opened a student hostel under the direction of Mother Paula Werhahn. She found another site in a section near the university where she established a meeting place for Sacred Heart alumnae.[84]

Making foundations in regions where Catholicism was firmly established limited the risk of failure or rejection. It was only shortly before the Second World War that the congregation went to Berlin. In February 1938, the French embassy proposed the creation of a French school for the children of the diplomatic corps credentialed to the Third Reich. Mother Werhahn, in charge of the new foundation, which was established in five small villas in the Grunewald, opened a day school for French-speaking children,[85] a hostel for university students and a residence for *grandes pensionnaires*. The foundations of Munich and Berlin had been approved by Cardinals Faulhaber and von Preysing.

The victorious countries of Western Europe did not experience the same dangers to their national life, but they had to bandage their wounds. Destruction had been massive in Belgium, in northern and eastern France and in the North of Italy. There were major human losses everywhere. Mobilization, introduced in countries like Great Britain that had never known it before, had affected more and more men from all age brackets. At Roehampton after the war, many little plaques were placed around the crucifix in the garden bearing the names of fathers, brothers and relatives

---

[of the Society of the Sacred Heart] down to our days."

[83] For a long time the official documents kept the spelling "Blumenthal."

[84] The house was aided by the family of Mother Werhahn and by Princess Paz of Bavaria who had been a boarder in Paris.

[85] Gen. Arch. C IV 2. Consequently the establishment benefitted by extraterritoriality. It took in children of members of the diplomatic delegations in the countries of South America.

of British nuns who had given their lives for their country.[86] The first visits the house in Amiens received in the 1920's were from English religious who were accompanying their students on pilgrimage to the battlefields of the Somme where the British regiments had suffered enormous losses.

Ireland, united with Great Britain since 1800, had gradually undergone a political evolution in the last third of the nineteenth century, although colonial government was maintained. In 1869 Prime Minister Gladstone had disestablished the Church of Ireland and redistributed its possessions to the Catholic and Presbyterian Churches. He had also reduced social tension by having the Land Act passed in 1881; it granted an indemnity to evicted farmers. On the other hand, the House of Commons and then the Lords had scuttled his plans for Home Rule. The increasing role of Irish deputies in British politics, then the radicalization of the island's move toward independence pushed the British to make concessions. Home Rule, finally granted in 1912, was to have been carried out in 1914, in spite of the opposition of the people of Ulster who just missed setting off a civil war. The declaration of war delayed it. Many Irish from the North and the South enlisted as volunteers in the British forces, banking no doubt, on the hope that the final victory would bring with it independence for their country. In their eyes a state that entered into a war to ensure the existence of Belgium and to fight to restore Poland would surely grant independence to Ireland.

During the First World War the Irish nation became a recognized entity, whereas earlier Lloyd George had characterized it as "artifice and imposture." Its soldiers, sometimes singing "It's a long way to Tipperary," fought on the Somme and in the Dardanelles with a courage that impressed the Allies.[87] In Ireland the insurrection of Easter Week, that lasted from 24 to 29 April 1916, left three hundred dead and thirteen hundred wounded and destroyed the center of Dublin. The revolt was crushed in a bloodbath and sixteen men sentenced to death were executed. After the armistice, the "Irish question" contributed to the crisis Great Britain experienced and the "four glorious years,"[88] 1918 to 1922, saw more confrontations. The government of Eamon De Valera proclaimed the independence of Ireland on 21 January 1919. The development of a war of independence that met with ferocious repression ended in 1921 in the partition of Ireland. From rebellion to guerrilla warfare,

---

[86] Grace Hammond, *The History of the England-Malta Province*, p. 80. It quotes the famous verse of Rupert Brooke: "If I should die, think only this of me: / That there's some corner of a foreign field / That is forever England."

[87] Irish losses were estimated at 25.34% of the number of enlisted volunteers.

[88] *Four Glorious Years* is the title that Frank Gallagher, colleague of Eamon De Valera, gave to the memoirs he published in 1953, under the pseudonym of David Hogan.

all of Ireland had been in the grip of civil war that had exhausted the country materially and morally, and it had to give up for a time the idea of territorial unity. The Society of the Sacred Heart did not suffer repercussions because until then it had worked mainly with the Anglo-Irish population and the "Catholics of the Castle."[89] These groups wanted to encourage Celtic culture and favored the autonomy of Ireland, even to its independence but without violence; most often they were unionists. The superior in Dublin had discreetly fed the people when the civil war added to the misery of the poorest. In the communities in Ireland not all the Irish religious had the same convictions or supported the same camps, while the English nuns deplored rebellion and suffered from being cut off permanently from Roehampton,[90] but the rule that forbade talking about politics in community was faithfully observed and kept personal conflict at bay.

Under the pretext of breaking up the vicariate of England, where the number of houses had increased and which covered England, Ireland, and Scotland, the Society of the Sacred Heart addressed this situation discreetly. In 1918 a vicariate including the houses in Ireland and Scotland was created.[91] With Newcastle in its midst it avoided a split that could have given the impression of support for the current political and national changes. The center of the vicariate was placed in Edinburgh. It was hardly possible to establish it elsewhere because of the troubles in Ireland. A novitiate was opened in Ireland in 1921, a short while after independence was declared. To keep Irish novices in England was no longer humanly possible. That became clear when one of the leaders of the insurrection of 1916 had been executed in the courtyard of the prison of Kilmainham at the same time that one of his sisters was a novice at Roehampton.[92] Was it reasonable then to send to the new vicariate the many Irish religious who were living in England? Henceforth the Irish belonged to two vicariates. The vicar, Mother Walsh, moved to Ireland in 1928, and the vicariate was named vicariate of Mount Anville. The house in Newcastle had been transferred to England, which avoided competition between its normal school and that of Craiglockhart. The memory of the contentious history between England and the countries that had given rise to the United Kingdom weighed heavily on the British Isles. In 1939, Irish students who were studying at Craiglockhart were accused of having "shaken their pretty curls and watched the pianist

---

[89] The civil and military authorities who governed Ireland lived in the Dublin Castle.
[90] Prov. Arch. England/Wales. Nuala O'Higgins: Summary of the History of the Province of Ireland/Scotland.
[91] The houses in Scotland had asked to be attached to Ireland.
[92] Testimony of Aideen Kinlen.

during the rendering of *God save the King!*"[93] In 1967, Mother de Valon proposed joining the novices of Great Britain and Ireland in England. The vicar, Mother Carton, answered her that though she understood that it was desirable to bring them together in view of their reduced number, yet she was opposed to the union of the two novitiates: she explained,

> Geographically the two countries are close to each other. However, there is a marked difference from the racial [*sic*] point of view that has been accentuated by the history of several centuries. I believe it would injure the Society in Ireland at this moment in the history of the country, if its little novitiate were moved to be joined to that of the vicariate of England.[94]

The vicariate of Mount Anville in both Ireland and Great Britain had to deal with three legal systems: Scotland, the Republic of Ireland and Ulster.[95]

---

[93] Prov. Arch. Ireland/Scotland, IRS.1.0030. Report of 26 April 1944.
[94] Prov. Arch. Ireland/Scotland, 1.0031. Letter of 15 August 1967.
[95] Prov. Arch. Ireland/Scotland, 1.0055. In 1942, the vicariate wished to have the young Irish nuns take courses in the normal school at Craiglockhart. The Minister of Education of Ireland let the archbishop of Dublin know that it was not wise for those who were going to teach in Ireland to study in Scotland because of the importance of the Irish language in schools and the "fact that an essential part of our system is the complete Gaelicization of the atmosphere and activities of our normal schools" (Letter of 19 May 1942).

Chapter III

Tradition, Evolution and Modern Life

The First World War put an end to a world that with hindsight appears more stable than it really was. Because of the millions of deaths and the destruction of all kinds that the war produced, it cannot be considered a parenthesis to be quickly closed. It fostered the emergence of transformations that constituted a background, whose characteristics demanded attention in the future. Everything had changed, even in England, where from then on one needed a passport, and to obtain it one had to supply information on oneself and one's family.[1] A new way of life was being born.

The Society of the Sacred Heart in the Years between the Wars

Effects of Social and Economic Transformation

One of the changes concerned the status of women. The human losses of the war had increased the disproportion between the sexes. Types of employment toward which schoolchildren had been directed disappeared. Domesticity became rare; work at home diminished. In the absence of their husbands who were mobilized, mothers of families had to manage their finances in addition to the education of their children. After the war widows had to take charge of businesses or farms. Women henceforth need instruction and qualifications to make them autonomous or capable of earning a living. Schooling allowed people of modest backgrounds a new standing in the marketplace. In 1928, the general congregation decided to modify the terminology used in its schools and replace the expression

---
[1] G. Hammond, p. 80.

"poor school" with that of *écoles populaires*, that is, schools for working class children. It suppressed the work of orphanages as no longer timely.[2]

The wealth of European countries had been largely engulfed by the war and inflation or by devaluation in countries in revolution or incapable of honoring their debts. The revenues of private citizens were compromised. The collapse of national currencies eroded estates and oriented toward work an upper middle class that until then had tended to live on its income and that now contributed to the spread of wage earning. The Sacred Heart experienced the backlash of this erosion of income; many families, obliged to reduce their life style, could no longer pay the expenses of the boarding school. Either they took their children out of school,[3] or they asked for a reduction in the fees. Houses had trouble meeting the needs of their charges and sending the tithe, the *dixième*, to the motherhouse. The crisis of 1929, as extensive as it was brutal, aggravated the situation even more; in the United States schools had to reduce their fees.[4] Families in both North and South America stopped sending their daughters to Europe.[5] Families of the nuns had difficulty paying the dowries or the income they had promised. Nevertheless, the Society of the Sacred Heart was able to maintain its program of purchasing property and of planned renovations, thanks to the savings in the general treasury, [*caisse générale*] and to gifts from its benefactors.[6]

It remained to be seen whether there could be evolution within the Society. The Code of Canon Law published in 1917 prescribed that congregations could no longer impose on the coadjutrix sisters a way of life completely different from that of the choir religious. At the Sacred Heart, the obligation to align the length of their aspirantship with that of the choir nuns provoked a stir. In February 1919, the motherhouse again asked each vicariate to establish a common novitiate for the coadjutrix sisters.[7] In 1922, the general congregation insisted on the quality of the formation to be given to them.

---

[2] Gen. Arch. C I C 3, Box 14. There was only one orphanage, the one in Saint Louis.
[3] The house in the Canary Islands was closed in 1922 because of the economic crisis.
[4] *Lettres annuelles*, 1958-1961, pp. 23 and 32.
[5] The house at Ostend that was supported by the work of the *grandes pensionnaires* experienced difficulties at this time.
[6] Gen. Arch. C I C 3, Box 15, 9 March 1935.
[7] Gen. Arch. C I A 7 B, Box 2. The cost of their trousseau was fixed at 200 F for the first year of noviceship and at 100 F for the second year. If a sister brought less than 1000 F at the time of entrance, the sum was to be allocated to the trousseau. For choir religious the trousseau was evaluated at 2000 F.

The novices are to be separated from the other sisters as far as possible; they are to receive thorough religious instruction, and the rule and the custom book [*coutumier*] must be explained to them in a simple and practical manner. Their formation to religious spirit and to the different employments must be the chief concern of the assistant who is in charge of them.[8]

In 1928, it was suggested that future sisters have in-service training as observers [*regardantes*] and service personnel[9] to prepare them for their employments.

Some coadjutrix sisters no doubt hoped that their situation would be radically modified. Although some congregations in the United States minimized the distinction between the two categories of religious, at the Sacred Heart nothing like that happened. In 1922 a link was even made between eventual demands for change, about which we have no details, and the ideological upheaval taking place in the world: "The socialist tendencies of our era require that the spirit and the example of Nazareth be constantly placed before the eyes [of the sisters]."

In 1926, a coadjutrix sister from the United States sent the superior general a long letter that revealed an undeniable malaise.[10] She said that she loved the Society and her vocation, but she drew Mother von Loë's attention to the distinction between choir and coadjutrix religious, the principle of which she challenged.

> I could never believe in the distinction, nor understand why it should exist in the House of God…. It always seemed to me that the only distinction in Religion should be age and authority. But it never affected me as it has in the last few years when I came to realize how much harm it was doing to the cause of God's glory and the welfare of the Society. It is keeping subjects from the Society, not only from the ranks of the lay sisters, but also from the ranks of the choir religious. We are continually being told that we are all one, that we are all working for the same end, will get the same merit and so on. Yet…we are certainly not treated as one. We get care, kindness, oh, yes, Very Reverend Mother, far be it from me to deny that, but I fear, in fact I am almost certain of it, that by far the greater number of us Sisters feel that it is like the kindness shown to servants and not as to members of the same family.

---

[8] Gen. Arch. C I C 3, Box 13.
[9] Gen. Arch. C I C 3, Box 14.
[10] M. Quinlan, *The Society of the Sacred Heart, 1914-1964*, 1995, pp. 188-199.

Where did she feel this difference of treatment? In the tasks given to the sisters and to the fact that they did not receive the same formation:

> What is there, speaking naturally, Very Reverend Mother, in our work that is congenial, uplifting, inspiring? Is it not depressing, uninteresting, discouraging, dirt and dust from one end of the year to the other? God often gives us talents and gifts but as Lay Sisters we must bury them beyond a hope of ever developing them. I do think that every one of the religious family should do a share of it [domestic work] and that our gifts and talents should be considered and developed just as other religious orders develop them in their subjects, and not tell them that there is no difference – we are all one family....

Other remarks concerned customs, the impossibility for coadjutrix sisters to talk among themselves,[11] the difference in treatment between choir and coadjutrix nuns at general gatherings,[12] the lack of leisure for the sisters.

> It is very often said that during vacation, the Society gives the choir religious all the rest and diversion possible, because their minds need it. But it has always seemed to me that we sisters need to divert our mind and rest ourselves just as much as they, after our year of uninteresting, uncongenial work. *And we certainly do not get it.*[13]...We could be allowed to go to interesting lectures about our country or some great character or the like which not only would divert our minds and hearts and instruct us, give us a love of the true and the beautiful, but we are not allowed or if not forbidden it is managed to be at a time when we cannot go.

She concluded her comments:

> I cannot see why a young choir religious because she has more "book learning," had a higher social standing and money when she was in the world should be called out and pass ahead of a dear old consecrated soul that has served God and the Society for forty or fifty years before the other one was even thought about.

---

[11] "All our recreations are general recreations, we do not have a chance to speak to one another like [*sic*] the Choir Religious have during the first half hour of recreation. Some Sisters have even been given permission by their Confessors to speak out to someone, for they felt that if they did not do so they would lose their minds."

[12] "When we go to the general recreations...we are often treated as if we were not there or did not exist."

[13] Underlined in the text.

The situation of the coadjutrix sisters was experienced differently according to the country. In eastern and southern Europe some of them had never been to school. Poland, Malta and Spain, which had many vocations, sent many sisters abroad. Those who made their noviceship in the new country did not have the means of learning correctly the language of the country that received them,[14] and initial formation was not provided in their own language.[15] Customs were also different. In Great Britain women who had not been pupils of the boarding schools, even those from Sacred Heart normal schools, were not admitted as choir religious.[16] The difference in treatment was no doubt accentuated in countries where there had been or still was an aristocracy. An Englishwoman, Winifred Wilson, after completing her studies at Fenham, entered as a postulant at Roehampton on 8 September 1928. Her memoirs corroborate the behavior stigmatized by the American sister whose letter was quoted above. This author situates them in the context of a country where the social structures were clear-cut:

> I had always been outwardly law-abiding, at home and at school, and at that level I did not find too difficult the whole ultra-formal code of manners and customs which governed every waking moment. At least it provided a protective covering for my rebellious reactions and my inward struggles to will wholeheartedly what I was required to do – to make God's will my free choice; this included the whole area of intellectual activity: henceforth this was not for me. I accepted that I had joined the servant class, and this involved such relatively small details: as referring to the children as "the young ladies" and addressing them as "Miss." It embraced all my outward relations with choir nuns (the youngest choir postulant was "Mother" to the most venerable "Sister").

Customs were regulated by the *coutumier* at Roehampton as elsewhere. Places in chapel, in the communion line, in the refectory and at recreation depended on the order of precedence defined by seniority in religious life or the offices held. "The sisters escaped all such subtle distinctions. In the general

---

[14] For a long time Montigny was a stopping point where Polish postulants studied French for about six months, but many of them were sent directly to Poitiers where the novitiate for the sisters was located. The Maltese were not taught English either, a lack that penalized them when they were sent to Great Britain or to the English-speaking missions of Asia.

[15] In Japan, a young choir nun acted as translator for the mistress of novices (Testimony of Ayako Kato).

[16] Testimony of Mary Roe.

arrangements they were simply 'the Sisters.'"[17] A choir religious always had to preside at their recreation in order to maintain decorum. Sometimes this task was confided to a new professed recently come from the motherhouse.

> This would be an informal session, telling us of an event that, as sisters, we would experience only thus, at second hand. Her enthusiasm and lively recollections would fan our filial interest. The General would be referred to throughout as "our Mother" and the tone was respectful. Invisible limits exercised restraints on free speech. Modes of expression, hallowed by usage, with odd French injection, helped to lubricate the exercise.
>
> On Sundays, minus vegetables[18] and in our Sunday habits, we joined the choir nuns for "general recreation." Its external arrangement awoke memories of glassy-eyed attention at school to expositions in history classes of the feudal system. Was this a faint survival of the baronial hall or, at least, of the later English manor, with the lower orders called in for an occasion? We, the sisters, sat in a block behind the "community" in the selective sense: we listened to the decorous converse – sometimes quite interesting, even amusing. A sister might be asked a courteous question. She stood up to answer and then sat again.

The narrator had felt among the sisters "a vivacity, an energy that emanated from the joy of a life centered entirely on God," but she added:

> I was conscious of the underlying system – procrustean and outmoded – a seamless ritual of received custom, habit that governed all activity. Official prayer periods were scaled down to the minimum required by the rule: the sisters' way of life was considered contemplative in itself. The spiritual scenario for this was the hidden life of Jesus at Nazareth. It was emphasised as a special and desirable privilege. The snag for me was that it had no discernible end.
>
> Toward the end of my first six months, I was told that if I wanted the habit, I must ask for it. This I did, beginning with the assistant, the only approved guide I had so far had. Rapport had been difficult, on both sides, sometimes impossible. On this occasion she asked flatly, "Do you want it?" I said with equal terseness, "Yes, of course." I continued my tour. The mistress of studies (of the vicariate) asked, "Can you give up books?" To this I said, "I have given them up." "Very well, I'll give you

---

[17] In the chapel the choir religious took their places in stalls; the sisters' places were in the pews.

[18] The coadjutrix sisters peeled vegetables during part of their recreation.

my vote." End of conversation! The mistress general of the [free] school was more communicative – very kind and human. She, surprisingly, had received an impression of inward happiness in my outward attitude.[19]

Did the letter from the American sister receive an answer? The General Congregation of 1928 addressed certain points it brought up, but the Society of the Sacred Heart was not ready to consider them.

> Some of the notes asked for changes in the sisters' habit that would bring it more into line with that of the choir religious. That would foster people's tendencies to rise above their condition: a tendency that cannot be placed at the basis of religious life and rather is harmful to it. One comes into religion to follow and imitate Jesus Christ, poor, humble, crucified.

It was decided that the fabric used in warm countries would be thinner and lighter than what was used in Europe and that the bodice would be washable.[20] But rising at 4:30 was "not completely suppressed." The sisters were not to have a meditation book for their use.[21] The members of the general congregation were aware that the working classes were evolving, but that awareness did not lead to a change in customs.[22] In 1935, notes sent to Rome requested an improvement in the health conditions in the workplaces and in the sisters' training for their employments. The general congregation recognized also that their spiritual formation was deficient. It recommended "treating them gently and kindly and not as servants.[23] It expressed the

---

[19] *Sister Winifred Wilson*, pp. 26-31. After her first vows in 1931, Winifred Wilson taught in the elementary school at Hammersmith in London. After a short probation and final vows, she was director of the practice school at Fenham, then of the elementary school at Hammersmith. The vicariate of England recognized her abilities and her competence and knew how to put them to good use.

[20] Gen. Arch. C I C 3, Box 14.

[21] "When it was judged apropos, a sister who was more advanced spiritually could be given a book, provided others did not see or know of the fact. Some pretext was to be found for her to make her meditation in private."

[22] "It is good to take into consideration that generally the sisters who join us now are better educated than formerly. Therefore, the assistants have to treat them differently, interest them, propose contests at recreation and on *congés* and questions to research in Scripture according to their ability...all the while maintaining them in their rank."

[23] As a consequence of the economic crisis, in Europe, the percentage of coadjutrix sisters was higher than the norm.

opinion that their novitiate should be located in the country and not in large cities "to avoid their having visits that could be a bad influence."[24]

The situation of the sisters was beginning to appear anachronistic. At the end of the 1920's, a young choir professed in Vienna, "very gifted and deeply attached to Jesus Christ, believed she should work for reform. She tried to persuade the sisters to ask to rise at five o'clock instead of four thirty," and she gained followers among the choir nuns. In the course of her visit to the vicariate, Mother Vicente learned of the case. These young nuns were given obediences for other vicariates and "calm returned."[25]

Apostolic Mission and Cloister

Cloister was an issue. In 1915, Mother von Loë had reminded that "visits from house to house during vacation are permitted to the religious from city houses to the country; even outside of vacation times it was permitted to assist at a ceremony or an instructive lecture." Some religious were making use of the school's bus to go shopping. Though it was allowed to visit a chapel in the city or to tour a building "to judge the general appearance," one did not have the right to enter to examine the operation of the machines and apparatus.[26] The question was taken up again in 1922. "The thought of our Constitutions is that we go out only to go to one or other of our houses. The times seem to require more, but permissions to be given are reserved to our Reverend Mothers Vicar," who were to call the religious to return to the letter of the Constitutions. Indispensable outings during the war to go to consulates, to banks, to consult business people and merchants were to be suppressed gradually. Superiors were to go to the bishop's office only if the bishop required it.[27] The religious were to be operated on in a clinic only if the surgeon refused to come to the house. It was not permitted to accompany the bodies of the deceased to the cemetery if it was outside the cloister. During journeys the obligation of cloister outweighed that of Sunday Mass. A dispensation was provided for, however, in the interest of family ties.[28]

---

[24] It also required that the sisters' novitiate not be placed in the same house as that of the choir nuns. This demand was not always carried out. The coexistence of the two could only accentuate the contrast.

[25] Gen. Arch. C IV, OSU. Testimony of Maria von Jordis.

[26] Gen. Arch. C I C 3, Box 13. General Congregation of 1915.

[27] It was up to the bishops to go to the convent, but it was the superior's responsibility to show willingness "to present her community and its works to his Excellency."

[28] "Generally it is permitted for a religious to go to another house to facilitate a family visit only for aged mothers and fathers, very rarely for other relatives,

Mother Stuart had asked herself whether cloister should be invoked to dispense teachers from activities useful for the apostolate.[29] In 1922, apropos of lectures organized for teaching religious, the general congregation thought that "if bishops request that we take part, we must comply, especially in Protestant countries. Sometimes we can arrange to have the lectures held in our houses, which is better." Visiting monuments, museums or factories is not authorized. But religious were allowed to accompany their students who had to go out for examinations. During the war, some houses had been visited by a superior officer. Henceforth, visits were to be limited to receiving heads of state and the examiners in university colleges. However, superiors and treasurers were permitted from time to time to have their houses inspected to examine the walls and the façade, but they should choose a moment when the nuns would be out of sight.

It took ten years after the war for cloister to be fully respected in the Society of the Sacred Heart. The General Congregation of 1928 enforced its application, the principle being that going out was to cease.[30] As a religious in the hospital was not allowed to receive visitors except her mother, to avoid all temptations, it was recommended that a sick religious should not have surgery in the city where her family resided. Religious ought not to visit a sick person who was in bed or profit by a visit to a hospital to do errands or to visit churches. However, cloister was lifted when religious had to study or to vote, and bishops were requiring religious to go to the polls. A list of places of interest that could be visited only once in the course of a change of house was established. Religious could accompany their students to Rome, but they could not enter the museums. Visits of families of religious were reduced to two per month and limited to one hour. Letters sent by the religious were judged too frequent and too detailed.

A veritable system of casuistry was being established. In 1930, Mother Vicente, who did not wish to see customs challenged, alluded to the inventive spirit some religious manifested to get around restrictions:

> We are asked too often for permission to go out to see or hear something, to assist at an educational meeting or a more or less important lecture outside the house, to go to meet with a certain official with whom it

---

even if these cover the cost of the trip."

[29] However, she reiterated Mother Digby's prohibition for the religious in Ontario to go out to study at the state normal school, as a law of 1907 required.

[30] Gen. Arch. Box 14, 23 November 1928.

would be useful to make contact, it seems, to go to the country to breathe fresh air, to assist at the First Communion of a niece outside the city where we live, to an aunt's jubilee. Our Mother Foundress wrote on a similar occasion: "If we gave in to all these caprices, we would always be on the highways!" What would she say now, Reverend Mothers and dear Sisters?[31]

In 1935, the general congregation authorized only outings that were "really necessary or seriously useful."

The Society of the Sacred Heart found it difficult to make use of the new modes of communication that were contributing to the creation of a truly mass culture. Some houses had bought radios without asking permission. In 1928 the general congregation found fault with listening to radio broadcasts because they were harmful to recollection and to the spirit of cloister and exposed listeners to hearing things that religious should not know about. "It is very pleasant to listen to a concert, but in entering religious life, have we not renounced this sort of enjoyment? That is not to say that we may not use the radio...from time to time for the children, for example." Listening to the radio was possible therefore for a "scientific experiment," [sic] but it was forbidden in community.[32] However, houses that had bought radios were allowed to keep them unless the vicar decided otherwise.

Old and New Fields of Apostolate

Mother Stuart used an image borrowed from Benedict XV to describe the work the Society of the Sacred Heart had to perform: "Education is today's battlefield and we must commit ourselves to it, not just at random but consistently." In 1910, the general congregation had decided to upgrade the juniorates in the United States and to establish them throughout Europe, even if it meant having recourse to the services of competent lay teachers. The Plan of Studies was revised.[33] The teaching of two languages became obligatory, but Latin was not required everywhere.[34] Change proved to be even more necessary as national policies concerning the education of women were changing. In some countries women could obtain the baccalaureate and then be admitted to universities other than as "auditors."

---

[31] *Circulaires de la T.R.M. Vicente*, pp. 55-57.
[32] Gen. Arch. C I C 3, Box 14.
[33] Gen. Arch. Box 12.
[34] On the other hand, it was encouraged in the United States, which helped in the creation of university colleges.

How was the Society of the Sacred Heart going to position itself with regard to an evolution that it had sometimes disparaged in the belief that its own programs took better account of the specifically feminine character than the new directions appearing in public education? Not all the vicariates had the same policies, and their execution was linked to the demands of the public and of the Church.

Appearance of Sacred Heart University Colleges

The first changes came from the United States. State laws allowed independent university colleges to grant degrees. The hierarchy wanted schools in all the parishes and institutions of higher education for women so that students would avoid going to non-Catholic or co-educational institutions, considered suspect for faith and morals.

The Religious of the Sacred Heart were not the first to open colleges for women,[35] but they took an interest in it.[36] The earliest were opened at Grand Coteau in 1914, in Cincinnati in 1915, in Omaha, at Manhattanville, at Lake Forest, in Seattle, at Maryville in St. Louis and in San Francisco. Manhattanville College, established in 1916 under the authority of the University of the State of New York, obtained a charter permitting the granting of academic degrees. In 1935, its inscription on the official list of members of the Association of American Universities was viewed as a proof of the excellence of the education given there.[37]

Between 1914 and 1919, the Sacred Heart opened ten women's colleges in the United States.[38] It had sufficed to transform the course of study of the last two years of the boarding school into a program for the first two years of college. Different states required different numbers of years of study in order to recognize a college. After the setting up of two-year colleges, hardly separate from the boarding school, the movement was toward fully autonomous four-year colleges, often affiliated with Catholic universities. Not all these establishments developed to the same degree, and some had to be closed.[39] The Sacred Heart undertook this adventure at relatively little expense. The schools had already become accustomed to

---

[35] M. O'Leary, p. 209. The first, Vassar College in New York State, dated from 1861. From 1897 on, some religious congregations started them.
[36] Patricia Byrne, "A Tradition of Educating Women: the Religious of the Sacred Heart in Higher Education," *U.S. Catholic Historian*, 1995, pp. 49-79.
[37] L. Callan, *The Society of the Sacred Heart...*, pp. 711-712.
[38] The last two, opened after World War II, were Newton College of the Sacred Heart in Massachusetts in 1946 and San Diego College for Women in 1949.
[39] That was the case of Clifton in 1935 and of Forest Ridge Junior College, Seattle, in 1937.

hiring lay teachers, and it was only necessary to set aside a few classrooms in the boarding school for the college students. In the 1930's, as the student bodies grew, and coexistence became undesirable, the colleges were separated from the schools, either by giving them separate buildings or by moving one or the other to a different property.[40]

Territories of the United States and English-speaking countries rapidly adopted the same policy. A university college was founded in 1935 at Santurce in Puerto Rico, and two years later, it was authorized to give university degrees.[41] Australia founded Sancta Sophia College in 1926, as part of the University of Sydney. A college began modestly at Stuartholme, at the request of the archbishop of Brisbane. Aurora College was opened in Shanghai in 1937.

In 1922, the general congregation took a traditional position with regard to girls' education. It recalled that the boarding schools were to be established and maintained in preference to every other apostolic work and that "university academies" were to resemble them as far as possible.[42] Six years later the reservations regarding university studies were still strong, for "these courses, above all philosophy, offer great dangers, with all the current systems that can trouble young intelligences and even cause doubts against faith." Therefore, it was necessary to follow up the students, "to be aware of the effect produced in their minds by the teachings and from time to time, if possible, obtain for them the opportunity for conversation with a professor of theology or of solid philosophy or some lectures during vacations."[43] The increasing number of colleges caused the setting up of a committee of vicars who had supported the original creations.[44] It was their chief task to seek to reconcile the new work with Sacred Heart education and semi-cloistered religious life: They believed, "It is best when the teaching and the diplomas are given in our houses," since cloister was then safeguarded. Otherwise, the students were to be assembled at the Sacred Heart where the religious "would provide an antidote to erroneous teaching and safeguard their faith." However, as they were not schoolgirls, it was decided that they could have "more freedom," the possibility even of

---

[40] At the beginning, the mistresses general and superiors had charge of the colleges. In the 1930's a different religious was named president of the college.

[41] *Lettres annuelles*, 1946-1951, p. 97, and 1958-1961, p. 171.

[42] Gen. Arch. C I C 3, Box 13.

[43] Gen. Arch. Box 14. Session of 22 October 1928.

[44] It was composed of Mothers Reid and Moran from the United States and Mother Salmon from Australia, along with Mothers Dupont, Perry, Guérin and Walsh.

"a few dances," where that was permitted, for in New York, the bishop had forbidden them.[45]

The American colleges grew strong as educational institutions by incorporating practices specific to university life.[46] As one religious of the Sacred Heart wrote,

> Seeing Manhattanville from the inside, one realizes how the spirit of the Society and the whole teaching power stored up in our fourth vow come to a happy conclusion. In this kind of work...one feels that Manhattanville is thoroughly American. It is because of the genius of the *Plan of Studies*, which lends itself to all manner of developments that this sort of work can be carried on.[47]

By accepting only small classes of students, the religious could keep the family spirit characteristic of the Sacred Heart. The American colleges were furnished with quality libraries and equipment, thanks to presidents capable of finding the necessary assistance to develop their activities. They fostered highly regarded instruction. Manhattanville founded Pius X School of Liturgical Music, which attracted students from many countries. Mother Grace Dammann, president before and during World War II, fostered a positive attitude toward racial integration and took steps to implement it in the college.[48]

The creation of the colleges developed the competence of the teaching nuns. In the United States for some time, some of them had had university degrees,[49] but vicars and superiors had to provide for those who were destined to teach in the colleges. They took summer courses given by professors from nearby universities, religious or not. Some religious did advanced university study.[50] In order to respect cloister, those who were studying at Stanford were driven there from Menlo Park, and they arranged to use a special room in the library to pursue their research.[51]

---

[45] Gen. Arch. 31 October 1928.
[46] M. O'Leary, pp. 209-216.
[47] M. O'Leary, p. 216.
[48] "Principles Versus Prejudice," a talk given at the Alumnae Meeting, Class Day, 31 May 1938, *The Tower Postscript 6*.
[49] P. Byrne, p. 59, notes that religious had obtained university degrees, one from the University of Iowa in 1899 and one from the University of Chicago in 1902.
[50] P. Byrne, p. 60. In the course of the 1920's, thirty-nine of them received a master's degree and nine, a doctorate. In the 30's forty-five master's and eleven doctorates were listed.
[51] P. Byrne, p. 62. Florence Moulton was the first Religious of the Sacred Heart to earn a doctorate in philosophy at Stanford.

Monique Luirard

Studies in Europe

From the end of the nineteenth century, the houses in the European capitals had been receiving *grandes pensionnaires* of many nationalities. These were young women who before their entry into society were sent to complete their education, visit the most famous cultural sites and learn foreign languages.[52] After World War I, the program proved successful. Ostend became a "league of nations" in miniature where Austria, Hungary, Poland and South America were represented.[53] As the war and the crisis of 1929 limited travel, some houses in South America created sections for *grandes pensionnaires*.[54] It was a task also to figure out what to offer those who wanted to pursue higher studies. Although in some countries parents were not yet ready to encourage their daughters to go to university, at the same time the question of higher studies arose for both the pupils and the religious.

In England, Mother Stuart had wanted future teachers to be able to acquire real professional, university approved competence.[55] In 1904 preparation for a teaching diploma for secondary teachers granted by Cambridge University was part of the program of the juniorate. The same policy was applied in the Commonwealth.[56] After World War I, the nuns took the examinations of the University of London. As that university had decided to create university colleges in the surrounding cities, the Society of the Sacred Heart had the idea of transforming Hammersmith into a college dependent on the university, but the experiment was of short duration.[57] In Ireland, Mother Walsh decided that her nuns had to have a diploma in education.[58] Those who were going to the university were not to speak about what happened outside except to the superior. During their travel,

---

[52] In Paris, the *Maison des Anges* on the Boulevard des Invalides was set up to receive them. The regulations provided for religious instruction in the evening and for their outings and correspondence to be supervised. These rules limited enrollment.

[53] *Lettres annuelles,* 1947-1952, p. 300.

[54] In Lima in 1942 the *Sophianum* began to accept them. The boarding school had been transferred there from León de Andrade.

[55] Information supplied by Mary Coke. Governmental directives made the same demands.

[56] Teresa McShane, who had been a novice at Roehampton, obtained the degree of Bachelor of Arts from the University of New Zealand in 1913 (*Lettres annuelles,* 1961-1963, p. 179).

[57] *The life and times of R.M. Archer Shee*, pp. 19-20.

[58] Prov. Arch. Ireland/Scotland, IRS 1-0010: "Unless we go to the university, we will perhaps have to close our schools, for they will satisfy neither the

they were to pray for those with whom they came in contact.[59] In Austria, Cardinal Piffl asked teaching congregations to bring their curricula into line with those of the state. The religious had to take a doctorate in philosophy or a licentiate in the other disciplines.[60]

Between 1929 and 1936, small communities were set up in university cities, in Oxford, Munich, Louvain, Milan, Dublin and Valença, Brazil, to allow Religious of the Sacred Heart to pursue higher study. Mother Vicente followed the movement rather than anticipating it:

> Today one speaks of knowledge, of university examinations, of careers for women. I am not opposed: we must keep *au courant*, force ourselves to have strong studies so that the Society keeps the place it has always had among the teaching orders. But let us not forget that we have a role as educators and that the first science we must teach our children is that of Jesus Christ.

This cautious attitude reflected that of pontifical directives equally mixed with the attitude toward higher education given to religious women. After the condemnation of 1907, an anti-modernist obsession had heavy repercussions in the seminaries and faculties of theology. The papacy was seeking perhaps to protect religious from these noxious influences, even more, as it was not generally thought certain that women had the capacity to always choose the right values! The encyclical *Rappresentanti in terra*, of 31 December 1929, had recommended

> sending on for university study only those religious who had given proof of solid religious spirit. That is why the superior general [insisted] on engaging in study only those of ours who already have a certain maturity of judgment and whose religious and intellectual formation is solid and enlightened enough to [allow] them to face study without prejudice to themselves or to their future apostolate."[61]

Religious in California were no longer going to Stanford and Berkeley, but because the fate of their college was at stake and the American Council

---

authorities nor the parents. It has taken me a long time to come to this conclusion, but I can no longer close my eyes to this truth."
[59] .Prov. Arch. Ireland/Scotland, IRS. 1-0010. 1923.
[60] In 1920, Maria von Jordis who was at Pressbaum went to Vienna three times a week to study for the examinations for a superior primary teacher, and she took supplementary courses in mathematics and Latin. In December 1928, she was the first Religious of the Sacred Heart in Austria to earn a doctorate.
[61] *Vie de la T.R.M. Vicente*, pp. 192-193.

on Education had accredited doctorates from only those two universities, during the 1930's, they were sent there again. Mother Rosalie Hill let the motherhouse know that Stanford's Department of English Literature was "safe," and the studies of the religious did not touch upon the contemporary period![62]

A different rhythm of life was required in the communities in which student nuns lived. At Oxford the first two students were not taking the same courses, and since they did not have the same schedule, they could not go together to the university. It was necessary to find two companions! As the distance between the two colleges was short, it was decided that a student could go by herself. The hours of meals and of the Office were adjusted so that the students could take part. Mother Archer-Shee, superior of the community, undertook to have religious from the United States come to study; that swelled the group. These houses were open to lay students also, most often to alumnae. The one in Oxford, where the nuns hoped to establish a university hostel, attracted few lay students,[63] probably because the rules discouraged candidates. The religious who had Oxford degrees contributed to the strengthening of studies in the vicariate.

In France, the basic question was the adaptation of the Plan of Studies to the state curriculum and eventual preparation of the pupils for the *baccalauréat*.[64] In 1915, not knowing whether it would be accepted by the authorities, the Society of the Sacred Heart had opened in Lyons a "family boarding school" [*pension de famille*] for girls over fifteen, called *grandes pensionnaires*. Then, realizing that the state was not going to interfere with the functioning of independent establishments if the religious were careful, the Society reestablished the boarding schools, except in Paris, where it carried on the work of the *grandes pensionnaires* at the Rue Saint Dominique.[65] Secondary education for girls had no legal status in France; therefore,

---

[62] P. Byrne, pp. 60-62.

[63] G. Hammond, pp. 21-22.

[64] Prov. Arch. France. At the time of the regular visit in 1912 to Rivoli, which was both the novitiate and the juniorate for the French, Mother Stuart suggested such a development and recalled that it was not a question of "immobilizing life on the excellent foundations of the past, which must be regarded as foundations and not completed works."

[65] In 1927, Mother de Neuville bought the château of Saint-Maur des Fossés in order to found a boarding school near Paris. In 1921 at Marmoutier, the fifteen pupils of the boarding school were sent away, and only *grandes pensionnaires* were accepted. As the French authorities had decided to maintain the legislation of Alsace and the Moselle before the annexation, the Sacred Heart still had its status as an authorized congregation and could have boarding schools as before, while the rest of the country was still under the laws of 1904.

as Sacred Heart schools reopened, they were declared to be primary schools with the addition of "complementary courses," which allowed for the offering of all kinds of subjects. The Sacred Heart kept its own curriculum but introduced Latin and the study of a living language, which allowed students to sit for the *baccalauréat*. After 1919, Mother de Lescure, mistress general in Poitiers, successfully prepared pupils for the *baccalauréat*. In the mid-1920's the same was done for the day pupils at the Rue Saint Dominique.

The curriculum reform of 1927, which placed the first part of the *baccalauréat* in the highest class, forced the Sacred Heart to incorporate the official curriculum into the Plan of Studies and to suppress Christian philosophy in order to avoid overburdening the pupils. However, "if in this pressurized race religious instruction is also sabotaged because of lack of time, what solid principles will remain in the heads of the children? Religious instruction, on the contrary, ought to be reinforced because the pupils can no longer study Christian philosophy and Church history and without these studies will lose the sense of the supernatural."[66] The Sacred Heart accepted only unwillingly the religious neutrality of the curriculum, for it "contributed powerfully to the secularization of minds that is the usual framework for religious indifference."[67] The General Congregation of 1935 decided that the Plan of Studies should be adapted to official curricula only if the demands of the state made it obligatory to do so. To avoid the appearance of the nuns' being secular school teachers, the general congregation emphasized that "religious instruction would be reinforced at the intellectual level of secular studies so that candidates for public examinations would be armed with religious knowledge at least equal to their secular knowledge, since ignorance leads to lamentable falls."

According to the French religious, the official curricula suited neither "the physiology of children weakened by the war [*sic*]" nor the wishes of the families, nor the traditional image of women.

> Parents do not make the financial sacrifices for the education of their daughters that they make for their sons destined to be heads of families whom they support by their work. Whatever she does, the woman is destined by her nature to be the companion of the man, to second him; it is not normally on her that rests the care of earning the family's living by a career. As a consequence, girls' schools must make sure that their pupils find within the school everything necessary for a complete education

---

[66] Report of Mother de Bournonville to the General Congregation of 1935, Second Part, p. 6.
[67] Report, p. 17.

for women. Then around seventeen or eighteen years old, if they wish to specialize, they will be able to do so easily, whether in the pursuit of university degrees or in domestic science schools, nursing schools, agricultural schools or quite simply – and this still happens – in staying home with their mother.[68]

Because it reflected the opinion of a social milieu that did not understand that a woman could exercise professional activity, the Society of the Sacred Heart did not push girls to pass the examinations for the *baccalauréat*. In addition, the religious believed that not all the students would be able to succeed, and they did not wish to group them according to ability.[69]

The adoption of official curricula upset the organization of classes, as understood at the Sacred Heart. The General Congregation of 1935 tolerated separate courses in mathematics and sciences but refused to give up the traditional system. When the families were not demanding that their children take the public examinations, there was no need to leave behind the educational tradition of the Society, for there was no progress outside it.

> We ought rather, while following attentively present advances, 1st, courageously pursue the development of our teaching in the direction of true intellectual superiority; 2nd, maintain our studies at a level that can respond to all reasonable requirements; 3rd prepare the nuns to teach the feminine disciplines that the families are beginning to demand; 4th, in proportion to the demands of the studies to reinforce religious instruction and moral development of the children; to give them good religion teachers; an advanced knowledge of the Gospel; not to neglect sacred history; at the end of schooling or in courses for young alumnae, teaching of Catholic social doctrine and preparation for Catholic Action, according to the wishes of the Church. The religious must also receive reliable and well-founded education in the true meaning of the encyclicals.[70]

But were the religious in France capable of preparing students suitably for the *baccalauréat*? Mother Stuart had wanted a few aspirants from Jette and Rivoli to take the *baccalauréat* in order to do university studies. From

---

[68] Report, p. 8.
[69] Report, Session of 12 March: "Let us not sacrifice the large number of children who are not capable of passing these examinations; they have the right to instruction that develops without overwhelming them; they have the right not to be deprived in the areas of manual work and the leisure arts, in which they are gifted by God. How do we know that later on they will not have more influence than our 'bachelors?'"
[70] Report, 15 March 1935.

October 1912 after a rapid preparation, two of them received the first level of the *baccalauréat*. They completed philosophy the following year and the licentiate in June 1914.[71] This ease in passing the examinations confirmed the Society in the idea that the studies at the Sacred Heart were at the level of the official program. Some candidates for the licentiate were sent to Lyons where they were to enroll in the Catholic university.

The university authorities demanded that they attend the lectures, at least occasionally; but because of cloister and because they were not relieved of teaching duties, they could not go to classes and take the examinations. In France higher study for religious appeared "useless and inopportune,"[72] since in the schools only the director had to have a diploma. It sufficed to have a few study in order to maintain the reputation of the Society, for it was "appropriate to be able to say ours have diplomas,"[73] and those who had diplomas could help those who did not. In the 1930's a few young religious passed their *baccalauréat* and took courses at Catholic universities, but the difference in treatment between the two groups was neither understood nor appreciated; and as it lasted beyond World War II, it left much bitterness.

The juniorate was the locus of formation for the young religious. In 1935, the general congregation judged that aspirants should receive intellectual training required by the present advances in studies. However, this culture did not replace

> formation "for us" according to the spirit of the Society, which makes of us educators and not just school teachers. These two types of formation can neither exclude nor replace each other: the juniorate cannot suffice for those who do not bring basic culture. On the other hand, culture already acquired does not replace the juniorate that forms to our spirit. And this educational formation must precede instruction proper as far as possible by giving direction to it.

Mother Vanderhagen proposed formation equivalent to one year of elementary juniorate for the beginning of the aspirantship in order "to strengthen the judgment, redress the frequent errors in modern minds and instill methods of work," and in preparing for the *baccalauréat*, the juniors would receive further instruction. Before probation, those who were destined to teach the higher classes would go to the superior juniorate where they would receive the "philosophical bases indispensable for

---

[71] At this time preparation for the licentiate required only one year of study.
[72] Report of Mother de Bournonville, p. 3.
[73] Report, p. 15.

maintaining the mind in the truth across so many dangerous currents of thought and more complete knowledge of educational methods." They would prepare for the second part of the *baccalauréat*. Mother Vicente clearly indicated that she would not permit them to undertake university studies, for "they would be exposed to never having the spirit left to us by our Holy Mother. They can aspire only to the *baccalauréat*," she concluded. But was this level sufficient? The juniorate was not really aimed at giving intellectual formation. Not all the religious went to the superior juniorate, and they did not have the opportunity to attend lectures given outside the convent or listen to the radio, or read newspapers or books not considered "safe." It is understandable that the rumor went around that upbringing at the Sacred Heart was excellent but the level of teaching was mediocre.

Caught between its desire not to be subservient to official programs and the necessity to maintain an appropriate standard to satisfy the families, the Sacred Heart did not systematically direct pupils toward official examinations.[74] Sometimes parental pressure necessitated *baccalauréat* preparation for fear of losing students. Many of these students had the feeling that they were presented for the examination only under duress.[75] The preference was at the end of studies to propose a year of domestic science, vocational courses, music and art lessons, typing, stenography to develop each one's aptitudes and "face up to the future."[76] Bishop de Durfort of Poitiers instituted examinations in religious education that allowed pupils of the Sacred Heart to obtain a diploma. In France, more than elsewhere, the anti-intellectual bias, which was contrary to the mind of the founder, created a dilemma. In the Society of the Sacred Heart, there was a tendency to see professional competence as somehow opposed to the quality of religious life.

In Italy, the adoption of official programs caused an increase in the numbers of students.[77] In Hungary, Mother de Galbert developed the *Sophianum* by reconciling the demands of the state and those of the Society. In Ireland, the boarders took school leaving examinations after 1931 and the teaching became more structured.[78] In Spain, Mother Garrido thought it necessary to adopt

---

[74] Mother de Bournonville insisted on the apostolic value of the *brevet*, which would allow alumnae to come to the aid of free schools, but the general congregation stated more prosaically that some alumnae were teachers in free schools by necessity.

[75] Testimony of Christine du Noyer. That was the tendency in the vicariate of the Midi (South) but not in Egypt.

[76] Report of Mother de Bournonville, p. 10.

[77] *Lettres annuelles*, 1958-1961, p. 28. Mother Boncompagni Ludovisi, who became vicar in 1928, had courses in classical humanities instituted in all the boarding schools, according to the directives of the ministry of education.

[78] Testimony of J. Stephenson.

official curricula and have the religious obtain state diplomas, but her views found neither support nor understanding. The fall of the monarchy forced conformity to state programs for fear of losing the institutions. In Zaragoza, seven religious then took courses in the normal school and prepared for the baccalaureate and the licentiate, "which saved the houses of Spain and the religious and the moral formation of the children!"[79] Some religious also studied in Madrid after 1933. Franco's government assimilated schools of religious congregations to those of the state on condition that the majority of the teachers had university degrees. A new plan of studies was adopted in 1941.[80] The boarding schools established preparation for the baccalaureate and were recognized as centers of secondary education.[81]

In Belgium, Mother Symon extended the classical humanities, which permitted studies at Louvain. After an unsuccessful attempt at Jette, she started classes in Greek and Latin humanities in Brussels.[82] In 1926 she gave Mother de Burlet the task of creating higher courses at Ixelles, suitable to prepare young women between seventeen and nineteen for their familial and social mission while offering quality teaching and providing "a transition between their life as a child and as a young woman and an apprenticeship in liberty by the progressive substitution of personal, interior discipline to the external discipline of rules."[83] It was not a question of creating a teaching method[84] but of pursuing the acquisition of general culture: "Our highest class is stronger, better adapted to modern requirements; everything converges toward the spiritual, intellectual, social, familial formation, complete feminine and Christian formation in a happy, fully Sacred Heart atmosphere."[85] These courses attracted young women from other European countries and from America. They contributed to the modernization of the work of the *grandes pensionnaires*.[86]

---

[79] *Lettres annuelles*, 1959-1961, p. 95. They even made sure that the way the girls dressed would not attract attention.

[80] *Lettres annuelles*, 1959-1961, p. 95.

[81] In Lima, the pupils of Chalet and León de Andrade took examinations before a national board for the first time in December 1932 (M. Recavarren, p. 61).

[82] *Vie de la R.M. Symon*, pp. 146-147. A complete section was established at the Rue du Cerf in 1935 and at Lindthout in 1941-1942. A section of modern humanities was instituted later at Lindthout. Similar programs were adopted in Congo.

[83] *Vie...Symon*, pp. 145-146.

[84] In Belgium, convents established to house university students were called *pédagogies*. They had to be approved by the rector of the university and keep university rules.

[85] O. Biolley, p. 88.

[86] The superior class at Lindthout was suppressed in order to foster the development of courses at Ixelles (*Lettres annuelles*, 1961-1963, p. 59).

Monique Luirard

In Austria Mother von Kuenburg, who became mistress of studies of the vicariate in 1926, reorganized the secondary school studies, basing them on sciences and modern languages. In collaboration with religious of other congregations, she edited literature and history textbooks that were adopted in the schools of the country. The quality of the studies to which she gave impetus in Vienna enabled the school to obtain a teaching license equal to that of the public high schools.[87] But Mother von Kuenburg "deplored the fashion that pushed women toward university studies, turning them away from the home, their natural field of action." In accord with a minister of public instruction who shared her point of view, she opened domestic science schools aimed at forming "truly complete women capable of meeting their obligations as mothers, wives and mistresses of the household." One is not very far away from the "feminine humanities" realized in other countries, but Mother von Kuenburg, who sought excellence in everything, set up a four-year course.[88]

Life in the Institutions

The boarding schools continued to recruit among the population that had always sent their daughters to the Sacred Heart. The uniforms might have changed in accordance with fashion; the education founded on the same principles as before still attracted pupils. As Mother Vicente wished, the Sacred Heart had to "hold to the good manners that must remain the distinctive mark of our children; not to allow slackening in discipline, silence, respect; that would be to lose our spirit."[89]

A description of the boarding school at Lindthout was given by a prestigious pupil and commented on humorously by a Belgian religious. In October 1919, Princess Marie-José of Belgium entered the fourth class, one of 152 boarders:

> She proved to be simple, cheerful, even naughty, distracted and disorderly; consequently, another pupil in her class was put in charge of keeping their two desks in the study hall in order.[90] Her success in studies was

---

[87] The gymnasium in Vienna had lay teachers from its beginning in 1926.
[88] *Lettres annuelles*, 1959-1961, pp. 252-253.
[89] Gen. Arch. C I C 3, Box 14. General Congregation of 1935.
[90] An apartment was set aside for her, but she used it very little, as she was almost always a day pupil. Sometimes her father came to call for her to her delight because King Albert allowed her to take her cage of white mice, which the driver refused! (*Lettres annuelles*, 1958-1961, p. 63). It seems that the royal couple's choice of Lindthout was due to the "tact, prudence and distinction" of the superior, Mother Jacquemin.

adequate, nothing more, but her presence attracted to the boarding school adolescents of the Belgian nobility while the French who were still numerous were flattered to be in such surroundings. On 4 July 1923, the princess was received as a member of the Academy of Leo XIII, founded in imitation of the one at Jette, and she gave a presentation on her trip to Lake Maggiore, already thinking about Prince Umberto of Italy, whom she was destined to marry. Finally, on 24 July 1924, she was received as a Child of Mary, at the point of death, and two days later, the 26th, her brother, Prince Léopold, presided at the distribution of prizes, as shy as the pupils to whom he was giving books and floral crowns. Religious and children had their eyes fixed on this 'charming prince' so young and handsome whose tragic destiny was as yet unknown!"[91]

During her exile, Queen Marie-José wrote her memoirs and described life at Lindthout thus:

The discipline was strict; every pretext was used to put us in ranks, and clappers gave the signal for general movement. The curtsey was part of the education of the girls. The courses were given exclusively by the nuns, almost all French, in their black habits and veils, their faces framed by a fluted white frill. Distinguished and cultivated, they inculcated in us an education that reflected the times: nothing too deep, a little bit of everything so as to shine in social life. However, I have good memories of those years at boarding school, but my father completed my general culture by numerous readings that I had to summarize.[92]

The Belgian religious concluded shrewdly: "She says nothing about the religious formation, which was also of the times, but which produced many vocations among her companions!"

At Craiglockhart in Scotland, life in the boarding school was not that of a public school.

They were two different worlds. The difference was social and there was a bit of snobbery. There was no real curriculum in the boarding school, no examinations either: they began just as I was leaving. Silence was obligatory, but we practiced it without even thinking about it. The difference between a Sacred Heart school and another was that at the Sacred Heart they gave more prizes and prizes that did not exist elsewhere.[93]

---

[91] Prov. Arch. Belgium-Netherlands. *Notes sur la maison de Lindthout*, pp. 6 and 7.
[92] *Albert et Elisabeth de Belgique, mes Parents*, pp. 322-323.
[93] Testimony of J. Stephenson.

The Prize of Excellence was rarely given because to be awarded it the student had to be first blue ribbon and first medallion, to excel in keeping the rule, to earn the highest number of points for daily work, to merit first place most often in the competitions, to merit the prizes of good conduct, of Christian doctrine, of distinction in studies and of diligence. All of this presupposed ease in studies, hard work, and the qualities required for excellence in conduct and school work. At Mount Anville,

> Certain religious were more friendly than others, but it was not difficult to communicate with them. We did not have much contact with the superior. We were sent to her when we had been really very naughty. The Mothers Assistant were always very friendly. The coadjutrix sisters were our great friends. They were so human.[94]
>
> It is claimed that Sacred Heart schools did not encourage friendships and that people lived anonymously there. That is not true. The truth is that in the boarding school no one referred to the family background of the pupils. Therefore, they were judged on their own merits. The rule was strict about contacts with the nuns. We were not allowed to have meetings with them one on one. That had to do with propriety, but we could have a talk with them if they wished it. I did not feel constrained in my relations with them. During recreation, a pupil used to play the piano and the others danced; a nun was there to watch us, knitting all the while. We could go and speak to her. I was not conscious of this rule when I was a boarder. It was only later when I entered the Society that I discovered it. Its strictness apropos of interpersonal relations was probably due to the Society's French origin and to the fact that the nuns had a real horror of sentimentality.[95]

There is little information about the day schools. After World War I in Halifax, talented directors organized book clubs and games for adolescents on Sunday afternoons to keep them busy and to prevent their getting into trouble. Some pupils learned music according to the method used at Pius X School at Manhattanville. Scouting appeared in 1921 and was opened to girls during the following ten years. The questions Mother Eleanor Sullivan used to ask her former students were along the lines of the following: "Show me your hands," for she wanted to know whether or not they smoked. "How long has it been since you went to confession?" Then she used to inquire about their progress in school.[96]

---

[94] Testimony of Mary O'Connor.
[95] Testimony of J. Stephenson.
[96] Isobel Page, *College Street Remembered*, n. d.

After World War I, the social milieu of the pupils remained approximately the same as before, but still there was some movement. The institutions in Budapest offer an example. At Durer sor, the pupils came from the upper class.[97] On the other hand, at the *Sophianum,* founded in 1917, where Mother von Schaffgotsch wanted to open a *gymnasium* and raise the level of the studies, the pupils came mostly from the middle class. At the beginning of the 1930's Durer sor became a language school that was not at first recognized by the state. The establishment developed and recruited pupils from the business and professional worlds.[98] In Halifax, the day school recruited most of its pupils from the middle class.

Development of Normal Schools

The Society of the Sacred Heart pursued the training of teachers. Some countries of Europe, North and South America and Japan[99] had normal schools. They were twinned with primary schools in which students did their practice teaching or with boarding schools, or else they were the only educational work of the Society in a given city or area. As the normal schools tended to grow, the result was to move the boarding school, a practice that allowed both to grow while respecting the specific nature of each. Some were of short duration. The one opened in 1924 at San Luis Potosí, Mexico, had to close because it did not obtain government recognition of its examinations. The apostolate begun at Valença in Brazil closed quickly.[100]

Normal schools evolved in relation to changes in legislation. In Peru, the training was redesigned by a British nun, Alice McVeigh, who had taught at the normal school at Saint Charles in London, where she had studied education. For twelve years, she implemented the curriculum of Saint Charles at San Pedro; she modernized the methodology and created a library.[101] On 23 June 1928, the Peruvian government transformed the normal school in Lima into a national teachers' college, the only one in the country. The Sacred Heart therefore trained both elementary and secondary school teachers. The alumnae/i who left it "worked efficaciously throughout the country. They held important positions in administration and influenced the education of

---

[97] From 1918 a baccalaureate class was held there. A free day school operated in the afternoon.

[98] The first baccalaureate was conferred in 1940.

[99] In Tokyo, the course taught in English lasted three years. It included religion and Japanese literature. History was added.

[100] The General Congregation of 1946 recorded its closing.

[101] At her arrival in Peru the books were still in manuscript (*Lettres annuelles,* 1958-1961, pp. 251-252).

thousands of students in the schools, colleges and major institutions"[102] of Peru. At Sarriá, students of the normal school created in 1925 also took courses at the University of Barcelona. In Tokyo, the *Semmon Gakko* founded in 1916 offered young Japanese the highest level of studies to which they could aspire. In the end, it had 300 students.[103] Starting from this normal school, after World War II the Society opened a university college in Tokyo.

Access to New Cultural Worlds

While continuing to progress in Latin America and founding new houses in Brazil, Colombia and Argentina,[104] the Society of the Sacred Heart developed in the Far East and in Southeast Asia and entered Africa.

Flowering of the Work in Japan

In Tokyo in ten years the boarding school had become mostly Japanese, populated by pupils whose parents had been posted abroad and wanted a western education for their daughters. In 1917, it grew by about fifty Russian exiles whose presence lasted some years.[105] The development of the works of the Sacred Heart, from Japanese kindergarten to normal school and foreign schools, unfolded during the Taishō era[106] when changes in policy and the culture of the country caused Japan to make a transition from tradition to modernity. In 1911, new treaties put an end to the unequal treaties of 1858. The industrial takeoff of the end of the nineteenth century increased the rural exodus. The appearance of the cities was still traditional. Aside from administration and commercial buildings in stone, the houses were almost entirely made of wood. The gigantic earthquake that destroyed the greater part of Tokyo in September 1923 accelerated changes in this regard.

---

[102] M. Recavarren, p. 59. 1118 elementary school teachers and 193 secondary school teachers were trained at the normal school in Lima before 1952. In 1910 the alumnae of the normal school formed an association that offered continuing education in the religious, social and professional domains and allowed them to maintain their family spirit.
[103] *Lettres annuelles*, 1961-1963, p. 181.
[104] A second foundation in Colombia, in Medellín, took place in 1930. It was rapidly followed by the one in Manizales. A novitiate was opened in Buenos Aires in 1935.
[105] Many White Russians left Japan for Shanghai.
[106] It coincided with the reign of Emperor Yoshihito, 1912 to 1926, and was followed by the Shōwa Era (1926-1989), the name given at the accession of Emperor Hirohito.

It happened that the vicar of Australia, Mother Salmon, was visiting at the time. The fires multiplied in a chain reaction fed by domestic hearths and by the collapse of vats of petrol in the harbor of Yokohama. At Sankocho, about forty kilometers from the epicenter, the quake began as the community gathered for adoration of the Blessed Sacrament. The steel supports of the brick walls of the chapel slowed down the collapse of the building and saved the lives of the religious. The walls shook, then fell down:

> Mother Sheldon seized the monstrance that was lying in the midst of the debris. She gave it to Mother Salmon who went down the one remaining staircase, followed by the community. A few of the nuns gathered up the office books as they passed; others took apples and bread from the tables in the refectory. Mother Sheldon went to get the ciborium and placed it beside the monstrance on a bench, while everyone knelt in adoration and supplication. The role was called: all were safe. The caretaker came in the afternoon when 222 small tremors were still shaking the city, which was on fire. The terror and suffering of millions of people who were crowded in the narrow streets were beyond description. A tidal wave from the bay of Yokohama brought with it burning gasoline[107] and further increased the panic of the dazed population.

The nuns camped in makeshift shelters and did the cooking under umbrellas. They had lost almost everything and were touched to see Jesuits appear to inquire about their fate and Japanese friends bring a little food, even toothbrushes, and invite them to make use of their houses, which miraculously remained intact. The earthquake was truly breathtaking. As Mother Salmon admitted later: "I was really happy to have been there at that moment, for I would never have been able to imagine from afar how frightening it was." The Australian government proposed repatriating its citizens, but Mother Sheldon decided that the work would continue.

School reopened on 1 October 1923, in borrowed houses or in huts.[108] Another earthquake on 1 January 1924 destroyed what remained of Sankocho. As Mother Sheldon summed it up, the event was a spiritual experience for everyone:

> If such a concern, borne together, has made us all so dear to one another, what must it be for the Lord? Now I understand better the words: 'I am with you in trials.' And who knows whether one of the reasons for what we have undergone has not given us a motive to love one another more?

---

[107] M. Williams, *The Society…Far East*, p. 60.
[108] About thirty pupils were sent to Mother Mayer's house.

The story of the past year shows clearly that our life here below is only a passage through exterior appearances that are not important.[109]

The Society showed its solidarity in sending things destined to help the religious in their daily life. The reconstruction of Sankocho, begun in 1925, continued for several years. In April 1928, it was finally possible to begin to use one building.[110]

The imperial regime was modernizing the country while relying on national tradition. Its doctrines and its institutions were centered on the person of the emperor, the *Tennō*, for the dynasty came before the state and the nation. In the past, the state and the nation had taken a moralistic religious tone and respect for the authorities, and they had as an ideal to ensure the well-being of the people. The monarchy was sacred. During her stay in Japan, Mother Stuart had recommended to the religious to be respectful of the customs of the country. When Emperor Yoshihito was crowned on 10 November 1915, two pines were planted in honor of the imperial couple. In the afternoon,

> Everyone assembled in the reception hall. We bowed in the direction of Kyoto; the *Kimigayo* was sung and the rescript of the deceased emperor read. Reverend Mother Heydon mounted the platform and congratulated the children on this long line of emperors, the longest in the world, that had governed Japan. She told them that the most sublime of all sacrifices had been offered that morning for the imperial family, and she presented loyalty as a duty toward all authority, correctly constituted, small or great. At three thirty, everyone went out to hear the cannon announce the precise moment when the emperor mounted the throne, to the sound of bells and the noise of whistles. Then Reverend Mother said *Tennō heika benzai*[111] three times and everyone repeated the acclamations.[112]

While the community accepted participating in Shinto rites in honor of the emperor, they did not do so without some problems of conscience. It was only in May 1936 that Pius XI permitted Catholics to take part in them, a year after authorizing the veneration of images of Confucius according to ancestral customs. The principles that the Sacred Heart was handing on, respect for political and familial authority and charity toward

---

[109] M. Williams, *The Society...Far East*, p. 62.
[110] As the Japanese government did not permit the building of a chapel for want of materials, Mother Sheldon made use of a stratagem. She had a large hall built into which she placed the stalls.
[111] It was the traditional viva; the meaning is: "Long live his Majesty the Emperor."
[112] M. Williams, *The Society...Far East*, p. 52.

the neediest persons,[113] were likely to be well received in Japan — although disconnected from their religious foundations — for they coincided with the *samurai* tradition. They also suited the middle class that was developing as a result of economic modernization based on the "way of the merchant," the counterpart of the "way of the warrior." Protected against foreign competition by the imperial regime, the middle class began to act like the Japanese aristocracy and adopted a level of life style and culture similar to it. Middle class families sent their children to the same schools as the aristocrats and created matrimonial alliances with them. The marriage in 1959 of an alumna of Sankocho and the Sacred Heart University, Michiko Shoda, a commoner, daughter of an upper class executive, with Prince Akihito was simultaneously an innovation, since it was the first time such a marriage had taken place in the imperial family, and the symbol of the evolution that had been going on for decades. The Sacred Heart was capable of accepting representatives of every social class in Japan as elsewhere.

Doubtless this flexibility in the face of a new cultural universe allowed the congregation to develop. A foundation made in Kobe in 1923 was transferred to Sumiyoshi and finally to Obayashi between Osaka and Kobe in 1926. The rebuilding of Sankocho did not allow further expansion, and foundations asked for at Okoyama, Fukuoka, Oizumi and Kyoto were refused or postponed. Although religious formation necessitated leaving Japan, Japanese were asking to enter the Sacred Heart.[114] The first Japanese professed, Kiyoko Iwashita, returned to Japan in 1926, and a Far Eastern vicariate was confided to Mother Sheldon. A religious from the United States was sent there in 1923. The vicariate was reinforced by Canadians, nuns from the United States and numerous Maltese.[115] It remained under Anglophone influence.[116]

---

[113] During the crisis of 1929, Mother Mayer, superior at Obayashi, had the Sisters of Charity come to Osaka, where the poorest of the population suffered particularly. Their charitable activity was largely supported by the *Seishin Gakuin* (*Lettres annuelles,* 1954-1958, p. 413).

[114] Testimony of Brigid Keogh. The first Japanese was accepted in Belgium, the second in England. Mother Salmon had not accepted them in Japan.

[115] Between 1926 and 1938 four French, three Belgians, two Germans, a Spaniard, three Irish, a Swede, one from Luxemburg, three Poles, two Hungarians and nineteen Maltese arrived in the vicariate. Some of these reached China. Seventeen of them died in Japan before 1982.

[116] Testimony of Hiroko Okui and Sawako Kageyama.

Monique Luirard

Entry into China[117]

Like many other Catholics, the Religious of the Sacred Heart dreamed of seeing Christianity revived in China. When in 1854, after the opium war and the opening of China to the West, Mother Barat had received a request for a foundation, she had not followed it up because the safety of foreigners was not certain, and she did not have at her disposal a person of Philippine Duchesne's moral fiber to send. A new attempt in 1867 failed. Bishops who visited informed the Society of the Sacred Heart of what was happening in China. They interested the pupils in their works, in particular that of the Holy Childhood in support of abandoned babies.

After the Sino-Japanese War that ended in 1895 with the dismemberment of China, an anti-Christian persecution broke out in 1897. The Boxers in 1900 took aim at legations as well as missions; it was apparent that in the eyes of the Chinese, religious and political interests, Christianity and western imperialism were confused. The rebellion was subdued and foreign powers further dominated the Middle Kingdom, circumscribing their zones of influence and reducing its authority to very few areas. A new appeal to found an establishment of English language in Canton was addressed to the Society of the Sacred Heart in 1909, with no more success than the earlier ones. Three years later, the disappearance of the Manchu dynasty and the proclamation of the Republic unleashed a cycle of violence that was to last for more than ten years. The central power, held first by Sun Yat-sen, did not succeed in prevailing over the warlords who, owing to the troubles, set up veritable fiefs where they maintained private armies and pressured the population. They had appointed protectors, British in central China, French in the South, Japanese in Manchuria and Soviets in the region of Canton. China was experiencing unprecedented chaos.

The concessions, foreign enclaves, were maintained. They constituted autonomous zones, benefited from extraterritoriality and offered guarantees to the Chinese who lived or took refuge there.[118] The capital of Jiangsu, Shanghai was a tripartite city, administered by an urban élite in the international concession, by a consul in the French concession

---

[117] Besides Margaret Williams' work, see Madeleine Chi, *Shanghai Sacred Heart: Risk in Faith, 1926-1952*, Saint Louis, 2001.

[118] It was in the French Concession in Shanghai that the first congress of the Chinese Communist Party took place in 1921. In the last years of World War I, France recruited many Chinese coolies to replace its labor force that had been mobilized. These workers and the students who had gone to France were exposed to communism. Zhou En-lai, the future official of the Communist Republic, was one of the group of Chinese who lived in the Paris region.

and by Chinese authorities in the part of the city that extended into the surroundings. It had become the principal center of modern industry in China, thanks to light industries and food processing. Its textiles and its workshops where silk and cotton were spun made it famous. The city had developed when World War I deprived China of imports from Europe. Shanghai dominated the industry of the Lower Yangzhi; it was the principal commercial port of China and an important financial market. The working class there lived in sub-human conditions. The local middle class was attracted to western civilization.

Catholic missionaries, often of European origin, were numerous in the center and South of China. They had developed parish life and founded many orphanages, while Protestant missions, often supported by the United States, had created social service and educational institutions at all levels including university that appealed strongly to the local population. In 1903 the Jesuits, who were in charge of pastoral care in Nanking, had founded Aurora University in the French concession in Shanghai. In the 1920's they sent out a new appeal to the Society. They envisaged the transfer of the Helpers of the Holy Souls to Nanking and proposed that the Sacred Heart take charge of the European school that the Helpers had been running up to that time. Mother von Loë authorized a preliminary exploration. Mother Sheldon, superior in Tokyo, and Mother Conchita Nourry, designated as superior of the foundation, went to Shanghai to make the necessary contacts and visit the house intended for them. In September and October 1926 eight religious arrived in China, five from Europe and three from Canada.[119] At first, they directed a day school.

The Society of the Sacred Heart entered China at the moment when Pope Pius XI consecrated the first six Chinese bishops, thus giving the country a native hierarchy. He recommended to missionaries not to support the political interests of their own countries. Central and South China were in full development. In Canton, the Guomindang had decided to reunify the country and eliminate the warlords. The *Beifa*, the great expedition toward the North of China begun in 1926, was accompanied by a series of peasant and worker uprisings and by anti-foreign agitation.

A general strike launched by the Communists in Shanghai in February 1927 turned to revolution. The safety of foreigners and of missionaries was not certain, and Mother Nourry thought about sending the youngest of the community to Japan. She welcomed the Helpers of the Holy Souls,

---

[119] Two French, Gabrielle Borson and Hélène de Guigné; an Englishwoman, Mary Foy; and two Maltese aspirants, Maria Camilleri and Josephine Fenech. The nuns from Canada were Sarah Fitzgerald, Florence Manley and Sarah Saint Arnaud.

who lived in a dangerous zone of the French concession near the Chinese city. During that painful period, the nuns prayed part of the night: "I think I have never prayed so much in my whole life," wrote Mother Nourry later. The Chinese troops respected the concessions. The rest of the Guomindang split into factions. In the course of a fierce repression, Chiang Kai-shek had thousands of Communists massacred, though he had been allied with them before. He transferred his capital to Nanking.

The mission of the Sacred Heart began in this context. The establishment inaugurated in 1928 was a foreign school recognized by the French authorities who assisted it financially in proportion to the number of French pupils it accepted, but they did not intervene in its functioning. It had two sections, English and French, and at its apogee in 1936-37, it counted two hundred and forty pupils of twenty different nationalities, two thirds of whom were in the English section.

The city of Shanghai, whose wealth was coveted both by the Nationalists and by the Communists, was undergoing complete social change. The fusion of the former literary elites with the business communities that had developed after the opening of the ports to foreigners had given birth to a middle class concerned about adaptation to the contemporary world. They sought to reconcile tradition and modernity and did not hesitate to have their children educated in foreign schools. The Chinese scholastic system was a composite marked by European and American influences. It was founded on a tradition that many intellectuals believed susceptible of reinterpretation in relation to the demands of each era. It was only in 1932 that the Religious of the Sacred Heart were able to open a Chinese primary school, recognized in 1934, whose head was a lay woman, Mme Zhang Aimo. Only one religious, Mother Ines Saint-Germain, taught in it. It was a day school with modest costs for middle class children. Shanghai was the very type of cosmopolitan city in which an international congregation could find itself at ease, above all if respect for tradition and family was one of its principles.

The Society of the Sacred Heart had plans for expansion. In 1932, it received a request for Canton that it did not consider because of the chronic insecurity in the South. The religious wanted to have a house close to Shanghai that would allow them to open another school and a place for vacation. The island of Zhoushan, a half day's journey by boat, was doubtless not the most suitable place for such a foundation. However, Hangzhou and above all Suzhou, with famous gardens and canals, half way to Nanking, where Chinese of high society liked to go, seemed possible locations for this foundation. The Society would open a boarding school for

Chinese. Finally, however, the motherhouse decided in favor of developing Shanghai.

From 1934 on the Jesuits were asking the Religious of the Sacred Heart to open a university college for Chinese girls who had studied in Catholic schools, for such an establishment did not exist anywhere in China. Aurora Women's College was inaugurated on the eve of the outbreak of the Sino-Japanese War in September 1937. It functioned on the American model. The following year the Religious of the Sacred Heart opened a Chinese secondary school whose graduates could go on to the college. The courses began to the sound of bombardments, and the walls of the college building went up in the light of the fires. As it was not prudent to accept boarders, the dormitories were occupied by some Franciscan Missionaries of Mary whose hospital had been evacuated.

Congo

The Congo was recognized by the Congress of Berlin as the personal possession of King Leopold II of Belgium and placed under his sovereignty. It became a Belgian colony in 1908, thanks to a royal legacy. Missions created by Catholic congregations of men and women and by Anglo-American and Swedish Protestant missions had squared off this vast territory. The Belgian administration granted indisputable support to the first. The Convention of Jonghe in 1926 transferred public instruction in Congo to the Church.

Mother Symon, the vicar of Belgium, was sensitive to the situation of families whose father, whether in military or civil service, lived in the colony without his family. The Sacred Heart was approached to open a metropolitan school, since the authorities thought that the assurance of being able to send their children to school would motivate the wives of colonials to go to Congo.[120] In 1925 stimulated by the missionary exhibit that had just taken place, Mother Symon went to Rome to lay her plans before Mother von Loë. After obtaining permission, she approached the Jesuits who were in charge of the apostolic vicariate of Kisantu and the ministry of the Colonies. Civil and religious authorities were favorable to the establishment of the Society in Congo, for there was an acknowledged lack to fill in what concerned the education of girls. The colonial administration promised a grant of six hectares (about fifteen acres) at Kalina, the residential section of Leopoldville, subsidies to assist in the installation and the loan of two houses until a building could be completed. On her part Mother Symon reflected on what life would be like for the

---

[120] Clotilde Meeûs, *Profil de l'histoire de la province du Congo*.

religious in Africa, for she realized that adaptation would be necessary in living quarters and in the habit. It was in Congo that Religious of the Sacred Heart wore white habits for the first time; afterwards they would wear white in any hot climate.[121]

The departure of the five founders,[122] accompanied by Mother Symon, cheered on by the alumnae, took place on 3 November 1926. On the quay at Antwerp, "there was a crush, for besides their relatives, the good religious had convoked delegations of pupils and teachers from all their houses in Belgium." It was a way of making known the fact that the vicariate from then on had the responsibility and duty of making this mission survive. Later, 17% of the Belgian religious had a longer or shorter stay in Congo.

The voyage lasted more than three weeks. Aboard the ship were religious of different orders; there were some Africans among the crew.[123] On 17 November, "We arrived in sight of the cliffs of Banana, the land of our desires!" wrote Mother Braun. "The rocks were overhung with poinciana, bursting with red flowers that the sun's rays rendered even more resplendent." At Boma, still the capital of Congo, the governor general of the colony and the inspector of education were hardly encouraging: "Ten years from now you won't have twenty children in your classes; Congo is not made for Europeans." The religious crossed the "cauldron of hell" that the ships went through at full speed and disembarked at Matadi, where they took a train in a tropical storm: "We were soaked to the bone; our caps offered a lamentable spectacle; impossible to stay in that state for thirteen hours in the train; it was necessary to take turns changing our clothes completely in the back of the car while the other travelers spontaneously turned towards the front." By stages they were lodged in missions and initiated "what could be a boarding school for black children." For Mother Symon the first shock was the silence: "We walk under a starry sky. The silence of Africa is impressive, one hears only the sound of insects, crickets

---

[121] Prov. Arch. Belgium-Netherlands. The work by Abbé Joseph Bubois, nephew of Mother Françoise Braun, one of the founders, based on her letters and memories, enables the reader to follow closely the first band of missionaries, thanks to a much more realistic account than the one in Mother Symon's biography.

[122] C. Meeûs, *Histoire de la province du Congo 1927-2000*. They were Françoise Braun, Clémence Claes, Alice Dethiou, Catherine Bleumers and Florentine Tinant. A reinforcement of nine religious arrived in 1931; five others were sent in 1935. One of the founders returned before 1931, and a Polish sister died at sea in 1937 on her way back to Belgium.

[123] "We have the joy of meeting them from time to time, and their good, intelligent faces light up at our smiles" (*Mitte me*, 1962, N° 2, p. 43). In fact, they met them the day they visited the machine room in the hold.

and others; I don't know which ones make a sound like little bells."[124] But Mother Braun alluded to insects, serpents and gigantic, venomous spiders. The Jesuits had them visit the existing missions. The new arrivals discovered the local customs and met Belgian nuns, some of whom were alumnae of the Sacred Heart. In Kalina the welcome of some of the male religious was hardly cordial; one of them said: "What have you come to do in Congo? There is nothing for you here. At least you can teach how to curtsey!" The founders had to manage on their own to find their land grant. They settled in two houses of twelve meters on a side divided by a hall with two large rooms on one side and a small room and a kitchen on the other. The day pupils had to be put in one room.[125] The administration lent the services of some Congolese imprisoned for not paying taxes to clear the land and build on it. In the group were some children seven or eight years old.

The Sacred Heart settled in Leopoldville a short time before the city became the capital of Congo. After three years the day school counted seventy-five children. "They arrive ignorant even to the sign of the Cross," wrote Mother Braun. "The parents have no time to take charge of them, and their stay is unfortunately interrupted by returns to Europe for holidays; it is a great obstacle to regular teaching."[126] A studio for women and a library for colonials were launched. The church, built in 1932, became a parish center for families of all nationalities who lived nearby. In 1936 the number of pupils had doubled, and a new wing of the building housed classrooms and a junior school. The school at Kalina accepted boys until the establishment of a school by the Jesuits. In 1937, it had a thousand pupils. The presence of the Sacred Heart in Congo encouraged colonization: "The question of education being resolved, colonists may now settle with their families in this part of Congo, an incalculable advantage, not only for family unity, but still more for the moral level and the future of the colony."[127] The objective of the foundation was "to awaken the mentality of Europeans to the understanding of their responsibility." "We will have accomplished a significant work, an indirect apostolate among Blacks by direct action with the Whites."[128]

In spite of the hesitation of Mother Vicente, who wondered if opening a school for the African population was not premature, Mother Symon

---

[124] *Vie de la R.M. Symon*, p. 155.

[125] *Mitte me*, 1962, N° 2, p. 44. The day school for white children was opened on 2 January 1928, with one boy and two little girls. Three months later there were twelve. It also included children from other European countries. Queen Elisabeth of Belgium visited it in July 1928.

[126] *Mémoires de l'abbé Bubois*, p. 6.

[127] *Vie de la R.M. Symon*, p. 163.

[128] C. Meeûs, *Histoire*, p. 1. House journal.

obtained authorization to open a station in the bush.[129] Land had been provided at Mbansa-Mboma, but it was at Kipako that the Religious of the Sacred Heart made a foundation in 1930: "It was less a question of creating something than of preventing the little that existed from falling into abandonment." The Jesuits had a few classes for boys, but they were occupied above all in instructing catechumens, a task all the more urgent as Kipako was the only Catholic center in a radius of twenty kilometers, and the population had been won over to Protestantism and to Kibanguism.[130] In Congo and in Rwanda and Burundi, there had not been a division of territory among different churches. The White Fathers, the Jesuits, the Scheut Fathers and the Spiritans did not hesitate to settle in proximity to Protestant missions in a strongly competitive spirit. Acting on the same pastoral logic, the Sacred Heart did the same.

Welcomed according to traditional rites and overwhelmed with gifts of chickens and eggs, the religious settled in their quarters, which they first had to clean and sanitize. When people saw them bravely at work, the prejudice that had preceded them fell away. Mother Braun noted:

> Kipako was truly poverty in all its rigor, not to say misery. The dwelling made of sun-dried bricks was covered by a thatched roof; it had no glass in the windows; when it rained, we had to close the shutters and move about in the dark cautiously, for the floor was open-work; the outside staircase had no handrail; anyone could climb at will, even those unbearable and indiscreet goats. But the view extended beyond the green hills to a wide horizon of blue mountains.

The boarding school lodged the pupils, not according to their ages, which they did not know, but according to their size. It provided religious training alternating with work in the fields. Lessons in household work took place out of doors. The nuns also undertook the training of monitors for the first primary class and after 1937 prepared girls for marriage in a program called the apostolate of *fiancées*. They organized retreats for adult men and women and opened a dispensary. At the beginning, "It consisted of a straw hut that lacked everything. The nurse pulled teeth with a pair of bicycle pliers. Soon we had a sort of hospital with twelve mats; the beds came later; a doctor visited our sick once a month."[131] In 1933, Mother Braun returned

---

[129] A month after their arrival in Congo, Mothers Symon and Braun had visited Kipako and Mbansa-Mboma.
[130] *Vie de la R.M. Symon*, p. 161, and Mémoires de l'abbé Bubois.
[131] Memories of Mother Braun, *Mémoires de l'abbé Bubois*, p. 7.

to Belgium; and by means of funds she collected, she was able to have a permanent building constructed:

> The atmosphere in our little community was joyful, happy and fervent; nothing of modern comfort; water from the spring was scarce; it was necessary to carefully collect as much rain water as possible; meat was rare; we hardly used canned food; it was only later that we could buy supplies in the European style market in Leo.

A year later the school had one hundred and thirty-seven pupils, day pupils and boarders, who did the cooking every evening around the fire.

From 1934 on, the motherhouse was being informed that a new project was in the offing:

> The government has given us a grant of one hundred twenty hectares to put to use before 1938. Besides the necessity of going forward vis-à-vis the government, Kipako is too small and the soil too worn out to nourish the present population of children. From the apostolic viewpoint, the region of Mbansa-Mboma has an extreme need of missionaries, for it is invaded by Protestantism.[132]

In 1939, the station of Mbansa-Mboma was inaugurated.[133] Mother Braun wanted to create an educational establishment there for young women called *évoluées* who had recently come from the bush. Its purpose was "to allow them to catch up with their future husbands who were already technicians and employees living in the city." The beginnings were modest. The nuns started by opening a primary school for village children. The mission included a large hall surrounded by arcaded galleries, quarters for a community of five, two rectangular pavilions with four classes in each, one for the girls and one for the boys. There was a boarding section in the bush flanked by a day school, which developed after the war. Toward the same epoch, the religious began to make a monthly tour of the villages, offering sewing classes, catechizing and weighing babies.

---

[132] C. Meeûs, *Histoire*, p. 17.
[133] When Mother Zurstrassen visited Congo in 1938, she realized how ingenious the construction of the house was: "What a task; in Belgium we have no idea what it takes. Everything has to be done on the spot: making the bricks, cutting down trees for wood for the floors; figuring out how to make the iron tenons to hold the metal sheets, finding workmen, teaching them the trade and furnishing the tools. It means being an architect, entrepreneur, mason, carpenter all at once. If scaffolding is needed, the Blacks take vines from the forest (27 June 1938).

The Religious of the Sacred Heart had entered into a new cultural milieu, and through their establishment in the bush they discovered the local liturgy that integrated dance and the sound of the drum. Mother Symon strove to fight against racism. It seemed to her that "the work with the Blacks has the characteristics that permit it to become a true work of the Society." In 1930, when Kipako was founded, she said to the nuns who were going to live there that their mission was

> to make the divine Heart of Jesus known and loved, to devote themselves to his glory; this is paradise on earth, said our holy Mother Foundress. Here more than ever, we must work to achieve this end. We must realize it by the constant, interior preoccupation that prayer develops, union with Our Lord in work. Not to let ourselves be overwhelmed by the external task, not to let ourselves be deterred by accidentals, to see beyond, otherwise *élan* disappears; not to let ourselves be limited, that is to say, absorbed in our own task, our own circle. See the world, Africa, Congo, the region, the whole Church. We must have a passion for his Kingdom, to be consumed interiorly, that is, to offer ourselves to his domination more and more radically, even to substitution; no more I, but him. Not to confuse exterior consuming of oneself with the interior. Devotedness is indispensable but insufficient; what he is waiting for in order to act is a pure, holy, immaculate oblation.[134]

In 1933, she gave the following directives to the religious who were going to live among the indigenous people:

> At the base of rapport with the Blacks, we must place the respect due to every human being; we must treat as human beings those whom we want to educate to be human beings. Still less may we treat without respect those whom we want to educate, not only as human beings, but as Christians. The message of Christ is a message of raising up the human; it is the announcement of royalty, of divinization.... And if we find ourselves faced with weakness, respect is all the more required, that respect of the delicate essence that resides in the noble soul and that elevates it by encouraging it. It is to imitate Christ the Savior. It is not enough to be devoted, even to kill oneself through devotedness, before all we must respect.

Respect comes about through knowledge of the milieu. Mother Symon recommended,

---

[134] *Mitte me*, 1962, N°2, p. 45.

Study the region, the race, the village, the indigenous customs, the reactions to certain events. Knowledge more or less prevents the *faux pas*, ill-considered actions, arbitrary measures, unnecessary confrontations. Know in order to take advantage of whatever in the race, the traditions, the characteristics, the attitudes is usable in raising them to the Christian plane. It is the whole person that must be Christianized, the whole life that must be placed on the Christian plane. The more one can rely on what exists already, the better it will be.... The Church used what she found in each country, in each race; she adapted to different characters.[135]

To bear fruit evangelization had to be realistic. The first Congolese vocations in 1946 came from the pupils.

India

Christian presence on the Indian sub-continent was ancient, above all in the South, in a line going from Goa to Madras. Even though very much in the minority, Christians were active. Since the end of the nineteenth century, their growth in numbers had been surpassing the natural increase of the population. Catholics outnumbered Protestants. Whatever church they belonged to, Christians had made a great effort in the area of education. Protestants had engaged more than others in higher education, including higher education for women.

The local hierarchy sent to the Society of the Sacred Heart appeals supported by the Propagation of the Faith. In 1935, the general congregation accepted a foundation in Bombay. On 20 May 1938, Mother Vicente informed the vicars that for India she was looking for

> persons in good health, who spoke a little English, who had the strength to overcome all obstacles and to tread underfoot all fears; devoted persons who did not fear giving everything in the service of the Society; who had the spirit of detachment, who held to nothing, who were somewhat optimistic, for pessimism is the evil of weak hearts; persons who are not inclined to regard the "I" who is suffering, but the Heart of Jesus who loves us and asks souls of us. I would like apostolic souls, full of God, who give him to others, lovers of prayer for they have the influence of an educator in their surroundings.[136]

---

[135] *Vie de la R.M. Symon*, pp. 171-172.
[136] *Vie de la T.R.M. Vicente*, pp. 316-317.

The foundation was entrusted to the vicariate of England for political reasons, perhaps. India had been a field of rivalries for western countries, which had established trading companies there since the beginning of the nineteenth century. In spite of periodic instances of native resistance, the country had been colonized by Great Britain, and after the fall of the Moghul Empire in 1858, it entered the Empire. In 1935, India had received a special status that provided for the organization of a federation with a central government and autonomous states and provinces, but the *British India Act* had not been received universally in India, and it was applied very slowly.

The three founders[137] left England on 31 December 1938. After a papal audience in Rome, they left for Bombay 4 January 1939. A second group from Britain joined them in October.[138] Their mission had different objectives from those originally foreseen. At the request of the Jesuit Archbishop Roberts, they were given charge of the formation of the Poor Sisters of Our Lady.[139] Mother Andersson visited women's colleges in Bangalore, Mangalore, Madras, Calcutta and Delhi. In May 1940, Sophia College was opened, and the University of Bombay recognized its first year on 20 June 1941. It accepted students of all religions and all castes. In June 1940, the Religious of the Sacred Heart also created a program of education in domestic and social culture.[140] World War II cut off relations between the community and the rest of the world, and it was only in February 1947 that the vicar of England, Mother Eleonora Bennett, was able to go to Bombay.

In the meantime, the works had known their ups and downs. When in 1941 the Religious of the Sacred Heart wished to extend the approbation they had received to a second year, the authorities caused problems: "We were women, British subjects and above all religious," they thought. However, affiliation of the third and fourth years was granted on 9

---

[137] The founders were Catherine Andersson, Norah Woellwarth and Dorothy Bullen.

[138] Winifred Ward, Mary Davis, Catherine Kenny. A Maltese, Marianna Camilleri, joined them later.

[139] Sara Grant, *Life of R.M.Catherine Andersson*, pp. 32-33. These religious wrote later: "We had neither rule book nor custom book nor traditions to follow, but the deep spirituality of our Mother Andersson and her fidelity to the numerous exigencies of conventual life were a powerful force to stimulate religious fervor in us. The three years of our very happy sojourn at the Convent of the Sacred Heart naturally drew us very close to the Society of the Sacred Heart, and we were proud to proclaim Saint Madeleine Sophie Barat our holy 'grandmother.'"

[140] S. Grant, p. 35.

February 1942. Shortly afterward, a grave danger presented itself causing rumors in the whole country through the campaigns in the press that followed. At a time when religious proselytism was strictly forbidden in India, the conversion and baptism of a Parsi student almost caused the college to lose its status. The threat was not carried out, but a second conversion in August 1943 aggravated the situation and resulted in the nuns being accused of infringing on the liberty of the students by using "moral persuasion." The university council tried to demand from them a promise not to assist a young woman in difficulty with her family in the case of conversion.[141] This double affair caused a decrease in enrollment in Sophia College, but the Jesuits and the local hierarchy supported the Religious of the Sacred Heart.[142] Finally, in April 1944 the university council proposed to the government to renew the affiliation of the college for three years. Recruitment of Indian religious rapidly came about, and the first Indian postulant, Gool Mary Dhalla, entered the Society of the Sacred Heart in 1945.[143]

---

[141] S. Grant, p. 41. One of them had taken refuge in the college to escape from pressure from her family.

[142] The account of these events has been reconstructed from the letter from Bombay that appeared in the typed series of *Lettres annuelles* for the years 1940-1943.

[143] Until 1956 when a novitiate was opened in Bangalore, the formation of the Indians took place in the English vicariate.

Chapter IV

PERSECUTIONS AND EXTREME IDEOLOGIES

In Europe and America, the aftermath of the war had been expected to be a time of return to normality. This dream was shattered by the crisis of 1929, which no country escaped. The years between the two wars were not peaceful. A new stage in world history was beginning: the twentieth century would prove to be an era of violence and of extremism.

Revolutions in Latin America

Latin American states tried to build national unity by using the force and prestige of Catholicism but with different political agendas, for not all the local churches held the same attitude regarding the economic and social state of affairs. The Sacred Heart did not have trouble in Chile, where in 1932 a political crisis put the lives of religious congregations in danger. Mexico, on the other hand, was the scene of a murderous confrontation between the state and the Church. Religious institutes, in particular teaching congregations of European origin, were battling in a conflict that went beyond them but was aimed at them. The Church counted on education to maintain its position and keep the loyalty of the people by attracting the elite. With the help of a liberal political regime, it had newly evangelized the country. The Society of the Sacred Heart had contributed to and benefitted from this temporary respite. By 1912 it had developed its outreach to the point of being able to enroll close to seven hundred pupils in its free school in San Luis Potosí.

The first signs of change appeared in 1909 when Porfirio Díaz wanted to angle for a new mandate. Economic development that had been given impetus during his long dictatorship had not contributed to a rise in wealth among the people. The insurrection, which began on 20 November 1910, won over the peasants, the miners and the Indians and gradually reached the whole country. Houses of the Sacred Heart were cut off from one another and were unable to communicate with Rome. Finally Díaz was forced into exile by Francisco Madero, who made himself the champion of democratic ideas and social reform. Two years later a coalition overcame Madero, who died in February 1913 during fighting between his partisans and his adversaries. However, the confrontations did not cease. In Monterrey, the nuns took refuge in the pupils' refectory; it was the only place safe from gunfire. They got off with a scare that time.[1] When the troops of General Alvaro Obregón took Guadalajara on 8 July 1914, in spite of the protection of the British consul, the Convent of the Sacred Heart was sacked and turned into barracks. On 9 July the forty-eight religious dispersed and went to private homes.[2]

The revolution took root and, in May 1914, ecclesiastics and religious were threatened with imprisonment or expulsion. Mother Stuart ordered the nuns to seek safety in the United States. On 31 August 1914, those from Guadalajara reached the coast in a special train accompanied by the British consul. They embarked with sixty priests and religious on a ship that normally transported Chinese immigrants and did not consider its passengers' comfort. After a voyage of seven days, they arrived in San Francisco and were sent from there to the Antilles, Peru, Colombia and Argentina.

Because Mexico was a federal republic, the fate of the houses of the Sacred Heart depended on the actions of the revolutionary troops. In August 1915 most of the nuns in San Luis Potosí had to take refuge in Monterrey and Mexico City.[3] Those who stayed in place opened a language school in another location, legitimized by the ministry of education. The house in Guanajuato remained open until December 1915; then the religious left for the United States and the houses in the Caribbean. The one in Mexico City suffered the least.[4] The nuns, who had hidden in the corner of a tribune, were not caught during the house searches, which the inspectors had no interest in doing thoroughly.

While confrontations continued more or less intensely between government troops and those of Zapata and Pancho Villa, a former governor of the time of Porfirio Díaz, Venustiano Carranza, assumed leadership of a "constitutionalist" movement. The constitution of Querétaro, which he had adopted in 1917, regulated the clerical profession,

---

[1] Gen. Arch. C III 2, Mexico. They spent the night of the 24th to 25th sitting on chairs.
[2] *Lettres annuelles*, 1947-1952, pp. 94-95.
[3] They had sought to obtain a reprieve in August 1914 through an interview with General Obregón when he passed through the city.
[4] It had been placed under the protection of France.

limited the exercise of worship and restrained the freedom of religious congregations to teach. But under the presidency of Carranza and Obregón there was no crisis. Therefore, in July 1923 ten religious returned to Guadalajara. "All began again as before." The pupils flocked to the boarding school and "the house was an oasis of peace and the center of a fruitful apostolate."[5]

The situation grew worse when General Plutarco Elias Calles took power in 1924. Considering Catholicism incompatible with the Mexican state and the struggle against the Church as a phase in the combat of light against darkness, he launched an extreme policy seeking without great success to give rise to a schismatic church. Then he unleashed against the clergy and those who resisted a violent and murderous repression, which was going to incite from 1926 on the popular uprising of the *Cristeros*. Sensing that persecution was coming, the vicar, Mother Lalande, gave up going to the canonization of Mother Barat.

The conditions imposed by the State on the exercise of worship and the functioning of private schools were equivalent to a direct confrontation with the Church. In January 1926, repressive legislation considered infractions in matters of worship as common law offenses and set the registration of priests with the Ministry of the Interior as a condition for the exercise of worship. The measure was aimed at reducing the number of priests and of eliminating those who were not Mexican from the clergy. Religious buildings became the property of the state. Priests and religious lost their civil identity. Worship could not even be conducted in private chapels.[6] On 14 February arrests of priests and religious began.[7] In Mexico City three days later the doors of the chapel at the Sacred Heart were sealed. Statues and religious pictures disappeared from the houses. As the superior at Monterrey wrote to the Mother General: "We are suffering very much at seeing Holy Church persecuted in our poor country. Our hearts are bitter, our Lord so offended, our holy, apostolic bishops under the weight of persecution.... We wish to console the Heart of Jesus, love him more each day."[8] On 22 February 1926, the ministry of education decided that instruction given in private institutions had to be match public school curricula, and it forbade religious congregations and ecclesiastics to conduct primary schools. Those in charge of Catholic education tried without success to counterattack. At the Sacred Heart, house searches increased.

---

[5] M. T. Guevara, pp. 75-76.

[6] A religious profession was celebrated in Mexico City on 12 February 1926, in the infirmary, which had been transformed into a chapel.

[7] Prov. Arch. Mexico. In one Sacred Heart boarding school, the chaplain had the pupils swear fidelity unto death before the Blessed Sacrament.

[8] Gen. Arch. C III 2, 18 February 1926.

A policeman was placed in the house in Monterrey. The bishops had the Blessed Sacrament removed for fear of profanation. Superiors encoded their letters. The religious gave up the habit and went out to church in small groups. Finally they left.

The legislation was not uniformly applied. In Guadalajara and San Luis Potosí classes could be resumed on 4 March 1926. But in Monterrey the nuns, who were not allowed to teach, gave courses in needlework and music to the pupils and organized games and readings, for they wrote, "We are told that the worst thing would be to send them away and we are holding out." On 11 March, the superior, Mother Tamariz, wrote to Mother de Lavigerie that she was expecting a visit from the judges: "I believe it is the beginning of a terrible torment, above all for the priests." She was taken to court for having incited the pupils and the alumnae to rebellion. She was accused of treason for having appealed for protection to the United States consul, of having stolen goods belonging to the nation, because she had hidden statues and objects of worship, and of failing to close the chapel at the first command from the authorities. Courageously the nuns began classes again without authorization on 5 April. They lived "abandoned in the hands of God, decided to struggle and to suffer to defend his rights and to save the souls of his children coveted by Satan and his allies."[9] In Mexico City, the nuns were obliged to close the free school: "That makes one's heart bleed," wrote one of the religious. The situation was paradoxical. "It is not a revolution," thought Mother Bermejillo, "it is persecution that wants to appear legal and takes the forms of civility and constitutionality. It is unhappily true that the Constitution of 1917 by its decrees authorizes a good number of the actions of the present government; for others they do not even have that excuse, but they wish to clothe them with the appearance of law; it is a truly satanic combination."[10]

When new dictatorial decrees appeared in June 1926, the Religious of the Sacred Heart, beginning to think about withdrawal, moved the examinations forward. In Monterrey they looked for a place in the city that could house them in case of expulsion, and they left precious objects and scholastic materials in the care of friends. Those in San Luis Potosí left on 25 June. Finally the bishops said they would have to leave the country because it was expected that worship would be banned by 31 August, and it was further anticipated that the government would leave no options

---

[9] Gen. Arch. C III 2. Letter of 9 March 1926. On 7 March seals had been affixed on the room where all the statues were collected, then on the doors to the chapel.

[10] Gen. Arch. C III 2. 13 April 1926 to Mother von Loë.

but submission or confrontation. The vicar ordered them not to resist.[11] Departures for Cuba and the United States took place during the latter half of July. A little group stayed at San Luis incognito to care for an aged mother who could not travel. The nuns of Monterrey and San Luis settled in the same house in Laredo, Texas, where they set about opening a boarding school for pupils who would cross the border, and they began to work with the local people.[12] Nuns from Mexico City went to San Antonio, then to the house at St. Michael's, which Mother von Loë put at their disposal in 1927 and where they accepted about sixty boarders.[13]

Some alumnae of Mexico with real courage[14] decided to watch over the houses of the Sacred Heart to prevent eventual confiscations. They took charge of the free schools and maintained the spirit of the Sacred Heart there.[15] Many of them took part in the spontaneous uprising that followed

---

[11] Gen. Arch. C III 2. Letter of 26 July to Mother von Loë. Prov. Arch. Mexico. *Journal de Monterrey*: "The practice of indifference is required. No comments. No desires."

[12] The two communities lived separately on different floors.

[13] Gen. Arch. C I A 7 B, Box 2. When the nuns took refuge in the United States, Mother von Loë wrote to them on 28 August 1926: "Now that I know you are in Texas, I hasten to come to tell you that we have taken part in the numerous sacrifices that God has asked of you. To remain so many months deprived of your religious habit, of the freedom to teach and above all of the presence of Jesus among you, are already very painful conditions. We continue to suffer with you. Now God has asked more: you have had to sacrifice your homeland, our dear houses and their beautiful apostolic works. I know you have made the sacrifice with generous courage and that your patience is sustained by the thought of repairing so many outrages against the divine King by an impious government. He judges you worthy to be persecuted for his love, dearest Mothers and Sisters. He keeps count of all the privations and troubles of the present moment, and his Heart forgets nothing."

[14] Gen. Arch. C I A 7 B, Box 2. Letter of 26 July from Mother Bermejillo to Mother von Loë: "Few in number, fear and dread of compromise paralyze wills and we feel alone." Already on 10 March, she had written to Mother Lalande: "Faith is less strong here than in other parts of the country, and it yields in the face of danger or material concerns. We are truly accompanying Our Lord in his Passion, always courageous, calm and even joyous...."

[15] The house of the Sacred Heart in Guadalajara was occupied by Dolores Palomar de Valencia and Clarisa Prieto de Hernández. Dolores Prieto opened a day school so the children could continue their studies in a house of the Sacred Heart. On the 25th of each month, the alumnae gathered for Mass and a literary meeting. At Guanajuato, where the house had been closed in 1915, the alumnae remained close to the "Mothers." They had a statue of Saint Madeleine Sophie placed in the basilica of Our Lady.

the inventories of religious institutions and the suspension of worship and then in the *Cristiade*, the instructional movement that started in January 1927 and lasted two years. The brutality of the bloody repression carried out by the army and of a veritable religious persecution encouraged the *Cristeros* to fight. Guadalajara and the center of Mexico were areas where the *Cristiade* had real success. Determining that the rebels could not be conquered there, the Mexican government had to settle with the Church, which had no interest in allowing the situation to continue. In June 1929, application of the anti-religious law was suspended. Worship was thenceforth tolerated and churches were reopened. Improvement in relations between the state and the Church allowed for planning a return of religious to Mexico, a step all the more necessary since the boarding school established at St. Michael's was having trouble recruiting, many Mexican families having been ruined by the economic crisis.

In August 1931 the Mexican religious in Laredo, then in October and December 1931 those from St. Michael's, began to return to Mexico without authorization, since religious were not allowed to enter the country. To cross the border they took advantage of pilgrimages organized on the occasion of the fourth centenary of the apparitions of Our Lady of Guadalupe. The vicar and her secretary, who were French, entered Mexico in December. They were threatened with expulsion and had to pay heavy fines; but thanks to the intervention of the French consul, in March 1932 they obtained permission to reside in Mexico. In 1934 the religious from San Luis Potosí, Mexico City and Monterrey who were not Mexicans left Laredo. A house was kept there until 1943, however, for the sick and invalids. That gave the nuns a post office box outside of Mexico.

The apostolic life of the religious unfolded under hitherto unheard of circumstances. The teaching of religion was forbidden. Education had to be socialistic and coeducational, and after 1935, had to combat fanaticism and initiate young people to a rational and literal knowledge of the world and of society. Religious "corporations," those involved directly or indirectly in promoting worship, were no longer allowed to teach. Sacred Heart institutions were turned into business schools or academies of fine arts. The primary schools were closed in order to avoid having to teach socialism. Religion could no longer be taught except by the spoken word.

The religious lived in quasi-secrecy and under the threat of exile.[16] The schools were officially directed by alumnae armed with the required diplomas. In Monterrey where the government practiced strict secularism,

---

[16] Prov. Arch. Mexico. An anonymous document contains the memories of a Mexican religious who lived in San Luis. It shows the kinds of difficulties the religious experienced, their efforts to conceal religious objects and even the

only the mistress general and a few surveillantes spent the night in the boarding school. In 1936 the authorities tried to turn the boarding school into a *Casa del Campesino*, then a *Casa del Maestro* [houses for local people]. The director of the academy tried to obtain a renewal of the earlier contract. As the goods of several congregations had been confiscated, the Religious of the Sacred Heart thought about leaving to avoid the violence that other institutes had suffered. In the end, they were allowed to stay in Monterrey.[17] In Mexico City the situation was still more troubling. About ten religious lived in a little house giving onto a tiny courtyard. At the beginning of 1935 the superior general allowed them to assemble groups of ten pupils in private homes. The nuns divided up and taught a few pupils every morning.[18] The vicar went from one place to the other to visit them. In 1936 Mother Vicente decided to send the youngest religious to spend a few months in Havana so that they could "live a normal religious life and wear the habit."[19]

In San Luis Potosí, where the school was officially recognized,[20] religious who had diplomas could teach. Because less pressure was felt there, a novitiate for the coadjutrix sisters was opened and the vicar settled there in October 1943.[21] The boarding school had pupils from all over the country. In January 1937, some religious from Mexico City, where the situation was dangerous, were sent there. Those who stayed in the capital could not find a site for the business school they had opened and continued to teach in the homes that were willing to shelter them. They had to go from one house to another; classes took place in different locations in the morning and in the afternoon, and the day pupils had to be transported from one place to another for the midday meal. There was no possibility of sending religious of other nationalities to Mexico. Therefore, the

---

pupils when there was an inspection, at least during the first year after the return to Mexico.
[17] Gen. Arch. C III 2. Report of the superior of Monterrey, January-July 1936. The Mexican authorities had trouble expropriating the houses of the Sacred Heart because they had been placed under the names of foreign religious residing outside of Mexico.
[18] *Lettres annuelles*, 1954-1958, p. 285.
[19] Prov. Arch. Mexico.
[20] Prov. Arch. Mexico. It was named for Juan de Dios Peza, Mexican Christian poet; it was a discreet way of recalling that the school was Christian since it had the name of God in its title. The name created no difficulty.
[21] *Lettres annuelles*, 1954-1958, p. 287 and M.T. Guevara, p. 42. In Guadalajara, the alumnae tried to have the house reopened. In 1938, they invited Mother Symon there and welcomed her with the words: *"Toujours, toujours!"* [Always, always.]

establishments in Mexico had a large number of lay teachers;[22] and in December 1938, for the first time the vicariate was confided to a Mexican, Mother Concepción Paredo.

Religious life had to be secularized. Taking note of the fact, Mother Symon said in Monterrey in 1938:

> At this moment circumstances impose sacrifices here. It is necessary to accept them wholeheartedly, without going back on them: these are means towards our end, which is the glorification of the Heart of Jesus. First of all there is the external. It must be a business school – secular in appearance. Therefore, agree to remove images, statues, etc., in order to be able to continue to put into the souls of the children – more important than putting it on the walls – the thought, the love, the imitation of Jesus crucified, the devotion to the most pure Virgin Mary. Then there is the habit. Here we must remember the means to the end. You are tolerated here only as laywomen. That is another sacrifice, but we must accept it and not go back on it. It is *given, given*…a contract already sealed with Him. Besides, instead of looking on this clothing as secular, regard it as religious "country clothes," in the words of a Spanish priest. It is greater, more impersonal to see only the service of Jesus Christ that requires this or that than to consider oneself even from the point of view of greater perfection. One of your bishops said: "You can perfectly well wear secular dress, when you consider that the Word of God clothed himself in our flesh!" This morning near the tabernacle I understood the same thing. *Et verbum caro factum est!* – Never will we experience self-abasement like his![23] [In Mexico the Religious of the Sacred Heart] were like those who keep the fire going in the lighthouse in the dark of night…. You are like the Tarcisius of every age, carrying not only the sacred species to give communion to your neighbor, but Jesus Christ in his teaching, his example, so as to aid in forming other Christs in the souls of the children. The Church counts on you. The pope, the bishops encourage you. You are at a post of honor in the Society. It is a choice grace.[24]

Mexico served as a laboratory for a new form of religious life without convent or habit. As Mother Symon said to the nuns: "You must keep the light of faith in all its splendor, all the more so as the external setting is like a veil that hides it. You have to watch over the flame of charity even more

---

[22] Prov. Arch. Mexico, *Histoire de la Province du Mexique, le retour dans la patrie*. [History of the Province of Mexico, the Return to the Homeland].

[23] *Vie de la R.M. Symon*, pp. 218-219.

[24] *Vie…Symon*, pp. 219-220.

as circumstances sometimes make life difficult. Finally you have to carry with a singular love and pass on to those who follow you the torch of our religious traditions."[25] The religious of Mexico as pioneers supported a life style that was going to be imposed on many others by the rise to power of totalitarian regimes. The situation improved in the 1940's to the point that they could reopen Guadalajara in 1941, install the center of the vicariate in the capital in 1943, and establish a novitiate for choir nuns in 1947 and a juniorate in 1948. Initial formation that had been provided in Belgium, Spain, Italy, France, the United States and Cuba could thenceforth take place within the country. In 1952 the religious could again wear the habit on Sundays.[26]

Political Crisis and Civil War in Spain

The Second Republic

The consecration of Spain to the Sacred Heart in May 1919 had solemnized Catholicism in a country where anticlericalism was the sign of the dechristianization of a part of the population and a means of expressing public and social controversy as well as nationalist aspirations. The Church that had supported the monarchy stayed off to the side during the military dictatorship of General Primo de Rivera.[27] Catholics feared a change of regime. Since 1928 the superior general of the Sacred Heart had been Spanish. Mother Vicente knew her country well enough to realize that it was important to anticipate rather than undergo trouble. Shortly after the proclamation of the Republic, she asked the vicar in Madrid, Mother Modet, to send the novices and those in the juniorate to Italy.[28] Mother Modet received the letter on 11 May 1931, at a moment when she did

---

[25] *Vie...Symon*, p. 220.
[26] *Lettres annuelles*, 1954-1958, p. 290, and 1958-1961, p. 140. Testimony of Patricia García de Quevedo and Soccoro Rubio. During the week in class they wore secular dress in black with long skirts. Their hair was in a chignon.
[27] The *Lettres annuelles* do not allude to Primo de Rivera. On the other hand, the account from Sarriá underlines the devotion shown by Alfonso XIII at the inauguration of the universal Exposition in Barcelona. He walked in procession behind the Blessed Sacrament. It comments on the dignity and greatness of soul with which he gave up his power (1929-1931, pp. 278 and 280). On the occasion of the death of the Queen Mother Marie-Christine, Palma de Mallorca presented her as a model queen, wife and Christian mother (p. 376). The queen was very attached to the house at San Sebastián, and her visits there enhanced the reputation of the school.
[28] At Chamartín there were fifty-nine choir novices and twenty in the juniorate.

not have time to open it. When she did, the novices' parents were already coming to take their daughters home. The same day convents were burned in Madrid, Valencia, Alicante, Murcia, Seville, Malaga and Cadiz. Chamartín was one of them. When Mother Modet and her companions, the last to depart, left the house, the "Reds" were dousing it with gasoline and a whole section was already in flames.[29]

The mistress of novices, Mother Sánchez de Alva, organized the departure of the youngest for Avigliana,[30] and the sick nuns were sent to France. The coadjutrix sisters' novitiate was moved to Montpellier. The French religious were repatriated by their embassy.[31] The nuns' flight was so rapid that Mother Modet was not able to find everyone. The Religious of the Sacred Heart returned to their house ten days later. The level of danger varied from city to city. Palma remained calm; the house in Seville, encircled by rioters, was saved by government forces; that of Bilbao was guarded during the night by the sons, brothers and husbands of alumnae. The religious rented a house near Chamartín, since they had to establish a foothold in order to avoid confiscation.[32] But by May 20, they resumed teaching and at the reopening of school in October, they gathered about fifty boarders in the part of the building that had withstood the fire. The statue of the Sacred Heart that remained intact in the entrance courtyard dominated the ruins.

Relations between the Republic and the Church underwent a variety of changes. Different currents were appearing at the heart of Catholicism: a liberal, social Catholicism began to grow.[33] But the hierarchy tended to denigrate the new regime and those, both nearby and far away, who supported it. This point of view, which was not necessarily that of the majority of priests or of the faithful, contributed to the development of anti-clericalism. Less than subtle pronouncements by both sides, led to troublesome actions. On 23 January 1932, the Society of Jesus was suppressed. In June 1933 religious instruction was cancelled in the schools. Religious congregations, forbidden to teach, were not allowed other income than that needed to maintain their members. At the Sacred Heart young

---

[29] Gen. Arch. C VII 2 c, Journal of Mother Castejón.
[30] Ninety persons left for Italy including six professed nuns and three sisters.
[31] *Lettres annuelles*, 1929-1931, p. 486.
[32] At Puerta Santa María, the governor ordered the reopening of the boarding school under pain of confiscation of the house. *Lettres annuelles*, 1929-1931, p. 525.
[33] In 1936 for the first time, sections of Catholic Action were noted in the accounts of the Spanish boarding schools.

religious studied to pass the examinations for teaching diplomas.[34] In all the cities with a republican majority, the quarters where the religious lived were isolated from the rest of the house. In Bilbao the nuns gave up wearing the habit in order to teach.

At the end of 1933, the Church succeeded in mobilizing the faithful and obtaining results during elections. Tensions seemed to have lessened and the respite seemed sufficient to Mother Modet to suggest the return of the choir novices to Spain. Mother Vicente refused but permitted the return of the coadjutrix novices. After a visit to Spain she wrote on 12 January 1936, "Since I speak of consolations, I will not hide from you that my last journey to Spain brought some in seeing how, after the revolutions and difficulties of all sorts, these houses maintain their fervor and flourish under the blessing of the Heart of Jesus."[35] But when she was asked her opinion on what was likely to happen, she replied shrewdly, "It seems to me that we are on live coals that are burning under the ashes."[36]

At a moment when popular agitation joined demands for regional autonomy to demands for social change, the participation of Catholic ministers in the government nourished antireligious sentiments. During massive strikes organized in the Asturias mines in October 1934, the insurgents took Oviedo, but the government stopped the insurrection at the beginning. Martial law was proclaimed throughout the country. In Bilbao, "the boarding school was dismissed. In the streets all traffic was stopped, not one vehicle; the silence was interrupted only by gunfire, either by the police or the revolutionaries. They occupied the roofs of houses and fired from those vantage points, police responding."[37] In San Sebastián, the military governor had the Sacred Heart guarded. In Barcelona a Catalan republic was proclaimed on 6 October 1934. The insurrection, fomented by the autonomists and the forces of the left was quickly strangled.

After the general elections of February 1936[38] and the constitution of the Popular Front government, instability increased, fueled by the provocations of the Falange[39] and by the left eager for revenge. In the

---

[34] In Bilbao, a Catholic association of feminine culture at the Sacred Heart provided training for teaching religious (*Lettres annuelles,* 1954-1958, p. 240).
[35] *Vie de la T.R.M. Vicente,* pp. 227-228.
[36] *Lettres annuelles,* 1935-1937, p. 359.
[37] P. 390.
[38] The nuns sometimes went to vote wearing secular dress. In Bilbao, there was an effort, at least in the centers where they went, to prevent from voting persons supposedly favorable to the CEDA, (Spanish Confederation for the Right to Autonomy), which grouped several Catholic organizations.
[39] It was founded in 1932 by José Antonio Rivera, son of General Primo de Rivera. Arrested by order of the republican government, summarily judged

communes where the authorities were favorable to the Popular Front, goods owned by the religious were tempting for those who thought that agrarian reform was a priority and who wanted immediate satisfaction. Several times in February and March 1936 Religious of the Sacred Heart left their house at the behest of the vicar or a superior who saw flames mounting from a church or a convent nearby. Rumors fed the apprehension on both sides. At Tetuan near Chamartín, the rumor circulated that the nuns were giving children poisoned candy. The mayor who wanted to take over their property was prevented by authorities in Madrid. In Zaragoza the convent was protected by volunteers and soldiers. At Santa María de Huerta the religious were able to teach until vacation.[40] Character assassination on both sides did not directly cause the insurrection, but was one stage in the process of confrontation. The army was openly preparing for a general uprising that broke out on 18 July 1936.

From National Movement to Civil War

Begun in Morocco, the putsch succeeded from its beginning in Galicia to the Balearic Islands and Andalusia, where the house in Seville served as base for the staff of General Queipo de Llano and where Granada was "an island of tranquility in the midst of streams of Marxists."[41] The Basque country remained faithful to the republican government. At San Sebastián Mother Garrido sheltered villagers who were fleeing the fighting, and she was respected by the Communists to whom she gave blankets for the refugees and provided food. But she refused to fly the red flag! The city was finally conquered by the Nationalists whose ranks included Carlist *Requetés*. Having hidden Nationalists, Mother Garrido saved republicans. Because of immediate and massive general mobilization, Madrid and Barcelona remained in the hands of the republic.

The National Movement was not a simple *pronunciamento* because throughout the country civilians took positions to uphold or oppose it. When the putsch failed, a civil war broke out that would last three years and take on the appearance of a crusade. The fratricidal tearing apart of the two camps, opposed to one another by their hopes for society and the country's economy as well as their concept of nationhood, turned Spain into a mass grave. Repression on each side was pitiless and even terrifying,

---

and shot at Alicante on 20 November 1936, he was called José Antonio by the Right. He was celebrated as a martyr by Franco's party, even though Franco did very little to save him.

[40] *Lettres annuelles*, 1935-1937, p. 583. In 1931, the villagers had promised to defend them.

[41] Pp. 515 and 571.

but the republican camp promptly betrayed an antireligious obsession that "[imputed] social oppression to religious men and women."[42] The Society of the Sacred Heart was one of its victims. Although the republicans violently attacked its members and interned many religious [43] or held them hostage, it had the good fortune to have counted no one among the dead.[44]

After the elections of February 1936 the two vicars set about looking for a refuge in Portugal.[45] The nuns from Seville, Granada, Pontevedra and Santa María de Huerta arrived in Lisbon, but they quickly returned to the liberated zone. Thanks to a superior officer, the vicar in Madrid knew when the insurrection was going to take place.[46] But the religious could not leave the capital because rail transport had been stopped. On 19 July, Chamartín was sacked just after the nuns left. The two houses in Madrid were invaded by "a multitude drunk with fury" that banged on the door screaming, "Open up, this house belongs to us!"[47] Three French nuns from Chamartín were repatriated by the consulate a month later. The Spaniards, dispersed in small groups, had to change hiding places several times. In Barcelona, after several convents had already been burned, the vicar, Mother Alcibar, ordered the religious to leave the houses in secular dress, taking with them only what was strictly necessary. On 7 August, the republican army seized the house at Bilbao. The region of Valencia, where the Iberian Anarchist Federation had been founded in 1927, had played an important role in organizing workers during the Republic and infiltrated the National Confederation of Work. It claimed the most victims among nuns,

---

[42] Pierre Vilar, *La Guerre d'Espagne*, Paris 1986, p. 108.
[43] There are forty-five internments on record. It may be that there were others, the memory of which has been lost.
[44] During or after the civil war the motherhouse asked the nuns to document what they had lived through. The Cardinal Protector, Eugenio Pacelli, requested those who had been imprisoned to write an account of what they had seen and undergone. These reports are collected in Gen. Arch. C I A 8 d, Box 3. Two accounts concern the vicariate of Barcelona, one concerns Godella, another, Madrid.
[45] Mother Elena Ytturalde had done research in Coimbra and Lisbon. The patriarch of Lisbon refused permission to open a boarding school. Upon her return she could not enter Bilbao. After a stay in Salamanca, she joined the community in Zaragoza.
[46] Mother de la Cavada was warned on the evening of 17 July by the father of one of the boarders who was to take part in the insurrection at the barracks in Montagna and who advised her to disperse her community "today rather than tomorrow," he specified, when the vicar hesitated because of the lateness of the hour.
[47] The house of Caballero de Gracia was awarded to the union of set designers; then it sheltered war orphans, finally militiamen of the War Department.

clergy and lay people engaged in pastoral and social work. Many churches were torched on 22 July. The house of Godella, where the city wanted to establish a public school, was spared; but the mayor asked that the religious prepare meals for two hundred unemployed Communists, both men and women. He did not want them, in their hunger, to cause bloodshed. The nuns left the house on 30 July; the eldest stayed in the village, and the others were taken in by friends.

In the republican areas religious men and women faced a dangerous fate, above all in Madrid. No religious ceremony was allowed, except in the Basque country. Worship was forbidden even in private; celebrants and those assisting risked their lives if they were discovered.[48] The failure of the National Movement gave the go-ahead for the arrest of priests and male religious, many of whom were massacred. The summary executions were especially numerous in the summer of 1936, less common after the overthrow of the anarchists in May 1937. In between times in Catalonia at least, the people's courts brought some assurances and prison replaced the death penalty. The persecutions began again in January and February 1939 when Franco's forces launched their final offensive.

While dividing up the religious among the shelters had been planned, the brutal unleashing of hostilities made it impossible to follow those arrangements. The civil war began at the moment when the families who had promised to help were on holiday. Some citizens expecting trouble had left early for vacation and had crossed into France. Servants opened a few doors. But in the large cities the militia checked on the doorkeepers and from them learned who was living in private homes. Most often the religious had to seek their own lodging and "go from door to door feeling their way."[49] Some coadjutrix sisters found places as domestics, cooks or nannies, thereby procuring shelter and earning their living.

Religious of the Sacred Heart were sometimes betrayed, but chance caused most of the arrests. The ferocious demands of the police and the people's militia created fear, and some religious paid the price. The repression was led by small, more or less independent groups, and the searches meant taking possession of anything of value. But the worst could happen if the militia discovered religious objects or symbols: "The triumphant Communists paraded through the streets in enormous trucks;

---

[48] Irujo, Minister of Justice in the Negrin government, stopped the persecutions after 1937 and sought to renew relations with the Church, hoping to go as far as to reestablish religious liberty. The negotiations were sabotaged by Torrent, the vicar general of Barcelona, who forbade all public worship in Catalonia and threatened priests who transgressed his orders with canonical sanctions. Reconciliation between the Church and the Republic proved to be impossible.

[49] Report of the vicariate of Barcelona.

they stopped their vehicles wherever they liked, set fire, pillaged, killed, without constraint. At any moment they entered private houses for these terrible *registros* – searches – when they first took away silver and valuable objects, destroying with satanic rage crucifixes, images and religious objects, and then took away people who seemed suspect to them and who generally did not return."[50] At the sight of relics or religious articles, "their fury knew no bounds. They threw everything out of the window, hacking, shredding, while in the streets children dressed up in church vestments and performed sacrilegious parodies of sacred ceremonies." The profanations and sacrileges they witnessed, not all of them by children, counted among the most painful events the religious had to face.

> At first, we were welcomed very well, but after three or four hours things began to change: the Reds conducted a search and if they discovered priests, religious men or women, they took out their fury on the buildings that they sacked, pillaged, demolished and on the brutally treated people who sometimes paid with their lives for their generous hospitality. The danger of compromising our hosts became such that we could no longer count on steady housing; many of ours had to change safe houses five or six times with great difficulty and spend whole days in the streets, wandering hither and yon aimlessly without food.

While the stress for the hosts never let up, most of them showed impressive courage.

Superiors could not protect the members of their communities. To someone who brought her one of her daughters, the superior of Godella, who did not know where to send her, said, "Take her to a bench on the boulevard for we no longer have anyone who can take us in!" Though she feared the responsibility, the person in question brought the nun to her home. Some religious who did not want to endanger their sisters no longer knew what to do. One of them in Catalonia,

> after hours spent alone without shelter, almost exhausted with hunger and fatigue saw night fall, and although she knew where her superior was hiding, did not dare to join her, knowing that there were twenty-four religious in the same place. She feared losing the whole group if she were detected on the way by the Reds. She succeeded in slipping into the house and said to her superior: "Mother, here I am, but if I am to jeopardize you, I am ready to return to the street." One can guess the response.

---

[50] *Lettres annuelles*, 1935-1937, p. 343.

Reverend Mother clasped her in her arms weeping for her who was more than ever her daughter.[51]

In Bilbao,

> several religious who had been sent out in the evening came the next morning to find the Mother Assistant: "Mother, where should we go? We had to leave the house we were sent to in a hurry." Where to go? That was the problem.... Finally they huddled together in a little rented apartment. Scarcely installed, we saw a friend running toward us: "Get out, there is going to be a search, you have been betrayed."[52]

The coadjutrix novices of Sarriá had been able to find refuge with their novice mistress and another religious in a location planned in advance. Their presence ended up attracting attention:

> The Communists of the quarter arrived saying that the house was requisitioned; they were not bad people, weak and fearful rather, for they advised us to hide our religious articles and to take precautions. We would have been able to stay if we had not had the young novices who were too much at risk from the visits. Three or four groups of Reds came at different times, amusing themselves with gross jokes that the novice mistress tried to stop. The last Communists who came were so wicked that they threatened to take away the novices. The mother who defended them with such courage had a gun pointed at her under the chin, while she explained that these girls were poor, that they were daughters of workers like them, confided to her care by their parents and that she was responsible for them. Finally the enraged Reds ended by consenting to her leaving with her daughters, giving her an hour to send them back to their families and evacuate the house taken by the FAI.[53]

In the whole of republican Spain it was dangerous to meet anyone in the street, for one could be arrested by the Civil Guard, militia, Communist or anarchist militants.[54] At best the risk was a thorough search and very

---

[51] Report of the vicariate of Sarriá.
[52] *Lettres annuelles*, 1935-1937, p. 391.
[53] P. 391
[54] Reactions varied according to the temperament of the people. Mother de Ymbert, superior in Barcelona, wrote: "On account of all the departures and changes of house, I had to go about a great deal in the city streets. I felt safer there, for in the houses there was always the fear of searches, but in the streets there were so many people that no one paid any attention to us."

lengthy interrogation. While they were wandering in search of shelter, some novices in Catalonia were arrested and kept at the FAI headquarters for several hours. Finally, after having been roundly insulted they were able to take refuge with a family. For security the religious were obliged to remain indoors. Not unreasonably, they "lived as if they were prisoners so painful was the terror of daily persecutions and the frightful anxiety of constant alarms in the area."[55]

By their presence religious could provoke the imprisonment or disappearance of their relatives, who risked the same fate as those whom they sheltered. Rosario Villalonga, assistant at Godella, found herself in prison with her mother in March 1937. Gloria Elió, superior at Madrid Saint Denis, who had taken refuge with her mother, was arrested with one of her sisters.[56] To avoid trouble for those who took them in, the vicariate treasurer, Mother Louisa Jacobs,[57] who was Belgian, finally made contact with her embassy. She lived in a place where religious and lay people of every nationality were passing through, all in danger of death.[58] The vicar, Mother de la Cavada, refused to take advantage of this refuge for fear of being totally cut off from her daughters. She hid with her family, keeping contact with those in prison, seeking shelters for her nuns and negotiating their departure with various embassies able to provide visas and organize convoys to the ports.

It soon became apparent that they had to leave Spain. The religious of Guipuzcoa were evacuated to France, 31 August 1936, in a German ship.[59] Before the siege of San Sebastián took effect, a French warship took some

---

[55] Report of the vicariate of Sarriá.
[56] On one search the militiamen found an insignia of the *Requetés*. They were part of a military organization of Carlist traditionalists. They were recruited chiefly in Navarre, so that when one coadjutrix novice stated at the time of her arrest that she was from Navarre she drew down insults upon herself from the members of the FAI who were questioning her.
[57] She related that the bags containing the valuables of the vicariate kept in a nationalized bank were found after the exodus of the government: "The intact deposit was returned to us at the bank in the presence of two notaries, a bank officer and our business manager; it was a moving moment. How many others did not have the same good fortune! Alas! The precious door of the tabernacle of Chamartín was returned to us only in part; the Reds had kept the interior, which was all in gold and brilliants with four artistically worked ivory medallions...."
[58] She stayed there 22 August 1936 to 26 February 1937, when she was able to get to Marseille through Valencia.
[59] *Lettres annuelles*, 1935-1937, pp. 391-392.

French nuns on board.⁶⁰ The vicars were no longer in communication with Rome, but they knew that Mother Vicente had ordered them to leave Spain. Italy seemed to offer the best chance for hospitality, because Mussolini was allied with the nationalists and had sent troops into Spain to support them. The vicar of Catalonia, Mother Alcibar, was able to obtain from the Italian consulate refugee status for sixty-two young religious who arrived at the port under the protection of the militia.⁶¹ After having arranged this first departure, she and her treasurer, Mother Pilar Verges, were arrested while in a tram and taken to Rabassada, the hill of executions near Sarriá. They were separated from each other, and while the treasurer was being interrogated "this poor Mother was subjected to all kinds of questions, so horrible and indecent that she cried out at this madness, 'Kill me! Kill me!' They cannot be repeated."⁶² Just as they were waiting to be shot, they were freed. Eight days later Mother Alcibar and fifty-seven religious from Barcelona embarked for Genoa. The evacuation of the aged and infirm nuns was difficult to arrange. They drew pity from the guards who had to carry them.⁶³ The nuns had to salute with raised fists!

For the thirty-one nuns of Godella who had received visas for Italy the formalities of registering at the office of the National Confederation of Labor, 7 September 1936, turned into a nightmare:

> The rumor went around that the religious were leaving. Then a terrible demonstration formed led by women, girls and boys fourteen to eighteen who surrounded the house where we were. Some of them climbed up on the window sills screaming and, worse, blaspheming. They did not want the religious to embark because they said, "They must go to the front and fight with us." "They are fascists," others said, "they are going to join the fascist army to kill us, to kill our sons." Others asked for gasoline to burn us; voices cried "*Al Saler*!" (It was the site of executions.) Other voices were heard saying, "Where are the friends who drove you to vote at the time of the elections?" We heard cries calling us hypocrites and other things we cannot repeat, painful lies: "We know the relations you have with the priests." The men were more moderate and seemed to wish to defend us or perhaps they feared being grouped with the women.

---

60 P. 483 and testimony of Vincenette d'Uzer. Normally this was forbidden: warships were not allowed to transport civilians.
61 Account of Mother de Ymbert, p. 5. The group embarked on 31 July 1936.
62 "A few Religious of the Sacred Heart of the houses of Barcelona...." pp. 15-16.
63 *Lettres annuelles*, 1935-1937, pp. 429-430.

Driven to the harbor station they could not get out of their vehicles because the guards feared a lynching, and they were finally kept for a month in the former convent of the Little Sisters of the Poor. There they became aware of the state of mind of the women of the militia, of their subjection: "I found in them," wrote the superior of Godella, "more ignorance than bad faith and real malice." For these women the revolution was revenge:

> Some of them had been in schools run by nuns; they admitted that their mothers prayed, that they had prayed also, but that now it was not necessary to do so because things had changed. A good number of these militia women who spent the day in the shelter slept on the floors occupied by the Reds, and they feared that if they lost this war, they would return to their sad life, not having enough to eat or adequate shelter.[64]

The Republicans identified the Church with the Nationalists. From the moment when, with the support of the Legion and the army of Africa, the Nationalists undertook the systematic conquest of Spain, the mob attacked the Church. It was accused of alliance with the Spanish upper classes, and congregations of teaching religious were said to be responsible for the widespread illiteracy of the masses.

The most critical case was surely that of Mother Elió. Arrested on 2 September 1936, she was incarcerated at the "Ceka"[65] of Fine Arts in Madrid. Saved almost by chance upon her arrival by a guard who hid her, she was pulled out of there four days later and sent without trial to the Capuchin sisters' convent, transformed into a prison that housed both political detainees and common law prisoners. She was compelled to work and lived there under painful conditions, food being scarce, the prison overcrowded, and promiscuity a trial. "How did I get out of there?" she wrote. "I don't know! I only know that after two months of imprisonment, the good God caused a new attempt at release to succeed in spite of the seemingly irrevocable adverse will to keep me until execution. One day they had us leave without warning, my sister and me, taking us to the Norwegian

---

[64] Report of the superior of Godella, pp. 1-2.
[65] The "*Cékas*" were committees of inquiry modeled on Soviet *Tchekas* and had in fact rights over life and death. In her report Mother Elió notes that the members of the tribunal before whom she had to appear were "Russians for the most part. On the spot they judged, condemned and executed. At the most they took the victim out into the country to shoot him. When by chance he was kept at the *Céka* he was made to suffer in every way possible."

embassy and from there to Paris by plane, where the minister of Foreign Affairs took charge of both of us."[66]

On 4 October 1937, the one hundred and fifty religious remaining in Madrid obtained their visas. Even so, some nuns were stopped at Valencia and Barcelona for almost a year. They were liberated thanks to the intervention of the vicar in England with the British Foreign Office, the British Navy and the ambassador of the United States to the Court of St. James, Joseph P. Kennedy, whose daughters were pupils at Roehampton. A British warship chartered by the United States took aboard the twenty-eight religious who remained and after a stop in Marseille transported them to Newhaven.[67] One of the conditions under which the British took charge of them was that they remain in Britain until the end of the war; they were dispersed among the houses of Roehampton and London. France and Italy sheltered most of the refugee nuns. Some Catalan families were taken in at Montpellier and Toulouse, some boarders in Genoa.[68] Between September 1936 and November 1937, more than one hundred religious passed through Marseille.

After the Nationalist armies had progressed toward the North of Spain, some religious were sent back into their country to support the houses that had continued or taken up their activities or that had taken in a field hospital. Many went to Palma de Mallorca but the greater number were sent to San Sebastián, which had become a refuge in the autumn of 1936 and whose boarding school was overcrowded: "From the last months of 1936 a good number of pupils of our houses in Madrid, Barcelona and Valencia and even Bilbao came to ask us for hospitality; they were children who managed to escape from the Red zone either with their parents, or often even alone with only one thought: to find their mothers and take up their boarding school life. They were welcomed with open arms and we crowded up a bit to make room for them." At the end of 1936 the numbers had doubled. During the summer of 1937 applications for enrollment tripled. The nuns' cells and dormitories were given to the school, the

---

[66] They were liberated on 26 October 1936, and went into Italy. In order to save them, Mother Vicente had France and Great Britain take action. Mother Ogilvie Forbes intervened at the Foreign Office and Mother de Neuville at the Quai d'Orsay. Finally it was the French consul who had them evacuated in a French military plane. Mother Vicente's situation was undeniably painful: "She suffered in silence from the tragic events of the civil war, from the misunderstandings and also from the situation of many of our religious in Spain," noted Mother Castejón.

[67] When the news of the liberation of the nuns detained in Barcelona became known, the motherhouse received letters from the whole Society.

[68] *Vie de la T.R.M. Vicente*, p. 295.

refectories transformed into study halls; meals took place in several sittings. "In the study halls it was a forest of desks, for the classes we had student chairs built that replaced tables and chairs at the same time." When the number had quadrupled, acceptances were halted: "Some mothers appealed to their very real titles of faithful and devoted alumnae of ours. Some made use of the influence of highly placed individuals: the Cardinal Primate, Jesuit fathers. After a refusal, one mother asked ingenuously: 'If I bring a recommendation from the Generalissimo, will you accept my daughter?'" The superior no longer went down to the parlor. "She said to a little girl one day, 'We have no more places in the refectory.' 'Mother, I will eat standing up.' 'We have no more places in the dormitory.' I will sleep standing up.'" Because the house was so full, it could no longer accommodate all the religious, who had to be lodged elsewhere[69].

The nuns also helped run field hospitals, on occasion as in Seville, or for the duration at the Aragon border where the fighting was intense and its outcome uncertain for a long time. The hospital at Zaragoza, opened on 20 December 1937, received wounded who had fought under General Moscardo. Sacred Heart alumnae and pupils cared for them,[70] the religious taking charge of attending the dying.[71] They noted the patriotism and fervor among the wounded and the relatives who came to see them.[72] In the reconquered zones houses were opened on properties lent by friends of the congregation. In October 1937 a colony of religious settled in Navarre at Villava, on the doorstep of Pamplona. The oldest or the sick remained there while the others were sent where needed. Seen at first as temporary,

---

[69] *Lettres annuelles,* 1935-1937, pp. 485-487.

[70] *Lettres annuelles,* 1959-1961, p. 50. The religious and the alumnae, trained by a military doctor and the hospital sisters, took complete charge of this hospital of five hundred beds. In order to provide for a night shift, the community operated on a double timetable.

[71] Gen. Arch. C I A 8 d, Box 3. Report of 8 February 1938.

[72] "A peasant couple, the wife in a classic fichu, came into the ward and one of wounded cried out, 'My parents!' and he burst out crying with emotion. The mother kissed him and said, 'Don't get any weaker! For God and for Spain this is little enough.' They are from Burgos. A Castilian appeared when his son had already been buried. The superior saw him and took on the fifth work of mercy, to console the sorrowful. 'The first thing your son asked upon arrival was to go to confession,' she said. 'I don't need to know anything else. That is enough for me,' answered this heroic Christian father." "A Few Echoes from Our Hospital," 8 February 1938. "A sergeant was very ill; he had just had an amputation: 'I'm going to die,' he exclaimed. 'No, you have many good deeds yet to do in your life.' 'I have already done three: first, being a good Catholic still; second, enrolling in the *Movement* from the beginning; third, having offered God my amputated leg.'"

the house was finally authorized by the motherhouse after the taking of Madrid.

At the end of the war, the roads were clogged with caravans of people returning home with their flocks; the battlefields were full of corpses. Returning was problematic because rail transport was far from being restored. In Godella on 30 March 1939, there were still red hospital personnel in the house, but on the balcony of the façade the Spanish colors had been put back. The return of the religious took on the air of a triumph. Although the vicar of Madrid in the end did not ride in General Franco's automobile,[73] the superior of Godella did use the one belonging to Cardinal Gomá, primate of Spain. "Upon our arrival," recounted the religious, "people looked at us, applauded; women came to embrace us and men to shake our hands; they took hold of our crosses and the medals on our side beads to kiss them."

It took patience to restore the houses that had been transformed into barracks or field hospitals or occupied by the army. In Madrid, the house of Saint Denis had been destroyed; Caballero de Gracia housed a social service center; Chamartín was occupied by the local inhabitants and there had been fighting in the garden and the cemetery. Temporary locations had to be found. The superior general made funds available to rebuild Chamartín and Sarriá. As soon as they reopened the houses received gifts from all over, in particular from England and Australia.[74] By October 1939 apostolic activity had been resumed everywhere. Gradually as the reconquest proceeded, the government of Franco

> abolished the sectarian laws, made religious instruction obligatory in elementary and high schools, restored the crucifix, prescribed the traditional Spanish salutation *Ave Maria Purissima, sin pecado concebida,* at the beginning and end of classes and in May the practices of the month of Mary. Coeducation was forbidden; text books had to be approved by ecclesiastical authorities. Teachers whose ideas or conduct did not seem entirely trustworthy lost their positions and were replaced by those who had been persecuted for their attachment to religion. In addition, laws were enacted, according to which civil marriage could be celebrated only after the canonical marriage; divorce was forbidden. The Society of Jesus was reestablished and everything that the Republic had confiscated was returned to them.

---

[73] Two of his daughters were boarders at Placeres.
[74] *Lettres annuelles,* 1959-1961, p. 175.

It was therefore with renewed hope that the religious took up their work with confidence that "the final triumph [of the Nationalists] had returned to the Divine Master all his tabernacles."[75]

Everything seemed to have returned to normal. But most of the religious had lost a father, a brother or a nephew in the course of the fighting or the assassinations that had been carried out. During her sojourn in Avigliana the mistress of novices had had to announce to her novices more than fifty deaths among their relatives.[76] The pupils found it hard to settle down to work after months or years of privation and anxiety.[77] The reconstruction of the buildings began in 1940, and their reopening took place in spring of 1941 for Algorta and Sarriá, in May for Chamartín. The Society of the Sacred Heart took advantage of the situation to make improvements in the facilities or carry through on projects that had been interrupted by the civil war. After 1940 the Franco regime contributed several new developments in the area of public instruction of women, recognizing the establishments of religious congregations on condition that they align their curricula with official programs, "very adaptable to our Plan of Studies," admitted the nuns in Bilbao. In Zaragoza, the free school was recognized as an official school, and funds were granted for the maintenance of the children. Chamartín benefitted from state subsidies granted to religious schools and was able to build a dining room in the free school.

The Sacred Heart in Germany and Austria under Nazism

Two months after Hitler took power, the German people were to know, item by item the *Gleichschaltung*, the forced standardization of all institutions and suppression of all opposition, imposed by the National Socialist revolution. The associations of the Catholic press were pursued under the pretext of fighting against political Catholicism, an accusation sufficiently vague to give the new regime the opportunity for various interventions. The purge of 30 June 1934, called the night of long knives, repressed all forms actual or potential of opposition. The persecution was speeded up in 1935 by the launching of legal repression. Because they were accused of taking orders from abroad and transferring funds there, leaders of religious congregations were hounded. The regime's publications underlined with exaggeration the aberrances to which the practice of the vows could lead individuals and the physical cruelty or sex crimes of which male religious

---

[75] *Lettres annuelles*, 1935-1937, p. 327.
[76] *Lettres annuelles*, 1959-1961, p. 27.
[77] *Lettres annuelles*, 1935-1937, p. 394.

had been guilty. Catholics were controlled by a policy that evolved from harassment to marginalization. The direct and indirect pressures exerted were many. *Hitlerjugend,* Hitler Youth, cultivated the young people and cooperated in social reorganization according to *Führerprinzip*. Catholic youth associations were gradually denatured and abandoned, and young people were prevented from going to church.

School was a sensitive area. From the beginning of 1936 the Nazis made a distinction between education, taken over by the state, and instruction, meaning teaching, that could still be practiced in private institutions. "The future is very uncertain, even very threatening, as the state is tending to concentrate the education of youth in its hands," as the vicar of Germany, Mother von Waldstein, recognized. At Saint Adelheid, one had to "to arrive at concessions required by the circumstances," the nature of which is unknown.[78] On the occasion of her visit in 1936, Mother Vicente received from the religious the promise "that being at a post of danger and of honor, they all wished to be faithful with noble and generous hearts on whom Our Lord can always count."[79] Nothing allowed us to foresee what form the eventual persecution would take, but it was not impossible to have some idea. In Bavaria the "deconfessionalization" of the school was declared on 1 October 1936, and backed by a plebiscite that appeared to Catholics a legal violation of the concordat, since respect for provisions of the latter was no longer obligatory when they contradicted the legislation of the Reich. The seminaries were closed in 1937 and some departments suppressed in Catholic university faculties. The Sacred Heart had to give up the day school in Munich. Petty objections were made to the inscription *Heim Nazareth* on the façade of the house, as it went against the anti-Jewish ideology of the Reich.[80]

The Nazis were clever enough to proceed slowly with their program of subjection. At the time of the regular visit in 1938 the secondary school had not yet been taken over by the state. A few large boarding schools remained: the house of Saint Adelheid was "still tolerated and even viewed favorably." But the vicar was aware that this tolerance could "cease in a short time. If the state lets it remain, it is and will be even more in the future crushed by taxes." For the studies, "the demands of the government, the perpetual modifications, and the various rulings require constant flexibility and a spirit of adaptation." In Munich it was becoming dangerous to teach religion, for "the burdens of the present time were more and more threatening.

---

[78] Gen. Arch. C IV 2, Germany.
[79] *Vie de la T.R.M. Vicente,* p. 230.
[80] *Lettres annuelles,* 1954-1958, pp. 181 and 183.

Parents could no longer exercise their most sacred rights."[81] Children twelve years old and older were granted their own choice regarding religion and some renounced it. Parents were urged no longer to give Christian names to their children. Children were encouraged to spy on their parents, which sometimes had weighty consequences. In 1945 the Religious of the Sacred Heart in Berlin became aware that many day pupils had never been baptized.[82]

From the beginning of 1938 the superiors in Germany encoded their letters and tried to send them to Rome with travelers. Mother Mathilde von Loë, who relied on male religious or Italian students who were returning to their country, was able to announce the closing of many Bavarian schools and describe the forms of anti-religious persecution:

> In the hospitals and other charitable agencies they have brought in many "brown sisters."[83] University professors have asked secretly that nuns no longer come to take their examination in their religious habits. In certain places no one can start anything without being a member of the party and that means leaving the Church. On the other hand, opportunities for work are being increased by immense building projects, among them large government schools. And the people are somewhat content because there is work.[84]

Six months later she gave news of the demolition of the synagogue and the Protestant cathedral of Munich, and she wondered if Catholic churches were not going to have their turn.[85] As relations between Germany and Czechoslovakia were on the point of rupture, Mother von Loë thought about sending the community of Munich to Italy or Switzerland. She alluded to the case of a religious whose congregation had been dissolved and who asked to enter at the Sacred Heart in order to continue her apostolic life. Religious no longer had the right to teach when their institution was closed or to be hired in a government school. After 1936 a patrimony law deprived them of their inheritance rights.

In Berlin, where the Society of the Sacred Heart was established in 1938, in order to avoid any confrontation with the authorities, Mother Werhahn was careful to obey government regulations, in so far as they did not affect conscience. There was a mandate never to speak of politics:

---

[81] Gen. Arch. C IV 2. The "deconfessionnalization" of teaching was not completed in the regions of Cologne and Aix-la-Chapelle until April 1939.
[82] *Lettres annuelles*, 1947-1949, p. 102.
[83] These were laywomen, not religious.
[84] Gen. Arch. C IV 2. Letter of 7 January 1938.
[85] Letter of 19 June 1938.

"This was a necessary caution, for among the girls who lived in the house, there could be spies."[86] All the same at Grünewald, Cardinal von Preysing read to the alumnae a plan for a pastoral letter on "noble intrepidity. They listened in religious silence; then spontaneously, everyone rose and intoned the traditional song of fidelity to the Church and to baptismal promises."[87]

While in Germany, the "bringing into line" had been gradual, in Austria it happened all at once and therefore seemed all the more brutal. In February 1938, in Graz, which was the general headquarters of the Nazis in Austria, "the atmosphere became heavier and heavier and the mothers of the council were visibly worried."[88] On 10 March 1938, German armored vehicles entered Austria and occupied Vienna two days later. Austria was "reunited" to Germany on 15 March. Before the proclamation of the *Anschluss*, the vicar of Austria, Mother Anna Kömstedt, on 13 March, wrote her first letter in code to Rome: "We have changed regime and we have a little difficulty in getting used to it. It seemed to go well with the old, strength was returning, there was progress. But the doctor found it good to prescribe this change, and we are trying to profit from it in order to be completely back to work."[89] At Pressbaum, a layperson, a home economics teacher, who was found to be a member of the National Socialist party, "set herself up as the officer in charge of the house. Standing on a platform before all the nuns and children of Austrian nationality, she scanned our faces, while we were obliged well into the night to listen to the speech the *Führer* declaimed in the imperial palace in Vienna, of which he had taken possession. In the boarding school there was a group of children related to the imperial family. Their behavior was beyond reproach. Their faces serious, their eyes lowered, they heard streams of insults to all that they loved and venerated."[90] On 10 April 1938, 99.73% of Austrians said that they were in favor of *rattachement*.[91] Cardinal Innitzer, the archbishop of Vienna, had asked major superiors to have religious vote yes to the *Anschluss*, and that request was complied with in religious communities.[92] After the vote, Mother Kömstedt summarized the situation, writing: "We

---

[86] Prov. Arch. Germany. Notice of Mother Werhahn, pp. 7-8.
[87] *Lettres annuelles*, 1954-1958, p. 125.
[88] Memories of Barbara Walterskirchen.
[89] Gen. Arch. C IV 2, Vienna. Mothers Maria Mayr and zu Salm-Salm went to Vienna several times to confer with the vicar, as the telephone and the mail were under surveillance (*Lettres annuelles*, 1961-1963, p. 137).
[90] Memories of B. Walterskirchen.
[91] "Reattachment" or "reunion" are terms that translate *Anschluss*.
[92] Memories of B. Walterskirchen.

have been able to say yes to what the good God has himself arranged."[93] It was surely only by considering it in the light of Providence that one could think about it with tranquility.

Pressbaum and Riedenburg had to house German soldiers, whose presence lent some security. Riedenburg received an order to fly the flag, and then learned by a threatening telephone call that it was not the Austrian flag that was to be raised but the swastika that had to be bought in the town. And it had to be displayed, not at the window but flown from the top of the bell tower.[94] This "spontaneous" decking out of Austria showed the enthusiasm of its people on the occasion of its change of status. The authorities kept Riedenburg and Graz under surveillance through a trusted person whom they chose from the teaching staff, clearly a member of the National Socialist party, or someone who wished to be in the pay of that person. At Pressbaum, the staff wore an armband with the swastika. A pupil threatened to turn in a religious if she continued to give the German salute carelessly, raising her arm but not opening her hand. In the boarding schools a few older pupils took charge of the *Bund Deutscher Mädchen*: they made the little ones do quasi-military exercises and taught them Nazi party songs.

Events moved fast. At Graz, on 7 May 1938, government delegates came to visit the place where they wanted to install labor offices. At the end of the school year, the director of the school was dismissed. In June, the kindergarten at Pressbaum was closed. Private schools were condemned to disappear because they no longer had the right to advertise. The house in Vienna was closed on 12 August 1938. On 29 August, a government school was installed at Graz; the director, a member of the National Socialist Party, was a former professor at the Sacred Heart. The boarding school at Pressbaum could not reopen. Riedenburg, where the kindergarten and the home economics school were closed, the boarding school, which was a "German school abroad,"[95] was reopened at the *rentrée* of 1938 and admitted Pressbaum students. But on 1 November, the chief inspector of schools of Voralberg, accompanied by a former Sacred Heart novice who wore the insignia of the Nazi party, came to order the institution closed.[96] The religious could continue to teach; the lay director visited their classes

---

[93] Gen. Arch. C IV 2, Graz. The superior of Saint Adelheid wrote to Rome: "What changes for our houses in Austria...."

[94] M. Benziger, p. 8. It was only in 1939 that the bell towers of churches in Germany had to fly the Nazi flag.

[95] Mother zu Salm-Salm had had this status recognized in 1929. Diplomas from a *Deutsche Auslandsschule* were recognized in Germany.

[96] M. Benziger: "It is the most beautiful day of my life," he said, "I have made Riedenburg fall."

from time to time. They thought they had gained a respite, but on 6 January 1939, the boarding school was closed. They did not even have the right to give private lessons.

In order to survive they sold everything they possibly could. The vicar decided to rent the houses when they could but to remain in place in order to be close to the pupils and to watch over the properties. In Vienna an advanced home economics school was established at the Sacred Heart. In the houses that were not confiscated the religious considered opening a residence for public school pupils and taking in lay persons. Because of a lack of funds they had to cut back on the number of domestics and take up work in the fields and gardens. They also had to reduce the numbers in the communities, and from October 1938 on religious were sent to Poland, Hungary, Holland, Italy, France, Great Britain and Berlin. As income became uncertain, the nuns in Vienna did knitting and embroidery for shops in the city.[97] At Pressbaum, they burned the old student desks and the stage scenery for heat. As the superior of Saint Adelheid wrote to Rome on 25 August 1938, "Our dear cousins are suffering painful trials." They went on for a long time.

In 1937 on two occasions the Holy See raised its voice against totalitarianism, of which Communism and Nazism could be considered effective manifestations. The almost simultaneous publication of the two encyclicals *Mit brennender Sorge* and *Divini Redemptoris* bespoke the pope's will to resist the deification of the state that Pius XI called state-olatry and that he presented as the new heresy of the century. Composed in German, *Mit brennender Sorge* was read, on 21 March 1937, in all the churches of the Reich, condemning its founders' principles. It denounced "the vain attempt to imprison God within the borders of a single people, in the narrowness of a community of blood, of a single race." *Divini Redemptoris* appeared on 19 March; it condemned Communism as "intrinsically perverse." The encyclical denounced the "atrocities committed in Russia, in Mexico and in a large part of Spain."[98] Nazism and Communism were two dangerous secular religions that must be overcome. In 1937 the struggle against the Church had not yet ended in Mexico or in Spain; in Germany and Austria the future was uncertain. The nationalism brewing in Europe and in Asia was heavy with foreboding and was preparing people for what was probably a prelude to war.

---

[97] They were aided by members of Marian congregations. Cardinal Innitzer asked the faithful to contribute to the support of religious deprived of their income.

[98] J.M. Mayeur, Ch. Pietri, A. Vauchez, M. Venard, *Histoire du Christianisme*, Vol. 12, Paris, 1990, pp. 39-40.

01 Statue of Saint Madeleine Sophie Barat by Enrico Quattrini; Erected in St. Peter's Basilica, Rome, 12 September 1934

02 Chapel of the Motherhouse, Paris, Boulevard des Invalides

03 Children's Uniforms, watercolor

1. Calais, 1868-1874: black dress, velvet shoulder straps, straw hat trimmed with blue ribbons
2. Roehampton, 1870: winter, black dress
3. Roehampton, 1870
9. Conflans, 1872: winter, black dress; summer, blue and white checked dress with collar
10. Beauvais, 1870: light coffee colored dress with pelerine and straw hat trimmed with white ribbons, blue tie
11. Beauvais, 1873: straw hat; grey alpaca dress, shoulder straps and bodice, blue tie
12. Santa Rufina, Rome, 1870 : yellow wool mousseline in honor of the Pope

04 Students of Montpellier, 1880-1890, wearing the ribbon of distinction; others, the medal of the Children of Mary

05 Centenary album presented to Mother Digby by the Vicariate of England and Ireland, 21 November 1900

06 Convent of the Sacred Heart, Roehampton, England, before 1940

07 Convent in Heliopolis, Egypt

08 Pupils' dining room, Sault-au-Récollet, Montréal

09 Student dormitory, Les Anglais, Lyon

10 Science laboratory in the boarding school, the Cerro, Havana

11 Students' monthly outing, boarding school,
Tijuca, Rio de Janeiro

12 Departure of Belgian religious for the Congo in 1927

13 Day school, Kalina, Congo, 1933

14 Mission at Kipako, Congo, 1933

15 Chamartín, Madrid, after the fire, 11 May 1931

16 Convent in Shanghai

17 Young Chinese religious, postulants, novices and aspirants in Shanghai, 1947

18 Arrival in Miami of the religious who left Cuba in 1961

19 Boarding School, Lindthout, Brussels, 1949

20 Pontifical Mass at Blumenthal, Netherlands, 1949-1950. Students are wearing white veils.

21 Manhattanville College of the Sacred Heart, New York, 1950

22 Audience with Pope Pius XII of *grandes pensionnaires* of the Trinità dei Monti, 1958

23 Religious of Rose Bay, Sydney, fishing at the end of the garden

24 Pupils' dormitory, Harigaon, India

25 Religion class in Marathi in the parish, Harigaon

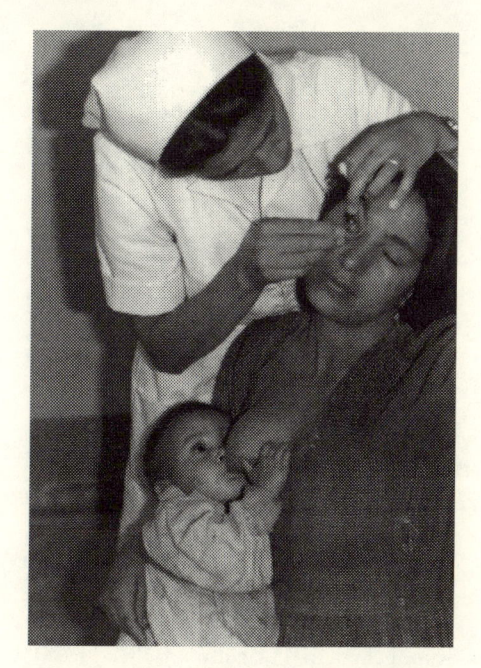

26 Dispensary in Upper Egypt

27 Hope Rural School for Mexican and Caribbean immigrants, Indiantown, Florida

28 School children, Huacullani, Bolivia, 1976-1979

29 Women's literacy class, Huacullani

30 Literacy class for men, Myky people, Brazil

31 Art class for children of Sankocho, Tokyo

32 Kindergarten, Guadalajara, Mexico

33 A community house, Redfern, Sydney, Australia

34 Chapel of the retreat center, Paju-Si, Korea

35 Clare Pratt, after her election as superior general, lighting the founder's candle in the oratory of St. Madeleine Sophie, Amiens, 7 August 2000.

A tradition in the Society: since 1865 each newly elected superior general lights a candle that belonged to the founder.

Chapter V

The Dark Years of World War II

Since the beginning of the 1930's annexations of one nation by another had been carried out in the East and the West, before which the League of Nations appeared powerless and the western countries conciliatory. They created speculation that there was a threat to the international balance so laboriously established after 1918.

Japan's annexation of Manchuria in 1931 was the prelude to the war that began in 1937. Hitler's military reoccupation of the Rhineland in 1936, the *Anschluss* – always presented in the *Annual Letters* as an occupation – the partial, then total takeover of Czechoslovakia by the Third Reich, in spite of attempts made to maintain peace at any price – these were so many upsetting elements that caused a haunting fear of a world war. The conflict broke out on 1 September 1939. Its direct cause was a dispute over the Gdansk corridor, that Polish enclave that gave Poland an outlet to the sea and isolated eastern Prussia from the rest of Germany.

Concerns of the Motherhouse

The government of an international congregation is subject to particular problems in war time. The Second World War affected all the countries in which Religious of the Sacred Heart were living, with the exception of Spain, Ireland and most of Latin America. The British Commonwealth and the United States mobilized in 1939 and December 1941 respectively, but the houses in America, India, Australia and New Zealand came out of the war unharmed, even though some of them were close to the areas of operation.

The motherhouse was gradually cut off from the countries at war. The Vatican helped it to get information about some of the houses. The network of Italian alliances gave it a way of obtaining news of countries in the Axis sphere of influence. The neutral countries played their role. Australia served as a relay station for messages transmitted by radio. But the isolation was intense. The few probations that took place in Rome during the war brought together only Italians and nuns coming from countries allied with the Axis. The aspirants from neutral countries could not get to Italy because of the danger of travel by land or sea. There came a moment when the motherhouse did not even know what was happening in Italy, military operations having reached the peninsula. The general council received news of destruction of the houses only after a delay of several months, and they did not always know whether or not there had been victims among the religious.[1] Financially most of the houses no longer had the means to contribute to the general fund. However, the treasurer general had saved what she could by having money transferred to the United States before communications were interrupted. Mother Bodkin had charge of redistributing funds according to need.

It was up to the vicars to make sure that religious life continued; they had the authority necessary to handle temporal matters, to admit to first vows, to direct probations and to receive final vows. They acted by presuming that the motherhouse would grant necessary permissions, and they knew they were supported. As Mother Perry wrote to Mother Sheldon in one of the last letters to reach Japan: "You simply have to make the decisions in urgent matters. Our Mother General understands that perfectly and God will guide you."[2] The vicars acted the same way with regard to superiors. The vicar of Belgium, Mother Zurstrassen, wrote afterwards: "My line of conduct vis-à-vis the superiors during the war was never to blame them for whatever they had decided in cases of complex problems. God alone knows the anxiety, the hesitation they experienced. And we must give our confidence to those persons whom we have placed in charge."[3] Pius XII said to Mothers Datti and Perry in November 1941: "We cannot see or predict anything from these sad events but confidence in God and constant prayer!"[4] To the extent that humanly speaking there was little one could do, prayer and confidence in God were the only true sources of reassurance.

---

[1] The motherhouse was informed of the bombing of Saint Adelheid, without knowing if the news was certain. It learned only six months later that two religious had been killed.

[2] M. Williams, *The Society…Far East*, p. 119.

[3] *Elisabeth Zurstrassen*, p. 3, 14 March 1946; p. 6, 2 April 1949: "During the war I always said to them: 'I will never blame you for a measure taken in a difficult and unforeseen circumstance. I know that you have always acted for the best where you found yourself.'"

[4] *Vie de la R.M. Perry*…. p. 118.

The government of the Society was troubled at the same time by the superior general's health, which could only deteriorate throughout this period. Mother Vicente had had pleurisy in October. She fell on 19 December 1940, and it was impossible to set the resulting hip fracture. From then on, it was clear that in her weakened state she could not govern.[5] The general congregation anticipated for 1941 would surely have taken action in this situation, but it could not be held because of the war. A vicar general had to be named. Mother Vicente had designated Mother Marie-Thérèse de Lescure[6] for this post, but the Holy See chose Mother Giulia Datti.

This assistant general had all the human and spiritual qualities required to take charge, but her nationality was the criterion determining her selection. No religious from a country at war with the Axis could be chosen.[7] Mother Vicente communicated this selection as coming from herself. She continued to decline, and after July 1942 she did not leave her room, living from then on in a state of periodic lucidity. Mother Datti's position was not easy. Certainly in the beginning she could collaborate with Mother Vicente; but when the superior general was no longer able to govern, she had a free hand in exercising the mission confided to her.[8] Mother Datti was assisted by a council whose membership could not be replaced or filled out. The assistants general were elderly, and the worsening conditions of life in Rome made them prone to illness. Mother Symon died on 12 August 1941. Mother Dupont continued to work; but she could move about only in a wheel chair, and she died on 21 February 1945, at the age of ninety. Mother Perry, seventy-eight years old at the end of the war, had lost her health because of the privations.

March toward Catastrophe

From crisis to crisis, from partial to general mobilization cancelled or sustained, Europeans became used to the likelihood of war. From 1938 on everyone awaited it anxiously, experiencing, according to the cruel but realistic saying of Léon Blum, "cowardly comfort" when the menace receded at the price of a new compromise for which one country had to

---

[5] *Lettre circulaire* of 21 April 1941, signed by Mother Dupont.
[6] Was the secret note really lost, as Mother Castejón leads us to believe? The assistants general were aware of this designation and had informed the person in question. Mother de Lescure never referred to this nomination except to one of the vicars of the North of France, if Sister Quinlan is correct. M. Quinlan, *Society of the Sacred Heart*, pp. 37-38, 83.
[7] Gen. Arch. C I A 8 d, Box 1. *Memories* of Mother Castejón.
[8] *Memories*...Castejón.

pay. As Mother de Burlet wrote on the eve of the declaration of war, "The setting is so calm, so beautiful, so peaceful that one asks if there really is a Hitler on this earth and a war in the air! Is it possible? But still we cannot continue to live with these sporadic fevers! One would like so much to finish with it once and for all. But will a means be found other than a bloody worldwide tragedy?"[9] No means was found.

Campaign in the East

The war against Poland was brutally launched, but it was not unexpected. During the preceding year, in the boarding schools there had been paramilitary exercises that upset the children,[10] and there were classes on avoiding suffocating from gas. At Polska Wies preparations were made to close the boarding school, and in May 1939 Cardinal Hlond suggested evacuating the oldest, the youngest and the sick nuns and putting valuables in a safe place. The vicar, Mother Zofia Günther, had rented an apartment in Warsaw to shelter them. On the morning of 1 September 1939, the religious of Polska Wies went out into the garden to greet what they believed were Polish aircraft: it was the Luftwaffe! That evening the superior had school equipment taken to Warsaw and sent the religious most at risk to Lwow and Zbylitowska Gora. They arrived at their destination after an eventful, stormy trip. Other groups that left later got lost on the way and had to return. The Polish army could not fight off the enemy's armored vehicles and aircraft. Warsaw capitulated on 28 September.

On 23 August 1939, Molotov and Ribbentrop signed a non-aggression pact with secret protocols that divided up Eastern Europe, a pact both stupefying and scandalizing.[11] It allowed Hitler and Stalin to recover territories lost during the First World War, because of the suppression of Poland, and to control the Baltic States and Bessarabia. On 17 September 1939, Soviet troops, urged by the Nazis to take possession of their booty, occupied Eastern Poland. The palatinate of Lwow, where the center of the vicariate was located, was in that zone. Germany annexed — except for Silesia and Western Prussia — Poznan and the Danzig corridor, which formed the *Reichsgau Wartheland,* according to a decree of 26 October 1939; the houses of Polska Wies and Poznan were part of it.[12] The rest of Poland was regrouped into a General Government, including Warsaw and

---

[9] O. Biolley, p. 107.
[10] Gen. Arch. Memoirs of Mother Antonina Zaleska, p. 3.
[11] As the writer of the house journal of Hammersmith noted, "Herod and Pilate, enemies that they were...."
[12] Poznan took back its German name of Posen. Polska Wies belonged to a commune renamed Forbach.

Zbylitowska Gora. When Germany declared war on the USSR on 21 June 1941, its troops took possession of the Soviet-occupied zone in Poland.

War in the West and the Collapse of France

At the announcement of the invasion of Poland, France and Great Britain declared war on the Reich on 3 September 1939. But there were only a few engagements in the West during the fall and winter of 1939-1940. Fearing massive bombardments of cities and the use of gas against civilians, after the declaration of war, western governments had planned evacuations of their people.

The British had most of the children in the London area sent to safer locations. Independent schools had to find safe places. The Sacred Heart occupied properties put at their disposal by families or rented from other religious congregations or individuals, including a hotel at New Quay. The evacuation was carried out in a hurry. The children, who had to be outfitted with gas masks, carried hand luggage and a name tag with their address;[13] they often did not have a change of clothing. The teachers had only whatever school equipment they could carry. Each group's destination was kept secret. When the expected attacks did not come, many parents took their children back home, and some religious returned to London; but most remained where they were until the end of the war. The nuns were sent to Kent, Cornwall, Wales and the Midlands. Some arrivals were picturesque. Madeleine Simon appeared at the convent in Oxford completely exhausted and famished, after settling all the pupils with the families who were taking them in. Marie Louise Schroen took her a warm drink, saying, "Don't ask me what this is." Two days later when Mother Schroen was leaving for the United States, she admitted, "It was Mass wine!"[14]

In the shelters those in charge had to be courageous in fighting rats, boiling water, finding food in neighboring farms and places for the classes. The children slept in corridors; classrooms were turned into dormitories for the nuns at night. The local people welcomed the evacuated children kindly; but in the regions steeped in stern ways that went back to Wycliffe, the atmosphere changed when they noticed that the children were Catholics and cared for by nuns, "women in black who never go out and do not go to church."[15] Eventually relations with the people and the Methodist minister

---

[13] *The Province Remembers, the Journey of Evacuation*, London, 1990. The work collects the memories of the religious who lived through it either as pupils or members of the Society.
[14] P. 26.
[15] Account of a religious who had taken refuge at Lutwyche.

improved. The religious supported the apostolate of the association of *The Sword of the Spirit*, whose goal was to make Catholicism known through lectures and various cultural activities. In the course of the evacuation they "felt that they had new and heavier responsibilities, new freedom, new mobility and a new kind of relationship with the children and their parents. The evacuation was a unique experience; it offered new perspectives and broke down barriers. We were all people together. Community life, very simple but real, infinitely flexible, adapted to this model. There were, however, limits to freedom of movement."[16] Although cloister was eased because of the circumstances, it persisted.

In France the people in the East and the North had to relocate toward the center and South of the country. Families lent villas and châteaux located on the banks of the English Channel and the Atlantic and in the valley of the Loire. The boarders from Montigny were sent to the château of La Bourgonnière. The community of Lille split into two groups; one went to Paris-Plage where they opened a boarding and day school, the other to Mayenne. A few caretakers remained at Rue Royale where proximity to the bishop's house protected them. The community of Bondues remained in place and took in a British field hospital.

Preceded by the occupation of Norway, the "phony war" ended on 10 May 1940, with the invasion of Belgium and the Netherlands. In six weeks the tide of Panzers condemned France to defeat. In Rome the beatification of Philippine Duchesne was being celebrated, but the vicars of Austria and Poland could not attend. Mother Zurstrassen left Rome twenty-four hours before the solemn celebration at the Vatican in order to get back to Belgium before the borders closed. The French vicars hurried home at the end of the ceremonies. Those from the United States and Canada brought back their probanists. With the vicars and superiors of Japan and Australia, they took a ship filled with nuns, priests and seminarians.[17] The British and Irish probanists who crossed France grappled with a train service completely disrupted by military operations. They took ship at Saint-Malo and completed their probation in their own countries. The superiors of Belgium and Holland who had not followed Mother Zurstrassen had to wait several weeks in the South of France before being able to return home.

At the time of the invasion, at the request of the vicar, the communities in Belgium remained where they were: "The risk accepted, we had the experience of the grace of state and had no reason to regret

---

[16] *Sister Winifred Wilson*, p. 41.
[17] Cited by P. Byrne, *History of the Society of the Sacred Heart in the United States*, unpublished chapter on the Second World War, p. 8.

the decision taken."[18] At Ixelles the Sacred Heart gave shelter to "two communities of Carmelites and a phalanx of Franciscan nursing sisters, panicked refugees" whom they had "to console, soothe, assist. The good God gave us the grace to be thus rewarded for not leaving our dear house. How happy we were!"[19] Ostend was abandoned at first then reoccupied.[20]

From the beginning of June 1940, preceded by a flow of Dutch and Belgian refugees wholly without resources, the invasion of France provoked a headlong flight toward the South. The exodus took place while the French campaign was underway and seriously interfered with troop movement. The arrival of tanks and targeted bombings increased the panic and made whole cities take to the roads. The religious in Bondues, who had wanted to get to western France, took in refugees from Tournai. At the approach of the Germans, they left the house with the English from the field hospital and went to Belgium. After much distress and a detour through Brussels, they returned to Bondues on 18 June to find their house pillaged as much by their neighbors as by the invaders. One part of the community of Amiens took refuge near Crotoy, while the other was able to join Marmoutier. The region of Tours, to which the French government had withdrawn, underwent intense bombardment. The novices left Marmoutier for the South, and after the armistice was signed, took refuge at Montpellier. The communities of Lyons and Grenoble went into nearby villages or tried to reach the South. They went back hurriedly, either because they were unable to find transportation to go farther, or because after the armistice, the French authorities ordered the people to return home. Mother Vicente, who feared Italy's entry into the war, sent the Spanish novices back to Spain just before Italy abandoned her neutrality.[21]

Great Britain's Resistance

Great Britain held its own. The battle of Britain, launched on 8 August 1940, led to intense, continuous, daily bombing of the South and center of the country. West Hill and Saint Charles in London were burned. At Roehampton, "night after night we heard wave after wave of our bombers flying out to deliver their deadly burden.... Night after night the sirens announced the arrival of enemy aircraft, usually about eight o'clock in the

---

[18] *Vie de la R.M. Zurstrassen*, p. 6. Mothers Symon and Zurstrassen had made a tour together of the houses in Belgium in September 1939 to decide what precautions to take in case of an invasion.

[19] O. Biolley, p. 110.

[20] Life was trying because of the incessant bombardments in preparation for the invasion of England. The house was completely abandoned to the Germans in August 1941. The nuns lived in a neighboring village until March 1944.

[21] Gen. Arch. Journal of Mother Castejón.

evening. That gave us time to have supper and to gather our supplies." The building had huge cellars that the nuns occupied: "Each one had her perch and with her pillow and comforter prepared for the night. Mother Shepherd thought that in spite of the risk the novices would be better settled above ground. The novitiate was set up first in the brown house, then under the theater. She had a statue of Our Lady, Seat of Wisdom, before which she placed a little night-light. When the bombing grew deafening and reached its target, she called upon it." The vicar spent part of the night visiting the buildings with the guards from the civil defense patrol. The house and the oratory where Father Varin, Mother Digby, Mother Stuart and Sister Lataste were buried were damaged. Mother Archer-Shee wrote:

> Our Lord has given us a wonderful gift of poverty. The community vestry was destroyed by the second incendiary bomb, not entirely, but as the cupboards were wooden, the shelves containing linens were lost. Not one of us was wounded and for that we are thankful. What had been saved from the first fire was lost during the second but nothing in the sacristy. The chapel also was saved, although the tiles had been blown off and there were holes in the roof. It can be restored, even though for the moment there is so much destruction. Each roof has a hole, with the exception of the two small wings and one of these has light and water. We spend our nights there for there is excellent protection. We spend all day cleaning and still the corridors are covered with mud. It is a very great privilege to have been the target of the enemies of God. Individually, of course, the enemy may be good, but the ideology of Nazism is so evil globally that one may believe Satan is behind it and that he uses it to wage his iniquitous will.

She concluded courageously: "All will be repaired long before the day of victory. A few months of ruins and then resurrection. It's the same thing in many places. London is magnificent; public transportation continues in the city, trains also, and everyone is full of hope and determination. May God enlighten us so that we can do his will fully."[22]

Bombings resulted in new evacuations in 1942.[23] These departures awakened admirable devotedness on the part of people who left their houses

---

[22] Letter of 3 November 1940. Communicated by Mother Hill to the communities of California. The Jesuit scholastics, by coming to help them move what could be moved and what was combustible, were an invaluable help. The novices were sent into Scotland to Kinross, the elderly nuns to Mapledurham and Levens. The others were placed in families.

[23] The normal school in London was installed at Roehampton, the novitiate at Stanford Hall, near Rugby.

to the Sacred Heart, sometimes free of charge, throughout the war.[24] At the abandoned properties caretakers looked after the day pupils, not all of whom had been evacuated or who returned in the autumn of 1942. West Hill lodged young women working for the government. Tunbridge Wells and Newcastle took in refugees; Saint Charles sheltered a child care center, and its fields were divided into garden plots. The nuns deprived of the income from the boarding school had to get along by themselves. Bonchurch took up raising tomatoes.[25]

The Sacred Heart welcomed those who could not leave Great Britain or who came to fight the war. Roehampton was an asylum for chaplains of the Allied armies and for various exiles. The Grand Duchess of Luxembourg went there with her daughters, and Madame de Gaulle[26] went there for a rest. The house also welcomed brothers and fiancés of alumnae from the United States, Canada, Australia and New Zealand. The houses located near military posts organized activities for the soldiers. Kilgraston was a welcome center for regiments passing through and for refugee Polish bishops.

From Italy's entry into the war in June 1940, the fighting moved toward the Mediterranean and North Africa. Malta was bombed from January 1941 on. The Sacred Heart's buildings sustained little damage, but the people lacked everything, because of submarine warfare, and famine was finally declared. School life was often interrupted, and in 1941 school authorities simply gave certificates of perseverance to the pupils. Saint Julian's and the Rosary were turned into hospitals. In 1941-1942, classes were held in a shelter dug out of rock where the children and the religious sometimes had to spend the night. The vicar considered an evacuation, but the chances of reaching Spain were slim, and the archbishop opposed the departure of the religious.[27] Life became nearly normal after the Allies took Sicily.

Life in North America

Canadian boarding schools welcomed refugee children from Poland and Austria[28] and later English girls evacuated during the Blitz. Because German submarines were patrolling the entry to the port of Halifax, the city lived under s a regimen of alerts and blackouts. The initial neutrality of the United States offered advantages for the Society of the Sacred Heart.[29] At

[24] Gen. Arch. C I C 3, Box 15. Report of the treasurer general.
[25] *Lettres annuelles,* 1941-1943.
[26] She was an alumna of Calais. The general's sister had studied at Lille, and two of his aunts had entered the Sacred Heart in Belgium.
[27] *The Life and Times of R.M. Archer Shee,* pp. 40-41.
[28] Eva Dolfuss, daughter of the assassinated chancellor, was a pupil at the Sault.
[29] The information on the United States is taken from the chapter on the Second World War in the forthcoming history of the Province of the United States by

the beginning of 1940 the motherhouse tried to have the houses in Poland placed under the United States, using an argument based on gifts from the American vicariates to Poland. After Pearl Harbor and the declaration of war on the United States by Italy and Germany, communications between houses in the United States and Rome were cut off. On 12 December 1941, San Francisco experienced the first alert. Religious of Japanese nationality were few in the United States. Two novices in formation at Kenwood were interned in the house.[30] Helen Condon entered the novitiate at that time; she remembered:

> Like the others I brought my ration card, which was given to the *dépensière*. We had twice as much to do because the war effort had taken workmen who had been employed earlier at Kenwood. Some of the novices and postulants had fathers, brothers and friends in the military, most of them overseas. We prayed a great deal for them. Kenwood had a siren and a shelter where we were to gather during alerts.[31]

The war effort brought about expansion in the western United States. Seattle was a center of wartime industry, and its many military bases created a population explosion that benefitted Forest Ridge. All the Sacred Heart schools and colleges saw their numbers increase however, either because the cities in which they were located grew or because they created specific programs to train young women in business or in nursing to replace men who had gone to war.[32] Scholarships were granted to refugees, and some schools employed exiled European teachers.

The Sacred Heart and the Swastika: Life in Hitler's Europe

In Austria, renamed *Östmark*, Nazi control tightened after its entry into the war. In Graz, on 2 March 1940, the Gestapo made the religious leave the wing of the building where they were living: it was not confiscation but a

---

Patricia Byrne, CSJ.

[30] Byrne, p. 16.
[31] Prov. Arch. United States, Helen Condon, "A Historical Perspective on Community."
[32] P. Byrne, "A Tradition of Educating Women…," pp. 13 and 15. Report of Mother Margaret Reilly, president of Barat College, Lake Forest, Illinois, for 1941-1942: "Without sacrificing what we believe to be the fundamental strength and specificity of our education, we are turning all our available resources now in view of the war effort of the country. A careful study of present conditions has revealed that there is no need to take more drastic measures; when a need clearly appears, we will spare no effort to meet it."

"forced relocation as a war measure." Three weeks later they had to leave after vacating, one after the other, the rooms they were occupying. The chapel was turned into a gymnasium.[33] On 7 May 1940, the property was seized because it was considered contrary to the good of the state and the nation. The superior of Graz was Mother Marie zu Salm-Salm. Since the *Anschluss* her relations with the new authorities had been bad. This German, who had met the Nazis bursting into her room without even getting up out of her armchair, wanted to resist. At the beginning she limited herself to verbal protests: "By being docile, I hoped to remain at any cost in the chaplains' house. If we had insisted, we would have been expelled immediately from Styria. The order our bishop gave to all the convents was above all not to leave the property. That was repeated to us by the Nuncio; the bishop and the lawyers advise us not to yield a meter of the land. Our house is now a mousetrap, and the garden has less than fifty-two square meters." She emphasized the courage of the nuns and was in contact with the local people: "Not a day passes without my having an opportunity to console, comfort and strengthen in the faith four or five dejected souls."

There was discussion at the center of the vicariate of the best steps to take. For Mother zu Salm-Salm to abandon the place

> was to hand over the rights of Holy Church. Elsewhere all the other convents only gave in when they were forced to have their eyes on us. And from whom would the faithful learn resistance to evil if we do not give them the example! These continual triumphs fortify extremely the present regime, which will probably decline only through evolution. Who will think of us again afterwards if we do not do all in our power to remain in place? It seems to me that even if nothing survives of our property, we would have to rent some rooms in order to remain in the city.[34]

She wished to yield only to force, even if it meant being expelled: "The expression is more frightening than the thing itself. The most likely outcome would be to spend a few hours in jail until the next train and to be sent to Vienna in a diplomatically sealed car.[35] That would do much good by strengthening the weak to whom it gives a very good example. In addition, this conduct has lessened esteem for the regime very much." She went to

---

[33] Gen. Arch. C III 2. "To give up our little church, that was the most painful blow that one could inflict on us, for it meant taking from us all our most flourishing works. Happily we were able to transfer them to other churches in the city."

[34] Gen. Arch. C IV 2. Letter to the Motherhouse, 22 May 1940.

[35] That is what happened to the Helpers of the Holy Souls.

Berlin to protest, but she could not return to Austria. At the same time, she admitted that resistance was exhausting:

> What costs me the most is to know that all those who remain in Graz, priests and religious, probably even the ordinary faithful will soon be facing open persecution, while I shall be sheltered, without being able to help them or suffer like them. There also one must see only the divine will.[36] It seems to me that one of the great evils inflicted on the Church in the present time is nearly to deprive religious souls of the possibility of a life of recollection and prayer. One does not have even one calm day. Happily interior peace remains.[37]

In spring 1940 Riedenburg took in some very elderly Franciscans of the Sacred Heart, evacuated from the neighboring city of Freiburg im Breisgau. Pressbaum sheltered mentally handicapped children[38] and military personnel. "One of the two tenants is reaching out more and more and watching us very closely," remarked Mother Kömstedt.[39] In the spring of 1941 the two houses took in a military hospital. In Vienna the community was relegated to the part of the house reserved for outsiders, and the sisters took on the heavy work of maintaining the home economics school installed in the main building. Since the tenants paid well, everything worked out better than anticipated.[40] "We are learning more and more to cut back, while holding on to the essential," Mother Kömstedt said. "The good God takes care of his own."[41] As communications between Vienna and Hungary were infrequent, a novitiate for choir nuns was opened in Budapest in August 1942.

In Austria religious activities were restricted or forbidden from the beginning of the war. Marian sodalities were suppressed. The religious provided days of recollection for between fifty and a hundred people and taught catechism. But that apostolate had to be handled cautiously. In Vienna, so as not to attract attention, the participants and the priests entered the Sacred Heart convent through the church, and to avoid meeting the personnel of the hospital, workers, entered the garden through a hidden door. These precautions did not prevent betrayals; and at the beginning of

---

[36] Gen. Arch. C IV 2. Letter of 17 June 1940.
[37] Gen. Arch. C IV 2. Letter of 1 June 1940.
[38] They were euthanized in the spring of 1941.
[39] Gen. Arch. C IV 2. Regular visit, June 1940. Two years later the Religious of the Sacred Heart "were tolerated in their residence" (Report of May 1943).
[40] Gen. Arch. C IV 2. Austria, 17 October 1941. Afterward they made slippers for soldiers.
[41] Gen. Arch. C IV 2. Letter of 25 February 1943.

summer, 1941, as "some undesirable persons" had been brought into the house, this apostolic work had to stop.

In Poland the kind of occupation in the zone where the religious lived determined living conditions. The *Gauleiters* [Nazi district heads] introduced German penal law in the Wartheland and Germanized it. The Poles and the Jews did not have the right of ownership; they were not to leave their place of residence and could be sent to "assembly camps" or industrial centers. Immigration of Germans coming from Baltic countries, from Volynia or Bessarabia under Soviet control, was encouraged. Teaching in the Polish language was forbidden. The fate of the Catholic Church was tragic; Governor Greiser tried a policy that after the war would apply to the entire Reich. The number of parishes was reduced to one or two per district. Worship, confined to Sunday, was limited to a few hours. Most of the churches and chapels were transformed into stores, hotels, stables or at Pobiedziska into a commercial warehouse. At Poznan the only church open daily was *Nur für Deutsche*, as indicated on a panel at the entrance, that is, reserved for Germans only. Another church was open to Poles only on Sunday. This policy, joined to the imprisonment and deportation of ecclesiastics, was so effective that there were no priests left in Polska Wies and Poznan in the summer of 1942.[42] To provide for the liturgy Mother von Schell obtained help from Silesians who spoke German and Polish or German Jesuits, who were not mobilized or apt to be mobilized because they were considered enemies of the Reich.[43] In May 1943 the nuns at Polska Wies tried to obtain permission to give one another communion. In spite of the many precautions they promised to take,[44] the Sacred Congregation let it be known that the pope had refused.[45] Undoubtedly Pius XII had not realized how difficult it was to provide for sacramental life in a uniquely feminine world.

Little by little convents were closed and wearing the habit was forbidden. In the spring of 1941, Greiser expelled the Religious of the Sacred Heart from Poznan. Unsure of the Germans' loyalty,[46] he had them sent back to Germany. A special concentration camp was provided for Polish religious. Not all the Sacred Heart nuns were sent there. Four remained at Poznan to provide service at their occupied house. A few

---

[42] Gen. Arch. C IV 2, 9 August 1942.
[43] She had to go as far as Katowice to find confessors for the coadjutrix sisters.
[44] Only the superior would touch the tabernacle door and replace the ciborium; the religious would communicate using a silver spoon and, of course, all would be done secretly.
[45] Gen. Arch. C I A 8 d, Box 5, 20 July 1943.
[46] His attention had been attracted by the activity of Mother Agnès Best who was helping Polish priests.

were able to go to Polska Wies, but the others were sent to Bojanowo, an old penitentiary where there were six hundred and fifteen religious from twenty-five different congregations and orders.[47].

Mother Helena Chlapowska, who had been superior of Polska Wies and of Poznan, was interned there. She was able to send out a few letters in which she described life in the camp. The food was limited; the nuns, deprived of the sacraments, could not go to Sunday Mass. The superiors were separated from their daughters, since all the religious were mixed together. In July 1941, Mother Chlapowska let it be known that she could no longer write more than one letter a month in German and that she could no longer receive a package weighing more than a kilo. Because of her age she worked inside the camp. Once at least Mother von Schell was able to visit the internees and bring them communion. She also took them some food supplements, vitamins and medicines. Finally, Mother Chlapowska was able to leave the camp under the pretext of lodging with her family without having to produce a document that was equivalent to abandoning religious life.[48]

The General Government did not enforce Germanization, nor did its authorities have as an objective the liquidation of the Catholic Church. There was neither massive closing of churches nor limitation of worship. But repression affected priests and religious. Because the Poles were limited to service work, teaching was confined to primary and professional education. In December 1939, at Zbylitowska Gora the religious were in charge of a public domestic science school. By posing as teachers in a sewing room they prepared about fifty pupils for the baccalaureate and taught catechism.[49] A new apostolic field opened when a Polish committee asked them to accept the children of evacuated families whose fathers were professional men.[50] In Warsaw also the religious maintained a public school and gave secondary and university training in secret.[51] The community had to be fed. At Zbylitowska Gora, educational fees were paid in kind. They cultivated wheat; the authorities bought part of the yield. In Warsaw, the nuns were nourished by the municipal kitchen and at soup kitchens for the

---

[47] Jerzy Kloczowski, *Histoire religieuse de la Pologne*, Paris, 1987, p. 472.
[48] Gen. Arch. C IV 2. Letter of 15 July 1941, from Mother Werhahn: "In this concentration camp they are trying to persuade nuns to leave their order; they take away the religious habit and after a few weeks place the nuns, one by one, in private families or in a hospital."
[49] Ludwika Skibniewska, *Souvenirs des années passées à Lwow* [Memories of Years Spent at Lwow], p. 25. A novitiate was opened here for choir nuns in August 1943, as well as a probation.
[50] Gen. Arch. C I A 8, Box 5. Letter of 9 July 1940.
[51] Information communicated by A. Merdas.

poor. Having to provide food for the evacuated families, they could thus obtain part of their own food.[52] But at Zbylitowska Gora, a German nun wrote: "Complexions are pale as alabaster. The superior lost her profession ring, her finger had got so thin."

Between September 1939 and June 1941 the house in Lwow was completely isolated. Upon the Soviets' entry into the city, it housed refugee religious from Poznan, Jesuits making their tertianship, and about forty nurses. Because the city was under the authority of the Ukraine, the teaching of Ukrainian was required. The curricula conformed to those of the USSR, and all religious symbols were prohibited. In January 1940 a school named "Red Army" was established at the Sacred Heart, which took in also Russian and Ruthenian schools, Ukrainian administrative offices and an acting troop. The nuns had to disperse and find work as domestics, governesses or caretakers of abandoned houses. The oldest and the infirm were placed in the care of the assistant, Mother Baillot, in a villa that was lent to them. Those looking after the convent lived for almost two years in two rooms in the basement, and they earned their living by embroidery and laundry work.[53] They were brought to court for illegal occupation of an appropriated building; but because the house had not been nationalized, they were allowed to continue to live there.[54]

In February 1940 the Soviets began imprisoning civilians or sending them to Siberia. Many alumnae were deported with their children.[55] Some religious would have wanted to follow them, probably not to "found the Sacred Heart in Siberia," as one report gave one to understand, but rather to pursue their apostolate and share the sufferings of their fellow citizens. They helped them when they left by having packages sent to them.[56] They feared that the nuns, the vicar in particular, would be deported.[57] Mother Günther hid; but believing that leaving the city was equivalent to desertion, she refused to leave Lwow.[58] The Red Cross, the German embassy in Moscow and the religious in Budapest all intervened to obtain a pass for

---

[52] Gen. Arch. C IV 2. Letter of 21 February 1940.
[53] When the Soviets devalued Polish currency, in the spring of 1940, it was necessary to have recourse to barter.
[54] Gen. Arch. C III, Poland, B, Krystyna Smigiel, "Lwow – Léopol – Lemberg."
[55] Gen. Arch. L. Skibniewska, p. 10. There was a respite after Sikorski obtained amnesty on 13 April 1941.
[56] Gen. Arch. C III. The vicar was content to say only: "I beg you not to get arrested by the Militia."
[57] Her kinship with General Haller, who had been one of the opponents of the Soviets at the time of the war of 1919, made her equally suspect.
[58] Gen. Arch. C IV 2. Letter of Mother Werhahn, 21 January 1941.

the nuns who lived there.[59] Some crossed the border secretly by using the "green line," according to the current expression, and arrived in the General Government zone, where they reinforced the community in Warsaw.[60] After the Reich declared war on the USSR, the General Government regime was in charge in Lwow. The Religious of the Sacred Heart returned to their house and resumed wearing the habit.

In Western Europe, the Reich did not apply the same policies in every satellite country. The Netherlands, administratively autonomous, was governed by a Reich commissioner, Seyss-Inquart. Until June 1943 the houses of the Sacred Heart could communicate with Rome. Blumenthal was coveted by the National Socialist Party, which wanted to set up a boys' school there, and by the German army, which wanted to establish a field hospital. It was the army that won out in August 1941. The house at Arnhem was seized in February 1942; the religious rented villas in a neighboring village and opened classes. The Hague took on a variety of works and also took in teams of football players and a group of Javanese. The number of pupils increased when in 1943 the government lengthened the time required in school.

After the capitulation of King Leopold, Belgium kept its head of state, government and national administration but under German supervision. Sacred Heart houses sheltered civilians and resistors who hid there. The farms produced their highest yields for the benefit of the communities and people in the surrounding areas. In the winter of 1942, Ixelles took in the school that the Jesuits had had to give up for lack of heat. In 1944 rooms were requisitioned for a military hospital.[61] Some religious in the vicariate were interned. Mother Barbara Napier, who was British, was arrested for the first time in 1940 and was taken by the Gestapo on 2 April 1941. She was deported to Friederichshaffen on Lake Constance, then to Liebenau near Dresden, to a camp for British and Americans. The camp, which brought together about forty nuns of fourteen congregations, had a thousand internees. Two or three times, she received a visit from Mother Tiefenbacher, dressed as a nurse, who came under the pretext of inspecting the camp.[62]

---

[59] Gen. Arch. Letters of 5 and 19 November 1940.

[60] It was thought that Mother Baillot, who was French, would be able to cross to Bucharest. It was not possible.

[61] O. Biolley, p. 111.

[62] Prov. Arch. Belgium/Netherlands. Mother Napier, who was liberated in June 1945, always refused to talk about her stay in Liebenau. During her captivity, she supported the religious interned with her so that in spite of circumstance, they could remain faithful to their religious commitments. Her sojourn in this camp was particularly painful.

France, which Hitler considered a corrupt nation, decadent and "negrified," was divided into four zones separated by lines of demarcation. Alsace and Lorraine again became German administered by *Gauleiters*. As "the French were illiterate" – most people of Lorraine could not speak German or chose not to speak it – instruction began to be given in German at Metz and Montigny beginning 17 July 1940. Despite that, the authorities consented to add instruction in French, evidence that they were somewhat realistic. Lorraine, destined for the Germans immigrants from neighboring regions, had to be vacated. On 16 August, under the pretext of a show of patriotic and religious spirit, the evacuation of the French began. They were sent by trainloads to the southern zone. The three youngest religious of Montigny left, surrounded by soldiers with fixed bayonets, without knowing where they were going or what was going to happen to them.[63] The others were expelled in November 1940 at the time of the second wave of departures. The vicar, Mother Bailliard, gathered a community at Marmoutier again. The community of Metz was installed at Nantes under the direction of Mother de Mondion.[64] In the end Mother Bailliard knew that she would no longer be able to return to Lorraine. She had to wait almost a year for a pass to visit the communities in Lille and Bondues, which were included in the "forbidden zone" attached to the military command of Brussels.

The zone called "free" covered the South of France until the German authorities occupied it on 11 November 1942, while retaining a "French state" under the increasingly theoretical direction of Marshall Pétain. The left bank of the Rhône and the Alps were placed under Italian authority; the Germans established themselves there on 9 September 1943, after the Italian surrender. The religious were locked in wherever they found themselves at the time of the armistice. Changing houses could only really happen after the complete occupation of France, when free circulation among the zones was reestablished in March 1943. Toulouse and Montpellier were places of refuge for many religious. At Montpellier Mother de Lescure was in charge of the novices and probanists, but she had difficulty in providing foodstuffs in a wine-producing region.[65] The nuns suffered from hunger when rationing became stricter and resources scarcer. The establishment of the Vichy regime brought with it modifications in the country's laws. The national Revolution abrogated the laws that had placed

---

[63] Testimony of M-T. Houdoy.
[64] Mother Bailliard left Marmoutier in August 1942, and the community of Montigny then joined that of Marmoutier.
[65] She had also welcomed some Carmelites. Some lay people in the region came to her aid financially.

members of religious congregations under special jurisdiction. The Sacred Heart took up again the management of its houses.

The "occupied zone" enveloped Bordeaux, Poitiers, Tours, Paris, Joigny and Amiens. In the summer of 1940, the Germans decided to expel foreigners who had settled in France after 1937.[66] In Amiens after several days of internment, the Polish sisters were found to be Germans, having been born in Poznan before 1918, and they remained in place. Bondues took in a German hospital until March 1941 but was able to reopen the school, whose numbers gradually increased.[67] Amiens, which sheltered some Poor Clares whose convent had been destroyed, took in Belgian civilian prisoners and French, Dutch and German workmen. The space left for the religious grew tighter, and in 1943 they could not even go into their own garden. The occupation of their house gave them the right to coal, which allowed them to heat the chapel. They tried to have an apostolate with the women who, voluntarily or not, had joined the German services. Marmoutier was partially occupied. Nantes was abandoned in March 1943, because the house had become a military hospital. A few religious continued to teach in parts of the house, including the garage. In September 1943, after the bombardment that destroyed the convent of the Visitation that was sheltering them, most were sent to the North and the Paris region.

In the annexed countries, there was an effort to preserve what could be preserved. During her transfer to the southern zone, Mother Bailliard had telephoned Rome to ask that German religious be sent into Lorraine.[68] The motherhouse had already given to Mother Werhahn, the superior in Berlin, the mission of managing the affairs of the houses under German control but without discharging the vicars who, because of their nationality, could no longer exercise their responsibilities except on the moral plane. The choice was undoubtedly a good one; besides her personal qualities, Paula Werhahn was the sister-in-law of one of the directors of the Siemens Company. She was able to mobilize a network of influential relationships in the army and upper levels of administration, in the diplomatic corps of neutral nations or those allied with Germany and in the German hierarchy, for she was related to Cardinal Frings. Armed with full powers from the motherhouse, she had influence in all the occupied or annexed countries. Mother Werhahn acted with authority, lucidity and competence but with

---

[66] In Nantes, six coadjutrix sisters and two choir religious had to leave.

[67] At the request of Cardinal Liénart, the house became a center of assembly for the movements of Catholic Action and of youth who could no longer meet at the Jesuits' spiritual center, which had been requisitioned.

[68] She had left Sister Kirsch, an Austrian coadjutrix sister, in charge at Montigny until help arrived. She wrote to Germany to ask for aid.

respect for persons. Aware of the realities of the occupation, she had the courage to inform the religious of Austria of the trials that she had happened to witness in Poland.[69]

> In autumn of 1939, Mother Werhahn went to Polska Wies:[70]
> She appeared humble and smiling, like a liberating angel. She presented herself as if she were a guilty person who wanted to make up for the evil committed by her own people. Perfectly aware of the immediate dangers threatening us, she nevertheless consulted the Polish Mothers on their defense plans, looked into all the problems and recommended a plan for an offensive based loyally on friendly relations with the German authorities, that is, the military. Aware of the risks she was taking on as protector of the Poles, she offered to facilitate understanding and agreements with the German authorities.[71]

The Polish religious appreciated "her unfailing nobility of soul, her generosity without regard to her own advantage, her delicacy of feeling, always attentive to the sufferings of others." She was really "an incomparable Mother."[72]

---

[69] M. Benziger, pp. 27-28: "Mother Werhahn came once to Riedenburg and at recreation she told us how frightfully the poor Polish people had to suffer. She told us that one day, during one of her visits to Poland, she had seen with her own eyes an enormous trench dug by the Germans (or by Poles on forced labor) filled with quicklime. She had then seen that a large number of Poles had been thrown alive into this trench. A few days later some of them were still moving. With an expression of horror, she added: 'I was ashamed of being German.'"

[70] Did she take the initiative in this action? Or rather was it at the request of Mother Chlapowska, the superior of Polska Wies, that she did so, as the memoirs of Mother Zaleska leave us to understand? (pp. 41-42). The documentation does not allow us to decide.

[71] Pp. 43-44.

[72] Pp. 56-57. Gen. Arch. C VII 2 C. She went to Rome in 1942: "She suffered intensely from the sufferings her compatriots inflicted on her Polish sisters, and she sought every means to console them and to show all the affection of the Society for them" (*Journal* of Mother Castejón). "She only passed through the house, but afterwards she remembered what we lacked down to the slightest detail. Only after her departure did we notice letter paper, stamps, sewing supplies. We were in the fields absorbed in our hard work when suddenly we saw a vehicle stop a few paces from us. To our great stupefaction we saw two Religious of the Sacred Heart get out. It was Reverend Mother Werhahn and her companion who were coming to our house for the first time. Face shining with joy, arms open, she came towards us and embraced us with

Monique Luirard

The first of her decisions consisted in naming Germans and Austrians to fulfill the functions of local superiors in the annexed countries. Mother Maria von Vittinghoff-Schell was sent to Polska Wies.[73] Mother Agnes Best was installed in Poznan, Mother Maria von Jordis at Kientzheim[74] and Mother zu Salm-Salm in Metz. They acted as weathervanes for the local superiors who were not approved by the Nazis. As Mother von Jordis wrote:

> For them I was the *Oberin* ["mother superior"]. As soon as they appeared, the portress gave the signal with a special bell. I went to ask the superior's blessing; she used to send me to meet them, saying 'Go, little one!' I was under the authority of the local superior and the French vicar on the one hand and under Mother Werhahn and Mother zu Salm on the other. That was a delicate situation as long as Mother zu Salm was at Metz. All that changed in 1943 when Mother Robert, the superior, and Mother Pinat, the treasurer, were expelled. Mother Bailliard let me know that I remained in charge of the house. I was acceptable to the Nazis, because as an Austrian, they considered me German. And for the Alsatians, because I was Austrian, I was not "*boche*." Besides, many believed I was French and did not notice my accent.

When she went to Rome in November 1942, Mother Dupont said to her, "Do not fear to sacrifice yourself for the sake of unity." "It was she who wondered if my position vis-à-vis the French superior was not difficult. But I was able to reassure her."

Mother Zalecka has left a beautiful portrait of Mother von Schell:

> She was a perfect Mother, created by the difficult circumstances we were in. Very straight, broad-minded, understanding, delicate and tender-hearted, devoted to our cause as if she were acting to defending the interests of her own country. At the same time a perfect guardian of the Rule and religious spirit, she knew how to win literally all hearts and had no enemies among the Poles.[75] At Lwow, she recounted how impressed she had been during her first visit to Warsaw by the state of the city destroyed by bombings: In telling the story, she had difficulty speaking;

---

all her heart without paying attention to our dirty work aprons. There was so much goodness and simplicity in that gesture of affection that I have never forgotten it" (Prov. Arch. Germany, Notice of Mother Werhahn, p. 10).

[73] Westphalian, she was related to Count Clemens von Galen, bishop of Münster. She had shown strength and diplomacy at the time of the *Anschluss*.

[74] She was first sent to Montigny where she was aided by Mother Biegeleben, an Austrian naturalized Frenchwoman. She was in charge of both Metz and Montigny after the expulsion of Mother zu Salm Salm.

[75] Werhahn, pp. 58-59.

tears were running down her cheeks. We said, "Mother, stop, we know that; it is costing you too much!" She answered us energetically, "I must make reparation for my compatriots, at least in this way, although it makes me suffer very much."[76]

As for Mother Best, she wrote to Rome: "To aid the Poles one must have a great deal of tact and an extraordinarily motherly heart: I am not up to the task." Clearly she had a tendency to undervalue herself because at Poznan, she helped a priest to escape from the fortress.[77]

The Sacred Heart's ownership of their houses came into question at once. Aided by judges and a lawyer in Berlin, Mother Werhahn tried to use for Poznan a counterattack she had used in other annexed countries.[78] As the Polish properties in Wartheland were liable to be confiscated, she made it known that those of the Sacred Heart belonged to an Italian congregation protected by an alliance with the Reich. At Polska Wies this operation was facilitated by the fact that the property had been purchased by the motherhouse; but the argument was difficult to maintain, for the house had been seized in December 1939. However, she saved it from confiscation.[79] So doing involved a constantly renewed effort, for the occupant tried to recover what was getting away from him. The same tactic was applied in the East of France. In Alsace, the *statthalter* was not trying to create problems, but in the spring of 1941 the Sacred Heart lost Metz and Montigny in Lorraine, where the Nazi party installed an experimental school to train kindergarten teachers.[80] The protection of the properties did not provide shelter for their occupants. Mother zu Salm-Salm was expelled from Metz in May 1941,[81] and Mothers von Capitain and von Loë also had to leave Lorraine where the

---

[76] L. Skibniewska, p. 18. Mother Werhahn had presented the religious come from Germany in the same way: "We are here to repair the evil that our country and our nation have done to you" (A. Zaleska, pp. 60-62).

[77] A. Merdas, pp. 23 and 25.

[78] Gen. Arch. C IV 2. Letters of Mother Werhahn of 18 December 1939 and 8 October 1940. In 1942, the objective was to demonstrate that the houses of the Sacred Heart were autonomous Italian houses and did not depend on the Vatican. It was feared then that a law might declare the possessions of religious orders under the rubric of "possessions of the Catholic Church," which would have caused them to be expropriated.

[79] Gen. Arch. C IV 2, 24 September 1941. A part of the house was returned to the Sacred Heart.

[80] Gen. Arch. C IV 2, 24 November 1941.

[81] Gen. Arch. C IV 2, 22 May 1941. "The Party is pursuing her personally. Her manner provokes their aggression." Mother zu Salm-Salm, believing that she was putting the houses where she was staying in danger, moved in momentarily

struggle with the Church was more direct than in Germany. The last French religious in Kientzheim were expelled in April 1943.[82]

Mother Werhahn took advantage of the Rome-Berlin axis to send some religious who were ill from Poznan to Italy.[83] That was all the more necessary as the Nazis were liquidating the gravely ill, the elderly and the mentally ill in pursuit of their policy of euthanasia. A Polish sister who was spending time in the hospital died of a lethal injection in 1939: "May the Lord pardon such crimes," wrote Mother Werhahn when she learned of it. She had another religious who was a patient in a psychiatric hospital return in time: "You know, perhaps, what we have to fear for those who have only limited strength or use of their faculties," she wrote to Rome.[84]

So that the houses of the Sacred Heart would not be targets of confiscation, the best thing to do was to make them useful to the occupation.[85] There were several possible ways of accomplishing this. One consisted of proposing to take in refugees of German origin driven out by the Russians.[86] The Poles of Poznan did not want the house to become a *Baltenheim*. But could one speak of patriotism when it was a question of "keeping the Society's possessions and carrying on an apostolate as far as possible?" wrote Mother Werhahn.[87] The nuns could also house those serving the German army. Polska Wies, the houses of Austria, Germany, the General Government and the Netherlands opened military hospitals. These were huge units that could have up to a thousand beds. These hospitals offered paid work for the communities employed in the kitchen and laundry.[88] The rental

[ ] with her family. But to avoid living in the château of her prince brother, she lodged in the gardener's house; she taught catechism to her nephews.

[82] There had been a preliminary alert in February 1941. Mother Louise Kintz, who was Alsatian, succeeded in maintaining a community at Kientzheim by threatening to no longer provide services for the occupation. After April 1943 the community was made up of coadjutrix sisters from Alsace, Lorraine, Poland, Germany and Austria and a few German or Alsatian choir nuns. The house took in aged German religious after the transformation of Pützchen (*Lettres annuelles*, 1958-1961, p. 49).

[83] An Italian, Mother Zabeo, obtained the necessary visas. When Italy broke off relations with the Third Reich she returned to Italy to avoid trouble.

[84] Gen. Arch. C IV 2, 24 September 1941.

[85] Gen. Arch. C IV 2, 21 January 1941: "In our day it is always good to be useful; that preserves us from eventual evacuation."

[86] From January 1940, the house in Berlin took in elderly women evacuees from the *Baltikum*.

[87] Gen. Arch. C IV 2, 1 February 1940. The operation was of financial interest, for the refugees paid for their lodging.

[88] The religious were not to give nursing care. In Netherlands and Austria the Germans had nursing sisters come in to care for the wounded.

contract signed by the army assured income[89] and food, for it provided that the religious employed would have the same diet as the German nurses. The use of the houses by the German army avoided the installation there of the Nazi party, the Gestapo or the SS; that would have been a dead loss, for those groups did not pay rent. The hospitals protected the religious they employed from probable deportation. Mother Werhahn took care to make contracts with the Luftwaffe, which had kept a certain autonomy within the German military structure.[90] This policy, aimed at saving people, risked appearing to the local population to be a form of collaboration with the occupation. In Lwow, it allowed the nuns to employ young Polish women in the hospital laundry and thus give them clandestine instruction.[91]

Working conditions were onerous. In the hospitals the sisters were in charge of cleaning the lavatories. The choir religious who spoke German were assigned – it was an honor! – to the laundry and the linen supply closets. They were all under the supervision of military inspectors.[92] Work in the laundry was not without risk, and epidemics spread in the communities. In Poland, the strongest among the sisters were assigned to farm work. They worked eight to ten hours a day according to the season:

> However they preferred this heavy work in the open air, exposed to bad weather but in the company of our peasants, to more sheltered work in the house, where they were subject to the insults of "Hitlerian supermen" and had to swallow them with stoic indifference. It must be said, however, that the Poles were well treated in the hospital and except for the moral pressure of humiliation as members of a conquered nation, they did not have to suffer real persecution like other women of the country, apart from privations of food, housing and clothing imposed on everyone by the war. Certainly here and there, there were national and religious animosities among Hitler's personnel and our sisters.

However, they did not come from ill will towards the Sacred Heart.[93] In Polska Wies the Religious of the Sacred Heart met Protestant religious who were nurses. Prayer in common united them. They gave Italian lessons

---

[89] Gen. Arch. C IV 2, 8 October 1940. 3000 marks per month at Polska Wies.
[90] She had friendly contacts with a general of this branch.
[91] K. Smigiel, "Lwow – Léopol – Lemberg."
[92] At Riedenburg, the sisters in charge of the laundry worked from six o'clock in the morning until ten at night. They had at their disposal, however, modern equipment furnished by the army, and the soldiers helped them (M. Benziger, p. 18).
[93] A. Zaleska, pp. 99-100.

to the doctors and officers who were to be sent to the southern front. Sometimes, but rarely, they could help the wounded spiritually.[94]

Common life among the German and Polish religious could have been sensitive. Testimonies indicate that the Germans were up to what was asked of them. At Polska Wies,

> ...the Polish mothers were zealous patriots, but touched by the devotedness beyond telling of the German nuns. Never was the *Cor unum et anima una in Corde Jesu* more perfectly achieved than in our little community during those terrible years. The German mothers came to us not to protect but to repair. All at once, all barriers of political rancor, national opposition, lack of understanding fell down. There was the most perfect exchange of mutual charity. The German mothers blended in with us immediately as if they had always been in the family.

The Germans never acted without the agreement of the Polish superiors.[95] They stood in solidarity with their sisters deprived of religious comfort, and at Poznan they refused to go to Mass in the churches reserved only for Germans. The youngest of the Germans worked in the fields and stables.

The Polish religious aided the resistance. In Lwow, Mother Elzbieta Walchnowska had formed bonds with "the boys of the forest," and she was an officer of the interior's clandestine army.[96] With the vicar's agreement, she procured for those in hiding food, clothing, work permits, the *Arbeitkarten*, bandages and medicines.[97] With the hospital's rubber stamp she created identity cards and travel permits for young Poles. She gave certificates of Aryan identity to Jews whom she sheltered for a few hours before turning them over to the resistance.[98] The superior in Warsaw, Mother Maria Mankowska, acted as a "mailbox" for the movements of the resistance. At Polska Wies, the nuns covered up the civilians' thefts of food, clothing, blankets and bandages from the hospital stores, and they even took part in them.[99]

---

[94] At Riedenburg they had been forbidden to speak about religion with the soldiers who helped them in their work. The Gestapo had had the crucifixes in the rooms removed, but the medical team was Catholic (M. Benziger, p. 15).

[95] A. Zaleska, pp. 60-62.

[96] A. Merdas, p. 32.

[97] L. Skibniewska, p. 19.

[98] Members of the *Judenkommando* were brought to the hospital in Lwow to clear the land. The nuns could provide food for some of them, and they were appalled to see the destruction of the ghetto in the city (L. Skibniewska, p. 25).

[99] A. Zaleska, pp. 133-134.

The role of the German religious was not easy, and perhaps they were shocked by the actions taken by their compatriots. As Mother Kömstedt wrote, "The four Germans in Polska Wies are courageous and full of charity. We feel only too deeply the evil done by our compatriots. Is it for that reason that we find the patriotism of our dear Poles exaggerated and as it were prized above everything else? This exclusive, strong patriotism is perhaps the greatest internal stress in our religious family." It was difficult to prevent the Polish from acting patriotically; and "there were also some less than frank proceedings that exposed the German mothers to great danger because they were not told the truth and therefore transmitted false information in good faith to the German authorities. Now everyone knows how that is punished." Mother Kömstedt recognized, however, that the conquered Polish had "suffering far too greatly to be overcome."[100]

In Germany itself the war effort imposed on citizens was somewhat delayed, for the *Führer* counted on the *Blitzkrieg* to minimize the need. Until the end of 1941, successive conquests, material supplies coming from the USSR, confiscation practiced on a grand scale provided the German people with adequate nourishment and a life style almost like that of pre-war times, since the occupation dispensed products, money and equipment necessary to the German economy. After 1943, on the other hand, the stagnation and then the setbacks in the USSR and on other fronts reduced productivity. The German people then experienced restrictions and had to be content with ersatz goods.

From 1939 on antireligious measures intensified, for Christians in general were not considered entirely trustworthy. The Reich still had as an objective to control or absorb the churches. The Nazis pursued their campaigns of calumny against the religious congregations regarding practices that they judged anti-natural. For fear of house searches Mother Werhahn advised the nuns to hide their instruments of penance and to destroy their spiritual notes, in particular those that were not written in German.[101]

In the winter of 1940 the authorities considered placing sick children or delinquents in convents or establishing in them schools for Hitler youth. The best countermove was to make them military hospitals. But while in the annexed countries religious could perform only auxiliary roles, in Germany they had to have real responsibility, for every German who could not justify

---

[100] Gen. Arch. C IV 2, Letter of 16 January 1941.
[101] In December 1939, Mother von Kuenburg was called to Saint Adelheid in order to help the German religious benefit from the experience she had gained in Austria in relations with the Nazis. She assisted them until spring 1940 when they had to close the boarding school (*Lettres annuelles*, 1959-1961, p. 255).

Monique Luirard

her position as useful to the nation was placed in a munitions factory. The novitiate program was altered,[102] and novices and aspirants had to study nursing or stenography before being assigned to the hospital opened at Saint-Adelheid in July 1941. As its personnel had to be self-supporting, Mother Werhahn had religious come from Austria. French and Russian prisoners of war were sent as workers to this hospital. Male religious among the wounded were not allowed to say Mass.[103]

In the spring of 1941, the Nazis tried to take possession of religious houses. As they did not exempt those that housed hospitals, conflicts developed between the party and the army. In spite of the protests of the ambassadors of Italy, Spain and Argentina and the nunciature and the bishop's office in Berlin, the SS confiscated the house at Grünewald on 26 June.[104] The school operating there was allowed to continue. Saint-Adelheid met the same fate in July 1941, and the religious had to continue to work without salary,[105] until the Gestapo left the house. The house in Munich was taken at the end of 1941, and the nuns were sent to Berlin and Riedenburg. Mother Werhahn had to find asylum for almost two hundred people. With the aid of alumnae she set up three shelters in the Rhineland, at Unkel, Aix-la-Chapelle and Mettlach. Nuns over seventy were sent to Unkel. As Mother zu Salm-Salm, who was superior, wrote, they did not wear the habit and they were deprived of the presence of the Blessed Sacrament: "Impossible to keep it without seriously compromising the family that has received us so charitably and without putting ourselves in danger of being regarded as a religious community and being put out anew. We are old ladies in a

---

[102] Gen. Arch. C IV 2, 21 January 1941. The Jesuits in Austria had closed their novitiate and assigned each novice a father master.

[103] Some French prisoners of war took part in the Mass celebrated for the religious in the basement. At Pressbaum on the other hand, the hospital was supplied with a military chaplain from October 1941, and he was visited by the military ordinary of the forces of the Reich in 1943.

[104] It had been invaded on June 4 in the course of a particularly spectacular operation, for the SS had entered through the ground floor windows, creating panic among the kindergartners (Memoir of Mothers von Chorinsky and Gielen and *Lettres annuelles*, 1941-1943). The house was searched by the Gestapo while Mother Werhahn was kept in her office. The nuns found refuge with the Sisters of Saint Charles Borromeo, the Servants of the Holy Spirit in Charlottenburg and the Sisters of Perpetual Adoration. Some religious were sent to Austria and some to Saint Adelheid.

[105] The memoirs of Mother von Chorinsky show that the relations of the religious and the doctors were satisfactory. Some of the doctors as well as the soldiers went to Mass. The religious provided nursing care and assisted the dying.

rented house." The villagers took care of them and sent them donations anonymously or approached them in the streets to ask them to pray for one of their sons at the front.[106] The younger ones among them worked in a factory making pins.[107]

In 1942, the Gestapo forbade groups of more than twelve to live together. Unless serving in the army, all Germans under forty had to work in factories. Mother Werhahn sent the eldest into Austria and Holland, keeping the youngest in Germany or bringing them back. She placed most of them in the military hospitals at Saint Adelheid and Grünewald, where she managed to return in the autumn of 1942.

The conditions of religious life in Hitler's Europe brought into question what personal or communal religious practices were possible. The religious were limited to a life that was no longer really conventual, and their apostolate had nothing in common with anything they had done earlier. The students and the nurses were not available to recite the Office or for recreation. In Poznan Mother von Schell did succeed in organizing the annual retreats.

> It was not without great effort on their part that the nuns subject to the law of compulsory work could make sure of their spiritual exercises. The working hours were strictly supervised. The mothers and sisters who labored in the fields were particularly overworked, especially in the spring and summer months. They had only a short time for meals, and they were so tired that they had difficulty being recollected and praying. They had to be in the fields at dawn, and they could not always go to Mass or make their meditation. In the evening they were dropping from fatigue. The mothers in charge did their best to encourage them and to give them rest on the rare holidays granted to those who were forced into military service.[108]

What was happening in the Reich brought up the question of religious life in a totalitarian country. In Germany and Austria the religious lived in constant fear of expulsion. Each one had her suitcase ready with clothes and identity papers on which was a photograph of herself in secular dress.[109] "I believe we are going to end up in a concentration camp, which will be hard for the elderly and the sick," thought Mother Werhahn in July

---

[106] Gen. Arch. C IV 2, 2 September 1941.
[107] Unkel had to be abandoned in September 1942, for the house was so cold that the religious could not have spent the winter there.
[108] A. Zaleska, pp. 192-193.
[109] M. Benziger, p. 35.

1941. There was no question of leaving the country, for Germans were not allowed to leave. The best one could hope for was to take shelter with one's family. Until at least 1942, Mother Werhahn had no doubt that the war would end in a German victory. Since in that case the Nazi regime would continue, it did not seem to her that the future of religious life was assured: "It is to be expected that they will secularize all of us after taking our works and our convents," she wrote to the motherhouse. "Many congregations no longer have homes."[110] In 1942 she announced that she was trying to adapt the Constitutions in case the nuns would be obliged to live in small groups, even alone. She thought it would then be a question of preserving the greatest uniformity possible. She wondered how to live poverty and respect cloister. Some discussion among superiors took place in Germany to consider this eventuality; not all were in agreement about the policy to adopt. The line of conduct proposed by Mother Nagant was "to do what everyone else was doing." She had said, "Try to gather [the nuns] as quickly as possible in small groups before that becomes no longer possible." Mother Werhahn added: "I believe it is not enough for a religious to live 'like everyone else.' Could we not say 'live as much as possible according to our holy rules?'"[111]

At the end of 1942 since all the men were mobilized, work in Germany proved exhausting for women to the point that Mother Werhahn tried to send some religious to Italy for a rest. Physical and mental health was deteriorating. Many nuns had vertigo or were subject to falls. Those who worked in the military hospitals had no rest.[112] The British and American bombings were an additional trial. In 1943 the civilian population was expelled from the Rhineland: "It is truly hell," wrote Mother Werhahn. "Many of our dear alumnae have died; many have lost everything."[113] In Berlin where the bombing destroyed sectors of the capital one after the other, the city gradually fell into chaos. On 1 August 1943, women and children were ordered to leave the city, which the diplomatic corps had already abandoned. The aged and sick nuns were evacuated to Austria. The others took charge of three day pupils and taught catechism to a few children in the neighborhood. Every two weeks a Jesuit came to give them a course in philosophy, offering some intellectual sustenance. They had to do manual work every week to meet their basic needs. They decided to remain in the capital "as long as possible to pray and suffer with the great

---

[110] Gen. Arch. C IV 2. Letter of 22 May 1941.
[111] Gen. Arch. C IV 2, 12 September 1942.
[112] They could not walk in the garden on account of the presence of the soldiers.
[113] Gen. Arch. C IV 2, 26 June 1943.

city."[114] They welcomed alumnae who had lost everything: "The good God manages to make it possible for us to help those suffering, by giving them food, keeping a few things they have been able to save and lodging them until they can find a new home. The classrooms have been changed into bedrooms for seven to nine women."[115] In March 1944 Grünewald was the victim of incendiary bombs.[116]

Reversal: toward the Liberation of Europe.

A military turnaround began to be seen in the autumn of 1942. From then on the United States had the technical superiority that allowed them to supply their allies with arms. The USSR was reorganized in the Ural and created industrial centers in Siberia. New types of cannon and tanks had been developed. The victory of El Alamein, 3 November 1942, halted the Axis threats to the Suez Canal and heartened the religious in Cairo and Heliopolis, who had dreaded the arrival of Rommel's *Afrikakorps*. Some countries, neutral until then, entered the war, as did Brazil in 1942.

The British and American forces landed in North Africa on 8 November 1942. On 5 February 1943, the surrender of Stalingrad pushed back the German armies. In the South the Anglo-American landing in Sicily in July 1943 led to the fall of Mussolini. Rome was declared an open city and occupied by the Wehrmacht. The Germans invaded Italy and resisted for a long time, but from the beginning of 1944 Mother Werhahn began to bring back the German religious who were living on the Italian peninsula. There was bitter combat between Allied troops who were trying to make progress toward the North and German troops who were trying to prevent their advance. The house in Catania was completely devastated. Out of fifteen Italian houses of the Sacred Heart, only two came out of the war undamaged. For the others the damage went from almost total destruction in Milan, Naples, Albano and Padua to more or less serious damage in Turin, Florence and Genoa. The religious took refuge in the villages. After the end of 1942 the vicar of Florence could no longer visit her houses. After 8 September 1943, she no longer had news from Rome and in 1944, from the North of Italy.[117]

The motherhouse was not spared when Rome was bombed. The raid on 10 March 1944 broke almost all the windows. The great worry then was how to protect the superior general who was utterly incapable of

---

[114] Gen. Arch. C IV 2, 9 August 1943.
[115] Gen. Arch. C IV 2, 7 February 1944.
[116] Gen. Arch. C IV 2, 17 April 1944.
[117] *Lettres annuelles*, 1958-1961, p. 33.

moving. At the request of the Vatican religious houses were opened to Jews threatened with deportation. The Sacred Heart houses sheltered a few women or hid their children among the boarders. They also housed the wives and children of civilians and military personnel pursued by Fascist authorities and people of all nationalities who risked being arrested.[118] The motherhouse welcomed the nuns from Albano, who were transported to Rome in a truck flying the flag of the Vatican.

In March 1944 to prevent Admiral Horthy from pulling out of the coalition, the Germans invaded Hungary. A reign of terror befell the people. The houses of the Sacred Heart no longer had contact with Rome and Vienna when in October Budapest was transformed into a base camp. A deluge of fire rained on the city. The *Sophianum* was put at the disposal of the Swedish Red Cross, which protected Jewish families. Refugees were hidden in the cellars, and the convent was not attacked either by the Nazis or by the Arrow Cross Party. The schools were closed but the pupils remained at the Sacred Heart. The *Philippineum,* which had already given space to a hospital, took in refugees who were fleeing the countryside: Jews, escaped French prisoners of war and hospital nuns of Notre Dame de Sion.

At the end of 1944 the troops of Marshall Malinovski began the siege of the city, and the street battles lasted fifty days. The defense of Budapest was nearly as bloody as that of Stalingrad. The *Philippineum,* guarded by three religious, was relatively preserved during this period. The *Sophianum,* whose superior, Mother Hildegarde Gutzwiller, was a Hungarian national, was at the heart of the fighting. It was under the protection of the nunciature and the Swiss embassy. It took in parents of pupils, friends who had lost their home or who could not leave the city, Poles who had crossed the border; lay teachers; some "English Ladies," nuns of Mary Ward's institute. More than a hundred persons lived in the "catacombs,"[119] "with Our Lord in our midst. The community spent nights in his presence, for there was no other place for us."[120] For months the nuns and their guests were confined to the house. In the *Philippineum,* "We were living like moles without electric light, with only as much water as helpful arms could pull from our well in the garden under a hail of bombs." The Germans, who were separated from the Russians only by the width of a street,

---

[118] The motherhouse lodged one of Roosevelt's nieces. *Lettres annuelles* 1954-1958, pp. 23-24, and 1951-1954, pp. 168-175.

[119] Gen. Arch. C IV 1, Boxes 3-5. *Le Sophianum aux catacombes. Petite relation du siège de Budapest vécu au Sacré-Cœur.* (The *Sophianum* in the Catacombs. A Short Account of the Siege of Budapest as Lived at the Sacred Heart).

[120] The only place they could find to place the tabernacle was the room where they did the dishes.

installed a radio on the roof of the *Sophianum*. The first of January 1945, the bombardments[121] and the fighting with heavy armaments gradually made the floors of the fire-ravaged building collapse.[122] Toward the middle of January the tension was such that the nuns did not dare to take their meals for "one would not like to die while eating," and slept without taking off their clothes for fear of the arrival of the Soviets, who inspected the rooms that were somewhat out in the open. The pipes broke and the nuns collected snow to melt. The Jesuits helped them save food and medicine, then sent a brother at night to ward off intruders.[123]

When combat ceased on 26 January 1945, the nuns of the *Sophianum* tried to send their guests away: "For the most part there was no longer any danger for them in living at home. The reasons they advanced for prolonging their stay here, lack of windows, food, heating, were even truer for us. We had to think of the future, of our children, of sustaining the strength of our young religious." When electricity was restored toward the middle of February, the religious were finally able to see the state of the house and of their personal effects. "The appearance of our caps was unbelievable!" They began to sweep up the debris. They left the basements on 19 February. The primary school reopened on the first of March, and teaching was resumed in April. After the feast of the Sacred Heart the first public Catholic demonstration in the neighborhood took place: "We decorated our ruins, which dominated the square, with a banner on which a large crucifix stood on a background of the Hungarian colors. It was symbolic. The crowd was alive with enthusiasm." An epidemic of typhus broke out, and in a few months fifteen nuns at the *Philippineum* succumbed.

Soviet troops, having jumped the Hungarian barrier, moved toward Austria. In Graz, the boarding school was burned during the fighting in April 1945. During the siege of Vienna, the religious had to abandon their

---

[121] Gen. Arch. C IV 1, Boxes 3-5. "Planes flew incessantly over the house. During the day a plane came by every eight minutes and dropped a load of five bombs. The planes were so low that we had the impression that at any minute they were going to take the roof off. There was constant machine gunfire. The walls were riddled with holes like a sieve. No one could go upstairs in the house any longer." Mother Gutzwiller wrote the same day: "Today eight bombs fell on our house and several on the Karoly palace. My good Jesus, what does confidence mean at this moment? I have counted on you unshakably, sure that you would preserve this house! Your will be done! Thank you for saving all our lives" (*Lettres annuelles*, 1959-1961, p. 216).

[122] The supply of potatoes was destroyed. Mother Gabriele Paradeis, the assistant, tried to recover what she could. She piled sheets and other linens under her mattress, which little by little rose to an uncommon height!

[123] Some priests and lay people also brought them food.

house. Riedenburg was close to Munich and Friedrichshafen where there was a Zeppelin factory. The Wehrmacht constructed a huge tunnel at the Sacred Heart. During bombings it served as both a shelter and a center of operations.

In Poland the religious worried about the future: "There is no longer any way to make plans; we live from day to day counting on divine Providence who will show us his will step by step," wrote Mother Werhahn on 18 March 1944. On July 19 the Germans evacuated the hospital in Lwow that had been retaken by the Soviets. In Warsaw, where the resistance rose up on 1 August 1944, the area where the Sacred Heart was located held on for eleven days. The German nuns could not obtain passes for the capital. Finally on 8 August, soldiers of the assault brigade forced out the nuns, whose crosses and rings they destroyed, and set fire to their house. With some lay women and the priest who lived with them, they were to be deported to Germany. On the way, thanks to her knowledge of German, Mother Gertrud Zurawska was able to convince the officers in charge of the column to detach her group. During their wanderings, the religious lived on money given to them by the resistance.[124] At the end of several weeks some of them settled in Grabow, a few kilometers from the front, in the country house that Mother Günther had bought in 1938. There they were joined by Mothers Werhahn and von Schell. Armed with safe-conducts they were sent to Polska Wies, then to Berlin and Pressbaum.

The Soviet offensive of January 1945 swept through Poland from East to West. The hospitals of Zbylitowska Gora and Polska Wies were evacuated. The German population, panic-stricken by the intensity of the fighting and by the tortures to which the Soviets resorted, withdrew toward the West beyond eastern Prussia. The German nuns left Polska Wies with the wounded on the last train from Poznan to Berlin.[125] In February 1945 the fighting caused incalculable destruction in Poznan. After the surrender of the city, the convent of the Sacred Heart was nothing but a pile of ruins.

In Western Europe events began to take another turn after the landing of 6 June 1944. The bombings that preceded it had no victims at Marmoutier, but the house in Amiens was partially destroyed. The nuns took refuge with their pupils in three small houses that were connected by the gardens.[126] The house in Metz became almost unusable during the siege of the city. Those in Ostend and Antwerp were preserved, but Arnhem was partially destroyed in September 1944. During the Alsace campaign the

---

[124] Information communicated by A. Merdas.
[125] They arrived in Berlin on 23 January 1945. Mother von Schell returned to Pressbaum two days later.
[126] They went out by turns to care for the wounded in the hospital.

nuns of Kientzheim "lived for seventy-one consecutive days and nights in the basement without undressing." At the liberation the house was without water; it had neither windows nor roof, and it had been ravaged by shells.[127] On 23 June 1944, the Gestapo burst into Ixelles and, after a thorough search, arrested Mother de Burlet, who was seventy-one years old. She had been denounced and was accused of helping a Canadian officer to get to England. Incarcerated for ten weeks in Saint Gilles prison and on the point of being deported to Germany, she was saved by the evacuation of Brussels by the Germans.[128]

The Allied troops moved towards Germany. On 11 November 1944, the house of Pützchen was bombed. The superior, Mother Elfriede Buch, Sister Felicitas Schröder and a postulant were killed. Mother Werhahn, who could not appoint the superior she had planned on to Pützchen, wrote to the motherhouse: "I will replace her, the hospital continues." It then housed more than a thousand people.[129] During the last months of the war the community lived in the cellar with the villagers and a community of Sisters of Saint Vincent de Paul from Cologne. The sick and the wounded were evacuated during a break in the fighting.

In Berlin after February 1945 bombings took place day and night. The noise of the artillery could be heard, and barricades were built in the city. A few nuns in poor health were sent to Riedenburg on 15 February. The community reduced to ten members harbored young lay women and contemplative nuns. It adapted life to circumstances:

> Every evening about nine o'clock, we have to go to the cellar. The priest goes to get the Blessed Sacrament, gives general absolution and the hours of torment begin. We are beginning to do the cooking and the laundry during the night, as we have no electricity during the day. And in the daytime, in between sirens, we repair the doors and windows, then help the poor who no longer have homes.

Gradually the circle closed around the city: "Almost no water, no electricity, more and more we settle in the cellar," which they would not leave at all after 22 April. Soviet and German troops surrounded the house. On 24

---

[127] *Lettres annuelles*, 1958-1961, p. 50.
[128] To a person who expressed her sorrow, after the liberation, at not having been able to go to prison in her place, she replied, "You would not have been able to bear it; 1917-1918 was like fresh dew in comparison to 1944" (O. Biolley, p. 119). Another religious, Marie-Thérèse Claeys-Bouvaert, was interned in August 1944 for three weeks in Saint-Gilles prison for listening to the English radio.
[129] She was named local superior by Cardinal Frings in the cellar of the house.

April, the first shell struck it. On 30 April, the nuns took in forty-five wounded and the house was placed under the protection of the Red Cross.

War in the Far East

Between 1914 and 1918 engagements in Asia had been few and far between. During the Second World War the Far East became a real front where the war, begun in 1937, became part of the global war at the end of 1941.

Prelude: the China Incidents

In 1914 Japan had declared war against the Central Powers to oust Germany from China and the Pacific. It had gained the Caroline, Mariana and Marshall Islands, but it had had to give up Shandong. The right of the Japanese empire to the occupation and exploitation of Manchuria had been affirmed in 1927, and the drive into China was at first economic. As a result of the incident of Moukden, Manchuria was occupied in September 1931 and Jehol annexed in 1933. When anti-Japanese movements grew stronger in China, war began in July 1937 because of the incident at the Marco Polo Bridge in the Beijing area.

A second front, opened in Shanghai, gave the Japanese the means to strangle the Chinese economy. Street fighting between Japanese and Chinese soldiers and bombings forced the Franciscan Missionaries of Mary to take refuge at the Sacred Heart.[130] The French Concession was cut off from the rest of the city, but from their terrace the nuns saw the fires caused by the bombs, and they learned from their guests of the horrors taking place in the city and the extent of human loss. Mothers Thornton and Mertens and Sister Katarina Sobota, prevented from landing in Shanghai, had to detour through Japan, but they were able to reach China in October 1937. At the end of the year the city fell. After going up the Yangtze and taking Nanking, which they sacked, Japanese troops occupied South China. Japan installed a puppet government. Guerrilla campaigns waged by the Nationalists and the Communists lasted for many years. The cities were calm again, but China was impoverished and despoiled.

From Pearl Harbor to Hiroshima

In December 1936 Japan had ratified the anti-Comintern pact. Nationalist propaganda engulfed the country from 1937 on. Archery became obligatory

---

[130] Their superior who was Austrian was an alumna of Riedenburg.

in girls' schools. However, nothing suggested that the Far East would be touched by war if it broke out in Europe.[131] The tripartite alliance between Japan, Germany and Italy was signed on 27 September 1940. It stipulated that "Germany and Italy would recognize and respect the authority of Japan for the establishment of a new order in the Asiatic East." Even before the signing, Japan had begun to send troops into Indochina.

In April 1940 a law forced religious associations to transfer their authority to the Japanese. Foreign bishops resigned. At the Sacred Heart young Japanese religious were named superiors, and at Obayashi, an alumna became mistress general. Not all the teachers agreed to collaborate with foreigners.[132] The nuns therefore gave up wearing the habit; they wore a grey coat and a head scarf. Crucifixes, religious statues and pictures were removed. Mother Sheldon no longer used her stall in the chapel except for ceremonies of *prise d'habit* or funerals. After the attack on Pearl Harbor the vice-vicariate of Kobe was separated from Rome and Shanghai. A novitiate was opened in Japan in January 1942. The move had been planned since 1939, but the war with the United States required it. The Japanese houses no longer had frequent contact with one another.

Those in Tokyo and Obayashi received their first house searches on 19 December 1941. In the summer of 1942, the "Path of Subjects," a text that condemned occidental cultures, justified the policy implemented in China since 1931. It presented the mission of Japan in Asia, expressed in the project of the "Co-prosperity of the Asiatic East," as of worldwide importance. The text was made compulsory reading. The Americans and Canadians were to have been expelled on 1 September 1942, but ships could not sail because of a typhoon. Finally on 16 September the twenty-seven western religious in Tokyo were sent together to an internment camp for Christian religious of both sexes, which had been set up in the institution of the Religious of Saint-Maur. Mother Sheldon, the vicar, had tried without success to have a similar one opened at Obayashi. On 22 September 1942, the police came to remove twenty-two "enemies of the nation." In Tokyo they had not arrested Mother Brady who was too ill to be transported; they did the same thing at Obayashi: the police did not take Mother Hamilton, and they decided that one nun could remain to care for her. That allowed Mother Sheldon to avoid being interned in Kobe. This decision made by her councilors did not alleviate her anxiety, for she

---

[131] In 1939 some Austrian nuns destined for Japan could not leave their country. Some Australians arrived in 1940.

[132] *Lettres annuelles*, 1954-1958, p. 415.

wondered whether she ought not to have followed her daughters.[133] In the end the Japanese freed the Irish because their country was neutral. As Americans of Japanese descent were considered Japanese, a religious whose father was American became the superior of Obayashi.[134]

In China the Japanese held the ports, but the French Concession in Shanghai had been restored to Chinese authorities. For a few months the Sacred Heart carried on its activities and also took charge of a summer school of social service attached to Aurora College. The number of students grew. The first three Chinese made their vows,[135] and the war did not stop women from entering. In March 1943 the Japanese arrested western religious. The ecclesiastical authorities chose the Sacred Heart as the site of an internment camp, which meant that religious from neutral countries and those from enemy countries lived side by side. The latter were subject to daily summonses, but they kept working in the school, which continued to function. Shanghai had the good fortune not to be bombed; but living conditions were frightful, and in the internment camp food was reduced to the plainest kind. Mother Conchita Nourry, the superior, needed a great deal of courage to uphold the morale of her community, while sustaining the nuns of other congregations whom she was lodging.[136] They lived together in real solidarity.

In the camp at Sumire, where the Tokyo nuns were interned, the living conditions were harsh and surveillance strict, but it seems that the nuns

---

[133] Prov. Arch. of Japan, biography of R.M. Sheldon. In 1952, she said to the vicar of Australia that she had hoped until the end that the separation would not take place. She reproached herself for not having sent her nuns back to their countries while there was still the possibility of repatriation. "How to manage the house? I could only cry out to God," she said. "Little by little, supernatural strength was given to me to enlighten my route and sustain me in daily anxieties." A Japanese religious who lived with her then wrote later: "For more than a year her expression was serious and her eyes were sad. Then suddenly there was a change in her exteriorly. A constant serenity enveloped her, a benevolent smile that did us good never left her lips; her heart seemed to open more widely to her daughters and to those near us who were suffering."

[134] Mother Ruby Gibbs was known from then on as Mariko Ito. Brigid Keogh recalled how loyal the Japanese religious were during that difficult period.

[135] Madeleine Chi, p. 77. The first choir religious were Tsung Luh, who entered the Society on 9 November 1941, and Renjing Chen, who entered 22 June 1943. The three first coadjutrix sisters, Leidi Gong, Fumei Loh and Yazhen Xu, entered on 19 March 1939; they came from rural families that had been Catholic for several generations. They were people of modest income and social position and had had little education. They were admitted upon passing a test in English.

[136] She died on 31 May 1945.

were not harassed. After January 1943, Mother Mayer managed to pay them a few visits. The nuns suffered from lack of space and food restrictions, so that some fell ill, but then they were cared for in a hospital. The invalids were finally sent to Sankocho, prisoners on parole. In Kobe where the surveillance was much less severe, the nuns could receive visitors, and they found safe ways to communicate with Obayashi.[137] But they also suffered from hunger.

In the autumn of 1943, the Japanese offered to let foreign missionaries return to their own countries. Archbishop Doi of Tokyo, who hoped that they could take part in future rebuilding, asked them to stay in Japan. The Religious of the Sacred Heart chose to do so.[138] Eleven of them therefore remained interned.[139] Probably because so many religious decided to stay in Japan, their conditions in detention improved. In October 1943 the internees from Sumire were sent to the Franciscan friary in Denenchofu. There they had no more space, but they could use the garden, have Sunday Mass,[140] and not be confined inside the camp. Finally they escaped to the minor seminary of Sekiguchi where Archbishop Doi took charge of them. They were less restricted there and could receive a few letters from Mother Sheldon and have daily Mass. They grew vegetables and did some sewing. The nuncio, Archbishop Marella, sent them food and money, and Mother Mayer was able to visit them more often. They said, "We were as happy as internees could be," which was a discreet way of saying how trying their time at Sumire had been.

On 1 July 1944, the sixteen internees in Kobe were sent to Nagasaki and installed in a Polish Franciscan seminary. They worked in the fields and cared for the house. Two religious from Obayashi were allowed to meet with them in the presence of guards. This visit provided contact with the vicar and was a comfort to them. They were there when the atomic bomb was dropped on 9 August 1945, but unharmed; some parts of Nagasaki, isolated from the target by hills, had been spared while the bomb completely destroyed the city center.

At Sankocho, the school had to carry on with fewer staff. When the arrest of the nuns was made known, some Japanese, including young

---

[137] Two of them were permitted to return for the funeral of Mother Hamilton, who died on 13 February 1943.
[138] However, Mother Mayer asked Mothers Britt and Nolan to leave Japan.
[139] See P. Byrne, pp. 17-18. Gertrude Schickel refused to be repatriated because she considered herself responsible for the eight Maltese sisters who were interned with her. She thought she ought to remain in Japan as long as there were any American Religious of the Sacred Heart in the country.
[140] They had been deprived of Mass at Sumire, when on another floor of the building, some priests were celebrating it.

women who had just finished their studies, came to offer their help in continuing school activity. Some German Jesuits gave courses in the normal school.[141] The nuns who remained took over the work of those interned. But the institution was gradually dismantled and the buildings occupied by a radiotelegraphy factory, a social service office and a factory where students made parachutes. The property was not confiscated. The pupils, working at tasks geared to national defense, no longer had daily contact with their teachers; they met only a few times a week. The grounds became vegetable gardens. Unable to feed the cows, the nuns were forced to sell them and replace them with goats. Some young women who wished to become Catholics helped the sisters in the garden and sold the produce. In the summer of 1944 a part of the junior school with five teachers was evacuated to Nasu, a small city in the mountains. The community in Tokyo lived quietly at a slower pace, often housed in the basement of the Japanese boarding school. The heating equipment had disappeared. Alumnae, knowing their distress, often helped the nuns by bringing food. In Obayashi where Mother Sheldon was living in hiding, only the Japanese nuns could take charge of the day pupils and the boarders. Gradually everything made of iron disappeared from the house, from the little name plates on the rooms to the staircase banisters, the elevator, the enormous radiators. Food became a fixation. An airplane factory was installed in the house. The older pupils were mobilized. Only the youngest stayed in school.

    The Empire of Japan reached its peak in August 1942. Besides Indonesia, Philippines, Thailand, Malaysia and Singapore, it had incorporated the Pacific archipelagos from the Aleutians to the Coral Sea and had come close to Australia. The school in Brisbane and the houses of Kincoppal and Rose Bay had to be evacuated, and their buildings served as American military hospitals. But the Japanese did not conquer Australia, and that was one of the turning points in the war in the Far East. After Admiral Nimitz took Saipan in the Marianas on 15 June 1944, American B-29s had a base from which to bomb southern Japan. Until October 1944, air raids were sporadic, but on 1 November the invasion of the Japanese homeland began, and until the end of the war there were raids almost every night. They became more intense when the Allies, after occupying the island of Iwo Jima, could reach the center of Japan.

    The Americans had perfected a plan of systematic destruction of Japanese cities, beginning with the most populated. It was unleashed on 10 March 1945. Incendiary bombs with phosphorous and magnesium devastated cities where most of the houses were wooden and often without cellars. Obayashi was spared, but the water pipes were broken. In Tokyo,

---

[141] *Lettres annuelles*, 1961-1963, p. 184.

where a whole section could disappear in one night, leaving no traces, the most fortunate lived in cellars. Many children and old people were evacuated slowly. During the night of 9-10 March 1945, three hundred and thirty-four B-29s poured tons of bombs on the capital. That nocturnal attack had one hundred thousand victims and destroyed the major part of the city. The following days, "the wind was crazy and the night was brightened by millions of flying sparks. The narrow streets surrounding Sankocho were transformed into a carpet of fire. The Semmon Gakko burned like a box of matches. The tower, which topped the central building and dated from the foundation, shone like an illuminated cathedral, then fell."[142] The chapel was saved. Each religious took what she could carry. Sister Hatsumi brought out the portraits of the imperial family, saying afterwards: "I did not think then to ask permission: they were imperial portraits!" Many people helped the nuns; the Jesuits gave them plates and other people sometimes brought them a little food, in fact, all they could afford to share.[143] This bombing was a very great shock for the country because it was a blind strike, without any fighting. The idea of a possible air strike had not been in anyone's mind.

The bombings were aimed at breaking Japanese resistance. Between 10 March 1945 and the end of the war, the number of civilian victims was double that of losses in the military during the forty-five months of combat. At the request of Japanese authorities and of Archbishop Doi, foreign missionaries left Tokyo where their safety could not be guaranteed. The Religious of the Sacred Heart took refuge in the Japanese Alps at Karuizawa, where they lived in cabins found for them by the alumnae.[144] They taught about thirty children. On 25 May 1945, what remained of Sankocho was destroyed by a new bombardment that caused the fire in the cathedral in Sekiguchi. The interned nuns, after making their way on foot, arrived exhausted at the hospital run by the Franciscan Missionaries of Mary.

In Tokyo, "15 August, when the guards learned that the Emperor was going to speak, they asked us to go to the chapel. It was there that we learned from the emperor himself the good news that the war had ended. We sympathized with our dear Japanese and we rejoiced quietly among ourselves." In Nagasaki on 17 August,

---

[142] Journal of the community, M. Williams, *The Society...Far East*, p. 127.
[143] *Lettres annuelles*, 1954-1958, p. 419. The religious promised never to regret the loss of personal belongings that just disappeared!
[144] *Lettres annuelles*, 1954-1958, p. 420. We had to cultivate a field in order to live. A French alumna, whose husband was in the embassy, declared: "From now on we will no longer call you the *Grandes Dames* of the Sacred Heart!"

...at one o'clock in the morning, the guards rang the bell and told us to go immediately to the refectory, without even finishing dressing. There was no siren. I found that strange. We went down in the dark, as usual, and found lights in the refectory. The officials, among whom were our guards, marched in and ordered us to sit down. The chief stood up, and when everything was quiet, he smiled graciously and said in Japanese: "Congratulations! The war is over. We have been beaten and you are the conquerors." There was simply an "Oh" and a long "Ah" on our part. We were dumbfounded. The official held out his hand and said, "Let us shake hands and celebrate the event!" Cigarettes, matches and wine were distributed abundantly. Everyone behaved properly; we would like to have withdrawn, but the officials seemed to want us to stay.[145]

A war is never over with the official end of military operations. In most of the occupied European countries, liberation had already taken place when the armistice with Germany was signed in Rheims, then in Berlin, 8 and 9 May 1945. On the other hand, in the Far East and in the United States, people had to wait for the emperor's surrender of Japan, accepted by General MacArthur on 2 September, to realize fully that a war that had lasted fifteen years in Asia was over. For the conquered countries, the end of fighting did not mean peace and, still less, independence. The Religious of the Sacred Heart had to rebuild and preserve union in the Society, which for many years had lived in an isolation that would disappear only little by little.

---

[145] M. Williams, *The Society...Far East*, pp. 131 and 139.

Chapter VI

From Chaos to Reconstruction

The aftermath of war weighs on countries that have undergone conflict for a long time. The Society of the Sacred Heart had to take up normal life again when the geostrategic echoes of the conflict were upsetting political, social and economic life. In a world moving toward profound, accelerated change, the Society had to remake itself in order to meet the challenges that were apt to appear.

The Traces of War

For a long time the motherhouse was unable to draw up a true account of the results of the war, and it did not know the fate of many persons.[1] But as Mother Datti wrote on 18 January 1946, "Our religious family has received much, in numberless graces, marvelous protection, that spared the lives of ours amid dangers of all kinds." The Society had not been the victim of internal divisions born of the confrontation of countries at war, and religious of different nationalities had been able to live together in real sisterly love. The division of the vicariate of Germany and Netherlands after the war was not caused by antagonisms, but by a logical development that allowed entrusting the German houses, most of which were located in the western zone, to a German superior and placing the houses of the Netherlands in the vice-vicariate of Blumenthal.

---

[1] In Japan, it took a long time for Mother Sheldon to learn that the religious interned in Nagasaki had not been victims of the atomic bomb. In the United States the news of the bombardment caused fear that the whole Japanese population was affected. The superior of Overbrook said to her community: "I have sent a message to Japan, just in case, but I wonder if our sisters are still alive and will be able to receive it!" (Testimony of B. Keogh). The vicariate of Japan did not get in contact with Rome until December 1945.

Monique Luirard

Although the deaths caused by military operations were few, we must take into account the comparatively high death rate due to malnutrition and epidemics. The psychological consequences of the war were passed over in silence because of lack of awareness of their extent or their effects. Many religious had not had news of their families for years. Nerves and health had been shaken by the conditions of the occupation[2] and the bombings. Eighty nuns left the Society between 1941 and 1946. That was relatively few for a congregation that numbered 6576 members, but the figure, higher than the earlier average, is no doubt explained by circumstances. In 1946 Mother Datti recommended not overworking religious whose health was poor; some of them had already undergone the privations of the First World War in childhood or adolescence.[3]

Students had experienced many traumas: long years spent with their father a prisoner of war; deaths of friends or relatives in combat; the economic ruin of their family; imprisonment or execution of their relatives during or after the war. Rare were the families intact. In Germany and Austria, the pupils scarred by Nazism did not seem "easy" to their educators. It took courage and patience on the part of the latter to "adapt to the mentality of the first pupils after the war, hardly out of their subterranean shelters, with rough manners, their heads full of criticism, still pained by the sorrows and anguish endured during the war"[4] and doubtless also of the exodus, the defeat, the humiliation in a country conquered, occupied and divided into zones. Those who had not lost close relatives had been deprived of their childhood and adolescence and the diversions considered normal by their elders. The trial had matured them and sometimes forced them to assume responsibilities beyond their years. It was difficult for them to follow the regimented life of a boarding school

---

[2] Thirty years later Doreen Boland heard Polish religious evoke their memories when she visited Warsaw in reconstruction: "How they lined up in the snow in the hope of having a little coal; how they had escaped from a building where they had been confined and which was about to explode. In the conversation automatically and in the most neutral manner came phrases like this one: 'When we were taken in a raid by the Nazis to be deported for work.... When my brother returned from Siberia.... When we were wading in the river by the border to save ourselves.... Twenty-three members of my family were killed or have disappeared'" (Letter of 7 September 1974), Prov. Arch. Ireland/Scotland.)

[3] After the death of a novice in Budapest, it was decided to review the pattern of life in the novitiates.

[4] Biographical notice of Mother Werhahn, p. 12. In Budapest, the family spirit and union had been reinforced by the fact that the nuns and the pupils had shared the same dangers, the same anguish and the same privations during the siege, then during the Soviet occupation.

or a novitiate, which did not seem to them to be in line with what they had experienced during the war.[5] The pupils of the Sault au Récollet were by thirds, English-speaking, French-speaking and Latin American. Conflicts were many between the first two groups, and verbal political fights broke out among the Latins during recreation.[6]

Travel conditions were precarious for a long time. In June 1945 it was almost impossible to go from one section of Rome to another. To go from Vienna to Graz was like an adventure.[7] In Holland there were no trains, and most of the bridges had been destroyed. When Mother Zurstrassen was named assistant general, it took her a month to find a military plane to transport her from Paris to Naples. Citizens of conquered countries could not obtain exit visas. In Italy the vicar of Florence visited her houses in a jeep. The religious stuck in Egypt were taken aboard English ships, by exception, ships otherwise reserved for the military.[8] To send religious to Congo, Belgium had to wait until ships were no longer reserved for troop transport. A nun from Austria summarized the general situation by writing: "In a word, we are alive."[9] That was already a great deal, for throughout the world the most immediate question was learning how to survive.

The armistices did not necessarily change the material conditions of the people. In France, rationing did not end until 1949. In the conquered countries it was not easy to provide the people with food. "One can make the children happy when for a birthday one can offer a crumb of bread." To sleep in a bed was a luxury for those who had lived in cellars. "They were grateful for every material improvement offered them, even the least."[10] Everything had to be rebuilt, or almost. In Europe it took months to repair the infrastructures crushed by bombs or destroyed when the German troops withdrew; and yet the unit commandants of the Wehrmacht had not always respected Hitler's orders for a scorched earth tactic. In Japan millions of people lived in the ruins, and vagabond children slept on the sidewalks. People talked there about "life like bamboo shoots"

---

[5] Testimony of Geneviève Bovagnet.
[6] Testimony of I. Page.
[7] One waited three months for an authorization; the trip, which could only be taken in British trucks, took fifty-six hours, for it was not possible to pass through the Semmering Pass.
[8] Testimony of Madeleine de La Hitte.
[9] Gen. Arch. C IV, 2, 2 June 1945.
[10] Gen. Arch. C IV, OSU, 1979. Testimony of Mothers Gielen and von Chorinski.

[*la vie en pousse de bamboo*] to evoke the human and material losses, "lost pride," a defeat for unknown reasons, and foreign occupation.[11]

Some houses of the Sacred Heart were in such a state that it was better to abandon them for the time being. Metz, Bois-l'Évêque[12] and Arnhem were given up. The religious left Metz because the buildings were too dilapidated to be kept. England bought the property of Woldingham to transfer the Roehampton boarding school there, and the novitiate was installed in Brighton for the moment. The normal school, Saint Charles, was moved to Roehampton and renamed Digby-Stuart College. New buildings were erected or old ones, not well adapted to educational work, were made functional, using the funds made available by the war damages and gifts that came from countries that had less material destruction.

The pupils were brought together where opportunity allowed. In Berlin the classes for day pupils were held in a building with partitions so badly cracked that one could hear what went on in two classes at once. Amusing incidents ensued. A little girl scolded her little brother who was in another room "because he had contradicted the teacher four times, which she had heard perfectly."[13] In Naples the school squeezed into the little that remained of the building in Via Crispi, and the day boarders went in groups to a borrowed villa. In Amiens, the *Berceau* had served as an arms depot and was clogged up with cannons and munitions. In Graz several people, including both religious and boarders, shared the same wash basin. The children carried their chairs from study hall to refectory. Most of the windows were stuffed with cardboard.[14]

Reconstruction took years and because of a lack of resources, as in Poznan, it was only partial. At Saint-Adelheid it was finished in 1947; in Munich it took until 1951. In Amiens in 1951, the lawn had returned to its ordinary, pre-war appearance, but the reconstruction was not finished. The day school in Berlin had begun in May 1945 in a military barracks and continued in a modest house in Charlottenburg, furnished with doors, windows and a roof, a rarity in the former Reich capital. It was moved to a building under construction in 1956.[15] In Budapest repair work was efficiently carried out. At the *Sophianum*, the pupils organized a group of *jeunesse ouvrière catholique*, young Catholic workers; they swept up the debris, making a chain from the cellar to the third floor to move reusable

---

[11] The repatriation of Japanese who had lived overseas and of prisoners in Siberian camps lasted until 1956.

[12] A house was opened at Le Sartay, near Liège.

[13] *Lettres annuelles*, 1947-1949, p. 101.

[14] *Lettres annuelles*, 1961-1963, pp. 139 and 141. The situation improved in 1948.

[15] Mother Werhahn was in charge of the reconstruction or construction of Saint Adelheid, of Munich and of Berlin.

cement and bricks:[16] "For months they worked this way, singing night and day the 'Hymn to Work' composed on a Russian air. One class after the other moved to the upper floors. They settled in at the end of a corridor emptied of the worst debris, then in a room where a few windows had been repaired."

In Japan the rebuilding of Sankocho, begun in 1947,[17] lasted almost eight years. A new foundation was projected in Tokyo. After much searching, for large intact buildings were rare, in January 1948, the Society of the Sacred Heart acquired a property in Shibuya that had belonged to the Kuni family, that of the reigning Empress Nagako. It had been transferred to an industrial group that wanted to get rid of it. This building transaction touched the Japanese religious because the birthplace of the empress was considered sacred.[18] It became *Miyashirocho* and was modified to house the international school and other works of the Society.[19] In Susono the immense property of the Iwashita family at the foot of Mount Fuji was left to the Society. It housed a novitiate that had about fifty novices of five nationalities. In April 1952 a school was established there.[20]

The network of Sacred Heart convents and alumnae associations facilitated the return to normal. As soon as they could, the houses located outside the combat zones had helped the others.[21] Those in the United States, Canada, Australia and New Zealand were instruments of providence for Europe. From 1940 on, some vicars in the United States had been sending money to England. All the houses there had tried to help those in Europe, even though some of them were not necessarily very well off themselves; and after 1942 civilians found many of their activities restricted.[22] After the United States' entry into the war, alumnae had asked

---

[16] Gen. Arch. C IV, OSU. Testimony of B. Walterskirchen.
[17] The *Go Gakko*, which became the International School of the Sacred Heart (I.S.S.H.), was reopened in September 1947. When in October Brigid Keogh and Odile Zeller arrived at Sankocho, where only one building was standing, it was not easy to find a place to put them.
[18] M. Williams, *The Society…Far East*, p. 158. The palace, a real jewel, remained.
[19] The Kuni palace was moved to the other end of the property (Testimony of B. Keogh).
[20] It was considered a substitute after the loss of the house in Shanghai.
[21] Some Spanish houses, to thank for the aid they had received during the civil war, sent oranges to England. Mother de Sicart sent foodstuffs to the houses of Italy and France that had welcomed the religious from Godella.
[22] When Mother de Lescure visited the United States, she was surprised at the state of disrepair of many of the houses. Mother Bodkin explained to her that there had been no repairs made during the war in order to save funds to assist other houses of the Society (Testimony of Anne Leonard).

their husbands or their relatives in professional or military deployments to take mail and learn the chief needs of the Sacred Heart. Beginning in November 1943, those in charge of the California alumnae associations banded together to collect gifts for an operation called "hands across the sea." The pupils organized fund raisers and kept up a real rivalry among the schools. Some gifts were spectacular.[23]

After the war ended, this aid reached the neediest houses. The American vicars had money sent to Europe, thanks to apostolic delegates or clerics who were going to Rome. The money was redistributed by the treasurer general or sent directly to Poland and Hungary. Aid to Japan was easier to send since the country was under American occupation. It is difficult to determine the extent of the aid given by the United States. In 1948 the alumnae associations had already distributed $15,000 to Poland, $13,000 to Hungary and $317,000 to the motherhouse. The contributions from the vicariates are not easy to calculate, but they were considerable. We have no means either to evaluate the gifts that came from Canada and Australia. All the aid, modest or magnificent, was proof of "a great devotion and sincere attachment of the alumnae to the Society.[24] The friends of the Sacred Heart appeared in every clime. The alumnae who followed their husbands to Europe or Japan often made connections with houses of the Sacred Heart.[25]

The contributions continued for a long time.[26] At the time of the General Congregation of 1952, the vicar of Canada, Mother Padberg, gave the vicar of Austria all the personal effects she had brought with her.[27] The communities received supplies of stationery with gratitude. The eight cows sent to Obayashi rebuilt a herd that had disappeared during the war. The ways of sending things were touching: "Quantities of chewing gum, wrapped in a little note in the pocket of sweater sent to poor children...."[28] In 1947 Amiens received goods of all kinds and medicines. Eden Hall also sent them used clothing and supplies that were distributed to their neighbors or their merchants. These parcels were received with great feeling: "This is the moment that the *Cor Unum* shows compassion and ingenuity helping those who it guesses are having a hard time. *Deo gratias.*"[29]

---

[23] Esther Rossi, sister of two Religious of the Sacred Heart, who had mobilized people of good will, collected several million dollars.

[24] Report of Mother Datti to the General Congregation of 1946.

[25] Those who lived in Berlin left the city in 1948 at the time of the blockade.

[26] Patricia Byrne has called it a Sacred Heart equivalent to the Marshall Plan, p. 30.

[27] *Lettres annuelles*, 1958-1961, p. 110.

[28] M. Williams, *The Society of the Sacred Heart, History of a Spirit*, 1979, p. 420.

[29] *Journal de la maison d'Amiens*, 5 May 1947.

The superior of Eden Hall, Mother Jean Levis, apologized for sending images of the Sacred Heart that were not in very good taste; she wrote "American piety is terrible!" Mother Sheldon answered: "Your images represent eight hundred acts of love made by the children every morning."[30]

Foreign Occupation

At the end of the war, some houses were occupied by Allied troops, who took over from the Germans.[31] At Yalta the Allies had decided that Germany and Austria would be divided into occupation zones, the two capitals subject alike to four-part occupation. The appropriation of the buildings lasted for various lengths time in the West. At Saint Adelheid it ended in 1946; but at Riedenburg, the French did not withdraw their field hospital until 1950.[32] Vienna housed the British. Mixing the army and the pupils was not desirable; the Allies, who had no interest in prolonging it, allowed Pützchen and Riedenburg to reopen a home economics school.

In the East the Soviet occupation was an affliction. Towards the end of combat the houses of the Sacred Heart had welcomed young women who had been undone by the behavior of soldiers who entered their houses demanding food and women and took both. At Pressbaum soldiers killed the farmer and an invalid housed by the community. A young nun was raped. The vicariate treasurer, Mother Muth, was able to prevent the capture of a young Polish sister by facing down the aggressor.[33]

Again Poland experienced a special fate. Occupied by the Red Army, that country dreaded the changed borders, because Stalin had made the Allies accept the territorial rights he had negotiated with the Third Reich in August 1939. At the Teheran conference in November 1943 he had insisted that the frontier be pushed back to the west. From January 1944 on, some Polish in Lwow had been deported. Ukrainian nationalism developed in an unhealthy atmosphere. After the armistice some religious from Lwow,

---

[30] M. Williams, *The Society of the Sacred Heart in the Far East*, p. 156.
[31] Mother Bailliard returned to Montigny in January 1945 and on 2 March she replaced the French flag in the chapel. But from 16 January 1945, the house was requisitioned by the Americans to serve as a recreation spot for the soldiers in Patton's army. The community reassembled however in April.
[32] In 1951, Mother von Kuenburg opposed the military authorities who wished to bury 1200 coffins containing the remains of soldiers killed during the war in the basements of Riedenburg. The French governor of Voralberg, when he learned about the affair, called a halt. He declared that "among his employees there was no one who could write his language as correctly as 'that superior of Riedenburg!'" (*Lettres annuelles*, 1959-1961, p. 262).
[33] M. Benziger, p. 47.

sent to Zbylitowska Gora and to Polska Wies to help reopen the schools, brought as much baggage as possible. In January 1946 the Uniate cathedral was given to the Orthodox. As Catholic congregations had to get back to Poland, Lwow was evacuated little by little from April on. Two elderly nuns, a French mother, Louise Baillot, and a Czech, Mother Jadwiga Wawra, had no passports. Mother Günther stayed on to the point of taking the last train destined for religious, 1 June 1946, hoping to have the matter cleared up; she had to leave them in the care of two Poles, Mother Elzbieta Walchnowska and Sister Maria Krupa.

Mother Walchnowska earned the living for the group by getting herself hired as sacristan of the Latin Rite cathedral. The little community, which made hosts for neighboring parishes, lived at the Sacred Heart until 1949, when the house was confiscated. The religious then settled in a small apartment near the cathedral. Mother Wawra died in 1949, Sister Krupa in May 1955 and Mother Baillot in October 1955. Mother Walchnowska could have returned to Poland; but Cardinal Wyszynski asked Mother Günther to leave her in Lwow, for she was helping Poles who remained in the city, where from then on there were few Catholic priests and few open churches. She continued to prepare children for First Communion, to make hosts and to copy the Ordo of the missal for priests deported into the USSR. She worked with some Basilian nuns, who had nursed Mother Baillot at the end of her life and who did the same for her at the end of her life.[34]

Japan, occupied by the Allies, came under the direct control of the United States through General MacArthur who took on the role of Shogun[35] without the title. The country's laws changed after the defeat. At the time of the surrender the emperor had accepted the "four freedoms," one of which concerned religion. On 15 November 1945, Shinto ceased to be the established religion. Christian churches were allowed to reopen; Japanese were baptized in large numbers, their conversion no longer considered treason.[36] Women were granted the right to vote. In 1946 an education law lengthened the course of study by a year; from then on it was modeled on the American system.[37] Each prefecture would have a university. Higher education for women became widespread. Schools had to

---

[34] K. Smigiel, p. 4. She died in February 1971.
[35] Jacques Gravereau, *Le Japon*, Paris 1988, p. 101, "The New Shôgun;" and p. 114, "MacArthur in his Kingdom."
[36] During the war conversion to Catholicism appeared as collusion with the civilization of the enemy countries of the West (Testimony of Tsuneko Takei). According to Sumiko Iba, "Catholics breathed after the war."
[37] From 1941, a reform of public schools had lengthened to eight years the obligatory cycle that had been six years before.

organize four-year college preparatory courses. The Society of the Sacred Heart, which benefitted from the experience of other vicariates, revised its plan of studies.

The greatest hardship in Japan then was food. Because of the destruction brought by the war, poor rice harvests and the reluctance of the peasants to sell their produce, the people were starving. After March 1947, the United States sent cereals and raw materials through LARA (Licensed Agency for Relief in Asia). In the meantime the houses of the Sacred Heart had been helped by the American Church and the army of occupation.[38] As Mother Mayer said to a military chaplain who asked her what she needed most, she replied, "Powdered milk.... The primary thing is to keep babies and the infirm alive."[39] Soldiers and American chaplains brought food and linens and all kinds of basic necessities that had disappeared completely and could not be found on the black market.[40] Help sent by the houses in the United States[41] and the Commonwealth and by the alumnae kept communities alive and allowed them to assist local alumnae often burdened with young children and reduced to misery following the loss of their husbands.[42] Malnutrition touched the entire population. Life only returned to normal in 1950 when Japan became the center of logistics for the United Nations troops engaged in the Korean War. Korea became independent again in 1952. The standard of living then surpassed that of pre-war times.

Renewal of the Central Government

On 18 January 1946, Mother Datti announced that a general congregation would be held in October. Mother Vicente died three days later: "Each of us, Reverend Mothers and dear Sisters, feels the importance of this event for the future of the Society," wrote Mother Datti on 24 May. This phrase was not simply a cliché, for the vicars general had always been elected superior general. That tradition was broken in 1946. It was in no way a rejection of

---

[38] M. Williams, *The Society...Far East*, p. 144. Archbishop Spellman of New York, chaplain of the American army in Japan, was generous to the houses of Tokyo and Obayashi.

[39] *Lettres annuelles*, 1954-1958, p. 429.

[40] Testimony of B. Keogh. The question was rather to divide the gifts between the Japanese and the international school. Numbers of international school pupils had fathers in the army of occupation and the school benefitted by that fact.

[41] Among Brigid Keogh's effects in 1947, there were foodstuffs, scholastic materials and a washing machine, which crossed the Pacific twice before arriving at its destination.

[42] Mother Mayer was a great help to many of them.

Mother Datti, but she was then seventy-eight years old. The choice fell on the vicar of the Midi, Mother Marie-Thérèse de Lescure. She was the first Frenchwoman to fill the office since the death of Mother Gœtz.

The election of 1946 took place under unusual conditions. For the first time since 1865, it seemed open, independent of the pressure exerted by the late superior general through the secret note. It took longer than had been expected, because as Mother Cubero, the vicar of Chile, admitted, "We had no direction whatsoever!"[43] The voting leaned toward Mother Zurstrassen, the only assistant general who could be named, and on Mother de Lescure[44]. After the election, a *Te Deum* of thanksgiving was sung in the motherhouse chapel in the presence of the community. The suspense lasted even longer than anticipated, because Mother de Lescure went right to her place while the vicars were accompanying the cardinal protector; and no one in the community turned around to see who was in the superior general's stall!

The general council was reduced to three assistants, one of whom, Mother Constance Perry, resigned for health reasons. It was completed by Mother Elena Ytturalde and Mother Ursula Benziger, superiors respectively of San Sebastián and Manhattanville. It was one of the few times when the assistants general were not chosen from among the vicars.[45] Mother Datti found herself in second place: "It was beautiful to see her so radiant with serene joy, so full of filial attention for her new Mother General! The latter relied on her, consulted her and on every occasion, showed her deference and gratitude."[46] Mother Datti's experience, her knowledge of the Vatican and of Roman society were invaluable for Mother de Lescure and allowed her to govern with some continuity, even though she had not been a member of the general council before.

---

[43] It had been more than ten years since the vicars had met.

[44] Gen. Arch. C I C 3, Box 15.

[45] There was even an amusing *quid pro quo* concerning Mother Ytturalde, for the telegram announcing her nomination was sent to Bilbao, which she had left two months before. It was through her replacement that she learned of her nomination; she therefore, awaited confirmation. It was only when she received congratulatory telegrams that she understood that there had been no mistake. But as she refrained from telling her community, the nuns learned of it from the lay teachers who heard it on the radio!

[46] Journal of Mother Castejón.

The Society of the Sacred Heart in the World of Its Times 1865 -2000

A New Geopolitical Context

The Cold War and the Iron and Bamboo Curtains

The generalate of Mother de Lescure unfolded in an entirely new world context. Although the westerners had promised before the armistice that free elections would take place in Eastern Europe, the countries occupied by the Red army were transformed into "popular democracies" and were gradually cut off from all contact with the world of the West.

Poland came out of the war decimated. Massive migrations took place. The Germans left the territories that had become Polish; the Polish held at forced labor in Germany returned to their country, and those who found themselves behind the eastern frontier took full advantage of their right to return home. The Eastern Poles did not have the same customs and dialects as the others, and adaptation was difficult. Despite that, the end was an unprecedented national uniformity. The issues of minorities that had poisoned the period between the wars had been resolved in a dire way.

From then on Catholics formed an overwhelming majority of the population. While the Communists newly in power had to neutralize the Church, they did so without violence. The agrarian reform of 1945 did not affect ecclesiastical properties; and at the time of the ending of the concordat, the government made a distinction between the Church of Poland and the Vatican. But when the new primate of Poland, Stefan Wyszynski, took office in 1984 after the death of Cardinal Hlond, relations between the Church and the regime began to deteriorate. The possessions of the Church were nationalized in March 1950. Convents and bishops' residences could keep only a few farms. At Zbylitowska Gora, the nuns kept only a garden and a part of a field and there and at Grabow, they built greenhouses and raised seeds and flowers. After the secularization of the state, Catholic educational institutions had been taken over by the state in 1949. But the student hostel in Poznan was not touched until 1954: the authorities bricked up the passageway between the hostel and the community quarters. The houses remained the property of religious congregations; the Society of the Sacred Heart took in lodgers whose payments could be used only for the renovation of the space.[47] The Society kept Polska Wies, called henceforth Pobiedziska.[48] It was one of nine Catholic secondary schools for girls in Poland. Up until 1955 it took boys. This school lasted only because it could measure up year after year to a rigorous inspection by the public

---

[47] A. Merdas, p. 43.
[48] A. Merdas, p. 50.

authorities. Instruction was free as elsewhere in Poland, and as the school did not receive public subsidy, the vicariate had to support it. It managed to hold on to the mission it had been given: making its pupils Christians capable of living in a popular democracy dominated by an atheistic ideology.

As they no longer had any other schools, the nuns turned to parish pastoral ministry and support groups, which were the principal apostolates practiced in Poland by religious congregations.[49] Most of them worked as catechists, sacristans, organists and nurses. They provided instruction in needlework, gave private lessons, taught Latin in the seminary at Tarnow, and in 1951 two of them were called upon to give lectures to women. Some houses of the Sacred Heart became diocesan spiritual centers. Social needs and the particular situation of the country caused the religious to go out of cloister. In the spirit of the extensive preparation for the Millennium of Poland launched by Cardinal Wyszynski, like many others, they contributed to helping the people with whom they came in contact to be aware of their national and religious identity.[50]

Because requests for passports were viewed with suspicion and could cause trouble, between 1946 and 1964, the vicars no longer went to Rome and probations were held in the country. The Iron Curtain was indeed a reality, and there was less and less news of the land of Saint Stanislaus.[51] In spite of the political changes effected in 1956 and Gomulka's rise to power, some areas remained volatile. In 1957 the religious of Zbylitowska Gora decided to open a home economics school; they had to give up the project five years later.[52] Material conditions were harsh: "Health is often tested," remarked Mother de Lescure at the time of the General Congregation of 1952. Mother de Valon, who went to Poland in 1964, had the experience of what life could be like in a people's republic: long interrogations upon arrival, police surveillance that required that the windows be open during meetings for fear that microphones had been placed in the room, being followed in

---

[49] Impressed by the extermination of the clergy, Mother Günther had, from 1944 on, organized courses in theology for her nuns so as to prepare them to teach religion in secondary schools.

[50] J. Kloczowki, pp. 540-541.

[51] *Circular Letters of Our Very Reverend Mother Marie-Thérèse de Lescure*, p. 151, 7 July 1953, and p. 213, 17 June 1955: "The last report was that both novitiates are increasing with good vocations, in spite of poverty within and threats without." "The families of Saint Stanislaus are valiant in their diversified and limited apostolate, their poverty, their courage, their touching union with the Society."

[52] A. Merdas, p. 44.

the car, poor food[53] from the new economic organization established in the countries of the *Comecon*, Council for Mutual Economic Assistance.

Hungary was put under pressure more and more after 1945. An agreement had been forged before the elections that, whatever the results, a coalition government would be formed. The Communists kept the ministry of the Interior. After the proclamation of the republic in January 1946, Ferenc Nagy, the head of the party of small landowners who had won the elections, ran the government, but was forced to resign under pressure from the Communists during the summer of 1947. From 1945 on, agrarian reform robbed the Church of its lands and destroyed financial support for its works. In 1947 religious education became optional.[54] Popular democracy was officially proclaimed in 1949. In Hungary persecution of the churches was much more direct than in Poland. The new authorities wanted to take possession of church institutions and confine religious activity to the interior of places of worship. State takeover of education began on 17 June 1948 and was felt all the more because Hungary was the Central European country with the most denominational schools, of which two thirds were Catholic. The Sacred Heart tried to have its schools recognized as the property of Italy, but in spite of the efforts of some government members to save them,[55] they were nationalized on 31 August and transformed into state schools.[56]

After the state takeover of faculty appointments, the Religious of the Sacred Heart were forbidden to teach. At the *Philippineum*, they had a few boarders in a program called "candidacy." They took in pupils and alumnae for language lessons, choir practice, days of recollection and sodality meetings. When the regime disbanded young people's organizations, young Sacred Heart pupils were pursued by the police and harassed.[57] Cardinal

---

[53] Testimony of Carlotta Leitner, who accompanied Mother de Valon, as her assistants general could not obtain visas. "We were hungry," she said.

[54] The demonstrations in celebration of the Marian Year in 1947 had great success. The primate of Hungary, Cardinal Mindszenty, had organized assemblies of Catholic parents to provide for and protect the education of the young. The Hungarian government doubtless acted on the pretext that it could consider it a provocation to launch its policy of state takeover.

[55] The minister of worship, whose wife and daughter had been saved from deportation to Auschwitz because they had been hidden in the cellars of one of the houses, intervened. The nuns received, therefore, advice from different ministers and from President Rakosi himself.

[56] The *Sophianum* became a Russian university called "Gorki."

[57] In her circular of 29 January 1949, Mother de Lescure alluded, without naming their country, to the courage of the young Hungarians who refused to sign "perverse" documents presented to them, knowing all the while that

Mindszenty protested against this situation, which was soon applied to the Church. He was arrested on 26 December 1948. His trial began on 2 February 1949, and the next day he was condemned to hard labor for life.[58]

It remained to be seen how the nearly one hundred Religious of the Sacred Heart were to be sheltered. Mother de Lescure sought the advice of Pius XII, who thought that, since their apostolates had been taken from them, the nuns ought to go to other houses of the Society, with the exception of a few who would stay as long as possible to provide spiritual support to the alumnae. They were simply to be careful not to put their lives in danger and to avoid deportation to the USSR.[59] On 20 September 1948, two Austrians left Hungary. On 15 November 1948, Hungarians, beginning with postulants, novices, aspirants, young professed and sick or aged professed, were told to leave.[60] After 6 March 1949, they had to bribe officials to obtain exit visas. On 5 April a letter arrived in Budapest in which Mother de Lescure asked all the religious to leave Hungary. The *Philippineum* was evacuated in May; a few caretakers remained, since the church was to stay open. On 18 June 1949, those of the two communities who remained moved into in a small house adjoining the *Sophianum*, in Museum Street. In spite of everyone's advice, a few nuns who were not Hungarian decided to remain so as not to abandon their sisters.

In May 1950 persecution against religious, both men and women, was unleashed;[61] they were to be sent to labor camps if they did not disband. Major superiors asked them to disband and to give up the religious habit. The Religious of the Sacred Heart decided to stay together. The arrests took place in three waves; the second during the night of 17-18 June involved the Budapest convents. Eleven Religious of the Sacred Heart were taken away in cattle wagons and found themselves in the early morning

---

they would not be admitted to their examinations. She cited the example of a twelve-year old pupil struck on the jaw for having answered to those who boasted about destroying the Church: "The Church will exist forever!" – "Do you believe that?" – "I don't believe it; I know it" (*Lettres circulaires...de Lescure*, p. 220). Erzsebet, to whom she was referring, had a dislocated jaw and had to be hospitalized.

[58] At the end of January 1949 the arrest of ecclesiastics and male religious was stopped, as authorities hoped to obtain from them testimony against the cardinal. Mother Edit Jarmai, the first Hungarian named superior at the end of the war, emigrated to avoid being summoned as a witness at the trial.

[59] *Vie de la T.R.M. de Lescure*, p. 260. She communicated these directives to the superiors in Hungary in April 1949.

[60] The novices, with their parents' permission, went to Avigliana.

[61] Major superiors had protested on 25 April against the obstacles placed to their apostolic activity in the parishes.

in a camp at Eger, which had been set up in the archbishop's palace. The archbishop's secretariat and some alumnae let Rome know. Mother de Lescure had a message of encouragement sent to them on 29 June. At Eger no arrangements had been made to accommodate a hundred religious. The dormitory consisted of straw laid down on the floor in a large empty hall. But neighbors fed the inmates and they could go to daily Mass.

Because religious were like a currency exchange in the negotiations taking place between the government and the episcopate, the bishops requested those of foreign nationality to leave the country. Mother de Lescure wrote to the superior of the *Sophianum*, Mother Gutzwiller, that she had to obey:

> You know every advice and decision will be made with love that you must never doubt because of the Heart that holds you in his care. If the big sister[62] must earn her living elsewhere, let the little ones not doubt Him who wills it and will take care of them in a divine manner. Let them count on the unceasing prayer of their mother.... Let them strengthen themselves by renewing their vows constantly: "Kiss the nails that attach you to my feet, to my hands and hold you to my Heart." At every instant throughout the world there is a paten waiting to offer them "through him, with him, in him...." and here every morning I place them there. I embrace you tenderly, with hope for the courage of each one and placing each one in the depths of the Heart that is everything for you and whose messengers you are. Your Madeleine Sophie.

Mother Gutzwiller left for Budapest on 21 July and began to look for lodging for her daughters, for the dissolution of religious orders was imminent. The eight Hungarians left Eger on 16 August 1950. The last two nuns who remained, two Austrians, one of whom was ill, were released three days later upon the intervention of their embassy.

On 7 September 1950, religious orders were suppressed. Religious were no longer to live in community; they had to secure work and lodging and give up the habit. Mother Gutzwiller reached Austria in October 1950 with the last Austrian nuns. In the name of obedience, a Hungarian had to ask for a permit to leave. It was a painful obligation, for in leaving their country, the Hungarians lost their nationality, and it was heart-breaking to abandon their apostolic works. Some of them felt they had deserted Hungary when they left.[63]

---

[62] The reference is to Mother Gutzwiller.
[63] When they were faced with the process of verification at the border, which took the whole day, one of them heard an official say: "If all the religious

Only seven Religious of the Sacred Heart remained in Hungary, three of whom were choir aspirants and three coadjutrix sisters, one of whom was an aspirant. The sisters could take shelter with their families or in other private homes. Some of the choir nuns were members of families whose property had been nationalized; they were under surveillance by the new authorities. They taught catechism and earned their living by giving private lessons. They were careful not to give their address, and they admitted no one to their house. In 1951 the aristocracy and the bourgeoisie of Budapest were deported in part to the eastern section of the country or to Siberia under pretense of purging pro-Nazis. The people, including the clergy, were afraid of any contact with the religious.[64] In 1952 they could not find a church in which to renew their vows on the feast of the Sacred Heart. The motherhouse sent them medicines and letters through the wife of the Italian ambassador. But the assistance could provoke suspicion of connections abroad. Two of them succeeded in escaping in 1952. One left Hungary, thanks to a priest who was helping nuns cross the border in the guise of his wife. She was the last to benefit from this subterfuge, for on the next attempt he was captured and executed.

Mother de Lescure look for ways to have all of them leave Hungary clandestinely, and she charged the Hungarian mistress of novices, Mother von Spee, with this responsibility. She approached a person whose business it was to get people out. But on 23 January 1953, the four aspirants were arrested following the imprisonment of this man, on whom was found a list of names and addresses. They were interned for almost nine months on the premises of the Avo, the Hungarian police force, undergoing endless interrogations, isolated or in a cell with other women. They were brought before a military tribunal on 6 October 1953 and harshly condemned. After an appeal the coadjutrix sister found her penalty reduced for "reasons of class." Two others also had a reduction of their sentence; only one, of aristocratic origin, did not. They underwent detention either in Budapest or in the country, in trying conditions, and were compelled to work on various construction sites. Among their fellow prisoners they met alumnae and members of Sacred Heart sodalities.[65]

---

leave, what is going to happen to us?" (Testimony of Magda Lengyel).

[64] M. Lengyel.

[65] Between 1946 and 1949, 15% of the Hungarian population came before the courts. In her circular of 17 June 1955, Mother de Lescure wrote: "News from Hungary is increasingly rare and laconic. The prolonged isolation of our dear children wrings our heart and cannot but make us anxious" (*Circular Letters*, p. 213).

One of them was freed on 21 November 1955,[66] another on 14 September 1956, before the end of their sentences. After the death of Stalin, a reaction against the previous way of handling ecclesiastical affairs was noticeable in the government as well as in the parties supporting it. No doubt the religious owed their anticipated freedom to this cautious thaw. They found work but could no longer devote themselves to any apostolic activity at all. Revolution broke out on 23 October 1956. In December the nuns tried to cross the border, but only one coadjutrix sister made it across. The others then took refuge with the family of a sister, but they managed to cross into Austria during the night of 6-7 January 1957. Those who had been sent to prisons and camps "with draconian regulations" had suffered from lack of sleep, body searches, hunger and cold; and they were surrounded by people who had no spirit of resistance.[67] This kind of detention left scars on its victims.

The last country to fall into the clutches of communism was China. During and after the Second World War the Sacred Heart had been invited to Soochow, Tientsin, Changsha and Yangchow to make foundations there. The house in Shanghai had expanded. In 1947 the university college enrolled 347 students, and the secondary and primary schools each had 500 pupils. With the 328 day boarders of the "foreign school" – renamed "international school" to counteract the nationalist movement – and the kindergarten, there were 1800 in all studying at the Sacred Heart. This growth required religious who could teach in Chinese, and some of them had begun to study Mandarin. They needed outside help, for the Shanghai community did not have enough religious. From every point of view the future seemed promising in China. In 1946 the Vatican had established a local hierarchy and named the first Chinese cardinal. Christianity was gaining converts.

President Chiang Kai-shek could benefit from the resistance he had led against Japan. In 1945 China came out of eight years of war liberated from the unequal treaties renounced two years earlier by the Allies and Japan. The country was recognized as a major power and named a founder of the United Nations Organization; it held a permanent seat on the Security Council. Not only did the expected reforms not take place, but the regions

---

[66] She wrote in the memoir that the motherhouse asked for, "When the good news arrived, I was no longer capable of rejoicing, not having the strength. That life had so exhausted me. It was difficult to begin a new life. I felt too weak. Especially in the streets I always had the sensation of someone following at my heels. The families were a little bit afraid of me."

[67] In probation they recounted that they had had to work without speaking, that laces and elastic were removed from their clothing, that they were not allowed to wear stockings. Their cells had no windows and were never heated.

liberated were controlled by corrupt officials, who prided themselves on their supposed or real anti-Japanese patriotism, and sought to profit by seizing Chinese goods commandeered by the Japanese occupiers. These were the methods of the Communists, who since 1944 had again begun to infiltrate and dominate the countryside, while the Nationalists held the cities. The USSR supported the Communists, while the United States backed the Nationalists. Against the Communists' guerrilla warfare, the Nationalists tried direct combat. They succeeded in holding the center and the South of China, where Communist penetration was too sporadic to snatch their areas of influence.

Until 1947 confusion reigned, but the balance of power called for negotiation on both sides and the fighting did not escalate. After the summer of 1947 the Communists began to drive Chiang Kai-shek's troops more and more toward the South, and civil war ruled again. In January 1949 Chiang resigned from the presidency of the Republic. Many foreigners began to leave the country, and the numbers in the international school reflected this withdrawal. On 1 October 1949, Mao Zedong, named head of state, established a popular republic and proclaimed China, henceforth unified after a century of occupations and humiliations, "once more on its feet." The decisive battle, however, did not occur until November. The Nationalists, who sought to keep Nanking and Shanghai, were beaten and withdrew to Formosa.

From the end of the Long March, the Communists persecuted the Christians in the territories of which they took possession. Therefore, in April 1949, the superior in Shanghai had five elderly, foreign religious leave along with fifteen young Chinese nuns. They arrived in Japan where Mother de Lescure had sent the novices. On 14 May cannon fire was heard first around the forts located on the estuary of Huangpu, then in the industrial cities that surrounded Shanghai. On 25 May, when the Sacred Heart community was celebrating the feast of the founder and the First Communion of six pupils, the city changed hands.

The establishment of "centralized democracy," efficient but cautious in its first appearances, was not accompanied by the feared excesses. Shanghai was cut off and foreigners could not leave. Communication with the outside was possible only by telegram and short telephone conversations, but the scholastic year ended peacefully. In the community some had a different view of the future from the optimistic one that the superior, Mother Fitzgerald, offered. They held the more moderate, even pessimistic positions expressed by religious who based their views on the effects of the policy that the Communists had followed in Shandong.[68] The policy of making the schools exclusively Chinese called for the replacement of Mothers Thornton and Lewis who directed the university college and the secondary school. They handed over their responsibilities to Chinese, lay and religious, who accepted them in order to help out. The sisters who worked at the front desk received a salary.[69] Foreigners could continue to teach, but it was clear that the goal of the new regime was to eliminate Christian education and to contest traditional values.

The first problems appeared at the *rentrée* [opening of school]. During the summer the buildings of Aurora College and of the Sacred Heart secondary school had been occupied by young progressives, armed with Communist goals who taught their comrades folk dances and the country's new anthem, "The East Is Red," accompanying them on traditional Chinese musical instruments. The Communists wanted to take over this stronghold where the first national Catholic conference on education in China had taken place a year earlier. When classes reopened, the secondary school pupils were told to turn themselves into "committees" in charge of scrutinizing the running of the school. They demanded scholarships and permission to bring in food. The teachers were accused of having got their hands on the students' school fees, causing disruption among the staff. The state exacted payment of heavy taxes.

The curriculum was "corrected." The teaching of languages, English and French, was stopped because it was "too cruel to ask students to study so many subjects."[70] Courses in dialectical materialism became obligatory. Religious education could no longer be given within the school building.[71] All religious pictures and symbols were removed from the building, which was heavily adorned with portraits of Mao. The progressive pupils, who had already had the Sacred Heart pay for their particularly loud musical instruments, tried to cause the nuns further trouble by demanding enormous quantities of paper on which to write slogans to post on easels that prefigured the *dazibaos* [propaganda posters] of the Cultural Revolution. Soon there were meetings to indict those in charge or who had been in charge of the schools. The religious, warned in advance, understood that above all they were not to attend. The

---

[68] It was known that the Catholic University Fujen of Beijing had lost all liberty of action after the taking of the capital by the Communists and that in the North of the country the Jesuits and the Helpers of the Holy Souls had had to abandon their missions and their schools.

[69] Prov. Arch. Japan. Letters of Mother Louise Bernard, 14 November 1951.

[70] M. Chi, p. 129.

[71] A reform of education based on the techniques of specialization and promoting generalization of literacy was promulgated in October 1951.

missionaries were said to be agents of western imperialism and accused of practices "inimical" to the Chinese people. A carefully organized system of informants had it that "a teacher was to supervise the religious, another teacher to supervise the teacher, and a student to supervise the second teacher."[72] Mother Bernard wrote: "I leave to others the task of describing for you the parades, the interruptions of class, the newspaper articles and a thousand other obstacles to discipline and to the exercise of authority, above all in Mother Lewis's section. We are praying fervently to hold out against the winds and tides, according to the *mot d'ordre* [watchword] of His Excellency, the Internuncio: 'Stay on,' he said to the Fathers of Aurora, who are even more harassed than we, 'even if they leave you only one room to live in.'"[73]

Bringing the Sacred Heart into line happened school by school. The situation soon became critical in the primary school, where the Chinese director, whether by opportunism or conviction, cooperated with the new regime and sidelined Mother Saint-Germain, who had been in charge until then. Elsewhere the loss of position of the religious followed the outbreak of the Korean War, which supplied new arguments for eradicating foreign influences. Sacred Heart property saw confrontations between communists and progressives and the Legion of Mary. On 8 December 1950, when the lily procession was taking place, students locked the doors between the college and the community quarters. As Mother Thornton explained later,

> The end was already coming. A new law announced that all land, buildings, books, funds, equipment were now the property of the "school." No one was able to tell us who the school was, but a committee of teachers, students and servants began to take an inventory and watched the doors day and night. One day we changed the locks on the communicating doors between convent and college. The next day, during the lunch hour the committee "sealed" them with paper, hoping we would break the seals. Warned in time, we locked the doors and insisted that the committee put padlocks on their side to forestall the accusation that we came at night to remove school property. As soon as the inventory was finished, we resigned.[74]

A bamboo barricade divided the garden. The Religious of the Sacred Heart had lost control of three of their schools.

---

[72] M. Chi, p. 130.
[73] Prov. Arch. Japan. Letter of 14 November 1951.
[74] M. Chi, p. 133.

Mother Fitzgerald had thought that the international school would be able to survive: she was to discover that it too was destined to disappear. From September 1950, foreigners were expelled and the Chinese were no longer allowed to attend a foreign school. The school could not even count on the children of foreigners living in China, since in May 1951 visas were reduced to six months' duration. On orders from Mother de Lescure, the international school ended its work in June.

Encoded letters sent by Mother Bernard to her vicar between 5 July and the end of the year 1951 show how precarious the fate of the community was. The religious could no longer live in their former houses, and they had to move out into a hostile environment. But they continued to receive in their quarters students who came with them. They allowed Catholic organizations that until then had been meeting in the school facilities to gather in the community part of the building. Beginning in April 1951 some nuns began to leave Shanghai. The last Chinese left before the authorities refused all departure visas to Chinese nationals. The departures continued in August and September by train as far as Hong Kong, then by ship to Japan, where the religious received new obediences.[75] Mother Bernard wrote on 5 July:

> We are economizing so we can stay longer, that is the general directive. Everyone is suffering, everyone is miserable. Only the children are laughing, singing and screaming with no care as to what is happening around them. Uncertainty being the rule at every hour of the day, we are all making great progress in patience and abandon; prayer is more intense when one feels the ground give way beneath one's feet. There is nothing else to rely on except on high.

While Rome was pressuring to speed up the departures, and the bishops of Shanghai were asking religious to defer their requests for visas, the authorities were trying to have Mother Fitzgerald rent the building that she had transferred to the diocese in June 1951 or give it to the association for resistance to America and of aid to Korea. "What to do on our side to help you," wrote Mother Bernard, "except to say wisely that we ask nothing for ourselves and we work our best so that we can make do on our own. We have rice, wood, coal for the whole winter until the February *rentrée*. Then we will see if our sisters retain any control of or sharing in the

---

[75] Testimony of Sawako Kageyama and Chinese sisters. The returns from overseas were badly managed, and nothing was done to have the Chinese learn Japanese. It is true that at that time the common language of the vicariate was English.

administration: it is very unlikely but it is not certain." In desperation, the authorities forced Mother Fitzgerald to leave China before 20 December.[76] On 8 December 1951, a last Mass was celebrated in one of the rooms that the religious still occupied. On 19 December, Sadie Fitzgerald, Elizabeth Duff and Salvina Xerri took the train for Hong Kong. Two Chinese postulants went back to their families. The other five were welcomed by religious of Xujiahui.[77]

Like others responsible for Catholic enterprises, Mother Thornton did not receive authorization to leave the country, because the school, the house, the finances and the student associations were all in her hands. No doubt to punish her for having created two *praesidia* of the Legion of Mary in her school and for having upheld their members' fidelity to the Vatican, but above all for being in some way a symbol of Aurora College, whose reactionary character was constantly pointed out, the emigration services did not want to grant her a departure visa. She could not hope for help from the authorities of her own country, for the new regime did not recognize British diplomats. She continued to wait in the house of the Sisters of Loretto, keeping contact with the alumnae and friends of the Sacred Heart, but doing so prudently in order not to compromise them. She filled her enforced leisure with prayer, reading and improving her knowledge of Chinese. Thanks to visits received and made, she was able to obtain details of the persecution that had befallen Catholics, on the phases of "correction" that had assailed the intellectuals and on the consecutive purges in the campaign of "Three-anti," then of "Five anti." These targeted, in the first case officers and members of the party or other bureaucratic officials, under pretext of corruption, waste and bureaucratic spirit, and in the second case the *bourgeoisie*, the financiers and businessmen as well as members of the liberal professions, under cover of struggle against fraud, diversion of public goods and tax evasion. She discovered also what courage the students could show:

> For a long time we have been searching for ways to give our Catholic pupils a sense of the Church, a little cultural minority without links to their great national civilization. What an experience for us during these last eighteen months to have learned ourselves from the Catholic youth of Shanghai that the sense of this life of the Church depends neither on time nor on tradition but on persecution and the Cross. For in a short time they arrived at full possession of this precious heritage. Those who

---

[76] Prov. Arch. Japan. Letter of 14 November 1951. The funds had been able to be transferred abroad in time.

[77] M. Chi, p. 143.

have had the privilege of being witnesses in their life at present all tell us: "It is like a revelation of the primitive Church."[78]

The whole Society of the Sacred Heart was praying that Mother Thornton would obtain her visa. That happened on 29 June 1952. She left China by way of Macao and Hong Kong on 7 July 1952. As she had announced by telegram to Mother de Lescure a little while before – "sacrifice consummated" – there were no longer any Religious of the Sacred Heart in China. The first cultural revolution had destroyed a work that for twenty-five years had manifested its efficacy, since the international school had had from its foundation 300 pupils, the primary school had educated more than 1000 little girls and boys, the secondary school had had 1000 pupils, while Aurora College had given a diploma to almost 500 young women.[79]

When the Society of the Sacred Heart made a foundation in Korea, the country had just experienced on its own soil the effects of the division of the world between two hostile ideologies. Following upon agreements signed between the United States and the USSR, Korea had been occupied by the Americans and the Soviets. The Republic of South Korea had been organized in August 1948 and been placed under the presidency of Syngman Rhee. One month later a Republic of North Korea had been created and directed by Kim Il-Soung. The claim of both sides to the whole country increased tensions. In 1950 a war began, stirred up as much by the new balance of power in Asia as by the developments of the cold war, in which many contemporaries saw the seeds of a third world war. Although that did not happen, the ongoing war between the people's democracies and the United Nations destroyed a country that was coming out of a long Japanese domination. The extremely brutal and murderous engagements left aftereffects for decades; families were dispersed and innumerable people disappeared because of the flight of civilians. The officials of the Catholic Church and members of religious congregations were victims of rampant, overt persecution that made martyrs of so many.

When the armistice of Panmunjom concluded the war in 1953, Korea was more divided than ever. Rather quickly, even before the end of hostilities, the missionaries returned to South Korea. Most of them were aware that the reconstruction of the country had to be brought about through education; this policy was even more necessary than it was

---

[78] *Mitte me*, N°6, p. 51. In 1954, it was learned that most of the alumnae of Shanghai had been or were still in prison accused of being guilty of counter-revolutionary activities (p. 70).

[79] M. Chi, p. 157. These numbers refer only to pupils and students who had had all their schooling at the Sacred Heart, not those who had spent only a few months or years there.

during the most difficult periods of its history, Korea had always sought to preserve its language and culture. In this context the apostolic delegate and vicar in charge of Korea, Bishop Paul Ro and Bishop Quinlan, a veteran of the "Death March" that in North Korea had decimated western missionaries, turned to religious congregations to reestablish their schools.[80] Their appeal quickly reached the vicar in Japan, who informed the motherhouse. They offered a college as poor financially as academically but which could provide a building block for the future.

The goal was to open a university college for women, because higher education was monopolized then by Protestant universities, directed by Koreans but supported by the United States. Creation of such a college would allow the Jesuits to give up the plan for a coeducational college that they had considered at first. But the Society had to think also of opening a secondary school in order to have a solid rapport with the local people and feed the future college. The emissaries had demonstrated that Korea was a country that offered opportunities for the development of Christianity. The seeds of Catholicism were already old and gave Korea the nickname of the "Ireland of Asia," a country capable of furnishing vocations in the near future.[81]

Mother Brigid Keogh made a request to Rome for a foundation on 5 August 1955.[82] After a quick trip to Seoul, she proposed the foundation of a university college there or that of a secondary school at Inchon, the port of the capital city, or the creation of two institutions, one after the other, with a two-year delay. Mother Keogh was aware that living conditions would be hard in a country utterly ravaged by war, whose culture was totally different from that of Japan. She foresaw "for the founders absolute poverty, almost unbelievable difficulties of language, of isolation, the possibility of a war, of communist persecution." But she added with good sense that the risks were not less in other Asian countries. Korea lacked running water and heating; but the people were eager for education and wanted to be taught in English. It remained to be seen where to make the foundation. Mother Keogh thought that the college proposed by the church authorities did not correspond to the requirements of the Society. She had visited a property on which a former seminary of the Foreign Mission Society of Paris was situated. Finally these half ruined buildings were chosen; Bishop Mousset

---

[80] Bishop von Furtensberg, the nuncio, had approached the Sacred Heart in 1951 for a foundation that was totally unrealizable because of the war.

[81] Gen. Arch. C IV, Korea. Letters of Msgr. Ro, 27 June 1955, and of R. P. Geppert, 27 August 1955.

[82] She was vicar of the Far East from April 1954.

agreed to rent them for twenty years for a token dollar with the condition that the Society assume the cost of the repairs.[83]

On 5 October 1956, Theresa Chu Mei Fen, a Chinese who would later take Korean nationality, and a Pole, Lucia Zielinski, arrived on the hill of Wonhyoro in Seoul, where a telegram from Mother de Lescure awaited them. The foundation was placed under the protection of Our Lady of Heaven and Earth.[84] A community of religious of six nationalities was rapidly put in place.[85] School opened on 1 April 1957, with eighteen pupils,[86] who were issued red uniforms. Korea was suffering then from a grave financial crisis. The New York vicariate furnished the guarantees required by the Korean government for the establishment of a school. An international school in English was opened in August 1957 for five foreign children living in Seoul; there were fifty-eight the following year. A kindergarten welcomed the first recruits in 1958 and expanded rapidly.

Material conditions were hardly easy at the beginning. Water and electricity were insufficient. They had to dig a well. "Often there was only one wash basin and seven people were waiting to wash their hands. Those whose hands were the least dirty washed first. There was no heat and often the water in the basin froze."[87] Very soon the first Koreans wishing to enter the Society of the Sacred Heart presented themselves.[88] They made their noviceship at Obayashi in Japan from 1958 on. A few years afterward, the Society settled at Chun Cheon on the border with North Korea, a city that had been taken and retaken thirteen times during the war.

Nationalism and the Rise of the Third World

On other continents the difficulties experienced by the Sacred Heart appeared modest in retrospect. In May 1948 a revolution in Colombia

---

[83] In 1957, Father Émile Froment proposed that the Society acquire the whole property.
[84] The Korean flag has symbols of the sky and the earth.
[85] The first religious were Sisters McHardy Flint, Guterres, Foy, Giesen and Loy. They were joined by Alice Atkinson and Catherine Rilley in 1957. The community comprised fourteen members in 1960.
[86] Forty-nine asked to enter.
[87] Agnes and Catherine Kim, *Early Days of the History of Korea Province*. Communicated by Kim Sook Hee.
[88] The first Korean to enter the Society of the Sacred Heart in Korea was Lee Jeong Sook. Two sisters, Kim Jae Soon and Kim Jae Sook, known in the Society by their Christian names, Agnes and Catherine, had entered in the United States. After her noviceship at Kenwood, Kim Jae Soon (Agnes) was sent to Seoul in September 1960.

forced the transfer of the coadjutrix sisters' novitiate from Bogotá to Medellín. New troubles in 1957 brought about a renewal of the consecration of the country to the Sacred Heart. In the meantime the situation in Argentina was discovered to be more serious.[89] Upon General Perón's assumption of the presidency in 1946, some Catholics and nationalists thought that he was going to free the masses of their attraction to liberalism, socialism and communism. But the governmental measures aimed at bettering the living standard of the poorest people were accompanied by a desire to deprive the former Creole aristocracy of its privileges. These measures sometimes seemed anticlerical, for Peronism, in trying to develop a populist mystique, sought support from groups that had been rivals until then and toward 1951 decided that Catholicism would no longer be the only basis for national identity. Anti-clerical waves of violence began, during which bands sacked the offices of political parties and churches. To defend "Argentinity" one had to struggle, to quote the dictator, against "the imperialism of the cassock."

On the economic plane, Perón froze salaries and prices and reduced imports, fostering the black market. The concession of Argentine oilfields to Standard Oil, deemed humiliating by the opposition, was one cause of the military coup that took place on 16 June 1955. But the anticlericalism supported by Perón was another. On 14 May 1955, the Chamber had decided to revise the constitution with a view to separation of church and state. After the news of Perón's excommunication became known the army revolted. On 14 July, he declared before Parliament that the revolution was finished and that he was no longer "head of the party but president of all Argentinians." In spite of this pulling back, the head of state could not right the situation. On 15 September, when Buenos Aires was in a state of siege after a general strike had been launched in support of him, the navy revolted. After the dictator fled on 22 September, a junta directed by General Eduardo Lonardi assumed power. At the end of spring, Sacred Heart novices had left Argentina. Their exile lasted only a short time, since after the fall of Perón the Church was paid back for the service it had rendered in mobilizing Catholics, and the military's success was said to be "the victory of Christ." The earlier anti-clerical laws were overturned, and in 1956 the Church obtained the right to open universities.

Without modifying its constitutional laws, Mexico seemed to want to end its policy of persecution. In 1945 the first stone was laid of the house of Plateros in Mexico City. Its works developed rapidly, and a school was begun in San Luis Potosí. The schools at Guadalajara and Monterrey

---

[89] *Circular Letters...de Lescure*, p. 213, 17 June 1955: "Argentina suddenly becomes a cause for grave concern and no one can foresee what the future will bring."

flourished and required new construction. A foundation in Chihuahua in 1950 was the sign of a general, hope-inspiring development. But religious of other nationalities could not yet be sent to Mexico. National policy had helped to isolate the vicariate from the rest of the Society and to perpetuate its conservatism.[90]

In Egypt, after the Second World War, the state tried to "eliminate the foreign element and to take over direction of industrial and commercial affairs that until then had been administered, for the most part, by European corporations. The Arabic language was imposed throughout; government schools, primary, secondary and even universities proliferated." At the Sacred Heart, teaching had to be adjusted "to devote more time to build competence in the language of the country." Free schooling at all levels had been mandated, except in foreign schools. The religious thought, "We are moving toward a new future that will without doubt be very different from the past."[91] Enforced holidays, multiple inspections, constricting educational laws and moving refugees to religious houses took place in 1948 at the time of the first Arab-Israeli War. But a fundamental change took place in 1952.

On 25 January, the British attacked an Egyptian police barracks. The attack caused about fifty deaths and unleashed riots in Cairo, the mob taking it out on everything considered symbolic of the power and way of life of the West: hotels, luxury shops, tearooms, cafes and nightclubs, apartments. Many places close to the Sacred Heart went up in flames.[92] "It is good and prudent to have protectors in high places; the good God has given us some," one reads in Cairo's house journal.[93] A curfew was imposed. Egyptian soldiers set up their headquarters in the Sacred Heart chapel, and the community supplied them with cigarettes and hot tea. Thanks to the intervention of the French embassy, the day scholars returned on 6 February, but not all of them. Many pupils had fled with their parents, who had lost their possessions. On 9 April the police took over from the army at the Sacred Heart, but the religious felt that they had to act wisely. The

---

[90] It was only in 1960 that a regular visit was made by Mother Bultó. After that visit the religious began to be trained in the normal schools of Mexico City and Guadalajara and at the catechetical school, *Sedes Sapientiae*. Relations with other congregations multiplied. In the communities lectures on Catholic Action and biblical courses were organized. After 1963, those in the juniorate studied social questions. The mistress of studies of the vicariate went to Europe in 1962 to make contact with her counterparts (*Histoire de la Province du Mexique. Les Années Soixante*, pp. 4-5).

[91] Prov. Arch. Egypt. *Histoire de la Société du Sacré-Cœur en Égypte*, 1950.

[92] Testimony of Marie-Josèphe Helly.

[93] The father of one of the pupils was the minister of public education.

processions held in the garden for liturgical feasts were carried out in such a way that "no one in the street would see or hear anything." During the night of 22-23 July 1952, the *coup d'état* of the Free Officers Movement put an end to the Egyptian monarchy. The superior in Cairo wrote to Rome: "Tanks are moving through the city inundated with soldiers; cannon and machine guns are posted at every street corner. Calm, stupor. No one speaks or stirs." Acting on what "the present circumstances or those to come may [bring] as to rapid and unexpected decisions with no recourse to Rome or Marseille," Rome charged Mother du Ligondes with the three houses in Egypt.[94]

All education, including higher education, became free in 1952. The new regime sought to support Muslim tradition and broadcast its affiliation with Islam more and more widely. As many families did not wish to send their children to public schools, applications for admission increased in the private school in Alexandria, which had become an island of prosperity since the end of the war. In addition, the vicar apostolic asked the Society of the Sacred Heart to open a kindergarten and primary school at Ramleh. But the religious had to give up the domestic science course and the boarding school,[95] which would have allowed them to reach a public beyond that of the capital.[96] In Cairo and Heliopolis the teaching of Arabic occupied a more prominent place in the studies than before. Many Egyptian pupils, whose parents were not Arabic-speaking or who did not agree with the emphasis on the use of Arabic, until then had been following the Arabic courses as a hobby.[97] After the revolution of 23 July they were no longer exempt from taking full part in them.[98] In 1954, three young nuns took courses in Arabic with the Franciscan Fathers. In 1955, private schools had to offer religious instruction to the pupils according to their individual status. The government let it be understood that the school had

---

[94] Prov. Arch. Egypt. Correspondence I, Cairo. Letter of 2 July 1953: "She would keep a record of the decisions made then in order to submit them as soon as possible" to the vicar of the Midi.

[95] Correspondence I, Cairo, Notes of 1953 and report to Cardinal Tisserant, June 1953.

[96] At the same time, the vicar of the Midi was even wondering if it was desirable to keep only one of the establishments in the Cairo area and to found in Alexandria.

[97] For the pupils of the Jesuit school of the Holy Family Arabic was not essential because one could not attach to it real practical utility or an image of modernity (Frédéric Abécassis: *L'enseignement étranger en Egypte et les élites locales, 1920-1960 : Francophonie et identités nationales*, Villeneuve-d'Ascq: Presses universitaires du Septentrion, 2001, vol. 3, p. 616).

[98] M. Lattif, p. 76.

to follow government curricula and that the state had the right to control the admission of pupils.[99] The situation became sufficiently serious that the Religious of the Sacred Heart began to take part in the meetings of directors and superiors of French schools,[100] whereas before they had been represented by other religious congregations.

For President Gamal Abdel Nasser, Egypt would achieve economic independence by upgrading its own region. Regulating the Nile seemed the best way to accomplish this goal. Still financial aid from western countries had to be procured in order turn this "pharaonic" site into the Aswan dam. Negotiations with France, Great Britain and the United States failed, leaving the financing of the dam in the hands of the Canal. On 26 July 1956, Nasser announced the nationalization of the Suez Canal Company. On 16 August, the conference of nations that used the canal, in which Egypt had refused to take part, proposed internationalization of the canal, administered thenceforth under the control of the United Nations. Nasser refused this plan on 28 August.

The motherhouse understood that there was danger of a showdown. Therefore, fearful that communications would break down, it speeded up the departure for Egypt of some religious who were in Europe. Those who had spent the summer on the coast of Alexandria and in Lebanon hurried back at the end of August. French and British forces converged in the Mediterranean. On 28 October, France, Great Britain and Israel made an accord, intending to engage in military operations against Egypt and after the victory to put a new "peaceful, friendly" regime in place. The same day a general strike broke out in Cairo: "The situation is tense; the pupils cannot come to school," one reads in the house journal in Cairo. On 30 October the Israeli army moved to attack. The Egyptian DCA began to fire during recreation: "The children were terrified. We had them come inside and moved up their departure by bus. In recent days we had felt that the situation outside was very serious, but we did not expect such a sudden outburst of hostilities. We learned after the children departed that the Israeli forces had invaded Egyptian territory." The 31st, "At nine in the evening the first RAF bombs were heard. We went down to the shelter prepared between the two school refectories, mysteriously baptized 'corridor of the dark night.'" In Heliopolis, the journal writer summarized the situation thus: "As for us, we handed ourselves over to divine Providence and to the Heart of Jesus who will take care of us. It is a time to repeat with great confidence: 'Your Heart is in this house and this house is in your Heart; we

---

[99] F. Abécassis, vol. 3, p. 709.
[100] *Journal de la maison du Caire*, 24 January 1956: "Given the gravity of the times, our Mothers went to them."

are safe.'" Heliopolis was bombed on 2 November: "We spend the greater part of our days in the cellar; we do not know exactly what to do, how we are to live."

On 4 November citizens of belligerent countries had to declare their nationality. An alumna of Heliopolis came to help the French and English nuns to fill out the paperwork. On 18 November, they were confined to their residence. On 23 November, they learned that the French and the British were going to be expelled from Egypt. Mother du Ligondes refused to abandon the place: "Let them expel us, if they wish, but we will not leave of our own will!" she declared. The announcement of possible expulsion panicked Christian families, many of whom wondered whether they had to think about exile. On 27 November, they learned that the measure did not apply to male religious who had obtained the protection of the Holy See and who were provided with special identity cards, but thousands of British and French were expelled and their possessions seized. Even religious who had spent from thirty to fifty years in Egypt and had even participated in the foundation had to leave. In the following years some elderly religious continued to return to Europe "to find a safer, calmer atmosphere."[101] A few nuns came from the United States to teach the English courses. The French returned to Egypt only in 1959 and in smaller numbers than before. In the meantime Belgians had been sent to Egypt to teach French. In 1957 the boarding schools were closed, thought to be burdensome and useless.[102] From then on everyone saluted the flag and the pupils had daily lessons in Arabic.

Prudent Openness[103]

At the time of the first general congregation after the war, there was an atmosphere of relief. The end of the conflict, the union shown in the Society all through the war, the election of a new superior general, all seemed to lessen the pressures that had mounted during the previous years of suffering. Civil society was evolving, but for Mother de Lescure,

---

[101] *Journal...Caire*, 10 May 1962.
[102] The Jesuits had made the same decision as of 1954 (F. Abécassis, vol. 3, p. 767). It was a question of not causing difficulties during Ramadan.
[103] *Circular Letters...de Lescure*, 13 November 1952. Pius XII had addressed to her on the occasion of the opening of the general congregation a letter in which he suggested "a prudent openness to the new needs of our day, the assiduous search for conditions best suited to the pursuit of the admirable work of education undertaken by your holy foundress" (p. 137).

Faced with the torrent of the world's needs, with the fever of apostolic activities and multiple methods for helping souls, the Society has no need to branch out into new paths. It has but to deepen the furrow opened up by our Holy Mother, a furrow wide, straight, rich in possibilities that are always at hand, by which the many souls who come to us from all parts may find their way to the open arms and the open Heart of Jesus.[104]

But the general congregation considered changes in relation to social changes. There was no opposition to accepting Jewish converts "and even" of young women of color. The recruitment of choir religious could be broadened to include the middle classes; but because economic and social life was drawing social groups closer without combining them, some feared the possible effects on community life of bringing together people who had different levels of education.[105] Many vicars thought it urgent to treat novices not like children but like already mature persons.

In what concerned the coadjutrix sisters, who "[underwent] more or less mental distortion from their social environment," the choir religious were to be

> all the more attentive to understand them, to have them feel the reality of our union, of our affection, of our equality on the religious and supernatural level. Let the choir nuns willingly share the sisters' labor. Let them be associated with the apostolic intentions of our works. Let the assistants watch closely not to overwork them, to safeguard their prayer life, to take care of their health, to be interested above all in their souls while maintaining them at a very supernatural level for a happy, deepened religious life.[106]

---

[104] *De Lescure*, 25 January 1947, p. 14. She expressed the same direction on 6 June 1952: "No General Congregation, in situations which at times were difficult, ever stressed the abrupt adoption of new ideas, but recommended that the Society unite in more generous efforts to deepen the understanding of its fundamental principles, recognizing its spirit, determined in its fidelity, and by that very fact, open to the interests of the Heart of Jesus at that moment" (p. 129).

[105] Notes sent at the time of the preparation of the general congregation by Spain and Australia. Acts of the 23rd General Congregation, p. 22: "It is necessary to find out whether the mentality of these subjects can adapt to the spirit of the Society and whether the level of the Society will not be lowered."

[106] P. 25.

Henceforth they could use a meditation book and a small spiritual library. Vacations should not increase their work but offer interesting activities and rest. They could be offered vacation courses "at their level." "Saint Alphonsus' room" [the sisters' community room] was to be light, airy, attractive. The sisters' dormitories were to be *healthful*. In the refectory "the sisters were to be served *like everyone else* with decent tableware, and the older sisters should be given chairs,"[107] if it was not possible for everyone to have them. But they were not to be given outdoor shawls [*de voyage*] and their chapel cloaks were not of the same fabric as those of the choir nuns. It was not obligatory to bring them together for probation. No doubt it was too soon to anticipate the suppression of the rank of coadjutrix. But was Mother de Lescure ready for it? Some members of the hierarchy had called her attention to the differences that existed among Religious of the Sacred Heart, "even to the habit." She experienced pressure from different countries. One witness noted, "I did not stop thinking that the difference between the two was too great. We were approaching a new era and, nevertheless, we were keeping the old structures."[108]

Some considerations from child psychology[109] were introduced into the Plan of Studies, for one had to "take the children as they were in order to render them what the Heart of Jesus wants them to be: apostles of their place and time." The structures remained but discipline was relaxed. Practical, doctrinal, social and apostolic formation should open up the pupils to service, "that is to say, to understanding and concern for others, to which egoism, individualism, heedlessness in all its forms are opposed." Visits to factories were added to visits to the poor.[110]

Hesitancy regarding official course offerings was lessening without disappearing.[111] Instruction in new subject matter by specialist teachers

---

[107] The italicized words are underlined in the original.

[108] Testimony of Josefa Fernández Hernández. She arrived at the motherhouse in July 1957.

[109] 23rd General Congregation, p. 37: "Instability of will, inattentiveness of mind, a certain unbalance of conscience, a growing tendency toward ease and compromise, a need of independence and initiative accompanied by a certain self-assurance, a diminished sense of respect and loyalty, are tendencies that conflict however in them with the desire for the best, generous impulses, need of support and of affectionate understanding that does not weigh on their independence."

[110] Pp. 38-39.

[111] In her conference for the opening of the Council of Studies, 3 August 1956, at the Villa Lante, Mother de Lescure said: "We must mistrust enslavement to [public programs], give them the value of means in view of a more general formation, infuse in them a spirit that imbibes the teaching of the sense of God and Christian solutions, give them a soul that creates an ambiance in

meant that a single religious could no longer meet all the needs of a class. At the same time, the Sacred Heart tried to maintain for some pupils a more specifically feminine teaching in its thinking and its curricula.[112] Higher education became so common that when Mother de Lescure, in January 1951, wrote a letter to the students of the Sacred Heart, she distinguished between "children" and "students." University colleges were autonomous to a greater or lesser degree according to the country. In India the University of Bombay granted the diplomas, but Sophia College gave the courses preparing for the examinations. In Sydney and Brisbane, students took courses at the university and received supplementary courses at the Sacred Heart. The Faculty of Arts of Medellín was annexed to the *Universidad Pontificia Bolivariana*. In Montevideo in 1952 the Sacred Heart opened an institute of Catholic professors of philosophy that did not plan to grant diplomas, which would not have been recognized in Uruguay, "but to conform minds to the truth."[113] In Peru, the national pedagogical institute left the old buildings of San Pedro for Monterrico in March 1958. A laboratory school for primary and secondary grades was added to it. In Mexico the improved political situation in 1955 allowed giving up the business division that had been an umbrella for the educational work. The division that led to the baccalaureate was attached to the autonomous university of Mexico, and a normal school was opened in Mexico in 1959.

Traditional works diversified. The free schools [*écoles*] tended to disappear, lacking enrollment; technical and commercial institutions increased. In Congo at Mbansa-Mboma a primary boarding school was opened for young women from the bush [*évoluées*], a model for other congregations. The domestic science sections at Kipako and Kimwenza accepted girls of different ethnicities who brought their own food every week and prepared it in the evening, as in the village.

In some countries where the institutions were receiving financial aid from the government, the Sacred Heart had to incorporate into its curricula "those aspects of the national civilization and culture that were compatible with a Christian vision of the world."[114] From then on, the spirit of education at the Sacred Heart remained in place while leaving to the vicariates complete latitude to set timetables, curricula and methods.[115] But traditions continued in the boarding schools. At Kenwood, the pupils had

which the fragile, new being that is confided to us will find the *vigor* proper to her total development: mind, will, heart and soul" (*Vie de la T.R.M. de Lescure*, p. 266).

[112] 23rd General Congregation, p. 42.
[113] 24th General Congregation, 1958.
[114] *Spirit and Plan of Studies*, p. 239.
[115] *Circular Letters...de Lescure*, 13 November 1952, p. 140.

a corner of the garden to take care of, and they drank the milk from the cows on the property: "We complained about the taste every spring when the cows ate onion grass."[116] In boarding schools in the United States in the fall they roasted corn and marshmallows on the hockey field.[117] In Canada in spring they went to taste maple sugar, and in Vancouver pupils helped gather honey from the hives. But in Halifax, and elsewhere no doubt, there were raised eyebrows when a pupil wished to borrow from the library Shelley's "Childe Harold," a suspect work. The works of Oscar Wilde, Henry Fielding, Victor Hugo and Tolstoy were off limits. Mary Robinson, a student at Mount Anville in the mid-fifties, was attracted by the austerity of the nuns who inculcated

> reserve and high moral principles, among them that of working for social justice. That influenced me very much. To be religious was to work according to the highest principles with personal commitment in favor of the poorest and most vulnerable. Mount Anville encouraged in me idealism and the principles of integrity. There was insistence on respect for one's word once given and on refusal to lie to avoid punishment if you had done wrong.[118]

But she had to fight to be allowed to read the *Irish Times*! The Sacred Heart had difficulty in keeping the sodality of the Children of Mary alive when there was competition from Catholic Action movements more open to the outside.[119]

The number of vicariates increased from twenty-two to thirty to include Belgium, Italy, England[120] and Australia/New Zealand; two vicariates of the United States were divided in two. In Latin America, Brazil was separated from Argentina/Uruguay; Colombia, Peru and Chile formed vicariates. The new structures, which responded to national development, only partially settled the linguistic problems. After the death of Mother de Pardieu, victim of an airplane accident in the Amazon forest, Mother de la Cavada became the first vicar of Brazil. "We have passed from French guardianship to Spanish," thought Maria Luiza Saade, "We have received

---

[116] *Journey of the Heart*, p. 108. Testimony of Marguerite Tate Taylor.
[117] Testimony of Brigid Keogh. That took place during the 1920's.
[118] Olivia O'Leary and Helen Burke, *Mary Robinson*, Dublin, 1998, p. 14.
[119] Note sent from Australia on the occasion of the preparation of the General Congregation of 1952.
[120] Congo depended on the vicariate of Jette; Malta and India, on that of Woldingham.

a great deal from our missionary sisters, but we were not yet a Brazilian vicariate."[121]

Could they modify the makeup of the general congregations and lessen centralization? In 1946 Mother Zurstrassen had thought about a more democratic government, which would have directed the Society's interest a little more toward administration. She wanted delegates to be present alongside the vicars at the general congregation. She spoke in favor also of "wisely giving more weight to what religious outside the governmental structure say sometimes. [She favored] more freedom for those in charge, keeping them respectful and submissive but not passive, that is to say, not thinking for oneself or expressing one's views with some independence, up to the moment when an opposite decision is given." Local experience was also to be considered: "How many conditions, climates, attitudes, governments, degrees of openness, of fresh air, make desirable, demand even, different things, granted with a great deal of breadth." But, she concluded, many decisions ought to be left to the judgment of the vicars for, "increasingly, differences are noted among us."[122]

Everything rested on the superior general's mode of governing. All her contemporaries were aware of Mother de Lescure's qualities, her lucidity of judgment, the firmness of her decisions, and her wisdom: "She grasped immediately the totality of an issue, its different aspects, its possible consequences, never acting until she had all the data in hand, waiting until the day the light would come and in the meantime she prayed."

She also had "an astonishing facility for work, the genius for organization, energy that never gave in to fatigue."[123] But she had a greater sense of absolute authority than Mother Vicente,[124] and centralization was affirmed during her generalate. Whereas Mother Vicente had wanted the motherhouse to be "an international house, open to all countries where the Society had a house, to their interests, their culture," but with an Italian ambiance, Mother de Lescure made it a French house.[125]

---

[121] Mother de la Cavada nevertheless gave her conferences in Portuguese. It was in 1966 that the first Brazilian vicar was named, Helena Maria Ferreira.

[122] *Elisabeth Zurstrassen*, pp. 23-24, letter of 12 October.

[123] *Vie de la T.R.M. de Lescure*, p. 253.

[124] Mother Keogh recounted that after her nomination as vicar, she was invited to Rome. She informed the motherhouse that the date chosen was not convenient because the jubilee of one of the founders of the vicariate was to take place then and the pupils would not understand why she was not present. Mother de Lescure answered her that it was not up to local superiors and vicars to tell the superior general if they could or could not come. They came when they were called.

[125] Gen. Arch. C VII 2 C. Journal of Mother Castejón.

The influence that this great religious exercised is undeniable. It was often thought burdensome by the French who stress the rigid authority she could show.[126] This characteristic did not go counter to her love of individuals. The firmness and vigilance that circumstances imposed on her could also be explained by her character and by the education she had received. Her love of the Society, her fidelity to the spirit of its origins, her attentiveness to the principles to which she always referred, her concern to control their application gave the impression of narrow conservatism; we shall never know whether it was real or not. In any case her stance seemed to her to assure "a basic security that allowed great audacity in faith so different from the spirit of adventure."[127]

It is not expected of a superior general that she be a revolutionary. Mother de Lescure was a woman of a generation in which religious life unfolded in a monastic milieu. She was not desirous by temperament or by personal affinity of practicing apostolic life apart from it. Many religious think that cloister was reinforced during her generalate. That impression drew on the fact that after the war, cloister was fully reestablished, while, to take up a formula of Maria Luiza Saade, "a new humanity was born." But, she added, "We did not see the importance of this change because of cloister!" Mother de Lescure reinvigorated the spiritual life of the Society, thanks to her superb writings, utterly unlike those from the years before the war.[128] She had the gift of finding striking expressions. She presented religious life as "a response to the love of the One who has first loved us,"[129] an expression often repeated.

Affirmation of Devotion to the Sacred Heart

While the canonization of Margaret Mary Alacoque in 1920 and that of Madeleine Sophie Barat in 1925 were signs that devotion to the Sacred Heart was more and more recognized, popular manifestations confirmed the importance that the Catholic world attributed to it. Allied soldiers during World War I had carried the insignia of the heart surmounted by the cross, displayed on regimental flags, except in France where it was forbidden to fly this emblem publicly, as it was considered a symbol of the restoration of the monarchy. In 1919 and 1920 Spain and Belgium

---

[126] Most of them, it is true, had been her novices or probanists. Marie de Monsabert, niece of Mother de Lescure, thought her aunt had a tendency to put pressure on probanists to obtain what she thought was for their good.
[127] *Vie de la T.R.M. de Lescure*, pp. 253-254.
[128] Marie-Antoinette de Torquat said how struck she was by the intensity of spiritual life these letters revealed.
[129] *Circular Letters...de Lescure*, 25 June 1954, p. 167.

had been consecrated to the Sacred Heart. On 6 February 1929, the feast of the Sacred Heart was established as a feast of the first class with a privileged octave. Two encyclicals treated the mystery of the love of Christ: *Miserentissimus Redemptor*, 8 May 1928, presented it as a synthesis of all religion and *Caritate Christi compulsi*, 3 May 1932, named the prayers and expiations to be offered to the Heart of Jesus. However, it was the encyclical *Haurietis aquas* of 15 May 1956 that gave the scriptural, patristic and theological bases to the spirituality of the Sacred Heart. It surpassed in richness all the earlier teaching and constituted a true treatise of the whole subject. If its publication could be considered a "royal triumph,"[130] it marked an apogee for the devotion to the Sacred Heart and indirectly for the congregations named for it. But the devotion, no longer contested in the Church, knew less success. The feast of Christ the King, promulgated in December 1925, was aimed at celebrating the social reign of the Sacred Heart, and it was on this new feast that the consecration of the human race was renewed.

The slight ebb in devotion to the Sacred Heart can likely be linked to the new relationship established between the faithful and the Eucharist and with the development of Catholic Action. Devotion to the Sacred Heart culminated in adoration of the Blessed Sacrament. With the changes that Pius X had encouraged in urging early communion, the Eucharist was associated more with the celebration of the Mass. Frequent communion came into use gradually and tended to prevail over adoration formally so called in liturgical tradition. Catholic Action movements, developed during the 1930's, had emphasized action rather than contemplation; and they had, rightly or wrongly, seemed directed toward relationship with the neighbor more than toward devotional practices, sometimes belittled as pious and individualistic.

Ten days after the appearance of *Haurietis aquas*, Mother de Lescure gave thanks for this "admirable encyclical" that could only give joy to a Society "completely consecrated to the Heart of Jesus" and for whom "the Heart was everything."[131] A year later a special issue of *Caritas* appeared, entitled "Devotion to the Sacred Heart in the light of the encyclical of His Holiness Pius XII." It reproduced extracts from the encyclical and presented scriptural or patristic references with the help of diagrams and quotations aimed at making it more accessible.[132] Added to it was the account of the ceremonies by which the Society of the Sacred Heart in

---

[130] Such was the title that Father Auguste Hamon gave in 1939 to Volume V of his *Histoire de la dévotion au Sacré-Cœur*.

[131] *Circular Letters*, p. 228.

[132] This work was carried out in great part by Mother Marie-Thérèse Virnot.

France, at the appeal of the pope, had celebrated the appearance of the encyclical and some echoes of the zeal of the religious, the pupils and the alumnae in spreading the devotion to the Heart of Jesus.

The full recognition of the Sacred Heart was a way of recalling the main characteristics of the mystery of salvation, but it was also the consecration of a devotion that could engage the whole person. Even though it was founded squarely on Church tradition, this devotion had in the past sometimes led to excesses; it had been reaffirmed at the end of the eighteenth century, thanks to the spiritual experience of a mystic. It is interesting to note that *Haurietis aquas* was composed in the pontificate of Pius XII, of whom it was said that he himself was gifted with extraordinary spiritual experiences. Still, after 1945, no doubt to avoid the downward spiral that can take place during and after periods of political and social troubles or unrest, the Holy Office reiterated the warnings or condemnations of revelations not approved by competent authorities. Several Religious of the Sacred Heart, between the two wars, had had experiences of this type.

In 1943 a small anonymous work appeared entitled *Cum clamore valido*, based on intellectual "visions" received in prayer from 1935 on by Amélie de Gibergues, who spent the last years of her life at Marmoutier, where she died in 1941. *Cum clamore valido* was "a call of the Redeemer to consecrated souls" and it contained "an instant and pressing supplication" received by Mother de Gibergues on 29 March 1936: "In order to save the world I need consecrated souls who will be true spouses and co-redeemers. I do not have enough of them; they are lacking. Give me these souls, be these souls. My Heart awaits you. My Heart begs you." Destined for priests and for religious, men and women, this appeal called for living with a more intense fidelity and in a spirit of prayer and intimacy with the Lord.[133] A note that accompanied the text suggested: "Understood and practiced, the 'supplication' would be a means by which the Sacred Heart would in the present save the world." The work was valued in Germany and the Netherlands but never officially adopted by the Society of the Sacred Heart, and it seems that it was published through pressure from Father Monier-Vinard. The Society of the Sacred Heart did not seek to obtain the beatification of Amélie de Gibergues. Nor did it that of another French religious, Anne-Marie Le Mintier de Léhélec, who, about 1926 in Poitiers, had an experience of a mystical kind and who seemed to have received

---

[133] It was published thanks to the insistence of the superior of Marmoutier, Mother Vanderhaghen, who believed the experiences of Mother de Gibergues were authentic.

commentaries on the Constitutions from Saint Madeleine Sophie. Mother de Lescure did not think it necessary to keep her notes.[134]

The war over, the Society of the Sacred Heart drew the attention of the Church to Mother Stuart and to Sister Josefa Menéndez in view of an eventual recognition of their merits. It was a matter of profiles of two very different religious. The one was a brilliant intellectual, a remarkable educator and a superior general. The other had spent her religious life "in the humble work of Martha." To propose them for beatification did not fly in the face of common sense, for the Church was continuing to add to the list of saints members of religious congregations and more and more women. After the canonization of its founder, the Society had obtained the beatification of Philippine Duchesne, both originally from France, "the mother of saints," as Benedict XV had called it. To introduce the cause of Janet Stuart, an English convert, and of Josefa Menéndez, a Spaniard, was at the same time to reflect the situation of an international congregation and to signify that each member of the two categories of religious could arrive at holiness by following her vocation and by carrying out the tasks defined by the rule. And from the recognition of the cause of Josefa Menéndez why not hope for coadjutrix vocations at a moment when they were becoming scarce? The process of gathering information on Mother Stuart took place in London[135] and the process was transferred to Rome in 1948. That of Josefa Menéndez took place in Poitiers in April 1947. Mother de Lescure was interested in both, but probably more in that of Josefa Menéndez with whom she had lived.

In February 1920 a Spanish novice who had entered a little earlier at Chamartín arrived at the novitiate of the coadjutrix sisters in Poitiers. Josefa Menéndez was almost thirty years old and had been a dressmaker. Soon she was having almost daily apparitions of Jesus Christ and of different saints. She confided in her mistress of novices, Mother de Girval, who thought, in view of Josefa's fidelity to what was imposed on her, that there was no trickery. Mother de Lescure was named superior in Poitiers on 12 August 1921. She was then made *au courant* of what was happening at the request of "Our Lord himself." Rather perplexed, she tried also to verify the authenticity of this spiritual experience by watching Josefa closely regarding her life in the community and the rule, her obedience, her indifference. On 28 August 1921, she decided to have Josefa

> write what she did, saw and heard every day in a notebook that I will translate accordingly. I said to myself before Our Lord that we may not

---

[134] M. H. Quinlan, *The Society of the Sacred Heart*, pp. 70-129.
[135] The first mention of the diocesan process figures in a circular of 5 January 1947.

demand signs of him.... If it is truly he, he remains the master. I will make use therefore of the lights of faith and of my reason to study, follow this child from near and far, day after day, at the same time that I will begin the work of translation first, then of reflection and prayer on the notes the sister has written in obedience to the Mother assistant.[136]

Without ever having a role in them, Mother de Lescure knew that these revelations concerned her, if only because of a sentence heard by Josefa: "I will help my Thérèse and I will guide my spouse so that she will enflame souls with my love." She was in a delicate situation: "These graces that have been greatly enveloping this house for a month: are they the sign of a very special presence of Our Lord among us?... His words about this house: are they *really* his? Does he meet love here?... If all of this is false, what a world of illusion! If it is all true, there is almost no place in the house where Our Lord has not been, walked, visited, and what are we in the face of this outpouring! And what am I, superior as I dare to be?"[137] Following a long series of diabolical temptations the novice experienced, in October 1921 Mother de Lescure got in touch with the diocesan exorcist and through him with the Dominican prior. They were gradually convinced, and they confirmed her in her conduct up to that time. The vicar, Mother Dupont, was informed and in turn informed the motherhouse. Mother von Loë took an interest in the situation and invited Mother de Lescure to come to see her in March 1922. The following year she asked her, under the pretext of making the superiors' retreat, to bring Josefa Menéndez with her. Josefa died on 29 December 1923, after making final profession in the Society of the Sacred Heart.

Mother de Lescure had done everything she could not to reveal what had been happening. Did she succeed? Opinions differ. It seems that other sisters had sniffed out a part of the mystery. At Marmoutier, where Josefa made a brief stay, her constant communication by letter with Poitiers surprised the superior. The boarders at Poitiers were astonished at the unusual character of her funeral.[138] Mother von Loë had asked Mother de Lescure the day after the death of Josefa to inform the community "that the sister we have just lost was a very privileged soul to whom Our Lord had appeared many times dictating to her messages of mercy for the world and for our Society. You will add that all of that will only be made public after a preliminary examination by ecclesiastical authority." Beginning on 31 December Mother de Lescure said in community "a word of Our

---

[136] *Vie de la T.R.M. de Lescure*, p. 63.
[137] *Vie*, p. 64, 6 September 1921.
[138] Testimony of Louise de la Taille.

Lord to Sister Josefa: 'I ask three things of my souls: reparation, love, confidence.'"[139] She continued doing so in the houses where she lived and in those with which she was charged after her nomination as vicar of the Midi, instilling in those for whom she was responsible the message of the revelations received by Sister Josefa. She used them also in her conferences and in the retreats she planned for her community. The Society of the Sacred Heart learned from Mother von Loë herself that

> a favor has been granted to our Society by the extraordinary graces accorded to a humble Spanish coadjutrix sister, Sister Josefa Menéndez, who died in Poitiers in the odor of sanctity last December 29. The favors of which she was the object (and which in her lifetime we surrounded with the most discreet silence) as also the instructions that Our Lord deigned to dictate to her for religious souls, in particular those of our Society, are at this moment the object of a minute examination by competent authority. When we are provided with ecclesiastical approbation, we will not fail to let you know of the mercies of the divine Master and the encouragement he has wished to give to the little Society of his Heart.[140]

On 29 January 1924, Mother de Lescure wrote: "Henceforth all our prayer is directed in this sense: that his Work may be realized, that his designs of love be accomplished and that his Heart itself prepare the path of his words toward all the souls that his mercy and love wishes to reach."[141] It remained to make known the message "dictated by Our Lord" to Josefa Menéndez. It was to Marie-Thérèse de Lescure that this mission had been confided in the course of one or more of the apparitions.[142] A first brochure, *Sister Josefa at the School of the Heart of Jesus*, had been composed by Mother de Lescure to be sent to communities, unlike the death notices usually dedicated to coadjutrix sisters. In 1926, a *Life of Sister Josefa*, destined for superiors was sent for examination to a consultor of the Sacred Congregation of Rites. It was only in April 1936, after the announcement of the cure of a sister in Cairo following a novena to Sister Menéndez, that Cardinal Pacelli, protector of the Society of the Sacred Heart, decided a work could be written and published beyond the congregation. A thin little book, *At the School of the Heart of Jesus*, composed by Mother de Lescure,

---

[139] *Vie de la T.R.M. de Lescure*, pp. 92-93.
[140] *Circulaires de la T.R.M. de Loë*, pp. 145-146, 18 January 1924.
[141] *Vie de la T.R.M. de Lescure*, p. 95.
[142] *Vie...* p. 105: Our Lord is quoted as having said to Sister Josefa, "When the Mother superior will be the vicar, she will have the obligation to speak my words; you, you will already be in heaven."

appeared in 1938, with a letter of recommendation from Cardinal Pacelli. The writer took to heart Father de Guibert's remarks to write a biography of Josefa that would insist more on the holiness of her life than on the extraordinary phenomena with which it was said she was gifted. This large work, entitled *The Way of Divine Love*, appeared in 1944 and, translated into several languages, became available to the whole Society.

How was the "Message" received? The question is difficult to answer. Many contemporaries said that they were at first attracted to the message but that afterward they pulled back from their earlier impression as a result of their own spiritual evolution. Marguerite du Merle, the biographer of Mother de Lescure, shows carefully that in the vicariate of the Midi not all the religious were ready to understand "the true character of the 'Message." Some who recognized in it Mother de Lescure's doctrine followed it through attraction to the vicar. "Others did not yet grasp the connection between the purest spirituality of the Society such that our holy Mother had left to it and what was appearing now, and they kept themselves somewhat at a distance."[143] There were reservations about the style, which seemed too effusive. At Montpellier and Mont-Villargenne, at the end of the 1940's the novices were being trained with the help of the Message, from which exercise [instruction in religious life] was drawn. Everything was perhaps a question of one's generation. The youngest, under the direction of Mothers de Lescure and Drujon, were drawn by *The Way of Divine Love* and touched by many of its pages. The older nuns thought that the Constitutions and the *Manuel du Chrétien,* used in their formation, were sufficient.[144] The reactions were not keyed to national culture; there were translations and laudatory comments arriving from many vicariates, showing that the Message was doing good. The apparitions at Poitiers and the role that Mother de Lescure had played contributed to her election, quite as much as her unquestionable qualities: some noted that she had been elected on 29 September, while Josefa Menéndez had died on the 29th of December.

Mother de Lescure's attitude toward the Message did not change after her accession to the generalate. From her first circular concerning the prayer of consecration for the first Friday of the month, she evoked the character of spouse and victim that was to mark a Religious of the Sacred Heart. She illustrated her remark with citations from the Constitutions, the Bible and the founder; but for the first time, she quoted from the Message.[145] Many of the following circulars included extracts or alluded

---

[143] *Vie....* p. 105.
[144] Testimony of G. Bovagnet who entered the novitiate at Montpellier in September 1946, shortly before the departure of Mother de Lescure for Rome.
[145] *Circular Letters...de Lescure*, p. 22, 13 June 1947.

to the Message's having been confided to the Society. Henceforth it was presented "as the normal development of the grace of vocation" of a Religious of the Sacred Heart. Just as the vicar of the Midi had spread it in her houses and among those whom she had trained, in the same way the superior general sought to spread it around the world by her circular letters and by personal correspondence. Her letters often took up phrases or expressions, with or without quotation marks, and without citing the source. For the one hundred fiftieth anniversary of the congregation, she proposed the "Chain of Souls,"[146] based at once on the letters of Mother Barat and on a "word" of 6 October 1923 "of Our Lord to the Society."

> What we know is that his Heart open to the Society has ratified the designs of his love, the same designs that he revealed earlier to our holy Mother when he plunged her into the abyss of his heart. By studying her writings, her letters, her conferences more assiduously, it has not been difficult for us to find, often in the same terms, the burning prelude to the Message.[147]

One had the impression that it was to Josefa Menéndez more than to Madeleine Sophie that the Lord had revealed his designs. While this way of presenting things was troubling, it was perhaps only awkward. It is true that the first step toward the beatification of Josefa Menéndez had been completed and that her cause had been sent to Rome.[148]

Mary Quinlan has written:

> While Mother de Lescure believed strongly in the validity of the experience [of Josefa Menéndez], she respected the liberty of each religious to follow the influence of grace in her spiritual life, a tradition going back to the founder. Consequently, she did not impose these revelations on anyone. In her journeys around the world, she gave an

---

[146] Pp. 81-100.
[147] Pp. 108-109.
[148] The French Jesuits whom Mother de Lescure had addressed from the beginning had reassured her, recalling, like Father Charmot, that the *Message* contained nothing that contradicted the Gospel of John, tradition, the teachings of the mystics or the desires expressed by Saint Madeleine Sophie: "Our Lord does not ask of you any innovation in your institute or even in your spirituality. He only wishes that the essential point of devotion to the Sacred Heart, the soul so to speak of your vocation, the deepest desire of the Heart of Jesus, do not become dead like ashes in an old hearth but be stirred up like a flame always more ardent and *bright*. It is a question of renewal, not of innovation" (*Vie de la T.R.M. de Lescure*, p. 289, letter of September 1942, communicated to Mother Datti).

impression of holiness, of affection for each person and of close union with God in prayer. If someone asked a question about Josefa, she answered, but she did not take the initiative in approaching the subject.[149]

But the Message "radiated through her whole person; in her conferences as in her direction, Mother de Lescure gave everyone the essential message."[150] Mary Quinlan added wisely: "The fervor of her own faith in the devotion to the Sacred Heart as she had seen it in the life and revelations of Josefa must have made it difficult for her to be objective about the reception of the Message within and outside the Society."

There were no unfavorable reactions within the congregation, likely because religious who were not at ease with the Message did not talk about it. Even so they found that Mother de Lescure's insistence on it to be excessive. The assistant general in charge of the probation, Mother Zurstrassen, was not convinced by the Message, unlike her assistant, Mother Raynaud de Lage. But she did not bring up the subject with the probanists before the death of Mother de Lescure. Outside the Society on the other hand, reservations were expressed from the moment *The Way of Divine Love* had been translated and widely spread among alumnae and in the schools.[151] Theologians, often Jesuits, criticized precise points of the Message that did not seem acceptable to them or certain "words" that did not give the impression of having been said by Jesus as he is represented in the Gospels. Some had even thought, upon reading the French text, that its publication was not desirable and that its circulation did not contribute to the spiritual development of the pupils. Some criticisms pointing to the parallels among expressions in the Message and in the writings of Teresa of Avila and Margaret Mary Alacoque questioned the originality of the contents.[152] Most theologians of all nationalities who gave an opinion, either by request or on their own initiative, suggested, like Father de Guibert, placing more emphasis on the holiness of Josefa Menéndez's life than on the extraordinary phenomena that had taken place. They were concerned lest such phenomena cast a shadow on the sister's cause, because the Holy Office was prejudiced against so many visions.

---

[149] *Vie*.... p. 86.

[150] *Notice de la R.M. Madeleine Drujon*, p. 9.

[151] Mother de Valon, in 1938, lent the boarders *À l'École du Cœur de Jésus* (Testimony of Solange de Pomyers). *L'Appel à l'amour* was one of the prize books given to the pupils (Testimony of Françoise Rollin).

[152] There were also parallels with the writings of Saint Madeleine Sophie, at which Mother de Lescure marveled, whereas she could have asked herself where they came from.

By accentuating the biblical and patristic foundations of devotion to the Sacred Heart, the encyclical *Haurietis aquas* brought into balance the ways of looking at it. But in the special issue on the encyclical that appeared in *Caritas*, the review published in France by the alumnae, there are extracts from the writings of saints, mystics or spiritual authors of all eras, some of whom were directly linked to devotion to the Sacred Heart.[153] Quotations are taken from the founder of the Helpers of the Holy Souls, Mary of Providence, no doubt because she was an alumna of Lille, from Louise Thérèse de Montaignac, the founder of the Oblates of the Sacred Heart, and from Mother Mary Saint Jerome of the Company of Our Lady, who in 1833 had established the "Month of the Sacred Heart" at the convent of *Les Oiseaux*. Extracts from Fathers Charmot and Lebreton, friends of the Society, were reproduced. Seven quotations from Saint Madeleine Sophie figure there as well. But taken together, nine passages of "Our Lord to Sister Josefa" show that 36% of the extracts used were drawn from the Message.

One could hardly do more! All the evidence agrees about the exchanges between Mother de Lescure and Mother de Valon at the time of the superior general's last illness. When she announced the death of Mother de Lescure, Mother de Valon wrote: "As I asked her two days before her death for her last recommendation for her daughters and especially for the superiors, she answered spontaneously: 'Tell them that I count on them, on their fidelity, on their gift of themselves to the work of Love until death.'"[154] Likewise, Mother de Valon had asked Mother de Lescure what her instructions were regarding the Message: "What shall we say when you are no longer with us?" "There is nothing more to say; I have said everything; there is nothing more than to do it." "And how shall we do it?" "By allowing the love of the Heart of Jesus to pass freely through us to souls."[155] That sent one back to the Constitutions. At the General Congregation of 1958, the councilors received an envelope containing twenty relics of Josefa.

Mother de Valon had become imbued with the Message during her religious life in the vicariate of the Midi, even referring to it in her prayer, including on the day she learned that she was named vicar general. It does

---

[153] In the order of appearance in the texts, the extracts are from Henry Suso, Saint Mechtilde, Saint Justin, Saint Catherine of Siena, Saint Frances of Rome, Saint Margaret Mary Alacoque, Origen, Saint Augustine, Saint John Chrysostom, Saint Ambrose, Ruysbroeck, Saint Lutgarde, Denis the Carthusian, Saint Teresa of Avila, Marie of the Incarnation, Bossuet. A citation is drawn from *De montibus Sinai et Sion*.

[154] *Lettres circulaires de notre T.R.M. Sabine de Valon*, p. 14, 1 January 1958.

[155] Letter of April 1965. The exchange is similar in *Vie de la T.R.M. de Lescure*, p. 326.

not appear, however, that she sought to address the last instructions of Mother de Lescure, maybe because she wanted to leave the glory of having spread the Message to her, or because it was not the supporting element of her spiritual life. After her election, she did not refer to it in her circular letters, and she kept a certain distance from religious of the motherhouse who were said to be favorable to it.[156] During her generalate, Mothers Alice Mallet and Marie-Emmanuelle Monrozier, who came from the Midi and who had been close to Mother de Lescure, were charged with furthering the cause of Josefa Menéndez. In spite of all the effort expended[157] and much supporting testimony, the work quickly came to an end. On 22 July 1958, the general council approved the suspension of the process and gave up having Father Charmot's work on the theology of *The Way of Divine Love* published, fearing that to do so would seem to contradict the decision that the Congregation of Rites had just made.[158] In 1959 through the influence of John XXIII the motherhouse tried to revive the cause, without result. It seems that Mother de Valon made no further attempts to take up the issue afterward. But at the time of the preparation for the Special Chapter of 1967, many vicariate assemblies asked for guidance on "a course of action regarding the Message and our duty to propagate it, so as to lessen the anxiety of many of us who are afraid that the importance given to the Message will be harmful to true devotion to the Sacred Heart." The summary report added: "Many ask to take advantage of it sincerely, prudently and tactfully."[159] Mother Bultó decided for poverty's sake to stop pursuing the causes of Mother Stuart,[160] Philippine Duchesne and Josefa Menéndez,[161] who was only third in line of Religious of the Sacred Heart

---

[156] Testimony of Germaine Dejean.

[157] At Pentecost 1958, Mother de Valon invited to the motherhouse all the Jesuits who were friends of the Trinità dei Monti, "the Mothers wishing by this means to extend the knowledge of the Society and of the Message" (Journal of the Trinità) of which they must not have been ignorant! Gifts were given also to those who could aid in advancing the cause.

[158] It was decided then to have *Cum clamore valido* translated into Polish, without the name of Amélie de Gibergues.

[159] Gen. Arch. C I C 3, Box 20.

[160] The cause of Mother Stuart continued to be supported during the generalate of Mother de Valon. In a letter of 16 October 1960, Mother Benziger informed the vicar of Ireland that the superior general wished to present it again to the pope (Prov. Arch. Ireland/Scotland, IRS 0073).

[161] Testimony of M.J. Bultó. It was thanks to a modification in the rules for the procedure of canonization, among others the reduction in the number of miracles required and thanks to financial support from the United States that the canonization of Philippine Duchesne could be celebrated in July 1988.

likely to be canonized. The Message continued to help people of all stations in life on every continent and to lead them to the Heart of Christ or keep them in his love: that was the essential.

When Marie-Thérèse de Lescure died on 31 December 1957, nothing suggested that profound changes were going to take place in the Society of the Sacred Heart. The succession had been prepared for in the traditional way by the nomination of a vicar general. The newly named religious was superior at the Trinità dei Monti, the "daughter house" of the motherhouse, but she was little known in the Society, for she had not been assistant general or vicar. Sabine de Valon came from the same country as the one who named her, as had been the case with Mother Gœtz and Mother Stuart. One wonders whether her appointment would overemphasize the French character that Mother de Lescure had given to the motherhouse at a time when internationality was increasing in the Society of the Sacred Heart.[162] All the vicars had backed this choice. Daughter of Mother de Lescure with whom she had lived in France, Mother de Valon had the same love of the Society and the same respect for her office. One could expect from her the same effort to make the congregation grow and to sustain its fervor.

---

[162] In 1967, at the time of Mother de Valon's resignation some Italian religious were relieved at the thought that there would not be another French superior general (Testimony of Eleonora de Guggenberg), while everything seems to suggest that Mother de Valon thought it would be a Latin American who would succeed her.

Third Part

THE SOCIETY OF THE SACRED HEART REFOUNDED
1958-2000

Chapter I

Innovation or Renewal 1958-1967

The desire for renewal that appeared in the Society of the Sacred Heart in the course of the 1960's was the fruit of an epoch in which change affected religious life. It was awakened also by the astonishing decision of Pope John XXIII to call an ecumenical council. The new superior general was a catalyst for change that took the Society in new directions of great importance, but it was not possible for Mother de Valon to see them through.

New Waves

"The times are changing"

A piece entitled *The Moving Times*, published in 1964 in London by Alexander Trocchi, took a step toward highlighting a counter-culture that was finding expression in the *avant garde* festivals of Edinburgh and London. A century earlier, when the "imperial festival" was spreading its influence throughout France, Mother Barat had written: "Times are changing...we must change our plan of studies!" In the congregation this formula became a leitmotiv taken up each time a modification seemed necessary.

The western world was experiencing vigorous economic growth. The social classes that had provided the pupils for the day schools of the Sacred Heart benefitted from this growth, and they demanded more solid instruction than in earlier days. Could they any longer be content "not to keep the best of our religious for the boarding school, to have the day school children take part in our religious feasts, to avoid making too much of social differences, and above all to force ourselves through charity to bring the classes together?" The students had to be able "to move from the free school to the boarding school," not by "an abrupt, complete assimilation" that would have met "much opposition in certain countries," but rather by means of more diverse curricula, so that pupils of both boarding and free schools could prepare for technical careers or for the liberal professions.[1]

Opposition to social exclusivity was all the more imperative as public policies were changing the ways in which instruction took place. In the United States, the GI Bill, which allowed veterans to pursue university studies, had transformed cultural and social standards. In France, the Fifth Republic had regularized the education of young people. Except in Alsace and Moselle, the financing of private schools had been the responsibility of the families who sent their children to them. The government of General de Gaulle legislated "contracts" with private education and took charge of paying the teachers, on condition that the school satisfied certain regulations as to the number and source of the pupils, the qualifications of the teachers and the programs. In Peru and Belgium free schooling had been established.[2] The length of schooling was extended. Coeducation became obligatory. New courses were offered. At Manhattanville, the number of college students doubled. The development of university colleges in the United States and the relocation of some boarding schools meant that because of cloister some religious could not continue their activity in parish schools.[3] These were transferred to other congregations or closed.[4] University colleges were opened in Colombia, Uruguay and Peru.[5] However, a school for social workers was not allowed either in Mexico or at Chamartín. The motherhouse did not consider such a project in line with the works of the Society. On the other hand, educational proposals answering to specific needs were increasing.

Technical progress and mass production were the order of the day; daily life was oriented toward speed, consumption, recreation and comfort. Could one still consider the automobile and record players mere gimmicks? It was possible to get along without them if one were poor, but it was

---

[1] Gen. Arch. Report of Mother de Valon to the General Congregation of 1958.
[2] "Free schooling will open our doors more widely to children of all social milieus, but the concept of the formation of the élite that our holy Mother wished cannot change for all that, for élite are found in all social classes," said Mother de Valon (Sessions of the General Council, 23 March 1959).
[3] "Poor schools" became parochial schools at the beginning of the twentieth century.
[4] At Manhattanville, Harlem Preparatory School brought young people in difficulty, often those of color, back into the scholastic circuit.
[5] In 1961, a university college was opened in Montevideo; in 1963, a women's university of the Sacred Heart, Unife, was opened in Lima.

clear that people of modest means had acquired them.[6] Aesthetic norms were changing and physical education was being emphasized. Because of better understanding of hygiene, people were giving more attention physical care.[7] Fashions, symbols of liberation or emancipation, began to confuse social and sexual identities and created a new look. Artists spread liberation in mores that contrasted with the prudish education that had carried the day until then. In France in 1954 Françoise Sagan published a novel in which a young girl, through jealousy, indirectly but willingly caused the death of her father's mistress. Looking back, one can see this work as tender and innocent as much as bitter and depraved. The fact that the author had attended the Sacred Heart school at Boisfleury shocked Mother Zurstrassen, who wrote to a correspondent: "In Belgium are they too talking about this book, *Bonjour Tristesse*, a masterpiece of style, but absolutely scandalous, written by a young woman of eighteen? Everyone is devouring it in France. She trades on the fact of having been our pupil and also of the Assumption. It is true that she was at our house in Grenoble for a trimester!"[8]

The new rhythms of pop music and pop singers were appearing and attracting adolescents. They were inflammatory and signaled a new social category that was taking shape, thanks to mass schooling. The young began to contest the authority of the state, the family and the Church. How could one give them benchmarks, educate them while at the same time allowing them more liberty? For young women who wished to enter the Society of the Sacred Heart, their formation was expected to be "very strong but in a climate of love and openness." Many young women were dumbfounded by customs that would have been better understood by their grandmothers.

Independence and National Politics

The experience of freedom resulted in legislative changes or outbreaks of violence. In Egypt in 1962, Christians could no longer teach Arabic. The motherhouse feared the confiscation or Islamization of its institutions. It placed Egypt under its direct authority and foresaw withdrawal if necessary into Lebanon, where the Society had acquired a property in May 1960.

In Congo the mission of the Society of the Sacred Heart, while making Jesus Christ known and loved, was to "hasten the integration of

---

[6] In October 1962, Mother de Valon and the nuns of the Via Nomentana followed the opening of the Vatican Council, thanks to the domestic workers of the motherhouse who lent their television set!

[7] From 1954 on, in Toulouse, the parents were asking for "fewer curtsies and more baths" (Testimony of Theresa Chu).

[8] *Elisabeth Zurstrassen*, p. 29.

all Congolese, white and black," a dream that haunted Mother Symon, "and may our eyes see it realized."[9] After attending a dance performance during which there was a waltz that had flabbergasted the young boys, the vicar of Belgium had written: "The difficulty is to find the happy medium between following European customs and keeping 'black' usages…for the moment."[10] After 1956 there was an African novitiate at Mbansa-Mboma.[11]

The development of the French and English colonies in Africa brought up the question of the fate of Congo. In 1955 a plan was made to lead to independence in thirty years, while preparing an élite to govern it on the English model of "indirect rule." For her part, the vicar thought that the process should go more quickly and bring the country's own people into it. After the triumphal visit in May 1955 of King Baudouin, who wanted a path toward independence "without useless delays or fatal haste," hopes for independence were fully evident. They were encouraged by the visit General de Gaulle made to Africa in August 1958. In Brazzaville he proclaimed the right to independence of the overseas populations. This declaration echoed loudly in Belgian Congo. The Pan African conference in Accra two months later showed the Congolese that other areas were moving more quickly and further than Belgium. Upon his return from Ghana, Patrice Lumumba claimed immediate independence. But the issue was tied up in the context of the cold war. The United States began to be interested in Central Africa, less locked in than before by France, which granted independence while seeking to keep its influence. Congo-Brazzaville, the Sudan, Burundi and Angola were captivated by Castroism and Soviet communism. Lumumba was not a Communist, but, like other nationalists of the neutralist camp, he ended up by accepting aid from the Eastern bloc.

Examples increased after January 1959. In March the orange trees at Kipako were uprooted "because they no longer wanted foreigners planting anything in the ground that belonged to the Blacks."[12] The prospect of independence soothed some, but the vicar, Mother Cruysmans, rode in a car with a Congolese seated beside the driver: "It is safer when a Congolese occupies the front seat of the auto, although the routes are not dangerous now,"[13] she wrote. One wondered what the fate of the religious

---

[9] 25 March 1955, C. Meeûs, *Histoire de la Province du Congo*, p. 11. In 1953, she had written that one must no longer speak of *"évoluées"* but of "young Congolese girls." But at Kalina until 1958 it was forbidden to admit Congolese.

[10] C. Meeûs, p. 13.

[11] In 1960, a *preparatorium* brought together candidates to religious life at Kimwenza. While pursuing their studies they led a kind of intermediate life between that of boarders and of postulants.

[12] C. Meeûs, p. 17.

[13] C. Meeûs, p. 18.

congregations would be when Belgium was no longer there to grant subsidies and what would happen to people if the Belgian army left the country.

Independence was announced on 30 June 1960. On 5 July, the Congolese troops mutinied, protesting against continued racial discrimination in the army and demanding that their officers be Africans. Two days later, they took the capital. Violent troubles broke out at Mbansa-Mboma in the night of 6-7 July. The families of Belgian administrators took refuge at the Sacred Heart. Women were molested by soldiers excited by a radio broadcast with the slogan, "The whites have violated our women; violate theirs." The religious were insulted and the Sacred Heart invaded; two lay teachers were taken and then released. Therefore, in the morning, the superior went to Leopoldville with the community and their guests. The nuns from Kimwenza arrived there also, thanks to some Belgians who came with them. All the religious of the diocese of Kipako were en route toward the capital under the protection of the bishop. Kalina became a shelter and transition point for 1500 Belgians waiting for evacuation; they included religious of different congregations, frightened families, wounded people, some gravely.[14] Mother Françoise Braun, who had been one of the founders of the mission, returned to Belgium because of her age.

The intervention of Belgian paratroopers, on 10 July 1960, to protect the endangered European population set in motion the internationalization of the "Congolese problem." The country floundered in civil war and was threatened with provincial secession. As Mother Cruysmans indicated in February 1961:

> Everything is the same and everything is changed! The future remains dark and uncertain; the present appears calm and orderly, but one has the impression that a mere nothing would suffice to cause a storm to burst! In any case education is privileged; they need teachers as they need bread. The authorities of this sector are more amiable and grant everything we ask for; the subsidies come from who knows where, but we accept them. The children, like the parents, are proud of the Sacred Heart *lycée* and parents insist strongly on placing their children there, even paying the rather high tuition fees. God willing, communism will not triumph. The truly great threat is from that quarter.

---

[14] In 1961, King Baudouin expressed to the superior at Kalina his gratitude for the welcome the Sacred Heart had accorded the refugees. The house served as a refuge again in 1964 to Congolese and foreign religious at the time that serious incidents took place in the North.

The arrival of UN soldiers[15] reassured the Europeans. Some Belgians returned, but they left their oldest daughters in Belgium. The *lycée* at Kalina was Africanized: "It is said that 1600 teachers will be required to respond to the need for education. UNESCO was alerted and promised to find 500. After many searches, they sent fifty, some of whom are Asians who speak barbarous French; they are pagans or Muslims." But as Clotilde Meeûs notes, some of the co-workers were from the Antilles; they were Christians, and spoke "a lovely Island French."[16] Archbishop Scalais asked the missionaries to adapt, not for political reasons, but out of love.[17]

In 1963, Mother Thuysbaert was given charge of the vicariate of Congo. Mother de Valon wrote:

> This separation only tightened the bonds between Belgium and Congo, for our dear missionaries will continue to need the help of the mother country, and our religious will always look with an envious eye on this dear mission where such admirable work is offered to their zeal. Both will show by their unity that there is no separation if the charity of the Heart of Jesus animates everything in our lives.[18]

Belgium remained the land of welcome for sick religious and for those in formation. At the very end of the century the last Belgians left Congo after having in some cases spent more than forty years there.

In the Third World, the struggles for independence were won by "a silent revolution." Identity became an issue for those who had lived under colonial rule, including in religious congregations. "Return to roots" was a slogan that could apply to dress, language and customs, but it was not used in the Society of the Sacred Heart before the Chapter of 1967.[19]

Political and cultural developments appeared in various parts of the world. In Québec – one no longer spoke of "French Canada" after the end of the war – more than ever language signified identity. The two Sacred Heart schools, which were offering an education in both French and English, underwent an important change. In 1962, the school in Montreal became Anglophone and the one at Sault-au-Récollet became Francophone.

---

[15] The "Blue Berets" had landed at Elisabethville, in Katanga, on 12 August 1960.
[16] C. Meeûs, pp. 21-22.
[17] C. Meeûs, 23 January 1961: "Whatever the difficulties the future has in store for us, let us keep in any case, our confidence in the vitality of the Church."
[18] *Lettres et circulaires de la T.R.M. de Valon*, p. 122.
[19] Testimony of Mary Braganza.

The Society of the Sacred Heart in the World of Its Times 1865-2000

The decision displeased the pupils as much as the alumnae.[20] In Eastern Europe the political climate in Poland relaxed. In 1963 the probanists and the vicar could go to Rome once again. They had not been seen there for ten years. Mother de Valon went to Poland in April 1964 and observed the hardships and struggles of the communities, which had to do without necessities. In Berlin life was equally hard and precarious.[21]

In Latin America conditions varied by country. Mexico had managed to prevent North American companies from taking root there; and thanks to the "Green Revolution," it had achieved food self-sufficiency and was selling its surplus outside the country. External debt was non-existent, and the development of industry gave birth to a large middle class. Nonetheless, government policies aimed at economic development more than at treating obstacles in the agricultural world. In Colombia after the assassination in 1948 of the head of the liberal party, Jorge Eliécer Gaitán, the struggle between the army and the liberals had resulted in deaths, a large rural exodus and the birth of guerrilla warfare. At the beginning of the 1960's those who spoke out against the extreme misery of a growing fringe of the population tried to bring about structural change. One of the best known was Camilo Torres Restrepo. Ordered by the hierarchy to abandon his priestly functions after participating in demonstrations, he joined the Army of National Liberation in October 1965 and was killed four months later during a skirmish. This warrior priest, who represented an extreme case, became an emblematic figure well beyond Latin America. The *Golconda* group, which brought together lay people and clerics, was concerned with pastoral renewal and increase of social justice. In 1966 to end the violence the liberal party and the conservative party formed a National Front and, reelected every four years, blocked alternative solutions offered by other political organizations. Elsewhere, beginning with Brazil in 1964, the military dictatorships that would come to power in the following years began to arise.

The Castro revolution had the most significant effect on the Society of the Sacred Heart. In 1960 the nationalization of education resulted in the closing of the houses in Santiago and Marianao and in the departure of the religious. As Mother de Valon wrote on 12 May 1961, "You can guess the sorrow of my heart in thinking that our two poor houses in Cuba have fallen into the hands of communists!... Houses pass!... They are not eternal, but souls. Poor souls of children, who are going to be deceived, turned from Our Lord; it hurts to think about it! Even so, we have to

---

[20] Testimony of Anne Leonard. It was the diminution in number of Francophone religious that explained the decision.
[21] *Lettres et circulaires de la T.R.M. de Valon*, p. 88, 31 December 1961.

thank Providence that our mothers have left." Two foundations, Caracas and Miami, brought together some nuns from Cuba as well as children whose parents had emigrated. The others were scattered throughout Latin America.[22]

Missionary expansion

During Mother de Valon's generalate there was unusual missionary momentum. Thirty-one foundations were made between 1958 and 1967. This expansion was a means of responding to the calls of the Church and the world.

Favorable Context

At the end of the 1950's a new way of thinking about mission, founded in a new ecclesiology, coincided with the geopolitical upsets occasioned by growing independence of colonies or countries under foreign control. This approach did not back all forms of nationalism, but it respected the demands for autonomy that were also evident in the religious sphere.

During the period between the wars the Church had fostered regional hierarchies. Later, the objective was to tie Christianity to national cultures. In the encyclical *Fidei donum* of 21 April 1957, Pius XII had proposed that western dioceses, above all European ones, "lend" priests and lay people for a time to Africa, Asia and South America with an eye toward their undertaking pastoral ministry at the request of the local churches. Religious congregations worked along the same lines. In 1959 in his encyclical *Princeps pastorum*, John XXIII addressed the clergy and bishops of mission countries and not the missionaries alone. He said that the Church had to be concerned with the salvation of human beings whatever their culture and history. The faithful were to "turn their zeal toward the missions and bring them effective support." Prayer and the dissemination of information on living conditions in mission countries would allow Christians to offer their help locally to churches.[23] Vatican Council II occasioned the redefining of mission.

During Mother de Valon's generalate the alumnae and the Church hierarchy continued to ask for foundations. Requests came from Sudan, Cambodia, Kenya, Ghana, Zambia and Fiji, and also from Sweden, Portugal and South America. Asia and Africa were given priority for

---

[22] Some very elderly Mexicans returned to the country they had left at the time of the persecution.

[23] Message to the bishops of Switzerland, 2 January 1961.

new foundations, because the motherhouse wanted to take advantage of opportunities offered by the development occurring in these areas.

New Methods for the Mission

The Society of the Sacred Heart had had a strong missionary consciousness from its beginning, and Mother de Valon was filled with it. The visits she made after her election reinforced her undeniable missionary zeal. In the Far East in the spring of 1961, she saw new cultures and became aware of the misery of developing countries to the point of thinking of ways to relieve it. Upon her return she announced a proposal to establish at the motherhouse a "mission office where information, offers and requests for service would be sent and where a publication, serious in style, which would give news of our current missions and treat questions of missiology, would be produced and sent to each of the houses."[24] She thought of introducing the essential elements of missiology at the beginning of formation, in particular in the international novitiate, opened in Italy at Frascati, that she hoped would nourish the missions.[25] The news of missionaries published in the *Annual Letters* had provided awareness of mission countries and awakened interest in joining them. The review *Mitte me*, whose first number came out in November 1961, followed in the Society's tradition. Its French title alluded to the words of Philippine Duchesne when she had begged Mother Barat to send her to America. Its goal was "to spread the love of the Heart of Jesus throughout the world."[26]

The review was assigned to Mother Marguerite du Merle. Thanks to quality contributions, she made it a publication that increased understanding and nourished reflection.[27] Some special numbers were dedicated to countries where the Society of the Sacred Heart had houses. *Mitte me* expected to "bring to light true missionary spirit, as distinct from its false versions, and to bring it about."[28] A booklet entitled *Are We Missionaries*, inserted in the magazine, was directed at pupils, to encourage their interest in the missions. It recommended beginning Philippine Duchesne clubs and contests among the schools. Mother de Valon suggested the

---

[24] *Lettres et circulaires*, 12 July 1961, p. 83.
[25] Testimony of Francisca Tamayo. While the vicars accepted sending their novices to Frascati, they asked to have them back after their first vows.
[26] *Mitte me*, N° 1, Introduction of Françoise de Lambilly, p. 1.
[27] Father Jerome D'Souza wrote an article in the first issue. He had been a member of the constitutional convention in Delhi and the representative of India to the UN. Father Arrupe's signature appears also on some articles. Pedro Arrupe was general of the Jesuits, 1965-1983.
[28] *Mitte me*.

creation of a missionary tax to be paid by the pupils of boarding schools in wealthy countries to finance the education of children in mission countries.[29] This proposal did not have much success. The boarding school costs were already rather high, and many parents were not willing to see them increased. However, Mother Benziger tried to interest the pupils in the construction of the house in Taipei and encouraged "Formosa committees."

In 1962 Mother de Valon launched the "Missionary Volunteers of the Sacred Heart." This project attracted young laywomen who would go "into mission countries to help the Mothers of the Sacred Heart, not to earn money, but to devote themselves to the educational and apostolic work in the jobs that they would be asked to do." This work was also assigned to Mother du Merle, who prepared the candidates during a period of theoretical and practical training at the motherhouse, at Grosse Pointe in the United States, Glen Iris in Australia, Belo Horizonte in Brazil and in Madrid. The volunteers could be sent anywhere in the world to fill a need, and they showed real generosity. Between 1962 and 1968, 146 young women of twenty-one countries served in Asia, Africa and South America.[30] They undertook activities that the religious could not provide because of cloister.[31]

Mother de Valon visited South America in 1965. She was deeply moved by the contrast between the wealth of the urban centers and the pitiful state of the *barrios*. In Colombia

> Ciudad Jardín in Bogotá touched her missionary zeal profoundly. In noting the distress, the financial needs of the area and the abandonment of little ones wandering about in the streets, she exclaimed, "Here we must make a foundation." That evening, surrounded by the Bogotá community, she commented on the words of Christ to the multitudes: "I have pity on the crowd." Cultural, material, spiritual nourishment were all needed. The pastor of the parish was touched by the generous gift he received because the Mother General gave him all the monetary gifts she had received in the course of her visits to the Colombian houses.[32]

She laid the first stone of the school.

---

[29] *Lettres et circulaires*, 12 July 1961, p. 83-84.
[30] 43.1% in Latin America, 33.3% in Africa and 24.48% in Asia.
[31] Gen. Arch. D I 3 e, Box 1. They taught, organized youth movements, occupied themselves with social work, worked in dispensaries, and visited families of prisoners and rag pickers in Monterrey. Latin Americans were trained on the spot to work in their own country.
[32] Testimony of Mother Salazar.

In Lima, after visiting the Agustino section,[33] on 20 April 1965, she wrote to the alumnae, whose associations were being reorganized,[34] a letter that would update and redirect their activities. This "appeal" took its departure from needs perceived in Latin America to incite the "army" of the alumnae to mobilize against desolation and illiteracy: "Not to know how to read, to know almost nothing of what can clarify thought, is a terrible evil; to know almost nothing of eternal life and of the ways that lead to it is a yet more horrible fate." In gratitude for the graces received, Mother de Valon encouraged them to be generous to "this Christ who considers as done to himself what one does to his own," to openness to the needs of the world, to inventiveness in developing projects that can be carried out where they are, but also to realism for, "if we do nothing to diminish the misery of their existence, they will be a prey to communism, we cannot doubt that."[35] Mother de Valon wished to involve the alumnae in the Society's mission, to utilize their ranks, their abilities and their resources.

New Places for Mission

The foundations of the 1960's differed as to the kind of people they included and the places in which they developed. There were eighteen Chinese religious in Japan and some Hong Kong Chinese had asked to enter. On 29 November 1958, Mother Keogh proposed to Mother de Valon that there should be a foundation in Formosa, because she thought that the Chinese would not be able to give their utmost except in their

---

[33] The alumnae had contributed in 1958 to the creation in this section of a parish under the title of Saint Madeleine Sophie; the school founded in 1963 was named *"Madre admirable."* In Colombia, certain ones among them made use of a diocesan radio relay station that evangelized the local populations.

[34] Although in the United States an association, the AASH, brought them together at the national level, they continued to meet by city besides. In 1959, the superior general sought to bring them together on the worldwide plane. A first meeting in Rome in 1960 had more than two thousand participants from twenty-eight countries. The world association of alumnae of the Sacred Heart, AMASC, was constituted in Brussels in 1965.

[35] A few months later, she said to the alumnae of Cairo and Heliopolis that she had seen in the outskirts of the city "people who do nothing because they are not loved enough, who do not rise because no one helps them rise.... And you, what are you doing? I know that there are some among you who make clothes for poor families. That is good. But it is not enough. Egypt is being tried, it's true; but it is not necessary to be wealthy to help. What is necessary is to give oneself. These people with such a kind gaze, these children who run up to us are not expecting money but love" (*Mitte me*, 1966, N° 10, pp. 6-7).

own language and on their own initiative: "They have more to give," she wrote. "China calls us. We know the heroism of the Chinese Catholics and the faithfulness of the alumnae of Shanghai; the Society cannot abandon them, even while awaiting better days." As the bishops had asked, she took on the project, opening a secondary school and a university college. After going to the island several times, she chose a property near the mountain of the Goddess, on the Tamsui. She praised its beauty, healthfulness and the price, and she insisted that the religious would be able to have an apostolate in the surrounding villages. The founders arrived in Taipei in May 1960.[36] Contributions from the international Society provided for the construction of the requisite buildings.

In Bombay and Bangalore, the Sacred Heart was providing education to an élite who could supply professionals with a Christian spirit to a society in the midst of radical change[37]. On 16 May 1961, a foundation was made among the outcasts. Located in the diocese of Poona, 300 kilometers from Bombay, Haregaon was a town whose population depended on a sugar plant that offered work only one month out of two. The Jesuits had established a parish center, opened a primary school and had had a well dug to allow for irrigation. They asked the Sacred Heart to take charge of a secondary school for girls.[38] The founders accepted Catholics, instructed a few catechumens and taught in the primary school. In Haregaon, they lived among malnourished people who had only a strip of cloth tied at the waist for clothing: "Our children are so poor that they spontaneously put the bath towels we give them around their shoulders, having nothing else to protect themselves against the morning cold. All their possessions fit into a little trunk that serves as a cupboard and on which they roll out their bedding: a blanket and a little rug. In the evening they stretch out on the ground in four classrooms."[39] The nuns lived by the light of oil lamps in Haregaon. The pupils and students of Bombay and Bangalore regularly brought them supplies.

In 1965 a mission was begun in the North of Peru at the request of Bishop Hornedo, a Spanish Jesuit, brother of a religious of the Sacred Heart, who was prefect apostolic of the Province of Marañon. Established at Jaén, a small city of 100,000 inhabitants, located on the other side of the Andes on the border of the Amazon,[40] it contributed to the opening up

---

[36] Archives of the superior general. File Brigid Keogh.
[37] *Mitte me*, 1962, N°3, p. 24.
[38] The foundation was made by an Irish nun, Mother Ivy Bourke, three Indian religious and an English and a Maltese coadjutrix sister.
[39] *Mitte me*, 1962, N°3, p. 23.
[40] *Mitte me*, 1962, N°3, p. 17.

of the country that the legal authorities desired.[41] To reach Jaén, one had to go by dirt roads bordered by precipices so narrow that one could hardly get across them. The population was composed of Indians and mestizos, all baptized. The Sacred Heart opened a school for children from the surrounding mountains.[42]

The Society of the Sacred Heart made foundations in 1962 and 1964 in two African countries that are completely different in their geographic, political and cultural framework. Called by Winston Churchill "the pearl of Africa," Uganda on the equator benefited from a climate moderated by the altitude, tropical vegetation and fertile soil. It was "a happy country where the life of its people in the countryside was easy and simple."[43] Chad, close to the Tropic of Cancer, was five times larger but its population, less by half, was not evenly distributed. It was a poor country, with a harsh climate, incorporated in French Equatorial Africa in 1910, while Uganda had been a protectorate since 1890.

Bordered by the long Islamized territories of Nigeria, Niger, Libya and Sudan and by Cameroon and the Central African Republic on their way to Christianization, Chad had undergone the influence of Islam and later of Christianity. The North was almost exclusively Muslim, the South animist. Preceded by Protestants who had established missions there, the Catholic missionaries from the Central African Republic and the chaplains of colonial troops had built the first missions in the 1930's.[44] Military chaplains had begun to evangelize the South and created a parish at Fort Lamy during the war. When the Religious of the Sacred Heart arrived, the church of Chad had been there for only twenty years.[45] The diocese of Fort Lamy, the largest in the country and in Islamic territory, was also the one with the fewest Christians and catechumens. Uganda had been Christianized in 1877,[46] and it was considered "the pearl of the missions."[47] More than half the population was Christian, a third of them Catholic; about thirty religious congregations were active there. Uganda has been independent since 1962 and Chad since 1960. The most important issues were those of

---

[41] *Mitte me*, 1962, N°3, 1965, N° 9, p. 14.

[42] M. Recavarren, *Raíces y Horizonte*, p. 178. The first superior, Concepción Vergés, came from Argentina.

[43] *Mitte me*, 1962, N° 2, p. 51.

[44] Paul Dalmais, "The Mission of Chad and the Diocese of Fort Lamy," *Mitte me*, 1966, N° 11, pp. 16-27.

[45] It was on 27 September 1964, a month after the arrival of the Religious of the Sacred Heart, that the cathedral of Fort Lamy was inaugurated.

[46] The martyrs of Uganda, the first canonized Africans, were canonized in October 1964.

[47] *Mitte me*, 1962, N° 2, p. 53.

the education of girls and the promotion of women. The Society could play a role in both.

The two foundations were initiated by bishops who hoped to attract new religious congregations to their dioceses. In the spring of 1961 Bishop Kiwanuka, the first African bishop, went to Dublin for the celebrations of the fourteenth centenary of the death of Saint Patrick. There he became acquainted with the Society of the Sacred Heart.[48] At Mount Anville, where he was given a biography of Saint Madeleine Sophie, he realized that the Society combined apostolic and contemplative life. On his way back, he stopped in Rome, on 7 July 1961, to ask the Mother General for a foundation.[49] His plan was to have the Society of the Sacred Heart develop a diocesan congregation of African sisters, originated by the Society of Mary Reparatrix, whom he wanted directed toward apostolic work. He wished also to hand over to the Society a normal school run by the White Sisters, which he feared would be seized by the government if it could not employ qualified teachers.[50]

The first contacts in Rome yielded no result. The assistants general were not favorable to this foundation for want of personnel, while Mother de Valon approved of it. A move by the vicar of Ireland/Scotland changed their minds. Mother Sherin proposed to Mother de Valon to contribute some religious if necessary. The foundation therefore was put in her care: "We are going to make for ourselves a small and very modest place in the heart of this great Africa, in spite of our littleness," wrote Mother de Valon. "I feel the energy in your vicariate for this undertaking and how happy I am! If I sent to Uganda all of your daughters who have offered, not many people would remain with you!"[51] Mother Veronica Blount, who directed the normal school at Craiglockhart, and Mother Winifred Killeen, who was to be superior of the foundation, made an exploratory journey in November 1961. It allowed them to make contact with the country, the local clergy and the religious congregations established in the region. During their visit in Rome, Mother de Valon said to them: "You are not going to give these Blacks the westerners' way of life, but only the wealth of the Gospel. You will have to understand them and to show them that we

---

[48] Some Ugandans had already visited the normal school at Craiglockhart.
[49] *Mitte me*, 1962, N° 2, p. 49. Mother de Valon wrote that she had seen in his visit a providential sign for he arrived at the motherhouse just when she had finished writing the circular letter in which she asked the Society to intensify the mission.
[50] Prov. Arch. Ireland/Scotland, UGK/2-9, Box 1 Letter of Bishop Kiwanuka to Mother de Valon, 11 June 1961, and letter of Mother de Valon to Mother Sherin, 3 August 1961.
[51] *Mitte me*. 4 September 1961.

admire them. I think it is necessary to love them, for when one loves, love gives insight."[52]

Winifred Killeen, Anna Mackie, Ita Ward, Kathleen Kennedy, Pauline Campbell of Ireland/Scotland and Anne de Stacpoole[53] of Australia/New Zealand arrived on 19 and 22 January 1962,[54] at Nkozi, sixty kilometers from Kampala, in a compound run by the White Sisters and by the two local congregations whose female branch they had founded. It included a normal school, a primary school for boys and one for girls and a hospital. The religious taught 300 normal school students while studying the local language, Luganda, as well as the country's customs and mores. As they lived in them, they discovered that the buildings were infested with rats. In addition, they learned that the ministry of education considered the location unsuitable for teaching because of the lack of water and the small number of schools in which the students could do their practice teaching.[55] Classes were added gradually, and in 1967 the school reached the maximum number of students it could accept.[56] Their families "live in very poor houses, huts of dried mud. The students are very refined and pose no discipline problems. They are avid to learn and it is considered a privilege for them to be able to read."[57] The founders took charge of the ongoing preparation of teachers, both religious and laywomen. They wrote textbooks, gave language courses and religious instruction to those who worked on the plantation and opened a club that a few women joined. The motherhouse sent three mission volunteers.[58]

The religious did not suffer from the divisiveness that accompanied the first legislative elections in March 1962, although the region was populated by a strong Muslim minority hostile to the missionaries. Mother Sherin came to visit Nkozi in September[59] and decided to found a house in Kalisizo, at the request of Bishop Ddungu of Masaka. Kalisizo, some eighty kilometers from Nkozi, was located on the road to Tanzania. Doreen Boland and Annie McGourty arrived from Ireland in June 1963 to go there. Two came from Nkozi, and Marguerite Cleary and Jacqueline Kearns from

---

[52] *Mitte me.* 19 September 1961. She gave the same advice to the founders on 19 January 1962.

[53] She was the first of the founders to leave the mission to return to her own vicariate for health reasons in 1966.

[54] Religious had been chosen who held university diplomas and were experienced teachers.

[55] Gen. Arch. C III, UGK/1. *A Short History of the Province from 1962-1984.*

[56] Prov. Arch. Ireland/Scotland, UGK/93, *The Society's Foundations in Uganda*, p. 1.

[57] Testimony of Winifred Killeen.

[58] Prov. Arch. Uganda, S2J3. Nkozi, 1962-1984.

[59] She had brought with her a religious from Uruguay, Ana María Escardo.

the United States joined them. They took charge of the secondary school of Christ the King, which had been founded by a Dutch secular institute. That group had asked Bishop Ddungu to find replacements for them.[60] The newcomers camped for nine months in four rooms in the middle of a school dormitory building. It was a "time of poverty, of inconvenience but also of joy and laughter," for they kept their sense of humor in spite of the lack of space. The building of a convent was financed by the motherhouse and by *Misereor* [German Catholic Bishops' Organization for Development Cooperation], which also contributed to the construction of dormitories, an infirmary, classrooms and laboratories.[61] The surroundings were superb: "Our property is invaded by crested cranes," wrote one of the founders. "They are magnificent birds with a crest of very fine feathers and measure at least a meter in height and they fly with unparalleled elegance. Who can prepare her classes with such birds promenading in the garden?"[62]

In 1965 Christ the King School received aid from the government that reduced the financial burden and allowed the recruiting of Ugandan teachers. The students served the underprivileged through scouting and the Legion of Mary. "They cleaned the parish church, no sinecure, for it had a mud floor. They visited the sick in the little local hospital and prisoners; they taught catechism, reading and writing to the children of surrounding villages who were not in school. From time to time we took them to visit the leper village near Lake Nabugabo."[63] Some episodes of school life were not without picturesque elements. The king of Buganda paid them a visit. The Religious of the Sacred Heart had been warned that in such circumstances he customarily chose some of the young women and installed them in the royal palace! Ana María Escardo took plenty of time and care to settle the students in the hall where the guests were to assemble. The plainest in appearance were placed in the front rows, and she hid the young beauties in the back. At the arrival and departure of the procession the nuns formed a line along the avenue leading to the building![64]

---

[60] For two years the Religious of the Sacred Heart took over the role of director and treasurer of the establishment, a delicate situation that demanded tact on both sides (Testimony of D. Boland; Prov. Arch. Ireland/Scotland, UGK/93, and Prov. Arch. Uganda, S2J3).

[61] "Kalisizo was more up market than Nkozi. We built a magnificent chapel and a convent. Everything was lost during the war. When I returned I found ruins" (Testimony of W. Killeen).

[62] Prov. Arch. Ireland/Scotland, UGK 125(12), Letter of 18 February 1964.

[63] Testimony of D. Boland.

[64] Shortly after the foundation of Kalisizo, Rome and the vicariate of Ireland had acquired at Nabugabo, at equal distance from Nkozi and Kalisizo, a property that served as a rest house.

The mission quickly produced vocations. The first Ugandan arrived in Ireland to make her noviceship in 1964.[65] The Religious of the Sacred Heart had to become accustomed to a new situation.

> The Ugandans did not make distinctions among congregations. The White Sisters had been the first missionaries, and often we were taken for them. They had never been cloistered; therefore it was supposed that we were not either. They went into the villages. When we did that it was somewhat unusual for us, but for the people it was normal, and it was what they expected of us. The association of religious of Uganda was formed after Vatican II and gave training sessions that accented *Perfectae caritatis*. It was a real stimulus for us all. To study the documents with other religious men and women created bonds and was a great support during the period of the changes.[66]

After Chad achieved independence, Fort Lamy, at first a fishing village on the Chari, became a capital city with a population close to 100,000 inhabitants. Archbishop Dalmais of Fort Lamy, a Jesuit, was the son and brother of alumnae of Rue Boissac in Lyons where he himself had made his First Communion.[67] He proposed a foundation to the vicar of France-Est, Mother Charlotte Blaire. A secondary school for girls was needed in Fort Lamy, because the first Chadian girls who had been to school were finishing primary school, and the first Chadian young men with diplomas were returning from France where they had done their studies and were not finding young women to marry whose level of education was equal to theirs. Archbishop Dalmais had asked other congregations without success. Mother de Valon wrote to him on 12 May 1962:

> Your letter of 5 May came to me as a real temptation. There is so much to do in that immense Africa, and I so desire to see our congregation take a modest place there. To begin a secondary school or even a normal school preparing primary teachers for the future would be a marvelous work. The present difficulty, you have already understood, is lack of personnel and the dearth of financial means. But I do not wish this double consideration to make me say another "no," all the more as you tell me you have had so many refusals already. It may happen that the lack of means is the most favorable situation to force divine Providence to

---

[65] She did not persevere.
[66] Testimony of Helen McLaughlin.
[67] Geneviève Bovagnet, *Trente ans au Tchad, [Thirty Years in Chad]*, Lyons 2002, p. 19.

intervene. Believe me that it would be an immense consolation to be able to respond affirmatively to your appeal. I believe that an "alumnus of the Sacred Heart," a devotee of Saint Madeleine Sophie, has special rights to her intervention with God.[68]

The founder must have made her power with God felt. Archbishop Dalmais, encouraged by this answer, promised to wait and to prepare for the arrival of the religious by having a building constructed. He proposed to make the necessary contacts with the government of Chad, international Catholic organizations, the French Ministry of Cooperation and to obtain subsidies from the Fund for Aid and Cooperation. France assisted its former colonies, and Chad was ready to provide subsidies to set up educational institutions. "Archbishop Dalmais says that the climate of Fort Lamy is good and that one can find what one wants, although the country is rather arid. Already he has had trees planted on the land he is preparing for his little girls' school."[69] The climate was perhaps not as idyllic as the archbishop suggested. As for subsidies the Chadian government had neither the ability nor perhaps the desire to provide them.

On 4 December 1962, Mother de Valon assigned the carrying out of the project to the vicariate of France-Est but with international personnel. Simone de la Hitte, who came from Egypt, was named superior of a community that included two other French nuns, Geneviève Bovagnet and Marthe-Marie Willoquet, two Dutch, Marijke van Eechoud et Magdalena Hensgens, a Pole living in France, Helena Strözyk, and a Spaniard, Juana Luisa Caro. They arrived in Fort Lamy on 17 August 1964.

Like many former colonies, Chad has as a goal to educate its population, especially the women. The Sacred Heart school was the first Catholic secondary school in Fort Lamy, where a public *lycée* for girls was already in place.[70] The nuns' mission was to open a school offering an education of the same quality as the other French schools of the Sacred Heart. French, although little spoken by the people, was the official language of the country, and the curricula were only somewhat Africanized. The school accepted two categories of pupils: Africans as boarders, nineteen the first year, who came from Catholic schools in the bush from Guéra, Bousso and Fort-Archambault and whose fees were paid by their dioceses; and daughters of *coopérants* [those doing National Service in a developing country] or of French army officers and those coming out of Syria, Lebanon, Egypt and Israel, all day pupils. The school grew, adding a new class each year. In 1967

---

[68] Gen. Arch. C III Chad. History, foundation.
[69] Gen. Arch. C III Chad. Report of 2 December 1962.
[70] A coeducational evangelical school was opened in Fort Lamy in 1964.

there was an equal number of African and foreign pupils. The number of Africans in the final year of school declined, for in Chad girls married young. It was "abnormal for them to be still in school at an age when many of their companions had already founded a household."[71]

After 1966 mission volunteers, then *coopérants*, supported the nuns. Besides maintaining the school at Chagwa, they took charge, with the help of translators, of catechetical instruction in the parish or in a village located beyond the Chari, which they reached by canoe. They taught literacy and gave sewing classes to the women. Starting with the first school vacation they began to learn Arabic. The first year ended abruptly. "In June we were peacefully continuing classes when downpours began to flow daily. We were immediately alerted: 'Quickly, you must send the boarders home. They must take trucks from the bush to return to their villages. With the rains, the routes will be cut off and no one will be able to get around any longer.' We did not know that the country had no paved roads except the one in Fort Lamy that crossed the city, nor did we know that the rains transformed the countryside into a quagmire."[72]

Life in Africa brought about changes in life style. To Clotilde Meeûs, "missionary life, despite its austerity, was more open than religious life in the Society in Europe."[73] As Helen McLaughlin, who arrived in Uganda in 1965, pointed out,

> Change was required by conditions in the country. We were already living in small communities and cloister was relative. Our communities were located far from the cities where we had to go to buy supplies. Therefore, we customarily left the property to go into the city when necessary. Because our communities were international, and each shared the news she received, we were fairly well informed of what was happening in other parts of the Society. Personal and community prayer was a priority, and for our annual retreat we went to a convent of another congregation, which was not done in Ireland and Scotland at the time. We had excellent retreat masters who came from Europe for a month. Sister Killeen had the gift of friendship and welcomed brothers and sisters of other congregations who came to visit.

---

[71] G. Bovagnet, p. 40.
[72] G. Bovagnet, p. 34.
[73] She notes that in Congo the coadjutrix sisters and choir religious lived together without distinction, and that there were frequent contacts with the Jesuit schools in Kalina, Mbansa-Mboma and Kimwenza.

Winifred Killeen has recalled that she was writing "all the time" to Rome or to Mount Anville to ask questions about what could be done. "The difficulty came from the fact that the answers were not always the same. I was in a dilemma about what to do. Later a superior general told me that I was too obedient! Then I had to make my own decision. My community always accepted what I decided." Circumstances led her not to observe cloister:

> One day I was sitting in the refectory with a White Father and an officer of the department of education who had come to inspect the school. We heard a howl and saw some African sisters beating the walls of the convent with their fists. They had learned that one of the elders of their congregation had just died. They packed their belongings and went to the funeral. The visiting priest told me that we had to go. I said that it was not possible, that we could not go out because of the rule of cloister. He repeated that we had to go. We went, Anna Mackie and myself.[74]

In Chad, cloister was strictly observed, perhaps because the community was located in the capital. However, from Christmas 1964 on, thanks to a Jesuit who made it clear that it was absolutely necessary, two of the nuns went "into the Bush" to attend midnight Mass in several villages. In that way they learned more about the life of their pupils' families and experienced another kind of celebration.[75] They were invited to Mass in a different parish every Sunday and welcomed by religious with whom they shared a meal.

The wearing of a religious habit, like that worn in Europe, with the exception that it was white, posed a problem: "The habit was very hot and became brown and red in ten minutes." We wanted to remove our outer skirts to avoid dirt but the Africans would not have approved. African women are enveloped in several skirts."[76] In Chad, the Jesuits made them understand that they absolutely had to make it lighter, but that would not happen easily.

The Beginning of the Reform

The Twenty-sixth General Congregation in the autumn of 1964 marked a new stage in the history of the Society of the Sacred Heart. Habitually called a "chapter," although it was made up only of members of the general council and the vicars, it was exceptional because of the decisions taken on

---

[74] Prov. Arch. Ireland/Scotland.
[75] Testimony of G. Bovagnet.
[76] Testimony of W. Killeen.

subjects that had been long discussed but never decided. It took place when Vatican II had already brought a breath of fresh air to the Church.

The Shock of the Council

The ecumenical council, which Pope John XXIII had announced shortly after his succession to the papacy, shocked the Church and local communities with the momentum of its renewal, whose consequences would not be seen for some time. The council seemed to concern primarily the Church hierarchy and only secondarily religious life. At the end of the second session, Mother de Valon affirmed in a circular:

> Yes, hope is certainly the virtue of the hour; our gaze is straining Godward; it is straining toward the future; something is coming to birth in the world, under the influence of grace; a star is shining in the night, the dawn is close at hand; we are awaiting the "tomorrow" that Love is preparing; tomorrow God will show his wonderful mercy and the eternal youth of his Church. It is the atmosphere of the Council that has raised this hope on the horizon; we do not yet know very much about its labors; we feel that they will be accomplished, no doubt under the sign of the Cross; but the Cross is good, and through it, the Holy Spirit is at work in the Church and in the world and will be able to renew the face of the earth.[77]

The Catholic world was waiting. There had already been some surprises: the openness of the sessions, the rejection by the Council Fathers of the schemas prepared by the Curia. Vatican II would not simply continue Vatican I but would draw on developments in theology to bring the Church and "the modern world" into accord. Its makeup also reflected the changes the Church had experienced over more than half a century, thanks to the progress of Christianity in mission countries and to the organization of local hierarchies. A third of the bishops came from Europe and 13% from North America, but 32% from South America, 10% from black Africa, 10% from Asia, 3.5% from the Middle East and 2.5% from Oceania. Non-Catholic observers attended the sessions, and their number tripled over the course of the council. Lay auditors were included and – a fact without precedent in the history of the Church – women.

At the request of John XXIII Mother de Valon had been asked at the end of 1962 to form an international union of major superiors of women's congregations on the model of the existing one for the men. After she had composed the statutes and had them implemented, she was named

---

[77] *Lettres circulaires*, 10 January 1964, pp. 139-140.

president.* In this position she became an auditor during the third session of the Council. There were fifteen women auditors, eight of whom were religious.[78] Mother de Valon was named "head of the women auditors" on 25 September 1964, and therefore she was introduced, alone, for a few minutes the next morning to the conciliar assembly. She valued the mission confided to her. She worked up her Latin and followed the proceedings of the assembly easily. She worked on the texts with the other superiors general and strengthened relations with experts and with conciliar Fathers from all over the world. The motherhouse served as a meeting place for some of the bishops. Mother de Valon thus reinforced her sense of the Church and her conviction that it was in Rome that modernization of ecclesial communities could be effected. Knowing what the Church thought was invaluable. However, as she spent part of her day at the Vatican during the general congregation, she grew increasingly fatigued.[79]

A Transitional General Congregation

The motherhouse had expected to put off the general congregation until the canonization of Philippine Duchesne, said to be imminent,[80] or the celebration of the centenary of the death of Saint Madeleine Sophie in 1965. Mother de Valon thought it would be good to wait for the decisions of the Vatican Council on religious life.[81] The Sacred Congregation refused an indult to postpone, but the preparation of the general congregation was so far advanced that the unexpected refusal was not an obstacle to its being held. To prevent the participants arriving in Rome "with thoughts so unformed that they would only drag things out," Mother de Valon had assigned preparatory commissions, modeled on those of the Vatican Council, composed of three or four vicars, and each commission linked to one of the assistants general.[82] On specific topics, they were "to make better

---

*   Further research has indicated that although Mother de Valon was instrumental in the founding of the UISG, she was not the first president. She had the title of Councilor. (Cf. Carmel McEnroy: *Guests in Their Own House: the Women of Vatican II*, Crossroad, New York, 1996.) [Translator's note]

[78] In 1965 it was increased and included ten religious, two major superiors of Eastern Rite having been introduced and thirteen laywomen.

[79] She wrote on 23 September 1963 to Mother Gabriele Paradeis that her nomination was "rather unfortunate, right in the middle of our general council which by this fact will certainly last longer."

[80] She was canonized in July 1988.

[81] *Lettres circulaires*, May 1964, p. 148.

[82] Mother Zurstrassen was in charge of the formation of choir religious and of coadjutrix sisters; Mother Benziger, of university colleges and normal schools;

known the present needs" of the world, "to assure to the Society of the Sacred Heart its inner strength and by that have a greater apostolic effect in serving the Church." Their reports formed the basis of the work of the general congregation.[83] At preceding assemblies the vicars had been seated in rank order as if they were in a classroom, facing the general council; the tables this time were arranged in a rectangle.

A Different Climate

The assembly began in a climate of confidence and energy. The Society of the Sacred Heart stood resolutely in the wake of a conciliar Church in the process of renewal. Like the Church it had to become more deeply aware of its original spirit in order to come to "renewed discovery of its relation to Christ:" "Has our consecration to the Sacred Heart of Jesus maintained all its strength? In principle, yes, but in practice, there are weaknesses; one is afraid to displease; we need to be on an even footing with today's attitudes. We must not apologize for being what we are; it is not apostolic enough." Renewal in the Society was the order of the day: "Moving forward today is more than ever a requirement and this requirement judges us, stimulates us, accuses us, supports us, makes us groan and pray, inspires us with hope and confidence."[84] New thinking and attitudes were perceptible among the vicars. According to Mother Zurstrassen, "The ensemble was certainly progressive; there was an abyss between this and the preceding one."[85] In the preparatory reports many vicars had asked for significant modifications in view of local circumstances. Afterwards the General Congregation of 1964 was seen to have been one of transition. Mother de Valon showed her good will in the way she communicated with the participants. She listened to them, and when possible, she sided with those whose opinion differed from hers.[86] Therefore the congregation did not give the impression of being manipulated, of being an assembly whose members simply aligned themselves with the positions of the superior general, as had been the case before. The vicars could make themselves heard.[87]

---

[83] Mother Lurani, of the boarding schools; Mother Bultó, of cloister and studies. Some supplementary questionnaires dealt with the qualities of those asking to enter the congregation, in particular their health, and with work, overwork and relaxation in communities.

[84] *Directives and Decisions of the 26th General Congregation*, pp. 2-4. Opening discourse of Mother de Valon.

[85] *Elisabeth Zurstrassen*, p. 38. Letter of 4 November 1964.

[86] Testimony of M.J Bultó.

[87] R. Cunningham, *Helen Fitzgerald*, p. 46. After the death of Mother Fitzgerald, Mother Keogh expressed the opinion that the vicar of New York had been the

The superior general revived missionary fervor at the assembly. When she took the floor, she pointed out developments in studies of the Church and the missions. She showed that the whole Society had to think of itself as missionary:[88] "The missions must not be regarded as *avant garde* in the Church nor the missionary undertaking as an "experience" or a "conquest." Therefore apostolic action in missionary countries was to be rethought: "Rather than conquest, we speak today of presence and of witness. It is not just darkness outside the Church. Grace exists in mission countries before the concrete presence of the Church. It is a question of a real meeting of the Church with cultures already worked on by grace." It is pre-evangelization of minds and hearts that the Church has to work on. This respectful approach will bear fruit because "in their contact with Christianity religions and peoples are transformed, evolve, mature, are enlivened and finally Christianized from the inside. In that way the conversion of peoples is prepared, through the conversion of individuals, the very aim of the Church's work of evangelization."[89] The Society had proved itself daring:

> We must not rest until this meeting of cultures takes place and bears more fruit, always more, following the example of Saint Francis Xavier. To hold back this progress through lack of generosity or through fear in order to establish a mission well, prudently, before going further, does not seem to be what the Church wants at present in its missionary work. The grace of God that fosters the meeting is also present in the fruits. Faith and hope must be the great supports of our missionaries.[90]

The missions were destined to become independent. The western religious were to step down in proportion to the attainments of the native people.[91] As the driving force of the Society was to be directed toward the mission, the chapter considered sending the youngest religious to the missions for experiences of at least some length.[92] Sacred Heart pupils were to be prepared to support the mission as well as they could. Information on the Mission Volunteers had been included in the statistics sent to participants. To insist so strongly on this global missionary orientation was a way of spreading the responsibility among all the vicariates and of

---

most influential personality of the general congregation.

[88] She was aided by the report on the missions made by Mothers Thuysbaert, Carton and Keogh, vicars of Congo, Uganda and the Far East respectively.
[89] *Directives*, pp. 50-51.
[90] *Directives*, p. 54.
[91] *Directives*, p. 50.
[92] *Directives*, p. 52.

disarming criticisms that came from those who thought they were "bleeding themselves white to provide missionaries."[93] An assistant general, Mother Meliá, was given special charge of the missions.

The Beginning of Renewal

Mother de Valon sought a renewal in the area of poverty, even though its practice was very strict in the Society of the Sacred Heart. From her own orientation and that of the Church hoping more than ever to be the "Church of the poor," she wanted to go further. Mother Lurani proposed that, following the example of Paul VI, who had given up the tiara given him by his diocese of Milan, the choir religious give up their gold rings. A chain would be made of them to be given to the Vatican for Latin America. Agreement was unanimous, and the vicars exchanged their profession rings for ones of silver. It was a chance to give the Society "a lesson in poverty that it certainly expects of us and to the Church the response of generosity that she is asking. The Society will only be more beautiful, more conformed to the divine model, Jesus poor, humble, crucified."[94] Mother de Valon also asked that schools sacrifice the year-end carnivals, because so much money was at stake. This sacrifice was hard to accept, for these festivals were a very old tradition in the boarding schools. The money collected went to support many good works and social service projects.[95]

New involvement in underclass milieus resulted in a radical experience of poverty. The religious of Sarriá understood it through an experiment in the Besos section of Barcelona.[96] For Mother de Valon the goal of establishing communities in these sections was to bring assistance to poor parish schools or to those founded by the alumnae, for

> we are not too well prepared for direct action in the slums, and we could lose our way, but we can teach the alumnae and accompany them often so that little by little the poor become used to seeing us. To train our alumnae in this social work will be still more faithful to the thought of our holy Mother and answer to the expectation of holy Church. Besides, if we wish to hold to our educational work, it seems that our direct action should

---

[93] *Directives*, Spain was in this situation.
[94] *Directives*, p. 85.
[95] Testimony of B. Keogh.
[96] The foundation of Besos dated from 1963, and the religious there undertook parochial service. The text of a report concerning the outreach into the popular milieu and social work was largely taken up in the *Directives and Decisions*.

be limited to what would be along this line: catechism, free schools, adult classes; leave the rest to our alumnae encouraged by their Mothers.[97]

They had to live among the poor in a small, "really poor" convent.

"To go toward" the poor, however, brought up the question of cloister. Mother de Valon was aware that the new apostolates could only be advocated if cloister changed.[98] The conciliar commission of Vatican II charged with preparing the schema on religious life had grappled with the distinctions to be set forth among congregations whose rules formed a veritable thicket. It wished to limit congregations to two groups, contemplative and apostolic. Those said to be "semi-cloistered" were a special case.

The General Congregation of 1946 had noted that some of the nuns had difficulty readapting to a cloistered world after the upheavals caused by the war. Respect for cloister led to specious reasoning, which hurt the nuns and was no longer understood by lay people or the clergy. An Australian who was an only daughter was allowed go out to deal with lawyers over her mother's estate, but she could not take charge of her funeral. A Franciscan told her superior that her father was hospitalized: she replied that the rule of cloister did not allow her to go to visit him. Just then, there was laughter in the corridor:

> The priest seemed surprised, and Reverend Mother explained that sisters were returning from a day of relaxation at Kerever Park since that was allowed by our rule. The priest exploded in anger. He railed against the inconsistency of the Society, which allowed nuns to go another house but did not let an only daughter go to see her dying father who was an unbeliever.[99]

Was maintaining cloister still compatible with educational work in a changing world? Some vicars thought it was a survival of another age and a brake on the apostolate. Mother Ogilvie Forbes had written to Mother de Valon that change was imperative: "Or we will continue what we are doing with the support of the clergy, of our old pupils and of our friends. They will note our schools, our flourishing houses. But we will not be responding

---

[97] *Directives*, p. 55.
[98] It was because she hoped that the Church would elaborate a document on religious life that would give clear indications about enclosure that Mother de Valon wished to postpone holding the general congregation.
[99] Testimony of Judith Hill.

to the needs of the country."[100] In February 1964 Mother Zurstrassen had written, after reading the preparatory reports: "The question of enclosure is much further along than I had thought, in one case after another. It is impossible for us to escape a significant change and our Mother is aware of it."[101] But the report of the preparatory commission on enclosure was not discussed in the general assembly. Mother de Valon simply stated: "The Council has just declared that there is no enclosure for apostolic institutes. Therefore we have nothing to discuss; we have only to obey."[102]

The superior general did, however, make it the subject of an intervention drafted in advance. Even though the Church asked the apostolic congregations to give up cloister, they had "to safeguard the value and authenticity of religious life," which the Council fathers had found difficult to define. The Sacred Congregation of Religious was still of a conservative mind in this respect.[103] If cloister could be eased, how far to go? The superior general and the vicars hesitated: To go more toward the world since the Church asks it, yes, certainly. To go toward the world without any restriction, no. They had "to be vigilant, to ensure a firm barrier to all the behaviors that, little by little, reduce the strength of the discipline, that is to say, the measures contrary to religious life." But how to be vigilant without being immobile?

> Our enclosure, until now, has been the guardian of our vows. Now, it is our vows that will safeguard our spirit of enclosure. Poverty will set limits; poor people cannot have every excursion, journey and pleasure trip, and neither can we. Our chastity will not allow us to go to every kind of meeting, or to share all our children's experiences. Our obedience must bow to the wise decisions of authority, even when they ask for very costly renunciation.[104]

---

[100] Testimony of Françoise de Lambilly. Joan Faber, *Sister Rebecca Ogilvie Forbes*, p. 21.
[101] *Elisabeth Zurstrassen*, p. 36.
[102] Testimony of Marie Mallet-Guy.
[103] In a letter of 29 February 1984, to Mary Byles, Mother de Valon alluded to the pressures being put upon religious congregations who were being asked to renew without abandoning their former character: "At the Council, many Fathers with whom I spoke said that it is very difficult to have to do the work of education of youth without seeing how they lived when one is cloistered. Afterward I consulted the Sacred Congregation of Religious. I was told: 'It is true that an educator has to see how her pupils are living and to be aware of the present evolution of the young; but that is not for you an obligation to give up your enclosure.'"
[104] *Directives and Decisions*, pp. 26-27 and 33.

The abandonment of enclosure was approved by a great majority. But as Mother de Valon wrote afterward, "When the chapter had finished, I submitted its decisions to the Congregation for Religious, and I was told, 'You have done well, it needed to be done. But keep to the spirit of cloister because it is in the spirit of your congregation.'"[105]

Outings ought to be "subordinated to the perfection of religious life and in the service of real apostolic necessities." Exceptions were training of religious in educational and apostolic work; carrying out apostolic work; business to conduct with religious, civil, medical and other authorities; family visits in the case of serious illness. Mother de Valon added: "I cannot list everything, but together we are going to try to work out the broad outline of these new rules without however pretending to predict every case. The essential is that we know how not to lose sight of the reason for the call of the Church and the spiritual meaning of our spirit of enclosure."[106]

The ending of enclosure undeniably allowed for apostolic development. One could get to know the cultural environment in non-Christian countries better[107] and foresee direct contact with the poor. It was a far cry from the time when Mother Mayer had the Daughters of Charity come to Obayashi to take charge of those left behind by the economic crisis, even to supporting them materially and having the pupils and alumnae of the Sacred Heart support their work.

In Egypt, the nuns took part in "popular missions" in various parts of the capital, where they met the alumnae, introduced the older students to social service work and worked together with other religious congregations. In August 1965, two nuns of Heliopolis, Esperanza Medina and María Teresa Arbeloa, accompanied seven of their students to Abu Korkas and Beni Ebeid. This mission, designed to prepare the children in these villages for their First Communion and to visit families, allowed students to get to

---

[105] To Mary Byles, 29 February 1984.
[106] *Directives and Decisions*, p. 33.
[107] Testimony of Betty Moriarty: "To teach in an international school was not easy, for the children came from various religions, and I knew nothing of the basic elements of those religions. We had no contact with people who could have shared their faith with us. It was imperative to learn something of the faith of these people, not from books but from themselves. It was through the heart that we experienced, as Vatican II asked, the work of the Spirit in the religion and culture of people. From the publication of *Lumen gentium*, I shared the main ideas with my pupils of fifteen years who welcomed them with enthusiasm. A girl came to me, eyes shining: "Now, after studying this text, I am proud to be a Catholic." A little while later, another pupil came to thank me because, she said, "Now I am a better Hindu.""

know the life of the Copts of the Saïd and was crucial for the two nuns. María Teresa Arbeloa felt that she had to live religious life in another context: "In the small chapel of Abu Korkas the call of God to live closer to the poor came to me, while I was still quite shocked by this first contact with Upper Egypt." This trip was also a step on the journey of Esperanza Medina, who had already had contacts with the founder of the Association of Upper Egypt, Father Habib Ayrout. She thought that the Society of the Sacred Heart should settle in the Saïd, that it was urgent to move away from a relationship with the elite minority to go toward the majority and thus offer "new horizons to all our religious."[108] She wrote to the motherhouse several times along these lines.

During the Council, the bishops of Assiut and Miniah had asked Mother de Valon to make foundations in their dioceses. In December 1965, she went to the Saïd where a house had been offered to the congregation. The general council, urged by the superior general, agreed to create a modest post in Samalout,[109] where the nuns took charge of catechesis, "because," she wrote, "we must have something that is quite in our line, namely, education."[110] The five founders[111] arrived at Samalout on 8 September 1966.

In Latin America, the nuns went into the barrios. Since 1963, the nuns in Santiago had been going into the *callampas* [shanty towns] at the time of First Communions, to encourage the alumnae who were investing in an association set up to reform the workers' housing. In January 1965, they participated in a mission in the suburb of Los Saldes.[112] In Brazil, they took part in "flying missions" with the missionary volunteers. In Lima, they intensified their work in the neighborhood of Agustino.[113] In Mexico, they led actions for justice in the popular districts of Guadalajara

---

[108] Testimony of María Teresa Arbeloa and Esperanza Medina.

[109] Prov. ArchEgypt. Correpondence I. Letter of Mother de Valon, 15 February 1966.

[110] Letter...de Valon, 29 January 1966.

[111] The group was composed of an Egyptian, Fawzeya Banoub, and four Spaniards, María Luisa López Arnais, Adela Blanes, Encarnación Schiaffino and Rosario Lemos. The following year they extended their apostolate to the villages of Abouan and Bardanoha.

[112] *Mitte me*, 1965, pp. 50-51 and pp. 37-53. On the evening of the first day, the preacher of the mission, who was however the chaplain of the school of Apoquindo, admitted to the vicar that this new type of contact with the nuns was a revelation to him: "Like many others, he did not know of their predilection for this apostolate among the poor."

[113] M. Recavarren, *Raíces y Horizonte*, p. 161.

and Monterrey.[114] In Puerto Rico and the United States they met new groups of the public through teaching the underprivileged, whether in summer schools or all year round. In Lyons, they took charge of Spanish immigrants. In Ireland, they ministered to persons with disabilities. Throughout Spain, they organized evening courses, and in the Canary Islands the founders of Fuerteventura opened a youth club. In Australia, a school was opened in 1966 at Sadleir-Miller, in the industrial area of Sydney. In Japan, the foundation at Amakusa, in early 1967, was partially intended for an apostolate among fishermen and rural people: "People liked these nuns who went about freely among them. Houses opened up; they brought Communion to the sick; they organized prayer meetings."[115] In Korea, a school under a tent was set up in the slum of Bongchon-dong, in 1965. At Chun Cheon, a nun gave lessons to girls who were selling apples on the streets and boys who shined shoes, all homeless orphans.[116] Parish activities put the religious in contact with other areas than those providing pupils to the boarding schools.[117]

With hindsight it is clear that one of the important decisions of the general congregation was the creation of a single group of religious, thanks to the integration of the coadjutrix sisters and choir nuns. Earlier there had been much reluctance to modify the status quo, deemed untouchable because it was addressed in the Constitutions. From 1958 on, with the recruitment of sisters becoming rare in Europe and in the United States, Mother de Valon had raised the question of whether to retain their status. She had rejected an "abrupt assimilation" that would have brought with it "a decline in our educational work and also in the standard for community

---

[114] *Histoire de la Province du Mexique, les Années Soixante*, p. 10.

[115] Brigid Keogh wrote to Mother de Valon, after her visit to the island in August 1966: "The kindergarten is not the only work. I have discovered that on this island there is the possibility of having a religious enter the public school as a teacher. That has always been one of my dreams. It is, I think, the model of the future for the work of education in Japan" (M. Williams, *The Society...Far East*, pp. 252-253).

[116] M. Williams: "The class was held in the space between the attic and the roof of a church. Very cold in winter; we had to use pencils because the ink froze. Not to mention our feet! We left our shoes at the attic door, but the wind passed through."

[117] In Korea, Brigid Keogh, at the time of each of her visits, brought the religious into the neighborhood: "Opening our doors signified opening to the poor and admitting them into our hearts. The love of the poor that Brigid transmitted touched the pupils." Under the direction of Catherine Kim Jae Sook, they dedicated time after class to bathing and teaching poor children (Testimony of T. Chu).

life. Experience has proved that people, capable but with a lesser degree of education, often found themselves ill at ease with us." She advocated a "slow assimilation."

> We are already being led to widen the field of recruitment of choir religious, and we will be so more and more. It is and will remain very certain that there are excellent choir religious vocations coming from the middle class, and there are also sisters who would not have been out of place among the choir nuns. By reason of circumstances, physical work is already being given to our choir religious and certain competent sisters can very well give courses to our religious and to our children. Thus this leveling must take place gradually.[118]

With a view to fostering this assimilation the General Congregation of 1958 modified certain points in the *coutumier*.

> Our sisters' morning prayer may be made in the chapel or in an oratory, provided they are in a group supervised by a choir religious. They may have the same spiritual books as the choir nuns for their own use, with the exception of the Office book.[119] They may have the book of the Constitutions in their library, which is to be well supplied with interesting spiritual books at their level. They may have a fountain pen or a ball point pen for their personal use. Take care not to say "the community and the sisters," for the community includes the sisters. Take care also to name them personally by their family names, as is done for the mothers; for example, do not say Mother X, Mother Y and three sisters, but name everyone. Give them an opportunity to talk among themselves and with the mothers from time to time. They may be placed at the same table in the refectory as the mothers and have call bells.

Mother de Valon decided that the sisters would have a name and devise for probation, and she asked that "a few sisters, very religious and reliable," be placed in charge of the linen room and the storeroom but not the infirmary or the sacristy "on account of sensitive dealings with the sick and with priests." She proposed that "a few capable sisters may be assigned to take examinations for diplomas and that they take surveillances [study hall supervision] and teach some courses."

In September 1958 the superior general asked that the religious instruction courses for the Polish sisters be continued, which indicates that

---

[118] Gen. Arch. C I C 3, General Congregation of 1958.
[119] Office was said in Latin.

they had been stopped. In May 1962, she insisted that they have a Sunday of relaxation every month, two weeks of vacation each year in a house other than their own and that the length of their prayer time be increased. Cardinal Wyszynski, it is true, had remarked that the two-class division of religious was a counter witness in a popular democracy and fueled anti-religious propaganda. This two-class division surprised candidates for religious life.[120] As one Chilean recounted,

> When I entered, I became aware of the differences existing among the religious: some wore a different habit and did not have the same kind of rooms as the others. Certainly I felt pain in the depths of my heart. It made me recognize my social position as a poor person. I learned to see myself more clearly in my own place, for I had never associated with people of another class. For me we were all equal. My eyes were opened and it made me appreciate more the simplicity of my place, my father being a simple workman. I realized that social differences existed also in convents. I can testify that the love of Jesus was stronger. He showed me his love in letting me know that he was also of a humble condition and that he was poor. Then I experienced such great joy that the differences had little importance.[121]

In 1960, Mother de Valon proposed making the religious habit the same for everyone:

> 1st, The difference in the habit is often misjudged in a world that seeks equality, even by priests who direct vocations elsewhere because of the apparent inequality. 2nd, Good vocations from our day schools go elsewhere instead of entering with us because they do not understand this outward difference. 3rd, Integration – harmony – would certainly reinforce charity and therefore good spirit. 4th, In some of our houses, the choir religious are already by necessity doing Martha's work; in others some of our more competent sisters are already at the head of certain employments, and some are puzzled not to see them in the habit of the choir nuns. 5th, We think that the majority of our sisters would be happy with this uniformity that would draw them closer to their mothers.[122]

---

[120] In Italy some members of the clergy discouraged young women who wished to enter the Sacred Heart, and they warned them that they would find there only princesses and the illiterate, which was exaggerated but showed that the Society was considered as having difficulty in recruiting from the middle class.

[121] Testimony of María Elvira Villaroel.

[122] Letter of 22 August 1960.

The vicars agreed. In the fall, the coadjutrix sisters put on the cap and pelerine and had a veil as long as that of the choir nuns.[123] But as some vicars had been reluctant to see them wearing the same cross and ring as the choir nuns, Mother de Valon did not give them those. In 1962 a juniorate was created for the sisters. Spain and England established professional training programs for them.

Radical changes were being promoted urgently, since the Sacred Congregation of Religious had indicated to Mother de Valon that it was receiving, especially from Great Britain, letters from coadjutrix sisters who complained of the discrimination against them. They condemned being limited to certain kinds of work, noted that the mothers were "on one side" and the sisters on "the other," that the food was not the same for all, that the mothers were hard on them and that the tombstones bore not only the first and last name of the deceased but also her class: choir religious or coadjutrix sister.[124] When Mother de Valon learned that the Church no longer believed it possible to keep the two categories of religious, on 16 July 1964, she asked the vicars to admit coadjutrix postulants no longer and to keep in the novitiates only those who were "absolutely reliable and capable after their vows of obtaining a diploma of some kind." In Colombia,

> the departure of twenty young women sent back to their families amidst general weeping was so upsetting that some hearts are still wounded. Maybe cloister meant that other alternatives for these young people had not been pursued. Some of them joined other congregations and succeeded at many tasks and gave the best of themselves even in positions with great responsibility. We hadn't enough vision for the future and the intuition and momentum that would have allowed us to offer a counter proposal.[125]

In Peru some novices entered other congregations. Some joined with the choir novices, but "afterward they were asked to go to another congregation because they were not made for educational work. It was a very sad moment."[126]

Agreement on integration was not unanimous, either in the general council or among the vicars or in the congregation. Therefore, it appeared that the superior general imposed it, while she was simply and promptly obeying the wishes of the Sacred Congregation of Religious. The consolidation had canonical consequences since all the religious of the

---

[123] The habit of the choir nuns was not adapted to the work of the sisters.
[124] Testimony of M.J. Bultó.
[125] *Histoire de la province de Colombie*, p. 3.
[126] Testimony of Gabriela Belón.

Society had to make the vow of education, whatever their assignments. Previously, coadjutrix sisters had been heads of schools or teachers without having made it, and some choir religious who had made it had not worked directly in education.[127]

Expectations of the Religious of the Sacred Heart

The Society of the Sacred Heart was then at its numerical apogee. The directives of the general congregation turned toward tangible restructuring of the makeup of the congregation itself and its apostolic mission. But the widespread changes produced an electric shock that caused as much resistance as boldness. What had been masked before came little by little into the light of day: the Society was in the grip of an internal ferment. The Council did not cause it but revealed it. The dissemination of *Lumen gentium* and *Gaudium et spes*, the publication of the conciliar constitutions on religious life, the knowledge of decisions made by the general congregation, even if narrowly understood in many vicariates, unleashed a torrent of self-examination both on what was being actually experienced and on what was wished for. The desire for openness was general, but it was more advanced in the United States where the religious had been trained in the social sciences and, because of the support of some vicars, were accustomed to act together and to take personal responsibility.[128]

---

[127] During the Chapter of 1970, taking into account this disparity of situations, two thirds of the capitulants spoke in favor of asking the Sacred Congregation of Religious for authorization to include the mission of the Society in the formula of profession rather than pronouncing a separate vow; this was granted *ad experimentum*. In 1982, the capitulants also asked unanimously that "our commitment to the service of education of the young be expressed clearly in our formula of profession rather than in the making of a fourth vow."

[128] R. Cunningham, p. 63. From 1965 on, at the request of the national conference of religious of the United States, Manhattanville welcomed each summer men and women religious, diocesan priests and some Religious of the Sacred Heart to pursue a master's degree in theology. The courses offered new interpretations in the fields of theology and exegesis. "During recreation and meals we discussed the contributions of the well-known lecturers like Henri de Lubac, Jaroslav Pelikan, John McDermott, who taught at Brooklyn College; William Alfred, playwright and professor at Harvard; Raymond Panikkar" (Testimony of Ann Conroy).

Troubles, Fears and Hopes

When the directives of a general congregation had been published, the vicars could begin to implement the reforms called for. However, promulgation of the decisions of 1964 was not guaranteed,[129] nor were they communicated with the same breadth of view, for in that era they were addressed only to the superiors.[130] Even if the changes were made, they were not necessarily explained: "The meaning of the changes was never clear in the communities; my contemporaries agree with me on this point," remarked April O'Leary. "No one ever mentioned those already made or to those to come. At Hove the superior announced one day to the community that there was going to be a walk and a picnic in Sussex. That meant abandoning cloister, and we had not heard about it. The principal changes that took place were looked at individually and not as part of a wider whole." Going out for study, shopping, or to visit one's family[131] were considered "permissions," and sometimes privilege, which was not understood by those who neither needed nor wanted them.[132] But the religious did not ask for explanations, having been taught in the noviceship that "asking questions was neither allowed nor even considered."[133] No clarifications were given about the change of the ring (the recommendation in England was not to refer to it), or about giving up the choir cloaks or about the small changes in the length of the habit and sleeves. "Symbolic in themselves, they also indicated that we were on a path toward evolution," recounted Marion Charley. The exchange of the rings was a significant and costly act for many religious.[134]

[129] In Mexico the sudden death of the vicar, Mother Carlotta Cabrera, three weeks after her return from Rome may explain the fact that the nuns did not learn what had been decided. The new vicar, Montserrat Espadaler, who came from Catalonia, modernized the vicariate. She established much warmer relationships with the former coadjutrix sisters. She did not hesitate to name nuns under thirty as mistress general or mistress of novices (testimony of Isabel Aranguren and P. García de Quevedo).

[130] Testimony of Jean Ford: "When I was named superior at Newton, Massachusetts, in November 1966, I learned that the text of the decisions of a general congregation was given only to superiors. That was the usual procedure then, but in the light of Vatican II, I found it rather astonishing." In Ireland and in Spain the young religious returning from probation were asked not to communicate what they had witnessed (Testimony of Moira Donnelly and Pilar Corral).

[131] Testimony of Mary Coke and Philomena Goddard.

[132] Testimony of Joan Faber and Monique Serpentier.

[133] Testimony of P. Goddard.

[134] Through obedience some had to give up a ring that had come from their family (Testimony of Ysabel Lorthiois). An Austrian considered it a *"renvoi."*

The atmosphere in the schools and colleges changed. The decision to abandon enclosure and the decisions of the general congregation allowed a greater openness to the world in general. Parents could attend events that took place in the school. Lay persons joined the religious in administration, although their role was not always well understood. Thanks to the Council, ecumenical activities were proposed. In Seoul Protestant pastors and teachers came to the Sacred Heart to learn about its educational practices at first hand.[135] In England, when Protestants were welcomed, the schools served as a "lightning rod, for no one in the community was sure how legitimate it was." This openness meant "reaching new frontiers, making contact with people of other churches, increasing friendships, mutual respect and understanding."[136]

As an expression of their desire to open their community to the world, some superiors encouraged the religious to extend their apostolate and introduced innovations in community life. At Woldingham they went to teach in the local primary school. Communities were permitted outings to the seaside or to the British Museum to see the Dead Sea Scrolls. Some religious obtained a driver's license.[137] In Rome, after 1966, the religious of the motherhouse took vacations and went to visit Subiaco. In the Eternal City there were more opportunities to go out because of religious ceremonies to which they were invited. Nuns from New Zealand and Australia remember the pleasure they had in being able to go swimming.[138]

Change affected many areas of religious life. In 1966, Office began to be said in the vernacular, which allowed the former sisters to join the other religious. From 1967 on the vernacular was used also in the Canon of the Mass. In England, where there was no agreement on this practice, there was a compromise: one group prayed in Latin, the other in English.[139] In Spain, it was only in January 1969 that the superiors decided to buy Office

---

"All that up to then had been valuable no longer counted. Get rid of it" (Testimony of Monika Schilgen).

[135] Testimony of Theresa Chu.
[136] Testimony of Joan Faber. "But the bishop who had tried to prevent such a meeting because an Anglican vicar had been invited to give the principal talk did not appreciate these changes, which riled the Religious of the Sacred Heart." The motherhouse encouraged communities to enter into contact with other churches and asked for reports on their endeavors.
[137] *Sister Dorothy Eyre*, p. 30.
[138] They recalled also with amusement how they had to get dressed behind the dunes so as to reappear in their religious habits.
[139] Testimony of A. O'Leary: "It was a decisive solution but one that added however to the numerous sources of inevitable friction in community and to new tension that was appearing."

books in Spanish so that everyone could say Office together.[140] In New York there were new ways of conducting the annual retreat. At Greenwich, on one occasion the retreat master did not follow the classic schema of the eight-day retreat: he encouraged discussion rather than silence and had the religious reflect on current problems in religious life.[141]

From then on aspirants could engage exclusively in study. Some juniorates were closed, and in the United States the young nuns studied theology in university centers. In France the juniorate was transferred to Paris where they could take courses at the *Institut catholique*, while being guided by a mistress of juniorate. Some communities, some of them international, were created for students. West Hill in London received aspirants from India, Australia and the Far East.[142] In Paris the community on Avenue de Lowendal welcomed Austrians. Australians were sent to Washington where they attended the Catholic University of America.[143] These opportunities became international experiences. Renewal took place, thanks to the contributions of lecturers who came to the communities or whom one could go to hear and who presented new directions in ecclesiology, dogmatics and exegesis or who spoke on psychology. Sometimes religious rendered this service in other vicariates.[144]

---

[140] Testimony of Maria Teresa Olmedo.

[141] R. Cunningham, p. 60. To cut short the criticisms, Mother Fitzgerald asked Father Cox to give a short session at Manhattanville so that the nuns could get an idea of his way of doing things.

[142] It was after Mother Tobin's visit to Australia that the decision was made to send young professed to study in England (Testimony of Esmey Herscovitch). The students of West Hill studied at Corpus Christi College, which had just been founded in London and which was advanced, with "people from different parts of the world, most of whom were avid for the new ideas that were being communicated to us in the lectures and discussion groups. It was a passionate, instructive time. I think some other religious were jealous, and understandably, of our freedom and our privileges" (Testimony of M. Charley). The life of the young nuns who had to combine their studies with a task to fulfill in the house did not offer the same advantages. Difficulties could also appear when professed and aspirant students were together in the same community (Testimony of M. Brennan).

[143] Testimony of M. Brennan.

[144] Australia welcomed two religious from the United States, Jean McGowan and Margaret Gorman, who excited much enthusiasm among their hearers by introducing them to a new approach to their subjects but above all brought "fresh air" into a vicariate that gave the impression of remaining for a long time apart from the rest of the Society.

More complex were the consequences of the "integration." One could welcome it as a liberation that put an end to a "destructive organism"[145] and appreciate "no longer having to chop up the coal, flute the caps, schedule the prie-dieu, starch the first communion veils, card and stitch mattresses" and having more time for prayer.[146] But if Mother de Valon's decision had the merit of a drastic action, it was very difficult to bring to bear.[147] There again preparation would have been advisable; but as the decision was implemented without being explained, "The years of transition reopened wounds."[148] In Chicago, according to Margaret Mary Miller, it "was a terrible blow to the sisters, because of its suddenness; today coadjutrix sister, tomorrow choir religious. Many former coadjutrix sisters told me their hearts were broken. Even if it was a good decision, they should have been helped gradually to see their vocation in a new way." Mary Braganza, who recognizes that she owed her vocation to their silent example of joy, peace and union with God, thought that at the moment of the consolidation sadness took over: "They were not educated but they were rich in the gifts of the Spirit. Our oldest sisters could not go back to school." Domestic tasks were not considered to be on the same level as the work of teachers, and the sisters' talents as housekeepers were not brought to light.[149] When the communities of the Far East stopped using English as their common language, some former sisters had to return to their own countries.[150]

The way in which the integration unfolded in England is all the more interesting to consider in that coadjutrix sisters had been members for a longer time than elsewhere, and many among them came from Malta and had only minimal education. "They had not been permitted to speak their language and we had done nothing to help them attain their true potential," was Vivien Bowman's summary. In the view of Andrée Meylan,

> This decision changed community life and the apostolate in ways that had repercussions for many years. There were even absurdities such as having the sisters called "Mother," then shortly afterward, the decision to call us

---

[145] Testimony of Sheila McAuliffe.

[146] Testimony of Leonor Yanez.

[147] At the motherhouse Mother de Valon had to take into account a certain reluctance, and she contented herself with giving the cross to the former sisters in her office, whereas she had planned a ceremony at which the whole community would have assisted (Testimony of Marie-Antoinette Renoux).

[148] Testimony of Fanny Martínez.

[149] Testimony of A. Kato and S. Kageyama. Some sisters who were carrying out their employments easily and successfully were full of anxiety and uncertainty (Testimony of Norah Glynn).

[150] Testimony of M. Braganza.

all "Sister." Italy kept the appellation "Mother" for years! The integration was certainly desirable, but its implementation was not easy. In England we took it to heart and to the letter, whereas it would have been better to put it off for a few months. It revolutionized the earlier forms of the apostolate based on the principle of "one community, one work." At the same time, public authorities were requiring professional qualification for all the teachers and the unbiased opening of positions. For certain community services, infirmarians, cooks, treasurers, the provincial treasurer had to enter invented salaries on the books so that her accounts were realistic.

"Integration was a real saga," remarked Vivien Bowman. The young saw it as an act of justice and a social necessity,[151] all the more as a certain rapprochement was already in place among their generation;[152] but the abandoning of accepted ways created unease. Each house managed as well as it could. At the beginning, Joan Faber remembers, there was

> confusion and bewilderment. Without discussion or understanding of what would have helped the integration, a subtle snobbery showed itself in not including the sisters during recreation, while they felt stymied and unable to express themselves or speak freely. We ended up ignoring the fact that no one felt happy or accepted. Some inflexibility was evident; the change of name and rank created confusion and uncertainty and the explanations were inadequate.

The integration sometimes took on the appearance of retaliation, and the pettiness went both ways. In Ireland some former choir nuns did not wish to sit next to the former sisters.[153] In the houses of Southern Spain people did not speak to them or told them, "You are not ours." "I felt," said an Italian, "a kind of jealousy on the part of the former mothers, as if the sisters were elevated and they [the mothers] were lowered because we were all called "Mother.""[154] At Monterrico in Peru no one understood why the new professed wanted to live in the basement with a former sister.[155] In Malta some sisters elbowed their way into the refectory in front of the choir religious. "Someone thought you had been lacking in charity or courtesy

---

[151] Testimony of Barbara Sweeney, M. Charley, Mary Barrow.
[152] Testimony of J. Faber.
[153] Testimony of Teresa Murphy.
[154] Testimony of Giovannina Russo: "I felt that the choir religious held to the distinction. Once when I was on the train, two alumnae, after greeting a Mother, turned to me politely and said 'Good morning, Mother.' The other immediately corrected them: 'No, she's a sister!'"
[155] Testimony of P. Tamayo.

during a conversation, and she went to complain to the superior. It was the word of the sister against that of the choir nun, and it was the former whom one believed."[156] Superiors did not always know how to manage the situation or maintain a balance between the two groups.[157] As no one dared ask the sisters to join in the housekeeping tasks, it was often the youngest who had to clean house without being freed from any of their own duties.[158] When the former sisters went to study, former choir nuns were annoyed. "The sisters have formed what they call OSA, 'Old Sisters Association.' It was taken as a joke, but it showed that the integration seemed imposed and was not satisfactory."[159] Some former sisters believed that they were no longer true to their vocation, and sometimes they discreetly avoided renewing the fourth vow. But the reactions also depended on personalities. As one Spaniard remarked, "I was helped by the way the mothers reacted. It seemed to me that nothing changed in my relations with them, or in the respect I had for them, for I entered to follow Jesus Christ in the Society, and I was going to follow him in the same way at this stage. I had entered knowing what I was committing myself to, and I continued to live in the same way."[160] If some of the Irish admitted having lost their bearings, one made it clear: "I received the news without turning a hair. I said to myself: 'We can't go backward; therefore, we have to go forward.' But it was hard. I wept for days for our family life was broken. Then I became accustomed to it and I was happy."[161]

The number of members in community gatherings quickly doubled. This was a considerable change if one remembers that before the choir nuns and sisters had different life styles under the same roof and met only for Mass, Benediction, morning and evening prayer and meals taken in silence, for the most part, and at separate tables. Both groups considered recreations less interesting. "The natural, human responses were missing. We were no longer on the same wave length in expressing ourselves."[162]

---

[156] Testimony of Mary Coke.

[157] As the community room at Roehampton could not accommodate all the aspirants' desks, the aspirants were installed in the sisters' room: "We had to work while they were peeling vegetables amidst conversation and laughter" (Testimony of Anne Hine).

[158] A. Hine: "We, the youngest, thought that our voices, that one hardly listened to before, were no longer ignored." It was after the setting up of small communities that housework was shared by everyone.

[159] A. Hine.

[160] Anonymous testimony.

[161] Testimony of Jessie Doyle.

[162] Testimony of M. Schilgen.

At the motherhouse they began to use Italian [instead of the customary French] during recreation to help integration along.[163]

At the time of the Chapter of 1967, some *desiderata* coming from former choir nuns indicated that community life had become painful in houses where there were many former sisters who were poorly educated, even unable to speak the language of the country where they were living.[164] The prefect of the Sacred Congregation himself inquired about the manner in which the integration had been carried out. Assimilation began to appear, but only gradually. Although not all the former sisters managed to adapt and some left the Society of the Sacred Heart, others appreciated the end of the discrimination they had suffered. But could one truly speak of a fusion? According to Mary Barrow, "The coadjutrix sisters were joined to the choir nuns; they did not fuse with them!"

Eddies, Revolt and Protests

Mother de Valon had planned to hold the Special Chapter in the spring of 1968, but it was held in the autumn of 1967, as the Sacred Congregation of Religious had ruled on the working plan developed by the general council more rapidly than had been expected. New ways to participate permitted professed to send their *desiderata* to the motherhouse, and in December 1966 and in January 1967 for the first time vicariate assemblies were held.

Rome had given no instructions as to their preparation or their process. In the Far East, Mother Keogh inaugurated the assembly that took place at Obayashi with these words of Saint Madeleine Sophie: "If I had my life to live over again, I would live it entirely under the influence of the Holy Spirit." She recommended that the delegates "look ahead. Let us only look at the past in order to see how the present has come about. Let us have a sense of history and of evolution."[165] In New York Mother Fitzgerald asked for

---

[163] Gen. Arch. C VII 2 C, Journal of Mother Castejón.
[164] Gen Arch. C I C 3, Box 21, Vicariate of Paris: "Prescribed by the Council – in the measure possible – the integration of the "sisters" is a very happy measure in what concerns the future. On the contrary, when it is a question of the elements actually and concretely composing the group of coadjutrix sisters to be integrated, the situation creates serious and multiple problems. No one would have the idea of mixing secondary school teachers and Polish immigrant laborers in the same Catholic Action group in France. Such however is the situation of our French communities. Community life has truly ceased to be viable...."
[165] M. Williams, *The Society...Far East*, p. 238.

an atmosphere of depth founded on charity, liberty and above all confidence. The way to live the *Cor unum* in these days is in openness of mind, united in love and veneration, one in glorifying the Heart of Christ in the task confided to us. We will then reinforce not only our bonds of unity, but we will open ourselves to the Holy Spirit who will render us capable of expressing different opinions, for diversity of views is good and expected, all without division or disunion.[166]

Because this kind of assembly was new, the religious took advantage of it to set forth their dreams for religious life. Their remarks surprised those who had not realized the breadth of the discomfort that had taken over when holding on to longstanding customs that promoted holiness appeared obsolete and well behind the evolution of secular society and other religious congregations. The criticisms did not come exclusively from the youngest members, whom one might have expected not to know fully the needs of the congregation and not to have a sense of "religious responsibilities."[167]

People became conscious then of the sufferings and dissatisfaction that had built up. Unheard of proposals turned the superiors and vicars upside down.[168] The outcry against the privileges that local councilors had enjoyed completely amazed them. Only then did they understand that *goûter* taken in the superior's room, while they conversed, was considered a breach of equality and had created anger and frustration![169] Hearing the desiderata embarrassed some religious who had done nothing but apply the directives they had received. For example, Mother Frances Allpress, who had been mistress of novices in England since the end of the war, was present when the vicar read the *desiderata*.

> When they came to those that concerned the noviceship, the wishes, hopes, desires – whatever name they were given – were concentrated on Frances. It was a raging fire of heartless criticism, apparently endless. In presenting negative experiences before suggesting reforms, they attacked her person with venom. We were astounded by what we were hearing, and the reading continued tirelessly. At one moment well before the end,

---

[166] R. Cunningham, p. 60.
[167] *Lettres circulaires de la T.R.M. de Valon*, 30 August 1966, pp. 191-192.
[168] Testimony Y. Lorthiois.
[169] Testimony J. Faber. At her return from Lumen Vitae in July 1967, she was momentarily left without employment. One of her contemporaries reproached her vehemently on that account, believing that she had been given special treatment because she had been a councilor: "It was one example that shows that the councilors were perceived as an elite." The privileges of councilors were also criticized in Mexico.

Rebecca Ogilvie Forbes looked up from the papers and said to Frances, for whom she had a great deal of affection: "Mother, this must be very hard to hear?" and Frances answered in an unforgettable tone of voice: "It is always good to hear the truth." Three of her former novices stood up to say that it was not the whole truth.

"Much later Frances told me," added Prudence Wilson, "that she woke up in the night thinking she heard Rebecca's voice continue the catalog without end."[170] This trial wounded Mother Allpress, and she took a long time to recover from it.

Many religious left the vicariate assemblies discouraged, as Mother Fitzgerald recognized in closing New York's:

> Many of us have felt that a sword was being put into the heart of the Society by all the new demands being made on religious life, because those of us who have lived in it for years, and loved it and its structure, felt that it was almost sacrilegious to touch it.... Somehow, it seems to me that something like this process of the opening of Our Lord's Heart is being done to the Society of His Heart.... It is hard for some of us, and less hard for others, but with the Society we should give what we have, as Our Lady and St. John did.[171]

For Jean Ford who took part in the Washington assembly, listening to the *desiderata* made it clear that the changes were already in the process of taking place.

The reports of the vicariate assemblies and the *desiderata* were sent to Rome. Mother Bultó said how astonished she was when she learned about them: "It's appalling! The floodgates have been opened wide. What criticism of superiors and assistants, everything. It was a real release of pent up feelings. It was very painful, even if it was good that everyone could express herself. How horrible! What bad superiors we have had! It is terrible what we have been able to make people endure!"[172]

Widespread Desire for Change

The synthesis of the reports of the vicariate assemblies produced in the spring of 1967 by an international commission shows how Religious of the

---

[170] J. Faber, *Sister Frances Allpress*, p. 45.
[171] R. Cunningham, p. 61.
[172] It was allowed to send the *desiderata* anonymously. Since then consultations have always been signed.

Sacred Heart saw their involvement in the Church and the world and how they imagined the transformations they hoped for. These reports can be considered a real sampling of what the congregation was thinking then.

All the vicariate assemblies were unanimous in asking that the glory of the Heart of Jesus remain always the purpose of the Society, while hoping that its scriptural and dogmatic basis could be outlined according to up-to-date theology, since there was no conciliar document on which to rely. Everyone insisted that the religious life of the Society must remain austere and strong, founded on prayer and interior life.[173] However, the Society had to face the consequences of its present-day circumstances as an institute of apostolic life. The religious had recognized a hiatus between the world and their way of living that did not result only from developments in civil society. Their religious consecration, which had been understood as separation from the world, had enclosed them in a sheltered life distant from reality.[174] Most people wanted to think positively about the values their contemporaries appreciated: openness to the ideas of others, respect for all without class distinction, solidarity, responsibility, competence. They wanted to share the concern about current problems, such as atheism, poverty, racial issues, political and international life in order to grow in personal responsibility and to help their students to face them.[175] Colombia asked that religious able to vote with complete freedom! Finally some assemblies in Europe and the United States believed that it was time to recognize the role of women in professional, public and international life and to work with a view to their advancement.

Worldwide, the apostolate was linked to education. However, there were proposals to open the institutions to everyone, give up all exclusiveness, suppress class distinctions, remove from the Constitutions all discriminatory expressions, no longer consider the poor as a separate category, democratize the boarding schools,[176] admit children coming from

---

[173] Chile specified: "Discipline is a defense of common life and of charity; it is a necessary element in all formation, for self-control, solid maturity and work habits. It must teach us to use freedom prudently and to proceed with responsibility and initiative, to collaborate with others. In necessary renewal, we must tend toward the perfect imitation of Christ, and not settle for what is worldly."

[174] The Paris assembly thought: "We do not know the world in which the young are developing, we speak a different language from theirs; we do not connect with them." Assemblies in Sydney, Grenoble, Saint Louis, Washington, Puerto Rico, Belgium and England expressed the desire to understand the psychology of young people.

[175] Vicariates of Mexico, Chamartín and Belgium.

[176] Reports from Brazil, Chile, Sarriá, Tokyo, New York, Canada and San Diego.

homes of divorced parents or those not married in the Church. To respond to the appeals of the Church and take into account the responsibility of the Society vis-à-vis the 80% of young people not receiving a Catholic education,[177] some religious were asking to teach in diocesan or public schools, to teach catechism, to work with the disadvantaged in poor areas, with physically, mentally and socially handicapped children, to open centers for young people and to intensify retreat work.

How could they accommodate a full, fruitful apostolic life bearing in mind these goals while maintaining vestigial forms of enclosure? How to act so that openness to the world did not end up as secularization? Until 1964, enclosure resulted from a strict or legalistic but regular reading of the Constitutions. In 1964 enclosure was understood as not canonical but disciplinary. In that case what should be allowed? To questions posed by the vicars, the motherhouse had answered in a restrictive sense. The religious were not to take meals with visitors or go on overnight school trips.[178] In Sydney they were not to join in celebrations organized on campus nor even have a cup of tea with the students, for "it is not in eating and drinking with our children that we will do them good."[179] Student nuns could eat their meals at the university but with their backs to the other students and without talking to them! One could visit one's parents when their state of health indicated that death was imminent, but what to do in the case of an aunt or older sister who had acted as a mother to the religious?[180] Individual cases were not taken into account and as "one looked back on permissions granted, it was worse than before."[181]

---

[177] Reports from Australia and Argentina.

[178] Response to some cases presented by Belgium. The vicar of Ireland, on 2 July 1965, thought that it was better to have the children accompanied by a lay teacher (Prov. Arch. Ireland/Scotland, IRS 1.0094).

[179] Testimony of Mary Shanahan.

[180] Mother Bultó recalled the case: "The Mother General said, 'Many people think that the religious should be able to go home when their parents are seriously ill. I answered No, for the Constitutions are very clear on this subject. It is No. What do you think about it?' All the Mothers [vicar] said: 'It's obvious, Mother! Of course not!' If it had been a matter of conscience, I am sure they would have expressed their opinion.... But they thought that the Mother General knew much better than they did."

[181] Testimony of Jehannine d'Hautefeuille. According to Mother Caracciolo, the question of permissions was at the heart of the discussions that at the chapter ended in the resignation of Mother de Valon. She even gave as one of the reasons for the hostility of some of the capitulants regarding the superior general: "Mother de Valon said that she had refused some permissions because she did not want to open the door too wide before the general chapter or go too quickly in the *aggiornamento*. The chapter reacted violently to her prudence."

All the vicariate assemblies thought that clarifications were needed. New York specified: "Our separation from the world must not be considered a flight from it or a protection against the its dangers but rather a 'distance' that allows us to face the world as it is now in the name of the world such that the Incarnation would like it to be." The broader understanding of enclosure was to be aligned with charity, the service of the Church, the demands of the apostolate, formation and strengthening of the religious' relationships with their families. The limits would be determined by the vows, the life of prayer and duty to the community. But did flexibility and independence have to play a role or could what was permitted or forbidden be firmly established? Five assemblies, seeing the ambiguity that was coming, opted for precise directives; eleven wanted vicars and superiors to be able to act according to circumstances.

The major innovations concerned government. The synthesis on obedience was introduced by a quotation from Father Arrupe who said that the principle of authority must remain intact, that dialogue between a religious and his/her superior tended to increase the sense of co-responsibility for the common good; but that "once a decision is made, adherence [was to be] joyous and prompt, in the true sense of what was called blind obedience." Everything indicates that obedience was not disputed in the Society of the Sacred Heart. But its meaning had to be deepened and broadened, to place the emphasis on its theological, ecclesial and apostolic aspects rather than on its juridical code. It must be considered as sharing in the Paschal Mystery, as the highest form of love of God, as an imitation of Christ in his gift to the Father and incorporation in his redemptive self-oblation and as placing one's talents at the service of the Church.[182] Obedience must be personal, active and responsible. It was not to be identified with a host of observances that had been linked to religious fidelity. The vicariate assemblies asked for recognition of the principle of subsidiarity, that the use of dialogue was not so much a right for those who must obey but a duty for those in authority.[183] "The Society of the Sacred Heart began to be aware that to obey includes responsibility; it wanted to move forward on this path. It was no longer simply 'this or that.'"[184] This understanding of obedience called into question the common top-down practice, since the pattern had been to invest the decisions of superiors with absolute power.[185] As Mother Fitzgerald wrote to Mother de Valon on 15

---

[182] The assemblies of Washington, San Diego, Netherlands, Bilbao and Sydney spoke about obedience to the community and not just to the superior.

[183] Report of Germany.

[184] Testimony of Barbara Hogg. She was a member of the preparatory commission.

[185] Testimony of M.J. Bultó: "We were not accustomed to expressing ourselves freely."

July 1966, "Our religious say that the professed are the Society, but that they have no role to play in decision making; that they are treated like children, not consulted, with no chance to defend their views, and if they express them, they appear disloyal."[186]

All the vicariate assemblies asked for decentralization, even though on the whole they had affirmed that the hierarchical principle was to be maintained and that authority was not delegated. New York asked that openness, responsible freedom and exactitude in giving an accounting characterize the actions of "all representative bodies, that the doctrine of charisms be respected at all levels." Chicago proposed "a reversal of the government as we have it in the Society: a pyramid in which all the power is centered in the person of the superior general" and advised "a power that rises in a spiral from each member to the general chapter, which is the real governing body of the Society. The superior general ought to be rather a center of unity than the center of power."

In 1964, "the excessive centralization" of the Society of the Sacred Heart had already been mentioned, but Mother de Valon did not wish to abolish a system built on permissions that in the last resort she could give or refuse.[187] The vicars held only partial responsibility because they had to seek authorization from the motherhouse for any decisions they had made. Therefore, to avoid being overruled, they tended regularly to have recourse to Rome even on questions that they could have settled themselves. Or else they limited themselves to informing Rome of the decision they had already made, thereby avoiding a refusal.[188] They were

---

[186] R. Cunningham, p., p. 59.

[187] *Directives and Decisions*, 1964, pp. 29-30. "Too numerous are the letters asking permissions often expecting immediate responses by cable or telephone, which is a waste of time and money. The vicars sometimes put the Mother General in the position of having to give answers when the circumstances are much better known by you than by her; this can have regrettable effects. When a permission is to be given and you do not know whether it would be granted or not, give it and have the courage to take on the odium of the refusal if the refusal comes. It is too easy to say, 'Our Mother General does not want it.' It is you, I repeat, who are responsible." That is how Mother Fitzgerald acted in 1966. She wanted the aspirants to be able to assist at the vicariate assemblies, which Rome did not wish. Mother Fitzgerald indicated the decision as coming from her and suffered the criticism"(R. Cunningham, p. 57).

[188] Mother Keogh proceeded thus on several occasions. When she adopted a Korean baby, she simply informed the superior general, who responded, "I laughed so much when I read your letter that I cannot scold you, but above all don't do it again!" In another situation, "One of the young nuns in my vicariate had to wear secular clothes in order to teach in a Japanese public school. That was something I desired and that I had had difficulty in

not always consulted on questions concerning their vicariates. During her journey to Latin America, Mother de Valon decided to create a novitiate in Colombia for the countries bordering the Pacific. As a consequence, the one in Peru was closed "without dialogue with the vicar. It was very painful for the latter, but as a good religious she obeyed. This dear Mother died just before sending the novices to Manizales."[189] In 1966 the motherhouse closed the house at Hove, even though Mother Ogilvie Forbes had expressed reservations about it, and the reasons for the closing had not seemed obvious in England.[190] In Ireland Leeson Street, Dublin, was closed for safety reasons, but the decision made quickly by Rome displeased the archbishop of Dublin and angered the parents even more, since the director of the school had authorized them to collect funds for the construction of a new building.[191] The system of "permissions" from then on shocked the Society of the Sacred Heart because it established a practice of inequality in an era when equality was considered a basic value. Religious whose vicar had broad views on how to manage daily life seemed to be better off than those whose vicar did not dare take any initiative. Mission countries showed that their apostolates needed independence. The mission called for the religious be able to stay in the villages. A white habit was not well suited to Africa and Asia where white was the color of mourning.[192] Even wearing the religious habit was problematic in India, where it was "regarded as a threatening sign of proselytism and confused with subversive activity."[193]

---

obtaining. I had spoken in one of my letters of secular clothes, but it had been overlooked in the reading. Mother de Valon, after someone reported to her that a Japanese religious was wearing secular dress, wrote to me: 'My dear daughter, I cannot believe that what I have heard is true. I know you too well to think that you could have done such a thing without consulting me. I am sure it is a question of a false report, but write to me to tell me that it is false.' I was very sorry about the dimensions this incident assumed in her mind."

[189] Testimony of G. Belón. When Peru became a vicariate in December 1951, the vicar, Mother Cubero, had opened a novitiate in Lima, thus ending the formation given in Chile and then in Colombia. The departure of the twelve novices and a postulant for Manizales, organized by the new vicar, Gabriela Belón, was painful for the vicariate.

[190] J. Faber, *Sister Rebecca Ogilvie Forbes*, p. 22.

[191] Prov. Arch. Ireland/Scotland, IRS 1.0130. Letter of the archbishop to the vicar, 31 August 1968. This closing was all the more painful as the establishment, open to middle class Irish society, had many good works in contrast to the house of Mount Anville, considered characterized by marked snobbery (Testimony of D. Boland and M. Roe).

[192] Testimony of Marthe Jacobs.

[193] Testimony of M. Braganza. Mother de Valon had authorized the wearing of a white or beige sari: "That really broke down the barriers that the religious

The most insistent requests to train personnel according to the cultural and social conditions of the countries concerned came from Asia.

While the vicariates were unanimous in asking for another form of governance, opinions differed on the process of nominating the superior general. Seven among them asked to abandon the "secret note" and the vicar general. Tokyo, Saint Louis, San Diego, Chicago and New York suggested that the superior general be elected by a general chapter.[194] Eleven vicariates wanted the superior general to continue to be elected for life. Sixteen others recommended a limited term but with the possibility of renewal.

With hindsight Mother Bultó could say how much these reports had revealed of a state of unrest. The weight of tradition in the Society of the Sacred Heart had little by little become so strong that one hardly wished to do anything new even in the name of the past. "We have never done that in the Society" had become an argument that cut short any desire for change. But the motherhouse was not the only obstacle to the process of evolution. She thought,

> Many vicars did not know about the changes that were taking place in civil society and in the Church. Some of them lacked critical sense; they were not just faithful to the motherhouse but docile. They had no plans for the future, and they did not even have a clear vision of the present. They held to continuity and they wanted to strengthen old values at any cost rather than consider the needs of the world.

This attitude had repercussions for the rest of the organization, for "the vicariate was a closed system. It seemed best to agree with the decisions of the mothers, the Mother General in Rome, the vicar in the vicariate." As vicars were not often changed, even after many years in charge, "everyone bowed her head and went along."[195]

This situation was all the more serious because the desire for change was stronger in some parts of the Society than in others. Mother Fitzgerald told Mother de Valon:

> Our religious who are most balanced, who have very much at heart the good of the Society, see clearly that if we do not do something soon,

---

habit had created and allowed us to identify significantly with our own people." Japan noted that it was costly to import the fabric necessary to make the habits since it could not be found in the country (Testimony of A. Kato).

[194] Chicago proposed that the membership of the Society present candidates for the office of superior general.

[195] She added: "In that era it was quite an affair to discharge a superior when she was no longer up to the task. And that depended entirely on the vicar!"

there will be some kind of division in the vicariate and maybe in the country. I am aware of these reactions because certain people have spoken to me about them. They are very worried about the future if we do not change, if we do not discuss these questions in community, if we do not make some experiments as other orders have done. I believe that the fear that we are not working hard enough to follow the advice of the Church about renewal of religious life is deeply rooted in their thinking. They have read and heard a great deal about the decrees concerning religious life, and they ardently hope that we will make some experiments before the next chapter. They say that the Society seems apprehensive about them. There are very few, if any, who want change for the sake of change. They want to support the Society in this moment so crucial to its future, and they think strongly that as adults, they must be consulted on the decisions to be made, and the time has come to change the structure of the Constitutions regarding authority, that subjects as well as superiors (the head and the members together) ought to take into account the decrees of the [Vatican] Council.[196]

But even those who knew the changes to be inevitable were frightened by them. In November 1966, Mother Ogilvie Forbes gave a conference to her community in which she said:

In 1836 Philippine [Duchesne] wrote to our holy Mother that she felt incapable of satisfying the demands of the general congregation that had just been held in France. If she was able to write: "These rules and these decisions frighten me," we will know consolation in the coming months when we are unsure of what the general chapter will bring us, and to do what she did we will, through faith, rely more strongly on God. Toward the end of the same year she wrote to Mother Barat: "Although the changes you have made have cost me, I accept it all as coming from Our Lord and from the Society...." We will have to accept as she did, the failure, maybe the feeling of insecurity, without bitterness and to go forward like the poor when some of our supports will have been taken away. We must not worry about what religious life will become, for our end is to render glory to the Sacred Heart of Our Lord in his life of humility, poverty and obedience to his Father, and nothing can go against that. Personally I am convinced that in so far as we hold to our community life and find our simple contentment therein, we will keep the true spirit of the Society.[197]

---

[196] R. Cunningham, pp. 58-59, 15 June 1966.
[197] Joan Faber, *Ogilvie Forbes*, pp. 22-23.

Mother Bultó recognized: "We were awaiting the chapter with some fear, even with some dread."[198]

Amid the inevitable friction during times of change, the religious expressed both the desire to live radically the charism of the Society of the Sacred Heart and some differences of opinion as to how to embody it in a manner that suits the common mission. The anxiety lest the congregation lose its soul was mingled with the hope of moving forward. The deepest unrest was institutional and had to do with the way authority and obedience were understood. However, nothing predicted the upheavals that would take place in the course of the special chapter and the shoals to be navigated in order to stay on course.

---

[198] But the assistants general knew changes were inevitable. Mother Meliá repeated to the probanists that if they did not feel capable of supporting change, it would be better to leave the Society (Testimony of A. Conroy who was part of the probation just before the Chapter of 1967).

Chapter II

From One World to Another

The special chapter that was convened in Rome in the fall of 1967 was called for by Church decisions and anticipated by the Religious of the Sacred Heart. For the Society of the Sacred Heart it was a mirror of what the Second Vatican Council had been for the Church. It overturned what had been presumed to be givens for more than a century. It was a source of joy, but the disturbance it brought with it brought the Society into a difficult period.

The Shock of the Special Chapter

On 1 October 1967, Mother de Valon opened the chapter referring to "the climate of uncertainty [that had] descended upon the communities; everywhere there is suffering, everywhere we aspire to recover that *cor unum et anima una* that in the past has been our greatest strength." It pained her to learn that Religious of the Sacred Heart sought another way to live obedience, and the suggestions presented by the vicariate assemblies had seemed to her a challenge to her authority,[1] which was not necessarily the case. It was not certain either that the religious of all ages, were "lured into thinking of those in charge of guiding them as the symbol of a bygone era."[2] But some vicars and the superior general felt their exercise of power challenged, and some of them were afraid of those who expressed "their rights as if they were their due, an attitude absolutely unworthy of the heart of a religious wholly abandoned to the will of God."[3]

Unquestionably the superior general feared this chapter, even though she had written: "We are going to approach this great task with confidence

---

[1] Testimony of B. Hogg.
[2] *Lettres circulaires de la T.R.M. de Valon*, 25 November 1965, p. 172.
[3] *Lettres circulaires*, p. 165, 15 June 1965.

and joy, that of knowing that it is the Holy Church that guides us."[4] This intelligent and sensitive woman was conscious that holding the special chapter was a risky undertaking for the Society of the Sacred Heart. How far to go to renew it without causing it to founder in worldliness and without provoking internal divisions? That question was pertinent, and it is understandable that it was asked of the one whose mission was to preserve the unity of the body, but there is no doubt that it became even weightier because Mother de Valon was not in a state to resolve it serenely. Her discomfort was linked to the state of her health.[5] Attacked on 12 March with a cardiac illness that had kept her from taking part in the meeting of mistresses of novices that she had convoked and from visiting the English vicariate,[6] Mother de Valon had rapidly fallen into a nervous depression. We will never know whether it was the cause or the consequence of the heart trouble. Her underlying condition was discovered later upon her return to France when she was diagnosed with severe hypothyroidism.

At first her fatigue was put down to overwork and in part linked to her attending the Council. But that was not the only cause of her condition. As Frances Gimber noted in her biography of Mother Marie Louise Schroen, Mother de Valon's participation in the work of the Council was gratifying, but

> was a source of deep anxiety and pain to her. She saw that she was going to have to initiate significant changes in the way of life of her religious as a result of some of the Council's decisions.... Mother de Valon heard in the debate on the Council floor denials of everything she had ever believed about religious life and the Society's particular understanding of it, which involved cloister, separation from the world, silence and a number of other monastic practices. These had as their purpose to safeguard the contemplative life of the religious, but they resulted in the diminution of their apostolic effectiveness. The Council decreed that

---

[4] *Lettres circulaires*, pp. 187-188.
[5] Monique Luirard, *Sabine de Valon*, Rome, 1997, pp. 245-261.
[6] The religious of the vicariate were pained, maybe even shocked, all the more as the schedule of the visit had been communicated to the communities, and England had not had a visit of the superior general since 1949. Mother Bultó went, but her visit did not replace the one Mother de Valon would have made. Mother Ogilvie Forbes, at the end of her life, wondered whether that renunciation was really linked to the state of Mother de Valon's health, or whether it was really explained by the trouble she experienced in a country whose language she did not speak and by her consequent powerlessness to control the situation. One sees by that how much the lack of information about Mother de Valon's state of health damaged mutual confidence.

religious congregations were to define themselves as either apostolic or contemplative and then adjust their life styles accordingly. It seemed evident that the Society of the Sacred Heart belonged in the apostolic category, but the consequences of recognizing that reality were far from clear or acceptable to everyone.[7]

Consequently, to try as she did to preserve the experience of the past, to maintain the unity of the whole but to avoid what appeared to be drifting off course, without however blocking modernization, was a formidable task. She wanted the development to be slow and gradual, led, not just undergone by herself,[8] but to promote that development could turn out to be an exhausting mission. Even though she knew that the Society of the Sacred Heart had to change, it is not clear that she could accept the metamorphosis that would inevitably call into question an office that she had received for life and that she wanted to keep unchanged, faithfully and honorably. Her spiritual notes from January 1966 show that she foresaw a change that appeared to her unavoidable but which frightened her in spite of her faith and her confidence in God.

Cared for at first in a Roman hospital, she returned to the motherhouse on 24 August 1966 after sojourns at Avigliana, the Trinità and San Vito Romano, north of Rome, for her convalescence. She had announced on 19 May 1966, that she had named Mother Bultó vicar general; then on 30 August 1966, considering herself cured, she let it be known that Mother Bultó had ceased to exercise that function.

Opinions differ as to whether Mother de Valon was cured or not. She had resumed all her duties and spent four weeks in Congo. But witnesses believe that even if her condition did not require specific care, she was not in good health. As evidence they note her tiredness, inconsistent judgment demonstrated by repeated counter-orders, lack of concentration and over-activity that was expressed by frequent trips until the summer of 1967. Another point at issue relates to Mother de Valon's awareness of her condition. In her circulars she referred only to heart trouble. It seems that her doctors and those around her never spoke to her about her depression so as to keep her from becoming more unstable, out of respect for her office or because she herself was simply not capable of admitting what the trouble was on account of her training. Whatever the situation, her assistants general wondered whether or not they had to refer to her health during the special chapter, but as they were not all of the same mind, they did not manage to settle the question. Mother de Valon saw the private

---

[7] *Woman of the Word*, pp. 148-149.
[8] Testimony of Carlotta Leitner.

meetings at which they had raised the question among themselves as a plot that caused her great suffering. In order to rebalance a council that she saw as divided and to know what was really happening, she decided, shortly before the special chapter, to name a new assistant general, Mother Teresa Caracciolo. Mother de Valon was also afraid to have a male religious present at the chapter, either a member of the Sacred Congregation or someone named by herself, while to do so seemed to be of capital importance to the majority of her assistants.

While the superior general's fears were legitimate and members of her council were not themselves fully at ease, the chief emphasis in the Society of the Sacred Heart was confidence in the forces of innovation that could allow the congregation to respond better to the needs of the time, always faithful to the Spirit and even more in accord with the inspiration of the founder. Moreover for the first time the Society of the Sacred Heart was going to have a real chapter since to the thirty-three vicars would be added forty-nine elected delegates.[9] More than a fourth of the capitulants were under fifty years of age.[10] The chapter would be truly international. For the first time Asians would participate.[11] Delegates represented their own countries. Maria Luiza Saade remarked:

> It was a cultural explosion! I realize that I was the delegate from Brazil because I am Brazilian. Mother de Imbert, the superior for a long time, was like the spiritual mother of the vicariate. Logically she ought to have been its representative. The chapter of 1967 was for me a unique experience: I knew the Society through our Constitutions, our documents, the obituaries of deceased sisters and our teachers who had lived in France before the war. All the myths fell away, and I met and loved a Society of flesh and bone, people from different cultures. The delegates represented our complex internationality, which until then was hardly even a matter of geography.

These capitulants however had "differing views on the present and differing expectations for the future, as much in the realm of hopes as of fears." In consequence "Communication required effort and was sometimes difficult."

The special chapter opened with a remarkable speech by Mother de Valon who began by surveying world developments, stressing the growth of

---

[9] Three quarters were superiors.
[10] Françoise Cassiers, delegate of the Vicariate of Jette, was only thirty-three. In 1964, the average age was sixty-five; in 1967 it was sixty-three.
[11] India had for a delegate Mary Braganza, one of the three youngest delegates. The Vicariate of the Far East had for delegates a Japanese, Mother Yoshikawa, and the superior of Seoul, Mother Chu.

scientific and technical culture and "the yearning for freedom, for human dignity, for culture [that] is felt in every class of society and in every nation." She pointed also to the uncertainties, worry and helplessness seen in the world. The Society of the Sacred Heart was to pursue "its apostolic work without losing its fundamental identity, not deviating from the mission that the Church has entrusted to it from the very beginning, but going forward with serenity even amidst danger." She recalled that the Society had strength: "Jesus Christ loved above all by a soul growing each day in supernatural freedom, which enables her to surrender herself completely to the service of humanity." This heritage was to be saved and "shown to the world without any weakness, or apologies meant to humor public opinion, but with the sole desire of being genuine. Our modern world is thirsting for such genuineness. In order that the genuineness of our life should be understood by [people] today," she posed the chief questions, which came as much from world developments as from the desires that the Religious of the Sacred Heart had expressed in the vicariate assemblies. She recognized that "henceforth there is to be a new way of governing…a new understanding of community life" and new forms of religious discipline. The adoption of a new mode of governance must mean for the whole Society, "a broadening, an enrichment, stemming from the responsible contribution of each member, but not a loss of unity, without which the work of the Society would be seriously impaired." About the new ways to obey and to command, she asked: "What shall we do so that all of us may always meet one another in one single supernatural search for the divine will?" About community life: "What shall we do that it may unite us, more than ever, in the charity of Christ, and be for us strength and joy?" About religious discipline: "What shall we do to preserve it in our communities so that they may be houses of peace, sisterly charity and zeal?" She concluded her remarks:

> Are we only to rush into the fevered race of the world, in order to preserve that social prestige, which, in times of faith, was granted to religious? Or rather, is it not more urgent to confirm by our witness – since religious life is a sign – that the spirit of the Gospel is always new, that it can solve all problems and that it will never be "out of date"? I think that our chapter must consider the world today through the Heart of Christ, in order to bring to it more faith, more hope, more charity.

The procedures developed by the general council[12] were adopted without any modifications by the Sacred Congregation for Religious. Some

---

[12] Mother Bultó recalled that it was after reflection on the way of acting of different congregations of religious women and of the Jesuits, but without

innovations had been expected. For the first time French would not be the only language of the assembly, and simultaneous translation in English and Spanish had been arranged. The superior general would preside at the plenary assemblies but would not act as moderator; four vicars, Mothers Drujon, Trias, Barcherini and Elizabeth Sweeney were to moderate in turn. Language groupings were arranged. A coordinating commission of six members that included vicars and delegates, named on 3 October, had the responsibility for the agenda and the direction of the work of the chapter. In some measure working groups on government and the treasury and finances would call on non-capitulants of various nationalities.[13] Finally, a great innovation, the votes were to be registered electronically.

There was some uncertainty about procedure. "Nothing happened for a week…a time of service to the Spirit. That gave the delegates the opportunity to talk. Concerns, conflicts, and anxieties about the direction were clarified; the result was division in the ranks."[14] The criticisms came not only from the delegates but also from some vicars who showed dissatisfaction, even displeasure, at the way Rome had been handling their requests.[15] In 1966, regarding cases submitted to the motherhouse, there had sometimes been orders and counter-orders, even on the same subject, in parallel correspondence from the superior general, one of the assistants general or the secretary general, giving different answers to the same question. Or vicars had not received answers to their requests about finances. This process did not follow earlier practice.[16]

As had happened at the Vatican Council, "When the work began, the procedure, so carefully planned, was rejected. The chapter was paralyzed. It was clear that neither the coordinating commission nor anyone else knew what might happen."[17] Mother de Valon's state of health caused the delegates to feel a weakness in the direction of the Society.[18] As the group was not organizing itself, the Canadians proposed having Mother Katherine McCaffrey come from Montreal to assist the moderators on questions of procedure. This Mother Parliamentarian was warmly welcomed by Mothers

---

copying them, that the general council had decided on it.

[13] Mothers Dillon (Scotland), de Vulpian (France), Hamilton (USA), Konold (Germany), Landivar (Argentina) and Nagamine (Japan).

[14] J. Faber, *Sister Rebecca Ogilvie Forbes*, p. 24. R. Cunningham, *Helen Fitzgerald*, p. 62, speaks of a climate of tension linked to the way the American delegates were proceeding; they were "strong advocates of change."

[15] Many of the vicars had been recently named. Maybe they were not used to acting autonomously in their management.

[16] Testimonies of Andrée Meylan and Mary Elizabeth Tobin.

[17] J. Faber, *Ogilvie Forbes*, p. 24.

[18] Prov. Arch. Canada. Biography of Alice Amyot.

Bultó and Tobin and coolly by Mother de Valon, who was not in on the suggestion. She had to teach the chapter members how to perform in a deliberative assembly, with methods and a vocabulary completely new to the majority of them.[19] She was finally accepted by the Europeans and the Latin Americans who felt that her presence allowed the chapter to move forward.[20]

These new processes undercut the capitulants who were not used to sustained, long discussions. They sometimes felt manipulated by those who spoke in the plenary sessions, on behalf of a number of others.[21] Those most at ease were the religious from the United States, who "expressed themselves more directly and more freely. They grew empowered by their organized reflection groups aimed at helping them develop their ideas and understand the course of events."[22] They met in the evening to prepare for the sessions of the next day, but they welcomed into their groups religious of other nationalities.[23] They had done the same thing before the chapter, profiting from those meetings to try to identify common ideas. A meeting of mistresses general in Montreal in April 1967 had been an opportunity for the delegates of the United States and Canada to get together. At the end they sent the motherhouse suggestions concerning the agenda of the chapter. This meeting, perceived as a national or international "mini-chapter" had created "some excitement"[24] in Rome and the fear that the Americans were trying to take control of the chapter.[25] It took time for some delegates to discover that work was being done in the corridors as

---

[19] She had to define what was meant by a motion and explain limiting their interventions. Toward 15 November the assembly was able to move with greater ease through the maze of the procedure (Gen. Arch. C 1 C 3, Box 21, procès-verbal of the sessions of the chapter). The activity carried out in 1967 by Mother McCaffrey was considered so useful that she was invited again to play the same role at the Chapter of 1970.

[20] Biographies of Mothers Whitehead, Amyot and McCaffrey.

[21] Testimony of Marie-Thérèse Carré. They also ended up forming a kind of pressure group.

[22] Testimony of M.E. Tobin. Mother Fitzgerald, in spite of her age (she was seventy-two), was a real leader of the Anglophone group.

[23] Testimony of Anne-Marie Guizard. The knowledge of English of certain Francophone delegates helped them then, although most of the English-speaking religious could speak French. Conversations in the evening among religious of the same nationality were facilitated by the fact that in the assignment of rooms delegates had been grouped by nationality.

[24] R. Cunningham, p. 62. Mother Fitzgerald wrote, on 11 June 1967, about these reactions that were in the air: "We thought that it was a good moment to exchange ideas, to be more and better informed about the thinking of others. We never thought about a national or international chapter."

[25] Testimony of M.E. Tobin.

well as in the formal sessions and that it was useful not to spend too much time in one's room.[26] Some of them did not understand that they could offer arguments different from those of the superior general.[27] As for the latter, she was ill at ease during the discussions and sessions, which seemed to her to drag on interminably. She was "reduced to silence," as she had often said and written during the preparation of the chapter. "The fact that Mother de Valon, who was presiding at the chapter, had to yield her place [to a moderator] while a parliamentarian controlled the discussion in the assembly was for her a major change, for nothing like that had ever happened before in the Society."[28] There were some awkward moments. On 26 October when the capitulants were going to attend the meeting of the pope and the patriarch Athenagoras at the Basilica of St. Paul Outside the Walls, Mother Fitzgerald proposed to Mother de Valon to hold a second session of the chapter, if necessary, "in the good old United States," as other congregations had done. "Mother de Valon was interested but she told me she did not think we would have two sessions."[29] That comment must not have eased her suspicions of the influence the capitulants from America could have or wished to have.

Mother de Valon's discomfort was evident, and her exhaustion increased in proportion. The question of her health was being raised more and more openly, chiefly by those in the chapter who thought they had to face reality. The testimony of Marthe Jacobs, delegate from Congo and member of the coordinating commission, makes this point:

> Thanks to my knowledge of English, I formed close contacts with our American sisters. Through them I learned the truth about Mother de Valon's health and could then see for myself the signs of the illness from

---

[26] It was Mother Dillon who encouraged the Irish delegates to act thus (Testimony of D. Boland).

[27] Testimony of Mary Braganza. "Three of us were sermonized by one or two of the oldest vicars who said firmly: 'When the Mother General speaks, you remain silent and answer respectfully "Yes, Very Reverend Mother,"' but other vicars like Mother Ogilvie Forbes and Mother Fitzgerald encouraged us to speak with the respect and conviction that the chapter merited." She continued, "Mother de Valon had shown special affection to the delegates from India; therefore, it was hard not to accept her comments. Often I had to take my courage in both hands and say what I was feeling because the vicar of India, Mother Winifred Ward, had chosen to keep silence. We were surprised and hurt when Mother de Valon called us one day and said: 'I have always loved India and the Indian sisters, but you have betrayed me.'"

[28] Testimony of M.E. Tobin.

[29] R. Cunningham, pp. 64-65.

which she suffered. When I was quite convinced, I spoke of it to my vicar, Reverend Mother Goffinet. What was my surprise to hear her say: "That is not correct. We had a meeting of the Mothers Vicar this afternoon. We asked about the state of health of our Very Reverend Mother. The answer was that she could very well continue in her office of superior general." One understands why dear Mother Goffinet could not believe my words.... There were differences in the way events were interpreted, and the mail that we received indicated the astonishment in the vicariate of Congo where the letters from the vicar and those from the delegate did not reflect the same opinion or the same state of mind. This is an example of the confusion probably felt in all the vicariates.[30]

At least in those who were told what was happening, which was not generally the case. Eleven years later, Marthe Jacobs said this about what had happened:

Objectively, it seems to me that in all these events, filial spirit and emotion had a predominant place to the detriment of a lucid, objective view of the facts that would have required a courage unknown to us then. Only the climate in which we lived can explain why, before the chapter, the Mothers assistant general had not sought advice from the Sacred Congregation of Religious on the subject of the government of the Society, which they knew to be hampered by the state of health of our Very Reverend Mother. If the chapter members had been informed quite clearly and tactfully, how much tension could have been avoided. Always, the patterns of an entrenched filial piety had to be taken into account to explain what, objectively, one would be tempted to consider mistakes in the matter of government.

One might well think that the assistants general had not fully played their parts. But could they have?[31] In the Society of the Sacred Heart every word of authority was accepted at face value, and the absence of discussion was a form of respect and obedience, even for members of the general council.

The question of government appeared quite soon to be the crucial one.[32] Mother Tobin wrote on the subject:

---

[30] Report written about 1978. Marthe Jacobs recounted also how in letters to her community she gave details, but not all of them in an effort to avoid what could have contradicted what the vicar was writing because she saw the events through a different lens.

[31] Mother Bultó thought it was impossible.

[32] According to Mother Tobin, the second worrisome question was that of flexibility of times of prayer. As Mother Bultó remarked, the principal

We all knew that one of the recommendations of Vatican II stipulated that a superior general was to be named for a limited term, six, eight or ten years. It was the question of a superior general named for life that was really the subject of the crisis that occurred during the chapter of 1967. A first schema on government had been elaborated, discussed, sent back to committee before another discussion in the assembly. Several proposals had been made: a term of four years, renewable once; or six years renewable once; finally ten years, not renewable. Following long discussions, Mother de Valon brought some members together and gave her opinion in favor of a ten year term renewable once. Never in the Society had a superior general governed for such a long time.[33] In fact, it was a way of proposing government for life in disguise; that was unacceptable to the chapter delegates. Then the question arose whether Mother de Valon was still to govern the Society in the future and whether it would really be possible for her to put into effect the changes recommended by Vatican II. The question provoked much discussion. It seems to me that this crisis of government in the Society caused the assembly of delegates to divide into two parties. A first party was composed of religious who, out of loyalty to the person of Mother de Valon, thought she ought to continue to govern the Society aided by assistants general who could second her.[34] They believed that loyalty toward a person was what the Society needed. Another party was formed by those who saw that Mother de Valon was no longer able to govern the Society. They saw that the Society had to enter a new era. For them loyalty to the Society outweighed loyalty to a person. Faced with the polarization of the delegates, we could not move forward.

The predicament affected everything. Opposition was strengthening, and the capitulants felt guilty of adding to a destructive atmosphere without wishing to do so. During this period Mother Ogilvie Forbes took an unheard of step. She had decided that Mother de Valon was not in a state to deal with the situation and that that she should resign. She confided in Mother Bultó who begged her not to do anything.[35] Disregarding this

---

questions for Mother de Valon were those of government and prayer: "For her, apostolic life was worth whatever prayer was worth."

[33] Except for the founder and Mother Lehon who governed the Society for almost twenty years but with serious difficulties at the end.

[34] Confirmed by C. Leitner and M.J. Bultó. Still one may wonder whether this was a tenable position and whether a superior general could continue to govern in case of serious illness.

[35] Testimony of M.J. Bultó.

sensible advice, the English vicar asked for a meeting with Mother de Valon. The interview was put off because of an outbreak of flu.

> When Mother de Valon was able to leave her room, I was ill myself. One day while I was convalescing, I was stretched out on my bed fully dressed. Mother de Valon knocked on my door and came in. I got up and fell on my knees. "No, no lie down again," she said. I said that I could say only on my knees what I had to tell her. I said, "I believe that you must be made aware of what is being said outside the meeting room; one hears much criticism there." I don't remember my exact words; I called it real distress. For a moment we spoke about it: "Then what do you think can be done?" she asked me. "Perhaps you could resign," I said. She seemed displeased. I added: "I ask you only one thing; it is not to take action that cannot be undone."[36] One of the assistants general told me later that she had told them that a vicar in whom she had confidence had advised her to resign.[37]

The prefect of the Sacred Congregation for Religious learned what was going on at the Via Nomentana, thanks to Father Molinari, S.J., who was fulfilling the office of advisor at the chapter and who supported some of the capitulants in the difficulties that were arising. Cardinal Antoniutti wanted the chapter to take place under the best possible conditions, given the influence that the Society of the Sacred Heart exercised in the religious world, and he wanted the procedure to be observed perfectly.[38] He invited Mother de Valon and her assistants general to come to see him. In the course of the interview, which took place on 6 November 1967, the cardinal brought up the question of agenda and among others,

> the probable increase in the number of assistants general, the suggestion that the current five resign to allow for the election of seven. When it came to the question of the superior general elected for life, Our Mother asked if it would be good to offer her resignation. The cardinal said it would be a beautiful gesture and quite in the spirit of the [Vatican] Council. Then they went on to discuss other terms of office; everything that concerned the chapter interested the cardinal very much.

[36] Testimony of R. Ogilvie Forbes, April 1991.
[37] J. Faber, *Ogilvie Forbes*, p. 25. It was doubtless Mother Bultó, to whom Mother Ogilvie Forbes was very close. Mother Bultó told that when Mother de Valon reported the contents of that conversation to her assistants general, Mothers Paradeis and Caracciolo cried: "Oh no! Very Reverend Mother!" She herself kept silence.
[38] Testimony of Paolo Molinari.

Upon returning "the Mothers talked about what the cardinal had said, and they thought of bringing in Father Molinari to ask him how best to proceed."[39] Some were leaning toward the resignation of the assistants general, but not necessarily that of the superior general. In any case, even if a collective resignation could be considered, nothing suggested that there would be a unilateral decision.

On 7 November 1967, when Mother Barcherini was moderator, the agenda included the presentation of a second report on the government. After saying the opening prayer, Mother de Valon asked to speak:

> What I have to say is serious and I desire that each one understand my words very exactly. For the greatest good of all of you, I offer my resignation as superior general. I repeat: it is for the greatest good of all of you. Let no one say that I am ill; it is not true. I am going to allow you to pursue the chapter without me; I will be happy to leave for the missions as soon as possible.

Then she left the room after handing the moderator the typed text of her intervention, dated the evening before. She had added by hand: "For the truth of the history of the Society." She had decided to resign without consulting the general council, who were astonished.

> The assistants general followed Our Very Reverend Mother out of the chapter hall; everyone was painfully stunned. When they came back after a few minutes that seemed like a long time, R.M. Bultó told us in the name of the assistants general that it was a painful surprise for them also, that the session was evidently over, and it was suggested that we go to the chapel.

She asked us "to pray much, to think of the Society, the good of the Society, of Our Mother who had worn herself out for the Society." In the meantime Mother de Valon had gone on foot to the Trinità.

This departure left the capitulants in a state of shock and utter confusion. "Many were angry and saddened that the superior general seemed so 'broken and sad' and believed that a disaster had befallen the Society. It was a difficult time to keep one's inner balance; few knew how to handle a situation beset by divisions and conflicts."[40] The situation was problematic, because without a president the chapter was considered interrupted from the canonical point of view. Mother de Valon had just

---

[39] *Procès-verbal* of 6-10 November 1967.
[40] J. Faber, *Ogilvie Forbes*, p. 25.

taken two actions that were going to weigh heavily in the following days. She had left the chapter without having asked for authorization. The consequent interruption of the work would permit the Church to intervene. Neither the superior general nor the assistants nor the capitulants realized that; neither did they foresee its effects. The Constitutions no longer had the force of law. The decision to be made concerning the resignation of Mother de Valon was no longer a matter for the Society of the Sacred Heart but for the Church alone. Religious of the Sacred Heart did not like to see the Church intervene in their government because of the autonomy the congregation enjoyed and the problems the founder had had to face. Therefore before anything else could happen, Mother de Valon had to come back to the motherhouse, as many of the capitulants were asking. It was also what Father Molinari advised; he thought the chapter's work had to continue, with the resignation of the superior general to be considered only at the end of the session. Finally it was decided that "a vote of confidence in our Mother General" be taken the same day at the end of the afternoon. Those close to Mother de Valon wanted it, and might be favorable; since as Mother Ogilvie Forbes thought, "many capitulants would have renamed her through pity."[41] When he was consulted, Father Molinari advised against it. The coordinating commission made the same request, because the serene atmosphere needed for a vote was not present. The vote was therefore put off.

In the course of the day, 8 November, Mother Bultó, who as dean of the general council presided at the chapter, took charge of the situation, asking the capitulants to take up the work in committees, since they could not hold plenary assemblies, to maintain "serenity, discretion, and according to the decrees, great mutual charity and to let themselves be guided by the Spirit of Jesus." It was likely that the assistants general were asked about the health of Mother de Valon in this session, "for we knew nothing about it," affirmed Mother Ogilvie Forbes: "They answered our questions as well as they could, and a statement made earlier by her physician clarified the matter for everyone. He had said [to the assistants general]: 'If the Mother General offers her resignation, do not put pressure on her to change her mind.'"[42] The delegate from Australia, Mother Mary d'Apice, had already raised the question of health in the Society of the Sacred Heart and of the means of helping those who were ill. She had said, "Sisters, the Constitutions remind us that sickness is a gift of God as well as

---

[41] J. Faber. Confirmed by Andrée Meylan who notes that "Certain delegates were saying that this resignation was a stratagem to ensure a reaction in her favor." She adds, "I don't believe that."

[42] Testimony of R. Ogilvie Forbes.

health."[43] However, Mother de Valon's health and the circumstances of her resignation were spoken to directly by the secretary general, Mother Andrée Meylan, who was infirmarian. Her intervention was crucial:

> No one asked me to say anything. During my adoration I felt very strongly that I had to say something. I asked for the floor at the plenary session facilitated by Mother Barcherini. I believe that what I tried to do was to show that this sudden resignation was not a lack of religious spirit but the consequence of a psychological state (I certainly did not employ this word!) that meant that she no longer had the strength to carry out her responsibilities. Not everyone understood my intervention. Several of the French mothers in particular held it against me during part of the chapter; but at the end they came very kindly to say good-bye and thank you. I had no experience; I had written nothing; but I know that several capitulants appreciated [my intervention].

The assistants general went to the Trinità to try to work out a solution with Mother de Valon, who "listened to them kindly but said that she had reached the limit of her strength and could return only after the acceptance or refusal of her resignation." No doubt they did not mention a proposal made to them at about that time, according to which Mother de Valon, if she were re-elected, would remain in office only for three years. In the afternoon the assistants general reminded Father Molinari that the Constitutions stipulated that the resignation of a superior general had to be accepted or refused by a general congregation. "The Reverend Father, who is not a canonist, cannot pronounce on the point, but he believes that the resignation cannot be decided upon during a special chapter, according to the Constitutions. He advises consultation with Cardinal Antoniutti."[44] He thought, like the majority of the assistants general, that since Mother de Valon had offered her resignation without conditions, the vote of the chapter could only be unconditional.

Just at the moment when the assistants general were getting ready to go to the Sacred Congregation to meet the prefect, the superior of the Trinità dei Monti, Mother Jeanne de Bodman, who was a delegate, telephoned from the Trinità to say that Mother de Valon was willing to go back to the chapter, since without her it could not continue its work. The assistants general therefore went to the Trinità. "They met with Our Mother, who was serene and ready to return." Mother de Valon returned to the motherhouse

---

[43] Testimony of M.L. Saade, who says that it was the next day after Mother de Valon announced her resignation.

[44] Report of the general secretariat posted but not given to the delegates.

in the morning after having been assured that the chapter would decide on the question of her resignation or remaining at the head of the Society.

The vote was planned for the end of the afternoon, giving the capitulants time to consult one another. The coordinating commission, believing that a meeting of all the vicars would not produce conclusive results, decided to consult some vicars who were "particularly open,"[45] but of mature age and well thought of by all: Mothers Ogilvie Forbes of England, Ward of India, Thywissen of Netherlands and Trias of Northern Spain. At the end of this meeting, they decided to ask Mother de Valon to delay the session until the next day, since the vote had not been proposed according to the procedure accepted at the beginning of the chapter. The objective was to gain time in order to allow some delegates to make a visit privately to Cardinal Antoniutti. Neither the assistants general nor the members of the coordinating commission would take part. Mother de Valon accepted this delay, "although that was painful for her,"[46] in fact, without knowing what was at stake in the immediate future.

The plenary session in the afternoon was dedicated to the examination of the following proposal: "Do you wish our Very Reverend Mother to take up again the government of the Society until the next chapter?" Confusion was evident in the wording, because Mother de Valon was still superior general in as much as her resignation had not been approved. Modifications were proposed: "Do you accept the resignation of our Very Reverend Mother?" or "Do you accept that our Very Reverend Mother govern until the next chapter?" The results would be decided by an absolute majority of the ballots "*placet*" or "*non placet*." Blank ballots were not to be considered in the count. Some capitulants hoped that a vote of confidence in favor of Mother de Valon would clarify the situation.

On the morning of 10 November the group delegated to visit Cardinal Antoniutti was composed of Mothers Ogilvie Forbes, Ward[47] and Thywissen; Mother Trias, who preferred not to take part because of her close ties with Mother Bultó, was replaced by Mother Concepción Camacho, a delegate. Mother Jacobs was the only member of the coordinating commission to join the group.[48] They wanted to inform

---

[45] Testimony of M. Jacobs.
[46] Report of the general secretariat. Gabriela Belón, in the name of the coordinating commission, informed Mother de Valon of it. "Later during a tête-à-tête, she told me I had made her suffer very much" (Prov. Arch. Peru).
[47] Mary Braganza insisted that she go to the Sacred Congregation.
[48] A question was raised for a long time about Mother Fitzgerald's presence at this meeting. Some of her contemporaries thought that she had taken part, others not. This last hypothesis is correct, for the religious from the United States were too much suspected of wanting to play a strong role in the chapter

the cardinal that they were not satisfied with the way the chapter was proceeding and to ask his advice on the subject of the afternoon's vote. The prefect said that in a special chapter the Constitutions are not applicable as they would be in an ordinary chapter. Therefore the acceptance of the resignation of the superior general was a matter for the jurisdiction of the Church. He told his visitors that he would come to preside at the afternoon session and that there would be no vote. Upon their return to the motherhouse they told Mother Bultó about their interview. She knew of their visit, but she asked that the interview with the prefect of the Sacred Congregation be reported to the assistants general all together. As Marthe Jacobs relates: "The Mothers thanked us. We left them at peace, for the matter was in the hands of Holy Church. But we absolutely had no idea how things were going to develop, except that there would be no vote in the afternoon. We agreed among ourselves that we would say nothing to anyone about our visit, but that we would inform the coordinating commission that there would be no vote in the evening. That we did."[49]

Cardinal Antoniutti asked that the dean of the assistants general get in touch with him. Mother Bultó immediately went to see him with the other assistants general.

> The cardinal told them that Father Molinari had informed him of the resignation, and he asked why this resignation had not been communicated to the Sacred Congregation. The Mothers had counted on coming yesterday, but Our Mother's return had prevented them from doing so. Concerning the question of the vote the cardinal said: "It is up to the Holy See to accept the resignation of the Mother General or not." And as the Reverend Mothers showed him our Constitutions, the cardinal observed that a special chapter is not governed according to the Constitutions and that the Holy See accepts the resignation of Our Very Reverend Mother. The Reverend Mothers returned with feelings one can imagine.[50]

---

for Mother Fitzgerald, whose prudence and wisdom all witnesses underline, to have taken part in a move that could have been considered compromising.

[49] Report of M. Jacobs. Upon her return to Congo, Mother Jacobs did not refer to her participation in this meeting. It was at the time of the Chapter of 1970, of which she was a member, that Clotilde Meeûs learned of it "from the mouth of several provincials who admired her courage."

[50] Summary of the session of 24 November. "Some delegates asked Mother Bultó if there had been approaches to the cardinal before the one in question. R.M. Bultó did not know but the general council had not made any. A conversation took place between Father Molinari and the cardinal; Father Molinari allowed it to be told. Here is the point of it: Father Molinari was

Maybe it was during this meeting that the assistants general provided the Sacred Congregation with a "memorandum of all the problems encountered up to that time"[51] Were there other approaches to the Sacred Congregation, coming from another "side"? The records are silent in this regard.

A little before five o'clock in the afternoon of 10 November, Mother Meylan came to announce to the chapter that Cardinal Antoniutti would preside at the session. The prefect met with Mother de Valon beforehand and informed her that he accepted her resignation. Then he entered the chapter hall with her. We read in the *procès-verbal* of the sessions,

> His Eminence spoke to us with great kindness, explaining that his visit was prompted by the sudden resignation of the Mother General, but that he would certainly have come at some point to be formally present at our chapter, as he does for all religious during renewal. He then said that he was among us as cardinal prefect of the Sacred Congregation of Religious to accept in the name of the Holy See the resignation of Our Mother, to tell her how edified he was by this act of humility that was such a beautiful example and a sign of openness to the spirit of the Church and of the Council, to thank her for all that she has done for the institute, her zeal, her devotedness, her spirit of sacrifice. The cardinal prefect said, "A special post-conciliar chapter has many powers, but it does not have that of accepting or not the resignation of a Mother General in the middle of the chapter. The Sacred Congregation therefore has studied all the aspects of this act of the Very Reverend Mother who has resigned and has accepted it. The general council remains in charge; the first councilor becomes vicar general; she takes over the direction of the affairs of the institute temporarily; elections will take place at the end of the chapter presided over by the vicar general." Then His Eminence gave us some fine recommendations concerning the work of the chapter

---

talking to the cardinal about other congregations and the cardinal asked, 'How is the general chapter going at the Sacred Heart?' Father explained that they were considering government structures and envisaging a term limit for the general. 'That's a good thing,' said the cardinal who had teased Father Molinari about the generalate for life of the father general of the Society of Jesus. After a few more questions Father noted that there was tension at the chapter and the cardinal suggested: 'Have the secretary general come. No, have the Mother General and the assistants general come.' The cardinal is following all general chapters very closely at present." It can be seen that Mother Bultó makes no mention of the visit of 10 November, about which she was informed but for which she did not take responsibility.

[51] Testimony of M.E. Tobin.

that would assure the renewal of the institute in the light of the Council while remaining faithful to the spirit of our founder, which is a spirit of humility, of sacrifice, of union with God, of consecration to the service of God in the Church. Having thanked Our Mother again, saying among other things, "Men pass on, but the works remain," [sic] His Eminence asked us to accept all the aspects of this suffering in a supernatural spirit and for the building up of the mystical body of which we are all members. After giving us his blessing, His Eminence wished to greet each of the Reverend Mothers of the chapter.[52]

When Cardinal Antoniutti indicated that the resignation of Mother de Valon had been accepted, Mother Drujon leapt from her chair with the Constitutions in her hand and tried in vain to speak, saying their provisions had not been respected. The cardinal paid no attention.[53] The cardinal's remarks had seemed interminable to everyone, and no doubt he was annoyed.

Mother de Valon left the motherhouse on 11 November, "profoundly broken."[54] While this departure was difficult to live through for her, it was equally troubling for the spectators, in spite of the bouquet given at the last minute. Mother de Valon stayed in Naples until 20 November; she then left for a short trip to Greece before arriving in Egypt where Mother María Josefa Ustara had offered to welcome her in Heliopolis.[55] She was greeted one last time on the evening of her departure by some capitulants who wanted to accompany her and whom Mother Bultó herself had encouraged to do so.[56] Mothers Caracciolo and Paradeis resigned from their office of assistant general and their role as capitulants. Mother Paradeis, who had written that on no condition did she want to remain at the motherhouse, left Rome on 18 December for Heliopolis, where she spent a month with Mother de Valon before going to Brazil.

Although a troubling situation had been settled, sadly the atmosphere at the chapter did not improve, because the visit of the five capitulants to Cardinal Antoniutti had not been understood. "For Mother de Valon and for the minority who were favorable to her this step and its result – the cardinal's coming to the session at which there was supposed to have been

---

[52] *Procès-verbal* of the session of 10 November 1967.
[53] Testimony of R. Ogilvie Forbes, L. de la Taille and C. Camacho.
[54] Letter to A. Las Casas, 11 November 1973.
[55] She was accompanied by Carlotta Leitner who had agreed to remain with her.
[56] Mother Bultó asked Mothers Ogilvie Forbes and Allpress to go to Naples to say good-bye to Mother de Valon: "I expressed," recounted Mother Ogilvie Forbes, "my gratitude for all Mother de Valon had done for the vicariate, but no allusion was made to what had just taken place."

a vote – appeared as a frustration and a betrayal."[57] Maybe because of the skimpy information that most of the delegates had about it, that step had contributed to the climate of suspicion that prevailed. Furthermore, it increased the sadness, even bitterness, of those who believed that an injustice had been committed against Mother de Valon, since she had not been allowed to express herself and to take back her resignation. The division between the majority and the minority was not based on national considerations; but, as Mother Ogilvie Forbes pointed out, maybe the French delegates were furious more because of the way events had developed than from personal attachment to Mother de Valon.[58] The minority was composed of almost all the capitulants from France, Italy, Austria, Germany, Ireland, Southern Spain and some representatives of South America. Mother Drujon was considered the spokesperson of this group,[59] which represented about one third of the chapter.

It was only on 24 November that the issue of the information to be given to the Society apropos of the resignation of Mother de Valon was brought up in a plenary session. It was a question of informing "with tact and according to the needs of each vicariate," the vicars giving the details they judged useful. Mother Bultó reviewed the history of the 6th and 7th of November and concluded her remarks with the wish that "we will speak no more of these events and that we will share the heart-suffering with Our Lord, for silence will certainly be very agreeable to him." The remarks she made afterwards show that the religious favorable to Mother de Valon thought that the Holy See had not really supported the former superior general. They were also critical of those among them who had gone to the Sacred Congregation. They felt that in taking up their cause Cardinal Antoniutti had not allowed Mother de Valon a way out:[60]

> When the Church exercises its unquestionable authority, we must accept it unconditionally; it is the expectation of the Church not to be disappointed. We must never challenge the authority of one of its decisions. Our Mother would never want that. The Church asks that we

---

[57] Testimony of L. de la Taille. Besides, Mother de Valon presented it as such afterwards.
[58] Testimony of M-T. Carré. For them the *Constitutions* had not been respected.
[59] Testimony of Eleonora Carloni.
[60] It is clear that Cardinal Antoniutti decided quickly to accept Mother de Valon's resignation. Although the assistants general were informed of the decision he had made before his arrival at the Via Nomentana, it may be that some of them believed in a reversal until the very last minute.

continue the chapter. The rule tells us: "Its fate is in their hands."[61] We must do everything to maintain our mutual confidence in one another and also the confidence of the Society in the chapter, so as to realize fully the *Cor unum et anima una in Corde Jesu*.

At the conclusion of the chapter Mother Bultó asked the capitulants to write their memories of these "incredible days" and required that these texts be kept in the general archives to be opened only after the death of the last capitulant. As a consequence, this writer did not have access to these documents, and in order to reconstitute the events, she has had to limit herself to the memories of those who were willing to share them with her.

A feeling of distress and aloneness was widespread in the two camps, to the point that Mother Ogilvie Forbes wrote toward the end of the Chapter that she hoped to arrive at the outcome so as to avoid more discussion.[62] As Mary Coke wrote humorously, "This chapter put an end to the *entente cordiale* between our two countries, France and England, for some time,"[63] since Mother Ogilvie Forbes was the first, perhaps the only, person who had frankly told Mother de Valon that there was a current of opinion unfavorable to her government and had suggested that she might resign. The strongest pressure was certainly exercised against Mother Bultó, but no one dared accuse her openly of having wanted to take Mother de Valon's place. She received letters from several vicariates from people incensed about what had just happened. In one, a religious from France wrote: "Have we gone back to the time of the Abbé de Saint-Estève and Mother Baudemont?" She was comparing the current situation to the one that nearly made Mother Barat an outcast from the Society of which she was superior general. With tact and good sense, Marthe Jacobs has explained the sometimes painful reactions that were then apparent:

> In a closed atmosphere like that of our chapter in 1967 and considering the feelings of a good number of capitulants who were little prepared to handle such events, it is not surprising that there were mistrust, suspicions and other signs of distress. We remain women.... But if we look at all the instances taken together, it is certain that each one did what she believed she must do for the true good of the Society.

---

[61] That is to say: the fate of the Society, [which] in the *Constitutions* is in the hands of the professed, is here in the hands of the delegates.

[62] J. Faber, *Ogilvie Forbes*, p. 25. She reinforced her bonds with Mother Fitzgerald and as token of union and friendship they exchanged rings.

[63] Letter of 13 April 1991 to C. de la Martinière.

As for Father Molinari, he told the delegates that the crisis made them suffer greatly because they loved one another greatly.[64]

When Cardinal Antoniutti was informed of the murmuring that was going on, out of compassion for the vicar general, he suggested holding the election of the superior general sooner than had been planned. Father Arrupe, who was of the same mind, asked one of his assistants general, Father Giuliani, to postpone a trip in order to preach the triduum prior to the election. On the last evening Mother Bultó met with him to ask the following question: "Do you think I may accept being Mother General if I am named?" Father Giuliani answered: "Not only may you accept, but you must, for at this moment to accept this office is nothing else than to accept a cross. And to refuse it is to refuse the cross of the Lord."[65]

The election took place in the presence of Father Molinari. Mother Bultó had to read the names on the ballots. The "minority" had found a candidate in the person of Mother Dorothy Eyre, who had shown a great deal of compassion to those suffering from Mother de Valon's resignation. Some votes went to Mother Drujon, or a Brazilian religious and a few others. In the hall emotion ran high and the silence deep. Mother Ogilvie Forbes reported the way the session unfolded: "I was seated in the first row, beside Mother Fitzgerald. She said to me that she would not count the votes but would say her beads. I answered that I was going to count; the first one to obtain sixty votes would be elected. At sixty I poked Mother Fitzgerald, but I think she had been counting too!"

Mother Bultó was elected superior general on 5 December 1967, on the first ballot with sixty-seven votes. "Poor Mother, she was seated on the platform, completely exhausted. After a few words addressed to the capitulants, they paid homage by kissing her hand, which was also a kiss of peace.[66] That was all, then the chapter took up its regular work."[67] Mother Bultó said that she would be superior general for only three years. Mothers Tobin and Meliá were re-elected. Three new assistants general were named: Mothers Barbara Nicholls, Kiyoko Wakamatsu[68] and Madeleine Drujon. A new secretary general was appointed in the person of Mother Barbara Napier.[69] These nominations showed that the Society wanted to have Asia

---

[64] Testimony of M.L. Saade.
[65] Testimony of M.J. Bultó.
[66] The ceremonial surrounding the election had been considerably simplified: the delegates were to recite the oath together, not to kneel at the moment of the election and there was not to be homage but a kiss of peace.
[67] Testimony of R. Ogilvie Forbes.
[68] Neither one was a capitulant. Mother Wakamatsu had been the first Japanese mistress of novices. Mother Nicholls was the superior at Chun Cheon, Korea.
[69] Mother Napier was mistress of novices in India.

represented in its government.[70] Mother Keogh had proposed a regional structure, spreading out from the central government and based on the recognition of "cultural blocs."[71] For Maria Luiza Saade, while the health of Mother de Valon had been "the material cause of division in the chapter, the principal cause had been culture shock." That shock had already been alluded to in a remark by the Japanese delegate who said publicly: "When I entered the convent, I left my family and my country but also my culture, my language to take on a western mentality."

Nominating Mother Drujon was a way to have the leader of the minority and, in a roundabout way, a French religious on the general council. This choice did not bother anyone, for Mother Drujon, who died in December 1969, had always shown her proven loyalty and love of the Society. Mother Bultó, at her death, rendered her this homage: "Reverend Mother Drujon has been an invaluable help to me through her unfailing loyalty, her wise counsel, her support in every circumstance. I guessed that she was very close to the Lord; her reactions were always supernatural. Her approach was always marked by simplicity and kindness. Always ready to help, to serve, she accomplished tasks given to her without the slightest delay. She worked in council meetings in that same spirit of service, that loyalty, that peaceful calm. She suffered with the Church and with the Society, but her confidence always prevailed."[72]

The Orientations of the Chapter

It is clear that there were two chapters in 1967. The first was marked by the unexpected events that took place during the first few weeks, and it ended, after a fashion, when the deliberations had to be interrupted after the resignation of Mother de Valon. It had put an end to a world. A second stage began after the nomination of a new chapter president. The work, which could then continue, resulted in Orientations *ad experimentum*, which were reported to all the communities, an innovation. They were voted unanimously minus one vote; the divisions around Mother de Valon's resignation had had no effect on their being approved.

---

[70] The choice of two religious from the Vicariate of the Far East was surely urged by Mother Keogh who had an undeniable influence in the course of the different general congregations and chapters in which she participated, in particular, in 1967 and 1970. Some expressions in the final text of 1967 come from her, particularly the definition of a Religious of the Sacred Heart as "poor, free, available, attached to nothing" (Testimony of T. Chu).

[71] M. Williams, *The Society of the Sacred Heart in the Far East*, p. 239.

[72] *Mère Madeleine Drujon*, p. 36.

Defining itself as a congregation of apostolic life, the Society of the Sacred Heart took as its starting point social needs, which varied from country to country. In light of this diversity a government had to be worked out to make service to the Church possible.[73]

> Consecrated as we are to education, ours is an apostolic institute whose life has its source in intimate union with Christ and serves "Christ himself in his members." Love of the Incarnate Word must inspire not only our life but its structure, and these should be oriented to our service in the apostolate.
>
> One of the duties of the Chapter is to remove anything that prevents our responding effectively to the call of the Church: identification with particular social classes, triumphalism, an air of self-satisfaction, the tendency to stress structures rather than persons, and a certain lack of charity among ourselves.
>
> Since the Church has trusted us with the work of education, we must respond by giving an individual and collective witness to justice, authenticity, freedom and love.
>
> We want to face facts: two-thirds of the world goes hungry; two hundred fifty million children lack education; the promotion of women poses its own problems. We must extend our apostolate to include all social classes.[74]

The vicariate assemblies had wanted to take into account the conciliar decrees. The orientations were based on *Gaudium et spes*, *Lumen gentium* and *Populorum progressio*. While in the body of the congregation social awareness had only emerged slowly, in 1967, the capitulants were influenced by powerful experiments already made and filled with a desire for works that offered a sometimes disturbing vision of religious life in the world.[75] As a result, in the course of their preparatory work, they had elaborated a schema entitled "The Society of the Sacred Heart, an apostolic institute in the Church and the world today," which found its place in the final document. In her inaugural speech, Mother de Valon took the same view. Later she had presented a study on the redistribution of personnel, urging her hearers to regroup their energies so as to respond to the needs of dioceses and growing urbanization. As Helen Condon recalled, one third of the lectures planned by

---

[73] Theresa Chu recounted that there was a discussion among the delegates, the more conservative wishing to define the identity of the Society before broaching the question of mission, the others wishing to present the mission first, then "clarify the identity in the light of the mission."

[74] *Orientations*, pp. 20-21.

[75] Cardinal Suenens' book, *The Nun in the World*, was one of those.

the general council dealt with social questions.[76] The chapter had explored the needs, hopes and values of the world and the Society's service in that light. "Gradually and painfully the final position paper evolved, a statement that expressed our opening to the contemporary world, recognized the Society's failures and called us to a more authentic, more realistic religious life...."

> The dignity of the human person, basic rights and values set forth in this first paper approved by the Chapter are key ideas more fully developed in the statement on Apostolic Life. This is a remarkable paper whose significance seems only recently to have been recognized. There is no hedging: God is calling us to broaden our educational mission and to work for social justice."[77] The Society of the Sacred Heart, in widening the apostolic field of its members as a response to calls heard in one or another country was directing itself toward "pluriformity."

The government evolved in its structures and in its spirit. The principles of subsidiarity, decentralization, co-responsibility and participation were presented as means of fostering growth, responsibility in obedience, adaptation to the new rhythms of life of the times, collective projects and consultation; for responsibilities would be shared "in spite of the risk of error." Common problems would have to be studied together: order of day, religious discipline, community life, our current and possibly new works and the financial situation. "This new form of government is not found in the Constitutions, but it is implied in the thought of St. Madeleine Sophie and its authority derives from God."[78]

The style of government was revised. Provinces replaced vicariates. Superiors were to be named after consultation with the religious. The length of their term was limited. Councils were created at every level. Their functions, their composition, the frequency of meetings were all defined. A renewal of offices was called for, with alternation between the service of government and "another duty," without clarity about whether the decision was applicable at every level. The return to the ranks was to

---

[76] One was presented by Frank Norris, a layman who had been an auditor at the Vatican Council and had worked for a long time in social service activity. Another on the means of social communication was given by the brother of a Religious of the Sacred Heart, Father Poisson, a Sulpician who worked in the secretariat of the Pontifical Commission for Social Communications. The other on poverty and its consequences was given by an American Jesuit, Philip Land, a member of the Pontifical Commission for Justice and Peace.

[77] Prov. Arch. United States, Helen Condon, "The Chapter of 1967 and Beyond: Some Insights."

[78] *Orientations*, p. 20.

foster an attitude of dependence on God's Will and availability to God's service; to secure a normal source of vitality and of renewal for the Society at the different levels of government; to allow more religious to participate more directly in the functioning and development of the Society; to allow superiors to be available for other apostolic tasks; to facilitate changing office holders without implying a lack of confidence.[79] The intention of this new style was to share authority.

All the general chapters would hold elections. Generalate for life was abolished, but re-election was possible, as in the cases later of Mothers Camacho and McLaughlin. "In the event of the death, serious illness or resignation of the superior general, the assistant who is longest in office will assume the government of the Society during the interim, which should not exceed six months. She will convoke an extraordinary general chapter." The office of vicar general was therefore set aside. Finally, recent events led to planning for crises that could affect the government: the superior general was to act in close collaboration with her council.[80] The divisions in the last general council had filtered through sufficiently for that phrase to be not just a pious wish. That phrase also showed a concern to break with past practice that had not always fostered close collaboration of the members of the general council or consultation that respected each one's mission.

Founded on prayer and the interior life, the Society of the Sacred Heart had translated its goal of contemplation into monastic practices. The special chapter underlined the apostolic character of prayer, from which "no one can dispense us, because no one can dispense us from God."[81] However, it said that "there are countless ways to pray, according to people, times, and life's challenges. God speaks to each one in an individual manner; the response must be personal and searching." Each one has the right to give to prayer the appropriate time and form and to have available an adapted liturgy and sacramental practice.[82]

The vicariate assemblies wanted the vows to be presented in a positive fashion. Regarding chastity, in the past one could be content to seek "the purity of angels," a concept that avoided giving information or details on the meaning of the vow. From the novitiate on, clear and complete instruction was to deal with its biological, psychological and theological aspects. Reworking of the paragraph of the Constitutions on particular friendships was requested. It was thought that "In an atmosphere of

---

[79] P. 31.
[80] P. 30. The crisis of 1904 was unknown to the religious, or at least they had only a partial understanding of it.
[81] *Orientations*, p. 35.
[82] It was a wish presented by the majority of the vicariate assemblies.

fraternal love, true friendships centered on God can develop. With understanding and acceptance, religious will reach maturity more easily and become more sensitive to grace."[83] Poverty was "love first, then renunciation." To be a "striking sign" it was to be translated into a life taken seriously under a dual personal and community perspective, simple and welcoming. But if religious had to live poorly, they must not hesitate to make use of technical means needed in their work. Obedience is "union with Christ, service of the Church and a sign of eternity." The Society must reeducate itself so that faith and love inform the new structures of government and of obedience. Dialogue was presented as a means of discovering the will of God in submission to the Holy Spirit. Its benefits were developed at length since it had not been the practice before. The chapter members were provided with extracts from interventions of Father Arrupe or conferences of Father Jean-Charles Bernard to gain a better understanding of the issues and go beyond the merely functional character of obedience.

The Chapter of 1967 elaborated a schema on community life, defined as "a fraternal community built up in Christ in the service of the world." The specifics of daily life, among others, order of day, use of the telephone, correspondence, silence, were approached after recalling the theological and mystical foundations of religious life and after pointing out their correlation with the charism of Saint Madeleine Sophie defined as "the love of the Heart of Christ lived through the consecration of our whole being to his service and to the service of all [human beings]." From then on, one could go out for relaxation, charity, education, strengthening of religious and family bonds, without restriction. In a number of areas the acts of the Chapter of 1967 only revisited decisions of the General Congregation of 1964, which had been pioneering in many regards. But this repetition was especially important because they had not been carried out in a broad-minded way and were not even known to everyone. Besides, the climate in which one approached the reality of religious life in 1967 was very different from what it had been before. The Religious of the Sacred Heart were seen as women who had made a particular life choice but who had to take into consideration their status as women. Because ongoing formation was insisted upon, they were looked upon as able to grow through what they had learned from their education and studies both before and after entering the Society. Psychological weaknesses, temperamental problems, even the effects of illnesses were hidden no longer.[84]

---

[83] *Orientations*, p. 42.

[84] Mother Whitehead, vicar of Canada, had asked the chapter to foresee psychological help for the religious. Mother de Valon had said she did not

The vicariate assemblies in mission countries had asked that the forthcoming Constitutions refer to the missions. Their reports had tried to capture the socio-economic and cultural environments of these countries or had examined the missionary vocation, which required special virtues: "unshakeable faith in divine power, faith that denies the impossible; openness to another culture, willingness to change one's ordinary way of doing things, of giving value to what appears to have none." A missionary must

> Be persuaded that one has much to learn from those whom one comes to evangelize; to wish at any cost to understand them in their language; to be ready to change habits in the areas of well-being, food, lodging, liturgical adaptation; to be happy to do without many things in the material, intellectual, artistic and spiritual realms; to know how to leave aside one's own patriotism and to understand political questions with the frame of mind of the people of the country.[85]

They had expressed a deep concern to become what would later be called "inculturated." Prompt learning of the language was indispensable for spiritual reasons[86] and in establishing the reputation of the Society

---

agree. But this proposal was introduced in the section on community life (Prov. Arch. Canada). Mother d'Apice, a physician, was asked to give a conference on "the health care that we must give to our religious." She believed that in religious life the demands of health care should not be inferior to what candidates had been accustomed to in the world, and she demonstrated that the expenses that would follow were largely "counterbalanced by the good resulting to the apostolate and by the aid thus given to those thinking of religious life." This conference considered religious life globally. When someone had advocated impersonality, Mother d'Apice recalled that "praise was a more efficacious means to humility than blame or humiliation." She pointed out that religious needed rest and that relaxation was not incompatible with community life: "One has suggested making our community rooms places of warmth and welcome. This is an excellent preventive measure; an example of possible relaxation, without great expense is to obtain for the community room armchairs and the rest. By going to secondhand shops, we bought furniture for a sum well below that of tranquilizers necessary for a few people for a week!" She informed her hearers also that mental illnesses were "ordinary" illnesses and that the more they were considered so, the better one aided persons suffering from them to take their place in their personal and community life.

[85] Gen. Arch. C I C 3, Box 21. Report of Congo. Mother Keogh gave the same advice: to be a missionary one must be astonished at nothing.

[86] Gen. Arch. C I C 3, "Our efforts [to master the local languages] will prove to the inhabitants of the country that we do not love them only 'for the love

in education, which would allow them to help promote national development.[87] Over all, this stance suggested the Africanization of religious life in Congo; in Korea, a "resolute and gradual 'Koreanization.'"[88] These reports were not taken up in the acts of the chapter, but Mother Wakamatsu was given special responsibility for the missions.

The directives of the special chapter were much appreciated. Many religious were satisfied with a better description of their consecration.[89] The vows were no longer viewed as renunciation but "as a gift of love."[90] Poverty no longer consisted of asking permission to give someone a pin and not to waste a scrap of thread. Chastity was perceived as the gift of the whole person to the Lord and to others. Obedience became the subject of discernment and co-responsibility. "The light that radiated from all these ways of understanding the following of Christ illumined the whole context of my religious life, made me more responsible, taught me not to make demands and to receive everything as gift," wrote an Italian religious.[91] For another,

> it was liberation from a life structured and centered on the interior. During my noviceship one had stressed fidelity in little things, respect for the order of day, punctuality, renunciation. That could come from the need to protect us. The moment had come to distinguish what was essential in religious life and what was not.[92]

Those who had always refused to show an exaggerated respect for authority and to what had "a sacred value" felt themselves "vindicated."[93] A new form of religious life was able appear in a Society of the Sacred Heart that wanted to be faithful to the spirit of its foundation.

---

of God,' but for themselves, as they are. In the eyes of God they are God's children the same as we are, therefore our equals, as rich as we in God's eyes, and having the same divine and human value. To believe therefore in their value, their qualities, to respect them. In coming to them we have as much to receive as to give them".

[87] Report of Bombay.
[88] "In the measure in which the religious of Korean nationality grow older and will be more numerous, the communities gradually and naturally will be capable of identifying more fully with the way of life of their people."
[89] Eleonora de Guggenberg appreciated the fact that the vow of poverty was placed second, that the vow of obedience was downgraded to third place and that the orientations were beginning to be lived *ad experimentum*.
[90] The formula was Brigid Keogh's (Testimony of T. Chu).
[91] Testimony of Marina Marino.
[92] Testimony of Angela Galetto.
[93] Testimony of Anna Lecciso.

Chapter III

The Opening 1968-1970

The directives of the special chapter were quickly approved by the Church.[1] Mother Bultó then had the difficult task of putting them into practice while preserving the unity of the body. The majority of the Religious of the Sacred Heart undoubtedly thought that the renewal of governmental structures was essential, but the new formulas were not necessarily easy to articulate or to carry out to the satisfaction of everyone. The first question to be raised, however, is that of the chapter's reception.

Reception of the Special Chapter

The question of reception had never come up before. After a general congregation the superior used to assemble the religious and say to them, "Let us rejoice, sisters, for we have seen that uniformity continues to reign in the whole Society."[2] The Chapter of 1967 brought about so many changes that that sort of reaction was no longer possible. The reception of the chapter was not the first concern of many who were grappling with demanding situations, as Giovanna Scarlata has shown very well. She wrote,

> I was then continually changing houses, cities, communities, activities: everything was new for me and absorbed all my physical, psychic and spiritual energies. It seems to me that I considered that period of change with much simplicity and serenity, maybe with a lack of awareness, but with fatigue, loneliness and suffering, especially when I was mistress of novices without a model or a person with whom to compare myself. I had to invent a totally new style, while trying not to lose sight of essential

---

[1] Pope Paul VI told her that he had followed the unfolding of the chapter "with respect, confidence and joy."
[2] Testimony of G. Bovagnet

values. I was hardly professed a year and not at all prepared for such a task.[3]

Some religious reacted with "indifference.... A page was turned. But we [the sisters] were the last wheel on the cart. We had only to listen and to keep quiet, without commenting! We were accustomed to that; it was life!"[4] In France a mistress general could say: "I could not understand why we were changing. I could not see it. We were swept away."[5] Another who said she was "at ease with the changes" believed that the question for her was rather to know "how far to go or not to go."[6]

The announcement of Mother de Valon's resignation came as a complete surprise, all the more as the news coming from Rome earlier had not given the impression that there was a revolution afoot. The vicars from the United States kept their houses au courant of what was happening.[7] In England, however, recounts Prudence Wilson, "We had absolutely no idea what was happening at the motherhouse, and the most bewildering was that the news that we did receive spoke about recreations and other trivialities. We had the impression of being isolated and relegated to another planet. We did not know whether our experience was shared by many other vicariates of the Society. There was not very much clarification after the return of the delegates." In Ireland the superiors received from their vicar, Mother Carton, a letter in which she wrote: "Earlier we had a superior general elected for life. Never before had there been a resignation of a Mother General! May the Providence of God guide us all!"[8] In Austria the treasurer in Graz wrote in her spiritual notes in November 1967: "The resignation of Our Mother is tearing at the heart of the Society. It is all unbelievable! One is aghast! What will become of the Society? Where shall it go?... Jesus, have pity on us! Dear holy Mother, save the Society!" The following year she added: "The imbalance in the Society seems strange. Something seems to say that the Society had lost the ground beneath its feet and has not yet found its new face. The soul feels repercussions: anxiety, uneasiness, confusion. We have to wait to see where all this will lead."

---

[3] Nancy Kehoe, from the United States, in 1970, felt more concerned with the closing of the house in Cincinnati than with questions on the provincial or international plane.
[4] Testimony of G. Russo.
[5] Testimony of Edmée Lesne.
[6] Testimony of M-J. Vié.
[7] Testimony of Ann Conroy. The vicar and the delegates from New York, Mothers Fitzgerald, McCormack and Coakley, sent a weekly communiqué.
[8] Prov. Arch. Ireland/Scotland, IRS 0111, Letters of 12, 16, 17 and 20 November 1967.

"Tension, confusion, anxiety for the Society. Is it possible that the Council has caused this trouble, this tragic shock? It is impossible that the renewal of religious life demanded by the Council is a decline, a descent, a lessening! A renewal ought to aim higher toward something greater, deeper, truer."[9]

News of the chapter was not reported to all the houses in the same way. In Peru Gabriela Belón assembled the nuns of her vicariate in Lima to share the directives of the special chapter.[10] In New York the vicar and delegates commented on them and distributed the text.[11] Chicago was "an open province in the sense that Mother Sheahan on her return told them everything that had happened, point by point, word for word."[12] But in Ireland after a meeting in Dublin with the vicar and the delegates the superior of Armagh announced that there had been no changes in the Society. Phil Kilroy remembered:

> That surprised me and seemed very strange. A long time afterward I understood and realized that in this province there was firm opposition to change even before 1967. Upon their return the provincial delegates had been instructed not to speak of what had happened and not to refer to the resignation of Sabine de Valon. These instructions were observed, and I know that they were hard on Sybil Swinton, the delegate from Scotland, who felt reduced to silence. This policy flowed out of a spirit of loyalty to the Society, but it came from the past and was an exercise in denial.[13]

Silence was the rule in France and Belgium.[14]

It took months, even years, for many of the nuns to learn what the atmosphere in Rome had been in 1967. Information came through participation in international meetings[15] or from the new superior general and members of her council. Various versions of the events circulated for

---

[9] Communicated by Eva Belle, 12 March and May 1968.
[10] Testimony of M. Recavarren. The community of Arequipa, of which she was a member, traveled in a bus in silence for ten hours to reach the capital. It was the first open meeting of all the religious.
[11] Testimony of A. Conroy.
[12] Testimony of Margaret Mary Miller.
[13] Even so, after 1968 Mother Swinton was able to speak of the chapter at Kilgraston, thanks to the superior, Margaret Ranaghan.
[14] Testimony of Thérèse Vercruysse. Françoise Cassiers, who had not had the same position as the vicar and the other delegate during the special chapter, was not invited to speak of the chapter in the communities.
[15] Testimony of Agnès Bigo and E. Belle who wrote in July 1971: "Although the Society is going through very difficult times amid great problems, it seeks to live the spirit of our holy Mother today. I experience great vitality in the

a long time including in the United States.[16] Mother Bultó's behavior during her journeys calmed many fears. "In observing her," thought Prudence Wilson, "I understood what the 'new' was, and I have always had a debt of gratitude toward her. The new was not different from the old. It was simply a matter of living love and forgiveness." At Manhattanville where Mother Bultó was received warmly at the beginning of 1970, "One felt from this visit that the Society had survived the crisis of 1967 and that we were in good hands."[17]

Chance sometimes contributed to increasing the difficulty of a situation that could have ended badly. In Austria the vicar, Mother Schilhawsky, who was ill, had not been able to go to Rome for the opening of the special chapter, and a replacement for her had been named. This deputy returned to Austria when the vicar was able to leave for Rome. The plan was for the vicar and delegates, when they returned, to tell all the houses what had taken place. However Mother Schilhawsky fell ill again, and the two delegates were not authorized to tour the province: "That is what caused so much pain in Austria. We were receiving news from here and there about different 'innovations' but no concrete, official information."[18] In England Mother Ogilvie Forbes suffered a traffic accident and could not personally give an account of the chapter's decisions.

The religious were surprised in proportion to what they already knew of expectations in the Society. In Paris, at least, the youngest of the delegates from the United States en route to Rome had circumspectly referred to the changes hoped for.[19] The probanists and the novices at Frascati, thanks to proximity to Rome, had learned about developments in the Church by Council fathers and theologians who came to speak to them about the Council documents.[20] Mothers Schroen and Meliá had referred to changes that might happen in the Society.[21]

The announcement of Mother de Valon's resignation was received with astonishment, however. At Frascati, it was "a storm. The repercussions were terrible: sorrow, confusion, disorientation; one no longer understood. It was a very hard period because contacts with different members of the chapter brought differing interpretations that did not help to get at the

---

Society in the search for new ways. The Society is not in the process of dying but of living!"

[16] Testimony of M.M. Miller.
[17] Testimony of A. Conroy.
[18] Testimony of E. Belle.
[19] Testimony of Hannelore Woitsch and Marie-Thérèse Deprecq.
[20] Testimony of Pilar Corral and Ippolita Marchetti.
[21] F. Gimber, Chapter 9, pp. 132-154, and testimony of A. Conroy.

truth."[22] Some religious from every country thought that Mother de Valon had wanted to align her action with the teachings of the Vatican Council and wrote to thank her for this act of obedience to the Church. The shock was strongly felt in many houses in the South of Spain, in Australia, New Zealand, and throughout Colombia, Ireland, France, Poland, Germany, Austria, Malta and Egypt. As Mechtild Büscher recalled, "It was an unparalleled event in the history of the Society."[23]

The issue of the resignation of Mother de Valon interfered with the reception of the acts of the chapter and got in the way of the application of the orientations.

> It was [on account of the resignation] that certain capitulants condemned the whole chapter whereas it had been commendable, and many of the documents had been signed by Mother de Valon herself. In addition, the chapter did not produce all the fruit it might have. Some provinces entered fully into its spirit, but the way others received it was limited to the point of view of the capitulants. Those who wanted neither changes nor innovations hung back, opposed it or did not accept it. The provincials of forceful character and authority went ahead and sometimes allowed things to happen that were really premature. Others stood back in fear, and thus, obeyed the letter of the law and things went badly.[24]

The changes that took place from 1968 on were understood to varying degrees, and sometimes appeared to be a relaxation of religious life. Rather than the chapter directives themselves, it was the awareness of changes occurring in various provinces that upset or worried the religious. Usually the modifications – when they were disapproved of – were blamed on the religious of the United States. In Ireland, "great mistrust of them was widespread and destructive for several years."[25] The nuns in the United States, however, were as surprised and sometimes as worried as others, and in some provinces or houses of the United States the changes occurred only after several years.

As the society had lived turned in on itself for so long without moving toward reform, "It was an opening of the floodgates, a real storm, in many places," as Mother Bultó recognized. "The Society was not prepared for

---

[22] Testimony of I. Marchetti who adds: "The news came by telephone direct from Mother de Valon to our superior: 'From now on I am no longer your Mother General.'

[23] The house in Hamburg, where she was living, was late in receiving the booklets containing orientations.

[24] Testimony of M.J. Bultó.

[25] Testimony P. Kilroy.

the changes. That is why the chapter was not a beacon that could be their light and guide their way. It could have fostered a path toward reform, but for some religious the reforms were reduced to ending the First Friday novena!" In France tensions were high between 1967 and 1972 but relaxed gradually later.[26] On the other hand, in Germany those tensions remained until the end of the eighties.[27] In some provinces there was neither a real examination nor application of the orientations of the special chapter. Therefore, the next chapter could not be appropriately prepared, and its decisions were met with confusion and hostility.[28]

Setting up New Governmental Structures

The change from vicariates to provinces was not just a formality, because a province had to be financially autonomous. Previously money moved from one vicariate to another in order to pay debts.[29] Treasurers now had to do whatever was necessary to make their vicariate autonomous and to change thinking. In the past, monies for investment realized by the vicariate treasury were managed by the central administration.[30] The reworking of financial policy and its implementation rested largely with the treasurer general.

Gisela Posada Gómez, the first treasurer general who was not French, was a Cuban.[31] She had both an understanding of the present and a vision of the future.[32] From 1964 on she asked that the accounts of the communities and institutions be separated and that vicariate treasurers seek

---

[26] Testimony of M-T. Carré. At Châtenay-Malabry where she was living then, the arrival of Mother de Valon, at the beginning of 1969, doubtless did not contribute to calming them.

[27] *Our Road to Emmaus*, 1994, report of the Province of Germany/Sweden, p. 33.

[28] Testimony of J. Faber.

[29] Testimony of Mary Henry. The deposit in the *caisse générale* in London, which was fed by Ireland and England, was divided *pro rata* by the number of religious and the inheritances received. "This was a painful process that made me aware of different aspects of the very sad history between Ireland and England in the recent past" (testimony of V. Bowman).

[30] Prov. Arch. Ireland/Scotland, IRS 0111. Letter from Mother Carton, 30 October 1967. In this province it was Mother Dillon who was in charge of the operation at which she succeeded (Testimony of D. Boland).

[31] She had begun law studies in Havana with Fidel Castro. During her aspirantship she studied economics at Manhattanville. She was aide to Mother de James, whom she succeeded in 1962.

[32] For Doreen Boland who assisted her in the general treasury from 1968, she was a "prophet." Vivien Bowman, who succeeded her in 1978, described her the same way. She adds: "We who knew Gisela and worked with her realized

the assistance of lawyers and qualified accountants, though her suggestions were not always followed. She played a major role in drafting the texts on finances adopted by the chapters of 1967 and 1970. She reorganized the general treasury beginning in November 1968 and charged a group composed of Doreen Boland, Malin Craig, Socorro Julia and Vivien Bowman with studying the financial implications of decentralization.[33] Gisela Posada had annual budgets established and had the financial affairs supervised by experts. She perceived that, through ignorance of the financial matters, the motherhouse was making decisions about foundations or works without worrying about or knowing whether or not it was possible to sustain them. She had projections made based on the age pyramid, and she called the general council to greater practicality.[34] She inaugurated short and long term planning and paid attention to national legislation.[35] Gisela Posada took charge of training provincial and local treasurers, who often had to face considerable changes in the execution of their tasks without sufficient instruction.[36]

These norms were implemented rapidly in the United States and Canada, where after 1968 the budgets of the institutions and the communities were separated. The teaching nuns began to sign contracts with the schools that employed them. Action was taken so that little by little persons and communities were able to set annual budgets responsibly.[37] Provincial treasurers took charge also of the care of sick and frail religious. They consulted with businessmen or followed the example of other religious congregations further along in this area than the Sacred Heart.

---

how alone she was in the considerable responsibility she had of orienting the Society toward a new era."

[33] They drafted a manual of financial administration that was proposed to the capitulants in 1970. Some earlier practices disappeared, like that of translating all the accounts into French francs before sending them to Rome.

[34] Testimony of D. Boland.

[35] Testimony of V. Bowman. "We were members of an international religious congregation and responsible for the whole, but our administration also had to be rooted in our national cultures."

[36] Doreen Boland accompanied her on trips between 1968 and 1970: "Gisela unquestionably aided them; she sought to put in place means that allowed each one to live her religious life at depth. She helped treasurers to understand that they were the stewards of the finances of the Society, at the service of the mission, but that did not mean that they were the guardians of the religious poverty of the communities. She was always directed toward others, very amiable and affectionate. Sensitive herself, she was sensitive to their sufferings."

[37] Testimony of Anne Leonard.

In the United States the nuns were impatient to see the new forms of governance put in place, for other congregations had already made changes, and the feminist movement reinforced them. In Chicago they took advantage of Mother Sheahan's absence to discuss at recreation changes to be introduced and even a possible merger of the provinces.[38]

> Developments were rapid, for the move toward a new type of leadership was growing. Many hoped to have as many people as possible participate in provincial government. All the sisters had to take on some responsibilities. At the provincial chapter in 1969 taking into account what she was hearing, Mother Sheahan resigned. Everything was changing. As religious were leaving the Society, Mother Sheahan thought that the Society was going in the wrong direction. She wrote to the Mother General; she was called to Rome and questioned on her actions and those of her province.[39]

A long range plan was created and a committee named COST, "committee open to the spirit of the times," was appointed. The name signified that the province knew that the changes would require costly effort.

> An important contribution to the construction of the province and of leadership was made by a "community of faith" focused on a community proposal carried out under the direction of a Jesuit. The Holy Spirit was at work but intelligence and courage were also tangible. The province was divided into groups for sharing; participants shared their faith and the story of their vocation and the gift of themselves with one another in the group "the seal of Christ."

The province proposed that each one make a directed retreat in the place of her choice or take advantage one of four retreats given by Jesuits. Margaret Mary Miller thinks that "This assembly of faith was a turning point for the province. These experiences brought about union, joy, peace, participation, taking charge of oneself." A provincial team was chosen, composed, besides the provincial, of three or four persons named after consultation with the religious, each one having charge of a sector of activities: communications, formation, planning and human resources. Adopted by the Chapter of 1970, this model served the whole Society.

Another decision made in North America had long term repercussions. Upon returning from the chapter of 1967 the vicars of the United States

---

[38] Testimony of Marianne Ruggeri.
[39] Testimony of MM. Miller.

and Canada decided to continue to consult with one another about what reforms should be carried out, for decisions made in one province affected the others. That was the origin of the interprovincial board that saw the light of day a few years later. The provincials had analyses made of their institutions by the same two consulting firms, which allowed them to use similar methods and to compare results. They took action to break down barriers between provinces, each with its strong identity, to reorganize resources, to adopt common practice in initial and ongoing formation and in finances and, finally, to exchange personnel.[40] After 1972 an interprovincial service formed by religious named after consultation was charged with assisting the provincial teams.[41] This organization drew the provinces closer and paved the way toward one province.

Throughout the Society there was a desire to strengthen unity and join forces. The number of territorial units was reduced. France moved from three vicariates to two provinces in 1968 and to a single province in 1971. The vicariates of the North and South of Spain, which had been subdivided in 1958, formed two provinces in 1969.[42] Italy had only one province after 1969.[43] This reorganization allowed for different staffing. In Canada, after the resignation of the provincial, the motherhouse named a team of five persons, three of whom were Canadians.[44] Shorter terms of office meant younger major superiors. The oldest of the vicars had held office for a very long time.[45] Some of them remained at their post in spite of poor health or old age; it began to seem that the office of vicar, like

---

[40] Testimony of Mary Mardel. "The five provincials met for a week three or four times a year. We worked at unifying our policies, created the Network of Sacred Heart Schools, gradually moved the five treasuries toward a single treasury. We did the same for ongoing formation and human resources."

[41] A Canadian consultant, Roger Gosselin, was involved in aiding this new structure to give the best service. After the Chapter of 1970, the meetings aimed at putting it into effect were bimonthly (Testimony of A. Conroy). It was in this framework that the decision was made to close a school in each province during the year 1972-1973.

[42] They were sub-divided again in 1976.

[43] Mother Caracciolo became provincial of the North of Italy and resided in Padua. In 1969, when she became provincial of Italy, she transferred the provincial headquarters to Rome.

[44] Testimony of A. Leonard. "The team of five developed a plan of government and helped to unite the province, which at the end of their term was capable of proposing names for the office of provincial."

[45] Mother Tiefenbacher, who had been the dean of the special chapter, had directed the affairs of Germany for twenty-three years. Mothers Ogilvie Forbes, Fitzgerald and Keogh had been vicars for fifteen years or more.

that of superior general, was for life.[46] India and Japan were governed by provincials from their countries for the first time.[47]

The provincials were to be named after consultation with the religious. It is not certain that the first nominations took place in that fashion. In France one of the two provincials had not been a vicar before; she was not unanimously accepted.[48] In Germany the delegate to the chapter became provincial. In England, according to Prudence Wilson,

> We knew that the vicar, now known as provincial, was to be replaced and that in some way we were all to have a part in the change, but we were led to understand that her successor was already designated. One spoke of her as the heir apparent; and even though she was perfectly acceptable, that put the new style of designating her completely in doubt; it made of it a sort of charade, rather than straightforward consent.

Joan Faber comments,

> If the directives could be thus neglected in such and such a province, what confidence could be given to what the provincials were supposed to promote? Some religious wrote to the motherhouse, and there was a troubled period during which there was a consultation, but it created tension and hurt. That must have been a difficult experience for Dorothy Eyre,

who had been named provincial. In Malta and some other provinces the religious did not understand the difference between a vicar and a provincial, and they were not given explanations that could have enlightened them.

The new provincials had the charge, and it was not an easy one, of making transitions or bridges "between a government of benign despotism and a government – the word was then fashionable – of collegiality."[49] As Fanny Martínez explained,

---

[46] Testimony of F. Tamayo and M. Recavarren.

[47] In Japan, Sumiko Iba was thirty-four years old when she became provincial. Afterward, older provincials were named, which indicated that the religious of another generation had not had the impression of being considered before. The first completely Japanese community was that of Sapporo (Testimony B. Keogh). Mary Braganza and Gool Mary Dhalla (Vandana) were the first two Indian provincials.

[48] Testimony of M-T. Carré and M. Serpentier.

[49] J. Faber, *Sister Dorothy Eyre*, p. 34. The formula is from Prudence Wilson.

We were coming out of an authoritarian model of dogmatism in which it went without saying that the truth was always in the superior, that is, in the one who found herself on a level of authority that placed her above me. It was a structure where the word of only a few counted, where information always arrived through only one channel.

The provincials were named for three years with the possibility of a second term. Their broadened powers allowed them to launch necessary experiments, which were to be adapted to the environment of their province.[50] They had to replace superiors who had served beyond the time appointed for their office, even though in some cases there was a decision to prolong the term of all the superiors to nine years.[51]

The change of superiors was an important moment in the life of a house, even of a province, for some of them were women of real power. They were women gifted with outstanding qualities and a real love of the Society, venerated both in the Society and beyond. They were strongly dominant in their communities, whose members considered them absolute authorities. If their way of presenting the chapter documents of the Society did not correspond to information coming from Rome or from the provincial house, the religious may have been shocked, but they succumbed to their influence. It sometimes took several years before such houses could be won over to the changes. We will take only the example of Châtenay-Malabry in France. It was a house "crowned with many Reverend Mothers,"[52] and which

> was considered by the provincial and by some religious as a bastion of tradition. Until 1971 the superior was Marie-Thérèse Virnot, former mistress general of studies, who had had and continued to have great influence. She was thought to be traditional. Around her were other thoughtful people who were not progressive but were good, intelligent religious who could raise questions: Hélène Serreau, France Deglaire, Mother Bailliard, full of wisdom, and others.[53] These persons viewed the exaggerations and the catchphrases circulating around the province with some anxiety. There were a number

---

[50] At the Chapter of 1970, it was they who gave the report of their provinces, which included the closings and openings of houses, as well as efforts at new apostolates, subjects that until 1967 had formed a part of the report of the superior general.

[51] In Austria this measure came to an end in 1971.

[52] Testimony of Alice Wasbauer. Several former superiors, vicars, mistresses of juniorate lived there, not to mention Mother de Valon.

[53] Testimony of M-T. Carré: she herself was part of the group "thinking types" and of influential religious.

of Polish former sisters who did not understand what was happening and wanted the status quo. There were also young nuns who represented the forward-looking wing but were not headstrong.

It would be wrong and unwise to believe that all the superiors who had influence or who did not necessarily desire radical transformations in the Society of the Sacred Heart fomented a sort of opposition, at least in spirit. Many received the decisions of the special chapter, including those that concerned them, with faith and obedience. The example of Marie-Josèphe Vié, who had been one of the mistresses of juniorate in France and who was superior of the Paris community, is enlightening:

> The Chapter of 1967 and the passionate year 1968 made me understand that I had to "detach myself from my little way of having the spirit of the Society." A bit haltingly we had to go forward. Knowing well that a general chapter is the first authority of any congregation, I had no desire to bargain with my obedience of judgment. But it was more difficult to explain to others the how if not the why.... Spiritual discernment was presented that year to all the mistresses of formation of the capital as the premier virtue of a religious moving toward the year 2000. And I knew that our holy Mother agreed.[54] Therefore untroubled, if not without suffering, I followed the path...until on a certain day and at a certain metro stop, God was waiting for me, for evidently I had not finished making room in myself for the charism. I opened a letter; it asked me for a particularly painful sacrifice. I murmured: "Yes, of course," and a wave of grace submerged me so completely that, there[55] in the noise and the crowd, I understood forever that union of wills makes union of hearts. And ultimately God alone knows in advance what in our future lives will be "the means in our power."[56]

Some provincial assemblies not only had to implement the chapter directives but also, according to Maria Luiza Saade, to "review the history of the province and dream about its future." They were the occasions of real emotional release, for as she recognized, "We were not prepared to speak freely and to accept liberating criticism." These experiences were painful in many places because, as in the vicariate assemblies that had preceded the special chapter, people did not always know how to channel

---

[54] She is referring to § 32, 43, 154, 240 and following of the *Constitutions* and to teachings of the founder on the Holy Spirit.
[55] She is referring to § 341 and to the end of the *Constitutions*.
[56] Prov. Arch. France.

criticisms that were directed at an office but reflected on the persons who exercised it. The process was burdensome. In England the workshops and assemblies never seemed to end. "Every word had to be scrutinized. Everyone could participate in these assemblies, but not everyone had the right to vote. If a non-voting member did not agree with a decision, she had to find a delegate who would listen to her. I am tempted to say we wasted a good deal of time," concluded Anne Hine, "but it was a means of returning to some structures, which most people wanted."[57]

From 1968 on some provincial assemblies decided to merge some boarding schools with free schools and open them to a wider public. One in Mexico chose to collaborate with other educational congregations.[58] So that poverty would follow the evolution of religious life, the province asked the religious to work eight hours every day and to have a life style similar to that of the salaried personnel. Each community was to agree on a minimum salary, convert income from investments into financial aid for students, share gifts, and re-evaluate the compensation of teachers and employees. Poverty was to be open to justice and result in service that brought the poor closer.[59] The religious participated more and more in consultations: seventy answered the requests of the provincial in 1968, 144 in 1969. As Mother Espadaler summarized in 1969, "There is no doubt that this form of government produced marvelous effects; among them, that of being able to share problems, responsibilities and hopes."[60] The introduction of democracy into provincial practice was a way of putting an end to earlier kinds of administration. In some countries where it did not operate in public institutions, it taught the religious to be on the side of oppressed peoples and to work to defend their rights.[61] The new modes of governance seemed to the greatest number of religious to be in harmony with the directives of the Vatican Council and the needs of an international society. Giovanna Scarlata remarked:

---

[57] According to Prudence Wilson (*My Father Took Me to the Circus*, p. 105), "In order to give means of practicing democracy, committees and commissions were multiplied, and at the same time so were the number of those who had not been named to one of these prestigious groups. At the same time the number of committees increased and also the sadness of those who felt alienated and profoundly rejected."

[58] In 1969, five teaching congregations of both men and women formed the University of Monterrey, with the support of the Church and the government of the State of Nueva León.

[59] *Histoire de la Province du Mexique, les Années Soixante*, p. 18.

[60] P. 19.

[61] P. 29. They proceeded to electoral campaigns and made use of secret ballots to nominate local councilors.

> I very much appreciated the understanding of authority as a service; the passage from a pyramidal government to a circular, democratic government; the application of the principles of subsidiarity, participation and co-responsibility and the means that could foster them (discernment, dialogue, chapters, open assemblies, consultations). My experiences of dialogue and discernment with my provincials have made me grow in an adult, liberated and responsible obedience.

Conferences were organized to gather provincials of the same country or the same continent. Mother de Valon had thought of them as an instrument of coordination for "a better regrouping of forces and in the future a more productive distribution of personnel." Between May and September 1969 provincial meetings for North America, Europe and Latin America took place in Saint Louis, Brussels and Lima. The superior general took part in all these meetings along with an assistant general or the whole council. The superiors general who succeeded Mother Bultó continued these assemblies, which allowed real regional coordination in Africa and Asia.

The Kaski Research

In order to have all the religious participate in the life of the congregation the general council solicited the services of Father Spruit, a member of an institute for socio-religious research at The Hague, the *Katholiek Sociaal-Kerkelijk Instituut*, Kaski. From his suggestions an international team of religious developed a list of sixty-five questions on understanding the charism, the definition, nature and desirable developments of the mission of the Society. This consultation had remarkable success with a response rate of 95.9%.[62] The general questionnaire was followed by a statement from each province outlining local differences.[63] The second questionnaire, a self-survey, sought to summarize apostolic activities and community life and thereby identify developments for the next ten years. Mother Bultó explained this use of social science.

> Our present task is research, both individual and collective, into the truth of our religious life. If we are really haunted by the desire to live the evangelical mission of Saint Madeleine Sophie today through a meaningful apostolate, if we have her concern for "littleness" and poverty, her thirst for making the love of Christ known among people then the

---

[62] M.J. Bultó, *Lettres circulaires*, p. 92, 14 March 1970.
[63] M.J. Bultó, p. 92.

study by Father Spruit cannot fail to meet a real need. A strong desire to be faithful to the Gospel and to the spirit of the Society is in itself the confirmation of our hope.[64]

The two inquiries were of paramount interest for the government of the Society of the Sacred Heart and for each religious, for as Fanny Martínez indicated for Colombia, "They allowed us to talk about everything that we never talk about. For me it was an interior liberation that put me back in a world that belonged to me, that I had to build with my own hands, where I had something to say that would be listened to." Some responses brought out the hope for unity in diversity. The synthesis developed by Father Spruit reflected tangibly on an epoch of transition and showed that the religious wished to base their life on the founding spirit to shed light on both the present and the future. The responses reflected a firm willingness to go back to the "personal experiences of the founder," the idea that the original charism, frozen in "institutionalism" could be recaptured "by radically accentuating the directions evident in the post-conciliar Church, directions in the line of the original inspiration of the Society."[65]

The results of the questionnaires were shared with everyone. That was a brand new practice along the lines of the desired democratization, but it could have some contradictory effects. The risk was to see opposition emerge in the Society of the Sacred Heart and consequently increase friction, and diminish understanding. Although Mother Bultó could write, "This work [of the preparation of the chapter] in which the Society has been engaged, seems to us to have been very real and very efficacious in creating union,"[66] some questions about the effects of diversity had been raised. The responses to the questionnaires showed that some provinces were better prepared than others to accept changes. In New York 55% of the oldest religious were favorable to dialogue. There was an abiding concern to participate in government.[67] Elsewhere, the responses to the questionnaires from Kaski made it clear that changes were in progress in the Society of the Sacred Heart and that they were desired. But some religious were troubled or were scandalized to learn

---

[64] *History of the Province of England*, p. 91.
[65] Pp. 91-92.
[66] Gen, Arch. C I C 3, Box 23, Report of the General Chapter, October 1970.
[67] R. Cunningham, *Helen Fitzgerald*, pp. 74-75. "The province encouraged diversity and action against social injustice. Its members saw the value of more freedom in community life, in the sharing of goods, local assemblies, exchanges among provinces. Their appreciation of values cultivated for a long time continued strongly: the need of prolonged contemplation, balance between prayer and work, special care for the elderly and the sick, charity for all."

that their province "was living on the margins of the Society."[68] The communication of the results reassured people that the Religious of the Sacred Heart remained attached to the essential: "I found my confidence in the Society again; for almost all of the religious, the place given to prayer and contemplation was the most important," wrote Marie-Louise Fabre.

Unity, Charity and Government

After the special chapter when the Society had seemed in danger,[69] a certain return to peacefulness took place, thanks to Mother Bultó's attitude. After her election she gave as her objectives to explain the chapter and to watch over unity, because "we were coming out of these events terribly shaken," she said afterwards. If the first objective was not always attained because "the life that was bubbling up was too strong to be controlled and there was too much effervescence in the Society of the Sacred Heart," the second was realized in a remarkable manner.

In its directives the special chapter had made charity the test of life in the Society of the Sacred Heart. Government was a "service of charity;" prayer was "the source of charity;" the work of education was "centered on charity;" community life was "the expression of charity."[70] This focus on the *Cor unum* was all the more necessary as the congregation risked entering a period of turmoil. In closing the chapter, Mother Bultó placed the coming effort in the context of the founding charism:

> Our holy Mother, who came to preside…during our moments of painful uncertainty,[71] will undoubtedly continue to follow us with motherly interest along the path we have begun to tread. What would she say to us at this turning point desired by the Church?
>
> She would beg us *to preserve and strengthen union of minds and hearts*. At this time when the signs of the times and the needs of the apostolate require of us a more flexible adaptation of what is accidental, we must seek the means not only to preserve, but to strengthen and make more authentic our *Cor unum*.

---

[68] Testimony of H. Woitsch. The communication of the results of Kaski was a cause of trouble in Canada (Testimony of A. Leonard).
[69] Testimony of Alice Amyot.
[70] Special Chapter, pp. 13-14.
[71] On 17 November it was decided to put the portrait of Saint Madeleine Sophie in the president's place.

The basis for this will no longer be uniformity, but confidence, love and the sole desire of working together in the apostolic work which the Church confides to us.

The pierced Heart of Christ will be the inexhaustible source and stimulus for this. Wherever we are in the world, this Heart will make us "one in him with the Father and the Holy Spirit."[72]

The new superior general held these convictions ardently. One of the first examples of their application was the way she treated her predecessor who had resigned. In her talks and circulars Mother Bultó was careful to associate Mother de Valon with the life of the Society. She also went to meet her in Egypt.[73] Mother de Valon did not want the interview, but it was indispensable in allowing her to go back over the recent past that had made her suffer and to help the Society to clarify a complex situation that was not well understood. The circular of 7 July 1968 addressed the real reasons for Mother de Valon's resignation,

> You know or you have guessed that the departure of Our Mother whom we love so much, who spent herself unsparingly in the service of the Society, was painful. We spoke of the cross and it was truly a cross that weighed very heavily on her whole being, above all on her heart. Our Mother felt that some of the capitulants did not have confidence in her, and wishing at whatever cost to preserve the union of the Society, she offered her resignation. She said to us: "I do so for the good of all of you." And the Heart of Our Lord, by very painful paths, accepted her sacrifice. For it was one of leaving, not an honorary office, but the work of direction of the Society at a moment of difficult developments, of exchanging an activity of her whole being and of every instant for a life without the responsibilities that government involves. Our Mother de Valon offered that and renews this offering each day from a heart

---

[72] Bultó, pp. 82-83. As Mother Drujon wrote to a correspondent who was not in agreement with the changes: "Continue to write to me everything you are thinking. You will ask, what good will that be? It enlightens us, allows us to hear the sound of several bells, orients us. I assure you that nothing is easy at this moment; we are really living the parable of the wheat and the chaff.... [W]hat has to be safeguarded at all costs is our union, for every house divided against itself.... The true renewal insists on one word: charity" (*Mère Madeleine Drujon*, p. 31).

[73] To ask for an interview Mother Bultó sent Mother de Valon a message in these words: "Mother, the desert is calling me; will you say yes?" (Testimony of M.J. Bultó).

captivated by that of Christ, totally given to serving him in serving the Society.[74]

Mother Bultó presented this meeting with Mother de Valon as "an immense grace" and "a favor of the Father of all mercy;" no doubt this was true, but the few days spent in conversation at Agami were not a happy occasion for either one of them.

Mother Drujon had told Mother Bultó that the former and the current superiors general had to write a combined letter to the Society to put an end to the "affair."[75] Mother de Valon agreed through "obedience." The contents of the paragraph she added was discussed so that it did not appear as a condemnation of the chapter but showed Mother de Valon's loyalty toward the Society of the Sacred Heart, no matter what she had suffered.[76] "Now I repeat to all of you what I have written to many since 5 December: 'Guided by the new Mother in whom I have complete confidence, let us be united and let us keep the Society strong in that union drawn from the Heart of Our Lord.'"[77]

In the interests of preserving the unity of the whole, Mother Bultó made it a priority to go to those countries that she knew to be hesitant in accepting the renewal or where attachment to Mother de Valon was strong.[78] Her first journey was to France where the majority of the delegates to the chapter had well-defined positions. The new superior general sought to meet the religious to reassure them. Mother Bultó told them that many of those who had sent her critical or provocative letters earlier now indicated their loyalty, their obedience and their confidence. Wherever she went she had to explain that the demand for change was not a sign that the Society of the Sacred Heart had proven unworthy.[79] The orientations were aimed at living the spirit of its origins with renewed intensity.

---

[74] M.J. Bultó, *Lettres circulaires*, p. 41.
[75] Testimony of M.J. Bultó.
[76] When she received the results of the election on 5 December, Mother de Valon cabled Mother Bultó: "Perfect obedience!" This was undoubtedly religious but lacking in warmth!
[77] M.J. Bultó, *Lettres circulaires*, p. 41.
[78] It is doubtless for this reason that she dedicated one of her first journeys to Ireland.
[79] "The renewal is in no way a condemnation of the past," wrote Mother Drujon. "The Society was not in decadence; it is fervent; it must return to its sources so that the *aggiornamento* may be made safely. *Aggiornamento* is certainly not an easy thing; it demands courage and prudence. The chapter is an act of obedience to the holy Church that wishes religious life to question itself and work to readjust certain structures to the world of today and to the young people who

Mother Bultó's first circular was addressed to the religious of the United States, whose delegates had taken such advanced positions that some people could suspect them of a desire for autonomy that could result in a schism. On the occasion of the 150th anniversary of the arrival of Philippine Duchesne in Louisiana, after recalling her personality and her action, Mother Bultó continued,

> Your country, dear Sisters, is now prosperous, enjoying technical and social advantages of which Blessed Philippine would never have dreamed. You are aware of the heavy responsibilities that this increase of wealth and power impose on you in the realm of social justice, freedom, peace. You are seeking the means of being neighbor to others, by struggling against poverty and loneliness knowing very well that every enterprise must be inspired by the Gospel. Enlightened and fortified by faith, may you go towards all people, the ignorant, the poor, those who suffer, and be Christ for them. It is for him that you have left everything, your father's house, those you love. You have given yourselves to him. You go with him to your brothers [and sisters]. Confronted as you are with so many needs, with such different needs…needs of the crowd that calls, ask him: "Who is my neighbor? To whom must our communities in America dedicate themselves?" He will show you! He has called you to religious life so that you may share this cooperative work and this loving aid, so that you may be neighbor to others. Go therefore, be neighbor to others…with him, because of him, in his strength and in his love, everywhere he calls you. Be neighbor always, to your sisters in community, to the students in your classes, to the people of color in the ghetto. Be Christ's neighbor in his poor, those who have need of him, those he loves.[80]

By positively reminding those who have received much that they must give much, but without blaming anyone, Mother Bultó opened new horizons. In the United States the Society of the Sacred Heart was able to evolve while remaining itself. Mother Bultó was sometimes surprised by what she saw during her journeys. She had the habit of saying then: "I don't understand you, but I have confidence in you."[81]

---

come to us" (*Mère Madeleine Drujon*, p. 33). Shortly before her death she wrote: "As Cardinal Daniélou said, a crisis is not a catastrophe, a defeat, it is facing up to different forces; great good can come out of a crisis" (p. 40, May 1968).

[80] M.J. Bultó, *Lettres circulaires*, p. 73.

[81] Testimony of D. Boland. That is what she wrote to the Society on 29 June 1969: "I dare to say, not only in thinking of the Lord but of each one of you, my dear sisters, 'I know in whom I have believed.'"

In all her circulars Mother Bultó tried to maintain and strengthen union in confidence and love. In September 1968 she recalled that charity had to show itself first of all in communities and that it was to be drawn

> from the open Heart of Christ, for the shortest way to love one another truly, courageously is to pass through Christ, to remain in him. We must be reborn to the Lord's way of loving, clothe ourselves constantly with his humility, his gentleness; for only meek and humble hearts converted by the meek and humble Master have the strength of love, the patience of love that is the true mark of strong persons. There is the decisive criterion of fraternal love. Does it give us the strength to suffer for our sisters, to love them to the point of giving our life? It is really a question of giving one's life, of losing one's life, of being worn out in the service of others, of taking others into our care, of carrying their burdens.[82]

Because she knew the dangers to mutual understanding that were possible in a time of experimentation, Mother Bultó voiced the risks of a breakup that could take place within the Society, and she repeated warnings to be on guard.

> I must admit that the circumstances in which we find ourselves at this turning-point in the life of the Church and of the Society have given rise within our communities to misunderstandings that could be divisive. I am sure that each one is seeking for the best according to her lights; on the one hand, those who, in a real concern for fidelity to what they identify as the spirit of the Society are reacting vigorously against all innovation, seeing in it a menace and a danger; on the other hand, those who, in the name of adaptation to the spirit of Vatican II, are anxious for radical changes and make others anxious too. The former express their love for the Society by keeping it in the forms which it has had up to the present; the latter, urged on by that same love and concerned for its future, are seeking and aiming to make it a dynamic Society, adapted to the needs and conditions of today's world. It is always possible to have differing points of view, but they should not lead us to take opposing positions; there are undreamt of riches, wealth in the construction of a "fraternal community built up in Christ." Therefore I would ask both groups to "consider at this moment the many needs of the Society and forget their own interests" (Saint Madeleine Sophie, 6 December 1836), in this case diverging points of view, differences in mentality, customs, and even formation, to penetrate beyond this outer shell and to seek only

---

[82] M.J. Bultó, *Lettres circulaires*, pp. 77-79.

what is essential in our religious life. Accepting that we are personally responsible, fully co-responsible for the unity without which we cannot go forward to meet the Savior, or work effectively for His Kingdom, let us listen with a new heart to Christ's prayer: "Father,...may they also be [one] in us, so that the world may know that you have sent me (Jn 17:21)."[83]

It was both an opportunity and a risk to no longer live uniformly, to accept diversity of cultures. Mother Bultó knew how to take advantage of the opportunity, while trying to arm the Society against the risk. She left the motherhouse after twelve years. During the three years of her generalate, this discreet woman, attentive to individuals, was able to imprint on the Society the "character of simplicity and union" that would characterize the Chapter of 1970.[84]

The Chapter of 1970

Careful Preparation

According to a proposal from North America the Chapter of 1970 was prepared during assemblies that brought the provincials together by continent. The one that had the greatest influence was the assembly of provincials of Latin America held in Lima in 1969. It introduced the Society of the Sacred Heart to the conclusions reached at the assembly of Medellín.

The Lima Assembly

Held in August 1968 shortly after Pope Paul VI went to Bogotá, the Medellín conference had for its purpose to apply the conclusions of

---

[83] M.J. Bultó, pp. 81-84. She expressed herself in almost the same terms on the occasion of the diffusion of the results of "Kaski," for "the period of experimentation rich in possibilities, includes as many risks as hopes" (2 December 1969, pp. 90-92). In her circular of 14 March 1970 (p. 92), she asks to read them "in a spirit that transcends all differences of age, province, nationality, mentality.... Let us think SOCIETY, not stopping at deploring what seems negative in our own or in other provinces; let us know how to rejoice in the good that we find wherever it shows itself: since we form only one body, everything belongs to all of us." It was a question of giving attention to all the currents without letting oneself be drawn in by one or the other (p. 64, 20 May 1970), of overcoming one's anxieties and one's own interests (pp. 98-99, 25 May 1970).

[84] Concepción Camacho, *Letters to the Society*, 28 November 1970, p. 1.

Vatican II to Latin America, but it went well beyond that. Noting the evolution that was already apparent, it elaborated a body of doctrine that caused a sensation and was a reference point during the following decades. Reflecting on the notion of "the Church of the poor" that John XXIII and the Council had underlined, it proposed — it was one of its original ideas — a new analysis of the concept of poverty, from which it drew consequences for pastoral action. At Medellín the poverty of Latin American countries was presented both as the consequence of underdevelopment and as the fruit of colonization, external and internal. In mining its natural resources at low cost and directing its economic life to their profit, the United States and Europe were exercising heavy pressure in the sub-continent. They were contributing to growing disparity between social classes and between the capital cities and the countryside and were leading to rural exodus, the misery of the poorest and the proletarization of the middle class. Whereas before, economic development was seen as the solution to poverty, Medellín showed that impoverishment was the consequence of political and economic exploitation. It was not so much underdevelopment as rigid social structures that must be fought.

The provincials of the Society of the Sacred Heart were aware of these arguments[85] and of the use Medellín had made of education in order to put an end to the unjust system. Taking up the thesis of the Brazilian Paulo Freire, they believed that the oppressed had to become the instruments of their own liberation. Freire affirmed that a new mode of education had to be put in place, for the oppressed to have the needed knowledge that would emerge through dialogue.[86] The educational system should not only impart knowledge but arouse creativity that allowed the oppressed to become the subjects of their own story. Instead of being dependent, the poor would become actors in a transformation that would be social, political and ecclesiastical. Community was a means of realizing liberation; it was in and through community that the organization of workers and of young people as well as the reception of the sacraments was to take place. It was with the poor, those preferred by God, that one had to make community.

The responses to the Kaski questionnaires coming from the Third World had shown that these positions had already been adopted. In the whole of the congregation, 80% of the religious believed that one of the functions of religious life was to confront the reality of the Gospel

---

[85] A priest gave them a lecture during which he showed that the impoverishment was due to capitalism, which was enriching a few countries and individuals, while in every country the greater number was suffering from the exploitation of their work and from structures that were in themselves a social sin that faith demanded to change (*Histoire de la Province du Mexique, les Années Soixante*, p. 36).

[86] Paulo Freire, *L'Éducation, pratique de la liberté*, Le Cerf, 1971.

and denounce oppression and injustice.[87] But while 52% of all religious were favorable to the idea of living and working with the poor, in Latin America the percentage was 90%. Some experiments in that direction had already been begun. In Peru where the revolution of General Alvarado was introducing a massive series of social reforms, including in the area of education, the province had decided to join the free school and the boarding school at Trujillo, to keep only one house in Lima and therefore to sell the *Sophianum*. The religious conducted socio-economic surveys of the families of their pupils and contemplated launching a new type of education with adapted pedagogical methods in working class neighborhoods and in rural villages, to work through missions and youth movements and to promote the education of adults and communities. In Chile sixty-two nuns who were running schools in working class neighborhoods and villages dedicated themselves to catechizing and lived in base communities. In almost all the provinces of Latin America the nuns were working in technical schools, visiting the sick, giving home care, working in centers for mother and child care.

At the Lima assembly the provincials decided to place communities in poor sections of cities and in towns and villages and to transfer to lay people the posts held by nuns in the institutions to give the latter the chance to work among the poor. They also proposed new ways of living poverty. The goods of the Society would be reserved for social works and missions. To learn the value of money the religious would receive a monthly allowance. The communities would be small so that they could adopt the life style of the poor. But the apostolic activities differed according to the provinces.[88] In Chile they came to believe that education was not the only form of apostolate the Society ought to have.

Preparation of the Chapter in the Provinces

In March 1969 the general council sent out a reflection on the formation of the religious, experiments already undertaken regarding government, apostolic life, life of prayer, community life, going out, the practice of poverty and the wearing of the religious habit.[89] An exploratory mission was confided to five international committees who were to provide the procedure to be used at the general chapter and to develop the schemas to

---

[87] Question N° 12.
[88] Final document of the Lima Assembly, quoted in *Histoire de la Province du Mexique, les Années Soixante*, p. 25.
[89] Gen Arch. C I C 3, Box 25.

be presented.[90] They worked from notes from the provinces and the results of the questionnaires developed by Kaski. In May 1970 Father Spruit summarized the problems that were being presented in the provinces under three rubrics. Some were due to the "questioning of the social context;" others were produced by the renewal of religious life; the last concerned the internal structure of the Society. Father Spruit thought that fidelity to Saint Madeleine Sophie was the only way to allow a renewal and to resolve the issue of unity at the heart of diversity. The will to live the dynamism of the founding charism in responding to the concrete needs of the epoch was evident in all the schemas that were drawn up.

The working groups did not arrive at a single document. Regarding government, two modes were proposed, one based on collegiality,[91] the other on subsidiarity;[92] but both modes maintained exchange of personnel among provinces to facilitate better service of the Church and the world. The committee in charge of formation leaned more on the profile of those responsible for formation rather than on the content of the formation program, but it recommended that the religious be formed as members of an international society, not just of one province. The committee thought that formation had to include initiation in prayer, formation through work, opening to social questions and maintaining a certain solitude. The schema on community life, deliberately brief, defined it as enabling meeting Christ in fraternal communion. The apostolate was to be oriented either "toward the poor" or toward the missions. There was agreement that one must be inserted in a milieu, to personify it and not to be identified with the masses, but education was not mentioned as a particular means of living the apostolate. The committee on finances reflected on the role of treasurers in the schools. It thought that it had to give to provinces the means of determining[93] whether their own funds were being well used and of adopting responsible planning. It posed questions that put finances in a new perspective: was it necessary to continue to sustain works that were not yielding results and to subsidize those aimed at the affluent? Did mutual aid among the provinces require the existence of a central fund? Could the

---

[90] Box 24, report of 23 May 1970. A working meeting brought together their members in Rome in May 1970. The documents of these commissions were addressed to the communities for study and amendment. The reactions sent to Rome were introduced into the schemas.

[91] It could not be total since at each level, responsibility was to be exercised by all; the final decision reverted to the superior.

[92] At the central level, the superior general governed with the assistants general who would be regional superiors and a council of "experts."

[93] Testimony of V. Bowman. It was a question of helping them to manage the costs of tuition and the salaries of the personnel.

contributions granted to the missions be extended to social works? How can we not appear allied with capitalism when we dispose of considerable sums of money? Ought we to consider that to put capital at the service of others is still capitalism?

The Work and Decisions of the Chapter

The chapter was held from 3 October to 16 November 1970. A third of the eighty-eight capitulants had participated in the preceding chapter.[94] A few religious had been invited.[95] Seven young professed[96] from France, Italy, Philippines, United States, Ireland, Congo and Peru were responsible to contribute "their knowledge of the problems of the world of today and the aspirations of youth." Thanks to Anne Mawete, who formed part of the group, Africa was represented for the first time by someone from that continent. The assembly was considerably younger than the Chapter of 1967, since the average age was forty.

Before the opening of the chapter the capitulants had to establish the objectives. The task proved to be delicate.[97] Based on the responses received the following synthesis was elaborated:

> To become aware of what the Spirit is demanding of us for a radically evangelical life, open to God today through prayer, committed to fraternal community, inserted in the world, as a liberating challenge integrated in international communion in the Love of Christ. Today that presupposes unity in diversity. The chapter will have to take a fundamental step in this direction. And in a world where change henceforth requires an interim dynamic, the chapter will have to create liberating structures that allow responding to the demands of the Spirit.[98]

---

[94] Thirty-eight were members *ex officio*.

[95] They were Françoise de Lambilly, secretary of UISG (International Union of Superiors General of Women), Doreen Boland, assistant to the treasurer general, Margaret Mary Miller, newly named provincial of the Chicago Province, Esperanza Medina from Egypt. Three others, Marie-Thérèse Virnot, Jeanne de Charry and Barbara Hogg, had produced studies on Saint Madeleine Sophie and the history of the Society.

[96] The term aspirantship was no longer to be used to name the period between first and final vows.

[97] One group found it preferable to determine the spirit of the Society and the ideal toward which all the members were tending: "To succeed in this, we asked one another why we were remaining in the Society," they wrote.

[98] Gen. Arch. C I C 3, Box 24.

The text made no allusion to any apostolic mission whatever,[99] nor even to any concrete facts of the religious life of the Society of the Sacred Heart.

Mother Bultó opened the chapter with a brief statement in which she urged the assembly to give "clear, calm, bold direction," which the Society expected and "which can draw us together and give us courage to go forward…..

> …I think we all want:
>
> To affirm again our determination to center our lives on CHRIST, and on His LOVE, that love for which the HEART pierced on the Cross is a permanently effective symbol. To deepen our fidelity to our religious consecration and to the vocation proper to us, diluting its demands in no way, and convinced that the Society's ideal will prove suited to any age so long as it keeps contact with the Gospel, and so long as it can combine total fidelity with a constant willingness to adapt and to grow. As we work, FIDELITY TO JESUS ought to be our constant care; our relation to Him must be the ultimate standard by which we set our priorities.
>
> This fidelity to Jesus will make us try with Gospel daring to live forcefully, effectively, dynamically, UNITY and DIVERSITY. Saint Madeleine Sophie who suffered so much to keep the Society ONE will be with us now, and we must try to move toward the same goal, but by different roads and at different speeds. To do this we must build an awareness of personal and group commitment. If we all fix our gaze on the same ideal, we will find the enthusiasm, the solidarity, the concern that distinguished the primitive Christian community and our own earliest communities.

The chapter also had to determine the spirit in which the mission was to unfold:

---

[99] Box 23. See for example the statement of one of the groups: "Jesus Christ is the center of our lives; he calls us to live the values of the Gospel in an absolute fashion in community, while responding to the needs of the world. The special charism of the Society of the Religious of the Sacred Heart is a loving interpersonal relationship with God and with other persons at the same time. The Society exists only in the measure in which each one gives herself totally and freely to Christ and to each member of the Society. The spirit of the Society rests in its members. In effect the incarnation requires that the Spirit take a body. Through our interpersonal relationships we give the Spirit to one another. Where interpersonal relationships are weak or lacking, the Spirit that unites us to one another is not transmitted; and in this measure the Society of the Sacred Heart ceases to exist. These interpersonal relationships demand mutual responsibility, which means that each one in the community is responsible to all the others and that the others are equally responsible to her."

As Religious of the Sacred Heart, how can we, both by our life and by our work, convey to the world the message of the freely given love of God, which is revealed in his Son? The task demands a courageous habit of listening, testing, searching; a broad vision of the world and of what is at stake in the Kingdom, which demands that we be detached, self-sacrificing, at the disposal of others. Our community life will have to be a sign of the Kingdom that is already here; a sign of the Fatherhood of God and of universal brotherhood in Christ. If these are the horizons to which we look, we can easily put aside useless debate....

Instead, we must interpret in the light of the Gospel various situations as they arise. This presupposes not only being aware of but accepting what is new. Does the Gospel not always, does it not ever remain the great innovation that upsets our routine, shows up our laziness, jolts our apathy? Unless we honestly meet this challenge of the Gospel, any action that we take will be superficial. We must have enough balance, courage and love to make the Society respond at a very deep level, with sincerity, and with one mind.

That response must not be hampered by undue timidity or by unchecked impatience. Nor, God forbid, by dissension. Our responsibility is a heavy one: THE RENEWAL MUST BE THE WORK OF ALL.

Mother Bultó reaffirmed once more her concern to unite a body that she knew to be more diverse than ever. Therefore she concluded her talk on an appeal to each one:

The basic living renewal of our community as a whole will demand of all its members a great effort of conversion in a spirit of humility, faith and trust, so that each may recapture the freshness, the inward power of her first meeting with Jesus, when He invited her to leave all for Him and for His Kingdom. May we not see this chapter as a new call, a genuine, demanding call of Christ to each one of us and, through us, to the Society?

May we, following in the steps of Our Lady and upheld by her intercession, share with one another what is best in ourselves so as to say quite sincerely to Our Lord: Here we are come together and the whole Society with us wanting nothing but to search out your will and to do it today.

Clarity, faith and hope were not to be accompanied by false humility, for "We have a rich heritage from which new life can spring. Let us go forward then," concluded Mother Bultó, "in an atmosphere of prayer, of wide and trusting union, of limitless love of Our Lord, strong in His peace and sure of His presence. Then, what can be wanting to us?"

The coordination commission had planned that after a presentation of the spirituality and fundamental values of the Society, the capitulants, starting from the priorities derived from the needs of the provinces, would seek to determine the form of government that could respond to them. After the election of the superior general, they would decide what options to take concerning apostolic life, finances, community life and formation. Even though it had been decided not to prolong discussion, no one could tell then when the chapter would end.

The atmosphere was good from the beginning, for much of the suffering following the special chapter had been alleviated. One felt a desire to go forward and to return to the sources of the charism.[100] The presentation of the reports by the provincials was instructive concerning the aspirations put forth, and it sometimes brought about a moment of great emotion.[101] However the capitulants quickly made it known that they did not intend to work on the prepared reports or even to create commissions charged with a particular theme, for everything was to come from the core. Neither did they intend to evaluate the way the directives had been lived since 1967. As for defining the identity of the Society of the Sacred Heart, although they knew that the Society desired such a definition, some of them wondered whether it was not necessary rather to treat the *raison d'être* of the Society. A definition appeared static to them and a statement of identity seemed abstract. They all met in the groups assigned and drafted texts, but their objectives were imprecise. They wanted to "give élan, a prophetic breath that gives confidence to the Society," to state or restate the great principles of our religious life," "to affirm ourselves clearly as a community that tends to live the Gospel in the diversity of local situations," "to give a certain number of criteria for the evaluation of the experimentation," but without specifying which ones, "to seek mechanisms to assure flexibility in the face of the reality of a changing life," "to rethink our apostolate in relation to life today," but without giving examples. They sought to define a "fundamental option" without success. But they were in agreement about "maintaining unity while respecting diversity" and "valuing the richness of the international Society while allowing each country to be completely itself." Because of the influence of Latin America, several

---

[100] Testimony of D. Boland.

[101] Bernadette des Francs, the provincial of France, gave an excellent report that reconciled many of the capitulants with France. Simply and humbly she showed that the Society in France was growing old, that evolution was in its beginning and was not unanimously accepted. Many capitulants thanked her in tears! (Testimony of Marie-Louise Leplat).

groups desired one of the objectives of the chapter to be to "decide to insert ourselves among human beings as a liberating challenge in the simplicity of the Gospel."

Two orientations emerged. Some capitulants wanted a change, but in the framework of traditional apostolates of the Society; others wanted "to go toward the poor."[102] The concern for the poor had been widespread since 1967.[103] At the heart of the chapter the Latin Americans formed a small group united by its desire to remain faithful to the teachings of Medellín. They made such notions as conscientization, liberation and liberating challenge heard; the last was defined as "the affirmation of a redemptive hope," deducing "the liberating mission through love" from the affirmation of the being of God and God's salvific love.[104] This language was new for most of the participants, and the words did not have the same meaning for everyone, as exchanges around the term "human promotion" showed. While for a delegate from the United States it referred to man going to the moon, others saw in the term the liberation of the human being in order to realize eternal destiny! Thereafter one had, and this was painful, to accept one another as different.

As Mother Bultó told it, "Days were passing and no one was saying anything to us because as each one was going along her own way; they were drafting summaries but there were no connections among what was being produced. There was no theme emerging."[105] Finally she asked Mother Camacho whether the central commission, of which she was a member, could not suggest to the groups some bases for reflection on which all could agree so that the chapter could make headway. "That was the genesis of the five options. Afterwards it was possible to continue reflection and the options were identified with much strength." The "values of secularization" presented as a socio-cultural phenomenon serving as a

---

[102] Testimony of M.J. Bultó.
[103] Testimony of Ana Ramírez Ugarte.
[104] Work of Group 5.
[105] If one refers to the summary of the desires expressed about documents to elaborate, the assembly wanted "a single document that gives a vision of the whole of apostolic community today. This text must express the requirements, the fundamental options and say how to live them. It must be centered on Jesus Christ, on the essential. It must take into account the ecclesial and world situation. It must take the form of a message addressed to all ages that challenges, calls into question and invites to conversion. It must give a prophetic élan expressed in dynamic terms, be short, clear, simple, cordial, in personal, evangelical and non-theological language." It was to reflect internationality without specifying the applications to be drawn at the provincial and local levels (Gen. Arch. C I C 3, Box 23).

background to the whole of contemporary life did not provide the material for a separate option.

The acts of the chapter were introduced by a quotation from the Gospel of Saint John (17:21-23), "May they be so completely one that the world will realize that it was you who sent me and that I have loved them," with this commentary: "This prayer of lasting power, the ground of our unity in diversity, has moved us to take several fundamental options, which converge in a single center: the Heart of Christ." There was a re-centering on the essential. The very brief text of the chapter can be summarized by the five options,[106] from which the Society of the Sacred Heart was going to live for a long time afterward.

The first option referred to the international community, "one and necessarily diverse," which the Society of the Sacred Heart was to be from then on: "In a divided world where the Church seeks evermore to bring about the reconciliation of all men in Christ, our unity will be a sign of fellowship open to all."[107] The second option was a reaffirmation of the educational mission of the Society as service in the Church "[a]t a time when the integral development of man is a task of special urgency." "It is the love of Christ which urges us to meet the needs of those weighed down by ignorance or servitude, and above all, the needs of the young who search for the meaning of life." This mission was to be carried out creatively in relation to the developments of the contemporary world: "Let us educate to a faith which will be relevant in a secularized world, to intellectual values, and to a social awareness which will impel to action." It required "examining the apostolic value of our institutions."[108] The third option affirmed solidarity with the poor by attaching it to the work of liberation of Christ, as it was expressed in the hymn of the Epistle to the Philippians: "Christ has made us his own: he emptied himself and gave his life to set us free. Henceforth we are caught up in a work which is essentially one of liberation. Wherever we are, a sense of solidarity with the poor should mark our lives: lives of hard work in which availability and a radical gift of self make serious demands."[109] The fourth option called for, "at a time when mankind hungers and thirsts for justice,...solidarity with the Third World that suffers poverty and oppression." Without giving precise information on places where one would exercise the option, it identified positions that could be put forward in different environments and countries: "This

---

[106] Testimony of M-L. Leplat, member of the coordinating commission. The term option was chosen rather than rule because it seemed less authoritarian and dictatorial.

[107] *Chapter 1970*, p. 9.

[108] *Chapter 1970*, p. 10.

[109] P. 11.

solidarity will, above all, shake us out of our complacency. It requires that all take whatever steps they can to ensure a more just distribution of this world's goods; it demands an appreciation of other cultures and traditions; it means an end to any attitude of power and paternalism. This option implies, according to needs and possibilities, the long-range planning of our works in a global perspective – planning that leads to resolute action. It should also lead us to take a stand against the dehumanizing structures of a consumer society."[110] The fifth option committed the Society again to the renewal of community life, "the one condition essential to the future of our religious life and to a genuine response to the summons of the Church and the world."[111] The perspective of self-government, largely dominant at the chapter, was respected since it specified that "each community will create its own life style, evaluated in faith, in the light of the Gospel."[112]

To the five options were added some "fundamental elements" that took up the objectives the capitulants had identified in their first meetings:

- a serious prayer life centered in the Eucharist and the Word of God;
  a contemplative outlook on the world, which presupposes times of deep prayer, both solitary and shared;
  an atmosphere conducive to the experience of God both for ourselves and for those about us.
- true interpersonal relationships, which give substance to our commitment to live the universal love of Christ;
- genuine acceptance of one another and sincere forgiveness, in friendship and joy.
- the sharing of all that we are and all that we have, in a life-style voluntarily simple, austere and welcoming.
- the common search for the will of God, in total availability, served by authority that is simple and evangelical.
- an effort of discernment which will open us in depth to the values of a secularized world where Christ is at work.
- true presence in the human community which we wish to love and serve.[113]

---

[110] P. 12.
[111] Marie-Louise Leplat remembers that the fundamental elements for apostolic community appeared revolutionary. It envisaged that the nuns would have personal budgets, already a practice in certain provinces. The Latin Americans were influential in the discussions on fraternal community and community of goods.
[112] *Chapter 1970*, p. 13.
[113] P. 14.

The acts conclude with confidence in Christ at work in the Society and in the world: "Strong in the faith that the Lord who calls us to this continual conversion remains with us, we can go forward in joy and hope."[114] If the capitulants had wanted to arrive at a text that took into account the *dynamique du provisoire*, the power of the provisional, they succeeded in elaborating a document that had that prophetic élan that they wished for.

Mother Bultó has told how worried she was when she saw that the term education was possibly not going to appear in the final document; "Everything had to be new, everything different." She asked to take the floor and said to the chapter, "I remind you that we are approved by the Church for education, which makes me wonder whether we may so easily withdraw that word." The capitulants then placed the option for education and for education of young people in their text.[115] In the course of the discussions three principal tendencies became evident. One group tended to think that education had to be carried out in the institutions. Others had contested this position saying that the religious ought to have less power and that we ought to leave the institutions in order to respond to the needs of the world and live among the poor.[116] The second preference was for a renewal in education, without eliminating scholastic establishments, along the lines of the experiments conducted in working class milieus. Taking up the arguments of Paulo Freire, who had been invited to speak at the chapter, it saw that instruction was liberation and pre-evangelization. The third preference was a desire to eliminate education from the mission of the Society, for it was based on the belief that the mission should be defined according to current times and needs. The apostolate could be a simple presence among the poor and an "apostolate of witness." An intervention of Marie-Thérèse Virnot helped to clarify issues. Basing it on *Perfectae caritatis*, she established that the works of charity proper to a congregation and confided to it by the Church formed part of the very essence of its religious life. Education that figured in the Constitutions and in the writings of Saint Madeleine Sophie and in the name her first companions had borne was the means of realizing the mission confided to the Society when it was recognized in 1826. While the Latin Americans had been unanimous during the discussions on the option for the poor and for community, they were divided regarding education.

The delegates from Argentina, Chile and Uruguay wanted to move away from the mission as it existed and transform the Society into a kind of

---

[114] P. 15.
[115] Testimony of M.J. Bultó.
[116] Drafts of Groups 2 and 5 on education.

"congregation of Little Sisters of the Poor," which Mexico did not want. Peru wanted an orientation more marked by training of public school teachers. Colombia held an intermediate position but close to that of Mexico. Puerto Rico did not insist on the political context. Venezuela was living according to its own rhythm. But there was unanimity in denunciation of the colonizing country of the first world,[117] namely the United States.

The option on solidarity with the poor was adopted without resistance. In drafting it the capitulants were aware of being in harmony with the thought of Saint Madeleine Sophie, since according to the Constitutions the only preference that a religious could express outright was that of being employed in a school for the poor. Many among them thought that the "true" schools of the Sacred Heart ought to have been those and not the schools for the children of the elite. They believed that because governments had gradually funded free education poor schools had little by little disappeared, unneeded. "Go to the poor" was a way to be faithful to the founding charism.[118] However this option could be a source of conflict between religious who were working in the schools and those who wished to "go to the poor," for from then on this concern was raised in a context outside the framework of the schools and scholastic works.

This option, alone at first, took into account every aspect of poverty. But was it possible to treat in the same option the latent poverty of developed countries where the life style was undeniably improving and the situations of misery that Religious of the Sacred Heart were facing in mission countries? As there was no African professed among the capitulants, the situation of the Third World was brought up by some Europeans who had lived there and who wanted a specific option to be dedicated to it. They were supported by the Latin Americans who had been made aware of the misery through their own discoveries, through the episcopal conferences in their countries and through political movements that appeared or developed during the 1960s. In Third World countries the Society of the Sacred Heart could contribute to the Church's moves toward liberation regarding unjust social structures as demanded by the Medellín assembly. It seemed that an option necessarily expressed the degree to which the Society wished to make that one of its priorities.[119]

---

[117] Testimony of Isabel Aranguren.
[118] Testimony of D. Boland.
[119] Doreen Boland remembers that those who spoke for the Third World received a very high level of listening from their sisters.

Drafting the options was hard-hitting. But they had to be developed to show their practical consequences so that they were not reduced to a state of mind or attitudes. For the first option a paragraph underlined that to desire unity and diversity signified that the Society of the Sacred Heart was to practice co-responsibility, sharing at the international level, and understanding of and respect for the reality of each country. These common efforts were capable of "strengthening the bonds which unite us in the same Spirit."[120] To the option of solidarity with the poor were added the following lines: "Some have a more direct and urgent call to work with the poor. Together we will seek the means to help them answer this call,"[121] which was an open door to implementing new apostolic activities that took into account individual vocations. The option for the Third World asked of the Society a new kind of sharing at the level of finances and of personnel. The options, like the decisions of the chapter concerning formation, government and finances, all had for their goal to "return to the Gospel, according to the spirit of the founder, to respond to the needs of the world."[122] Marie-Thérèse Virnot had shown that Saint Madeleine Sophie, in order to make known the love of God revealed in Jesus Christ had been attentive to the needs of her time and had adapted to developments in society. By fulfilling these triple conditions it would be possible to contribute to the renewal of the Society of the Sacred Heart in fidelity to the Church and to the spirit of the Council.

The conclusion of the acts of the chapter shows how matters demanding attention and identified little by little during the assembly were unified "in this central theme of our Constitutions: union and conformity to the Heart of Jesus."

> To contemplate this Heart, we need not turn our gaze away from this world, the home of the living God. Christ is here, hidden at the very heart of the world. Here, where he died, his risen life springs forth and is gradually penetrating the whole of history. He is there in that unconscious expectation that is working in the whole of creation, here at work in man's efforts to build a world of justice and brotherhood. It is up to mankind, whose fears, solitude and love he shared, to manifest his glory.
>
> At the deepest level of our vocation this call resounds today to contemplate the Heart of Christ through the pierced heart of humanity. This union and conformity with Jesus makes us determined to be present in the world as he was, close to his brothers and available to them. "Let

---

[120] *Chapter 1970*, p. 9.
[121] P. 11.
[122] P. 44.

this mind be in you which was also in Christ Jesus." Our presence in varied spheres of life at a time when national spirit is asserting itself and when our uniformity is disappearing, will surely accentuate our pluriformity. One might think that unity in the Society for which Saint Madeleine Sophie had prayed and suffered so much, would thereby be weakened. But we can affirm through our experience of the Chapter of 1970 that instead of dividing us this diversity has strengthened and enriched our unity. Now that certain exterior resemblances have vanished, the essential reality seems all the more clear. The effort to achieve this deeper unanimity in respect and understanding of this pluralism has given new life to our unity and is for all of us a sign of hope.

Thus in order to remain faithful today is in a sense to change. It is to go beyond precise laws to rediscover their spirit and life. "The times change," wrote Saint Madeleine Sophie to Mother Duchesne in 1831, "and we too must modify our views." For her the only thing necessary was to make known the love of God revealed in Christ. For us too, this is the sole criterion of our renewal.[123]

The capitulants had not wished to produce a text of theological import. But they had arrived at expressing in accessible language a "theology" of the religious life at the Sacred Heart, without going into details but offering a new way to speak of a spirituality founded on Scripture. It was a shock for many religious. "It was a moment of liberation and of a true 'return to the sources,' to the intuitions I had been aware of since my youth," recalled Hannelore Woitsch. As Mary Shanahan wrote, "The Chapter of 1970 presented more of a challenge. I think I still try to live its vision." For Helen McLaughlin, delegate from Uganda,

> This chapter changed me for life. I became aware of the strengths and weaknesses of the Society. There was formidable confusion about the future of religious life; the hopes of the Latin Americans were very different from those of the Europeans, and the Americans differed from the Asians. The chapter was very long, but we needed all that time to direct the whole Society toward the future. It was a painful experience, and like the others, I passed through darkness, but it was magnificent at the end to see what we agreed on and how we were going to grow together. It was like living the paschal mystery. The documents of 1970 are the fruit of suffering, of much prayer, of search, and the manner in which the Spirit was at work was not always recognized then. I changed very much during

---

[123] Pp. 44-45.

that chapter – it was the experience that formed me the most – and I was full of enthusiasm to communicate the results of our deliberations. Everyone in Uganda was open, inflamed by what had happened at the chapter, and I had no difficulty in sharing it. There was no resistance at all to what was new.

The election took place on 16 November 1970. The choice of Mother Camacho undoubtedly marked a turning point in the history of the Society of the Sacred Heart. For the first time a superior general who had not been vicar general was elected for a limited term. As a Spaniard succeeded another Spaniard, people wondered if Mother Bultó had not designated her successor. She denied it strongly. Even less did she wish to intervene in the nominating process, since she did not want to exert pressure that would have given the impression of a return to the earlier practice.[124] Concepción Camacho had spiritual and human qualities sufficient to impress the chapter. She had learned in 1967 to take on responsibility. After the special chapter she had been provincial. When Mother Bultó advised the provincials to go to a country other than their own so as to see what the reactions to the changes and experiments had been, she went to the United States where her personality had much impact. At the Chapter of 1970, as a member of the central commission, she had real influence on the capitulants of all nationalities.

Her election went smoothly. Although three names had emerged, soon only two remained on the ballot, hers and Mother Bultó's. The latter had made it clear that she did not wish to be renewed in her office.[125] As Maria Luiza Saade recalled,

> The eve of the election the provincial of Italy, Mother Barcherini, made a comment that contributed to the direction of the vote the following day: "Sisters," she said, "at this moment the Society has greater need of hope than of experience…." The next day Concha Camacho was elected!

She was forty-two years old. After the founder she was the youngest superior general of the Society of the Sacred Heart.

---

[124] Mother Bultó recalled that Mother Camacho had not consulted her on the eve of the election.

[125] Some pressure had been exerted on her in view of re-election, including by Mother de Valon. She was able to resist, relying on the statement she had made at the time of her election; she slid under the doors of the capitulants a letter that she had reviewed with Father Molinari, in which she indicated that her decision was firm. Thanks to her tenacity, generalate for life was not re-established in a discreet disguise.

Chapter IV

Turbulence

Calling on the memory of those who have lived through the events is the best way to discover the reactions of members of a group when what constitutes its life is called into question. The answers to the same questionnaire sent to all five continents[1] portrayed extremely diverse circumstances. There had to be an appraisal at the beginning of the 1970s, since Mother Camacho during her generalate had to oversee the changes taking place in the Society of the Sacred Heart.

Varied Pathways

At the end of the 1960's the identity of a Religious of the Sacred Heart was vigorously affirmed. As one Austrian nun put it: "I entered a congregation in which everything was uniform; the aim was to glorify the Heart of Jesus. We were charged with the education of girls from kindergarten on, and our communities were designed to implement that objective. Our way of life made room for prayer, community life and the apostolate."[2] Cloister had reinforced the cohesion of the group without necessarily destroying one's personality, for around the world the religious gave proof of their

---

[1] M. Luirard proceeded by individual interviews in Japan and Mexico, by group interviews in Peru and through a questionnaire sent to the whole province in Australia, New Zealand, Belgium, Ireland, Scotland, Great Britain, Italy, France Southern Spain, Chile, Colombia, Canada and the United States.
[2] Testimony of M. Schilgen.

individuality.[3] But they had been undervalued because "the iron clad structure had not allowed them to make full use of their gifts."[4]

While there had been a culture of uniformity, the provinces did not look the same. Australia and New Zealand, on account of their distance, had not had a regular visit since 1913; they had maintained modes of religious life that already seemed obsolete to Mother Tobin in 1965.[5] Persecution in Mexico had resulted in a respect for tradition that Mother Bultó tried to bring up to date.[6] In the largest countries distances made governing difficult,[7] and in the United States the character of the houses depended on the state of the Church and on local school policy, the region determining to some degree the kind of education offered. Between 1921 and 1946 the general council had not had a representative from the United States. A certain distance regarding the motherhouse had resulted, all the more as the annual reports of the councilors had to be written in French. When Mothers de Lescure and de Valon went to the United States, they had not visited the whole country, not even all the houses of the vicariates through which they passed.[8]

The changes resulting from the Special Chapter did not affect the whole congregation in the same way. Although some provinces implemented them rapidly, it was only after the Chapter of 1970 that the transformation became widespread, and even in the same province

---

[3] Testimony of Joan Scott: "One of the reasons that attracted me to the Society was that most of the nuns I met were well balanced, intelligent, educated, spiritual. They were hard workers, sometimes a little eccentric, often holy women. Whatever the faults of the system, it produced remarkable women, or at least it did not destroy them!"

[4] Testimony of P. Corral.

[5] She said she had found the religious "still more French than the French!"

[6] Testimony of P. García de Quevedo and S. Rubio.

[7] The vicariate with the greatest extent was that of Canada, where the Society extended from British Columbia to Nova Scotia. The Washington Vicariate extended from Miami to Boston. The New York Vicariate was divided: because most of the houses centered around New York City; Detroit appeared to be separate. In California because of few houses, rotation of personnel was inadequate. In St. Louis the attitudes were traditional as in civil society. Manhattanville was "the intellectual center" that "set the pace of thought in the province" and perhaps in the country (Gen. Arch. C III, USA, Report of M. Tobin, 1968).

[8] Mother Tobin distinguished between a regular visit and a passing visit in which the superior or an assistant general spent time in a house without examining its functioning or having visits with the religious. This second type of visit did not contribute to an understanding of the culture of the country and its evolution.

not all the houses evolved at the same pace.[9] In Australia, New Zealand, Ireland and Malta the ecclesiastical hierarchy was not encouraging changes in religious congregations and did not approve them when they appeared in the Society of the Sacred Heart, which was often the first group to make changes. For the Hungarians who had suffered persecution and for the Polish who lived in a totalitarian country, to defend religious life as it had existed was a way of affirming faith and courage. Some aged local superiors had been in office too long and were not aware and appreciative of developments in civil society; they held back the process. Finally, in certain mission countries the first generation of indigenous religious had so assimilated the culture of the congregation that they were not able to return to the ordinary practices in the culture of their own country.[10]

From 1968 on innovations symbolic of a change of attitude were taking place. As the religious were allowed to organize their own time, they were given alarm clocks. Reading in the refectory was abandoned as well as the chapter of faults, which had already disappeared in Uganda and in Chad;[11] silence was no longer observed as before. In Asia and Africa culturally sensitive liturgical celebrations were developed. In Bombay, where Sophia College was a center for Indianization, prie-dieu were kept in a part of the chapel, but rugs allowed the religious to pray in new postures. A low table, behind which the celebrant was seated cross-legged, served as the altar. Gestures, use of incense, light, flowers, fruits, water and traditional *arati* were introduced into the liturgy. Hymns[12] and liturgical music were interpreted with the cithara, bells and drums.[13] Yoga was used in the novitiate and in community prayer. The communities adopted a vegetarian diet. In Japan they began to use chopsticks at meals.[14] In Congo there were two dietary regimes.[15] In Uganda traditional instruments were used during liturgical celebrations conducted in the local languages.[16]

---

[9] In Japan change was rapid in Tokyo, slower in Susono and Sapporo (Testimony of Hiroko Okui).
[10] Testimony of B. Keogh.
[11] Testimony of D. Boland and G. Bovagnet.
[12] They were due to Gool Mary Dhalla.
[13] Prov. Arch. Ireland/Scotland, UGK 169. Letter of D. Boland, 1 March 1970.
[14] Testimony of H. Okui.
[15] Testimony of C. Meeûs.
[16] Testimony of W. Killeen.

The Crisis of Authority

The practice of authority required some adjustment. Before, there had been such constraints that now the religious wished to enjoy more liberty, but many did not know how to discern what was possible or desirable. Some religious were leading their own life without accounting to anyone.[17] The youngest were coming home late in the evening and openly opposing the superior when she expressed disapproval.[18] Decisions of provincial chapters had little importance for certain religious.[19] Resistance to authority grew, and those in office were no longer respected.[20] According to the picturesque description of Dolores Díaz-Varela, "Meat is good but if it is given to a baby, the body does not tolerate it." In the United States the aversion to authority was correlated with the counter-culture born of the Vietnam War. As Joan Faber noted,

> Suddenly everyone was supposed to be trained and interiorly directed in what was unprecedented conduct. The elders did not understand and often did not appreciate the new ways. There was no model for the young who were living through a transition because structures were different from earlier ones. Traditional values like silence were questioned. More flexibility and personal choice occasioned criticism. If there was no prescribed time of formal prayer, were people praying? Was it possible for everyone to be personally responsible for her prayer life? How to manage friendships? What was understood by a life that was simple, open and ordinary? How to judge whether one was a true religious? Answers differed and that worried people. There were tensions between the young and the old. Still one had to listen to the young and to have confidence in them.[21]

The reactions to superiors revealed a crisis of authority. While some superiors succeeded in fostering initiative, communicating with transparency what they knew of discussions in the congregation and allowing each

---

[17] Gen. Arch. C III, USA, f. 30. Report of M. Tobin.
[18] Testimony of María Teresa Olmedo.
[19] Testimony of Moira McCourt.
[20] Testimony of Nancy Kehoe.
[21] The new situation that privileged the youngest members to the detriment of the oldest was a source of frustration for the intermediate generation "bound by the principles, usages and customs of the past. Before everything was for the older sisters; they were surrounded with assistance, with services given with affection and deference. Then everything was for the young. One took interest in them, questioned them as to their preferences and desires. They could organize their lives and their apostolate" (Testimony of Marie-Thérèse de la Rochère).

one to find her own place,[22] most of them were not able to carry out their role because they had no models to follow. Whereas before 1967 they had contributed to stability by their character and their behavior, now they gave the impression of being overcome by uncertainty.[23] They became mistrustful.[24] Or else they tolerated everything and appeared naive. Provincials seemed to be merely administrators. It was difficult to reconcile this situation with the concept of responsibility proper to religious life and to the vow of obedience. In England frequent meetings were held to help superiors explore through role play the psychological factors that were at work.[25] But where there had previously been a climate of confidence and dialogue between the superior and the religious, the changes were not so noticeable.[26]

Finally there were communities without superiors, as vicariate assemblies in the eastern United States requested.[27] But this phenomenon emerged gradually. In 1970, 76% of communities had a superior. The percentage changed to 61% in 1972 and to 44% by 1974. The provinces most rapidly and fully affected were those of New York, Japan, Chile, Peru and Puerto Rico. By 1973 there were communities without superiors in Austria, Germany, Poland, Uganda, Chad and India. Two years later this organizational pattern had spread throughout Europe, had reached Mexico and had become the norm in Argentina, California, New York and Chicago, which had spearheaded the movement. In the United States the

---

[22] Testimony of M-L. Fabre and Solange Teisserenc regarding Mother Peyredieu du Charlat.

[23] Testimony of Beatrice Brennan: "Between 1962 and 1967, when I was assistant at Manhattanville, I knew what was expected of me. But in 1969 when I became superior of a small community at Bloomfield Hills, I was no longer sure. We were searching for ways of living religious life in a circular manner rather than on a pyramidal model without knowing very well what that required. Persons were encouraged to make responsible choices without consulting the superior each time." She was challenged by some tricky situations: "One morning I found at my door a note in which a nun told me she was leaving the Society to marry a priest who was the chancellor of the diocese!" She concluded, "In spite of the mistakes we made and our uncertainty, I felt the deep love of most people for their vocation and their sincere desire that the future Society be modeled on the spirit of Saint Madeleine Sophie."

[24] Testimony of Barbara Crombie.

[25] Testimony of J. Faber.

[26] Testimony of H. McLaughlin.

[27] Testimony of Ann Conroy. As Mary Henry remarked, it was also a solution inasmuch as it became difficult to find superiors capable of doing what was expected of them.

South maintained local superiors longer and even sought to establish the role in the small communities as they were organized and brought together religious from other provinces.[28] In countries where foreign religious had been superiors, the responsibility given to each religious appeared to be a liberation in contrast to "the domination of the French and Spanish sisters who had created a kind of guardianship that made us minors. Communities without superiors motivated the religious to share community responsibilities."[29] In France the phenomenon was not so widespread. In the communities without superiors "some religious who had been somewhat overwhelmed in the past or those who were very independent appreciated feeling more free. But the fear of being seen as a leader paralyzed some initiatives or proposals."[30] In certain provinces, the result was a lack of authority at the local level.[31]

The changes that affected local government furnished arguments for those who believed that the Society of the Sacred Heart was in the process of losing its traditions. The Sacred Congregation for Religious alluded to them.[32] The changes were not universally approved in the Society. The preparation for the Chapter of 1976 revealed concern about local government: "No one knows clearly who must give an account of what; at the local level, there is little community leadership or spiritual and apostolic fresh air; it is not clear what authority a person has when she is given a responsibility. We have not yet found a balance between the participation of individuals and the concerns of the whole. We must clarify the difference between authority and responsibility and establish their relationship in

---

[28] Testimony of Marianne Ruggeri.
[29] *Histoire de la province de Colombie*, § 59.
[30] Testimony of Christiane Chazottes.
[31] Testimony of M. Mardel.
[32] Letter of Cardinal Antoniutti, 20 April 1971: "The 'life style' created by each community ought to refer clearly to the end of the Society and to the intervention of major superiors in view of assuring a life and experiences conformed to that end. In what concerns government the chapter seems even to envisage the possibility for certain groupings not to have a superior. As for the local council, if there is no objection in small communities to having all the sisters form part of it, nevertheless experience shows that in larger houses a limited council remains necessary at least for the more important affairs. Of course, the superiors general must govern more and more with their collaborators and their councils; the fact remains that having 'to render an account for the souls confided to them,' they cannot abdicate the share of personal responsibility confided to them by the Church. It is the same, all proportion guarded, for the other superiors."

the spirit of the Gospel and of religious life."[33] Japan asked that there be superiors in each community.[34] However, the changes regarding responsibility were energizing.[35] As Elizabeth Basset believed, "We have not arrived at educating each one in individual responsibility, but maybe one can get there only by experience." Vivian Bowman remarked, "The psychological adjustment required to accept new liberty was considerable. It takes a long time to develop confidence in oneself and to be able to profit by it."

Major Changes

Returning to the Family

The change most widely appreciated was the opportunity for religious to visit their families. In 1964 a family visit was authorized only in the case of serious illness of one of the parents. The Chapter of 1967 allowed religious to go home on the occasion of ordinations, funerals, weddings, baptisms, First Communions, but they were not to spend the night. After 1970, a religious could stay with her family.

Some people saw this as a return to the past.[36] Others were fearful at the thought of meeting relatives whom they had not seen for a long time or whom they did not know. But the joy of their relatives helped them establish normal relationships with them. One religious recalled with emotion how her mother got out her best tableware![37] Sometimes the return became a collective celebration. Leonor Yanez recounted, "My father was waiting for us at the door. He was laughing and crying with joy. At Mass the following Sunday the pastor placed us in red armchairs. He asked me to ascend the pulpit to greet the parish and then to say the Our Father in French!"[38] Some religious had scruples about the cost of the journeys; but as a superior said to one of them, "Don't you want to make an act of charity for your poor old mother?" Nuns whose parents had not approved of their entering religious life were touched to see how happy they were to

---

[33] Gen. Arch. C I C 3, Box 26.
[34] M. Williams, *The Society in the Far East*, p. 281.
[35] Testimony of M. Shanahan: "I had to put in place certain structures, but for me the main thing was that they be flexible. What I came to appreciate – and sometimes it was difficult – was realizing that to live a life of commitment to follow Christ was not to make a choice at a given moment but rather to make it every day. To listen to the Spirit became the reality of one's whole life."
[36] Testimony of Monica Barudi.
[37] Testimony of Patricia McMahon.
[38] She spent the greater part of her religious life in France.

have them back. This change was particularly well received in non-Catholic families.

For the most part family relations were simplified and became more humane. A Spanish nun wrote: "It made me aware that I had been living in a bubble, on the margin of the problems my parents were facing. They had never spoken to me about them because the visiting time was too short."[39] These relationships gave everyone a new responsibility toward their families[40] and allowed them to better "adjust to a non-cloistered life."[41] Even the religious most attached to tradition appreciated being able to renew contact with their families.[42] Those who had lived outside their own country for a long time could return for short but regular visits. In Africa most congregations set an annual leave of two weeks with the family. Presence at times of mourning was an obligation, and the communities took part. In Congo taking nieces of the religious in the boarding school had to be regulated, because the demands of the families could be difficult to reconcile with the understanding of poverty as sharing.[43] Visits to families were a means of exploration, for one had to learn to balance investment in the community with being present to the family. Relatives and friends were also welcomed by the communities. The Constitutions of 1982 recognized these bonds of "a new affection for our family, a love that is true, tender and faithful," while maintaining the availability religious commitment demanded.[44]

Religious Life and Appearance

For many religious it had been a real sacrifice to take the habit in the first place.[45] Some modifications had already been made, but their adoption had varied by vicariate.[46] A new habit was worn for the first time at the

---

[39] Testimony of P. Corral.
[40] Testimony of Virginia Henao.
[41] Testimony of A. Conroy.
[42] Testimony concerning some Austrian religious.
[43] Testimony of C. Meêus.
[44] § 65.
[45] Testimony of E. de Guggenberg who took the habit in 1953: "A few days afterwards, I was making the way of the cross at Frascati. I remember at the tenth station saying to Jesus: 'Lord, they have taken off all your clothes. They have made *me* put them on. I accept it only for love of you.'"
[46] In England at the end of the 1950's nylon was introduced in the caps, but these had the same shape as before. France followed and the nuns who had permission to drive cars arranged their caps so as to have better vision

motherhouse on 8 December 1966: "At eight o'clock in the morning, we met for breakfast, all newly clothed, in silence, eyes down, in perfect self-control. For me this change was a veritable liberation, above all because of its practical and hygienic aspects; I did not know how to thank God and the Society," remarked Giovanna Scarlatta. It was washable and with it one could ride a bicycle and drive a car safely, but it was not comfortable and the nylon caps were too tight.[47] "We detested this 'modified' habit," commented Mary Coke. "It looked like nothing in particular." "It was no longer our habit," added Andrée Meylan. "Therefore, when at the international or provincial level it was felt that some diversity in dress was necessary, it wasn't so painful." During the Chapter of 1967 discussions had taken place about religious dress.[48] The situation evolved more quickly than had been expected, noted Mary Braganza regarding India, for "it was time to consider the 'apostolic potential' that the religious habit exerted in a sacralized society and the place it had in the public life of the Church and in a country that had already entered into a definitive secularism."[49] Going out of the convent and engaging in sports and leisure activities made wearing the habit in its traditional form questionable.

From the winter of 1967 on, six religious of the Chicago Province asked and received permission to wear secular clothes, promising to return to the religious habit if they experienced hostility on the part of the parents and pupils.[50] The following year during an inter-provincial assembly in the United States and Canada, at which Mother Bultó was present, it was decided to have a different costume for winter and summer, and colors and styles were chosen.[51] Different provinces kept the habit while opting

---

(Testimony of M. Coke). The reason for the changes in the habit was not explained to the religious. "From time to time we were called to the vestry to be measured" (Testimony of P. Goddard).

[47] Wearing this cap caused loss of hair for many.
[48] *Orientations*, p. 93.
[49] She adds: "Secularity in India does not correspond to a complete eradication of expressions of the sacred. In our understanding of secularity religious professionalism has a unique place, as have other spheres of professional, social, religious and cultural life. India believes that all religions are equal, that no religion can say in public that it is the unique and only way to God. Tolerance has always been a part of its heritage. This understanding of religious liberty and tolerance is not only preserved in its constitution; it is a precious legacy that has come to us from time immemorial."
[50] Testimony of M. Ruggieri.
[51] Gen. Arch. C III USA, Box 30, 6. In Chicago, "We were experimenting with what we wanted to wear. Some suggested a suit like those worn in banks or by flight attendants but in different colors. But some nuns said that because

for new colors; however, the change from black to gray made it hard to get rid of ink stains. Finally blue was chosen. In 1970 Mother Bultó asked capitulants to wear the habit to the chapter; everyone complied. But for the first time, the gathering did not have a uniform dress, for some, in particular the Germans, kept the black habit with a long veil. Some North Americans were in beige verging on coffee color, while the Australians were in blue.[52] The chapter defined the dress of a Religious of the Sacred Heart as "the expression of a person close to her brothers [and sisters] who has made an evangelical choice,"[53] without giving further information about what it was to be. But it authorized wearing secular clothes. The delegates from the United States were struck by the fact that the provincial of India, Mary Braganza, had to wear the habit during the chapter sessions but put on her sari to participate in an international meeting of teaching congregations.

After 1971 giving up the habit gradually became general. Wearing secular clothes was first authorized for vacations, then extended.[54] The cap was given up for a veil of the same color as the habit.[55] Some religious wore secular clothes but kept the veil, "so that we resembled old-fashioned grandmothers," according to Anne Hine. The question of uniform dress came up. "In England," reported Andrée Meylan, "we examined different models of a very simple dress without a veil. Because we could not come to an agreement on the same pattern, even in different colors, we settled on a navy blue suit for ceremonies and the habit for those who wished to wear it."[56]

This development brought with it tension and unhappiness, first of all in the congregation. For religious from Eastern European countries it awakened painful memories among those who had been forced to take off the habit because of the political situation or during their imprisonment:

> of the figure and size of some religious a suit was not desirable. In certain provinces it was decided to shorten the habit just below the knee. Others were wearing striped cotton dresses down to the ankles. One of our nuns was in charge of helping us find clothes that could suit everyone. She had coats and jackets made out of our winter shawls" (Testimony of Catherine Seiker). In New York, some religious took off the habit at the beginning of the school year 1969 (Testimony of A. Conroy).

[52] Testimony of I. Aranguren.
[53] *Actes*, p. 28.
[54] Testimony of Dorothea Hewlett.
[55] Testimony of E. de Guggenberg, who distinguished nine changes of appearance and color! In this regard a relative remarked to Henriette Raynaud de Lage, "Every time I see you, you have taken off something else!"
[56] In Australia, one religious had designed a green and purple habit, but "thank heaven, it was not adopted" (Testimony of E. Herscovitch).

"On the part of their persecutors, it had been a way of humiliating them, of showing contempt for the value of their persons and religion. Therefore wearing a secular costume was considered a sign of fear, a refusal to witness, even by one's clothing, to one's faith and belonging to the Church and to Jesus Christ."[57] Worldwide, the eldest were shocked by this development and let it be known. Many of those who wished to keep the habit, young or old, indicated that giving it up was equivalent to rejecting religious values and that it was a first step toward leaving the Society. In Chicago, at Woldingham, at Marmoutier and in Canada, some religious refused to speak to those who were no longer wearing the habit. The provincial of France, Bernadette des Francs, was welcomed with "Good day, Madam," by the mistress general when she visited Kientzheim.[58] The clothing issue interfered with the reception of the changes that had occurred since 1967,[59] and in international communities, it emphasized the differences among religious.[60]

Outside the Society reactions were mixed. The nuns' families appreciated this change in appearance as long as the clothes worn were tasteful.[61] On the other hand, giving up the habit caused problems with the hierarchy in India and in Australia.[62] In Ireland, "the fight to keep the religious habit was particularly fierce, and the visit of Pope John Paul II in 1979 showed that there was still a long way to go. Even though now it is ancient history, our archives are full of reports showing how bitter the discussions were and what filtered through to the Vatican as well as to the motherhouse."[63] In Congo "those with the African sense of the sacred hardly admired our varied costumes."[64] At the grass roots, on the other hand, the religious were often supported by priests[65] and those with whom they worked. As for the alumnae, many were pained by this development and in certain countries let it be known loudly.

---

[57] Testimony of E. Belle.
[58] Thérèse Vercruysse, in Belgium, was gratified by a "Good morning, Sir," when she wore trousers, "which were more correct in my work."
[59] In the Canaries, it was the appearance of a religious with "a skirt up to the knees and hair out of the cap" that was the sign of changes taking place henceforth in the congregation (Testimony of Otila Pacheco).
[60] In Japan the American nuns shortened their skirts while the Japanese remained faithful to the habit (Testimony of H. Okui).
[61] Testimony of A. Hine and G. Bovagnet.
[62] Testimony of M. Shanahan.
[63] Testimony of P. Kilroy.
[64] Testimony of C. Meeûs.
[65] Testimony of Mercedes Santillan and Jacqueline Janssens.

The reactions were even livelier because the underlying discussions were related to the group's identity. To decide on appropriate clothes would have required reflection on the true spirit of the vow of poverty and on a simple life style.[66] The religious did not have much "experience or taste. I remember," recounted Andrée Meylan, who was provincial in England, "being taken aside by the archbishop in Malta because one of our sisters was wearing a bright pink pullover and another who taught science was wearing trousers during geological excursions." Actually there were some exaggerations at the beginning and not only in the realm of color. The 1960's saw the appearance of miniskirts. At Woldingham Mother Eyre posted a notice in the community room that only skirts mid-calf in length were permitted.[67] Some religious who had entered a long time earlier did not know how to dress. When they were given the opportunity of wearing secular dress, they spontaneously reverted to the styles and colors of their youth. It took time to realize that a woman of forty or fifty should not dress like a girl of eighteen.[68] Certain outfits were "a source of dismay and bewilderment, but also of hilarity,"[69] coming from trunks in the attic after long past *prises d'habit* or thrift shops. It took time for the religious to find the right tone, to choose clothes that were neither too luxurious nor too poor nor too fashionable. The excesses of some were cause for thought for others.[70] Giving up the habit meant also taking care of one's appearance, one's hair and of wearing suitable undergarments. In Congo, "When our African sisters adopted the *pagne* like most African religious, it was soon evident that it had to be uniform lest families be tempted to make gifts of them to their daughters."[71]

There were different reasons for abandoning the habit. Wearing clothes like those worn by the people among whom one lived seemed the normal outcome of the end of cloister.[72] The religious habit was now likened to "a uniform like that of ecclesiastics" and seen as "a cause of separation, not consistent with the conduct of Jesus of Nazareth."[73] "I changed out of conviction," said Hannelore Woitsch. "The young people with whom I was working confirmed me in my decision by telling me that they no

---

[66] Testimony of M. Braganza and T. Vercruysse: "In Belgium the sisters regarded us with a disapproving eye. Afterward, some felt it necessary to justify wearing secular clothing: 'It was given to me,' 'It was not expensive,' or 'It's secondhand.'"
[67] Testimony of T. McCarthy.
[68] Testimony of D. Boland.
[69] Testimony of B. Crombie.
[70] Testimony of Isabel García.
[71] Testimony of C. Meeûs.
[72] Testimony of M.M. Miller.
[73] Testimony of Mary Hinde, Mary McKeone and T. Vercruysse.

longer felt the barriers of a life far removed from reality." The appearance of the central team in secular dress was seen as an encouragement to do the same.[74] But some religious in the United States and Ireland felt pressure from their superiors either to give up the habit or to keep it.[75]

For the pupils the change was a surprise: "The first evening I was in surveillance in the ten-year-olds' dormitory. I was sitting on one of the beds, and they were telling me what they had done during vacation. Suddenly I felt a little hand gently touch my hair. I remember the name of the one who did it, and I recall that experience very clearly."[76] Secular dress was imposed on religious whose apostolic activity was carried out in public schools or those run by non-Catholics.[77] In Ulster the Irish appreciated wearing it when they were crossing rough districts where Catholics were the targets of the other camp.[78] It allowed closer contact with the surroundings; it gave the feeling of "more equality with others;" it "removed barriers and fostered greater confidence."[79] People spoke more easily to those who were no longer wearing the habit,[80] which seemed like a sign of another era[81] or encouraged privileges.[82] Giving it up allowed many religious to "recover the image of themselves as women."[83] In hot countries it was a liberation. In India the sari allowed the nuns to mingle more easily with non-Christians, and wearing the sari in Asia was a meaningful move because it was made of

---

[74] Mary Catherine McKay arrived in Rome in secular clothes. The whole team was in secular dress by the summer of 1972. If it was a shock for the members of the motherhouse community (Testimony of Margaret Byrnes), it gave a stirring example: "If it is a step that the Society has taken, I take it with her" (Testimony of D. Varela Sanchez). "I said to myself that I do not have to hold to my own opinion when before my eyes I have the example of those who govern the Society" (Testimony of Margaret Tindal). In Colombia, the arrival of the central team in secular clothes was a sign of the new governance and provoked displeasure among the alumnae.

[75] Testimony of Helen Donohoe and Sheila M. Hayes.

[76] Testimony of M. Charley.

[77] Marie-Thérèse Deprecq, who went into the Latin Quarter in the habit in May 1968, during the confrontations between the students and the forces of order, understood after a blow that the religious habit near the barricades could be considered a provocation.

[78] Testimony of Kathleen Friel.

[79] Testimony of Teresa Agius.

[80] Testimony of Nazarena Debono, Helen Hoffman, Dorothy Bell: "A student said to me: 'It's much easier for me to speak to you now that I know you have knees!'"

[81] Testimony of D. Díaz-Valera.

[82] Testimony of Joan Stephenson.

[83] Testimony of C. de Clock, Pilar Cumba Zabaleta, Jacquette de Cadolle.

less costly fabric than the habit.[84] But those who were sent to Egypt wore the veil, for in that country "women always have their heads covered. If we did not do the same, we would have been taken for tourists."[85]

While the question might appear pointless, it is not. Clothing in religious life expresses consecration; it is a sign of a relation to the whole that had never been questioned in the Society of the Sacred Heart. It was the object of dispute with the Sacred Congregation, who saw giving up the habit as an indication of a worldly life and of rampant secularism.[86] Although it can appear anecdotal, it was nevertheless one of the most important issues that arose during Mother Camacho's first term.[87] The article in the new Constitutions dedicated to the habit was the one most lengthily and bitterly discussed. The Religious of the Sacred Heart had to redefine their identity: for a long time the religious habit had brought them immediate recognition. They had to express their vocation in another way and to show by the simplicity of their manner that they had chosen a life style rather than one in which clothing was an ostentatious sign of opulence.[88] As Mary Braganza rightly summarized it, "Much time elapsed before we could arrive at a varied but simple, suitable dress that continues to be a sign of our presence to the world."

Apostolic Activities and Community Life

Education and Sacred Heart Schools

Until 1967 the schools had been the framework of the apostolic life. Many religious continued to work there, but Sacred Heart establishments were less homogeneous than before because they accepted pupils of varied social classes and introduced new directions in curriculum and pedagogical methods. The institutions evolved under the pressure of national and Church policies. In Malta the government financed private secondary education.[89] In Peru the revolutionary government of the Armed Forces initiated reform in national education. In Austria Cardinal König took charge of schools that religious congregations could no longer sustain because of a dearth of vocations.[90] Far and wide bishops asked congregations to found schools in the fast growing fringes of the cities and, in Latin

---

[84] Testimony of Maria Xuereb and A. Kato.
[85] Testimony of B. Brennan.
[86] Memoir sent by Cardinal Benelli to Mother Camacho, 29 October 1977.
[87] Testimony of D. Boland.
[88] Testimony of B. Brennan.
[89] Testimony of T. Agius.
[90] Testimony of Andrea Szakonyi.

America, among the indigenous populations.[91] In Peru, after the violent 1971 earthquake that devastated the Ancash region leaving innumerable victims, they asked congregations to make foundations there.[92] In 1981 after an appeal from the Mexican episcopate, the Sacred Heart made a foundation in Nicaragua. Religious of the Sacred Heart adapted to new circumstances and made more contacts than before with the outside world.

The events of 1968 had to have repercussions in North America and Europe. "A week after my return from probation and walks in the motherhouse garden saying my beads," recounts Ann Conroy, "I found myself at the University of Maryland, amidst the smell of marijuana and listening to the drug guru Timothy Leary talking about the benefits of 'grass' and of the plunge into other drugs. Families broken by divorce, drugs, unwanted pregnancies, abortions, suicides and alcoholism were the preoccupying issues of society. Could a person faced with all that cling to 'principles?'" In Grenoble the pupils thought that the education they were receiving was passé.[93] France was undergoing the upset of a second secularization. The private school, associated with public service, appeared more secular than before. The establishment by the state of the *carte scolaire* [school system] obliged institutions under contract to merge with other private schools. The issue was important for the Sacred Heart, which went from "a relationship of competition with other establishments to one of collaboration and mutual assistance," a development strongly criticized by the alumnae.[94] For the nuns working in the schools created by the mergers, it was "a beautiful time. There was life, an opening, a dynamism, for them and therefore for the congregation."[95] Those who were employed by another congregation discovered that each institute had its own way of educating, of understanding discipline and of directing a school.[96] Relations between religious and lay women became friendlier: "We were invited to their homes; we visited with their husbands and children. I felt," testified Marie-Louise Fabre, "that through that I was revealing more of the love of the Heart of Jesus than I had by my reserved and even distant earlier relationships." But the assignment of religious to these new schools created in the province, especially when the assemblies and chapters convened, "a certain separation between those who had stayed in the 'pure Sacred Heart'

---

[91] M. Recavarren, *Raíces y Horizonte*, pp. 258-260.
[92] Testimony of F. Tamayo.
[93] Testimony of C. de Clock: "They told me that I was making them live dishonestly because as soon as they crossed the threshold, out of my sight, they put on trousers and smoked, and boys were waiting for them."
[94] Testimony of M-L. Fabre.
[95] Testimony of M.L. Leplat.
[96] Testimony of S. Teisserenc.

and the others. Some found it troubling. It was somewhat like the quarrel between the Ancients and the Moderns. It settled down gradually as those in the merged schools gradually retired."[97]

Worldwide the Sacred Heart renewed its apostolic works. At Chamartín they opened a residence for working girls.[98] Some schools were transferred to the suburbs, which brought with it a change in the student population. The school in Rue Saint Dominique in Paris moved to Châtenay-Malabry: "The house was new, highly regarded, and functional. We opened technical sections, an innovation in that era, and accepted students of more modest circumstances than those of the *VIIe arrondissement*. From the apostolic point of view we were rather in the forefront," wrote Marie-Thérèse Carré, but this move was not unanimously approved in France. The boarding school, El Valle, in Seville was reopened in Aljarafe, a section where housing projects were being built and where there were many young couples with "problems." These transfers allowed the nuns to become acquainted with subcultures unknown to them. The mix of pupils from different social classes was most often a challenge.

Upon their return from the special chapter the vicars of the United States and Canada had had a survey of their institutions made by consulting firms, with the objective of close and factual examination in order to offer better service[99] and to reorganize resources so as to "face up to the basic problems of the nation." But because schools in the United States had been maintained to carry on religious education in each region, it was decided to close those that were not financially viable and those that could not attract middle class students or people of color.[100] In fewer than four years the five provinces closed twelve schools,[101] without consulting their staffs.[102] Three colleges

---

[97] Testimony of M.L. Leplat.
[98] Testimony of María Padilla. After the closing of the boarding school some religious from Caballero de Gracia were sent there.
[99] Testimony of M.M. Miller.
[100] From April 1968, the nuns in New York worked out new directions for their schools. They wanted "to make a radical change in the social, racial and economic composition of their schools in view of total integration" and for themselves they inaugurated formation on "the race, culture and history of African Americans." To achieve integration in stages, at first each school was to recruit at least one person of color on the faculty and all the communities were to support Harlem Preparatory School (Gen. Arch. Sacré-Cœur, C III USA, dossier 30).
[101] In 1968, closing of City House, Saint Louis, and Duchesne College, Omaha; in 1969, closing of Eden Hall, Overbrook, Rochester, Grosse Pointe; in 1970, closing of Clifton; in 1972, closing of El Cajon, Elmhurst, Noroton, Buffalo and San Francisco College for Women.
[102] Mary Charlotte Chandler: *Supporting the Social Identity*, p. 166.

were closed between 1968 and 1978, three others became independent, and another merged with a similar institution.[103] Although the reason for these closings was explained to the families and the children had been admitted to other schools, the shock was intense.[104] The youngest religious had difficulty in finding rewarding apostolic activity.[105] From the end of the 1960s,

> ...schools in the United States had given up many of the practices common to the Sacred Heart and were recognized as part of the world of independent schools. They had kept the uniform, the system of notes and the distribution of prizes. But among the teaching and administrative personnel, lay persons outnumbered religious. The curriculum varied from one part of the country to the other, but there were always religion courses. We had discovered a new way of being: we were Catholic without being attached to parochial schools, private, not affiliated with the state, and our tuition costs were in between those of other private and public schools.[106]

In 1972 informal meetings of mistresses general resulted in a decision to coordinate nationally. In 1973 they held their first official meeting in a move toward the creation of a network for an education in freedom, justice, peace and faith. The following summer the Stuart Conference held in Cleveland raised the following questions: what a Sacred Heart school was, what made it possible to be one, what participation in a network meant. Because neither the presence of many nuns nor the preservation of traditions was seen as a primary condition, "goals and criteria" had to be developed. Elaborated in 1976, they reflected and preserved the vision and educational philosophy of Saint Madeleine Sophie. Every five years each school was to be evaluated by a team from the network with a system unique to each

---

[103] The colleges had been the chief source of vocations in the American vicariates. In 1999, 81.9% of the religious who had entered the Society before 1975 had studied in one of the colleges (Chandler, p. 167).

[104] The cooperation taking place at the beginning of the 1970's among the provinces of the United States allowed for mutual consultation about the closing of schools, at the request of the provincials of New York and Washington. They showed that the closing of schools in one province had repercussions in another (Testimony of M. M. Miller and Anne Leonard).

[105] Testimony of Mary Roe.

[106] Testimony of A. Conroy.

province.[107] "But it took many years for our lay colleagues to see themselves as equals with the Religious of the Sacred Heart."[108]

Some of the closings were not well managed. In Canada all the institutions were unstable and did not have the means to pay adequate salaries to the teachers unless they accepted state support. The Sault was closed in 1970. The province decided to leave Winnipeg in an effort to save the other establishments in the province, but the closing was not carried out "with tact. The feeling was that those responsible for the decision were all from the East and had not the slightest idea of the needs of the West." This affair served as a lesson, for when Vancouver was closed, the nuns had recourse to the mediation of a priest: "Some Canadian nuns have never been resigned to closing Winnipeg; they have never forgotten the pain and misunderstanding" they experienced then.[109] The closing of the kindergarten in Tokyo brought on strong resistance in Japan. The families who entrusted their children to the Sacred Heart tried to have the decision reversed, even trying to involve the Vatican. The decision, made rapidly by Mother Keogh,[110] displeased the Japanese religious who thought that formal education was key to evangelization and that alumnae sometimes asked for baptism a long time after their school days.[111] The tension was such that Mother Keogh asked Mother Bultó not to come to Japan so that she would not have to face the antagonism.

In Latin America there evolved an effort to cooperate with the desire for change expressed by most of the national episcopates. Chile decided in 1968 that the school at Apoquindo would be opened to the poorest pupils through

---

[107] Talk by Catherine Baxter, published in *Journey of the Heart, a bicentennial anthology*, Saint Louis, 2000, p. 67. "In 1990, the Goals and Criteria were described as 'ageless...the five elements that have been the framework of Sacred Heart education since its beginning in 1800. They express the values, the intentions and the hopes of the Sacred Heart tradition, sharpened to meet the needs of a rapidly changing world.'" The five goals are: "to educate to a personal and active faith in God, to a deep respect for intellectual values, to a social awareness which impels to action, to the building of community as a Christian value, to personal growth in an atmosphere of wise freedom."

[108] Testimony of A. Conroy. "In some cases the alumnae were hostile to these changes. Elsewhere they supported them. Our institutions suffered and some still suffer from lack of financial support from the alumnae. Still today some of them or our colleagues cannot call us Sister; they continue to call us Mother and cannot bring themselves to use our first names."

[109] Testimony of Shelagh Deegan, who was provincial treasurer. "I was an alumna of Winnipeg, yet the responsibility of selling it fell on me!"

[110] She told M. Luirard that it was the only decision that she regretted having made. All the non-Japanese nuns were favorable.

[111] Testimony o f S. Kageyama and H. Okui.

scholarships and would develop a social sense in the pupils through a special program. Two free schools were founded.[112] Peru took the same direction but in a different context, since there were already projects among the working class in schools recognized by the state. In Lima, where a merger of Chorillos and the *Sophianum* was hoped for, the acceptance of pupils from modest families was encouraged by scholarships and the cost of board made proportionate to family income.[113] In Colombia, in 1973, it was estimated that the schools were justified only if they implemented a strong pastoral dimension.[114]

After the Chapter of 1970 many provinces engaged in long range planning that consisted in evaluating the apostolates of the religious and having them express their hopes and concerns. In Ireland they balanced activities carried on inside the institutions with those outside them. In Australia a national committee on education was linked to the provincial education office.[115] The opening of technical programs altered the image of some schools. There was a new atmosphere in the most elite European schools. For Anna Lecciso:

> The proposal to give preference to the least advantaged social class was clearly indicated, but its deep meaning was sometimes difficult to understand. I agreed with it to some extent, but I understood how important it was to our institutions to educate students who would fight on the front line for human rights, because they had been given the most authentic possible knowledge of social justice and had had experience of sharing their lives with different social classes. For the students most aware of these questions, I set up friendly contacts with disadvantaged people by offering tutoring services, *goûter* and meals together, not at the Sacred Heart but in the homes of the new friends. Each one had something to contribute.

In countries where there were sharp social contrasts, mixing together pupils of the boarding schools with those of the day schools for working class children proved touchy. The boarders' families did not want their daughters to have a second-rate education and did not appreciate this change; neither did the parents of the day pupils who were sometimes in service to the families of their new fellow students. In the Canaries where integration was not a success,

---

[112] Testimony of Esperanza Calabuig.
[113] M. Recavarren, p. 199.
[114] *Histoire de la province de Colombie*, § 58.
[115] The Scott Report led to the closing of certain schools and the mixing of pupils (Testimony of M. Brennan).

the pupils came from extremely different social classes and needed a longer preparation. We hadn't a suitable method or tact or, above all, time. This caused serious problems: the day pupils were ashamed of their families and their homes; to keep up with the boarders they used to lie about their weekend activities. They even began to steal. I taught the boarders to associate with and get to know the others. At the beginning this method seemed good to me, but when the children asked their parents to cut back their expenses in order to share with those who had less, their families reacted![116]

In Chile there were violent reactions that translated into "an avalanche of attacks and accusations. We tried to give our reasons, to justify our position, but the tide of public opinion about the goals of the school at Apoquindo was opposed to our plan."[117] It is true that socialism was coming into power. However, in Zaïre the merger of the boarding school, where teaching was in French, with the *mavula*, which took in the children of the villages, took place in 1969 at Kimwenza and in 1972 at Mbansa-Mboma. The closing of some boarding schools was said to be the result of unworkable mergers or shortage of personnel, just as additional choices appeared for the apostolate.[118]

New Apostolates

After 1967 nuns went outside the institution in order to work in public schools. In Alsace, where the Society of the Sacred Heart was one of the recognized congregations, thanks to the maintenance of the regime of the Concordat, they taught catechism in the public schools and were remunerated by the State.[119] Because of an error concerning the term "educator," Chantal de Clock studied for a diploma in group leadership. "Through study and contacts with social workers already in the field and the leftist climate of this profession, I discovered an entire universe," she thought. Christiane Chazottes had charge of adults in a center for continuing education attached to the state university and partially financed by its employers: "This training was very important in the department *du Nord*, where most of the French workers and immigrants had been

---

[116] Testimony of Otila Pacheco.
[117] Testimony of Margarita Hurtado.
[118] In Colombia, the first school sold was the one in Manizales in 1977. In Peru, the *Sophianum* in Lima was not sold, as had been planned, and the school at Arequipa was finally handed over to another religious congregation. A community remained at Arequipa to minister to the alumnae.
[119] Testimony of Marguerite-Marie Bernard.

to school only until the age of fourteen. I worked in a state organization with people of all political persuasions, all religious denominations, all kinds of environments, a secular organization where I was asked not to do any proselytizing." "Little by little aspects of religious life, those we are tempted to call 'spiritual,' and those of our mission became intertwined."[120] In Uganda the nuns went into the bush on Sundays to prepare for Mass and to teach catechism to children who were not in school. Then some of them worked full time in the parishes.[121] In Chad classes took place in the morning; in the afternoon the nuns went to the parishes or into areas of N'Djaména to teach catechism and literacy, as well as sewing to women and singing to young people.[122] In Zaïre, they worked in the parish of N'Djili in Kinshasa; new communities were opened at Kasongo-Lunda in 1971, at Kisenko and Kimbanseke in 1973. Wherever they were, the religious added parish activities to teaching; they visited the sick and took care of the poor. In England apostolic activity outside the institutions first addressed abandoned children or recovering alcoholics during holidays. New professional areas opened up, like psychotherapy, which had been looked upon with mistrust and suspicion for many years.[123] New ventures were already beckoning. But while the Kaski report had shown that 83.2% of the nuns wished to work in education, it appeared in certain provinces that the youngest members were interested in other activities.[124]

"Insertions"

As some religious moved from large cities to their outskirts, to smaller cities, even villages, some experiments took place. The name "insertion" was given to these foundations, often very different depending upon the country and the time. The movement that began after the Special Chapter of 1967 or after that of 1970 involved small communities whose members had varied apostolates and lived "with the poor." It sprang from individual creativity but was supported by provincials who made sure it would succeed.[125] In Latin America it echoed the dream of education beyond schools that had been the hope of the Medellín conference.

In the beginning the nuns settled in apartments in a working class or disadvantaged neighborhood rather close to a Sacred Heart school to

---

[120] Testimony of F. Martínez for Colombia.
[121] Testimony of H. McLaughlin. In 1970, she was giving homilies.
[122] G. Bovagnet, p. 44.
[123] Testimony of J. Faber.
[124] Four provinces of the United States were among the eight provinces of North America, Africa and Spain where this direction was manifested.
[125] Testimony of M. McCourt.

accommodate those who wished to continue teaching there.[126] Foundations of this type appeared at Aluche, Tetuan and other outskirts of Madrid. Some religious taught in public schools and in neighborhood associations.[127] Those in Granada who went to live in working class sections of Chana, Virgencica and El Zaidin[128] worked in a center for young people and in a cultural center for the women of the area, and they organized summer camps for disadvantaged children.[129]

In France the first community of nuns in varied ministries was that of Petit Châtenay, opened in 1968, close to the school. The others appeared after 1970. One in Amiens, established in a former parish rectory, brought together three Religious of the Sacred Heart and an Ursuline[130] who worked at the Sacred Heart; they had charge of parish catechetical work and were active in either a hospital or a center for endangered women. Other such communities were opened in Lyons in 1972 and in 1975, in Lille in 1974, Tourcoing in 1975, and Vénisseux in 1978. In a suburb of Lyons in 1976 volunteers replaced some Spanish nuns in an insertion begun two years earlier at Saint-Priest. There they had "very simple relationships with the people who saw how we lived, at the market and elsewhere. Marguerite du Merle played marbles with the little boys on the sidewalk."[131] Following other appeals some religious took part in activities at two spiritual centers run by the Jesuits at Fontaines, Chantilly and at le Châtelard near Lyons. Others engaged in pastoral ministry at la Madrague near Marseille, among a population of fishermen and other workers. In 1973 the bishop of Montpellier asked for a community to be sent into a rural area:

> The call was heard after many hesitations – "We are not rural," although a good number of us are of landed families! – In August 1974, we were inserted in a village rectory closely linked with three priests who had chosen to live in a team consisting of some lay persons and the religious. Our own mission was to live the daily life of rural people: their environment, work – grape harvest, housework, night watch, household help – parish commitments, closeness to people – listening, welcome,

---

[126] Testimony of María Socorro Duaso.
[127] Testimony of Dolores Bermejo.
[128] "We read the Gospel with other keys; we heard the clamor of the poor, better still the call of Jesus for them" (Testimony of Manuela García de la Rasilla).
[129] Testimony of Manolita Martín Juarez. In another disadvantaged section at Fondillo, near Tafira, an insertion began in "a poor house amidst the poor" (Testimony of Pilar Jiménez-Carléz).
[130] Testimony of Jacqueline Rousselon.
[131] Testimony of H. Reynaud de Lage.

friendship, sharing – attentiveness to the least fortunate, community life – a poor life style in which welcome and sharing were the priorities.[132]

In Italy around the same time insertions were made at Miano, a suburb of Naples, and in Ivrea. In Belgium a small fraternity was opened by the Union of Religious to offer hospitality during a time of readjustment for some who had left or who were leaving their religious congregation. Two Sacred Heart nuns went to live there in 1971, then joined a fraternity that opened in the province the following year.[133]

The movement toward "insertions" was a result of the Chapters of 1967 and 1970: "Certain words gave us joy: preference for the poor, justice, encouragement to become more human, insertion in the world," but words or trends that were not universally accepted: "We must say that after years of cloister when we had been cut off from people's lives, it was with full hearts that we opened ourselves to the world, its life, distress and very obvious needs." Since it was not always possible to share these discoveries in communities not yet ready for change, they had to find other forms of community life. In Belgium the change of apostolate

> was slow but very real. Awareness of the human and Christian values among lay people came about gradually; it took time to accept, even ask for their collaboration in our works, to try to create new ones. Then carefully we saw our way to join existing social or spiritual groups by inserting ourselves into services that we had not founded. We passed from rejoicing in the gift we were bringing to the joy of sharing mutual values.[134]

In Latin America the insertions were born of theological reflection that grassroots communities had awakened. "Without much preparation but with the mystique of being on the side of the poor," many sisters spread out in small communities in working class areas, in general, to "use their educational expertise in the schools and to evangelize in the parishes. Others began to study and participate in popular movements, which were very much in vogue at that moment. Little by little close relationships with the people revealed that everything we knew was of no use here."[135] The objective, as Isabel Aranguren succinctly expressed it, was to have "the

---

[132] Testimony of C. de Clock. This mission lasted thirteen years with four nuns, then with two, finally for seven years with one nun attached to the community of Montpellier.

[133] Testimony of T. Vercruysse.

[134] T. Vercruysse.

[135] Testimony of F. Martínez.

greatest possible insertion among the poor and the weakest possible in the bourgeois world."[136]

In Chile the first insertion was at Entre Lagos. When Esperanza Calabuig arrived in the country in 1972,

> the renewal was in progress as if we had always lived like that. Communities were small, spread throughout the country, inserted among the poor. There were few religious in the schools. Closely united with the Chilean Church and the Church of Latin America we jumped joyously and boldly into research. The first small communities had eight to ten people. From that came other communities of two or three who were inserted in the poorest places.

Many religious assisted in diocesan administration and did pastoral work. "As we were concerned with faith education, we saw no division between popular education and pastoral work."[137] In Brazil, it was

> Vatican II as read and interpreted at Medellín and Puebla with the option for the poor; the local Church urging insertion into base ecclesial communities (CEB), using the felicitous and fitting expression the "Church of the poor;" reading the Bible according to the method of the CEBI [*Centro de Estudios Biblicos*] and [pondering its] underlying spirituality; the political reality of the dictatorship that we experienced in our daily life; the strength of our martyrs and so many of our imprisoned comrades. This called for a change of location and of activity and a community in solidarity with the people, a new fabric of relationships, experiences of lived faith.[138]

The first insertion took place in the Northeast in the diocese of Itabira in 1969: "We were beginning to understand that our place was on the margins with poor, down-to-earth people. We also recognized that a change of geographic and social location presupposed a cultural change, which in turn was producing a new spirituality. For us it was a return to the sources of the Society."[139] In Argentina/Uruguay, the nuns had been "struck by the conditions of their people, their struggles and hurdles, their wounds and their hopes. Little by little we were able to fashion a simple life style by trying not to be the main players and by giving priority to relationships

---

[136] *Histoire de la Province du Mexique, les Années Soixante*, p. 25.
[137] Testimony of Paz Riesco, in Frances Makower, *Towards Tomorrow*, pp. 131-132.
[138] Testimony of Heloisa M. Rodrigues da Cunha.
[139] Testimony of Elizabeth Amarante, in F. Makower, p. 123.

and commitment to the poor and the life of the people."[140] In Colombia "an exodus to the outskirts" took place in 1970 with the foundations of Minitas at Barranquilla, Ciudad Jardín in Bogotá and the University of the Sacred Heart in Cali.[141] Between 1971 and 1976 five foundations were made successively in Venecia, south of Bogotá; at Santa Marta, Cali and Barranquilla.[142] At Ciudad Jardín the community combined work in the school, pastoral ministry in the area, participation in parish life with different forms of evangelization already adopted by the young people: "Work in the school, taking charge of catechetics and responsibility for groups constituted one of the most successful missions." Later the young nuns were trained in centers set up by the religious congregations.[143] A "Philippine Duchesne missionary team" of three members visited places in the department of the Magdalena and stayed with a villager. The team went to Manizales then to the area of Santander. It wanted to support "the rights of the villagers, their struggle for rights and for the dignity of women, for the renewal of faith and the opening of a place in the Church as well as in the life of the people."[144] In Mexico foundations were made or developed at San Pedro Garza García, near Monterrey; at Meseta del Nayar; at Ciudad Pemex, a city born of oil drilling near Tabasco; at Santa Cecilia, north of Guadalajara. In Peru, where the Society had been confined to Lima for a long time, the insertions extended its geographical presence.

Religious of the Sacred Heart sometimes lived in mixed communities with priests, religious men and women of various congregations and with lay people.[145] In Brazil reflection on the conditions of evangelization of local populations led to the creation of an indigenous missionary council, which the country's episcopal conference finally took charge of. In this context, after discernment by the whole province, Elizabeth Amarante went to live among the Myky of the Iranxe nation in 1977. In Colombia, in

---

[140] *Religieuses du Sacré-Cœur*, p. 41.
[141] *Histoire de la province de Colombie*, § 26-27: "The fraternity of the University of the Sacred Heart (CUSC) in Cali, was given impetus by Anne Marie Paternot, a Brazilian who worked very hard for the opening up of the province. It was affiliated with the University of Valle: it was admitted that its diplomas for women only brought an important contribution to the young women of Cali as well as to the Religious of the Sacred Heart who studied there."
[142] After the Chapter of 1970 developments were not sufficiently prepared. The five options were applied in a manner that seemed brutal to the directors of the institutions of the country.
[143] *Histoire...Colombie*, § 47.
[144] *Histoire...Colombie*, § 49 and 50.
[145] The one in Itabira around 1973 included two Religious of the Sacred Heart, the bishop, a Carmelite and a member of a secular institute.

order to become closer to the poor, a community was installed at Cascajal, a section of Cali where a marginalized black population lived, among whom the nuns had been working for several years.

In Egypt insertions developed in the Nile valley beginning with Samalout, where the community worked in the school and the dispensary of the Association of Upper Egypt. Missions followed in nearby villages; then foundations farther south were made: at Beni Abeid in 1971, Abou Korkas in 1972, Dairout in 1974, El Ghanayem in 1977 and Bayadeya in 1980, at the initiative of Esperanza Medina, named provincial after the Chapter of 1970. The first religious who dedicated themselves to this work came from Cairo and Heliopolis. They were joined by sisters from Malta, the United States, Great Britain, Netherlands, France and Spain. They taught children, taught literacy to adults, conducted workshops and small dispensaries, taught catechism and visited families. Day after day they made the eye medications, ointments, syrups and oils that the people needed. They lived in villages that had "in common misery, poverty accompanied by ignorance, under-development and lack of hygiene."[146] At Abou Korkas, they became aware that the pace of life could not be sustained for any length of time. The nuns started the morning at the school, then went in the afternoon to the villages, which they sometimes had to reach on foot and only to return early, because there was neither transportation nor electricity late in the afternoon. Duties followed the needs of the place. The foundation of Dairout in the Assiout diocese established the Society in another diocese and allowed the Catholics there to have a church.[147]

In Zaïre, Marthe Jacobs, the provincial, was able to make use of a team of Spaniards who wanted to live in small communities in a poor environment. However, the foundation of N'Djili, where the Bakongos from Kinshasa were grouped, was made by two Belgians, Anne Poncelet and Marguerite-Marie Hanquet, who had lived in Lower Congo. The Spanish spent more time in the social apostolate than in the schools. Carmen Sivatte began prison work in Makala and intervened in the courts to move trials along. The work consisted of feeding the prisoners, having them cared for, listening to them, teaching them catechism, making contact with their families and housing them, if necessary, upon their release from prison.[148] In Chad and Zaïre, people did not always understand why the

---

[146] *Interfrat*, N° 15, 6 January 1973. Testimony of Reyes Callis.
[147] Testimony of Hedwige de Cadolle.
[148] Testimony of C. Meûss and *Connections*, 2, 1992. Clotilde Meûss adds: "Kimbanseke still has a parish commitment: catechism and social work, but there is no longer presence of RSCJ in the dispensary or in nutritional education, while the dispensaries of Mbansa-Mboma and Kipako have developed. Outside of Kinshasa there was a foundation at Kasongo-Lunda

European nuns lived in uncomfortable quarters, in a dwelling like that of the locals. The Zaïrois considered it "play-acting because they knew that 'Europe' was there to support them."[149] The Chadians understood only that the nuns came to share the poverty that they themselves wanted to escape.[150] The insertions were no doubt better accepted when the communities understood the local people. But in Colombia, recounts Fanny Martínez, "Those who welcomed us showed their affection; I heard it said once that in a community of Blacks our presence was a sign for them that they had value."

The change of outlook in the Society of the Sacred Heart was such that the entry into the Philippines in 1969 took place without the founding of any institutions. The young professed, who had been trained in Japan and who took charge of it, began programs for young people often supported by a non-profit foundation created in 1971 and named for Saint Madeleine Sophie. Aided financially by Japanese pupils, it obtained scholarships for poor students.[151] An Australian, Betty Moriarty, who was studying at the East Asian Pastoral Institute in Manila, decided to work in the city prison. With the assistance of alumnae she undertook to have the women detainees make artificial flowers. A second project, supported by the government, had them make dresses with supplies and material from local merchants.[152] Some Spanish religious went into Bolivia in 1970; they took charge at Aimara of rural advancement and education. In 1976 a community, attached to Peru, was set up at Huacullani with a Spaniard, a Peruvian and a Chilean.[153]

Work among the disadvantaged followed the personal development of the religious. As one French nun put it,

---

on the border with Angola, where our sisters who are doctors and nurses dedicated themselves during an epidemic of sleeping sickness. Another foundation was made in the heart of the forest at Kole where our sisters support a school for dressmaking and work in a hospital."

[149] Testimony of Claire van de Velde. In the community criticisms were equally lively: "They are the enlightened who believe they are poor among the poor. But we are as poor as they are!"
[150] Testimony of G. Bovagnet.
[151] F. Makower, p. 52.
[152] The Minister of Prisons and members of the Senate consulted her in view of eventual reform: "If I had been an American, they would not have listened to me. If I had been a Filipina, I would have been killed. But as I was only an Australian, they listened to me and acted accordingly."
[153] M. Recavarren, p. 261.

> During the first years of my religious life, I sought to succeed in the tasks given to me in our schools, both middle and high school. I spent some happy moments. But deep inside me something was not satisfied. I had difficulty doing my work with joy, for my heart was made for something else. There was an attraction for a consecrated life closer to those who are so far removed from having, from knowing, from power. Something inside me was not leaving me in peace. I understood it but not precisely.

In 1976 she experimented with a month of trying to be "contemplative while working in a hospital laundry that could just as well have been in a factory!" She stayed there nine years.[154] For others after the Chapter of 1970 remaining in the institutions did not appear to be consistent with the options.[155] Thanks to a broader understanding of the educational mission, a growing number of religious turned toward pastoral and social work. Marie-Louise Leplat remarked, "There was a displacement, as it were. At the beginning those who engaged in social work were marginalized. Little by little it was those who remained in conventional education who worried about what others thought of them."

Developments in the social and political realm account for these new pursuits. Qualification requirements for teachers changed in Great Britain.[156] When the boarding schools were transformed into day schools or closed altogether, some former coadjutrix sisters who had served in them found themselves unemployed. The youngest in Great Britain, Ireland, Spain, Malta or Austria studied to be nurses. No doubt the expectation was that they would practice among the elderly sisters or in Sacred Heart schools, but they were employed also in hospitals and public and private schools. In Colombia they asked to be sent to Peru, Cuba, Argentina, Puerto Rico, Venezuela and the United States, where they were helpful, "thanks to their personal qualities and their aptitude for service."[157] In Egypt the Spanish former sisters who came from country families rapidly became acclimatized to the Saïd and proved to be of great help in the dispensaries and the workrooms.[158] But adds Andrée Meylan, "We also became more aware of the privations we saw around us and of ways to use different gifts and talents, but always with an eye toward the Kingdom."

---

[154] Testimony of Jacqueline Teisserenc, *Religieuses du Sacré-Cœur*, 2007, pp. 3-4.
[155] Testimony of Anne-Marie Kalbacher. She studied to be a social worker.
[156] Testimony of A. Meylan.
[157] *Histoire de la province de Colombie*, § 13.
[158] Testimony of Rosine Baboin.

New Forms of Community Life

The renewal called for by the Chapter of 1967 brought with it other ways of thinking about the community. There was concern to remove any hint of monastic spirit and to split into smaller units the houses that had become cumbersome with too many people and too great a mix of ages. Shortly after her election, Mother Bultó formed a community with the members of her council; the other nuns at the motherhouse formed another.[159] The shift to small communities was sometimes linked to a particular circumstance. In 1970 the community of Monterrico in Lima included thirty-six people. Groups were set up to work on the preparatory document for the chapter. One turned into a small community of eleven members. The provincial, Gabriela Belón, created another.[160] In the United States small communities began experimentally in 1968.[161] The movement spread between 1970 and 1976 in the Society where the number of communities increased from 250 to 375. The communities thus subdivided represented 33.9% of communities in 1970. In 1974 there were only about ten communities of more than thirty persons. Those with six to twelve, which formed almost half the communities in 1975, had become the norm.

At first communities were designed to provide the young with a life style compatible with their studies, to experiment with life in small groups and to establish new kinds of relationships among them. Tried first in Great Britain, this style of living spread. In Austria, the young professed who were studying at the university "found no support at all on the part of the community and experienced much criticism." A small community was formed for them in the provincial house.[162] At Compostela a community of five students was set up in a university residence.[163] In Chicago the provincial, provincial treasurer, another nun and the students moved into two apartments on different floors of the same building.[164] A community

---

[159] That was not appreciated by the contemporaries (Testimony of Lilian Amato).

[160] "From the chapter we kept this *mot d'ordre*: small communities must be formed immediately. The nuns chose to live with others – no one was living alone. The provincial team (of Chicago) and the provincial encouraged the project. The small communities did not have a local superior" (Testimony of M.M. Miller).

[161] M. Recavarren, p. 203.

[162] Testimony of H. Woitsch.

[163] Testimony of M. García de la Rasilla.

[164] "We had a large dining room and two bedrooms. Our bedroom also served as an office. We had no oratory. We did the cooking. We went to Mass in the morning or the evening in the neighboring parishes. The two students lived on another floor. We had no superior. Finally we had made a community for the two students with the other nun who was the driver and one who worked for the diocese.

bringing together a few professed with young professed students was opened in Lyons. In Ireland the first small communities were composed of those returning from probation.[165] Problems could arise when it was not possible to create a community with religious of compatible age and activity. At Tunbridge Wells the only young nun who worked outside the institution wondered how she could go to evening meetings outside and return before the doors were locked, how to reconcile her activity with community life since she could no longer participate in Office and meals, how to have relationships with nuns of her own age when they were occupied in the evenings with surveillance in the dormitories: "As I was looking for companionship, I took to going to visit with them in the dormitories in the evenings, which was not really approved. We began talking at meals, but at breakfast there were two tables; at one we talked, at the other we kept silence. One religious remarked that the Society had lost all sense of discipline."[166]

Trials were made of small communities alongside large ones or of fraternities within large houses.[167] All kinds of groupings were possible, from fraternities whose members separated for meetings and prayer but took their meals with the others in the house, to fraternities that led a completely autonomous life but within the same house. Often the first fraternity was created by volunteers,[168] sometimes in a conspiratorial atmosphere, in the United States and in France, "after long discussion among a few about what we wanted and how to ask for it."[169] Most people wanted to make smaller groups "in view of the common good and without any malice."[170] At Bondues an autonomous group formed in 1971 with the consent of the provincial: "It was bold," thought Marie-Louise Leplat. Some religious decided to stay in the large community to support the

---

Afterwards we bought a house for the provincial house. This time there was an oratory and our bedrooms and offices were separate" (Testimony of C. Seiker).

[165] Testimony of M. Henry.

[166] Testimony of B. Sweeney.

[167] In 1971, the Trinità dei Monti was subdivided into four fraternities, to which was added the novitiate, and five *responsables* were named, "but it was soon seen that there was a need for a single superior responsible before ecclesiastical and civic authorities because of the school and canonical decrees" (Testimony of E. de Guggenberg). At Châtenay-Malabry, the new superior of the house settled in the fraternity formed at Petit Châtenay (Testimony of A. Wasbauer).

[168] In Montpellier, religious were grouped according to responses to a questionnaire.

[169] Testimony of C. Chazottes.

[170] Testimony of Louise Marie de Bellefonds.

superior who had been obliged to accept what she considered a tear in the fabric of community:

> The community that remained faithful looked askance at the separation. The French seemed to want to defend or protect the superior and did not approve of our way of proceeding or of the changes we wanted. The others understood nothing of what was going on and thought we were losing our religious spirit. We were staying a long time at table, we were not going to all the readings; we were going out.[171]

While the break-up of large communities pleased the young, it was harder for the oldest, who felt rejected and had the impression, in Mother de Valon's words, that it was painful and cruel to be forced to live in "a home for old people." The young realized that the new style of community deprived them of the wisdom of the elders.[172] As small communities were being presented as a way of bringing religious life into a new era, the impression created was that the earlier life had been onerous and that it was outmoded.[173]

Some provinces remained somewhat apart from the movement. In Austria sisters firmly against separation stayed together without forming small groups. Others tried, with more or less success, to share in groups while maintaining good contact with the large community. They wanted to engage in the process

---

[171] Pressure groups aimed at supporting the superior existed as well in Montpellier and Kientzheim, where a traditional group formed around the mistress general and obstructed efforts of the superior who was trying to make things evolve (Testimony of Marguerite Depierre).

[172] Testimony of M. Charley.

[173] Prov. Arch. USA, H. Condon, "An Historical Perspective of Community." She recalls that while in the era of cloister, "Some of the activities and customs hard to endure were the pressures of insufficient time for needed work, a closely structured life, having to obtain permission for many things, a lack of independence, and so on.... Other customs and activities offered opportunities for enjoyment: conversation, entertainment, occasional 'free time,' games, congés, sharing tasks. The age span of the community can be particularly interesting and stimulating, with wonderful older women who gladly share their experiences. Sometimes reading aloud by one of the community was enjoyable – biographies, the annual letters from the past, significant spiritual books. New members of the community bring new insights and experiences. Despite restrictions, friendships we formed have lasted through life, a bonding blessed by the Lord who cherished his friends on earth." The reactions of mistrust regarding "small communities" were not all the result of age; some religious by temperament felt more at ease in the former structures of community life.

step by step, while the progressives wanted to deepen the renewal: "There were many clashes, problems, even fights. When the progressives formed an autonomous group, it was helpful to them and the others who could then regulate their life according to their own rhythm. Small communities were founded in Innsbruck and Vienna-Heiligenstadt."[174] At Mount Anville three communities of five to six persons were called "the moderns, the traditionals and the radicals."[175] In some houses the tension lasted a long time:

> When Craiglockhart was divided into three communities the superior was caught between her loyalty to the Society that was asking for the changes and the firm resistance of a few nuns. Later there were only two groups and we took our meals separately. Gradually the situation evolved and relations became more cordial. But before that happened, I remember the feeling of hostility when the provincial or the superior general visited, testified Sheila Hayes.

The creation of small communities also grew out of apostolic demands. In England in 1969 the first one brought together two Religious of the Sacred Heart and four Faithful Companions of Jesus in East London. They lived amidst longshoremen and working men in a population that new immigrants had completely transformed. "It was an adventure," commented Joan Faber, who was part of it. Quite as reckless was another insertion in Southall, an area that included more Asians and people from the Antilles than "non-colored" English.

> That opened us to inter-religious contact. It was the beginning of a simpler way of living in close contact with the parish, the priest and the faithful. It was a shock for those who knew us as the "Ladies of the Sacred Heart." Then a community was opened in Hammersmith to extend the works of our schools. People came to the house for a weekly Mass and for catechism. The local apostolate allowed for community unity, which the division of the large communities attached to our schools would have made more difficult, for many did not see the need for small units or for exploring new ways of living our life. Therefore, the most open minded and the youngest were the ones creating these new forms.

---

[174] Testimony of E. Belle.
[175] "The mods, the trads and the rads!"

In Italy after the Chapter of 1970 large communities began to be divided. Mother Camacho created the first autonomous small community on the peninsula in Turin.[176] The house in Genoa split into two groups,

> where everyone sought to participate and share. There was the beginning of a community project that took into account both the community environment and the apostolic work. The boarding school became more homelike. But there was some tension in the direction: the new was pushing and the old holding back. To put it better, the community ought to have been the place to live and grow cooperatively, the superior being more democratic.[177]

But at Villa Peschiera the group that met separately, even though supported by the superior, was not accepted by the greater part of the community:

> Its members were called separated brethren, *fratelli separati*, but at the same time several religious of different ages moved towards the small group in which the members were trying to live by faith with participation, sharing and fraternal correction, while accepting contradictions in an ongoing effort to be useful, charitable and serene. The birth of small fraternities inserted in a normal human setting was not appreciated; they were seen rather as a betrayal of the great institutions that were losing their most promising features. The most widespread opinion was that the small fraternities were created by difficult religious or by those for whom the community had become too narrow. A very small number of religious believed in and supported them. Some, even though interested, were afraid of innovations.[178]

But for those who accepted taking the step, life in fraternity was one "of their most beautiful experiences." In Turin, recounts Giovannina Russo, "I felt at ease, satisfied. It was an experience of seven sisters united in real sisterly love. It was a fraternity where there was no jealousy, where nothing belonged to this one or that one, where we shared all that we had and all that we did."

The question of fraternities did not come up in Africa where the communities had never included more than about ten people. Where a move from large to small communities, like the changes in apostolic activity, was seen as a decree from Rome or the provincial, preparation was sometimes

---

[176] Testimony of E. de Guggenberg.
[177] Testimony of A. Cavallari.
[178] A. Cavallari.

provided. During the year preceding the closing of El Valle in Seville, the nuns were divided into communities of seven or eight, thereby facilitating the next step of insertion in working class areas.[179] In Malta the superior, Honor Davidson, said that it was an experiment that would be evaluated at the end of a month. Consequently, there were many applicants and those who were not accepted felt hurt.[180] Later new communities were opened to welcome the Maltese who were returning from England, the United States, Japan, India and Taiwan. At the end of the 1970's in Malta there were plans to establish communities in local parishes.[181] The same thing was tried in Ireland.

The move to small communities called for considerable training, for some nuns had "to learn how to be women, how to cook and care for a house."[182] Thanks to sharing household tasks, the distinction between former coadjutrix and choir religious really was minimized. But getting used to different personalities was not easy. One had to take risks,[183] "to give and receive, to accept one's own weaknesses and those of others."[184] This life was schooling in reality:[185] "We experienced how difficult it is to communicate every day."[186] But at Oxford in 1968 the nuns seemed

> more natural. The community was small, composed of a superior, two or three other mature religious and a few students. There was a sort of informal character, of spontaneity and relaxation, which helped study

---

[179] Testimony of R. Carbonnel.
[180] Testimony of B. Sweeney.
[181] Testimony of T. Agius. 1972: Dar is-Sliem, built on the property of Saint Julian; Fgura intended to provide a house for elderly sisters coming back from abroad; 1973: an apartment after the closing of the normal school at Tal-Virtu (closed a year later); 1977: Pieta, a house; 1978: two communities in parishes, one at Senglea (closed in 1986), the other at Zejtun; 1981: Floriana, provincial house; 1988: two houses at Zurrieq (closed in 1999) and on the island of Gozo (closed in 1996); 1996: Lodge House, on the property of Saint Julian (closed in 1999).
[182] Testimony of M. Kennedy and C. Chazottes. Jacqueline Rousselon told how lay people helped when the nuns had to buy supplies for the kitchen. "I had studied before in a home economics school, but the years in cloister had completely erased all my knowledge of that field."
[183] Testimony of M. Martín Juarez.
[184] Testimony of V. Henao Botero.
[185] Testimony of T. McCarthy. Testimony of Maria Socorro Duaso. Some religious who committed themselves generously to the experiment asked afterwards to live in large communities when they saw the material constraints (Testimony of S. Kageyama).
[186] Testimony of M. Connolly.

and serious reading. We still wore the habit and the veil, but we were able to form enduring friendships with the professors of our university college and with others, which we would not have been able to do before.

Long refectory tables were replaced by tables with three to six places, making exchanges less formal.[187] Meals were scheduled according to apostolic activities. At Montpellier, life became much more sisterly. "We began to address one another informally. We began also to speak of our childhood, our family and to share concerns. We began to watch television regularly. Meetings, discussions, exchanges were interesting"[188] because of the variety of personalities[189] and apostolic commitments.[190] Small communities allowed for the separation of work and community life. Shared meals replaced the recreation of earlier days.[191] As Mary Hinde remarked,

> For a long time I was not living in a small community, only in a fraternity located in an institution, which I found strange, difficult and artificial, a little as if we were playing a role. When I went to a real small community in a poor area in the outskirts of the city, that made a great deal of sense and I was happy.

Small communities were a transition to a new form of religious life. "The old monastic structures had not prepared us for the give and take of interpersonal relationships," remarked Bea Brennan.

> Our differences of character became obvious when the rule of silence that had covered them was abandoned. We did not know how to receive each one's awkward efforts to make herself known as a human being. Failures and the difficulty of feeling accepted and understood caused some people to withdraw as far as they could from community life and to find friendship elsewhere. We tried to pray together, but sharing tended to be intellectual at best. When I went to Upper Egypt, I had an experience of small community living at its best. Since we had different languages

---

[187] Testimony of A. Hine and A. Conroy who added: "That sometimes caused the loss of lively discussion on various subjects and limited horizons."
[188] Testimony of M-L. Fabre. In England, "We stopped calling one another sister and began to use nicknames before deciding to use first names" (Testimony of A. Hine).
[189] Testimony of T. McCarthy.
[190] Testimony of P. Corral.
[191] Testimony of J. Xuereb.

and cultures, and we could not find diversion outside because of the restrictions on women imposed by the culture, we were thrown back on ourselves. Each day we had to face new challenges, and we helped one another to answer to what we received as a call from God. We prayed together; we laughed at our mistakes; we shared our successes and our failures.[192]

New Ways of Expressing Sacred Heart Spirituality

The Chapter of 1967 had given the religious the freedom to regulate their own spiritual life. The first instance concerned the time and place of daily prayer. When Mother Sheahan announced in Omaha that the nuns had responsibility for their times of prayer, "at the end of recreation many did not go to the chapel for night prayers as we were accustomed to do but walked around the campus."[193] Those no longer living in the institutions went to Mass in parish churches as it suited their schedules. Sometimes because of the obligations of their work they were even unable to participate in daily Mass. Spiritual exercises made in common fell into disuse little by little, except in the communities of the elderly. But after the Chapter of 1970 various provinces emphasized the importance to community life of prayer and the Eucharist, which created "a climate in which each one was enabled to live a life of contemplation."[194] In Ireland/Scotland and Mexico, religious, while believing that the Office was an excellent form of prayer, recognized the freedom of each community to choose the way of saying it or to replace it with another form of common prayer.

Each one managed her prayer life most often by trial and error, for the changes were a source of both liberation and challenge. Some felt relieved to no longer be required to say Office and the Rosary, to have spiritual reading in common, to make the two daily examinations of conscience. They nourished their prayer through Bible study and books that were not necessarily classified as spiritual reading.[195] As Helen Condon wrote,

---

[192] On her return to the United States, she noticed a change: "We were more accustomed to sharing our lives. A new Society was beginning to take shape."
[193] Testimony of M. Ruggeri.
[194] Assembly of Australia/New Zealand. Same comment from the assembly of Ireland/Scotland in 1976. It referred to a formula of the Chapter of 1970 on the life of prayer. In Canada, where many religious ardently desired a profoundly and really spiritual life, prayer at the time of the provincial chapter of 1976 was presented as a priority.
[195] Testimony of B. Brennan.

Responsibility for one's own prayer life and greater personal freedom enabled us to deepen and share our prayer. Some may remember how two or three would gather for a morning hour, intent upon the same scriptural passage. One or other might occasionally share an insight or a need, a hope, a moment of joy or pain. The silence too was a bonding, a drawing closer to one another and to the Lord who teaches us to pray.[196]

The creation of small communities helped in sharing prayer,[197] as did ways of praying drawn from the charismatic renewal, which became widespread. The support of spiritual direction was encouraged in all the provinces.

To preserve the tradition of the Society founded on the interior life, there had to be a new link between the apostolate and the life of prayer. From what she heard, Mother Camacho knew the difficulties people could experience. She repeatedly spoke about the duty of personal prayer, the urgency of returning to the source that was the Heart of Christ, the demands of the vocation to the Sacred Heart "to live by, with and in Jesus Christ."[198] She insisted strongly on the need for prolonged prayer and renewal, believing it all the more necessary as apostolic activity was changing to maintain fidelity to the Spirit and to live under the Spirit's inspiration,[199] in order to be in union and conformity with Christ:

> Of you, the youngest, who entered a short time ago, whose sensibility is close to today's world and its problems, I ask that you give first place to prayer, to listening, to openness of heart, so as to discover and comprehend what faith in love demands. I ask you to continue learning about this interior life, which has to be the soul of the response you want to give to our brothers' and sisters' needs. And you who are fully active and are responsible for conserving the primitive inspiration,

---

[196] Prov. Arch. USA, *A Historical Perspective of Community*, p. 2.
[197] Testimony of H. Okui.
[198] C. Camacho, *Letters to the Society*, p. 2, 12 March 1971.
[199] C. Camacho, 25 May 1971. Fidelity to the Holy Spirit is an omnipresent characteristic in the different communications of Mother Camacho. For her, as for the founder, it was a question of the very essence of the vocation to the Sacred Heart (20 October 1972, p. 24). To be faithful to the Spirit was to be in accord with the charism of Saint Madeleine Sophie, to seek the will of God in a climate of prayer, of liberty, of self-discovery. As it was a question of "being attentive to discerning the action of the Spirit in history," this fidelity demands also a habit of personal and communal discernment (18 June 1971, 20 October and 15 December 1972.) Evaluation was to be a constant practice to allow the religious to "tend to unify prayer and life in order to arrive at being in Christ a living prayer" (Message, August 1972).

which vitalizes our mission: make the disciple's attitude central in your life. In every event, every situation, in the simplest things of daily life, look long at Christ so as to respond according to his Heart. Thus our mission will bear the traits of Jesus, simple and humble, but powerful in love.[200]

The nearness of Christ, realized and experienced among others through and in prayer, makes the disciple.[201] It is after experiencing and tasting it that one is able to be sent on mission. The Chapter of 1976 recognized "unanimously that our congregation has an ever living call to contemplation and communion. The call to contemplation as gift and to adoration lays hold of our whole life. Thus from our contemplation springs up a force for conversion and transformation for the mission."[202]

The charism of the Society – the use of that expression was just beginning – was to be expressed in the context of the times. Although the Second Vatican Council had not referred to the devotion to the Sacred Heart, some theologians, along the lines of the work undertaken by Father Hugo Rahner, had shown that "It is nothing other than a concentration on the Paschal Mystery and from that invokes fully the core of Christian faith,"[203] uniting Christology, pneumatology and ecclesiology, which the encyclical *Haurietis Aquas* had also highlighted. But two approaches to considering the Heart of Christ were distinguished more clearly than before. The one based on the revelations of Paray-le-Monial, which were no longer universally accepted because too conditioned by the culture of the nineteenth century and too tied to "practices,"[204] tended to give way to another perspective based more radically on the Bible. In the spirit of the school of spirituality of Bérulle, which Saint Madeleine Sophie had known and espoused, it was a matter of contemplating Jesus so as to be imbued with his ways of living and working and to reproduce them.

The Heart of Christ became the meeting place with Jesus Christ as understood in the wholeness of its mystery, with God and humanity, with cosmic reality, with and in the history of salvation. The provincial chapter

---

[200] C. Camacho, 8 September 1981, p. 105.
[201] C. Camacho, 1 July 1973.
[202] *Chapter 1976*, p. 6.
[203] Joseph Ratzinger, *Ils regarderont Celui qu'ils ont transpercé*, Paris, 2006, p. 57.
[204] At the time of the provincial chapter in Mexico in January 1970, among the practices called into question and presented as coming from Saint Margaret Mary were visits to the chapel, celebration of the First Friday, adoration of the Blessed Sacrament and the repetition of ejaculatory prayers aimed at "consoling Jesus solitary in the tabernacle and suffering from lack of correspondence to his love."

in Mexico in January 1970 drew four conclusions from this. Drawing near to the Heart of Christ urged one to interiority and personal prayer, oriented one towards charity and through this lens contributed to new strength in community life, and revalued commitment to the world in which the Lord was present.[205] The pierced Heart of Christ determined a new relationship to the world and disposed one to compassion towards those suffering and living in difficult conditions. It challenged the one who gave herself to it, inclined her to what the Society of the Sacred Heart called "union and conformity." Interiority did not result in turning back upon self, for it was only "authentic if it went out toward others for whom Christ died and to whom he addressed his message. It signified that making our home in the Heart of Christ urged us to go to meet all the requests of suffering humanity; in other words to try to restore a civilization of love."[206]

The expressions used to evoke the Heart of Christ reveal an evolution that was not just semantic. In her conference opening the Chapter of 1967, Mother de Valon had said: "I think that our chapter must consider the world today through the Heart of Christ, in order to bring it more faith, more hope, more charity."[207] The capitulants were seated in a hall where there was a picture of Fra Angelico's crucifixion. In it the painter had represented the scene of the piercing with the lance. At the time of Mother de Valon's resignation, the chapter had an experience marked by the cross. In closing the chapter Mother Bultó took up Mother de Valon's formula, linking it explicitly to the piercing: "The orientations *ad experimentum* are the fruit of that gaze fixed on today's world, seen through the pierced Heart of Christ, so as to bring it more faith, more hope, more love."[208] Although no conscious decision had been made in this regard, the introduction of the *Orientations* and the parts concerning prayer, the vows and apostolic life contain direct allusions to the pierced Heart. Toward the end of the chapter the capitulants went to the Villa Lante where Mother Bultó renewed the consecration of the Society to Our Lady of Sorrows. She inserted the following words into the usual formula: "May the piercing of his Heart be for us forever the sign of that love of the Son of God, come to give life to the world and the pledge of that new life springing up from his Heart."[209] In her first letter to the Society she evoked the "Heart wounded by love of humanity."[210] Six of her circulars contain the expression "pierced heart" or

---

[205] *Histoire de la Province du Mexique*, p. 30.
[206] C. Camacho, *Conferences*, pp. 223.
[207] *Special Chapter*, p. 6.
[208] P. 82.
[209] Prov. Arch. USA. Helen Condon, *The Chapter of 1967*, p. 2.
[210] In a sentence in perfect agreement with the new exegesis: "This heart that the Spirit has handed over to us."

"open heart." In introducing the Chapter of 1970 she expressed the desire of all "of reaffirming our decision to place Christ and his love at the center of our life; his Heart opened on the cross remains the meaningful symbol of that love."[211]

Some elements of the founder's intuition were stressed because of the needs of the times. Some new formulas appeared. The "Heart of Christ at the heart of the world," – which we owe to Bernadette des Francs – was one of them. This formula, which rapidly came to be seen as the original call of the vocation to the Sacred Heart, signified that a religious had to give a response of love completely centered on the Heart of Christ, by discovering and confronting her personal call with the needs of the world and the true values of religious life. These two efforts were possible only under the action of the Spirit. An expression often associated with Mother Camacho was the "contemplative outlook," which she used beginning with her first circular letter. Seen first as an attitude of prayer[212] that allows one to discover "the hidden gifts in others and Christ's love in them, our hope,"[213] the contemplative attitude was presented as committing one

> to live as Jesus lived. We can learn only from his Heart how to look at the world, to listen humbly to what he tells us about the realities of the world and to approach it in a truly human and friendly manner. Long stretches of time, listening to his Word, fixing our gaze on Jesus Christ, for the knowledge of whom we have left everything, will enable us to discover the Gospel values that will confront our lives and exact a critical awareness of the world, inspired by humility and the hope that the Kingdom is already among us.[214]

In several of Mother Camacho's circular letters the expression "contemplative attitude" is synonymous with contemplation.

At the opening of the Chapter of 1976 she related the expressions "Heart of Christ" and "heart of humanity," saying that "in communion with and in obedience to the Spirit," the assembly had to "discern as a body how to glorify the Heart of Jesus Christ suffering in humanity."[215] The chapter wrote that "at its depth our vocation echoes today this call to contemplate the Heart of Christ through the 'pierced heart of

---

[211] *Chapter 1970*, p. 3.
[212] C. Camacho, *Letters to the Society*, 28 November 1970, p. 1.
[213] 12 March 1971, p. 2.
[214] 21 November 1974, p. 43. On 25 May 1977, she proposed it as a means of "seeing life in the light of faith," pp. 62-64.
[215] *Chapter of 1976*, p. 42.

humanity.'"[216] One of her texts on the charism shows the evolution that had taken place in the understanding the Sacred Heart: "Saint Madeleine Sophie, in listening to the calls of her times, saw the Body of Christ 'outraged' by 'impiety;' today we contemplate the wounded Heart of Christ in humanity torn by the injustice in the world; and our charism urges us to be in solidarity with people in their suffering and in the search for a more just and fraternal world."[217] It is no longer a question of consoling a lonely Jesus but of experiencing the sorrow his heart is feeling in the world and in the poor, the suffering part of it. This understanding of the Heart of Christ was influenced by liberation theology. In the same way that Christ through the incarnation came into the world, the Society of the Sacred Heart was to place itself among the poor. Beyond concrete insertions it was to express its life in terms of solidarity, liberation and challenging presence.[218] These two currents – opening to the world and the devotion to the Sacred Heart – came together between 1967 and 1976, according to Helen Condon. The opening to the world through the pierced Heart of Christ brings to life a new awareness of our charism and our mission today. The call to reveal to others the love of Jesus Christ, constant in the history of the Society and in the vocation of each religious, is equally a call to compassion and a call to work for justice. The Chapter of 1976 thus expressed this commitment: "Seek justice with the heart of an educator."[219] And the Church has established that "action in favor of justice is a constitutive dimension of preaching the Gospel."[220]

This interpretation of the spirituality of the Sacred Heart replaced the earlier way of understanding reparation. For a long time it was seen as a compensation for outrages inflicted on the Lord in the Blessed Sacrament in particular, as a sort of "reimbursement" and making up for evil and injustice. "From then on the emphasis was placed trying to make the flagrant injustices of our time disappear, the wrongs done to our sisters and brothers. Victimhood became translated into a more direct service of others and into solidarity rooted in love. Justice became the new name for

---

[216] P. 58. Again, it was an expression of Bernadette des Francs.
[217] P. 6.
[218] *Histoire de la Province du Mexique*, p. 37.
[219] *Chapter 1970*, p. 13.
[220] H. Condon, *The Chapter of 1967*. All the same some provinces wanted consecration to the Sacred Heart to be reaffirmed "because in the 1970 documents the section on union and conformity with the Heart of Jesus underlines contemplation of the Heart of Christ through the pierced heart of human beings. But there was no mention of the contemplation of the Heart of Christ in himself, in his life with the Father, which is also a part of our vocation" (*Living Pages*, 1976. Province of India).

reparation."[221] This vision concurred with the thought of Saint Madeleine Sophie, who had not introduced particular practices to express reparation, believing that it was by their ongoing efforts that Religious of the Sacred Heart would accomplish it. The contemplative attitude and the Heart of Christ perceived in the pierced heart of humanity enabled movement from one vision to the other, from one culture to another.

The Society of the Sacred Heart changed its emblem. On its original seal were the two Hearts of Jesus and Mary, the image following the way in which the devotion was spread after the revelations of Paray-Le-Monial.[222] After the Chapter of 1970 the California province was looking for a new emblem and appealed to Victoria Seidel, a young professed who was an artist. She designed a stylized heart surmounted by a cross.[223] Ten years later Oonah Ryan of the New York province, at the request of the general council, produced an emblem that could be given to the people at the chapter:[224]

> The heart moves dynamically: it is open, (so as to suggest the wound) ready to collect, to gather. But above all there is the world fully present with the cross planted in its midst. The domain of contemplation is considerably enlarged. It is not only the Eucharist that one contemplates in adoring Christ, but the world also becomes the object of our contemplation in order to discover him there: "Christ is there, hidden at the heart of the world where his death has buried him and whence his risen life springs up over time penetrating history.[225]

As Gabriela Cavassa summarized it, "the Society of the Sacred Heart was committed to loving and serving the Lord more than just admiring him and undergoing his sufferings."[226] This back-and-forth conversation regarding

---

[221] Testimony of Rosario Valdeavellano: "That demands confronting the structures of social sin and seeking to transform them, to commit oneself to the transformation of policy and of ways of making policy."

[222] *Religieuses du Sacré-Cœur*, Agnès Bigo, "History of the Emblems," p. 14.

[223] Testimony of M. Phelan. Towards the same epoch Korea had a similar design executed in silver-plated metal in the form of a pin.

[224] Communicated by F. Gimber. The provincial, Anne O'Neil, had had cards made with the image and sent them to the nuns in her province and to the capitulants, thus spreading knowledge of the design.

[225] *Religieuses du Sacré-Cœur*, A. Bigo.

[226] Testimony of P. Cardó: "Since 1970 I have understood the mystery of the open, wounded Heart of Jesus in our world of today. The option for the poor is the same option Jesus made and our charism to discover and manifest this love attracts me more and fills me with joy." R. Valdeavellano: "The option

the Heart of Christ and the world, seen from the viewpoint of those who suffer violence and who are wounded by the economic, political and social conditions imposed on them, was a source of inspiration for many religious.[227] For others, this way of considering the spirituality of the Sacred Heart corresponded to their own experience, to sufferings they had had or had witnessed and which had made an impact on them.[228]

Communities inserted among people who lived in utter poverty and had to face subhuman situations adopted their life style. At El Ghanayem, the founders recounted, "We lived like the people of the village. To telephone, we went next door to the neighbors' house. There was no shower in the house. We had set up an oratory under the stairs, and when we were in there we heard the noises of the neighbors' animals. Even the Lord was in a corner."[229] At Bayadeya there was so much malnutrition that premature babies whose mothers died were placed in the room of one of the nuns who was a nurse so that she could feed them drop by drop to give them a chance to survive.[230] In Latin America the nuns welcomed the people and shared their house and their food with them.[231]

When they were not able to speak the language of the country, to understand the local mindset and traditions, the religious experienced their own poverty. In turn they became momentarily illiterate, depending on others, "poor in being unable to give a religion class or any training and to have to be content to teach them sewing and knitting."[232] Where there was contact with people the sense of mission changed. In the section of Agustino in Lima, "We were trying to help them and alleviate their needs, but what we were doing raised questions for us. Was it paternalism? How to help them grow? How to give them a sense of their personhood?"[233] In

---

with the poor to build another society, another possible world, that is the key. That changes the way of reading and understanding life, spirituality, the Scripture, studies."

[227] Testimony of M.L. Leplat: "In Joigny in 1971, for the first time, I heard contemplation in action and a contemplative attitude spoken of. The explanation gave me a great light that helped me to unify my life and to free me from my monastic ideal."

[228] A double survey was made among the nuns of Chile, Peru, Mexico and Brazil and among nuns living or having lived in Egypt. For it seemed interesting to weigh the human and spiritual repercussions on religious living in their own country or on those in a country other than their own.

[229] Testimony of Kamelia Nassif.
[230] Testimony of Cecilia Van Zorn.
[231] Testimony of Violetta Jaimes.
[232] Testimony of M.T. Arbeloa.
[233] Testimony of V. Jaimes.

Upper Egypt, "How many times in my contacts with the poor, have I not wanted them to be 'the ideal poor,' as if I were refusing them the right to have their defects and their ambitions."[234] The religious discovered that the poor were evangelizing them, and that among them and thanks to them they were meeting the Lord.[235]

> We were going to the poor while believing that they needed so many things. We learned through cooperative relationships that the poor are just what we are missing most in religious life and in the Church! We cannot get along without them to enter into relationship with God and follow Jesus. The sense of humor of the poor refreshes and challenges our joy. Our sense of receiving a gift keeps growing. It helps us realize that we don't need money, but only the least hint of it…to deal with "our masters the poor," as they said in the Middle Ages and with this Jesus whom they reveal to us continually. Although sometimes the desire to cry, "My God, my God, why have you forsaken me?" spills over, we accept solitude as an offered treasure that gives rise to a new and stronger life.[236]

Daily life caused the discovery of a country's values, for example, the popular religion of the Andeans and Amazonians or of the mountain people who came to live in the shanty towns of Lima.[237] The widespread *machismo* encouraged growth in womanliness. Language, symbolism, feelings and the ways of expressing them were also enriched by experience.[238] The way the poor lived was an occasion for both surprise and thanksgiving:

> Faith in providence brings about small miracles. The courage of the women who have to find ways of feeding and caring for their children and sending them to school. Their strength in supporting difficult husbands, unbearable situations, their cleverness in living on little nothings, in making use of everything, in getting along without the anything extra. Humility in asking and in thanking, in taking with good grace what others refuse. Gratitude for every gift received and above all for friendship and hospitality. The will and the capacity to grow and to get ahead, to give their children an education and an environment that they themselves have not had.[239]

---

[234] Testimony of M.T. Arbeloa.
[235] Testimony of V. Jaimes. *Religieuses du Sacré-Cœur*, p. 41.
[236] Testimony of R. Valdeavellano.
[237] R. Valdeavellano and Elizabeth Bazán.
[238] Testimony of Lilian Crosby.
[239] Testimony of Rosaria del Vecchio.

"The poor have given me lessons in hospitality, generosity, solidarity and abandonment to the Lord, which, even if it is influenced by Muslim fatalism, has its roots in faith."[240] Feelings about the other changed:

> I learned to understand their weaknesses, to love them as they are with their smallness, their limits, and their defects, to pass over appearances: it is the heart that counts. I learned to believe in the other and to have confidence in him/her. I learned that the value of the person is greater than that of work or of success.[241]

Respect grew with closeness because each person was to be accepted and loved such as she was: "I became freer about norms; the person was more important and charity became the ultimate touchstone."[242] Entry into another rhythm of life offered an opportunity to do things less hurriedly, "to take time to contemplate nature and the action of Christ in the Church, expressing itself according to the character of each people."[243] Being totally immersed in the midst of a people led to another kind of spirituality of Nazareth. While before it had been reserved to one group of Religious of the Sacred Heart, later it seemed to be intended for everyone, and it directed one toward the contemplation of Jesus, "man of his times," who had chosen the simple life of Nazareth, who let himself be approached, who had been "one among others," one of his people.[244]

As close relationships were formed the nuns were able to look "with sympathy and humor but without misgivings at the old lessons about religious life that had separated us from our brothers and sisters and that forbade any show of affection. That brought with it an interior apprenticeship in a new form of meaningful friendship, no stranger to risks, with the people with whom we worked." Circumstances were changing and one's feelings about them as well.

> New opportunities arose to bring us into closer and more natural contact with persons of the opposite sex, politics, the world, with families, with our colleagues. Personal and social conflicts arose that we had never before experienced. These situations of risk and of violence strengthened our convictions and allowed us to discover the passion for Jesus and the Gospel without theorizing about them.[245]

---

[240] Testimony of M.T. Arbeloa.
[241] Testimony of Adela Blanes.
[242] Testimony of E. Bazán.
[243] Testimony of Christiane de Rousiers.
[244] Testimony of Magda Khalifa.
[245] Testimony of R. Valdeavellano.

At the time of the assembly of Latin American provincials in 1969, Chile described the repercussions of the new apostolates on prayer, which henceforward took on "a collective dimension." Some religious in Mexico were praying in the streets and in the market while contemplating the life of the poor.[246] Prayer was taking its point of departure from reality "with great faith in the presence of the Spirit in people and events."[247] Some religious in Saïd, from the verandah of their house, contemplated "everyone's tired faces, from little children to old men; their enduring such a hard life; in the dispensary the tenderness of the father for his child and the sad but serene face of the mother."[248] For religious whose prayer had been before "very enclosed, hardly related to what was happening outside,"[249] to pray starting from the truths of everyday life brought about "a liberation." One person said,

> My prayer became more inclusive of the world in which we were living. I try to look at it with the compassion of Jesus. It was as if God and I, the Lord Jesus and I, we are looking at all the scenes that come before us and offering them to the Father. I try to look at them with his eyes, with his kind, merciful heart; he loves justice and the right and asks us to make him present in these realities, almost always with a springing up of hope.[250]

"Once people have entered into my prayer, they no longer leave it; they come into it more and more," said another.[251] "First of all my image of God has changed. Little by little I have learned to find him in life, not only in mine but also in the suffering reality of my people, in the faces of my brothers and sisters to whom life has not given the opportunity to grow and to get ahead."[252]

> My prayer has become very simple and not centered on myself. To live this close to such suffering, poverty, primitive or instinctive ways of living keeps one from thinking about what one is experiencing. I sometimes feel powerless, unable to help with such suffering, but I feel very strongly in the depths of my being that God is there and with me always.[253]

---

[246] *Histoire de la Province du Mexique*, p. 27.
[247] Testimony of V. Jaimes.
[248] Testimony of R. Callis.
[249] Testimony of G. Cavassa.
[250] Testimony of A. Ramírez Ugarte.
[251] Testimony of E. Bazán.
[252] Testimony of P. Cardó.
[253] Testimony of A. Ramírez Ugarte.

Because of the internal upheaval implied by insertion in another culture and in a people other than one's own, "God becomes absolute."[254]

There was a new and different closeness to others and to God. The mission brought us "close to the Lord by living in the midst of this people chosen by God."[255] "The opening up to other relationships and to other ways of looking at life and of celebrating it removed the distance in my relationship with Jesus. I became familiar with him."[256] "The relationship with the Lord becomes more a matter of feeling *'sensible.'* It is like a tonic that renews you at the deepest part of yourself." Esperanza Medina related an experience she had one day at Bayadeya:

> In a very personal and visible fashion I felt the infinite love of God for the human being. A poor old man was dying alone, deprived of everything; his destitution complete: thrown on the ground, covered with a dirty rag, owning nothing. Around him was total emptiness, there was nothing in his room; it was not even a room, just a little doorway. I sat down next to him and suddenly I felt a light, as it were, come upon him: I felt palpably the immense love of God for him: God loved him and that was everything for him. He had nothing but he had everything: created by God in his image, what greater richness! Nothing was necessary since the Trinity lived in him; he was richer than any man; he was entering heaven rich in the love of God. I felt very strongly the value of that man and of every human being, with no distinction whatever; and the love of the poor grew in my heart. The more miserable they were, the more I saw the love of God in them all.

The communities shared their prayer and their home liturgies with their neighbors:

> The people's presence, their expressions, refreshed and gave new form and new content to our community prayers. It also put pressure on us for more honesty, authenticity, more consequences for oneself, because our mental plans were shaken up as well as the behavior that we had absorbed through traditional religious formation.[257]

---

[254] Testimony of E. Medina.
[255] Testimony of Fawzeya Banoub.
[256] Testimony of E. Bazán.
[257] Testimony of R. Valdeavellano.

Sharing could bear on what was most intimate: "My prayer ceased to be taboo for others. The simplicity of heart of the catechists in living their faith was contagious."[258] The meaning of liturgical feasts looked different:

> Before, I experienced Christmas with much joy and devotion to the image of the Infant God. That no longer suits me. Now it is the enormous scope of the mystery of the incarnation of the Son of God in these human realities – "He became one of us" or "Let us make the redemption happen" of Saint Ignatius – that comes to me. And Easter that has always resonated forcefully in me is now the certitude that all death is for life and that we in our turn must bring our little grain of sand so that this life becomes a pathway.[259]

The developments in the spirituality of the Sacred Heart expressed little by little by the general chapters were fostered by leaving a cloistered life, by the experiences the religious were living and by the study of the real world.

> It was clearly a question of discovering first the love of God revealed in Jesus in order to show it forth. Our experiences of daily *relecture* [re-reading], the loving presence of God in our lives close to the people supported us and encouraged us to express it. Feelings of indignation in the face of injustice, of admiration in the face of the solidarity of the people, their resistance, their faith, their capacity for celebration and hope brought us to a more contemplative prayer. It was a joyous surprise to experience very sincerely that we were invited to discover the sentiments and predilections of Jesus in harmony with the poor. To celebrate with the people, to have days of recollection with so many people doing the same work and having the same objective, men and women religious, lay people, a few priests, groups and associations, opened our eyes, our heart, our life.[260]
>
> A spirituality of the open heart now marks the way I relate: to remain vulnerable, to let myself be affected by people's joys and sufferings, to have an attentive presence. I try above all to live with fidelity and compassion. Community life is more than an interior framework from which I live our spirituality; it is rather a place where I experience how God guides me with and through others. To live the spirituality of the heart is to go to the depth of things and events. It is to offer to others the time and space to express the depths of their heart. It is to forgive and

---

[258] Testimony of E. Bazán.
[259] Testimony of A. Ramírez Ugarte.
[260] Testimony of H.M. Rodrigues da Cunha.

to ask forgiveness. Wounded hearts have a tendency to close up to avoid further wounds. But the Heart of Jesus remains open, and mine must open itself also. It is a space in which all can meet "among themselves." This heart offers me the capacity of welcoming even those who are very different from me. All of that helps me to have a prayer that is closer to that of Jesus and that occupies my day.[261]

"The spirituality of the Sacred Heart for me took flesh; I understood that in order to live it, I had to be a sister to men and women, to love them very much, to express my feelings, to share their concerns. People had to feel the closeness of God, his interest and his mercy, through what I was for them."[262]

The spirituality of the Sacred Heart, become "heartfelt," was extended until it took on

> unsuspected meaning and dimensions: adoration of an absolute God, beyond all ritualism or fetishism. Life leads us to adore continually in "spirit and in truth" and to uproot the idolatry that sometimes springs from a false understanding of perfection and a preoccupation with behaving irreproachably in the eyes of our sisters. The Eucharist has become more firmly the celebration of life: pardon, life given, sharing of bread, thanksgiving and the sense of blessing and praise. The creation of community takes on a greater dimension as we foster and go hand in hand with down-to-earth, urban groups, as we take on more commitments for the transformation of society. Mercy is not just the pardon we receive for our sins but that which moves us to the depths; we feel so weak and so human that we need the compassionate gaze of God, and we cannot see others in any other way.[263]

The mission resulted in a revolution, differing by country and culture, but always consisting in "making human beings grow in all aspects: faith, health, and social, economic, cultural, and artistic life." It was "a peaceful revolution," Céleste Khayat could say. "We were fighting against the injustice in which Egypt was plunged, a struggle in silence to build up men and women who could stand on their own feet. What a mission! I felt I was taking part in a great divine work." During the Chapter of 1970 Mother Camacho felt that the Society of the Sacred Heart had to live

---

[261] Testimony of Teresa Lecaros.
[262] Testimony of E. Bazán.
[263] Testimony of R. Valdeavellano.

what the prophet Micah proposed: "Act justly, love tenderly, walk humbly with your God."[264] She shared it often during her travels. It was a way of saying to Religious of the Sacred Heart that the insecurity of their life had meaning and their only guarantee of security was the love of God.[265] Most of the religious experienced this. As the province of Mexico/Nicaragua summarized it in 1994 in a fictional dialogue with Saint Madeleine Sophie:

> Sharing the life of simple, believing people has gradually transformed our spirituality. God has shown us his tenderness and his fidelity through the daily expressions of our people in sharing, celebration and feasting. We have also discovered that we are women alongside other women, and we recognize and celebrate the presence of the Spirit in struggles, strength and wisdom.... You who now see things through the eyes of God, help us to understand the mystery of God's love that embraces our history.[266]

---

[264] Mi 6:8. Testimony of C. Camacho.
[265] *Correspondence of Mollie Ahern*, Christmas 1975, p. 10.
[266] *Our Road to Emmaus*, pp. 81-82.

Chapter V

GREAT HOPES

After 1970 a new Society of the Sacred Heart emerged. Unlike most former superiors general, Mother Camacho had not been part of central government. She was freer in the positions she took and had to put into operation new governmental principles.

Another Kind of Governance: Collegial Government

The Chapter of 1970 had specified that the Society would be governed by a "legislative body," the general chapter, and by a "central team" composed of the superior general and the councilors who would not be assigned to geographical regions. It described the aims and obligations of the central government[1] before stating that the superior general had the final responsibility before the Church and the Society.[2] The method by which they were chosen was different for the superior general and for the general councilors. The superior general was elected by the chapter for six years with the possibility of re-election for another six-year term. The members of the central team had a three-year term renewable once; they were named by the superior general, after consultation with the chapter. In comparison with other congregations, whose chapters elect one council member after the other, the Society of the Sacred Heart showed

---

[1] To the Acts of the chapter was added a sheet that gave the meaning of the terms govern, legislative body, dialogue, subsidiarity and authority.
[2] The local community was presented before the provincial community and the superior general, which was a way of showing the reversal in the way the Society operated. The power no longer came from the top but from the base (Testimony of M. Braganza).

its originality.[3] It was the end of vertical government and the beginning of government by a team.[4]

In 1970, Mother Camacho gathered her team with two Europeans who had been present at the chapter, Doreen Boland and Françoise Cassiers, and with two from the Americas, Mary Catherine McKay and Maria Luiza Saade, neither of whom had been there. The first, an Irish woman, had lived for many years in Uganda; the second was Belgian; the third was from the United States and the fourth was Brazilian.[5] The personal bonds that Mother Camacho had formed during the Chapters of 1967 and 1970 and during her earlier journeys most likely accounted for these nominations.[6] In 1974, after Françoise Cassiers resigned for reasons of health, Mary Braganza, provincial of India, joined the team.[7] "The presence of an Asian was for us and for the Society a new element that brought us a different vision, another way of thinking, other values and new possibilities for deepening our religious life," thought Maria Luiza Saade. The second team in 1976 was composed of Alicia Hughes, who had been provincial of Argentina and had lived in a poor area,[8] Mary Shanahan, former provincial of Australia/New Zealand, and Judith Garson, who had been headmistress of two schools in the United States. Europe was represented by Mary Cavanagh from Scotland.[9]

In sharp contrast with preceding governments the first team was on average forty-one years old; the oldest member was forty-five and the youngest only thirty-six. "I think," thought Françoise Cassiers, "that a younger councilor [than Mother Camacho], someone who she felt was on

---

[3] Testimony of P. García de Quevedo. The chapter nevertheless determines the criteria for the nomination of councilors.

[4] Testimony of M.L. Saade.

[5] M.L. Saade: "It seems to me that with my nomination the chapter heard the cry of Latin America." Mother Camacho said that she had not had complete freedom of choice in 1970, since some of those she considered were not available because of their responsibilities.

[6] Testimony of F. Cassiers.

[7] According to her own account, she had relationships in different milieus of all nationalities and religions and had lived in the United States at two different times, where she felt recognized as an Indian and lived on an equal footing with the American religious.

[8] Testimony of A. Hughes: "At that moment it was something new, and for some provincials that was important."

[9] Mary Cavanagh thinks that the necessity of speaking the three languages of the Society was felt from then on and that the Mother General, a Spaniard, needed another European on her team rather than someone who was English-speaking.

her wave length, could appear to be an asset when she wanted to create a government that mirrored community and that in any case moved forward. At the same time, I am sure that I was the last councilor chosen and Concha's own choice, for many delegates would have preferred someone older and more reassuring." The team's youth facilitated its life style and its particular characteristics. The superior general was the only one to have been a provincial, a short time "to have had the experience of exercising authority, but she had an innate wisdom and a facility for discernment. Her free spirit, her *joie de vivre*, without any authoritarianism helped us very much to form a united group."[10] The second team had the same age range; the youngest, Mary Cavanagh, was only thirty-six and professed only five years.

The first circulars to come from the motherhouse gave indications of modernization. They were signed by the members of the team from then on. The use of first names or nicknames became frequent. The members of the government had to form a team, have a sense of teamwork and create a real community; for the superior general did not want to live in community only in the motherhouse. They had to invent everything, having no model to follow. Mother Camacho had chosen women who could relate to one another,[11] because to make a community, relationships among the members had to be possible.

Community of Government

The goal was to bring together a community of sisters and to show that it could happen.[12] "To work as a team was easy for us," recounts Maria-Luiza Saade, "thanks to Concha's personality. She let each one be herself. Each one had her space. The differences of temperament enriched our life and our work. We spoke French among ourselves, but during discussions each one inadvertently spoke her own language!" The central team reported to the Society how they used their time[13] and the outcomes of the workshops

---

[10] Testimony of M.L. Saade.
[11] Testimony of M. Shanahan: "I think that my gifts are in the area of relationships, and I suspect that was one of the reasons I was chosen!"
[12] Testimony of D. Boland. In the course of the first two years of their term they were assisted by a social psychologist, a specialist in communication, Michel Séguier, by Michel Leconte and by Father Pasquier who told them that they had "to hand on their experience. If you do not live what you say…" (Testimony of C. Camacho).
[13] C. Camacho: *Letters to the Society*, p. 3, 12 March 1971: "We have Eucharist in the meeting room where we gather for both work and prayer, and we hope to do the same every week." "House" Eucharists were not very frequent at the time, but here they are presented as a possibility.

or retreats in which they participated. Sharing the results of a workshop or a group dynamics session was a way of letting the Society know that the "best service" came about through the knowledge and sharing of each one's strengths. A governmental community had to know how to distinguish work time, time for religious life itself and time for relaxation, just as it had to know how to differentiate among "decision-making meetings, meetings for exchange and sharing and prayer meetings."[14] "The Society still had to learn to live a radically different kind of community life" from what had been before and "how to govern in a new way. 'As a team' was a concept more difficult to explain than to express: it had to be experienced in order to be understood."[15] In 1976 Mother Camacho thought that this community life was one of the strengths of her mandate.

> We set about creating honest, sisterly relationships and serious times of prayer, and that gradually opened the way. The obstacles to integrating the different personalities and temperaments, the different cultures and distinct points of view sometimes seemed invincible. There were some painful and uneasy relationships. To live the truth in charity demanded a great deal of asceticism, of solitude, of individual and shared prayer. The way one lived encouraged the others, strengthened us, and made "tender and sincere love"[16] grow among us. Accepted in faith, the obstacles themselves constituted the basis of a sincere, real community.[17]

The members of the team set challenges for themselves. One of these was the monthly sharing of an *examen* [or self-inspection] that helped them pay attention to interior stirrings. It allowed them to know one another better, to be united and to govern differently.

> We were aware that we could not move the Society forward toward new types of community life that put the emphasis on interpersonal relationships, faith sharing, community prayer and simplicity, if we did not force ourselves to form such a community ourselves. We were convinced that this was the way that we would become a community that discerns and that if we did not do it, we would not be a government that discerns.[18]

---

[14] C. Camacho, pp. 4-5.
[15] Testimony of J. Garson. The expression *"en équipe"* is in French in the [English] text.
[16] Summary of the Constitutions, XIII.
[17] Gen. Arch. C I C 3, Box 26. Report of the Superior General, p. 4.
[18] Testimony of D. Boland in F. Makower, pp. 153-154.

Thanks to the spirit of openness in the group each one was able to show her vulnerability.[19] The sale of the motherhouse on the Via Nomentana demonstrated the will to form community; at the new motherhouse[20] the team and the staffs of the general treasury and the general secretariat formed three communities.

Their common life facilitated their work. "We were never obliged to wait to have a quorum since we were always together," said Doreen Boland. "Sometimes people asked us if there were not five 'Mothers General.'" Maria Luiza Saade then answered: "If there had been a fly on the wall during our meetings, it would not know who the Mother General was. But we knew very well! We knew at every moment that Concha had the right to make a decision in spite of what we might think."[21] Thanks to mutual confidence, community life enabled them to avoid letting strong emotional responses interfere too frequently in the course of discernment. When a decision was to be made, the team decided not to settle the question if one of the members was reluctant; the question was taken up again after a delay and recourse to prayer. Decisions were made by consensus, never by majority vote.

The central team learned that community life was important in apostolic life. Its members traveled together, not only to learn how things went in the provinces, but to show that they experienced the same joys and the same difficulties as others, that they shared the challenge of creating a community of sisters at that moment when a new kind of community life was being forged, sometimes painfully. According to Mother Camacho, a gauge of her government was "to be aware of the importance of relationships, to be vigilant so that they will be genuine in moving toward freedom" and to grow in harmony. The members of the two teams have underlined the character of Concha Camacho's relationships and her concern to arrive "in truth, at creating union among religious and provinces. With confidence and much supernatural spirit, the fruit of prayer, she met success everywhere!"[22] "One of the memories that stays with me," Mary Shanahan wrote, "is that of the community in which I lived. Concha Camacho, Alicia Hughes, Judy Garson, Mary Cavanagh became real friends of mine and they have remained so. We worked well together and we supported one another well." Mother Camacho's qualities helped to explain

---

[19] Testimony of C. Camacho: "One can then speak of one's own shadow side and the others can accept it."
[20] There were several apartments, each with a specific function.
[21] F. Makower.
[22] Testimony of A. Hughes.

her triumphal re-election in 1976.[23] She herself recognized, "I would not have been able to live out my responsibility without my team."

New governmental practice appeared in the provinces, to some extent modeled on that of the central team. The provincials constituted a team[24] that sometimes included young religious[25] and whose members took charge of a region or an area of the life of the province.[26] The teams settled outside of the institutions in houses that were centers of community life and government.[27] As the central team was doing in its own realm, they "experienced what the search for new ways meant, with trial and error and many questions."[28] In Italy the task of the first provincial team consisted of "living together, paying many visits to communities, having frequent interactions with the nuns in the province, organizing assemblies and meetings by categories of religious and by age groups in order to connect better with one another."[29] It was a mark of this provincial team government that the central team met with provincial teams, not just the provincials.

In the multi-national province of the Far East, councils were organized in Japan, Korea and Taiwan.[30] To allow better communication with the communities in France a "council of wise women" served as a link between

---

[23] She was re-elected unanimously with the exception of one vote and one abstention.

[24] In Mexico, Isabel Aranguren, in 1971, chose them from among those who had received 10% of the nominations at the time of the consultations.

[25] In Austria and in Belgium, the teams included young professed.

[26] In Mexico, Isabel Aranguren was in charge of communities, of planning, of the finances and of communications; the other two members of her team handled formation at all stages and the apostolate.

[27] Eleanor Whitehead, of Canada, was the first of the North American provincials to do so. In France, Maryvonne Keraly decided after a few years not to live any longer with her councilors who joined other communities in Lyon. In the Chicago province, a laywoman was appointed secretary (Testimony of C. Seiker).

[28] Testimony of E. Belle.

[29] Testimony of I. Marchetti and A. Lecciso, who recalled that the goals of the team included two focal points: "To follow up and intensify the education of the former sisters by having them study for diplomas if they wish and to respond to the new needs for evangelization by opening small communities in modest or poor neighborhoods."

[30] M. Williams, *The Society...Far East*, p. 275. They had all the powers of a team except that of accepting candidates. The provincial was a member of each one, but the council could meet in her absence. In the provinces of Ireland/Scotland and Australia/New Zealand a member of the team lived in each country in the province.

the communities and the provincial team. It had no decision-making power and those who participated in it ended up wondering about its utility. A team for "research and prospects" joined forces with some lay people to lead reflection and created a veritable laboratory of ideas and projects. It contributed to transforming ways of thinking and to create openings to other aspects of the real world.[31] In England, at the request of the provincial team, a permanent commission had the task of discussing questions and topics suggested by the membership.[32] In the United States the provinces reflected on their works with lay people, both women and men.

Knowing the Provinces Better

At the Sacred Heart, the superior general's visits to the houses, accompanied by one of the assistants and sometimes the treasurer general, had been a governmental procedure from the beginning. However the growth of the Society had never allowed a superior general to visit every house. During Mother Camacho's first term, the central team succeeded in doing so in three years. The great innovation was to have the whole team make these visits and to make them a tool for governing. It was important to experience the life of each province as a central community and "that to grasp that reality through ten eyes and ears, to reflect and share together, was different from hearing a report from a single person."[33] Doreen Boland wrote, "During these years I came to know and love the face of the Society, or rather, the hearts of so many sisters, trying generously to incarnate the charism of Saint Madeleine Sophie in such a variety of circumstances and cultures. They were ready to share with us; they allowed us to question them and they questioned us as well."[34] The team became aware in this way of the responsibility the Society had to recognize the richness of each country and "to develop it and thus contribute to the growth of the Kingdom."[35]

The kind of visit Mother Camacho inaugurated provoked both surprise and interest:

---

[31] Testimony of M-L. Fabre.
[32] Testimony of A. Hine.
[33] C. Camacho, *Conferences*, p. 47 and *Letters...*, p. 7: "We see more clearly that to travel together in this way is a real value in achieving that communion desired by the chapter. Nothing replaces personal contacts, discernment together, sharing life." She adds: "Mickey, Maria Luiza, Doreen and I have had the experience of both (travels together and travels alone). It is not the same thing."
[34] F. Makower, pp. 153-154.
[35] C. Camacho, *Letters*, p. 6.

Monique Luirard

> We were received with great joy in the provinces and with a certain curiosity because of the novelty of the situation. But the personal relations of the team with each religious and Concha's charismatic personality changed the atmosphere. We also lived through some difficult situations in a few provinces that did not accept our life style, the shared authority and above all the five options of the chapter.[36]

The team built its way of governing on communication and concrete relationships with the religious,[37] "contacts that were the source of real communion,[38] for she had discovered that government and communication are one.[39] She sought more contacts with communities than with individuals because she wanted to "understand the relationship and the searching among the members" of communities.[40] Even though the visits were brief, they allowed the team "to grasp the life of the Society in its diversity, its complexity, its richness."[41] In accord with the planning in the provinces, the team met with members of the clergy, those in charge in the schools, some communities of young people, all of which gave them the opportunity to become acquainted with the local reality and "to give priority to people over institutions."[42]

The visits were much simpler than before, without elaborate ceremony.[43] They opened the visitors to the truth of the Third World; that was one of their goals. According to Françoise Cassiers, those were "shocking encounters with the world after a cloistered life." Judith Garson remembered her arrival in Zaïre. "I had never seen so many children and such beautiful children!" "I was already interested in the Third World after my studies at Louvain," remarked Françoise Cassiers,

> but to enter the shantytowns of Peru, to glimpse the violence of the dictatorship in Argentina, to cross the streets of Mumbai jostling the bodies of those who had only the streets to sleep in, to enter the miserable huts of the Egyptian peasants, that was something else! I drew from it that injustice is universal and that the important thing is how we respond to it. One can undergo it fatalistically or ignore it and let it continue because one is among the privileged, consciously or

---

[36] Testimony of M.L. Saade.
[37] C. Camacho, *Letters*, p. 2, 12 March 1971.
[38] C. Camacho, *Letters*, pp. 4-5, 5 April 1971.
[39] C. Camacho, *Letters*, pp. 6-8, 17 May 1971.
[40] C. Camacho, *Conferences*, p. 49, Assisi, 1975.
[41] Gen. Arch. C I C3, Box 26. Report of the Superior General, 1976, p. 4.
[42] Testimony of F. Cassiers.
[43] F. Cassiers

not. One can also try to fight it; for followers of Jesus this most often means to place oneself voluntarily on the side of the suffering with all the consequences that implies. In this sense in most of the provinces I met sisters who were completely generous and courageous in their initiatives.

Religious from the United States during their journeys in Latin America were confronted with the sufferings inflicted by western policies. But, remarked Judith Garson, "People knew that I was not representing our government. All the same it was painful to see the results of these policies. Because I had seen how our sisters were living in so many countries, I considered my own country differently when I visited the United States as a member of the central team." To discover the unjust state of the world was a striking experience because at the Sacred Heart cloister had been reinforced by the social background from which its daughters came.[44]

These numerous and long intercontinental travels were made easier by improved air transportation during the last years of the twentieth century; but though the draining pattern of life was bearable because the members of the group were young, it was hectic[45] and "often beyond our strength," as Maria Luiza Saade recognized; it caused the resignation of Françoise Cassiers. This practice had its down side. The trips were expensive; the central team was absent from Rome for long periods; it seemed that administration was being neglected, even though the team always kept a part of the morning free to attend to general business.[46] The members of the Sacred Congregation of Religious had difficulty in understanding the purpose of these visits. Mother Camacho tried to make them understand that the point was learning at first-hand what was happening in the countries where the Society was established. Mother McLaughlin afterwards showed them that exploring government issues was a priority, and that was the point of the visits, government being based on real life issues.[47]

The travels of the central team were not without other hazards. One of them just missed being tragic. To cross the Andes the team had embarked in a six-seater plane that was caught in a storm. The plane was bouncing around wildly and, as Doreen Boland recounted,

---

[44] Testimony of C. Camacho.
[45] Testimony of F. Cassiers.
[46] Testimony of M.L. Saade.
[47] *Process of Approbation of the Constitutions...*, p. 28.

It was not comforting to hear the conversation between the young pilot and the control tower with which he was still in contact. He was advised to keep the aircraft as high as possible so as to avoid crashing into the mountain! The flight should have taken twenty minutes, but at the end of an hour and a half we were still in the air. Finally we landed on a strip near Pereira and had to return to Manizales in a taxi across the mountain. Upon arrival we shared what we experienced with the community who had believed we were lost! Personally I was concerned for the provincial of Colombia who was going to have to announce to the Society that the whole general council had been annihilated![48]

During Mother Camacho's second term the visits were not regularly made by the whole team. Their purpose was to give the team members the chance to understand living conditions and cultures other than their own and to let the provinces know them.[49] Most of the journeys included either the superior general and a councilor or two to three councilors. This pattern was followed during the generalates of Helen McLaughlin and Patricia García de Quevedo.

Other developments had repercussions on the government of the Society. Decentralization that fostered co-responsibility was accentuated to the point that sometimes the provinces had to be reminded that Rome ought to be made aware of what was happening. It could have adverse results including a weakening of the bonds with the center of the Society. If the provinces arrived at a kind of autonomy, the internationality of the Society would lose its relevance.[50] The history of strong centralization was one reason the provinces sought to affirm their autonomy. But sometimes it was unclear how a provincial was meant to function. Some provincial teams asked that their responsibilities be more fully defined.[51] If the relations between the provinces and Rome were

---

[48] F. Makower, pp. 153-154.
[49] Gen. Arch. C I C 3, Box 29. Report of the Superior General, 1982, p. 5.
[50] Testimony of C. Camacho and Gen. Arch. C I C 3, Box 26. Report of the Superior General, 1976, p. 6. After the assembly of provincials in 1972, "Many of the provincials were faithful to informing us about developments in the province, and this exchange really helped us to follow somewhat the situation of the province."
[51] The team in Chicago suggested "searching for simple, adapted structures" in order to arrive at "reinforcing the corporate sense, so necessary for the realization of our common call."

sometimes interrupted, the motherhouse did not try to create a structure to remedy it.[52]

The continental assemblies created by Mother Bultó continued. Thanks to assemblies of provincials in Rome and Assisi, co-responsibility moved forward between the "center" and the provinces and among the provinces themselves. These assemblies made possible an updating between general chapters and allowed provinces on the same continent to move toward "interculturality."[53] They did not set up the delegate assemblies required by the Chapter of 1970. But in 1971 an assembly of formation personnel of Europe and Africa took place. Regional assemblies met to study a particular issue or to prepare for the general chapter.[54] The one in Rio laid the foundation for a process of unification among the South American provinces.[55] A meeting of the provincial teams of Africa took place in Kenya in October 1978. In July 1980 a meeting in Chile of provincial teams and mistresses of novices of Latin America allowed for an examination of political and ecclesiastical issues in those countries. An assembly of teams from Asia and Australia and New Zealand, which was held in the Philippines in 1981, included time for the participants to experience the country itself, to pursue biblical and theological reflection and to learn to use different analytical tools. The European teams assembled in Brussels in July 1981 to search out how the life and mission of the Society of the Sacred Heart could be a source of hope for the world.[56]

Communication came through newsletters with a new tone. They no longer contained only official documents, reports of conferences or articles by members of the central team but essays that shared life. A communications team set out to create the "new style of communication and information" asked for by the Chapter of 1970.[57]

---

[52] Gen. Arch. C I C 3, Box 29. Report of the Superior General, 1982, pp. 5-6: "It is perhaps a point to review now."

[53] M. Williams, pp. 281-2. A propos of the assembly held in Manila in June 1975, Ambuja, the provincial of India, thought "that the meeting had allowed for deepening the understanding of Asia and of interculturality, it was really the penetration of a culture by Jesus and his Gospel." Sumiko Iba, from Japan, expressed it thus: "Since I have been provincial, I have suffered somewhat apropos of our internationality. What does internationality mean when we are Japanese, Koreans, Chinese, or Filipinas? Internationality and the nationality of each one must not be juxtaposed, even harmoniously, but must form an organic unity, each developing and informing the other."

[54] Gen. Arch. C I C 3, Box 29. Report of the Superior General, 1982, p. 5.

[55] *Histoire de la province de Colombie*, § 61.

[56] Gen. Arch. C I C 3, Box 26. Report of the Superior General, 1976 pp. 6-7.

[57] Gen. Arch C I C 3, Report…1976, p. 5

Challenges and Tensions

The Causes of Conflict

Even though the changes came about as a result of reflection and prayer,[58] they were not accepted without confrontation, no doubt because the psychological adjustment required was considerable and to build confidence, according to Mother Camacho's expression, took time. The definition of the five options and the opening of new fields of the apostolate had altered the way the Society functioned in the world. But the options appeared to be mutually exclusive:

> Not everyone understood the Chapter of 1970 in the same way. There were religious who wanted this new direction, who lived it interiorly and entered into it fully in fidelity to the Society. There were those who took it on with élan and obedience but were not mature: they entered into it more deeply than they could follow through on it. A small number sincerely resisted it.[59]

In the United States the central team had to remind the nuns that it was not a matter of choosing among the options,[60] because they had their beginning, their end and their paradigm in union and conformity with Christ. "It was a question of five avenues, five strategies, five energies that flowed from the same source, the Heart of Christ to the heart of the world."[61] But as Mother Camacho pointed out in 1972, if "this close bond between the options and our purpose was clear to those who had experienced the Chapter of 1970, many in the Society had not had that experience; and we found may things to look into, as your responses also echoed."[62] She recognized, "We have not been able to find a way to communicate that meets the needs of these people."

Some tensions arose about the way to define community life. Small communities were seen as "cliques;" free discussion and impromptu meetings, so unlike the ways of earlier religious life, brought on much distrust and unrest.[63] Within them conflict could arise around liturgy,

---

[58] Testimony of E. Calabuig.
[59] Testimony of C. Camacho.
[60] A difficulty in vocabulary may explain this misunderstanding. The term option means different things in French and in English. In English it may signify making a choice among several possibilities.
[61] Testimony of C. Camacho.
[62] C. Camacho, *Letters*, p. 20, letter of 3 July.
[63] Testimony of Barbara Crombie.

communal prayer, use of the car, free time or dinner invitations.[64] Some of those who had opted to join a small community – another point at issue – tried to find solutions to calm others down. But it took many community meetings with facilitators to ease community relationships.[65]

The chief problems came from notions about apostolic life. In Madrid,

> We were several nuns working in the secondary school at Rosales, but divided. Some still valued the essentials of education, and others defended a radical change in every sense of the word. They preferred lay persons to religious; they began to leave the schools to go to work elsewhere, and we who remained were accused of being reactionary and of not loving the poor.[66]

In France there were also tensions around teaching – in the North they held to it more strongly than in the South, according to Marie-Thérèse Carré – and around work and places to live:

> A good number of religious did not see why it was suddenly necessary to go to live in HLM [low-income public housing]! Some, and this even when we began to have contracts, suffered consciously or unconsciously and, it seemed justly, from not having an active apostolate that would have shown them to be of value. They rejected the past and were full of criticisms.[67]

Those who went to work in a lower class environment were judged unfavorably: "What are they doing? They are wasting their time! That is not for us. Being what you are, you would be able to do more good…."[68] In the United States there was also tension between those who worked in the schools and those "who worked only with the poor" or those who lived in a poor neighborhood:[69] "Those who remained in the institutions believed that there they developed leaders who could make the world a different place

---

[64] Testimony of Mary E. McLean.
[65] Testimony of A. Conroy: "Too often those who expressed themselves better dominated the group. The differences of generation, of life style, of level of education were challenges that the facilitators helped us to meet."
[66] Testimony of P. Corral.
[67] Testimony of M-T. Carré and M- G. du Penhoat.
[68] Testimony of C. de Clock. The reactions in Egypt were similar: "You spend hours taking care of sore eyes, whereas you are vowed to education" (R. Callis, *Interfrat*, N° 15, 6 January 1973).
[69] M. Ruggeri indicated how a nun whose apostolic activity was in prisons could be afraid of living in a dangerous neighborhood.

and that to abandon this mission would cause the projects among the poor to fail."[70]

> The option for the poor was seen as a rejection of quality education. To leave formal education was equivalent for many among us to leaving the service of education. We thought that the Latin American nuns had had too great an influence at the chapter and that we were being asked to live a reality that was theirs, not ours. In that era we really were not conscious that a class system existed in our country.[71]

Isabel García remembers the pain she experienced in these confrontations, for in Chile to work in the traditional schools was considered by many religious as a betrayal of the Gospel.[72] In Colombia, "the division between the 'schools' and the 'poor' continued to be accentuated, and it even happened that some among us went on strike during a provincial assembly because of decisions in favor of the poor,"[73] remembers the director of an institution.

Wherever one looked, the needs were great and the personnel limited: that fanned the fire, as an example from Egypt indicates:

> Right from the beginning, one sympathized with those who for a long time had wanted to be inserted in Upper Egypt. But when the needs of new foundations grew, and the schools of Ghamra and Heliopolis had to send young people to these foundations,[74] there was an understandable and sometimes painful tension that seemed in some people's minds to pit the capital and Upper Egypt against each other. For some it was as if what

---

[70] Testimony of Janet Reberdy.

[71] Testimony of A. Conroy who adds: "It was only in 1974, after spending a month in Latin America and taking part in an assembly of provincials that I really understood the importance and the opportunity of the Chapter of 1970." With hindsight that opposition between those who held for the option for the poor and the others in the United States surprised her: "I am baffled by it for Madeleine Sophie's concern for the poor was being expressed in community service projects by students and alumnae in our schools and colleges. Financial aid for those who could not pay tuition costs was traditional in our institutions."

[72] She lived in the communities of the schools of Apoquindo and Renaca. She was hurt by certain harsh and excessive judgments of the alumnae who, after all, she said, had been formed by the Religious of the Sacred Heart!

[73] *Histoire de la province de Colombie*, § 57.

[74] Esperanza Medina had asked the houses of the Delta to send nuns into the Nile Valley.

was given to the Saïd had to diminish what it was possible to accomplish in the schools, while for the others real devotedness and real apostolic work were to be found only among the poor.[75]

Mother Camacho referred openly to the prejudices, the lack of trust among sisters engaged in different apostolic tasks, a tendency to "do our own thing" that could spread,[76] to be in community as if in a hotel, without really being engaged in the growth of the others[77] and the temptation to put the individual ahead of the group. In 1976 she posed the following question: "Have we thought seriously enough that the strength of our common mission depends on the response of each one in obedience and availability to the plan of God for us as a Society? And that, as the Province of Northern Spain has said so well, 'we have delegated part of our autonomy to the charism of our congregation.'" In 1979 she reminded everyone of the significance of having the courage to dress with great simplicity and to wear the distinctive cross of the Society.

Innovation in apostolic activities and in life style could trouble community life. Prayer suffered from incessant activity. As one Spanish religious put it picturesquely, "During these first years, we ought not to have run around so much. The image I have is that of the bull when the gates of the bullpen are opened, and he comes racing out, hardly seeing anything. We ought to have had a slower process, preparation for change." Mother Camacho reported on the breakdown of the life of prayer that she had sometimes noticed. Daily Eucharist, morning meditation were sometimes abandoned. Humorously she referred to religious who, relying on "the most beautiful theological arguments, say that 'all is prayer,'" and that they no longer had the need of times of formal prayer: "I can believe it for the Blessed Virgin!"[78] she concluded. Collaboration with men, whether or not they belonged to a religious order, for which the religious had no preparation, was a source of reflection on the meaning of religious consecration, but it sometimes led to abandoning religious life.[79] "I really think we made mistakes during the first years after the changes: too casual relations with the opposite sex, perhaps through reaction against the past; too much preoccupation with 'doing' at the expense of the spiritual," commented a religious who lived in an insertion.

---

[75] *Interfrat*, N° 16, 11 March 1973. Testimony of Rosario Mendez and Marie-Cécile de Viviers.
[76] *Letters*, p. 68, 8 September 1977.
[77] *Conferences*, p. 21, 25 July 1973.
[78] *Conferences*, March 1975.
[79] *Conferences*.

Finally there were tensions that came from political circumstances. The international context was marked by the gradual withdrawal from a rigidly bipolar world. The disarmament treaties signed by the two major powers, the break-up of the Communist bloc as a consequence of the Sino-Soviet conflict, the entry of the People's Republic of China into the UN and the resumption of relations between Beijing and Washington allowed one to believe that a new peoples' springtime was possible. But destabilization emerged in the economic domain as well, with the end of cheap oil in some parts of the world. Europe was not shielded from sudden rampages and lived through "leaden years" especially in Germany and Italy at the mercy of extreme leftist terrorism that aimed at urban warfare.

A take-over by the army did not mean the same thing in every country. The military dictatorships of Marcos in the Philippines and of Park in Korea brought with them mail and telephone censorship. In the Philippines in 1971 some religious participated in Sonia Aldeguer's electoral campaign for a seat in the constitutional assembly, which she won. A year later martial law was imposed in the country. In Latin America military regimes had different policies and different developments. In Peru the putsch of 1968 had for its purpose to fight "against established economic powers both national and foreign that wielded so much authority and that, by frustrating the people, sought to maintain an unjust social and economic order that preserved the benefits of national wealth for the privileged classes, while the majority of the population was suffering from marginalization and assaults on the dignity of the human person."[80] Gasoline was nationalized and the infrastructure of the country changed by agrarian reform, teaching reform and a law of "social ownership." But widely varying popular reactions took place after 1977 against the military dictatorship. The nuns participated in long and massive strikes organized by the educational workers' union.[81] The first presidential election after twelve years of military regime took place in May 1980. The same year the Shining Path began its guerrilla actions. In Argentina, on the other hand, where the military held power from June 1968 on, the violence of the dictatorship could be seen everywhere. In Uruguay a *coup d'état* took place on 12 June 1973, and the military regime lasted eleven years. In Colombia the liberal president, Julio Cesar Turbay Ayala, elected in 1978, launched "a wide-sweeping repression and governmental policy that opened the doors to drug traffic. In 1979 in Nicaragua the Sandinista

---

[80] Manifesto to the nation of the revolutionary government of the Armed Forces, 2 October 1968, in M. Recavarren, *Raíces...*, p. 197.

[81] M. Recavarren, p. 240. After 1975, the military regime returned to certain measures that had had as a goal State control of the economy. The people who were organized in labor unions, which were growing in numbers, staged serious strikes.

revolution triumphed, undoing the dictatorship of Somoza. The witness given by revolutionary Christians gave hope to people committed to justice on the continent."[82] In Colombia in 1979 the group M-19 took over the embassy of Santo Domingo and for two months held ambassadors and politicians hostage, one of whom was the apostolic nuncio. Its members then took refuge in Cuba.

Chile had a long democratic tradition, a sense of dialogue between different political positions, and a moderate Communist party faithful to Moscow. The reforms introduced by President Eduardo Frei and the Christian Democrats had not been strong enough to improve economic and social development, and in September 1970 elections brought to power a government of popular unity under Salvador Allende. In Talca a shed belonging to the Religious of the Sacred Heart was used for neighborhood meetings. It served as a center for young people, for catechism and for liturgical celebrations: "The president of the Junta, a Communist, paid 1% of the money for the liturgy; he insisted on doing it! That is what our terrible Communists did."[83] Some religious took part in the activities of the movement Christians for Socialism. But in Santiago many families hostile to the movement toward socialism in the country and to innovations in the programs at the school in Apoquindo did not understand positions taken by the Society of the Sacred Heart. The killing off of "Chilean socialism" on 11 September 1973, then the ongoing power grab by General Pinochet, who became, on 16 June 1974, the supreme head of the nation and in charge of the executive for an undetermined length of time, changed living conditions in Chile. With the denationalization of copper, the large mining companies returned to their former owners; the stadiums were transformed into prisons, and the regime outlawed political parties. The very day of the *coup d'état* the army took possession of the Sacred Heart school at Apoquindo, near the residence of President Allende, then at the end of September confiscated the community quarters.[84] The Society of the Sacred Heart decided to leave the place before the end of the scholastic year. Supported by Cardinal Silva Henríquez, the local Church and the faculty, the religious moved to other houses in the country.

In Congo, renamed Zaïre in 1971, education was nationalized "in a climate of anti-Christian struggle."[85] The Sacred Heart schools were taken

---

[82] *Histoire de la province de Colombie,* § 73.
[83] *Connections,* 2, p. 31. Testimony of Adela Guzman.
[84] "The administrative council of our school had denounced us," M. Hurtado, *Connections* 2, p. 13. Was it then that the Constitutions of the Sacred Heart were burned in public in a kind of *auto-da-fé*?
[85] C. Meeûs, p. 9.

by the regime and then returned.[86] In 1974 religion classes were suppressed in the schools. The only party in the Popular Movement of the Revolution strove to destroy youth movements and any kind of religious activity in the schools as well as in parishes and seminaries. The Religious of the Sacred Heart then encouraged the movement called "Young People of Light,"[87] inspired by initiation rites, sometimes providing coordination at the local level; and they prepared volunteer mothers for family catechesis.

In Spain the death of General Franco on 20 November 1975, did not necessarily mean the end of Francoism. But from December 1976 on political parties were granted legal status, and on 9 April 1977, President Adolfo Suarez legalized the Communist Party. In the preceding years some Religious of the Sacred Heart had been steered toward work with militant Communists. The youngest, desirous of evangelical radicalism, were going further in their concern for openness to the world. At Vigo and Santiago de Compostela, where "they seemed to run everything," they had sold all the valuable objects including the flower vases from the sacristy and the wrought iron at the entry. Through solidarity with the people of the neighborhood, when the Communist Party was still illegal, they allowed a party meeting at the convent. The leaders put the hammer and sickle on the balcony. The police arrived very soon, but the organizers and the participants had disappeared. The event was fortunately without consequences, for in that era many militants of the extreme left were rotting in Franco's prisons or in the luckier cases had been expelled.[88] The progressive departure of a brutal and entrenched regime helped the religious to live through political changes with the hope that the poor would be able to obtain more rights.[89] At Huelva, where they were inserted, "the residents who had come to the city for a better life found misery when they left their villages. The neighborhood was the sewer of the city. It was called the 'lawless city.'" When Mother Barcherini passed through there, she exclaimed "What a sight!"[90] At Aljafarenear Seville, "there were neither shops nor buses, nor hardly any social services." In the Canaries the

---

[86] *Correspondence of M. Ahern*, 23 January 1980, p. 56.

[87] *Histoire de la province du Congo*, p. 15. The reference is to "Bilenge ya Mwinda," the BYM.

[88] A law in 1959 allowed challenging "whoever commits or has the intention of committing an act contrary to public order." Two who were condemned to death, Julian Grimau, director of the clandestine Communist Party, executed on 20 April 1963, and the militant anarchist, Salvador Puig Antich, strangled on 2 March 1974, became symbols of the tortures of Francoism.

[89] Testimony of Carmen Fabiani.

[90] Testimony of Pilar Puig de la Bellacasa.

hovels destined for seasonal workers were permanently taken by the local populace. They were tiny, without water, facilities, electricity or windows."[91]

The mission was sometimes expressed in protests that the nuns had not received sufficient training to lead. In Colombia two religious of the missionary team were arrested: "The rest of the province did not fully understand the positions they took and manifested disagreement with their actions. However, the provincial continued to support them and was present with the two 'Cecilias' when they were obliged to leave Santander."[92] From then on

> It was not possible to understand religious life and the life of the Society without trying to grasp something of what was happening in each country, whether in national politics, church politics, attitudes toward religious life, important philosophical and theological currents that were beginning to appear. When we were preparing to visit the provinces, I was touched by the efforts of the provincial teams to give us information about what we were going to discover.[93]

Politics, about which no one spoke before, became pervasive. Still people had to be warned against the contagion of *"tout politique"* for in certain Latin American countries, the new apostolates were sometimes taken to be the same as political activity by lay people or clerics.[94] Mother Camacho acted prudently, reminding the religious that political commitment was not an absolute and that one had to keep a safe critical distance through prayer: "If our communities become politically involved without a truly evangelical spirit, without a very explicit sense of the Kingdom, our prophetic value is diminished, even while we may think ourselves to be real prophets. It is for others to see this prophetic quality in us." One had to avoid being dazzled by political systems or falling into "a messianic activism."[95]

The issue was not easy to resolve for women who reacted with their hearts in the face of injustices they witnessed. Those who were living in

---

[91] Testimony of Clara M. Rodríguez Izquierdo.
[92] *Histoire de la province de Colombie*, § 50.
[93] Testimony of J. Garson.
[94] Testimony of F. Martínez for Colombia: "They saw us as a danger and linked us with the movements that were disturbing Latin America, calling us communists without much information on the goals of the ideology out of which we were operating. They regarded us with suspicion, even within the Church. Doors were closed to us." In Chile some small "inserted" communities were closed because the pastors were hostile to the form of apostolic activity of the nuns (Testimony of M Hurtado).
[95] *Conferences*, pp. 57 and 102.

countries just coming out of colonization or in countries where destitution was endemic found it difficult not to place their hope in regimes that were promising progress and prosperity. Theology itself had evolved as a result of the insights of the "Basic Christian Communities." But the reactions of religious who lived under socialist regimes also had to be taken into consideration. During the Chapter of 1970 some Polish delegates had thought that Marxism was invading the Society of the Sacred Heart.[96] The very term "team" revolted them,[97] no doubt because it must have recalled for them the Soviet *troikas*. The central team discovered in Poland what life was like under a Communist regime: "Convinced Communists? They seem to be very few. Faith is often expressed in traditional forms, for example, processions, but that is the only form these courageous people have found to express it." A certain leveling was at work: one did not see extreme wealth or poverty, "but a dreary similarity. A few models for houses are allowed by the government and are often built by people with little talent. A lay person with whom we spoke said she thought the system had produced mediocrity rather than equality. It has certainly not produced liberty, and that is the people's greatest suffering."[98] Some religious from other countries were afraid that a new understanding of politics was contaminating the Society: "Let us return to the Gospel in all its radicalism, in complete loyalty, without trimming it to our measure, without accommodating it to our intentions, without weakening it or using it to justify the infiltration of every kind of ideology into the Society," wrote a Spanish religious to the Chapter of 1976.[99]

While the superior general had encouraged the Religious of the Sacred Heart to discover in prayer and in fidelity to the Spirit new apostolic methods "allowing more creativity to commit ourselves with Jesus Christ for a more just world,"[100] she asked them "to remain in Christ:"

> Let insertion in the world, necessary for the mission, not diminish the strength of our consecration. Let us listen to the constant invitation "to remain in his love," Let us not forget it: this personal unification to be lived in a realistic fashion supposes centering our security and our need to love and be loved on the experience of the love of Christ; keeping in mind in our choices our brothers [and sisters] in need; walking with the Father constantly turning on the world a contemplative gaze. All that requires

---

[96] Testimony of Brigitte Tribot-Laspière and I. Aranguren.
[97] Testimony of M. Braganza.
[98] Prov. Arch. Ireland/Scotland, 160. Letter of D. Boland, 7 September 1974.
[99] Gen. Arch. C I C 3, Box 26. Letter of M. Luisa de la Arena, 1 October 1976.
[100] C. Camacho, *Letters*, pp. 27-28, 15 December 1972.

personal discipline, interior calm, simple austerity, that will help us ward off too much stimulation and give us a more serene perception of reality.[101]

Malaise and Sorrow: the Case of the House in Florence

Some houses were considered "difficult," quick to dispute the directions determined by the central government.[102] It was Florence, however, that created a real crisis. On 15 August 1973, Mother Camacho informed the provincials that the Church had granted it the special status of "homogeneous house," which allowed the members to lead "a kind of life more in accord with their concept of religious life."[103] This decision responded to a situation that had deteriorated gradually since the eve of the Chapter of 1967.

According to the testimony of Mother de Valon herself, relations with Florence were uneasy. The house was the center of a vicariate and on the eve of the special chapter had more than thirty religious. Its boarding school was renowned, and its superior, Mother Eleonora Carloni, brilliant and spiritual, was one of those superiors who exercised indubitable power in the community and in her native city. Vicar of the South of Italy after 1957, she had always resided in Florence, with the exception of one year spent in Naples. At the beginning of the summer of 1967, Mother de Valon thought that to allow a religious who had major offices in the house to remain there for such a long time was not consistent with the Society's tradition.[104] But because of preparations for the chapter, Mother Caracciolo, the assistant general in charge of Italy, could not make the appointments needed.

Mother Carloni accepted neither the resignation of Mother de Valon, which she saw as a weakness[105] and a "defenestration,"[106] nor the interview that the delegates had requested of the Sacred Congregation and that she considered "unclear,"[107] in any case, coming from "a small group that by illegal processes had manipulated the situation."[108] The acceptance by Cardinal Antoniutti of Mother de Valon's resignation seemed to her a complete contradiction of the Constitutions. Florence did not accept the election of Mother Bultó or the orientations of the special chapter.

---

[101] *Letters*, pp. 39-40, 21 June 1974.
[102] M. Braganza spoke of "the silent ones of Florence," who did not accept the changes, but did not go so far as to confront Rome.
[103] Gen. Arch. C I A 12.
[104] Testimony of Teresa Caracciolo.
[105] E. Carloni to M. Luirard.
[106] Gen. Arch. *Brève histoire de la maison de Florence*, translated from Italian. Document presented to P. García de Quevedo.
[107] To M. Luirard.
[108] *Brève histoire de la maison de Florence*.

Later Mother Carloni stated in public that the Society of the Sacred Heart had lost its validity when it had changed direction in 1967 and that it had floundered even more radically in 1970. That meant for her that henceforward its authority was no longer legitimate. She did not accept visits from members of the central team, and she acted without informing the superior general or the provincial.

In 1968 the Italian vicariates came together as one province under Mother Caracciolo. At the time of the provincial assembly in 1969, redirection of apostolic activities and a plan for changes that were probably going to occur by reason of reduction in personnel were decided upon. The fate of the schools, one of which was Florence, was part of the equation.[109] The decision of the special chapter concerning the length of the terms of the local superiors had to be implemented, and that caused the first confrontation. The situation in Florence was a true test case because Mother Carloni had had two six-year terms as local superior. Mother Caracciolo decided to send her to Turin, a move that appeared "to the community" as a desire to punish her because she was not following the new orientations of the Society and as the proof of an authoritarianism without precedent. The archbishop of Florence intervened so that she could remain in Florence, arguing from the fact that she had an office as inter-diocesan secretary.[110] Cardinal Antoniutti made a similar approach to the superior general. Mother Bultó, after going to Florence to obtain Mother Carloni's acceptance of her new position, ended by leaving her there but discharging her from her office of superior. The one named to replace her could hardly exercise her mission in a house where the authority continued to be wielded by Mother Carloni.[111]

In December 1971 the community of Florence asked the new provincial, Mother Marchetti, to separate the community and the school, the community continuing to belong to the province and the school being placed under the authority of the diocese. Mother Marchetti refused.

---

[109] *Brève histoire…* "1968. The communications speak of the suppression or of the reduction in number of our institutions. The new orientations direct religious who are qualified to state schools or to works outside our institutions. We are informing Cardinal Florit of these innovations."

[110] *Brève histoire*: With reference to the same document, the religious who went to visit him explained that "the experiments in process in other communities prove to us that once the superior is replaced very rapidly conditions are created for the closing of the house and consequently for the suppression of a work."

[111] In 1971-1972, Mother Carloni and Mother Platania, who had been sent to Florence to be superior, were responsible for the two groups established in the house.

Then several religious in Florence let it be known that they wished to be placed directly under the authority of the motherhouse, an arrangement that contravened the organization of the Society by provinces. In January 1972 Mother Camacho and two members of her team were welcomed courteously at the Poggetto;[112] shortly afterward, however, the situation grew tense.

In February 1972 the director of the school told the provincial that she had no intention of following provincial directives concerning the schools. From then on, it was not only the relationship of the house in Florence to the province of Italy that was in question but more deeply the acceptance of the decisions of the Chapter of 1970. Florence moved from confrontation to open rebellion. There was so much tension, and the authority of Mother Marchetti was so openly disputed that some religious asked for new assignments.[113] Finally, supported by the archbishop, in July 1972, Mother Carloni presented to the Sacred Congregation in the name of five religious of her house a request for autonomy. It will never be known what arguments then held sway. The one publicly stated was the desire to continue the traditional life style and apostolate of the Society of the Sacred Heart. But other houses in other provinces had done the same without demanding such a status. Mother Carloni had a monastic concept of religious life in the Society wherein houses would be autonomous entities simply linked among themselves by charity and without a superior general. But that opposed the structure of the institute maintained by Saint Madeleine Sophie from the beginning, the body of the professed forming one whole, which required the obedience and availability of the religious, with the general council as the visible sign of this unity. Mother Carloni, however, always maintained that she wished to remain faithful to the spirit of the founder.

The house in Florence acted autonomously even before it had been allowed to do so, since the provincial's authority was no longer recognized, and the local treasurer refused to send to the provincial treasury her assessment for the old age pensions of the sisters. Negotiations were even harder to achieve because autonomy had been granted to this house without the Italian provincial or the superior general being informed of it. On 31 July 1972, the decision to establish Florence as an autonomous house was directly communicated by a representative of the Sacred Congregation to the religious of the Poggetto, some of whom were hearing about it for

---

[112] The name given to the house in Florence.
[113] On the other hand, a nun in Florence, whom those in authority wished to remove from the house to give her the possibility of taking some time for reflection or to have a *recyclage*, refused her obedience.

the first time. Seven religious decided to leave after the first of August, followed a little while later by two others who were not at home then.[114] Mother Camacho wanted this experiment in autonomy to be limited to one year. Her request was not granted.[115] In the autumn of 1972 Mother Carloni was elected local superior. Attempts by members of the central team or by provincials to bring about a reconciliation had no effect.

After 1975 a very few religious, some Italian and Spanish, a Puerto Rican and a Cuban asked to live in Florence or went there without authorization.[116] The house was allowed to accept recruits from other houses after July 1974; on 3 July 1975, the nuns of Florence invited other Religious of the Sacred Heart to join them, arguing the prerogative that had been conferred on their house by the Sacred Congregation. In November 1979 the Holy See allowed them to open a novitiate. With an eye to appeasement in 1976 and in 1982 the central team invited representatives from Florence to the chapter with voice but no vote. Mother Carloni, who was present at the Chapter of 1982, did not take part in the ceremony of obedience that followed the election of Helen McLaughlin.[117]

Florence's situation was painful for the Province of Italy and for the whole Society. For Mother Marchetti, it was "a great cross that weighed on us during a period of commitment and enthusiasm." It was, according to an expression of Mother de Valon,

> a dropped stitch in the fabric of the Society, up to then intact! How painful! What will come out of that? I am quite sure that the five people who wanted that had "valid" reasons since the Sacred Congregation, which said no at first, ended by acceding to this request.... I admit that, carrying in my heart great suffering at no longer living the vocation that was mine forever, nevertheless, I would never have thought of abandoning the Society, for I love it too much.... Is this house going

---

[114] Of the nuns who refused to remain in Florence, three had lived there less than five years, four from five to ten years, two more than ten, one had been there for forty-three years.

[115] The constitution as an autonomous house granted for one year was prolonged for three years, then on 27 July 1977, for "at least five more." On 26 June 1980, it was erected as a special delegation *ad sexennium* with a special statute, by sovereign concession of Pope John Paul II.

[116] Two of them left Florence in 1975, one in 1977, three in 1978, one in 1979; three were exclaustrated in 1976 and 1978.

[117] Testimony of M. Keraly and H. McLaughlin.

to abandon the Society? Or if they have vocations, is it going to be the beginning of new congregation?[118]

In December 1977, she referred to her suffering from the fact that the Sacred Congregation authorized "some professed to join Florence." She herself refused to go there, and she thereby rendered real service to the Society. According to Judith Garson, "In the course of our travels, people everywhere asked us, 'What is happening in Florence?' In spite of the anguish this affair caused, it was certainly not the most important question we had to face. I believe that Florence claimed a great deal of time and attention out of proportion to its importance, but it was not possible to avoid it."

The Society of the Sacred Heart as a whole stood together with Mother Camacho in this case and supported her in the ordeal.[119] In May 1975 Mothers de Valon and Bultó came to Rome a week apart to meet with Cardinal Mayer, secretary of the Sacred Congregation, "to give him additional information and thus help him understand how the problems of this house [were rooted] in an already distant past."[120] Religious from different provinces wrote to the Sacred Congregation to inform it of their full agreement with Mother Camacho's government and to condemn what appeared to them to be deviant or schismatic leanings. It was a time of exhaustion, psychological, physical and spiritual, and for many religious a test of "thinking with the Church Militant."[121] In spite of all the memorials composed by the religious of Florence to underline the wrongs of the "new" Society of the Sacred Heart in its way of interpreting the charism and of living religious life and in spite of their criticism of successive chapters, the documentation and the testimony of contemporaries offer evidence that the archbishop of Florence pushed the religious to separate from the Society and that that separation was encouraged by the Sacred Congregation. One can see in this story a new avatar of attempts led by many ecclesiastics to take over the authority of a house or a congregation of women religious. The Society of the Sacred Heart had already been in the grip of such situations in the nineteenth century. But undoubtedly it

---

[118] Letter of 4 September 1973, to A. Las Casas. The house in Florence tried unsuccessfully to make a foundation in Cuba.
[119] According to M. Braganza, "The fear spread that there would be other, undeclared, 'Florences' which would lead to a schism in the Society."
[120] Gen. Arch. Memoir on the house in Florence, p. 7.
[121] Ignatius Loyola, *Spiritual Exercises*, § 352-370.

suffered more in a Church that during the Vatican Council had wished to break with certain earlier behaviors.[122]

The Chapter of 1976

The mission required serious examination. In spite of the divergences in the ways of carrying it out, the charism was not in dispute. To test it was to rediscover the original vision, for the Society of the Sacred Heart had not been founded to "do" something, to accomplish tasks, but to "be," and even to "be with." But in the exhilaration of innovation one ran the risk of not distinguishing the mission from the apostolic tasks that could be accomplished, and also of confusing charism and mission. There had to be "a common basis that would support different kinds of life."[123]

Chapter preparation was in the hands of an international commission that developed reflection sheets for the communities on the "educational mission." The answers were collated under the title "Living Pages" and sent to communities for amendment. "Mixed expressions of pain and joy, fear and hope sprang from these pages." The commission studied them

> in the light of the Bible and the reality of today's world. We have sought to discover whether there was a united spirit that was giving strength and cohesion to the whole body, and we have uncovered the way it is expressed today. We know that our first intuition was right: our problems with our educational mission are symptoms of a deeper, global issue, the problem of human beings in the world of today.

As the Canadian province expressed it,

> in a world in which a steady fulcrum has been overturned, the very image of the human being is in trouble. The Christian steeped in the prevailing mindset of today and dragged down by contemporary intellectual uncertainty is tested by an identity crisis that spares no person or place. Human characteristics, Christian and religious, are linked to such a degree that when crisis and dismay touch one, they touch the others.

"It is useless therefore, to seek solutions if we do not have the courage to engage in that level of reflection." This was the thinking of the commission

---

[122] J. Garson wrote: "I was astonished at the seriousness with which the 'official Church' in Italy regarded the situation of Florence."
[123] Gen. Arch. C I C 3, Box 26. Opening of the Chapter of 1976 by Mother Camacho, p. 8.

that marshalled its conclusions around the identity of the religious, of the charism and mission of the Society and of fraternal community.

Many of the "Living Pages" asked for a clarification of the meaning and value of the vows. Referring to tensions and frictions in the congregation, Peru proposed research on whether the problems were operational, organizational, or structural. There was a general desire to clarify what identifies a Religious of the Sacred Heart. But Brazil and England thought that the term "religious" was ambiguous and that its definition varied from person to person. Venezuela preferred to speak of "a believer." Belgium specified that the radicalism of the gift of self to God was not the monopoly of religious.[124] Chicago called for

> bypassing the vocabulary of "religious life" and acknowledging in some way the fact that all Christians are struggling to understand what it means "to be Christian" in today's world. Because we try to live the Gospel consciously, we are aware that a conversion must be as broad and as deep as the human race. We are only a sign of what Christ awakens on the face of the earth.

For Ireland there was a conflict between the juridical and charismatic aspects of religious life: "In the present renewal of the Church, we are set the challenge of deepening this aspect of the mystery and the mission of the Church, of developing the contemplative and charismatic dimension of the Church, complementary to its hierarchical structure." While some provinces wanted clarifications of a juridical type, others were expecting "the chapter to be an experience of discernment, of communion and an encouragement to live the Gospel in the radicalism of religious life. The need to deepen our sense of identity as religious is universal."[125]

Some provinces tried to highlight the essential aspects of the charism. For India the cornerstone for everyone "was born of the contemplation of the Heart of Christ in his life with his Father." The San Francisco Province wanted to change viewpoints: "Maybe something is missing from our service of the world as members of the Church, in as much as we have not been touched deeply enough to want to change the life that most human beings lead." For Venezuela, secularization had values that appealed to the

---

[124] "Why is it that there is a kind of fear of being known as religious?" (South Central Spain/Portugal). "Let the chapter take cognizance of the fact that for most people the image that we religious give is the following: someone who is easily discouraged, who is confused, who has too much security, who has an attitude of superiority that renders her tedious" (Venezuela).

[125] For Austria it was a question of "contributing so that the Spirit may be liberated anew in the Church."

real ideals of Christianity and not to religious conventions. Religious there thought that one acquired an identity in the measure that one confronted worlds different from one's own. "God is one, as his creation and the history of salvation are one," thought Peru. "However, we have looked at our religious life and its different aspects in a fragmented way, outside the context of their history and creation. That has led us very often to reduce God to our splintered understanding of reality. Our effort to achieve integration is a recent one."

Mother Camacho opened the chapter by showing that contemplation of the Heart of Christ through the pierced heart of humanity had made Religious of the Sacred Heart more conscious of oppression, injustice and the suffering of their brothers and sisters:

> And at the same time we feel more strongly the inadequacy of our response to this challenge. That is why we wish to reaffirm with new vigor the decision to place at the center of our lives the love of Christ; to contemplate anew his Heart open on the cross, a symbol that still expresses today what it is to love humanity even to the end."[126]

In order to give momentum to the mission, she asked the Society to study the appeals and the dynamics that were driving it.[127] "There is something that must be healed in the Society. We must neither manipulate the Word of God nor be afraid of it, but be true to it."[128] The superior general gave spiritual energy to the chapter by beginning each day with an extended meditation.

The first paragraph of the documents of the chapter characterized the charism as an agent "of unity, of continuity and of change." In the same way that the founder, "conscious of the call of her time, saw the Body of Christ 'outraged' by 'impiety,' in the same way we contemplate the pierced Heart of Christ in humanity torn by the injustices of the world, and our charism presses us to be one with others, suffering and searching with them

---

[126] Gen. Arch. C I C 3, Box 26, Opening of the Chapter of 1976 by Mother Camacho, pp. 8-9. D. Boland gives the same testimony; she recalls that from 1970 on the team had a concern to center religious life on adoration: "It was only when we were living it that we could build communion and seek justice. That linked the five options. Justice was no longer 'aggressive' but all that was lived in communion and in the spirit of the Gospel."

[127] Three invited experts, Maria Tereza Latgé, Mary Quinlan and Sara Grant presented reflections on the charism.

[128] Gen. Arch. C I C 3, Box 26, env. 4, verbatim and account.

for a more just, fraternal world." The members of the Society of the Sacred Heart were to be "witnesses to the love of God for all people."[129]

> The call to contemplation in freedom and adoration has laid hold of our whole life. Christ is present in our world and draws us to find him in his Word, in everything around us, and in our innermost selves. The life of Jesus in us draws us into his movement toward the Father and gives us a contemplative outlook on the world in which we live. We must let this life take hold of us if we are to look upon and love the world with the same love with which Christ looks upon it and loves it.... This asks of us a style of life in which prayer comes first and enables us to look for God in all that happens.[130]

Contemplation was becoming the first aim the Society was setting itself in preparation for its mission.[131] It allowed for authentic discernment, assured the *Cor unum*, made possible "being available to allow oneself to be challenged and changed by others and to take on *as a body* the apostolic choices of other provinces and communities so as to show forth together the mystery of God's love." It nourished the "educational dimension" of the mission, the way of living the vows, the style of governing and of putting goods at the service of mission. In the measure in which the charism unified the five options, it appeared sufficient to define six "goals"[132] to help each one to update it, to "respond to the evangelical demand of justice and of the integral development of human beings, unify the efforts and the life of the whole Society, give common direction and facilitate accountability."[133]

---

[129] *Chapter of 1976*, pp. 5-6.
[130] *Chapter of 1976*, p. 6.
[131] *Chapter of 1976*, p. 13: "By being open and welcoming to the mystery of God's gift, we wish to seek and find the presence of Christ in his Word, in circumstances and events, in ourselves and in everyone, and to allow ourselves to be touched and transformed by this Word and this presence at the heart of the world."
[132] *Chapter of 1976*, "To live the demands of contemplation. To build communion. To seek justice with the heart of an educator. To share our goods with a view to our mission, not only among ourselves but with those in greatest need. To test by discernment whether our choices are consistent with our contemplation. To continue our formation whatever our age." A final objective was to participate in communication in order to share and reinforce the life of the Society in conformity with the six goals of the chapter.
[133] *Chapter of 1976*, p. 18.

While experimentation in the apostolate was increasing and the image of the Society as tied to the boarding schools was diminishing, the chapter affirmed the past while strongly linking education to "the call to work for justice:"

> As an international apostolic community, called to spread the Gospel, we see that our service to the Church has always had an educational dimension. For a century and a half we have, among other means, given preference to the education of youth. This educational dimension and the state of today's world have opened to us new ways of fulfilling our mission to show forth the love of God revealed in Jesus Christ. Caught up ourselves in the unjust and dehumanizing structures of our world, we feel the need to "embrace all the means in our power" to proclaim the Father's love. The educational dimension of our mission is, in fact, inseparable from our call to work for justice. In a world that does not reflect the call of the Kingdom, in which people are often impaired, used as tools, frustrated both in their basic needs and in their deepest longings, we pledge ourselves to seek solidarity with the poor, with those who live on the margins of society, and to work together for our mutual liberation, which is growth in faith and love.[134]

Human Maturity and Formation

The Need for a Fresh Start

Her travels around the world had shown Mother Camacho that some religious had had difficulty in adapting to new and necessary ways of relating interpersonally. Community meetings that resulted in decision-making no longer had any resemblance to the exchanges that used to take place at recreation. Some religious were not able to manage their new freedom. Some provinces had trouble adapting to the directives of the

---

[134] *Chapter of 1976*, pp. 7-8. See the assessment of M. Ahern: "I found treasures in the texts of the general chapter. Before, we had more or less understood that the world was God's business, not ours, that we were to leave it to him since we were contributing to it through our vows. I tried to do that, supported by a strong sense of the paradox of Christian wisdom. I experience no regret at all in the face of the new way of thinking. The interaction between the contemplative life and action suits me better than contemplation behind walls. I savor the vision that the recent chapter has given us of 'solidarity with the Third World.' Please God, 'yes and amen' to the hope that maternalistic attitudes are fading. 'Yes and amen' to loving the truth of the other" (*Correspondence…*, p. 21).

chapters. The central team, which had not found adequate ways to transmit the message,[135] looked for a solution.

There was a proposal to apply principles from the social sciences, practiced at the central level, to the whole Society, and the motherhouse provided questionnaires for evaluation.[136] Discernment became one of the leitmotivs of this era. From the beginning of her generalate Mother Camacho insisted on its centrality:

> The method may vary and the one used here will be modified from country to country, but the preliminary conditions for any discernment remain the same for all: only the person who prays personally can discern; only the one who is open and available to the will of the Father can discern. Insofar as we grow in individual discernment we can grow in communal discernment. If we are open to the Spirit, He will ask for us what we do not know how to ask for. He will touch us with the living power of the presence of Jesus.[137]

She specified, "Often the choice offers a risk: a religious or a community must be able to take on the insecurity of making a mistake and come back on a decision badly made. Is that not a form of poverty that we must take on?"[138] In Assisi in 1975 she presented discernment to the provincials as a "strategy."[139] To be responsible each one must learn to know herself. The emphasis here was on formation, but discernment was seen as something that varied individually, sometimes according to one's psychological makeup.

In the United States in order to understand better their own and their sisters' behavior, after 1968 the religious were helped by group dynamics. At Lake Forest, psychologists came to lead sensitivity workshops at which the nuns were invited to express themselves about the way they related to others.[140] In San Francisco adaptations of life style, customs and expressions of feelings were facilitated by a Catholic psychiatrist who met weekly with small groups of nuns. Presence at the sessions was optional, but almost all the nuns took part for four years.[141] Some training in pastoral work was also a great help.[142] In France after 1968 a *recyclage* session based on the practice of "Personality and Human Resources" liberated many

---

[135] Testimony of C. Camacho.
[136] C. Camacho, *Letters*, pp. 9-10, 13-14, 28.
[137] *Letters*, p. 27, 15 December 1972.
[138] *Letters*, pp. 12-13, 20 October 1971.
[139] *Conférences*, pp. 48-49.
[140] Testimony of M. Brennan.
[141] Testimony of M. Mardel.
[142] Testimony of M. Connolly.

religious by showing them that they could modify the way they prayed[143] and enter into better self-knowledge: it was for many a "rejuvenating experience."[144] But such efforts were not made everywhere, and in 1976 Mother Camacho recognized that "the weakest point and the cause of many other weaknesses" was initial and ongoing formation, which was not sufficiently directed toward the requirements of the mission.[145] The provinces were asked to send their proposals to the motherhouse, and in the fall of 1977 a commission developed guidelines that offered reference points for different stages of religious life.

Initial formation, which had already been addressed in continental assemblies, was taken up again in December 1979 during a meeting of mistresses of novices that had as its purpose to standardize the program.[146] The participants agreed that the main elements were discernment, biblical study and deepened understanding of the spirituality of the Sacred Heart, while underlining the importance of intellectual training. In 1982 Mother Camacho remarked that that meeting had made the central team understand how the responsibility of mistresses of novices extended beyond their province to the whole Society, for autonomy must not lead to division. In South America, regional needs were given priority to the point that it was sometimes forgotten that the Society could ask someone to serve outside her province or at the central level.[147] A regional assembly there considered formation. The resulting plan laid out requirements so that, while the training incorporated what the country needed, it would be marked by the charism and the mission of the Society.

---

[143] Testimony of C. de Clock.

[144] C. de Clock: "Several discoveries: I possess good qualities…not just defects! The faultfinding carried on by several superiors is harmful. I am responsible for my health, for money. The word 'blind' was disappearing as a modifier of obedience." Agnès Bigo referred to this session as a time of liberation.

[145] Gen. Arch. C I C 3, Box 26. Report of the Superior General, p. 8.

[146] Testimony of B. Tribot-Laspière. The office of mistress of novices had been suppressed as such at the Chapter of 1970, in spite of very strong opposition. According to Joan Faber who was a member of the probation team at that time, "Authority was understood very differently; some young religious had no knowledge at all of Scripture, and individualism ran counter to those who were still seeking a 'Mother' Superior and to the infantile behavior that resulted." She concluded, "It's a miracle that the Society survived, and maybe it is in part because the changes came from the top, which avoided a clash between the young, those who wanted to question, and authority."

[147] Testimony of J. Faber.

Some religious now needed training because they had received very little earlier. In Mexico in 1970, former coadjutrix sisters had asked for it at the provincial chapter in order to make a real integration possible. Through workshops about thirty of them were able to begin or finish their studies, acquire some professional training, prepare to teach catechism by studying the Bible, Church history and the Council documents. In Colombia, where half the nuns were former sisters, a training style named "exodus" gave participants some elements of psychology, spirituality, catechesis, literacy, apprenticeship in kinds of work that would prepare them for an apostolate in a parish or in insertion among the poor.[148] In Tokyo evening courses were set up for the former sisters.[149] Creating small community groups of former sisters was another training tool. In France Marie-Josèphe Vié brought together a few of the Polish former sisters. One of them said, "You have pulled me out of nowhere. When people spoke, I had some ideas, but others spoke ahead of me. Now when we speak, sometimes people listen to *me*!"[150]

At the Chapter of 1976, Carmen Hornedo asked that training be provided specifically for the former sisters, because the Society of the Sacred Heart that wanted to promote justice ought to exercise it at home. This proposal, supported by Latin America, rapidly became a "serious obligation" for the whole Society.[151] *Recyclages* led by religious of different nationalities and languages took place from 1977 on. The program for the first one, held at Bambamarca in Peru, served as a model for the others[152] and took up self-knowledge and personal integration, communication, the mission of the Society, the influence of the vows on life and growth in prayer. In 1979 to celebrate the bicentennial of the birth of Saint

---

[148] *Histoire de la province de Colombie*, § 44 and 46. This formation that had as theme "Israel wandering in the desert for forty years" was provided after 1972 by Lucía Escovar and Alicia Merizalde: "The province lent everything: house, sisters, financial means, personnel" (L. Escovar). "SENA assisted us with sewing machines and instruction in how to use them. The University of Antioquia helped us with literacy so that we could work afterwards in the surrounding areas." According to F. Martínez, this effort of professionalization made a great contribution to the province.

[149] Testimony of A. Kato. Some refused to participate, saying, "I am not made for study." The more gifted were sent to university colleges.

[150] Testimony of M.J. Vié.

[151] Testimony of A. Lecciso.

[152] Gen. Arch. C V 4. Mother Camacho came to conclude this *recyclage*, the success of which decided the continuation of the experience for the next three years. In 1978 the provinces were consulted on its appropriateness and most of them were favorable to it.

Madeleine Sophie, the motherhouse organized renewal sessions worldwide. Ursula McAghon and Carmen Hornedo, who had been in charge of the first *recyclage*, trained about fifty leaders who directed thirty sessions in small international groups on all the continents. These lasted usually three months and brought together twenty-five people of different nationalities. These sessions helped to lessen the conflicts and tensions that had developed at the time of the integration. "It was a very rich experience; it brought much to each one through its content, the elements of renewal, a wider vision of the world, of the Society's mission and of the Society itself, thanks to meeting and sharing with sisters from other countries."[153] Between 1979 and 1981 almost 500 religious took part in these *recyclages*.

Some sessions for everyone also took place at the provincial level and were adapted to the needs of the participants. Leadership by facilitators from different continents helped to reinforce the *Cor unum* by doing away with hesitations and preconceived ideas.[154] Some religious came from India to give retreats and workshops using yoga and initiated their western sisters in alternative spiritualties.[155] Some probations were held outside of Rome: in South America, in Asia and in different European countries. They were sometimes open to professed who took part in them for renewal. Many chose spiritual direction, a directed retreat or making or remaking a

---

[153] *Histoire de la province de Colombie*, § 68. See also the assessment of Misao Shimamoto who was one of the three leaders of the sessions that were held in Taiwan, Sydney and Taytay, near Manila. They allowed "each one of us to become anew living persons in the Lord with the help of each one. Before, we knew little about one another, but through the sharing of lives in the group, we have received and shared our deepest selves in profound respect and love. On this basis, we experienced the creative working of the Spirit of life that brought us a new life. We understood in another way the spirit of the Society, especially humility and generosity, and we have experienced the dignity and beauty of the human person. We hope that in the future formation will be more and more personalized and relational, allowing openness and confidence in the Lord who is master of our growth" (M. Williams, *The Society…Far East*, p. 285).

[154] Testimony of P. Kilroy and K. Friel for Ireland and different testimonies for Australia. In both cases it was religious from the United States who offered formation in theology. Kathryn Sullivan's visit to Scotland was useful there: "She helped me modify, even change completely, my way of seeing what was happening in the Society" (Testimony of S. Hayes). Bessie Chambers' workshops were a source of challenge, depth and great originality (Testimony of K. Friel).

[155] Testimony of K. Friel: "These presentations on prayer based on yoga suited me in my search for a prayer integrated into my life that was asking to be balanced whether I was teaching full time or whatever my activity was."

thirty-day retreat.[156] Many also decided to undertake study and to follow workshops whether in the secular or religious area. It was a way for them to enter into the renewal, to understand better the development of the world and the Church and to deepen their vocation.

A Case in Point

Undoubtedly it was their faith in the consideration that the women living in the country had given to the issue that the motherhouse decided not to give orders to leave when a situation grew tense. Uganda experienced a series of political upheavals that degenerated into bloody conflict. In 1966, the abolition by Milton Obote of the semi-autonomy of the old kingdoms had caused the revolt of the Buganda. The Kabaka, the head of state since independence, had been forced into exile. Obote became president. The favors granted to his ethnic group and the announcement of the inauguration of "Ugandan" socialism through nationalizations brought about much discontent. On 25 January 1971, Idi Amin Dada staged a *coup d'état*. "When he came to power we could hear the people's joyous cries from seventy-five kilometers away," recalled Winifred Killeen. But the fighting had serious consequences: "To be attacked meant to be abducted. It could happen to us, given the presence of religious, nurses and pupils. I wrote to Rome and the bishop to ask what to do if a nun was abducted. The convent in Nkozi was not attacked. The presence among the pupils of two Muslims whose fathers were influential spared us."

Idi Amin Dada maintained a policy of Africanization aimed in the first place at Indians and Pakistani who controlled half the commerce and industry of the country and were forced to depart, leaving all their goods behind. Their departure caused a real economic disaster. In compensation for petrodollars received from Arab countries, Amin decided to Islamize the country. Catholic and Protestant missionaries were enumerated and some were expelled.[157] Administration of the Sacred Heart schools was transferred to a local congregation. But because there was a risk that the nuns would be forced to leave, a foundation in Kenya was decided upon. Different foundations were made there, some for a short time; those made in 1973 and 1974 at Eldoret and Chekalini, where three nuns were in charge of a mobile dispensary and a secondary school, were permanent.[158]

---

[156] *Histoire de la province de Colombie*, § 81.
[157] The Catholic archbishop was imprisoned; the Anglican archbishop was assassinated by Amin himself. Six Religious of the Sacred Heart were expelled, according to Pauline Campbell.
[158] According to Pauline Campbell, whose comments were reported by M. Ahern (letter of 10 March 1975), the arrival in Kenya was the sign "of a clear policy

A little earlier in order to give the community in Chad a new framework for its activity and to respond better to the country's needs, the provincial of France, Bernadette des Francs, thought it ought to be self-governing. After a visit from Mother Camacho in 1972, the Uganda/Chad Province was formed.[159] The next year Elizabeth MacGinty, Margaret Conroy and Paulina López Ridruejo, who had not obtained return visas for Uganda, arrived in Chad.[160] In 1975, President Amin declared that Uganda had enough language teachers. Some Religious of the Sacred Heart had to leave the southern part of the country for Karamoja. At Naoi, which had been established in 1972, "I found," wrote Mollie Ahern, "an international community of my Society, reflective, devoted, established in a place where basic human needs, as we understand them today, were scarcely met."[161]

Shortly after its independence, Chad had begun to be shaken by rebellions, partially because of government negligence. Abuses of all kinds pitted the Toubous and the Goranes of the North and East against the Saras of the South, from which President Tombalbaye came. The presence of French troops prevented the worst, but the conflict degenerated into insurrection. Colonel Kadhafi's entrance on the scene in 1968 marked a new stage. Copying what had been done in Zaïre under General Mobutu, Chad inaugurated a "return to authenticity," which consisted in giving up foreign names and titles. Fort-Lamy became N'Djaména. Although the Sacred Heart school did not suffer, and with reason, from the effects of the new period of initiation because it was imposed only on men, it had to redo all its rolls to record the new names.[162] But when Tombalbaye took on the army, a *coup d'état* erupted on 12 April 1975. Although the confrontations took place in the presidential sector near the Sacred Heart school, its buildings were hardly touched.

---

that consists of going where the need is greatest to form others so that they can replace us to go elsewhere." The first Kenyan postulant was accepted in 1981.

[159] The provincial and the provincial treasurer of Uganda/Kenya used to go to Chad twice a year.

[160] Some religious who found French difficult to master left Chad in 1977. Helen McLaughlin sought to internationalize the community in Chad by sending Spaniards and an Italian.

[161] *Correspondence*, p. 97. The parish in Naoi had been established by the Comboni Fathers in 1971: "The Society gave part of the money realized from the sale of the motherhouse on the Via Nomentana; the difference between the sale price and the purchase price of the new motherhouse was allocated to projects in the Third World" (28 February 1975).

[162] G. Bovagnet, p. 71. Foreigners called *dopélés* were systematically attacked by Chadian propaganda, but the missionaries were not included.

President Félix Malloun, who was a Sara, neither won over nor conquered his opponents. The departure of French troops in 1975 meant sixty fewer pupils in the school but contributed to its becoming a Chadian establishment. Educational reform that took into account the circumstances of the students, some of whom were already mothers, was put in place. French was taught as a foreign language, and textbooks adapted to Africa gradually replaced what had been in use. The boarding school, no longer essential because schools had been opened in the bush, remained open until 1978 for pupils from Guéra. The building thus freed up became a center for women and girls who were studying in the public schools:

> Educational reform and our open door policy for women of the area [took up] all our time and [allowed] our imaginations to develop activities adapted to the needs of the moment. We [formed] an educational team with the same goal. Committed lay people were added: two households of French *coopérants* living in our compound, six Chadians, two from Cameroun and five young French women, whose husbands were working in the city for the French *Coopération* [foreign aid service]. With them or alone, we organized weekend educational meetings at Bakara.[163] Outings to the bush, invitations to visit homes, and days in the desert [broadened] our horizons.[164]

In spite of efforts at reconciliation, some regions of Chad had become off limits because of the rebellion. The troops of Goukouni Oueddei had left the Tibesti Mountains while Hissein Habré troops held the East. Mediation by Sudan, Niger and Libya in 1978 did not bring peace:

> Each one [of us] carries on with her life as do all the civilians. But classes are disturbed more and more because parents who are civil servants keep close watch on military movements. At the slightest alarm they come to take their children away. Then fear runs through the classes, and we can do nothing but let the children leave, class by class or home district by home district, depending on the rumors.[165]

War broke out on 10 February 1979. The school was closed from March to June. The community remained in place, but the religious had to leave N'Djaména where the school was looted.[166] The community was dispersed,

---

[163] The reference was to a Jesuit spiritual center about twelve kilometers from the capital. In 1978, three Religious of the Sacred Heart worked there.
[164] G. Bovagnet, pp. 78-79.
[165] G. Bovagnet, p. 82.
[166] Some of them had arrived in Cameroun.

and some religious taught in the high school in Bongor. The school in N'Djaména reopened only in 1984.

Under the military regime of Idi Amin Dada life in Uganda deteriorated because of the forced departure of the country's political and economic officials and the transfer of confiscated businesses to incompetent and dishonest staffs. Some Ugandans were massacred; life for foreigners became dangerous. At the beginning of 1977 the British and the Irish were warned that they risked being taken hostage. The central team wondered "whether the Religious of the Sacred Heart ought to leave Uganda because of the seriousness of the situation. We decided to leave the decision to each one there, unless one of them could no longer make a decision because of the horror she experienced."[167] The team wanted to "respect the freedom of each religious to choose to remain with the people for whom in a sense she had already given her life, provided she felt after sincere discernment that was what she had to do."[168] The provincial, Helen McLaughlin, asked each one to speak out and everyone wanted to stay.[169] This pattern became standard from then on.[170]

The colonizers had drawn borders intended to limit conflicts between European countries but without considering the interests of the local people. In February 1976, Amin reclaimed a territory that had been transferred to Kenya in 1902,[171] but the affair did not go beyond declarations of intention. In September 1978, on the other hand, his troops moved into Tanzania where many Ugandans, one of whom was former president Obote, were exiled. The attack was checked. But in mid-January 1979, a counter offensive was launched against Uganda. The artillery fire was so intense that the five nuns in Nkozi had to withdraw to Kampala.[172] The new provincial, Doreen Boland, with no news of those who were caught behind the front lines at

---

[167] Testimony of M. Shanahan.
[168] C. Camacho, *Letters*, p. 60, 1 April 1977.
[169] Testimony of H. McLaughlin. Only three sick nuns left Uganda.
[170] At the time of the war in Chad, the nuns decided what they thought would be best for themselves: to return to their own country for the moment or to remain (Testimony of G. Bovagnet).
[171] It was the territory of Nakuru at the heart of the Great Rift Valley. Kenya forbade transport of merchandise between Mombasa and Uganda, and the traffic was detoured toward the Sudan.
[172] When the Religious of the Sacred Heart were able to return to Nkozi, they found their school looted and destroyed. It was rebuilt, thanks to the generosity of several organizations in Europe whom Pauline Campbell approached: "It wasn't easy. The Society came to the rescue. The motherhouse and different provinces did what was necessary so that there were enough beds, furniture and a few books to reestablish a semblance of normality." But

Kalungu, tried for three weeks to get in touch with them without success.[173] "We had God, we were together and we had a sense of humor to help us live through it," remembers Carmel Flynn. In April 1979, the military regime fell. The remains of Amin Dada's army were pushed back to Jinja, then toward the Sudan and Zaire and then rampaged in Karamoja. Obote returned from exile and took power again in May 1980.

The elections had been rigged, and the adversaries of Obote won in the bush where a former defense minister, Yoweri Kaguta Museweni, formed the National Resistance Army, the NRA. Tribal struggles contributed to the deterioration of conditions in the province of western Nile near Sudan, which was Amin's stronghold, then throughout the country and caused more shifting of the population. In 1983 the novitiate was transferred to Nkozi, so risky was that area. Confrontations between the regular army and the guerrillas increased at the end of 1985, and the two communities of Nkozi and Kalungu were once again cut off from the rest of the province.[174] The National Resistance Army took control of Kampala in January 1986. Makerere University,[175] where thousands of refugees flocked, was at the heart of the battle.

> The National Resistance Army gradually provided security, and committees took charge of administration, public service and security. In a few months the NRA controlled the entire country, although some governmental practices were alarming, like enlistment of young boys and the requirement for men and women of all backgrounds to spend three months learning to bear arms, to study the history of Uganda from an anti-colonial point of view opposed to the kind of Christian teaching that most had received.[176]

Yoweri Museweni was named president in January 1986.

The civil war between 1980 and 1986 resulted in half a million dead and an incalculable number of torture victims. The communities were isolated from one another and cut off from Rome and from the countries

---

the effects of this disaster were felt for several years (Prov. Arch. Uganda/Kenya).

[173] Testimony of Carmel Flynn. During the occupation of the Tanzanians it was necessary to send the boarders away so that they could find food. Soldiers entered the school to steal or to take the pupils away.

[174] Mary Roe was isolated for four months. To get to her it was necessary to cross Lake Victoria dotted with military patrols in an unprotected vessel.

[175] Doreen Boland and Patricia Coyle lived there.

[176] Conclusion of M. Ahern, *Correspondence*, p. 97.

from which the religious came. Locally personal safety was at risk. Doreen Boland recounted:

> Three times I found myself in the crossfire of cannons, and the fourth time I tried to joke a bit with a drunken soldier; he was brandishing a grenade through the open window of his car. The onlookers, petrified, couldn't help us! Many people were robbed at gunpoint. To resist was equivalent to certain death. As provincial I had ordered submission, even though resisting myself the first time I was accosted. That happened one day when I was coming back from the city. I noticed that I was being followed. I could not shake off the thieves who cornered me in order to take the car and all its contents. Another time we were driving in an uninhabited area when three bandits ran out of the bush. We had to stop and lie down on the muddy road, faces to the ground. While the thieves were stripping the car, we were praying aloud, "Sacred Heart of Jesus, we trust in you." They took everything but not the car, which allowed us to get out of there. Such were the events that people experienced every day during those years. To undergo such experiences seemed to us the natural consequence of our solidarity with them. The word of the Lord, "I am with you always" gave me, gave us strength. The adversity and insecurity that overwhelmed us at some moments cemented among us deep love, union and support.[177]

As Mollie Ahern could write: "Our Bugandan sisters said: 'You must leave. What are you doing in Karamoja? Leave!' In my heart, I responded: 'They are telling me we are dead, and look, we are alive!' None of us wanted to abandon them."[178]

In 1979, famine broke out in northern Uganda, where there was a severe cholera epidemic. The process of obtaining vaccines was long and hazardous. An unnamed sickness was spreading: it was HIV-AIDS, which would decimate the population of East Africa. The mood in the communities was oppressive:

> These months of famine, then of less dramatic hunger, were a period during which we all had something to endure. It is easy to explode under those circumstances. The infirmarian is always treating desperate cases. The rest of us have less pressure and some work to do that gives us hope,

---

[177] F. Makower, p. 72. The last episode took place in 1983.
[178] F. Makower, p. 79. It is in this uncertain situation that the secondary school in Kangole was reopened in October 1980.

but we all have our own challenges, confronted daily by signs, stories, and evidence of tragedy. Keep us in your prayer.[179]

During the assembly of provincial teams held in Kenya in October 1978, the provincials asked Rome to pay particular attention to Africa. Mother Camacho proposed naming a coordinator who would be based in Rome. This mission was given to Helen McLaughlin.[180] She "was to share African values and priorities with the whole Society." Her role at first was to be a link between the central team and the provinces and also among the provinces of Africa, without modifying the structures and responsibilities at the provincial level. As Mother Camacho stated in 1982: "For the central team this experience has been very positive. We are conscious that we have been helped not only by this arrangement, but above all by Helen's constant care to remain in contact with us." Born of the unique circumstances in Africa, this arrangement had been "a great help."[181] In 1978, Chad was given a special status, since the communities there were isolated; communication with the other African countries was difficult and the situation of the local Church very different from that of Egypt and East Africa.

In 1979, "the triumph of the Sandinista revolution brought hope to all of Latin America. We in Mexico joined in the suffering, the struggle and the victory of the people of Nicaragua."[182] The confederation of religious institutes of Mexico, the CIRM, had asked congregations to go to Nicaragua to stand with the people in their struggle and to help with the reconstruction of the country. Some Religious of the Sacred Heart went to spend a month there. Then the Province of Mexico decided to take part in a national literacy campaign. But in the face of such urgent needs there were many tasks to be undertaken. In Esteli, a largely leftist city, food had to be distributed, the wounded card for, and liturgies celebrated. Contacts with the people made the religious aware of the harsh struggles:

> Some families had been able to remain in place during the war; the others returned from the mountains where they had taken refuge and found their houses looted. The people spoke of what had hampered survival, of bombardments, loss of those close to them, the courage of the young, almost children, who joined in the struggle for a free Nicaragua. Talking about it was their therapy. They were happy to have a foreign religious

---

[179] F. Makower, 2 August 1980, p. 61.
[180] Testimony of H. McLaughlin. As there was no direct connection by air between Uganda and Chad; each time she went to Chad, she had to spend several days in Zaïre. She was called "the woman from Africa."
[181] Gen Arch. C I C 3, Box 29. Report of the Superior General, 1982, p. 9.
[182] María del Socorro Rubio Marchan, *25 años en Nicaragua 1980-2005*, p. 5.

listen to them and join forces with them. I became aware of what a community of believers was, like that of the early Christians, because they shared the little they had and they sought to find solutions to the problems as they came up.[183]

A community was begun in 1980 in Nicaragua at Jalapa, in the war zone near Honduras by two religious from Mexico[184] reinforced by the arrival of other Mexicans and religious from the United States.[185] Jalapa, which produced corn and tobacco, was considered the breadbasket of Nicaragua, and its mountains had been covered with trees: "Today we cannot say the same, the exploitation of precious materials, the war, forest fires have all changed the countryside."[186] The community of Managua was launched by a nun from Argentina and a Spaniard who came from Brazil.[187] Between 1980 and 2005 twenty-eight Religious of the Sacred Heart, seventeen of whom were from Mexico, worked in Nicaragua[188] in popular education or at the University of Central America.

Peace Returns

A New Approach to Education

The Society of the Sacred Heart began to make a clearer distinction between its mission and apostolic tasks. As Mother Camacho had remarked, sometimes, because of scant training or through excessive professionalism, the nuns were not living the mystique of the mission. But were the means set forth by the Constitutions of 1815 to glorify the Heart of Christ always pertinent? "We are beginning to be aware that social justice is a dimension of our mission of communion and liberation," said the superior general in 1976.

> The conviction is unanimous. However, we can distinguish very different emphases in the ways we live it: Some work for justice by concentrating on raising the consciousness of the students in the schools, on training "agents to change structures," in preparation for a more just world. They run the risk of theorizing, if in some way or other they do not have

---

[183] *25 años*.... p. 6, testimony of Elena Anaya.
[184] The founders were Marimer Cepeda and Esperanza Orvañanos.
[185] Lisa Fitzgerald and Mary Catherine McKay.
[186] *25 años*.... p. 14. Testimony of Consuelo Armida Moran.
[187] Esther Sastre and Pilar Repullés.
[188] One from each Argentina, Brazil, Colombia and Cuba; three from Spain, three from the United States, one from the Japanese province.

direct contact with those who are poor or oppressed. Others seek to be in solidarity in a special way with those who are oppressed and to struggle with them to change their circumstances. They run the risk of losing sight of the true liberation of persons and of sowing hatred rather than love. Others finally emphasize their option for the poor by sharing their simple life. They run the risk of neglecting their own development and consequently that of others. Without training it is easy to foster passivity among the oppressed and to be naïve when faced with unjust situations that require action and risk-taking.[189]

The Chapter of 1976 had discussed the spirit that ought to animate the mission, underlined its "educational dimension," and had looked at education in connection with justice. But what were the means to take? Should all the institutions be maintained, at least to some extent? Or rather should we be educators taking on other roles? After 1976, education had to be reconsidered as to both its founding principles and its practice. The assembly of provincials held in Mexico in January 1979 helped to clarify the "educational approach" of the Society of the Sacred Heart.

Announced on 19 March 1978, the assembly was given the assignment of drawing up the criteria for guiding the choice of apostolic tasks in order to respond to the world's needs and the spirit needed to carry out the mission. An international commission made a study of the existing endeavors and the needs to which they responded. They studied the responses of the local churches and of the Society in the face of injustice. They echoed the responses of the provinces to their founder's insights as expressed in her writings and in the Constitutions. They sought to distinguish between those issues that affected the congregation as whole[190] and those that concerned individuals but had repercussions on the whole.[191]

---

[189] Gen. Arch. C I C 3, Box 26, Report of Mother Camacho, pp. 6-7.

[190] Responsibility towards our institutions and other activities; the need to educate in depth and the great number of needs; spiritual values and the need of material development; the sacred and secularization; Christian education and the dominant philosophy of the country; spontaneity in responding to needs and the needs of prudence in planning; the sense of mission and a repressive government; the sense of mission and a reactionary hierarchy; different ideologies among religious in the same community; those who remain in the institutions and those who are oriented towards new apostolates; westernization of countries of the Third World and the development of local cultures.

[191] The apostolate as it existed at the time of entrance into the Society and the changes that occurred; the desire to respond to one's own call and the limits to achieving that response.

The provinces looked at their educational practices in the light of Mother Barat's concern to mold a complete education, to embody a preference for the poor and to use every means to glorify the Heart of Christ.[192]

In Mexico they took as their starting point the experiences of the provinces, "in union and conformity with the Heart of Jesus, in concern for fidelity to Christ, to the Church and to the person of today."[193] Held shortly before the second general assembly of the Latin American bishops that took place in Puebla, this assembly was marked by liberation theology. The provincials affirmed the desire of the Society of the Sacred Heart to remain faithful to its founding charism. The Heart of Christ, contemplated in humanity torn by injustice, impelled the Society to solidarity with an eye toward a more just and more fraternal world: "This vision of the world demands of us a serious effort to respond better along the path of our shared vision. It questions our faith, engages us in working together for the growth of humanity in Jesus Christ and teaches us that the search for justice is the way our mission expresses the love of the Incarnate God."

The educational direction of the Society of the Sacred Heart was defined as "education for justice in faith," a synthesis of the options identified in 1970 that ended confrontations seen among those who were continuing to work in formal education and those who had moved away from it. It meant

> regarding the world with the preferential love of Jesus for those who were poor and marginalized, a preference that must mark our lives wherever we are. To see human beings as children of God and brothers of everyone in Jesus Christ, called to live and grow compassionately according to the Gospel. To live by a faith inseparable from engagement in reality.

The provincials agreed that the choice did not have to be made for formal or informal education, for the young, women, families, facilitators or base communities. It was enough to prefer "the least favored" and to seek out those who could respond to that education in justice with a transforming dynamism.

The assembly defined some criteria that aimed at consistency between apostolic choices and the educational direction. Every endeavor was to "try to develop the whole person with an attitude of respect and love toward the person considered unique, in a relationship of reciprocity and sharing. It required "that there be a community where people educated one another." It was

---

[192] Gen. Arch. C I C 4 d, Box 24. Introduction to the working papers on education (September 1978).

[193] Assembly in Mexico, p. 1.

to enable the person to be the agent of his/her own growth in a dynamic process, develop detachment and solidarity, the service of others, the responsibility and meaning of commitment, liberty and a critical sense that fostered choices in accord with the Gospel, creativity in the face of the real world, allowing the person to be an agent of transformation and to seek to build a unity lived out in forgiveness and harmony.

Each province had to find a way to reach this goal. The assembly pointed out the value of ongoing formation, evaluation and accountability, deeper understanding of the word of God, study of the theology of the Incarnation and ecclesiology. It also recommended taking finances into account when deciding upon apostolic commitments. "At this assembly," concluded Mother Camacho, "We have committed ourselves to discern diligently the choices of our own provinces and as a whole to take on those of other provinces."[194]

Some religious were assigned to share their competence and expertise in the area of formal education with teams of educators who wanted to revise their techniques. Catherine Collins from the United States crisscrossed Austria, Germany, Ireland/Scotland, Malta, the Far East, Australia and New Zealand to give lectures or workshops on continuing education. Shona García from Peru was called on as an expert by groups in Bolivia and Nicaragua that were reorganizing the educational systems in their countries. Renewal and reflection continued during the following generalates and provided for the refinement of the options set in motion in the provinces.

At the Mexican assembly the provinces of the United States had presented a shared report. In February 1979 the five provincials decided to form a single province.[195] While this choice may have seemed unexpected, it was probably influenced by the growing unity of the preceding years, represented by the decision not to present five separate reports at the Mexican assembly.[196]

---

[194] Assembly in Mexico, p. 4.
[195] Meeting in Bolinas, California, letter to the five provinces, 28 February 1979: "A single province with appropriate areas and area authorities seems to be the best way to sustain our mission as a body today. We want to share with you very simply our conviction, although the details have not yet been worked out." Testimony of Clare Pratt, who was the provincial of Washington: "We came to this meeting with the intention of reflecting on alternative models of restructuring the five provinces. During our discernment it became clear to us that only one single province could carry out our goals."
[196] The fusion actually took place in September 1982. The country was then divided into twenty geographic areas, with an area authority in charge in each

Monique Luirard

Toward New Constitutions

The Church required that new constitutions be drafted. It was necessary to comply. As Helen McLaughlin, Francisca Tamayo and Hannelore Woitsch noted,

> In the Society of the Sacred Heart of Jesus we were very attached to the Constitutions left to us by Madeleine Sophie. We recognized in them a unity and depth that were so strong that it made it difficult for us to modify them without first having had a sufficiently long period of experimentation.[197] The interval between the Special Chapter of 1967 and the General Chapter of 1970 was too brief to allow for an accurate and realistic evaluation of our renewal. Because of this the period of experimentation continued. It was during the 1976 General Chapter that the Central Team was asked to form a commission to revise our Constitutions.[198]

In December 1977, the motherhouse asked permission of SCRIS [the Sacred Congregation] to defer the revision until the Chapter of 1982; the response was favorable. A commission of five former provincials from different cultures came together: María Antonia Blanes, from Northern Spain, Jean Ford, United States; Bernadette des Francs, France; Sumiko Iba, Japan; and Margarita Hurtado, Chile. They were to begin a process that would result in a new text. The new constitutions were to integrate the contributions of the renewal chapters, but they were to take as starting point the earlier Constitutions, which had "allowed many generations of religious to achieve the unity of their life."[199] Since the entire Society had to participate in the revision at the request of the commission, the Constitutions were reprinted so that each religious could have a personal copy in her own language: "This was especially significant because until

---

> one; a government plan was established in 1987. While this development was generally approved by the nuns, some regretted the loss of the special character that the five earlier provinces had had and feared that from then on contacts with a provincial in charge of 700 persons would be less easy than before, when the numbers in each province were at most around 200. For several years workshops, various gatherings and retreats allowed the religious to get to know one another.

[197] These are the terms of Mother Camacho's letter of 22 February 1978, *Letters*, p. 71.

[198] Helen McLaughlin, Francisca Tamayo and Hannelore Woitsch, *Process of Approbation of the Constitutions of the Society of the Sacred Heart of Jesus, 1982-1987*, p. 9.

[199] Letter of Mother Camacho to the Sacred Congregation of Religious.

then each religious had a copy of only part of the Constitutions, and the whole text was not translated into all the languages spoken in the Society."[200] For eighteen months the nuns individually and in community reflected on the Constitutions, trying to absorb their strength and their spirit[201] and using a questionnaire to identify the key points needed in the new text. In several countries religious gave talks on the Constitutions. There was interest throughout the Society: "This in-depth process of prayer and study inspired in each RSCJ a deep invitation to and desire for renewal of religious life in the Society of the Sacred Heart."[202]

For a better understanding of the tradition some writings on the Society were published and some already published were translated.[203] Among the most significant we can cite *The Society of the Sacred Heart, History of a Spirit*, by Margaret Williams, and above all the canon law thesis of Jeanne de Charry: *The Definitive Constitutions and Their Approbation by the Holy See*, the first volume of which, *The Formation of the Institute*, was the first real history of the origins of the Society. At the time of her defense at the Gregorian University, Jeanne de Charry had underlined four elements that she considered essential: "A spousal consecration to the Sacred Heart; a disposition towards adoration and reparation that presupposed a deep interior life; the apostolate of education that gave preference to the poor but rejected no one *a priori*; an institutional structure modeled on that of the Society of Jesus, in which unity was manifested in the general congregation and the superior general."[204] Marie-Thérèse Virnot edited the journal of the first novitiate at Poitiers that we owe to the founder herself. Religious of all nationalities were assigned to research the ways that the charism had always been accompanied by renewal of what seemed to them to be the "soul of the Society"[205] or modifications that might have been introduced into the Constitutions.[206] As the provincials meeting in Cairo in 1986 wrote, "The

---

[200] H. McLaughlin, F. Tamayo and H. Woitsch, p. 10.
[201] Gen. Arch. C I C 3, Box 29. Report of Mother Camacho to the Chapter of 1982, p. 7.
[202] H. McLaughlin, F. Tamayo and H. Woitsch, p. 10.
[203] *Travail et prière* of Father Brou and Pauline Perdrau's *Les Loisirs de l'Abbaye* were translated into Spanish. The life of Saint Madeleine Sophie was translated into Italian. Jeanne de Charry began to edit the correspondence of Saint Madeleine Sophie with Father Varin and with Philippine Duchesne.
[204] This extract was used on 6 December 1977 by Mother Camacho in a meeting with Msgr Caprio.
[205] Gen. Arch. C VI 3, Box 3. Studies of Marguerite du Merle and Mary Quinlan.
[206] Gen. Arch. C VI 3, Box 4. Charlotte Blaire, Elisabeth Charvet, Françoise de Lambilly, Marguerite du Merle and Marie-Josèphe Vié determined that there had been no essential modifications with the exception of the ones required by

obligation to rework the Constitutions has awakened a great interest in and esteem for our primitive Constitutions."[207]

In 1980, the constitutional commission drew up a proposal to be sent to each religious. In January 1981, the communities' responses were taken up by a synthesis group[208] who sorted out the amendments. The commission[209] identified the points on which provincial chapters had to give input in order to draft a second proposal that would also be sent to the whole Society. It collated the suggestions from all the provinces. From the responses it became apparent that one of the concerns bore on the expression "to the glory of the Heart of Jesus" that many proposed replacing with "manifesting the love of God made man." Father Arrupe, who was consulted, advised caution, persuaded that the change of expression went beyond the revision of a term and would signal the end of the Society of the Sacred Heart.[210] He proposed consultation with Father Calvez, one of his assistants general.[211]

The commission, reinforced for a time by Françoise Cassiers, drafted a working document preparatory to the general chapter; it was sent to capitulants and to communities at the end of March 1982. It was from this text, assembled from their amendments, that the chapter began its work in Frascati in July 1982. Although it was presented as only a sketch, its approval by the Church, after having been reworked by the chapter, was taken into account. It was created from "all the 'living words' sent in by the provinces." In that way all Religious of the Sacred Heart could contribute to these Constitutions and to "infuse into them the spirit that [animates the religious]."[212]

---

the decree of 23 May 1851, and by the publication of the Code of Canon Law of 1917.

[207] H. McLaughlin, F. Tamayo and H. Woitsch, p. 57, letter of 25 February 1986 to SCRIS.

[208] Composed of Mary Hinde, María Parrella and Chantal Goullin.

[209] A sub-commission was composed of Jean Bartunek, Keiko Iwai and Felicitas Mastropaolo.

[210] Testimony. S. Iba.

[211] Gen. Arch. C VI 3, Box 3. The commission was advised also by Father Vanhoye on the exegetical aspect of treating in a biblical perspective the Heart of Christ, the covenant, the Heart and the Spirit, seeking conformity and the spousal imagery in speaking of the relationship of the religious with Christ. For Father Calvez the glory of God was equivalent to the "joy of God." "Our lives, whatever their circumstances, must be given to God 'to seek to please him, to seek what would give pleasure to his Heart'" (Testimony of S. Iba).

[212] *Constitutions of 1982*. Proposal, avant-propos, p. 7.

The Chapter of 1982

Prayerful reflection on the Constitutions had rallied the Society of the Sacred Heart for four years. This "work constituted a great moment in the renewal of essential values of our religious life and of our affection for Madeleine Sophie and among ourselves" said Mother Camacho at the opening of the chapter. But it was not just a matter of composing a text. As Saint Madeleine Sophie had done and faithful to her inspiration, the Constitutions had to "to answer to the desperate needs" of the last quarter of the twentieth century and to move on to a re-reading of the life experience in the Society during the last twenty years, "fruit of the intuition of our Mother founder and the continuation of our entire history."

> We will try to write Constitutions that are more than a description of what we are, more than a law that we must obey, more than an expression of a desire or an ideal. The Constitutions give form to the body of the Society, sustain its life and its vigor. They are the essence of its life, its sap, its inspiration, its radiance, and they express our shared life, our story. We recognize ourselves in them and others recognize us in them. They translate our life concretely, foster the growth of new insights, and bring about new ways to serve the world that are more adapted to the needs and sensibilities of our time. The Constitutions express our commitment to follow Christ with the sentiments of his Heart.

The center of the Constitutions was "always the Heart of Christ, symbol and source of his love, the Heart pierced on the cross." The dynamic of the piercing, which went back to the birth of the Church and the Eucharist, was to be linked to the needs that had arisen during the last years: "Our sense of the Church; the sense of personal responsibility; ongoing formation; internationality seen as diversity; educational direction; preference for those who are poor; prayer and discernment." The capitulants had to consider the whole life of the Society as well as the self-expression of the cultures of the countries where the religious were working, and the insights of the two preceding chapters.

Individual and community reflection in view of the preparation of a new normative text had given everyone the opportunity to re-appropriate a rich congregational tradition and to look for words to express the charism. Some of the rediscovered elements found their way into the text. The image of breath, breathing in and breathing out, to signify the union of contemplation and action had already been used by Mother Stuart.[213] Some

---

[213] *The Society of the Sacred Heart*, p. 134.

new expressions came to light. There were references to heart rhythms and to *diastole* and *systole*. Jeanne de Charry suggested evoking the union between action and contemplation by the expression "a single movement" that had held an important place in the writings of Saint Madeleine Sophie and that figured in the Constitutions. The vocabulary was enriched also with words taken from conciliar texts.

On the eve of the Chapter of 1982,

> the capitulants were very conscious of their responsibility and of their desire to be loyal, which helped them live the chapter in an atmosphere of prayer and discernment. This union, so evident in the collaboration and sensitive respect for our internationality, fostered a mutual attentiveness, thanks to which each one was free to express herself in the commissions as well as in the general assemblies. They became aware that the task at hand was to write new constitutions and not just revise the original ones of 1815. The decision to do this was ratified by the vote of the general assembly. Thus the new constitutions became the fruit of the growing and deepened awareness of our spirituality…in the light of the Gospel, and in response to the request of the Church and the needs of the world. The unanimity of the final vote was a clear expression of the "union of minds and hearts" that constitutes the great richness of our Society and our mission.[214]

According to Helen McLaughlin,

> There was in the Society tremendous hope and an extraordinary interest in what would happen afterwards. The Society was at peace and ready to receive new Constitutions. The provinces understood one another better.[215] The chapter was easy to lead because one knew where one wanted to go and the delegates, well chosen by their provinces because of their experience in formation, government and the life of the Society, had prepared carefully for the chapter. In the course of these weeks they showed a real desire to draft a text in a short time. They gave evidence of fantastic commitment in the groups. There was never a complaint when they had to finish editing a text at night.

---

[214] H. McLaughlin, F. Tamayo and H. Woitsch, pp. 10-11.
[215] She believes that relationships among Americans were less strained and that religious from the United States had come to understand the desires of the Latin Americans.

The capitulants had to decide on 9 July 1982, whether or not to create a new text. They were almost unanimous in deciding not to touch the Constitutions of 1815[216] but to write a new text. Agota Baternay recounted

> The chapter set to work using a method inspired by the experience of Puebla.[217] This plan that fostered intense interaction among groups working on different themes and greater participation of all the members of the large assembly went hand in hand with the development of ideas and the drafting of a new text. For eight weeks the capitulants worked hard to find the right expression of the Society's charism and the essential elements of its spirituality.[218]

The Sacred Congregation had sent as an expert a Benedictine monk from South America who was not used to this kind of gathering of apostolic religious. He was replaced by Father Patrick Mallia, a Maltese Augustinian, who assisted the chapter especially in the area of Canon Law.

The capitulants were divided into five commissions, which, in the first days, were to share their thoughts on the section that was to become "End and Mission of the Society." As one of the participants, Moira Donnelly, reported,

> What surprised and delighted us during these days was the degree of correspondence that emerged in the five reports. All the drafts began with the loving initiative of God sending his Son into the world. The charism of the Society was situated in the salvific mission of Christ and in the Church, people gathered by the Spirit. From a linear presentation we came rapidly to a circular or spiral view to express the dynamism inherent in the mystery of the love of God.

The capitulants had spontaneously referred to Scripture texts, in particular the Gospel of John,[219] for which Father de Tournély and Saint Madeleine

---

[216] In community discussions phrases in the Constitutions that best expressed the spirit of the Society were brought out but also passages that had become obsolete.

[217] Helen McLaughlin, who had been named facilitator of the chapter, had decided, during her visit to Peru, to employ the methodology in use in meetings of CLAR.

[218] Gen. Arch. C I C 3, Conference to the Chapter of 1994: "A rereading of the life and development of the Society during the last thirty years."

[219] Gen. Arch. C VI 3, Box 3: "The Making of the Constitutions of 1982:" "In the same way that the prologue of John's Gospel presents the principal themes of the gospel, so in the section 'End and Mission' we have the essence of the whole of the Constitutions. Like the prologue of John, it suggests what

Sophie had special love and from which they drew their love of the Heart of Jesus. Some stages were especially significant as the chapter unfolded.

> Reacting against the literal conformism of the past, many delegates underlined the need for interior liberty without which one could neither have co-responsibility nor be in a position to make a lasting commitment. One wondered whether liberty and the law were concepts opposed to each other by their natures. It was then that Philippe Bacq gave a homily on the law and the prophets. As we realized from it, the greatest part of the law is in fact a distillation of the teaching of the prophets on the fidelity and tenderness of God. Therein lay in part the challenge of renewal: to accept at the same time both the law and the prophets but always interpret the law according to the prophets and never try to constrain the prophetic spirit by the law.

They succeeded in integrating into the Constitutions the contributions of the fifteen preceding years. Discernment appeared throughout the text and there was no hiatus between action and contemplation. An anonymous commentary entitled "Double Movement" appeared in parts of paragraphs 7, 8, 11 and 30 of the new Constitutions: "We want people to grow in human dignity, as human beings and as children God." "This grace of vocation is a way of conversion and of apostolic fruitfulness. The pierced Heart of Jesus opens our being to the depths of God and to the anguish of humankind. Jesus draws us into his movement of adoration of the Father and of love for all, especially those who are poor." "…that they be enabled to encounter the love of Jesus [and] that they let their lives be shaped by an active faith." "Gathered together in community…to live in communion among ourselves and with others…." "It is the twofold rhythm of the heart, a double movement that leads us ceaselessly from the interiority of a presence to the exteriority of a message. To discover this faithful and merciful love for ourselves and manifest it to others and in manifesting it to continue to discover it. That is what it means for a Religious of the Sacred Heart to glorify the Heart of Christ." The Constitutions no longer described specific works but defined outlooks and a shared approach to education. They strongly affirmed solidarity with the poor that could be expressed in different life situations and in all apostolic activities.[220]

---

is to come and links it to what has already taken place. For John the loving tenderness and faithful love revealed in the Old Testament become enfleshed in Jesus. In our 'End and Mission,' the concepts developed since the beginning find their fullness."

[220] § 36: "We wish to live simply so as to express our solidarity with those who are poor." § 56: "Within a Church which longs to be poor and to serve, our

A supplement provided guidance from earlier years in the choice of apostolates.

The new Constitutions, adopted unanimously by the members of the general chapter, were received with joy by the Religious of the Sacred Heart who saw how well conformed they were to the spirit of those of 1815. The summer of 1982 marked a new stage in the history of the Society. The identity of the Society had been redefined and reaffirmed, thanks to the reflections of the preceding years, at once on the nature and forms of religious life at the Sacred Heart, on its mission and on its charism. One could hope that the crisis of confidence in authority or in the institutions was going to fade away. However, the new text had to meet the expectations of the Church be and approved by her. The Society of the Sacred Heart drew new energy from that realization.

---

communities seek to be places of joyful sharing and open-hearted welcome where all can feel at home. Our life style – housing, food, clothing and recreation – while allowing the community to fulfill its apostolic commitments, will be simple and unpretentious. We shall strive to reduce our needs, to have less in order to share. Upon being sent by the provincial we assume the demands of serious work, and are faithful to the mission proper to our Institute. When helplessness, deprivation or insecurity in life bring us to greater poverty, we shall have the joy of following Jesus more closely in his poverty."

Chapter VI

The Return to "Ordinary Time"

Helen McLaughlin and Patricia García de Quevedo governed the Society as superiors general during the last twenty years of the century. The first had had extensive experience in East Africa. As coordinator of the provinces in Africa she had formed close contacts with representatives of the Church and religious congregations. Patricia García de Quevedo was the first superior general from the Americas and the first since 1968 to have been a member of the general council. Mother McLaughlin composed her first team with Hannelore Woitsch, Francisca Tamayo and Rita Karam, former provincials of Austria, Peru and the southern United States respectively and Sonia Aldeguer of the Philippines. With an average age of forty-six, the group was comparable to those that had preceded it. During her second term she brought into the council a Japanese, Keiko Iwai; a Mexican, Patricia García de Quevedo; Jean Ford from the United States; and Marie-Guyonne du Penhoat from France. In 1994 Mother García de Quevedo named more Europeans than had Mother McLaughlin: Marta Jiménez from Spain, Mary Hinde from England, and Maryvonne Keraly from France.[1] For the first time there was an African councilor, Ursula Bugembe, but no Asian, a change from the preceding generalates.[2]

---

[1] Only Patricia García de Quevedo and Maryvonne Keraly had been provincials before. The presence of a French religious on the Council could be useful, since in the framework of the bicentenary that would take place in 2000 some celebrations would necessarily take place in France.
[2] Maybe there would have been a difficulty in choosing a single representative for all of Asia. For as Patricia García de Quevedo recalled, Asia is a mosaic, like Europe.

Monique Luirard

Re-appropriation of the Identifying Characteristics

Approbation of the Constitutions

The unanimity among the capitulants in 1982 "could be seen as an effective breath of the Spirit" and the new Constitutions "as a fruit of discernment, of mutual listening to our differences of culture and ways of thinking." The general council had to get them approved while remaining "faithful to the spirit of the Chapter, to the charism of Madeleine Sophie and the living tradition of the Society, to the Church in its search for the characteristics of apostolic religious life, to the reality of the world where we have to live and where we have to carry out our mission."[3] This approval was unexpectedly called into question.[4]

The presentation of the new Constitutions to the Sacred Congregation took place on 20 October 1982, the feast of *Mater Admirabilis*. For the general council these Constitutions, which had been well received in the provinces, would "reinforce unity in the whole Society, foster its renewal, allow a deepened understanding of the charism and the sense of mission in the Church."[5] The Sacred Congregation granted transitional norms regarding some religious who had been previously committed to the Society by a promise as well as regarding the establishment of provinces according to the list submitted. But on 21 February 1983, while recognizing "the seriousness with which the work had been accomplished as well as the love of the Society for Saint Madeleine Sophie Barat that [was manifested]," the doctrinal richness of the texts expressed in language adapted to the present time, the valorization of personal responsibility in the life of the institute, "the desire to be docile to the inspirations of the Holy Spirit and the wish to be submissive to the universal law of the Church," the Congregation presented twenty-one comments. These last concentrated on the mission, on the place of education that appeared insufficiently focused and on the fourth vow, on "religious values" judged to have been minimized in favor

---

[3] Testimony of H. Woitsch, who cited the report of the general council 1982-1988, p. 11.

[4] H. McLaughlin, F. Tamayo and H. Woitsch, *Process of Approbation...*, p. 12: Again Cardinal Pironio, in receiving them "did not conceal the fact that our situation was very difficult, given that there were influential persons opposing us."

[5] *Process of Approbation*, p. 12. Through workshops the religious sought to make the text their own (Gen. Arch., C VI 3, Box 3). These meetings were accompanied by Bible study and theology of education and concluded with a time of prayer and discernment using the following questions: "What is asked of me? What responses can I give? How can I put them into practice?"

of sociological values, on the life of prayer and community, on the vows of obedience and poverty and on government.

While some of these comments could be accepted as given or with only a slight modification, others called for serious study. The general council decided to get the advice of experts in theology and canon law. The experts thought that the Constitutions of 1982 were insufficiently prescriptive and presented lacunae regarding the practice of authority at the local level.[6] The motherhouse decided to consult the provincials before presenting each new alternative[7] and to ask for the prayers of the communities but without sharing the content of the observations, a good way to preserve peace of mind. Mother McLaughlin, in presenting the spirit rather than the detail, proposed to each religious to reflect on three questions that seemed to her "a challenge for us at this moment in our history: What is the educational quality of my service in the Church in response to the needs of today? How do I accept the service of authority, and how do I live co-responsibly the search for and acceptance of the will of God? Are my choices in harmony with the call of the Lord and with the public character of our consecration?"[8]

In order to provide documentation to support the discussions, some Religious of the Sacred Heart were asked to examine the characteristics of the mission of the Society of the Sacred Heart from its beginning.[9] By comparing the texts of 1982 and 1815, in referring to the decisions of general congregations and to the statements of superiors general, Mother McLaughlin showed that the Society had always made a distinction between education and instruction, that works aimed at working class environments had grown and that, beginning in the early twentieth century, the retreats that the founder had hoped for had been increasingly focused on. Regarding the "fourth means," she referred to a statement by Jeanne de Charry, who had written that the Society was perhaps "the only institute that had had the boldness to inscribe in its constitutions conversations in the parlor as a means of apostolate. The mention of this fourth means

---

[6] *Process of Approbation*, p. 17.
[7] Gen. Arch. Report 1982-1988, p. 11.
[8] Helen McLaughlin, *Letters to the Society*, 5 May 1983, p. 16.
[9] Gen. Arch. C VI 3, Box 3 and C I C4, Box 23, env. 5. Gabrielle Husson, Mary Quinlan, Margaret Williams, Bernadette des Francs, Claude de la Martinière, Mary Roe and Mary C. Wheeler researched the works carried on outside the boarding schools and the development of educational projects of the Society. Dominique Sadoux took charge of studying what in the text of 1815 could or could not remain normative. Their contributions were utilized by Mother McLaughlin in the letter she addressed on 3 September 1984 to the pro-prefect of SCRIS, Archbishop Hamer.

Monique Luirard

enhanced the possibilities of openness in the future as new contacts would extend the apostolate beyond the convent parlors."[10]

The Sacred Congregation continued to receive criticisms from various sources as to the behavior of some members of the Society. These came from people outside the Society, but also from religious who complained about the failure of the Chapter of 1982 to impose wearing the habit, about a life style that they considered worldly and secularized, about the lack of religious discipline and the closing of some schools.[11] As to the habit, there were only rear guard actions because some provinces had decided to adopt a navy blue outfit with or without a veil for official events. As the superior general remarked during an interview at SCRIS, "in general the experience of recent years is positive, and the cross allows us to be easily recognized as Religious of the Sacred Heart."[12] As to the schools, information sent by third parties to SCRIS was sometimes inexact for, although some of them had been closed for financial reasons or because of lack of personnel, their total number had increased worldwide, and beyond that, the scope of the educational projects meant that many more young people and adults from a variety of environments were connected to the congregation than before.[13]

The text of the new Constitutions had to be reworked. While continuing the dialogue Mother McLaughlin asked the religious to put all their best "efforts into living them, since their value will prove itself more in life than in words."[14] At the time of the second presentation of the text, 3 September 1984, she asked all the communities "to live this moment co-responsibly," with prayer and fasting. She ended her letter with article 9 of

---

[10] Gen. Arch. A IV 3, Box 5, 1982, env. 8.
[11] H. McLaughlin, F. Tamayo and H. Woitsch, p. 25.
[12] H. McLaughlin, F. Tamayo and H. Woitsch, p. 34.
[13] Gen. Arch. A IV 3, Box 5, 1982, env. 8. Letter of H. McLaughlin, 3 September 1984 to Archbishop Hamer. Some closings are explained by developments in national legislation and had resulted in the opening of other schools where there were none, or to respond to calls from local churches. If one refers to the study of March 1984 made by Francisca Tamayo (C I C 4, env. 3), in 1983, there were 211 educational institutions, of which 186 were schools. Out of 1675 active religious (there were at that time 5040 Religious of the Sacred Heart), 46% were carrying out their mission in a school; 18% were employed in pastoral work and faith accompaniment; 9% were engaged in the promotion of justice and development. 85 institutions existing in 1963 had changed their form of management. 98 establishments had been opened in response to new needs. 114 of the old establishments were continuing to function and 72 others had appeared. 186 institutions (93% of the total) were schools.
[14] Gen. Arch. A IV 3, Box 5, 1982, env. 8, p. 26. Letter of 4 January 1984. This letter is not included in *Letters to the Society*.

the Constitutions, which she turned into a prayer: "Mary, woman of faith among God's people, live close to us, and to all that incarnates the life of your Son. As Society, we confide ourselves especially to you, whose heart is united and conformed to the Heart of Jesus, so that you will lead us to Him."[15]

At the beginning of 1985 SCRIS, requested another typed draft of the Constitutions. In exchanges with members of the Congregation, it appeared that the points in the text that were causing difficulty were the concrete aspects of the mission, in particular formal education, the fourth vow, the wearing of the religious habit and the renunciation of goods. The paragraphs that were the object of the most modifications concerned the habit and obedience; SCRIS believed the latter was not sufficiently specific regarding superiors. New drafts of the disputed paragraphs were sent in January, June, August, October and November 1986. But on 14 January 1986, SCRIS announced that the Constitutions of 1815 and of 1982 were both to be regarded as authoritative. Consequently, the very nature of the Constitutions of 1982 was in question, since they were considered "constitutional norms" and a simple updating of those of 1815.

The decision made by the general council to share all this information with the provincials was carried out at the assembly in Cairo in February 1986. The general council let them know where the negotiations were and what issues were in dispute. The provincials unanimously believed that, even though the Constitutions of 1815 could no longer have normative value, they must "remain forever a source of inspiration for the Society."[16] On 25 February, they addressed a joint letter to SCRIS showing that it was not possible to have two authoritative texts without causing complications in government and creating confusion and real problems of conscience for the religious:

> The 1982 text was in no way written with this idea in mind. We wanted to write new constitutions, precisely to avoid the ambiguity of a double normative reference. We wished rather to compile a text which, in itself, had its own consistency, based on the spirit of 1815 and taking into account the new perspectives opened up by Vatican Council II and the responses of the Society of the Sacred Heart to the needs of the world.... For the Society, the text of 1982 is considered our rule of life, since it is the fruit of the General Chapter, our supreme body of government. Since 1982, the many positive responses from our religious of all ages and every generation have only confirmed this conviction. We are thinking especially

---

[15] *Letters to the Society*, pp. 28-29, 8 September 1984.
[16] H. McLaughlin, F. Tamayo and H. Woitsch, p. 53.

of so many elderly sisters who have expressed their joy in finding here the spirit of the 1815 and, on the other hand, of the candidates, novices and young professed who have come to the Society and wish to remain, drawn by the 1982 text.

Therefore the provincials were asking the superior general to make an appeal: "It is the example of our holy mother Saint Madeleine Sophie's responsible obedience, love and loyalty to the Church that inspires us today. If our appeal is rejected we will submit and help the Society to do the same, believing that this trial will contain its own promise of life."[17] They wanted the general council to reconsider with SCRIS the decision concerning the fourth vow and to pursue dialogue relative to the different points at issue.

Mother McLaughlin informed the communities of the content of the last communications from SCRIS and of the positions taken by the general council echoing the support she had received from the provincials. The situation was delicate:

> In our poverty, in our weakness, we are invited to be totally dependent on the Spirit, relying solely on God; he is the one absolute in our lives. Everything we do is through him, with him and in him. The sign that we are living these events in the spirit of St. Madeleine Sophie will be the communion among us, that communion which was her main concern in moments of difficulty.[18]

She asked them to intensify that communion and recalled that it was "the responsibility of each one not to allow anything that could break it." The *Cor unum* was evident in the support of all kinds that flooded into the general council, but also in the messages sent to SCRIS, in which Religious of the Sacred Heart showed that they supported the positions that their major superiors had taken. Maybe it was this concrete, public expression of the *Cor unum* that prompted the final decision.

On 20 May 1986, SCRIS decreed that the text of 1815 remained the fundamental document giving the thought and spirit of the founder, but that the text of 1982, drawn up according to the prescriptions of Vatican Council II, contains the rule of life. The two texts were to be published in the same volume, and the final decree of approbation would cover both. The first remained the source of inspiration of the Institute, but the

---

[17] H. McLaughlin, F. Tamayo and H. Woitsch, pp. 55-56.
[18] *Letters to the Society*, pp. 43-44, 25 February 1986. H. McLaughlin, F. Tamayo and H. Woitsch, pp. 59-60.

Constitutions of 1982 had the force of law.[19] SCRIS gave some ground regarding the fourth vow and took note of the changes effected after the proposals of January 1986, but it still demanded sixteen more modifications of the text. The point that remained up in the air the longest was that of the habit. Finally the formula that Cardinal Hamer himself had suggested was adopted in a new version of article 45: "[Those] who have kept the veil may legitimately wear it and the sisters who, having removed the veil, wish to wear it again will be supported in doing so."[20]

On the morning of 2 January 1987, Mother McLaughlin learned that the decree of approbation had been signed the day before. Ten days later, she informed the Society:

> The assurances of your union at this historic moment in the Society's history have made me feel deeply the vitality of our COR UNUM. I want to express my gratitude to each one of you for all that these years of waiting, prayer, suffering and sacrifice have meant, for it is this which has led us to be able to rejoice together in the approbation of the *Constitutions*.

A new stage in the history of the congregation was opening up. It was a question of making the Constitutions "live through a fidelity that is constantly renewed."

> The question that springs from this call is not so much "What must be done?" as it is "Where must we put our heart?" To follow Christ according to the *Constitutions*, to glorify his Heart, will lead us to love in a new way, and this will be our best response to the challenges of the world. This love will become an effective and prophetic sign of the Kingdom, of this Kingdom present in our midst, and at the same time, always in the process of becoming. Is it not love incarnate, visible, among ourselves and towards all our sisters and brothers; that is to say, the witness of love in all our relationships that must be the characteristic of a religious of the Sacred Heart? If we live our *Constitutions*, we will be signs of love in the world, and we will find ways "to reveal the strength and tenderness of Jesus" love for each one'.[21]

On 15 June 1987, the provisional norms for the fourth vow, the renunciation of goods and the habit were approved. This decision brought

---

[19] H. McLaughlin, F. Tamayo and H. Woitsch, pp. 60-61.
[20] H. McLaughlin, F. Tamayo and H. Woitsch, p. 63. These were the terms used by the cardinal in a letter of 2 July 1985.
[21] *Letters to the Society*, 12 January 1987, pp. 49-50. The quotations refer to § 180 and 62 of the Constitutions.

to an end a process that took longer than that for other congregations that had been required to revise their rule of life; in the course of the process the Sacred Heart had been required to make changes that were not asked of other institutes. Was it because, as many experts in theology and canon law thought and said, the Society of the Sacred Heart was so well known and so widespread?

The International Education Commission

After the meaning of the educational mission had been refined during the assembly in Mexico, the Chapter of 1982 recommended establishing guidelines suitable for the whole Society. It was a definite change, since during their conversations the capitulants had agreed that the discussions, while promoting provincial participation, would have to be directed by the "center." The process had to be attentive to the diversity of apostolates and of cultures while identifying the spirit and character of the educational service of the Society of the Sacred Heart in order to lay the foundations of a pedagogy and train the religious.[22] The commission in charge of leading the discussions, working closely with the general council, included religious who had worked in various geographic and apostolic areas.[23] In each province a committee was named to guide and coordinate the task of research and renewal. Regional meetings, which took place in Lima, Madrid, Mbansa-Mboma, Washington and Bombay, refined the working methods in accordance with the religious, political, cultural and economic conditions of the countries in those regions. Their results were communicated to the Society in March 1987 by means of special issues of the review *Communications* and taken up at the provincial level. In February 1988, a booklet summarized the work accomplished at various levels of deliberation and dialogue.

These studies constituted a full survey of the mission[24] and revealed a new way to approach the apostolate in an integrated global vision. While there still remained some traces of a "cloistered" mentality, expressed through ignorance of politics or through privileging the Church in the area of education, many provincial committees went beyond a description of their activities and asked themselves if they were at the

---

[22] Gen. Arch. C I C 4, Box 24, env. 4. Letter to the provincials, 10 July 1985.
[23] Catherine Collins, Judith Garson, Marie Noronha, Shona García, Ada Martínez, Isabel Rodríguez and Marie-Guyonne du Penhoat.
[24] Some collaborators of the religious participated.

service of the individual and the community[25] or of interest groups and what the consequences were of state intervention in the functioning of the schools. While the apostolates varied considerably, they were concentrated in schools, health and pastoral services, and they had an educative dimension. Education was not only accepted but viewed as a fundamental condition of apostolic commitment. The broadened interpretation of education gave the religious "renewed energy, conviction and confidence in the certainty of the call to be educators." They moved beyond "a common work" to a mission constituted "by the sum of individual calls." But since needs seen as urgent differed, depending on whether the religious were working among the middle class or among those who were poor, could they educate the privileged in social justice and not risk contributing to "a continuing domination through charity or dependence?"[26] How should we define excellence in education and imagine the role and position of its leaders? Does education involve deliberate or intentional action? How to educate in countries where the religious and philosophical bases were not Christian? Was Sacred Heart education possible only in countries or cultures that had a common religious base? Most provinces believed that a new image of women had to be part of education.[27]

The action encouraged by the international commission promoted looking beyond the needs and conditions of each country.[28] It contributed to transforming educational practices at the local level and gave rise to training that would allow the religious to develop and introduce a "liberating pedagogy" into the schools.[29]

---

[25] Belgium, from the situation of migrants and young people permanently out of work, wondered whether it was not time to refashion the mission in relation to the radical changes that were appearing in Europe. Argentina/Uruguay, deciding that education had a leveling and dehumanizing tendency, believed that it made as much sense for a Religious of the Sacred Heart to work in public schools as in establishments of the Society.

[26] Egypt, Peru, Belgium, the United States wondered if one could teach solidarity in Sacred Heart institutions when they were private or supported by the state but located in areas that were economically and socially privileged.

[27] Reports of Egypt, England, Chad, Spain South, Philippines, Colombia, Cuba, Nicaragua, Venezuela, Korea, Ireland/Scotland, Uganda/Kenya, India and the United States.

[28] Testimony of M.G. du Penhoat. Some provinces envisaged for their members the possibility of working in countries other than their own.

[29] C. Meeûs, p. 39.

Poverty and Financial Management[30]

While the question of money had been considered taboo in the Society of the Sacred Heart, a new way of thinking about the vow of poverty and the introduction of salaries in apostolic activities caused it to be regarded differently: keep a non-possessive attitude toward it, put all resources in common and, thanks to sharing of goods, come to the aid of provinces that could not be self-sufficient. Because the religious in the West were aging as a group, providing pensions and planning care for the aged became issues. The Chapter of 1976 had given orientations on the spirit of communion, sharing and co-responsibility that were to form the basis for financial decisions in the Society and had specified the responsibilities of the central government in this area.[31] A consultative committee of experts, formed by the provincial treasurers, played the role of a broadened council for the central administration.

The question of the renunciation of goods proved to be complex. Before 1967 the renunciation made at profession was obligatory but conditional. Afterwards it became optional but absolute. The application proved not to be easy. In some countries, one could not renounce in advance what one did not yet possess. For those who chose not to make the renunciation, it had to be determined how their goods would be administered, since the vow of poverty forbade a religious to do so herself. This situation, arising from canon law, had financial repercussions at the provincial level. The Chapter of 1982 rendered the renunciation of goods optional but absolute.[32] The putting into practice of the renunciation of goods was sometimes delicate. In response, a new edition of the booklet entitled *The Religious of the Sacred Heart and Patrimonial Goods* was sent out in June 1993.

The congregation had to have a financial policy to know, for example, what to do with funds after the sale of property.[33] It was a challenge to have an investment policy when religious values differed fundamentally from those of the business world:

---

[30] This paragraph is based on the testimonies of two successive general treasurers, Vivien Bowman and Monique Fabre.

[31] Gen. Arch. C I C 3, Box 29. Report of the Central Government 1976-1982, p. 10.

[32] That created a difficulty during the process of acceptance of the Constitutions by SCRIS.

[33] Testimony of V. Bowman: "In countries where there was no stock exchange, our sisters had to find solutions, for example, buying apartments and renting them, which brought with it many legal problems. One province bought a mountain on which to raise deer whose antlers they sold for their medicinal properties."

We needed to extend our portfolio to provide for pensions and for the needs of provinces that did not have sufficient income. Ethical investments were an attractive option since our capital was working for those who were in need. We determined criteria for investing according to justice, while knowing that no enterprise is exempt from negligence. Another challenge we had to face was finding a balance between prudent supervision and the risks taken to come to the aid of those less comfortable than we. We had to share our resources so that the Society could develop in countries that were not financially self-sufficient. An attitude of non-possession was important when we were diversifying our activities and receiving salaries and benefits.[34]

All the provinces had to face these challenges. If in Latin America where the sense of community was strong, sharing goods, space and money was accepted; in northern Europe, North America and Japan, an individualistic mindset could reduce the sense of sharing; and while one had to provide for the future, one had to admit that the religious had more security than the majority of the population. In Africa, which depended on finances from outside but where family cohesion was strong, it was not easy for religious enjoying financial security not to want to share with their families. "When I look back, I realize," concluded Vivien Bowman, "how much we have changed in sharing financial responsibility. It was an important moment for me when during a chapter we acknowledged that most of the decisions we were making had financial implications and that it was not always up to the treasurer to be responsible for their consequences."

As the responsibilities of provincial treasurers grew,[35] adequate training in management proved indispensable.[36] The general treasurers hoped that they had simple, easy relationships with their superiors, their sisters and their associates.[37] Some provincial treasurers had begun to meet

---

[34] In 1988, the chapter affirmed, "In a world that is hungry and thirsty for justice, our following of Jesus Christ demands that we take positions and decisions that lead us together to more evangelical poverty."

[35] Testimony of V. Bowman: "We had never imagined that we would have anything else to do except to manage the schools and provide for a large number of nuns."

[36] In 1985, they were invited to Rome for a meeting that had as its purpose fostering mutual acquaintance and the importance of solidarity among the provinces and with the most disadvantaged.

[37] Testimony of M. Fabre. At the time of their nomination, on which she was consulted, she attached as much if not more importance to the quality of their relations as to their financial competence.

informally.[38] The treasurer general brought them together by continents. The goal of these meetings was to provide mutual training. Thanks to sharing a common mission, each one received the support and interest of the others.[39] In November 1991, an international finance committee of four religious was named to study the solidarity proposals submitted to the central administration, to develop principles to assist provinces in matters of real estate and to reflect on some general problems, such as external debt. It proposed to the general council that the whole Society take a stand in favor of solidarity and justice.

Towards Uniform Formation

Initial formation had to be looked into. In February 1987, the general council brought the mistresses of novices together in Rome to examine what it meant from now on to be a Religious of the Sacred Heart and to identify the formation to be offered upon entrance into religious life. The group thought that the noviceship should include sharing the life of an apostolic community while benefiting from spiritual exercises and the study of Sacred Scripture and that formation should continue throughout life.[40]

Formation was the dominant objective of the Mother McLaughlin's second term. International *recyclages* took place in Rome and in some provinces. The formation of young professed had been discussed by the Chapter of 1988 but there was no unanimity on the policy to adopt. To review the programs in the light of the Constitutions and to provide more unity and continuity among the various stages of formation,[41] the general council organized two meetings in Barcelona and in Rio in 1990, at the end of which the participants accepted the fact that the programs were not uniform. In March 1992, a booklet entitled *Its Fate Is in Their Hands* expressed the synthesis of the directions and convictions at which they had arrived. The text underlined the continuity that should exist among the different stages of religious life and suggested that a vocation ministry might be developed.

During the generalate of Mother García de Quevedo, the general council gave attention to the consistency, continuity and human

---

[38] Testimony of F. Rollin.
[39] The meeting of provincial treasurers of Asia could not take place in Philippines for reasons of security. A meeting in Cairo brought together the provincial treasurers of Europe and Africa.
[40] Report of the General Council 1982-1988, pp. 26-28.
[41] Report of the General Council 1988-1994, pp. 14-15.

dimension of the formation plans,[42] to their ability to initiate candidates into the charism of the Society, while respecting a country's culture, to a standardized formation for the whole congregation[43] and to the profile of candidates who had often had responsibilities before entering religious life, but who were also "in a stage of apprenticeship and in the position of a disciple."[44] The council was concerned also with the characteristics of the communities into which candidates, novices and young religious were being integrated and which should at the same time respond to the expectations of the new generations and to the requirements of formation.[45] They emphasized that the newly professed had to be welcomed and supported on their return to their provinces,[46] as well as their need for ongoing formation during the first years after perpetual profession. Ongoing formation was also seen as important at the time of a new apostolic commitment, and the need for life-giving support in communities of elderly sisters was stressed.

In the world's current circumstances, internationality had to be integrated into formation.[47] It had a "wider and deeper meaning than the simple fact of being present in a number of countries and cultures or of being sent in mission to another province." It had to be "at the service of the mission and a characteristic of the life style of communities." In the last years of the twentieth century, attitudes changed little by little from "internationality" to "multiculturality,"[48] which required "growth in tolerance of and respect for other cultures, religions, nations" and which could appear only when the difficult historical circumstances that various European and Asian countries had confronted were faced directly.[49] The building of the international community required learning languages. Both international novitiates and more numerous contacts among the religious, in particular the youngest, strengthened it. In Europe the presence of young professed in almost all the provinces, the relatively small number in the

---

[42] Report of the General Council 1994-2000, p. 36. It approved fourteen formation plans.
[43] Testimony of M. Keraly: "In the Society we are all in agreement in concern for the most needy, in prayer, in the contemplative outlook, but how to live these and express them in daily life?"
[44] Report of the General Council 1994-2000, p. 18.
[45] Testimony of M. Keraly. The formation community does not have to be "made up of professed who are models of perfection but by a sufficient number of religious in such a way that it is not just one person who is in charge of formation."
[46] Report of the General Council 1994-2000, p. 37.
[47] Report of the General Council 1994-2000, p. 16.
[48] M. Keraly believes that "interculturality" was little spoken of at that time.
[49] Report of the General Council 1994-2000, p. 17.

novitiates and the increased exchanges among the provinces encouraged other types of collaboration. A common novitiate for Belgium and France was set up in Brussels in 1996. Annual meetings among the young professed of Belgium and France resulted in a common formation plan for the two provinces for that stage of religious life.

Separation of the House in Florence

Mother Carloni had hoped that the election of a new superior general would bring about a transformation in the relations between Florence and the Society, and maybe she believed that some of the former customs would be restored.[50] From the beginning of her mandate Mother McLaughlin tried "to take all the steps necessary to keep a cordial and sisterly relationship with the community in Florence," which, after March 1982, was using an internal rule composed according to the directions of Vatican II but based on the Constitutions of 1815. In June 1983, accompanied by Francisca Tamayo, she was received at the Poggetto as superior general. She was able to hold a group meeting each day and to have visits with individual religious, in the course of which she commented on the new Constitutions, the text of which she had received in Italian. After that visit the general council tried "to send [to Florence] with more punctuality the communications that went out from the motherhouse to the communities." The two visitors, who had also made contact with the new archbishop of Florence, Archbishop Piovanelli,[51] informed the alumnae of the state of things.

The climate later disintegrated. The atmosphere during Mother McLaughlin's second visit in March 1985 appeared "a little tense."[52] Was it because Florence had accepted an Italian into its novitiate? "In 1986 there was no visit, lacking a propitious climate. The approbation of the Constitutions seemed imminent and Cardinal Piovanelli advised us to wait." The house in Florence was aware of the difficulties the Society was having in getting the Constitutions approved, and no doubt it hoped for a refusal, which would have rendered those of 1815 normative again. In February 1986 some communities of the Society received letters from the Poggetto, in which the text of 1982 was commented on unfavorably. But in the

---

[50] Testimony of F. Tamayo.
[51] Testimony of H. McLaughlin and report of the general council. "During the whole process we remained in contact with him, benefiting from his kindness and wisdom."
[52] H. McLaughlin: "The management of this issue demanded energy, including physical energy, for the communication with Florence was not easy, and the superior general felt a lack of confidence."

expectation of an eventual approbation of the Constitutions, in June 1986 the special status of Florence was not renewed.

In January 1987, Cardinal Piovanelli went to announce to the religious of Florence that the new Constitutions had been approved. He took the final text that Mother McLaughlin had had sent to him. This text caused "great perplexity," because not only were they seeking "in vain continuity and integration" between the Constitutions of 1815 and those of 1982,[53] but above all because they were wondering what their position would be in the future. Cardinal Piovanelli and Mother McLaughlin had "organized the steps to go through to allow the sisters [in Florence] to move forward, with the time they needed to understand the spirit of the decision and to have the essential elements they needed to make a personal decision. From that moment on the provincial of Italy took a more active part [in the process], in view of the integration of the community into her province.[54] In 1987 Cardinal Piovanelli went to the Poggetto several times to exhort the religious "to forget the past" and to prepare to "return" to the Italian province. On 19 April, he presented them with the three possibilities. The first consisted in having the special delegation renewed but in a more institutionalized and definitive manner, which would permit the house in Florence to remain in the Society of the Sacred Heart. He made them understand however that there was little chance that this status would be granted. The second was to "return unconditionally to the Society of the Sacred Heart, *hic et nunc*, by accepting the new Constitutions." The third came down to "being in the Province of Italy," any relationship with the superior general and the provincial being carried on through the mediation of the archbishop.[55] At that point eleven religious opted for the first solution. Following a new visit from the cardinal, on 14 May aided by a canon lawyer, they wrote a petition to the pope.[56] But they soon understood that even though the archbishop of Florence was willing to send it to the Vatican with a favorable opinion, he was opposed to this step.[57] From then on they could only consider giving in.

---

53   Doubtless it had been hoped that the modifications of the text would be more significant than they were.
54   Report of the General Council 1982-1988, p. 33.
55   *Brève histoire de la maison de Florence*.
56   *Brève histoire*, p. 5: "On 20 May, the petition addressed to the Holy Father was read in community. All listened. It was then left in the community room until the next day so that those who wished could sign it. On 22 May the petition was taken [to the Vatican] by the archbishop. There were eleven signatures.
57   *Brève histoire*: "It remained for us only to submit but with what bitterness before what seemed to us a game rather uninvolved in our lives."

Without the special delegation and feeling that the petition to the pope would not be granted, the religious who favored autonomy wanted to negotiate the conditions of their return to the Society of the Sacred Heart, even to obtain a special status, which was not possible for the congregation. They sought ways of countering but without success. On 3 September Cardinal Piovanelli wrote to Cardinal Hamer that the community of Florence welcomed

> the desire and the invitation of the Congregation for Consecrated Life to accept the approved Constitutions according to the letter and the spirit that SCRIS [had] indicated and that they [asked] to be considered fully sisters of the unique Society of the Sacred Heart; that they [wished] to take together a path of growing communion among themselves and above all towards the congregation and they were asking to be assisted by the mediation of the archbishop of Florence.

They had finally opted for the third solution. On 22 September, Cardinal Hamer charged Cardinal Piovanelli with continuing to follow the community to guarantee the freedom of its members and to assist in the resolution of its relations with the Society. Two Italian religious were sent to Florence and one from Florence went to Villa Peschiera.[58]

The exchanges between Florence and the Province of Italy began again. The visits of the provincial, Anna Maria Catelani, and the superior general took place in a relaxed atmosphere. Mother Carloni's resignation had yet to be tendered. The question, put off at first in order to keep things calm, hardly seemed easy to settle. In 1989 there arose the matter of the final profession of a young professed. The house in Florence asked SCRIS if she could make her probation there, not in Rome with the other religious of the Society and without having to spend time beforehand in another community of the province. It was becoming clear that since 1968 the evolution of the religious in Florence "had proceeded along their own lines. Their autonomy was so integrated into their style of life that it was no longer that of the rest of the Society."[59]

A division within the community came with the nomination of a new superior. In June 1990 thirteen religious said they were in favor of maintaining Mother Carloni in office; five asked for a change of superior. If the change was carried out, there was a risk of rupture, but if it was not done, it would become impossible to do so later. It finally took place in the summer of 1990 after the provincial of Italy discussed the matter with the

---

[58] H. McLaughlin, *Letters to the Society*, p. 67, 10 November 1987.
[59] Report of the General Council 1988-1994, p. 21.

archbishop. But on 20 September a religious from Florence wrote to the pope to ask for a juridical definition of the house and the possibility of having a novitiate, "in order to be just" towards the young religious who had entered the delegation of Florence and not the Society of the Sacred Heart and "in order to safeguard her vocation." They were on the road to separation.

When Cardinal Piovanelli had informed them of the approbation of the new Constitutions, the religious of Florence had wondered if one could

> annul with a single stroke of the pen, fifteen years lived in complete obedience to the directives of the Church? Can we suppose that in fifteen years the discrepancy has not grown still greater between the two paths followed, one by the Society of the Sacred Heart, the other by the community? Is it possible that the vows pronounced by a young religious the year before must be nullified because we are dragged by force in one direction that no longer answers to the commitment freely assumed by our religious profession? How can the directions of Paul VI and John Paul II requiring the transformation of the Society of the Sacred Heart be annulled?[60]

The resumption of relations with the Society and the Italian province had not lessened the impact of these questions.

In December 1990 the provincial of Italy and the general council undertook consultations with the archbishopric of Florence and the Vatican to arrive at a solution acceptable to all. Two months later fourteen religious in Florence proposed to form a sort of monastic branch within the Society of the Sacred Heart or to separate. On 11 May Mothers McLaughlin and Patricia García de Quevedo, who was the council member in charge of Italy, went to Florence to communicate the decision of the general council not to grant a special status and to initiate a process of separation that would spread out over a year during which the house in Florence would be under the authority of the motherhouse. Two days later the Italian provincial, Maria Finocchiaro, came to give assignments to those who did not want the special status.

> From July to December Marie-Guyonne du Penhoat and Patricia García de Quevedo met several times with those remaining in Florence to discern and search with them how to respond to the question of autonomy. During these meetings the community ended by realizing that it could not achieve the two objectives that it was pursuing. It was not possible

---

[60] *Brève histoire de la maison de Florence*, p. 4.

to reconcile the desired autonomy with belonging to the international Society. Finally the sisters recognized that their desire for autonomy was stronger than their desire to continue to belong to the Society.[61]

"I really worked at communion with them in the spirit of the *Cor unum*," believes Mother McLaughlin, "but the best means of living communion was the separation." For Marie-Guyonne du Penhoat, the process that ended in the division was exemplary:

> We were able to understand and make the sisters understand that they saw the Society as a federation of houses or provinces, with a certain fidelity to the spirituality of Madeleine Sophie, considering the superior general as a sister among sisters and not as a person having authority in the government of the Society. They themselves used the image of the Po, which before flowing into the sea divides into several little rivers totally different but having the same source. They refused in particular the possibility of having an obedience for another house of the province of Italy or of the congregation. They finally understood by themselves that if the Society refused to become a federation of provinces, they had to ask for separation.

She adds: "Notwithstanding, I have kept great feelings of friendship for those sisters with whom, little by little, the sharing became free from distrust and even cordial."

In January 1992 the Congregation for Institutes of Consecrated Life gave its consent in principle for a separation that had juridical and financial implications. On 11 May total autonomy was granted to the religious in Florence, who became the *Religiose del Sacro Cuore di Firenze*, "a religious community *sui juris* of pontifical right, belonging spiritually to the religious family founded by Saint Madeleine Sophie Barat and confided to the special care of the archbishop of Florence."[62]

> Mother McLaughlin wrote on 15 June 1992:
> We believe that in presenting this request the sisters of the community of Florence are seeking sincerely to follow the will of God according to a way of life that has been theirs. We respect their way of life, and while this brings with it the suffering of separation, we have supported their request to the CIVCSVA.... We are confident that the suffering, which we have all felt, and very particularly the province of Italy, will be life giving.

---

[61] Report of the General Council, p. 22.
[62] Report of the General Council, p. 22.

[We remember] them with affection in our prayer, confiding them to Saint Madeleine Sophie, who will be our special link with them.[63]

The separation that Florence had finally asked for was also the result of the Society's affirmation of an identity and a form of corporate unity that seemed foreign to the house of Florence.

The Weight of Politics

A New International Situation

In the 1980's there were political upheavals in Latin America. Between 1980 and 1985 civilian power was restored in Peru, Argentina,[64] Uruguay and Brazil, and in 1982 Colombia ended a state of siege. In Chile the "protest movements" begun in 1983 lasted four years.[65] Participants blocked the roads with barricades:

> The measures taken in response were harsher: At dawn we heard helicopters flying over our houses, people were brutally turned out of their homes, and nearly all of their belongings were destroyed. The protests cost many lives, usually of innocent people – a child going to buy bread, a young person climbing up to see what was happening. The helicopters fired shots to right and left. There were also detentions, tortures, continual persecution, threats. Uncertainty and fear reigned everywhere."[66]

But democracy was not guaranteed. In Colombia the drug cartel had the Minister of the Interior assassinated. In 1985 members of M-19 occupied the ministry of justice in Bogotá and, after the intervention of the army, massacred the Supreme Court justices. In Peru, the Shining Path, a movement with Maoist leanings, begun in 1980 in Ayacucho, was making progress. In 1982 the government decided to re-establish the state of emergency in seven provinces.[67] In 1984, the revolutionary group Tupac Amaru, named

---

[63] H. McLaughlin, *Letters to the Society*, p. 114.
[64] The War of the Malvinas (Falkland Islands) distressed the religious of Argentina and England whose provincials were friends, but it had no repercussions regarding the relationships between the two provinces.
[65] *Connections*, vol. 2, N° 1, 1992, p. 152. The article refers to a demonstration in 1987 in a place near the provincial house, organized after the death of young protestor.
[66] *Connections*, vol. 2, N° 1, 1992, p. 135.
[67] The capture in 1992 of its founder, Abimael Guzmán, and of its chief directors caused it to decline little by little. It had had an impact in the province

after a notable Inca whose insurrection was considered to have led Peru to independence, undertook its first actions in the southern part of the country.[68]

Steps toward liberation often began in ecclesial communities. The evolution of Oscar Romero, whose commitment to the Church of the poor led to his assassination by a death squad in 1980, was typical of a change that had led the hierarchy to distance itself from dictatorships. In Chile during the Pinochet years,

> Church groups were almost the only means of meeting and of training.... Together with instruction in the Bible and doctrine, people learned how to lead groups, to participate, to organize themselves, to choose their representatives and leaders. It was the only forum for speaking out with relative freedom. At the time of the Referendum of 1989 these groups formed a valuable contingent able to set up a national campaign network, first by making people aware that they could enroll on the electoral register (the old one had been burned by the dictators), and then by working to remove the fear of voting.[69]

Religious of the Sacred Heart participated in the protests during which religious, priests and lay people recited the Rosary and psalms and chanted freedom slogans. They supported fast days and days of prayer organized by the local Church; they contributed to caring for the wounded, whom one could not think of sending to hospitals; and they supported families during wakes and funerals. "In these hard times the Passion of Christ was truly re-enacted." At the time of the national Referendum, the base communities took charge of making sure the rights of voters were respected. "On the eve of [voting] day, all of us gathered in the chapel of the base community for a liturgy of sending. On the altar was the Chilean flag, a ballot box and ballots, flowers, the Paschal candle, the Bible and a broken chain." On voting day,

> The Lord had decided once more to listen to the cry of his people and free them. Those who had lived under repression for many years consoled the supporters of the regime that night; there were few of them, and they were frightened. The poor had only their Bible, their celebration song, the fraternal embrace of a people seeking freedom. After sixteen years, we had learned to say no: no to injustice, no to death, no to violence. Together with the base community we learned to value simple gestures.

---

of Cajamarca where base communities were organizing the population.
[68] It declined after 1996.
[69] Testimony Adela Guzmán, *Connections*, vol. 2, N° 1, 1992, p. 32.

Although poor, they were well organized, and we learned to discern from their perspective; we learned to be people in the midst of a People.[70]

In Uruguay after the end of the military dictatorship, a national commission sought to boycott an amnesty law aimed at ignoring crimes committed previously. The school run by the community in Paso Carrasco opened its doors to neighborhood association meetings intended to raise consciousness:

> It was obvious to us that we should take part given the extent of the impunity and the objectives of the organization.... Also we felt that we had to, out of fidelity to those we supported in prison and the hope that such violation of human rights should not happen again. These activities required that we would give time and space to this work and that we would talk about and reflect on what had happened.... All the RSCJ in Uruguay were keenly interested in the issue. Many took an active part. In 1988 the repeal of "law that prohibited the State from taking punitive measures" was not obtained.[71]

Central Africa was in the throes of troubles also, both before and after 1988. In Uganda after a few years of temporary improvement, the situation again became precarious. As a consequence of the volatility and insecurity, half the provincial assemblies had to be postponed between 1988 and 1994, because of a lack of fuel or the closing of the border with Kenya. The assembly that was to prepare for the Chapter of 1988 could not take place. Communications were difficult, and the telephone rarely worked.[72] In Kenya nepotism and tribal favoritism made trouble for the apostolate of religious who did not share their ethnicity.[73] Chad, impoverished by successive droughts, faced a new civil war in 1989, while the conflict with Libya, which had lasted since 1978, was coming to an end. War and difficult geographical conditions made this country, where those under twenty represented 51% of the population, one of the poorest in the world. Its wars had caused deaths and migrations and had weighed largely on women.

General Chapter of 1988: the Political Dimension

The theme initially planned for the Chapter of 1988 was "Our Apostolic Vocation."[74] Some provincial assemblies identified strongly with the witness

---

[70] *Connections*, vol. 2, N° 1, 1992, pp. 135-137.
[71] *Connections*, vol. 2, N° 1, 1992, pp. 151-152.
[72] Report to the General Chapter of 1994.
[73] Testimony of C. Flynn.
[74] Prov. Arch. France. Letter of H. McLaughlin to the provincials, 2 February 1987.

internationality could give that unity was possible among people and communities of very different nations or even of some in conflict with each other. But to opt in its favor was to desire that the voice of one's own country and culture be listened to and that "biases be avoided in apostolic projects of a global scale." The questions posed by the provincial chapters showed that the religious were concerned to embody apostolic life in the new economic and political circumstances:

> What new aspects does the need for inculturation give to our internationality? What challenges does our intercultural world throw out to us? What structures must we create for a dialogue among cultures, to approach the problems of our world: human rights, justice, peace, respect for creation, migration? What must be the role and the attitude of the Society in the different socio-economic and political systems?

But there was "marginalization, domination, colonialism even in our own Society," and some provincial chapters proposed that the Society use a common currency other than the dollar for international payments in favor of the Third World. Some continents were of the opinion that their voice was not sufficiently heard. Asia was one of them.[75]

Thanks to the dialogue carried out under the leadership of the international education commission, the Society of the Sacred Heart had become aware of the implications in the religious realm of the general conditions of the contemporary world. Some provinces living in different cultural worlds[76] felt that they had to think about "the necessity for some of ours to take a political position publicly in the context of our mission itself" and even suggested arriving at "a vital and prophetic synthesis between the compatible elements of Christian humanism and Marxist anthropology." Some wanted the Society to make a pronouncement against capitalism and the chapter to treat injustice in the world.[77] Canada, Egypt, Latin America and Europe evoked the preferential option for the poor: "Each time we meet and share about poverty and our service to the poor, we feel guilt, anguish and confusion. To be rich Christians in a world where

---

[75] Testimony of S. Iba, H. Okui and M. Braganza.

[76] England, Austria, Belgium, Brazil, Colombia, Korea, Puerto Rico/Cuba, France, India, Malta, Uganda/Kenya, Poland, United States, Venezuela, Zaïre.

[77] Belgium, Brazil, Spain, Holland, Ireland/Scotland, Japan, Philippines, PuertoRico/Cuba, United States, Venezuela, Zaïre. A nun from the United States, Anne Montgomery, spent several months in American prisons for her anti-nuclear activity. Involved in an ecumenical group of militant pacifists, Christian Peacemaker Teams, she participated at the time of the Gulf War in several actions in Iraq and the Middle East.

The Society of the Sacred Heart in the World of Its Times 1865-2000

many are poor is a constant challenge for us." Congruence among that option, religious life and the service of education had to be established.[78] Some provinces wondered "How can we continue to deepen our knowledge of the historical development of our peoples and participate in it? How can we penetrate further into popular piety and its values, and be evangelized by them?"

The discernment that Puerto Rico proposed at the beginning of the chapter was symbolic of the thinking at the time. Should we respond to the needs of the Third World by making a foundation in Santo Domingo or to those of the poor in our own country?[79] The situation of Chad was demonstrated by a map that showed the multiplicity of ethnic groups, the division between Muslims and Christians, the threat of war and drought. The United States described a discernment to decide whether we should take a public position in favor of Central American refugees and give them asylum, which would have meant embarking upon illegal action. The Philippines referred to "the popular revolution lived by the Religious of the Sacred Heart as an experience of faith and of *Cor unum*." For Françoise Cassiers, who had assisted at many general chapters, the atmosphere was new, and she felt during the chapter

> ...an explosion of life. We are free now of the looking inward on ourselves in 1982 when we had to define ourselves; now we can embrace the world. Each one gave the impression of bringing here the sufferings and hopes of a whole people. It seems that the work of the chapter will be to discover concretely how our very diverse cultures are ways to the Spirit and at the same time how the Gospel transcends all and leads them even into the Paschal mystery. Would that be the meaning of our internationality?[80]

On 18 July the delegates decided to treat the central theme of the chapter from the point of view of the charism and spirituality of the Sacred Heart, by looking at the political, ecclesial and financial implications for its ministry of education and to deepen above all the international dimension, since it was the result of each one's insertion in the world. The assembly determined to "start with the cries of the world." Some working groups were formed around sub-themes, the first of which concerned "the political

---

[78] "To make our way toward a simpler life style, to respond to needs that are not satisfied regarding education, to make a gradual exodus towards outlying and rural areas where marginalized people live."
[79] Chapter 88, News, 11 July, 2-4.
[80] Chapter 88, News, 11 July, 2-7.

implications of our commitments."[81] As Agota Baternay remarked, "This chapter can be qualified rightly as 'political.' Not only because of the intense study of the encyclical *Sollicitudo rei socialis*,[82] but because each of the sub-themes brought forward in a very concrete fashion the political dimensions of our life in mission."[83] But situations varied. Could one still speak of "the young" when "life for some young people [could] be characterized by a more or less elevated level of well-being already achieved (study, relaxation, travel...) while life for most of the others [was] a struggle to live a life with death close at hand?"[84] Consensus was difficult to attain in the working groups where sometimes fifteen nationalities, a dozen countries, and eight languages were represented, and where one tried to take into consideration the cultures, ideas, experiences and concerns of each of the participants.[85]

The reflection was "political" in the measure in which the theme, treated for the first time in the Society, was born of its apostolic life. As Father Ricardo Antoncich, who accompanied the chapter, pointed out afterwards, "The difference did not lie in whether or not we were with the poor, but in a contrasting perception of the causes of poverty." Among these were the "structures," the laws, the exercise of power and participation in decision-making. The final text of the chapter showed that politics led to a deepened understanding of the spirituality of the incarnation, which was vital for understanding the charism of the Society, and that the proclamation of the Kingdom and the ethical evaluation of political and socio-economic structures of the world could not be separated.[86] One of the acts of the chapter was given over to inculturation,[87] an important question for Asia and Africa, whose cultures were little known in the West. But thanks to the religious from India, the chapter had become aware that it was important in a theological perspective.[88] Openness to the world had led the Religious of the Sacred Heart little by little to identify

---

[81] The others treated young people, women, the world of migrants, the poor and oppressed, inculturation.
[82] It had been sent out six months before the general chapter.
[83] Chapter of 1994, opening conference.
[84] Chapter 88, pp. 5-6.
[85] Chapter 88, News. Testimony of Lita Walker and Marguerite de Thélin.
[86] "A Chapter for Mission," p. 10.
[87] Father Antoncich, in Chapter 88, p. 23, notes that it was the text most laboriously worked over.
[88] Acts, p. 1. When one wished to proclaim starting from faith in Jesus the love of God that extends to all humanity, was it necessary to place the accent on the incarnation by using a Christian perspective or on creation and then begin a dialogue with the other religions?

themselves with local cultures. From a "transculturation" that appeared as a form of colonization they moved onward to "liberating inculturation."

The same goal, conversion, appeared regarding migrants, a concern of the European provinces, where their numbers were increasing and whose poor the religious were meeting. The final text proposed a reflection on the kinds of relationships to form with migrants. But it also called for an examination of racist attitudes, past or present, in the congregation itself: "Society, history, theology have been addressed from the 'center' of Western culture. It is important to contrast this perspective with others from its outer edge." On the eve of celebrating the fifth centenary of "the discovery of America," a notion that caused a stir among the Latin Americans, Father Antoncich suggested that "People born in America continue to think with a European mentality and consider that their history begins with the 'discovery' of those who arrived there, as if all the earlier life and culture were of no importance."[89] So it was surely independence from European culture that non-European provinces wanted when they asked that their style of religious life be taken into account.[90]

The theme of women was introduced by the United States, England, Australia/New Zealand, Brazil, Venezuela and Zaïre. Although the Society had always been interested in the lot of women, it was coming to the realization that women's conditions of life were imposed by the culture and the social, economic and political structures of their countries.[91] The final text denounced the marginalization of which women are often victims. A course of action called for "working for the promotion of women through every educational method, formal or informal, to ensure that all our educative work enables women to take their rightful place," without naming civil life or ecclesial life that the delegates saw as a place where the status of women was little recognized.[92]

While every general chapter is marked by the calls of the Church, that of 1988 was particularly attuned to the teachings of the Holy See after Vatican II. It coupled them to the new expression of the charism in 1982, saying in the introduction: "We let the world set our agenda."[93] It also referred to the "real faces of young people, of the poor, of migrants, of women, all those who in many cultures live in conditions of inequality, even

---

[89] Chapter 88, p. 18.
[90] H. Okui notes that the formation given in Japan was considered insufficiently respectful of Asian values. Afterwards, *Connections* ("Inculturation," vol. 3, 1993) published the reflections of religious from Uganda, Kenya and Egypt on this question.
[91] Chapter 88, p. 20.
[92] Chapter 88, pp. 22 and 19.
[93] Chapter 88, p. 1.

of oppression." (The introduction worded it as "to have been woven on the loom of the world.") Afterwards the Society of the Sacred Heart shared the experiences of its members and an analysis of those experiences through a publication entitled *Connections*. The three volumes, which appeared in 1991, 1992 and 1993, were devoted respectively to *The World of Migrant Peoples*, *Politics Behind the Utopia* and *Inculturation: Not One Way*. They aimed at giving Religious of the Sacred Heart "a planetary consciousness."

The Collapse of Bipolarity

A year after the chapter a new world order came in to being. The unexpected end of the Cold War brought about in Eastern Europe a "return of the nations." Many thought that there was "no leadership in the so-called ruling nations of the world."[94] People were not yet aware that a superpower, one alone, had surely appeared. In a few months the world had become different. The disappearance of the USSR brought about the rise of neo-liberal economies, and misery was just as widespread as it had been in the poorest countries, in particular in Sub-Saharan Africa. In 1988 the delegates had prepared a text on young people. They had reflected on those who were confronted with drugs, violence, homelessness, maltreatment, abandonment, HIV-AIDS and crime in all its forms: "Children for whom all that we experienced as children is foreign, children different from those with whom we have worked in the past" and who "were already running disturbing risks."[95] But in the following years the world learned that the police were killing them in the streets at night in several Latin American countries, that

> children of eleven years of age in violent Washington were preparing for their own burials. Children were running around picking up landmines that looked like toys, planted in their school yards by guerrillas. We know the violence of the Skin Heads and the resurgence of neo-fascism. But who had foreseen the "ethnic cleansing" of former Yugoslavia or of Rwanda?

Who would have imagined that children would be enrolled in regular armies in Africa and elsewhere? The migrants of 1988 came from Third World countries: "Who could imagine that a year after the general chapter the new world wave of refugees and migrants would be coming from Eastern

---

[94] Report of the General Council 1988-1994.
[95] Marilyn McMorrow, "The Change of Structure of the International System," p. 1. Presentation to the General Chapter of 1994.

Europe?"[96] In the summer of 1989, the opening of borders between the popular democracies was a sign that a thaw was in progress. East Germans moved to the West with tourist visas by crossing through Hungary and Austria. The suppression of travel restrictions for those coming from the German Democratic Republic brought with it, in November 1989, a rush toward the Federal Republic of Germany, Austria and Czechoslovakia.

After the fall of communism, life changed in Eastern Europe. In 1988 the Polish delegates had said what it meant to them to freely elect a superior general when they had no experience of free elections in their country. They had it from then on. Some "new" countries like Russia, Ukraine and the Baltic countries had become Poland's neighbors. Divided Germany was beginning to think of a possible reunification. Jean Ford was in Germany when the Wall fell: "I had a very moving experience then," she recounted. "With Margret Fühles, the provincial, I went to Berlin on the first plane from the Federal Republic that was permitted to land. Her excitement and emotion touched my heart." At the same moment, Marie-Guyonne du Penhoat was in the Netherlands and remembers the sentiments experienced by herself and those around her: "Astonishment, great joy and uncertainty about the immediate and far-reaching consequences" of the event. Shortly afterward a day spent in Budapest allowed her to witness "the creative dynamism of the Hungarian nuns who were rediscovering their country in the rebuilding around newfound liberty."

Some returns or new insertions proved to be possible in countries to which access had been forbidden for a long time. In September 1989 Mother McLaughlin and Hannelore Woitsch went to Budapest on the occasion of the centenary of the *Sophianum*. Discussions held with the local episcopate had to do with the eventual restitution of confiscated institutions:

> The bishops thought that we should ask for the restitution of at least one of the properties. Our alumnae in Budapest were strongly of the opinion that we ought to reclaim our property and reopen a school. But the age of our Hungarian religious and other factors made such a decision inadvisable. We reclaimed the *Sophianum* but left the use of the school for ten more years to the Piarist Fathers who had been running it for several years. We took steps to obtain some compensation in exchange for the *Philippineum*.[97]

The Society of the Sacred Heart presented to the Hungarian government a request for official recognition, which was granted in January 1990. That

---

[96] M. McMorrow, p. 2.
[97] Report of the General Council 1988-1994, p. 20.

same month a community was opened in Budapest with three religious. Several Hungarian candidates had asked to enter the Sacred Heart; consequently a novitiate was established in Budapest in April 1992.

From 1990 on a few Religious of the Sacred Heart lived in Moscow. It was an unheard of situation, since the Society had never succeeded in settling in Russia in spite of Mother Digby's desire to do so. The first, Maria Stecka, obtained a work permit to teach young Poles who were living in the capital. She was joined by religious from Poland and England. To go to a country slowly coming out of an atheism that devastated the national church and that was finding again its cultural and orthodox religious roots could look like a very unecumenical takeover. For the general council, it was not a question of "going to convert Russia" but rather "to assist where necessary in training personnel and to collaborate with groups already present, including a Catholic university" that had just been founded. The Moscow community was attached to the Province of Poland, but the general council was responsible to supply the personnel.[98] Marie-Guyonne du Penhoat, who went to Moscow three times in less than two years, realized that rapid changes were taking place: "Freedom would create the poor or more likely would create the rich and differences of social class."

Some dictatorships had their backs to the wall, for Perestroïka had destabilized single party systems. In Zaïre, on 24 April 1990, President Mobutu promised a multiparty system and democracy after a brief transition. But a few weeks later the single party was reestablished under pressure of the regime's privileged class: "Very quickly our illusions fell," admitted the nuns. "Little by little corruption destroyed the élan of the sovereign national conference, which only reopened at the price of a peaceful march by Christians. A group, called Amos, tried to educate people in evangelical non-violence."[99] The people tried above all to assure its survival. The visit to Congo carried out after 1994 figures among Marta Jiménez's significant memories: "These were dramatic moments for the people and for our sisters. To be sent to be with them, to bring the affection, solidarity and support of the whole Society was unforgettable for me."

Manuela Valle had returned to Santiago de Cuba in 1970 with a residence permit for family reasons; she had been active in a parish and on a diocesan catechetical commission. Two years later she was joined by Raquel Pérez. They lived isolated from the rest of the Society in a country suffering from malnutrition, where milk was reserved for infants and old people.

---

[98] Report of the General Council 1988-1994, p. 24.
[99] C. Meeûs, p. 32. The Religious of the Sacred Heart participated in a peaceful march on 16 February 1992.

The Society of the Sacred Heart in the World of Its Times 1865 -2000

When religious activity was restricted, "It took a great deal of courage to dare to place a religious object where everyone could see it. However, sometimes we noticed images of the Sacred Heart and of Mary through the shutters of houses."[100] The Canadian provincial took the documents of the Chapter of 1976 to them in August 1977. An Argentinian, Florence de la Serna, joined them in 1979, and in 1980 Mother Camacho was able to visit them. The community was gradually reinforced by the arrival of Cubans returning from exile. A second community was established in Havana and a novitiate opened at Catalina de Güines in September 1990. Marie-Guyonne du Penhoat discovered in Cuba "a climate to dream about, magnificent countryside," "a country that suffered from real poverty but a country not contaminated or polluted by consumer society."

Politics and the Society of the Sacred Heart

The Chapter of 1994 bore witness to "the situation of a world shaken by profound change" and took note of "the forces of life and of death always present with their continual uncertainty."[101] For the first time a general chapter took place outside the country where the motherhouse was located. Canada welcomed it at Aylmer, near Ottawa. It was prepared according to a plan founded on the Gospel of Luke. As the Risen Christ had the two disciples whom he approached recount the events they had just lived through, the meaning of which they had not grasped, communities and provinces had to journey through their own "road to Emmaus," to remember experiences that had left their mark on them, to weigh their discouragement and disillusion in the face of a difficult or hostile situation and to explore where to direct their energies.[102] Some provinces

---

[100] F. Makower, p. 17. In the tiny house where they were living they kept the Blessed Sacrament hidden behind a picture of the Sacred Heart. The correspondence sent through different channels took more than three months to arrive to and from Rome. They knew nothing about the Chapter of 1976 until it was opened. Then they received a letter from Mother Camacho promising to send all the preparatory documents and asking them to send a report on their experience.

[101] General Chapter 1994, p. 1.

[102] After receiving the "Road to Emmaus" from all the provinces, districts and areas, the religious were to contact another province to ask after reading what had made their hearts burn, what lines of action of that province challenged their life, what they perceived of the reality of the world situation, what were the sentiments of Jesus that responded to the cries of the world thus heard and what were the underlying values of this communication (Letter from the Preparatory Commission of the Chapter, 3 March 1994).

were creative. Ireland/Scotland made a mandala. Australia/New Zealand brought out the difficulties of a province where the life of the religious was complicated by distances, individualism and the fear of not being understood:

> As they walked and discussed together
> Jesus himself came up and walked along with them
> by the pools of silence....
> And he showed them how to see in all their experience,
> and in the calls of the world,
> all those things that are of concern to himself.
> For he had been homeless and they had received him.
> He was in the Dreamtime reverence of their Aboriginal people
> and in the sacred covenanting of the Maori,
> and they found him at the still heart of the turning worlds.
> Women, choosing to include and empower one another,
> had known his Spirit in the wine of the *kairos*,
> that Spirit at work in and through all the cultures of their countries....
> He showed them their place in the sweep of the ages,
> and the star stuff at the heart of all things.[103]

In Mexico/Nicaragua, it was Mother Barat who approached two religious while Philippine Duchesne was visiting the community that remained in "Jerusalem!"

> "We dreamt that we were going to change the world," the two disciples said to her, "to create just and fraternal structures, to build political and economic relationships that would construct equality. We worked side by side with many others and with great hope coming from the new winds of Vatican II, Medellín's fire, and the prophetic vision of the Chapter of 1970 and the confirmation of Puebla. We lived years of idealism and creativity, years of risky search for new ways of living apostolic community...." Sophie exclaimed: "What a deep experience! And now?" "When we thought our dream was going to come true, our world, our story, our hopes were all shattered. The year '90 was very hard for us: the Sandinista project, for the promotion of the Nicaraguan people, was brutally arrested. In Mexico, a government project that would be the death of the people was built up. Have you heard about 'neoliberalism,' Sophie? It is too hard for us to understand it, but in Latin America as a whole we are suffering from it — a devastating effect. Previously,

---

[103] *Our Road to Emmaus*, p. 7. The text was illustrated with boomerangs.

there were poor and marginalized people. Now they are really excluded, rejected, just a nuisance, it doesn't matter that they die if that helps the rich and the powerful." Sophie questioned them on their relation to the Church: "After Vatican II we felt joy in realizing that we are the Church, it isn't only the pope, the bishops and the priests, all of us, the People of God. It's sometimes difficult to accept that the power structures are so strong that they don't leave space for the Spirit. Love is the Gospel criterion by which we recognize Jesus' disciples. This is what you taught us above all, you wrote it in the Constitutions. But sometimes there are conflicts because some of our bishops have other priorities. In all this the church as People nourishes our hope. Among them there are prophets and martyrs, communities that struggle. That is why we sing gladly:

"Simple Church, seed of the Kingdom,
Beautiful Church, heart of the people."[104]

The first document of the chapter was "Our Response as Society to a World in Profound Transition." Confronting the vision that had been identified in 1988 and the events that took place afterward, it took note of the collapse of communism, the end of apartheid in South Africa, the destruction of some nuclear arms that had begun after agreements signed by the United States and the USSR, but also the rapid development of communications technology, the resurgence of pacifism and nationalism, ethnic cleansing, the spread of neoliberalism and the strengthening of religious fundamentalism: "We have hardly begun to comprehend the implications of these transformations. The stripping away of familiar international structures and landmarks, along with the ideologies that sustained them, has left us alternately elated or despairing, and often without a compass."[105] Faced with a world that was becoming unfathomable but in which individuals and groups were seeking to build a new civil society and an authentic democracy, the chapter wished to "rekindle our hope and keep it alive," while trying to go to the roots of inequality and the negation of liberty. Religious of the Sacred Heart were to "be there with the poorest

---

[104] *Our Road to Emmaus*, pp. 81-82. The province had undergone some repercussions from the policy set in motion by the Vatican. Formation institutes where young religious were studying, the Jesuits' institute of philosophy and the institute of theology of Mexico, had been closed. The province was not able to open a house in the State of Oaxaca, ranked third among the poorest states. The bishop of León, where the novitiate was established, showed some lack of trust in the Society.

[105] Acts, pp. 6-7.

and the marginalized and be evangelized by them."[106] Living the prophetic role of religious life in building the Kingdom of God, they were invited

> ...to recognize and foster in the human rights movement the biblical call to protect the bruised reed, to care for the widow and the orphan, the homeless beggar at the gate...in the work of small and large social movements, within and beyond borders, the multiplication of the loaves and the talents,...in the ecological movement the gospel call to be faithful stewards of all that has been entrusted to us.

They had to question themselves also on their part in collective sin: "What is our own role in new efforts among our peoples to rectify corruption by acting honestly and justly in daily life? When the political and economic solutions or ideologies to which we have given allegiance have failed to accomplish their purposes, can we find the courage to recognize the fact?" Strategies were proposed to answer the call of Africa. Besides a means and methodology by which the members of the Society could deepen "their understanding of critical issues of justice and peace," the chapter proposed to link the Society at the international level to groups working for justice and peace.[107] The text concluded with two pages of notes that defined notions that, until then, had hardly ever appeared in the acts of general chapters, such as absolute poverty, external debt, or structural adjustment policies.

The contemplative outlook on the world linked henceforth macro- and micro-economies, macro- and micro-histories and encouraged alternative policies. The new global or regional conditions had not eliminated wars or social conflict. In "our deeply wounded and divided world where change is rapid and far reaching" the Religious of the Sacred Heart were called "to nurture life by educating to reconciliation"[108] and to be "women of communion, women of compassion, women of reconciliation." This call, which was to be lived in every circumstance and every undertaking, gave new strength to the educational direction identified at the time of the Mexican assembly and articulated it further. It required acting in respect, truth and the search for justice:

> Respect demands welcoming the richness of differences:

---

[106] Acts, pp. 8-9. "The constant effort of our inserted communities to discover with their people more human ways of living is as essential as action for justice at an international level."
[107] Acts, p. 12.
[108] Acts, p. 16. Title of one of the chapter documents.

- letting ourselves be challenged by the values of other cultures;
- accepting the call to change our stereotypical attitudes, our inferiority and superiority complexes towards other persons and different mentalities.

Truth requires:
- confronting conflicts and sufferings without negating them;
- going to the roots of issues, believing in the capacity of persons to search for just solutions and to forgive.

The search for justice requires:
- looking at the world through the eyes and feelings of those who suffer any kind of poverty or marginalization;
- being aware that there are structures that oppress and destroy humanity;
- growing in sensitivity to the suffering of those who have neither voice nor power;
- educating to a deeper commitment to justice.

The search for reconciliation and peace calls us:
- to develop methodologies based on non-violence;
- to foster relationships where there is participation and reciprocity.

For this to be possible we need to create spaces that give welcome, to be in solidarity with persons so they can live,
- value the meaning of life,
- discover their own worth and
- be open to the gift of faith.

This course of action was to be followed in openness and vulnerability, in collaboration with others, "our sisters and brothers of every age, race, creed and social condition" from whom we must learn but also with whom "we wish to share the richness of our charism and the educative intuition of Madeleine Sophie handed down through history and lived today in greater internationality."[109] A new way of envisioning relations with lay people was beginning to emerge.

Refocusing Regarding Government

From a Central Team to General Council

After 1982 there were changes affecting governanc%oe that were not necessarily desired. In their report in 1988, Mother McLaughlin and those

---
[109] Acts, pp. 18-19.

who governed with her referred to their life and work as "team-council." This new expression indicated a change from the preceding structure. For the Vatican Congregation for Consecrated Life the term "team" left room for various interpretations, with an emphasis on solidarity, while "council" makes clear who is ultimately responsible. The consulters had also thought that the Society of the Sacred Heart was insisting on the role of the team even though the superior general chose her councilors. But the semantic change was not to mean "loss of the content, which is essential to the spirit of government of the Society at every level. We can say that we have looked at the way we serve in a constant effort to live and work as a discerning community." Councilors' testimony shows that work as a team truly took place during the successive generalates and created lasting bonds among its members.[110]

The mission of the councilors was reviewed in the sense of a sharing of responsibilities, by geographic regions and by duties. This division, which should not "diminish the quality of discernment and of co-responsibility" and which provided material for regular accounting was created in the interest of efficiency. It made for continuity and allowed for more direct contact between the provinces and the central government.[111] After 1988 a "link" was established between the motherhouse and the provinces[112] through charging each councilor to be in contact with a group of provinces. To be a link, Maryvonne Keraly thinks, is to be "what the Christian communities said of Barnabas, a servant of encouragement." But the general council refused a division into regions that could have led to a "subtle form of decentralization."[113] Links with the general treasury, the probation, the general secretariat and the community of the motherhouse were also provided by the general councilors. The administrative work was facilitated by the transfer of the motherhouse from Via Adolfo Gandiglio

---

[110] Testimony of M. Keraly. "The general council was really a team, with what that represented of difficulties and richness. I had been used to working on a team, but when one meets with different nationalities, the challenges and difficulties are greater; and I believe that, while maintaining our differences, the team to which I had the joy of belonging had its cohesion, and the fruit that we gathered, once our term was over, is great friendship among us." Ursula Bugembe summarized it thus: "We were very different, but we valued the gifts that each one had and that she brought to the team."

[111] Gen. Arch. C I C 3, XXXI, Report of the General Council 1982-1988, pp. 5-6.

[112] She followed the business to be handled and provided continuity between visits. The councilor "link" kept in touch as far as possible with political, economic and social events that could have immediate repercussions on the life of the nuns (Report of the General Council 1988-1994, p. 7).

[113] Report of the General Council 1988-1994, p. 7.

to Via Tarquinio Vipera, a little nearer to the center of Rome. To move from a collection of three apartments in two large buildings and two small houses to a single house called for reorganization[114] but consolidated operations. In 1988 the various communities regrouped as a whole. Prayer together for the international Society continued daily.[115]

Development of Administrative Structures and New Foundations

At the beginning of the nineties, the general council created areas "to set up a governmental structure suitable for small numbers of religious."[116] It was in response to problems arising from geographic distance from the center of the province, from the absence or frequent interruption of ordinary means of communication and from the need to make decisions on the spot by reason of government instability or restrictions.[117] Each area had a superior named by the general council after consultation with the religious. Her authority was delegated by the superior general, and she served with a council.

Korea was a separate district after 1976,[118] and this juridical situation had been confirmed in 1982. Malta, which had been an area, and the Philippines became districts in January 1984 and January 1987 respectively. In January 1990 the general council approved the decision by common agreement of Japan and Taiwan to separate; they were the last of the four countries that had constituted the Province of the Far East. Taiwan became an autonomous area. On 7 June 1991, Korea became a province. Chad[119] and Cuba became areas. In the Netherlands the religious considered becoming part of another province or having a non-resident major

---

[114] Testimony of M. Fabre.
[115] Before 1982, it was prepared in turn by each of the communities. Then it was decided that it would be silent: "We worked and prayed for the international Society" (Testimony of H. McLaughlin). Report of the General Council 1994-2000, p. 5: "That symbolizes our mission at the service of the international community."
[116] Statute of the Area, November 2000. Article § 581 of Canon Law provides that "the division of an institute into parts, whatever the name, to erect new ones and to join parts erected earlier, or to define them in another manner belongs to the competent authority in the institute in accordance with the norm of the constitutions" (communicated by C. Pratt).
[117] Report of the General Council 1988-1994, p. 18.
[118] Testimony of S. Iba who prepared for the separation of Korea for three years so that there could be agreement about it. The communities of the province that were hostile to the separation at the beginning accepted it afterwards.
[119] A third community was opened in 1992.

superior. They leaned toward the second solution, which was ratified *ad experimentum* by the general council.[120]

Proposals for foundations continued to be made to the Society of the Sacred Heart. In February 1989, following a request from the bishop of the capital of Indonesia, Anne O'Neil, from the United States, went to Jakarta to teach at Atma Jaya University. For while religious were not allowed to enter the country as religious, they could obtain work permits for jobs that could not be fulfilled by Indonesians. An international community formed slowly, living with the Ursuline nuns during its first year, then moving close to the university, where the role of Chizuyo Inoue contributed to creating a Japanese section. English courses for teachers from a social institute directed by the Jesuits and a contact with groups of street children allowed for work among the poor and opened the door to other types of apostolate.[121]

As the "Stroessner years" were coming to an end, two nuns from Brazil, Odette Mattos and Pilar Repullés, and Margot Bremer from the Province of Argentina/Uruguay, began a new community in Asunción, Paraguay, in 1988. Reinforced by Maria Luiza Saade, it was attached at first to Brazil. As this province by reason of its own personnel needs could not support those in Paraguay, the community was finally linked to the Province of Argentina/Uruguay.[122] Supported by Puerto Rico, Mexico/Nicaragua, the United States and Canada, a foundation was made in Haiti in January 2000. The project, joined by Cuba, was set in motion by the provincial of Puerto Rico who had the responsibility for coordination and final decisions.

Communication in the Society

Promotion and intensification of communication in the Society were presented by the Chapter of 1994 as aspects of international co-responsibility. During the last twenty years of the century communication was carried out both by classic means and by new technologies.

---

[120] Solange Teisserenc, who had been provincial in France, took on this service. Report of 1988-1994, p. 19: "She remains a member of her own province and carries out her apostolic activity there. At the same time she has the ultimate responsibility in all that concerns the Province of Netherlands and provides the link with the central government. She visits the province three or four times a year and works with a council of three members including the treasurer, the superior of the retreat house and a sister living in The Hague."

[121] Report…, p. 23. A novitiate was established on 21 November 1999, in Jakarta.

[122] Odette Karmy from Chile and Lastenia Fernández Maldonado from Peru were sent there.

Visits

Visits to the provinces remained a key aspect of government. Mother McLaughlin, who felt that the primary objective of her mandate was to explain the Constitutions and to calm anxieties,[123] decided to visit the entire Society within three years and to close each of these visits with a continent-wide meeting with the provincials.[124] As before, these visits, held with communities in their own settings, were to allow the general council to observe different life styles and to be better able to answer the criticisms of the changes that were being transmitted to the Congregation for Religious Life. They were also a means of keeping the Society united. After 1988, the councilor specially charged with a province always participated in the visit.[125] Mother García de Quevedo decided to pay special attention to Asia since there was no one from Asia on her council. Council members planned travel to the Far East and India; these visits forestalled oversensitiveness and put aside regrets at not having a representative on the general council.[126] Each province and each district was visited several times.

In 2000 the general council turned to the various concerns that came up during the visits. They intensified "the awareness of the whole body. They offered the opportunity to get some distance, to see beyond provincial horizons, of reflecting on the local situation in an international context and to welcome questions." Costly in time, energy and money, they were "the means to greater understanding of the mission of the Society," but they required careful preparation. The council noted, "Sometimes we regretted not having more contacts with people other than the Religious of the Sacred Heart, which would have allowed us to place the province in context of the church and the country." The visits helped them to grasp the geographic, social, political and ecclesiastical milieu of the provinces, and

---

[123] Testimony of H. McLaughlin.
[124] Report of the General Council 1982-1988, p. 17. They took place in Argentina, in Joigny, in Nairobi, in Saint Louis and in Taiwan.
[125] They were carried out by groups of two, the whole council meeting to participate in the meeting by continent with the provincial councils. Beginning in 1986, visits by a single council member were more numerous than before. During her second mandate Mother McLaughlin finally gave up visits by continent.
[126] In October and November 1995, Marta Jiménez visited Korea and Japan which, during the first trimester of 1996, received the visit of Patricia García de Quevedo, Mary Hinde and Maryvonne Keraly. Patricia García de Quevedo and Mary Hinde also visited the Philippines. In November 1996, Ursula Bugembe went to India. As Mother García de Quevedo noted, "In the end they were happy!"

one could discover when on the spot the influences at work on people and their ways of thinking.[127]

They were "moments when we thank God for the great things God has done and does in the life of the people of God and in the members of the Society. There are moments when we are challenged and humbled by the generosity of so many of our sisters. We get to know the Society in its best and sometimes also in its most fragile and sinful aspect. We are a part of all of this and we come as sisters to support and encourage."[128]

Facilitated by the democratization of air travel, visits increased after 1982. But their purpose was not really understood either within or outside the Society. Jean Ford wrote about this:

> When someone objected to the considerable amount of time we spent traveling, I always answered that the visits were indispensable so that we could have firsthand experience if we wished to be capable of situating ourselves, even briefly, in the context of the life of the members of the province. That did not necessarily mean that we always made the best decision, but that gave us the necessary context for the decision we had to make.

Members of the Roman Curia believed that a congregation ought to be governed from the motherhouse. Mother McLaughlin had to make them understand that the visits provided knowledge of how life was really being lived in the provinces.[129] Thanks to the visits the members of the council learned of the relationship slowly being established between "internationality and inculturation. That was already felt in our work: the way of conducting meetings, languages, thought processes, attitudes towards the law. Their preparation and their organization helped me," wrote Hannelore Woitsch, "not to be seen as a 'visitor.' Thanks to these visits the Society has always remained for me a concretely international community, composed of a great number of known persons, living in countries and situations that touched my life." Jean Ford noted,

> What surprised me is that the welcome was the same everywhere, and I had the experience of feeling at home everywhere. In spite of feelings that United States policies could inspire, I was welcomed everywhere as a Religious of the Sacred Heart and not as an ugly American. Even our

---

[127] Testimony of M. Keraly.
[128] Report of the General Council 1988-1994, p. 20.
[129] H. McLaughlin, F. Tamayo and H. Woitsch, *Process of Approbation...*, p. 31.

Latin American sisters came to make a distinction between us and the United States.

She was in the North of Spain when the war in Kuwait broke out, in the South of the country when the presence of an American base near two Sacred Heart communities caused much distress: "Our nuns and, I suppose, many Spanish people were totally opposed to our presence in that place. Who would not have been?"

"When I was visiting the provinces," recounts Maryvonne Keraly, "I was sometimes asked 'What strikes you when you visit the country?' I responded with the title of a book by Father Varillon, *The Beauty of the World and the Suffering of Humanity*. That is what I retain of the visits to countries where the Society is present. I have had the opportunity of seeing landscapes of stupefying beauty: the world is beautiful! And at the same time of encountering the people's suffering. But what I added, which is not in the title of Varillon's book, is that I always saw groups and individuals rising up so that things changed, sometimes in an extremely modest manner. There was a will among them that things change." Marie-Guyonne du Penhoat was sensitive also to the contrast between misery and opulence perceived during a visit to Asia: "I traveled from India to Japan on the same day in 1991; from a country where life hardly counts at all, to a country where safety measures are an absolute. On the same day I passed by corpses on the pavement and workmen armed with helmets, masks and gloves while working on a building in Tokyo." Marta Jiménez characterized her experience of that time thus:

> I received a great deal and I lived it as a gift, as an unexpected and enriching surprise for my vocation as a Religious of the Sacred Heart and a world citizen. I have a living memory of many free and intimate meetings with people. I cannot forget it, for from each one I received and learned so much about her life given over to the mission of the Society. In many countries I had the opportunity of touching the suffering of the people, of street children, of women. Their faces remain with me; they live in me. These places where it was given me to tread are a holy land that now accompanies my life.

Visits to the provinces seemed so important to the members of the general council that Mother McLaughlin suggested that the treasurer general also visit.

Relations between the Provinces and the Motherhouse

The style of government established in 1967 also accounted for the importance that Rome placed on the visits. Since the creation of provinces, much was carried on at that level, and the superior general had relatively little to decide.[130] Under those conditions the nomination of provincials was one of the most important acts of government. With these nominations in mind, some provinces set up a consultation in several stages. The general council also visited a province during the consultation.[131] But because of the number of provinces and the length of the term of the provincial, this process recurred often. Hannelore Woitsch has remembered it as a "shared and authentic search based on the needs of the province concerned, of people's abilities, and finally what appeared to us to correspond best to the will of God. In most cases we were able to arrive at a consensus, even if we started from different points of view." For Jean Ford the time spent by the council on these nominations and the care given to them were considerable: "Once we invited two people to Rome to discern with them. Another time when I was visiting a province with Helen, we discerned with two people to learn whether one or the other of them wanted to be provincial. It took time and patience to come to a final decision."

The general council had to approve provincial government plans. Some provinces had to be encouraged to draft or revise theirs.[132] The new style of governance placed importance on regional or international meetings and in particular on assemblies of provincials.

> At the time, one or two provinces would have seen the move to a certain federalism in the Society as a good thing. There was a real risk of seeing the central government lose all authority, the superior general being just a sister from whom one expects only interest and friendship, without for example any right to question and challenge. With decentralization and the desire to give value to the different languages and cultures, this risk was

---

[130] Testimony of M-G. du Penhoat. The consultors of the Congregation for religious life thought that the provinces enjoyed exaggerated powers, that the dealings of the provinces with the motherhouse were seen through the lens of equality and that communication was carried out with an attitude of dialogue (H. McLaughlin, F. Tamayo and H. Woitsch, p. 15).

[131] Report of the General Council 1988-1994, p. 40.

[132] Testimony of H. Woitsch. Report of the General Council 1982-1988, p. 44: The plans did not result in a juridical enumeration of details of government but had "most often grasped the spirit and the needs of the province at a specific moment of its life." Between 1989 and 1994, the general council approved a dozen of them (Report of the General Council 1988-1994, p. 21).

not negligible. It was a challenge to assure that provinces and provincials take responsibility while allowing the central government to work to maintain the Society in its unity, which is a fundamental characteristic for us. In connection with that question we have emphasized this slogan of Father Carrier, which has been criticized by some: "To govern is to communicate and allow others to communicate among themselves."[133]

In 1983 Mother McLaughlin decided to bring the new provincials together, as is done in the Society of Jesus, to allow them to have contact with others who were also beginning their term of office. These meetings let them get to know the members of the general council, the community, the activities and services of the motherhouse, to learn the responsibilities of the treasurer and secretary general directly from them, to discuss the problems of their provinces, to meet the general archivist and to pray together. These meetings took place every two years and yielded a blend of information sharing, theoretical presentations and reflection.[134]

Halfway through its term during an assembly of provincials, the general council gave an account of its service and asked for communication from the Society. That meeting, which took place in Japan in 1991, marked a new stage in the way of developing this kind of gathering. It was the first time that a meeting at which the whole Society was represented was held in Asia. The participants were encouraged to visit another Asian country beforehand. They had an immersion experience in the city of Tokyo before the assembly that allowed them to understand internationality better, which was one of the objectives of the meeting. This assembly reinforced "the sense of community among the provincials."[135] It opened up a new understanding of internationality as "good news" and generated enthusiasm to respond to the appeals coming from different parts of the world. The one held in Chile in October 1997 was the occasion of celebrating the length of time the Society had been in South America and Anna du Rousier's role in the foundation in Chile. The general council wanted to choose the theme of the forthcoming chapter together with all

---

[133] Testimony of M-G. du Penhoat.
[134] Report of the General Council 1988-1994, p. 13: "In the course of a general meeting we were treating of the importance of finding appropriate means for each one not to go beyond her strength in her work."
[135] Report of the General Council 1988-1994, p. 39: "The provincials took the responsibility of continuing to build this community by relationships based on open, sincere exchange and on the effort made to understand differences without being content simply to accept them. Their efforts have at the same time deepened and extended the understanding of community in the Society and shown new pathways to collaborate in the future."

the provincials, as had been the case before, more or less.[136] Each provincial had to present the priorities of her province for the mission by means of three slides. Because the presence of religious among young people and the educational dimension of their commitments appeared clearly,[137] the theme of education was self-evident.[138] The general council made "Our educational mission a pathway to discover, a space to announce the love of the Heart of Jesus" and of "apostolic community, which brings us together and sends us to a common mission," two of the priorities of the second half of its term.[139]

During the generalate of Mother García de Quevedo meetings of "priority areas" were added to the meetings of new provincials and provincials and provincial councils, In July 1996 a forum on Europe and migrations took place in Budapest. The heads of European Sacred Heart schools met in Amiens in July 1998 and those of the whole Society in Joigny in April 2000. The general council encouraged the three workshops on reconciliation that were held in 1998 in Austria, France and Spain. Sixteen Religious of the Sacred Heart participated in the Fourth World Conference on Women in Beijing in 1995.

Other Modes of Communication

At the beginning of the eighties there was an international commission in Rome in charge of communications. One of its members participated in the continental meetings that the motherhouse organized, so that the members of the Society could learn about them.[140] During her second term Mother McLaughlin sent her letters to communities via cassette recordings. She thought that these would be more easily used by the elderly.

At the end of the century communication was enriched, thanks to electronic mail. The internet was in its first stages in the Society of the Sacred Heart. While the United States had a provincial website and a site for the Network of Schools was being planned, there was no general site for the Society. Through experience, it was determined that e-mail was really useful in provinces where access was difficult by ordinary means

---

[136] Testimony of P. García de Quevedo.
[137] Report of the General Council 1988-1994, p. 25.
[138] Testimony of M. Keraly. It was a great joy for the general council who desired it.
[139] Report of the General Council 1994-2000, p. 25.
[140] Testimony of H. McLaughlin. In order to present the context of certain of the questions brought up, she was able to have interviews with the provincials.

of communication,[141] in particular in Africa.[142] But it required everyone's discernment to avoid being submerged by messages, to keep some distance and reflection, so as not to succumb to the temptation to material over- consumption.[143]

The general council wished to encourage "horizontal communication," that is to say, exchanges from province to province, from person to person. The results were limited because some provinces were more isolated than others, or they used minority languages, or had few means of communication or geographic distances were such that it was difficult for them to meet other provinces.[144] To make internationality good news could be realized also by solidarity, interdependence and the exchange of services. Sharing personnel and resources was one way. Between 1994 and 2000 forty-eight religious were sent to serve in other provinces.[145] As the Chapter of 1994 had asked that Africa be made a priority in the sharing of resources, fourteen of them left for African countries. Six others worked in Africa with the Jesuit Refugee Service and Caritas. Sending religious temporarily was a means of providing workshops and retreats in other provinces. The Solidarity Fund and various gifts contributed to sharing of financial resources.

Responsibility regarding the international Society required an exchange of information so that the needs or the generosity of one province might be communicated to the others. In a congregation whose numbers were diminishing, priorities had to be discerned, urgent internal needs evaluated, calls from outside heard and nuns sent, even those who were the most needed in their own province. The general council tried to regulate exchanges by clarifying the decision-making levels and by asking for the use of normal lines of communication, in order to avoid plans being made directly by an individual religious with the country asking for her or with the motherhouse.[146] Those planning to serve in another province were to be prepared by studying the country, if possible by learning its language, by

---

[141] Report of the General Council 1994-2000, p. 7.
[142] Testimony of M. Keraly. When serious troubles broke out in Congo, it was the only means of contact between the motherhouse and the province.
[143] Report of the General Council 1994-2000, p. 8. "We are aware that the spread of communications media concerned only a small number of people since the telephone is accessible to only 50% of the world population and internet to only 3%."
[144] Report of the General Council 1994-2000, p. 9.
[145] Twenty-two provinces received some religious; twenty sent some.
[146] Testimony of M. Keraly.

psychological and spiritual orientation and by progressive inculturation.[147] But because it was becoming common to remain only two or three years in the receiving country, the expenditures and efforts needed for adaptation seemed sometimes to be wasteful.[148]

Another form of solidarity and exchange consisted in vitalizing interprovincial projects. Two recent foundations saw their status evolve. Paraguay was on the point of being incorporated into the province of Argentina/Uruguay. In Europe the province of Belgium/Netherlands began in 1997. The provinces of Austria/Hungary and Germany drew close to each other, even to considering the formation of a new entity.

The International Commission for Justice and Peace

In the last years of the century, some "crises of civilization" affected the world. Egypt experienced the aftereffects of the growth of fundamentalism, and terrorism touched the Saïd. The Religious of the Sacred Heart were stranded in Dairout for months. Assassinations claimed victims among their relatives at Abou Korkas and Beni Ebeid.[149] The migration of Christian families towards Cairo brought about, at the request of the Catholic Coptic patriarch, the opening at Ezbet el Nakhl of a community to serve them. The effects of the neo-liberal thrust were felt in developing countries. In Peru, Colombia and Brazil large sections of the population were victims of denationalization, of the precariousness of their jobs or of unemployment. The inclusion of Paraguay in Mercosur [the Southern Common Market] was a factor in impoverishment.[150] Pressure from the IMF and the World Bank on several states to make them pay the interest on their debts had catastrophic consequences in Uganda and Kenya, where the governments made drastic cuts in the education and health budgets.[151]

---

[147] Report of the General Council 1994-2000, p. 10: "We are sometimes too self-sufficient and unrealistic. We would profit by learning from other missionary congregations who are often more sensitive to the need of preparation than we are. It would be helpful if the province receiving could make more explicit its plan to incorporate the new arrival."

[148] Testimony of M. Keraly.

[149] Report of Provincials 2000, p. 45.

[150] Report of Provincials 2000, p. 145.

[151] Report of Provincials 2000, p. 132. "This situation has modified many aspects of our life. Our salaries covered our current expenses before; that is no longer the case, and we are more dependent than ever on the motherhouse. Where teaching is given in overly large classes with a minimum of scholastic equipment, priority is given to discipline rather than to the personalized

In 1994 the chapter recommended the establishment of an international commission for Justice and Peace. Named in 1995[152] with a five-year mandate, it had as goal "to stimulate and fortify the commitment of the Society to work for justice and peace as an expression of our charism to manifest the love of the Heart of Jesus and as an expression of our educational mission." Its mission was "to facilitate investigation by looking carefully into situations of injustice and violence; to encourage reflection rooted in our spirituality and in contemplation on the causes of injustice, of inequality and the denial of liberty; to establish a communications network and to commit the Society of the Sacred Heart to action, in collaboration with other organizations but without losing the special characteristics of our contribution as educators, women, Religious of the Sacred Heart."[153]

For the first time a network went beyond the frontiers of the provinces and worked at regional and international levels.[154] The commission sought to familiarize the religious with the interconnection of worldwide social structures that perpetuated injustice. It launched activities in Sacred Heart institutions. The most significant were the campaign for the cancellation of foreign debt, the initiative for which came from Mother García de Quevedo, and the dissemination of information about the crisis in East Timor, which had repercussions in the Philippines and New Zealand. At the end of its term, the commission believed that it had given more attention to justice than to specific questions of peace and the integrity of creation; that internal training had to be a priority in the congregation, and that coordinated action with other organizations was indispensable for greater efficiency.[155] The Society of the Sacred Heart had to make itself heard in international forums, in particular at the United Nations, alone or with others.

Another Mode of Development

Thanks to the approval of the Constitutions by the Holy See, the Society of the Sacred Heart moved toward the end of the century peacefully. It

---

attention to each child. It becomes very difficult to find work or to move someone who needs another experience."

[152] It was formed of five regional coordinators, Cornelia Bührle, Maribel Carceller, Joan Kirby, Solome Najjuka and Carmen Pariente. Mary Hinde was the link between the commission and the general council. Its report of activity was appended to that of the general council at the Chapter of 2000.

[153] Report of the General Council, 1994-2000, pp. 13-14.

[154] Report of the Commission, p. 4

[155] Report of the Commission, p. 4. "We must enter into world structures if the voices of the oppressed are to be heard at the highest levels, for example, in the United States."

looked on its circumstances with truth, simplicity and in peace.[156] In twenty years the Society had been cut by nearly 30% of its strength. In 2000, with as many religious as in 1865, it was again the "little Society" that Saint Madeleine Sophie Barat called it.

Reduced Numbers

New demographics emerged in the last quarter of the century. Before 1982, 98% of the professed of temporary vows were under thirty-five at the time of their first commitment. Six years later the percentage changed to 88.5%. From then on, women were entering religious life later. A new age pyramid was at work. In 1967 the largest group was those in their forties. At the end of the century the average age was sixty-seven years.[157] A smaller number of persons able to take responsibility hampered local government and sending religious outside of their original province. But while aging also complicated the way community life functioned and diminished apostolic insertions, it did not slow down the apostolate. In Malta all the religious under eighty were engaged in an active apostolate. In Canada the province had aged, but the religious were lively and involved in the educational mission: "We are standing up committed to significant apostolic work as long as that is physically possible," noted the provincial.[158] Septuagenarians directed themselves toward new apostolic fields, especially towards the marginalized. Some physically inactive religious continued in dialogue with others through correspondence and conversation.[159] But fewer numbers weakened visibility and the corporate sense, and brought with it lessened influence, but while it affected individual and collective vulnerability, it "opened us to the power of God who works in weakness."[160]

Aspects of Demographic Decline

The decline in numbers that the Society of the Sacred Heart experienced was largely shared by most religious congregations of apostolic life. But the Society at least had the opportunity to receive vocations and to be able

---

[156] Testimony of P. García de Quevedo.
[157] In France, 17.7% of the religious were under 65. In the United States, 50% were under 50 in 1969, 7.4% in 1999 (M. C. Chandler, p. 176).
[158] Reports of Provincials to the Chapter of 2000, p. 21.
[159] Report of the General Council 1994-2000, pp. 56-57. "The lives of aged and sick persons question our values and our need to prove what we are in what we do."
[160] Report of the General Council 1994-2000, p. 57.

The Society of the Sacred Heart in the World of Its Times 1865-2000

to open or reopen novitiates, for entrances were high in some provinces.[161] Between 1969 and 1976 the questioning of the apostolic mission and the decisions made in some provinces concerning initial formation[162] had coincided with a decline in the number of novices.[163] But after 1978 entrances had picked up. At the end of the century the proportion of young professed was greater than it had ever been since 1967. Between 1994 and 2000, 111 religious from twenty-four different countries made their final commitment in the Society of the Sacred Heart.

While there had been a crisis of vocations in the Society of the Sacred Heart, many more left than was the case earlier. At Vatican II the place and the role that the laity could and should fulfill in the Church had been highlighted. Religious life was not the only way of perfection, of fidelity to God and of service to the Church. It had never been so, but doubtless it had never been said so openly as in the years following Vatican II. Between 1964 and 1967 departures doubled, which in such a short time could not be the result of chance. The phenomenon, significant in Latin America,[164] affected the United States deeply[165] and Europe to a lesser extent, except in Spain and England.[166] Twenty-two professed and seventy-four aspirants had left the Society.

---

[161] In the United States, 17.6% of the religious were in initial formation in 1969; 2.2% thirty years later (M.C. Chandler, p. 176). Ursula Bugembe, who came from a country where vocations were numerous, was surprised by the small number and the age of novices in certain provinces she visited.

[162] In many countries the office of mistress of novices had been given up after 1968. In Chile, "the mistress of novices did not belong to the formation team, and one had to consult her by telephone," recounts Isabel García who was a novice. "But I could participate in all the activities and that gave me the possibility of active incorporation in church life. For me that was a gift of God." In Colombia, the novices had been integrated into the apostolic activities of the community of Ciudad Jardín. Later they were registered in formation programs organized in common by religious congregations. Their formator had them do "internships in missionary experience" in isolated places on the Pacific Coast. Often, as in Argentina in 1976, the novitiate was established in a working class neighborhood.

[163] In Peru, between 1965 and 1979, there were thirty-six entrances into the novitiate, none in some years between 1970 and 1979 (M. Recavarren, *Raíces...*, p. 198).

[164] Six religious from Brazil, three from Argentina, four from Chile, three from Mexico and three from Peru left then. In Puerto Rico, there were thirteen departures; one third of those who had entered in thirty years.

[165] There were eighteen departures in 1966 and 1967.

[166] England lost eight and Spain seventeen religious.

The movement toward secularization accelerated after 1970. Some former coadjutrix sisters were not able to join new apostolic activities.[167] Some religious, who did not feel ready to take on the options of the chapter and the new forms of community life, seemed to find themselves in a congregation different from the one they had entered.[168] But others left because they believed that the renewal of the congregation was not rapid enough.[169] The dispensations from vows reached its peak in 1971 and 1972. The redefinition of mission in 1976 and the drafting of the Constitutions no longer provoked further questioning.[170] But between 1968 and 1993, 913 religious left the Society, 13.7% of the number in 1967. The movement hardly touched Africa[171] and did not affect all the provinces to the same extent. Dispensations from vows, calculated on the numbers of 1967, concerned 11% of the religious of the United States and 13% of the Spanish but 6.8% of Italians and 4.4% of the French. In Latin America departures appeared greater as the total numbers were small. In Mexico seventy left the Society.[172] Half the religious who left the Society before 1976 were under forty years old and were professed fewer than ten years. The departures of young professed are explained also by canonical changes that prescribed temporary vows. While before 1964 it was in the novitiate that decisions were made, after that time departures took place when a definitive commitment was at issue.[173] Some provinces were devastated following these departures. In Puerto Rico, for example, in 1976 there was only a small number of young people, and the majority of religious were over fifty-five years old.

---

[167] Gen. Arch. C I C 3, Box 28. 20.8% of the departures.

[168] That was the reason for 35.4% of the departures.

[169] 10% of the departures. Prudence Wilson, in *My Father Took Me to the Circus*, p. 105, believed that some left also who should never have been allowed to make first vows and who, if the changes had not opened the doors and legitimized their flight, would have lived "a diminished half-life." For Mary Henry, the departures were numerous above all in provinces where the novitiates had been populated before by an elevated number of novices whom the mistress of novices could not follow up in their discernment. Chamartín counted more than 100 novices at the beginning of the sixties. Kenwood had been planned by Mother Bodkin to accept ninety novices from the United States and Canada (F. Gimber, p. 65).

[170] In Austria and Peru there were almost no more departures after 1975, in Spain and the United States, after 1977.

[171] For religious serving in the missions, departures from the Society were handled in their province of origin.

[172] Testimony of P. García de Quevedo and M. del Socorro Rubio.

[173] Testimony of H. McLaughlin.

While all the departures were traumatic, those that affected the age group of thirty to forty, on which hopes rested,[174] and those of well-known religious were the most difficult to bear. An example was the departure before 1970 of four religious from the United States. One was the mistress of novices; another, the president of Manhattanville where the two others were teaching. But the move of superiors to a contemplative order[175] had devastating effects on the public. These departures resulted in a lack of support for new generations. In provinces with reduced numbers and limited and aged personnel there was a risk that flexibility and innovations in apostolic life would be difficult. The recovery that took place at the end of the seventies allowed for improvement in some of these situations.

New Spaces, Contrasts and New Faces

A major difference from the situation during the nineteenth century: the Society of the Sacred Heart was henceforth present in forty-three countries, on all the continents[176] and its nuns spoke twenty-six languages. These were women whose development included contributions from various geographic, political and economic milieus. Some women found in themselves deep echoes of Christianity but also of Buddhism, Islam, Hinduism, Shintoism, Shamanism, Animism that some of them had practiced or with which they were familiar, because of the cultures of the countries where they lived or from which they came. "[They were] convoked to be a people within the people of God, within the people of the country where they were living."[177] Symbolically for the bicentenary, Virginia O'Meara, from the province of the United States created a new emblem in which the Heart of Christ was surrounded by the names of all the countries where the Society was present. The requests received and world affairs had contributed to unprecedented geographic expansion and had brought about new communities with very few members. Four religious were living in Moscow; they formed the only Sacred Heart community "in that immense Russia where Catholics are in the minority. For me it is truly the little grain of mustard seed, sown, buried in the earth, which bears fruit. This way of making the society, its charism and its mission present is new and rather extraordinary," stated Maryvonne Keraly.

---

[174] H. McLaughlin.

[175] That happened in Colombia, Chile, Peru and Germany.

[176] In 1967, the Society of the Sacred Heart had houses in thirty-four countries, and the nuns were from forty-nine nationalities.

[177] Gen. Arch. C I C IV, Box 28/31. International Education Commission, "The Face of the Society of the Sacred Heart Today."

In 2000 more than half the Religious of the Sacred Heart were European.[178] But the diminution of forces in some countries called for rethinking provincial combinations. The Netherlands, already provided with a non-resident major superior, joined with Belgium to form the Province of Belgium/Netherlands in September 1998. The provinces of Germany/Sweden and Austria/Hungary undertook a process of rapprochement.[179] These needed evolutions made clear how much "the uncertainty about the future, our histories, our stereotypes, the great diversity of life styles, of community and of government among the provinces, including those on the same continent, could give rise to opposition and fear." Two neighboring provinces could be different in social, cultural and religious contexts; such differences had consequences for community life, governance and even spirituality.[180] During a visit of the general council Ireland/Scotland and England/Wales organized a "kind of pilgrimage of reconciliation," which consisted of three days of reflection around the identity of national stereotypes.[181] Having a common language facilitated the activities gradually developed by Belgium and France; German was a factor in the rapprochement between Austria and Germany, which included however the religious who spoke Hungarian and Swedish. Some of these new gatherings showed weaknesses associated with their national structures and their history.[182] It seemed even more important to consider some rapprochements among provinces as the political reconstruction of Europe was in process.[183]

---

[178] The religious of the two provinces of Spain formed the most numerous national group in the Society and represented half the European religious.

[179] In 1999, the religious of both provinces prepared for the general chapter by meeting in apostolic groups in different places but working on the same themes.

[180] Reports of Provincials 2000, p. 16, Belgium/Netherlands: "It would be good to be enriched by our differences. The North more in contact with Protestantism, the South marked by devotion to the Sacred Heart could have a constructive dialogue on the theme of the Eucharist."

[181] Report of the General Council 1994-2000, p. 20.

[182] Besides, in Hungary, the weak point was the disparity between the number of professed and that of religious in formation, as well as age differences between the two categories.

[183] *Our Road to Emmaus*, 1994, report of the Province of Germany/Sweden, p. 35: "The unification of Europe acquires for us an ever greater significance. Unanimously, we want to live in the Society itself the positive aspects of the idea of Europe and its political and cultural dimension, going beyond its economic objectives. For us the essential is the values of solidarity and fraternity in a society where people of diverse cultures live together. In this movement of development in Europe, our province values relationships with neighboring provinces." The provincial chapter of Austria/Hungary envisaged

In the rest of the world, transformations were also at work. Unification of the provinces of the United States resulted in the largest province in the Society in number of members.[184] Latin America ranked after Europe in number of religious, and after many years without recruitment, it became second with respect to the number under forty years of age. Insertions in underprivileged areas had drawn to the Sacred Heart a new public from geographic areas where the Society was newly established and they came from more modest social milieus than before. In Peru, Colombia, Chile, the Society of the Sacred Heart had more women of color than in the middle of the twentieth century. In Mexico there was a young religious of indigenous origin.

In Asia, only 5.6% of the religious were octogenarians. But the age pyramids varied according to the age of the foundations. While Japan's profile looked similar to those of Western countries, Korea had an average age of forty-three years. In India, vocation ministry was developed in new regions of the country and in new cultural milieus.[185] The educational system there had helped to reduce the marginalization from which the *dalits* and forest people suffered; some of their members had become physicians, nurses, architects, engineers and technicians. The novices were now coming from this new élite of Indian society, and they received professional and spiritual training in view of the work they would have to take on. "They will not be the future heads of our schools and colleges," remarked Mary Braganza, who had taken part in this evolution, "but they will do a fabulous job in the framework of development and of awakening of rural people, and this is the need of the hour."

In Africa from which 4.5% of the members of the Society come, those under forty represented more than a quarter of the whole. Uganda/Kenya had the greatest number of young professed of the entire Society. Chad finally had some people enter.[186] In Egypt vocation ministry organized in the Saïd was bearing fruit. The youngest religious did not always come

---

a "European federation," governed by a single major superior and regional responsible persons. Short term it proposed the formation of "an area" with the province of Germany/Sweden having a common administration (p. 88).

[184] The United States and Canada formed 15.47% of the numbers of the Society and Australia/New Zealand 2.82%.

[185] Reports of the Provincials, 2000, p. 67: "Since our recent vocations come from the poorest and least educated backgrounds questions arise about the direction of our apostolates in the future."

[186] Reports of the Provincials, Chad, p. 128: "It is the sign of a greater adaptation of our communities to the milieu. The young see us closer to them, simpler, more accessible."

from the institutions, even in the provinces that have held on to them.[187] More and more those in charge are African. Congo has had a Congolese provincial since 1979.[188] The "Egyptianization" of that province had begun in 1986 with the nomination of an Egyptian mistress of novices; then, the provincial treasury and the business offices of the schools at Ghamra and Heliopolis, the stages of formation, vocation ministry and the province had been entrusted to Egyptians.[189] In Uganda/Kenya Africans formed 39% of the people in the province. But the ten years of war and instability reduced the number entering[190] and slowed down the Africanization of those holding office.[191] Doreen Boland could say: "Because I arrived in Uganda a year after the foundation, I feel I took part in forming a new family of Religious of the Sacred Heart in Uganda and Kenya. I had the privilege of living in a very international province, which in itself is a sign of the universal love of the Heart of Jesus. It was important to be a sign of fraternal life in countries where tribalism reigned."[192]

Consequently, the Society of the Sacred Heart was able to grow in Africa and Asia. The general council noted:

> Maybe in the future, there will be a "reversal of missions," that is to say that persons of so-called mission countries will be called to the older provinces in response to the needs of migrants who are looking for a new life outside their countries of origin. In this way our internationality would be at the service of populations obliged to move in search of work to earn a livelihood for their families.[193]

A first Ugandan religious had been sent to Venezuela in 1997. The first Korean missionary left for Chad in 1999. But as personnel needs were

---

[187] Reports of the Provincials, Congo, p. 33.

[188] The first was Anne Mawete Mukoko from 1979 to 1987. Those following were Albertine Fila Wumba from 1987 to 1990, Marie-José Nsenga Fwakwingi from 1993 to 1999, then Christine Mukoko Ngudi Mpasi from 1999 on. Mercedes Eguilior was provincial from 1990 to 1993.

[189] In 1998 the first Egyptian provincial, Jeannette Hanna, was named.

[190] A generation is missing between the African religious and those who came from outside. To answer socio-economic necessities and even to be able to earn a salary, the young religious undertook long professional studies.

[191] In 1998, the provincial treasury was confided to a Ugandan. Hilda Bamwine was named provincial in 1999.

[192] *Religieuses du Sacré-Cœur*, Province de France, 2006, pp. 3-4. In 1994, the African religious came from eight tribes. The others came from twelve countries of Asia, Australia, New Zealand, North and South America and Europe.

[193] Report of the General Council 1994-2000, p. 56.

considerable in Africa, a third of the religious who left their provinces between 1994 and 2000 were sent to countries of that continent.

Internationality was developing. At the end of the sixties, some religious were carrying out their apostolate in new places, even in isolation. In 1968 Marie Louise Schroen, at the request of the superior general of the *Ancillae Domini*, worked in formation with those sisters in Papua New Guinea. She spent a year among populations "completely foreign," more than three thousand kilometers from Brisbane, the nearest house of the Sacred Heart.[194] Brigid Keogh was recruited as a professor of English at Beijing University. Her initial contract was not renewed, but she returned to China to teach at Yan-an University. A few religious had an apostolate as "itinerant rabbis," while seeking to keep links with a community.

The foundations made in geographic and cultural areas hitherto unknown presented a double challenge. The establishment of a community in a part of the world where there was a good chance that it would remain the only one was a recent phenomenon. The question, observed Maryvonne Keraly, was to know how these communities could remain linked with the Society and "have what was necessary to feel part of the whole." Opening communities in countries where the geographic conditions were constraining and insecurity endemic meant that the location had to be determined carefully.[195] Community life that brought together women from all horizons and all cultures, united by their common religious life but holding multiple identities, required openness and flexibility.

One Mission and Many Apostolates

The glorification of the Heart of Christ through education was always the goal of the Society of the Sacred Heart. At the time of the assembly in Chile in 1997, the general council remarked,

> It was a joy when we could repeat to one another that our educational mission is intimately linked to our charism and that we have to live it

---

[194] F. Gimber, p. 187.

[195] In Peru, a community had been founded in 1989 in Altiplano, at Ayaviri, at the request of Bishop François d'Alteroche. Ten years later it was transferred to Layo, a village of 350 families, located in a very isolated region deprived of religious congregations, at an altitude of 4200 meters. The presence of a community in Tinta, less than two hours away by car, permitted the nuns in Layo not to feel too separated. At the request of bishops, foundations in the interior in Chad were made after 1992. The communities of Moulkou and Guelengdeng, situated on the highway N'Djaména-Bongor, formed a single "community in mission" (Report of Provincials, 2000, p. 128).

starting from contemplation, which gives it the faith dimension and interiority and which opens it to the calls of the world, by giving priority to young people, to women, to those excluded and disadvantaged."

The kind of visibility that the Society of the Sacred Heart had had through its renowned boarding schools reserved to a social élite had disappeared. The numbers in the Sacred Heart institutions had increased, and the religious no longer had the means to exercise in them the kind of influence they had had in boarding schools where there were rarely more than 100 students. But as the founder had wished, the Society continued to develop the students' capacity for leadership[196] and aimed at educational excellence. Through their educational practices the provinces sought to build bridges among contrasting cultural worlds. The Latin American network of popular education began with the needs of young people and adults to build its programs,[197] which could be carried on through formal and informal education. In Peru where the educational institutions remained the norm, a network based on the same principles operated a university, schools, a college of education, parish schools and an experimental program in popular education among rural people.

While "deinstitutionalization" was complete in only certain provinces, worldwide religious were present in the most diverse areas: in schools and other educational centers; among children and young people, adults and the elderly, people with special needs, refugees and migrants; in poor neighborhoods, in villages, mountain hamlets and cities large and small; in base communities, in centers for workers, for young people; universities, parishes, catechetical groups, churches and ashrams, in care centers, hospitals and mobile clinics in villages, in houses of formation and spirituality centers, in associations, in prisons, and refuges for the homeless.[198] Some provinces opened workshops and schools for young people who had no work or education. Education was carried out through

---

[196] In the United States, in 1999, only 5.2% of the religious thought that education was *not* the means of realizing the charism of the Society (M.C. Chandler, pp. 226 ff.).

[197] *Religieuses du Sacré-Cœur*, p. 41. In Argentina/Uruguay, "in the programs the emphasis was placed on self-reflection so that they could search together for the steps to take and from that to organize apprenticeships. They were the protagonists themselves. And all the work aimed at the growth of persons and the formation of communities through research into justice and solidarity, through reflection on the Word of God, work together, the sense of the Church as 'people of God' and learning to live together as Jesus wished."

[198] Gen. Arch. C 1 C 4 b 28/31. "The Face of the Society of the Sacred Heart Today."

various professions. The diversity of ministries was henceforth recognized as a sign of strength,[199] but it had helped to alter the visibility of the Society of the Sacred Heart. The general council, during their visits, had observed that the religious were giving themselves to the mission creatively in response to requests. "Thanks to the two weeks I spent in Korea," recounted Marta Jiménez, "I learned much about their life, the faith of their people, their generosity in dedicating themselves to the poorest people, of the seriousness of their formation in religious life." Mary Hinde remembers particularly a visit to a community living in a very poor neighborhood in New York. After the Medellín conference, Argentina/Uruguay "had tried to let itself be transformed by the option for the poor, as much in community life as in apostolic work" to the point that in 2000 all the communities, except those for the elderly, were located in working class areas.[200] Throughout the world the religious coped with the urgent needs of those who were marginalized or neglected.

Did the diversification of apostolic activities bring with it the risk of fragmenting the mission and increasing individualism? The shared mission was a subject of concern for many religious. Maryvonne Keraly observed,

> There are some conditions that favor it, others not. The general council does not see diversity of apostolates as an obstacle at all. We wondered rather how the community was situated; what conditions it set up to make a shared mission out of this diversity. One point worried me. The variety of contexts, better understood on the spot, showed that there was an immense challenge for the whole to remain united, conformed to the mission of Christ, to his preferences, his priorities, and that as local community and as part of the Society we have visibility and that we make manifest the Heart of Christ. We live out this tension between the diversity and the center, for in the Heart of Christ there is a centrifugal force toward the world. But while the center can be everywhere, there is a center even so!

Living the mission through new and different works, in institutions or through individual presence, is efficacious in responding to needs and can make for closer touch with the world of the excluded, but it can create "distances and misunderstandings among various insertions. A mission lived with generosity meant crowded schedules, full agendas and excessive work."[201] That did not produce joyous and peaceful lives; it complicated

---

[199] Reports of the Provincials, 2000, p. 8, Australia/New Zealand.
[200] *Religieuses du Sacré-Cœur*, p. 41.
[201] Report of the Provincials, 2000, pp. 54-55. Northern Spain.

Monique Luirard

community life and gave priority to work. This life style did not come close to "a God who is guiding history mysteriously" but rather put religious "in touch with their own plans, their success and failures." Delegates from the North of Spain who made this statement felt called to draw their apostolic dynamism from contemplation, in which their religious life finds its moving spirit.

Religious of the Sacred Heart have always had relationships with lay persons, whether with the parents of their pupils or their co-workers. The opening to the world had reinforced these. In 1994 the chapter expressed the conviction that the spirituality of the Sacred Heart did not belong only to the religious but was a gift to be shared, "a treasure others help us to discover. With them, we want to continue to search how to live and express it for today, how to proclaim with hearts burning within us that we have recognized the Risen Christ in the breaking of the bread."[202] Marta Jiménez remarks,

> The strength of our charism and our sharing it with lay people in many countries has struck me. They are called Associates, Friends of the Sacred Heart, Lay Family. My whole experience can be summarized as a strong feeling of communion, of solidarity and interest in one another, from one end of the earth to the other, shown among persons, communities and provinces. The *Cor unum* is lived; it is a reality that gives life to the charism.

Some provinces entered "with enthusiasm into collaboration with others," not only because their frailty imposed it but also because of the contributions of everyone.[203] Collaboration with the laity was happening everywhere the religious were present and through projects in many provinces. In the United States, Associates, men and women, joined Religious of the Sacred Heart in prayer and recollection and took part in some of their meetings. In that country and in Australia and New Zealand school administrators who are part of a network of Sacred Heart schools familiarize themselves with the Society's educational philosophy and contribute to maintaining its influence. Alumnae/i meetings were occasions of sharing. At the time of the congress of the worldwide association (AMASC) in San Luis Potosí in 1998 Mother García de Quevedo gave them the following message: "Saint Madeleine Sophie spoke of the importance of educating women, 'called to live in the world, which they should edify.'" She underlined the importance of their influence and their example in the

---

[202] General Chapter, p. 30.
[203] Report of the Provincials, 2000, p. 8, Australia/New Zealand.

family, the Church, the world; this with a single aim: to glorify the Heart of Jesus, and with a single mission: to discover and manifest his love.

> As alumnae of the Sacred Heart you are called to share with us and to spread the mission of discovering and manifesting the love of God revealed through the wounded Heart of Jesus. To carry out this difficult mission demands not only cultivation of interiority, but also effective action in favor of life in a world deeply wounded and divided by injustice. The measure of our individual and collective commitment to transforming this wounded world into a world conformable to the desires of God is the measure of our union and conformity with the wounded Heart of Jesus. It is also a manner of making explicit the profound meaning and raison d'être of the mission and spirituality of the Sacred Heart of Jesus in our world of today.... I would like to invite all of you gathered here to renew your commitment in favor of life in a world that begets death, to work for reconciliation in a world deeply divided, to educate for justice and peace in a world plagued by war and oppression. I am sure that the profound conviction of the blessing of Saint Madeleine Sophie on this collective effort will be a pledge of the fruitfulness of your commitment.[204]

Thanks to their tradition, the Religious of the Sacred Heart had a treasure in which lay people asked to share. They experienced it during the preparation for the celebration of the bicentenary of the Society. Lay persons participated in international meetings that took place then.[205] Groups wishing to be linked in one way or another to the spirituality of the Sacred Heart were formed.[206] For the first time, lay persons were invited to the General Chapter of 2000.

Return to the Source

During the last years of the century several events provided an opportunity to go back to the past and, in particular, to the convictions that had motivated the founder and her first companions in order to find new momentum.

---

[204] *Religieuses du Sacré-Cœur*, p. 29.
[205] At the meeting of heads of Sacred Heart schools in Joigny in April 2000, of the eighty-four participants forty-four were lay persons.
[206] Report of the General Council 1994-2000, p. 19: "Has the moment come to create a juridical structure that can express to some degree belonging to the body of the Society?" Some provinces wanted research in this direction to be undertaken.

Monique Luirard

The Unexpected Canonization of Philippine Duchesne

On 23 October 1987, Pope John Paul II signed the decree of approbation of the miracle attributed to Philippine Duchesne[207] that opened the way to her canonization.[208] It had been requested and obtained by the Archdiocese of Saint Louis in the United States and was received as a gift by the Society, which had ceased to pursue it. The celebration that took place, on 3 July 1988, in St. Peter's in Rome brought together several hundred religious from around the world and many alumnae. It occasioned various celebrations throughout the world and better acquaintance with the life of the saint. On 3 April 1988, Mother McLaughlin had invited the Society to plant an oak tree, "somewhere significant in our provinces, in the community garden, on our school campuses…symbolizing our own desire to sink our roots into our earth and to reach up and out to touch life and to give life, to shelter it, to nourish it, and to stretch our vision ever upward to the Light of Life." Is not the planting of our tree in honor of Philippine "a call to confident patience, to profound trust, to courageous gratuity and to great love? As we dig deeply into the fertile darkness of the earth, as we let the silent gentle soil cover these tender roots of promise, and as we surrender our control over the life of the tree, let us ask the Lord of the Harvest to bring us to the same abandonment and transformation in Him that will bear fruit of unity and peace for our world."[209]

Philippine Duchesne had been "the woman who was always praying" a strong, simple, austere woman on fire with love for Christ and for the world. Her life was a reason to celebrate hope:

> Her courage was that of an evangelical woman, inspired with a passion to proclaim the Gospel, who lived in faith the élan of a hope without limits. Philippine offers, especially to us her sisters, strong lessons for our lives as apostles.… Philippine knew how to look with the eyes of the heart, how to see beyond the needs of post-revolutionary France; and this look, courageous and full of love, on the "New World" of her time has not been extinguished. Philippine speaks to us of leave-taking, of going forth, of going beyond ourselves, of living in faith…faith [that] was not a routine matter; it was love in action. She lived this faith in a difficult and painful tearing away of all security, of all that she had known, of all that

---

[207] It was the cure of Marguerite Bernard, a French nun who had been a missionary in China and Japan. When she had been operated on for cancer of the thyroid in the United States in November 1951, the surgeon had declared the operation unsuccessful. She left for Japan in March 1952; she died there in 1970.

[208] H. McLaughlin, *Letters*, p. 66, 10 November 1987.

[209] H. McLaughlin, *Letters*, pp. 72-73.

was familiar. She consented to live within herself a leave-taking that was dispossession, stripping, poverty. It was the strength of this faith always at work in her which, little by little, transformed her, liberated her heart, to make room for the divine initiative. Philippine is still teaching us to witness to hope. This woman, always young, who unceasingly gives birth in sorrow and in joy to a new humanity made one in Christ.[210]

In 1993 the Province of Mexico/Nicaragua had described its "Road to Emmaus" in the form of a parable during which Philippine shared some of the convictions that inspired her:

"On that Holy Thursday night, for me like a new day, I knew for certain that the salvation that Jesus brought us has to reach the five continents of the world. The presence of God is very clear in the process and the history you have lived. He wants us to look at reality with new eyes. To use our senses for new intuitions so as to hear the calls and the possible responses. He wants us to use our hands to recreate this world with audacious love, our feet ready to walk new paths, our hearts burning with new hopes. From the depths of our lives and our hearts let us bring about signs of new life, which will enable us to reinvent a world that God can recognize as his." As they listened to her, the "disciples" once more felt their hearts burning.

They included in their project, the "coming together with the indigenous people" that Philippine had so much desired. "And our spirituality, Philippine? How shall we renew that?" "According to what you have told me of the world today and my own experience in the struggle for justice, for peace, for life, your wish to live heart to heart with Jesus' pierced and merciful Heart will give you the ability to discover and make the Kingdom present in daily living."[211]

Mother Duchesne had led the exciting but austere life of a missionary. A contemplative, she had established the Society in America, dreamed always of going farther west toward the Great Plains and the Rockies, wanted to educate Blacks in the South; and she had embodied the genius of the frontier that characterized American society of her time, which was "to be open to the future,"[212] but she had desired also to live among the Indian

---

[210] H. McLaughlin, *Letters*, pp. 77-78, Feast of the Sacred Heart 1988.
[211] *Our Road to Emmaus*, pp. 83-84.
[212] Sharon Karam, "Philippine Duchesne and the Frontier," *Philippine Duchesne 1818-1968*, quoted in *A Spiritual Journey*, p. 58.

tribes that were beginning to be dislodged from their homes. She could help the Society in reflecting on its apostolic vocation:

- Philippine had a clear and dynamic vision for the Society, which gave her life direction, enthusiasm, fortitude, which captured all her energy. What is our vision today? Do we bring to it this twofold dimension of an apostle, a profound life of prayer and joy of mission?
- Though distances were great and communication extremely difficult, Philippine adapted as she could to the new circumstances and was indefatigable in her efforts to keep this mission united to the body of the Society. How do we give concrete expression to our desire for union while assuring true inculturation?
- Philippine's dream was to be one with the Indians, to live with them. After years of waiting, she went to the Potawatomi whom she loved dearly. Who are our Potawatomi?
- Her love for the poor, for the most abandoned was clear and strong. What place do the poor have in our life?"[213]

In October 1989 the Congregation for Divine Worship gave its approbation for the Masses of Saint Madeleine Sophie, of the Sacred Heart, of the Immaculate Heart of Mary and of Saint Philippine.[214] The Society of the Sacred Heart thus had at its disposal liturgical sources that were a means of unity and renewal in depth.

The Bicentenary of the Society of the Sacred Heart

The preparation for the bicentenary offered the Society of the Sacred Heart the opportunity for an individual and collective renewal while revisiting the circumstances of its birth. Sister García de Quevedo wrote: "We want the celebration of our bicentenary to be above all an occasion of renewal and deepening of our charism in the service of mission: to celebrate and remember a significant event while making it present again, with the certainty that the experience of two hundred years of history gives us and for which we give thanks."[215]

---

[213] General Chapter 1988, opening by Mother McLaughlin, pp. II-III, 11 July 1988.
[214] H. McLaughlin.
[215] Patricia García de Quevedo, *Letters and Conferences*, pp. 46-47.

Several projects were set in motion to achieve this spiritual renewal. Besides the letter that the superior general traditionally wrote for the feast of the Sacred Heart, letters were sent to the Society every year for 21 November, the anniversary of the first consecration to the Sacred Heart of Sophie Barat and her first companions. The letter in 1995 asked each one to regard the founding event of 21 November 1800, as

> a source of new life and spirit so that in turn the Society of today may commit itself to a process of refounding. Everyone is called to participate, whatever her age or the moment in her history, wherever she is. Let no one remain by the side of the road. Let each one hear the triple call of the Chapter to follow Christ, to open our eyes to the reality of the world, to deepen our roots. The charism is alive in each one and each one is responsible for it.
>
> Today we need to be seized once more by what Madeleine Sophie and her three companions did almost two hundred years ago: they gave their lives to the Heart of Christ and made their own his passion for the world.
>
> The commemoration was to be a celebration with several facets:
>
> To celebrate the bicentennial is, therefore, first of all to return to the freshness of our original vocation, to that heart-space where our first great desire to love and serve God was born. It is to surrender our lives for the salvation of a world thirsting for meaning and for justice, for our people in search of unity.
>
> To celebrate is to wonder at the trust God has placed in each one of us and to give our trust in return.
>
> To celebrate is to give thanks that we are not alone, that we live our call together in the Society.
>
> To celebrate is to remember the life of the Society yesterday and today and to recall those religious of the Sacred Heart who are dear to us because they accompanied us and enlightened us along the way.
>
> To celebrate is to discern in the signs of the times that paths that need to be opened up in fidelity to our apostolic vocation, sure that the Spirit is at work in the world with a renewing and creative power.[216]

It was a question of a "eucharistic journey: conversion, listening, thanksgiving and apostolic generosity." The following letters developed these themes; the one in 1999 took the form of a sending forth.[217]

---

[216] P. García de Quevedo, p. 47.
[217] Testimony of M. Keraly and M. Jiménez. The 21 November letters were prepared together by the general council, and the time given to the writing

An international team of five religious[218] prepared *A Spiritual Journey* to help members of the Society to undertake "a year's journey of profound prayer and contemplation for the sake of our mission."[219] Both individually and in community, the prayer was to build communion and be integrated with life.[220] "The most important call is to travel the road together, seeking ever deeper conformity with the attitudes and sentiments of the Heart of Christ," recalled the superior general in her introduction to this booklet. The goal was original, since it was "to give everyone a shared momentum in living the path of preparation," in the light of "spiritual exercises in daily life."[221] The *Journey* suggested Scripture texts, quotations from the writings of the founder, from chapter documents and from letters of the superiors general. It suggested original forms of prayer: touch the ground, enter into dialogue with creation, practice breathing in the spirit of Zen meditation, choose a mantra, dance, pray while walking in the street and observing how those who are poor live. It was a way of honoring the many cultures represented in the Society, of being open to new theological and spiritual intuitions, of reading the Bible differently.

A publication entitled *Religious of the Sacred Heart*, the oversight of which was entrusted to Marie-Guyonne du Penhoat, presented the Society in its history, tradition and spiritual characteristics but also the aspects its mission was taking on now in different places. Both *A Spiritual Itinerary* and *Religious of the Sacred Heart* were translated into the twelve languages spoken in the Society of the Sacred Heart.[222] Some other works also gave new expression to the spirituality of the Sacred Heart.

Thanks to the bicentenary, Saint Madeleine Sophie and the places where she lived were rediscovered. A biography of the founder, written by

---

contributed to the solidarity of the members, for lengthy sharings gave them a chance to compare their points of view on religious life at the Sacred Heart based on their own experience.

[218] Barbara Bowe from the United States, Françoise Greffe from France, Han Soon Hee from Korea, Christine Mukoko from Congo and Carmen Pisano from Argentina/Uruguay.

[219] *A Spiritual Journey*, p. 7.

[220] *A Spiritual Journey*, pp. 8-9. Five themes were proposed, each forming a stage during the year 1999-2000: "Return to the freshness of our original vocation; women of communion, women of reconciliation; to give our lives day by day; enter into the sentiments and preferences of his Heart; a passion to proclaim the Gospel." Overall they reproduced the paths of the Exercises of Saint Ignatius.

[221] Testimony of M. Jiménez.

[222] In French, English, Spanish, Italian, Portuguese, German, Polish, Hungarian, Arabic, Japanese, Korean and Chinese.

Phil Kilroy, gave her story a new lease on life and made her more human. The house in Joigny where she was born was renovated and became a center of spirituality where international meetings brought together Religious of the Sacred Heart as well as their co-workers.[223] Amiens, the "cradle" of the Society was chosen as the location of the General Chapter of 2000. In Rome a "heritage room" at the Villa Lante near the archives housed the collection of objects that had belonged to Mother Barat, to the superiors general and various religious. Several meetings were held in places of symbolic significance to the Society in France[224] and elsewhere. In Chicago there was a conference of Society theologians. Workshops in Japanese and Celtic spirituality were offered by the Japanese and Ireland/Scotland provinces. All were a form of *recyclage*. The renewal became "a transversal axis that gave color and opened a new horizon to the religious and drew them to their common mission with renewed energy from their original inspiration."[225] The last years of the century were "a time of grace and joy"[226] for the Society of the Sacred Heart. In celebrating its foundation the Society was solidly refounded, always oriented toward the glorification of the Heart of Christ, seen as the discovery and manifestation of the love of God and expressed in different but receptive cultural worlds.

---

[223] Besides the director of the spirituality center, Brigitte Combier, an international leadership team included two nuns from Spain and Puerto Rico, Carmen Hornedo and María Clemencia Benítez. They collaborated with the Joigny community in welcoming the participants to events organized in Sophie's birthplace. 387 religious of all ages and nationalities took part, either in workshops offered to everyone or in meetings of particular categories: mistresses of novices, archivists, artists, heads of Sacred Heart schools.

[224] *A Spiritual Journey*, p. 17.

[225] In Poitiers a workshop on "The Exercises and Spiritual Accompaniment according to our charism" took place in 1998. Other workshops on the spiritual exercises were held in Hungarian and in German. Nuns in Korea created a forty-day retreat.

[226] Testimony of P. García de Quevedo.

CONCLUSION

Every human group is confronted in the long term with the need to renew itself continually to avoid extinction. Between 1865 and the eve of the twentieth century, the Society of the Sacred Heart underwent a test of real life. Its history shows both continuity and rupture and can be seen as a series of challenges overcome, thanks to the determination of its members and to an individual and collective reclaiming of its founding intuition. As a consequence, calm periods alternated with brief troubled ones in connection with world events and the thrust of the Church, but also with times of reflection on the mission that enabled redefining the apostolate and the observances of religious life.

At each epoch, under the impulse of the general congregations, the institute carried out an internal reform. Its first concerns were personal growth and improvement, but in some special moments, because of unexpected crises, the whole Society had to question itself about itself, to discover, intensely sometimes, shadows and frailties that did not all flow from the Society itself. These stages were difficult to go through, but because of deep rootedness in faith, they permitted the Society to discover at the heart of the body tangible human resources and a real energy to put at the service of the mission. The structures of the congregation have evolved toward a flexible form of government,[1] seeking to preserve bonds of dependence and weighing the risks of separation and autonomy. Reform of the ways to carry out the goal of the institute, the glorification of the Heart of Christ, was guaranteed. The very contemplation of reality, from the Heart of Christ to the heart of the world, from the pierced Heart of Jesus to the pierced heart of humanity, has set in motion a new way of being a Religious of the Sacred Heart. As Mother Bultó often recalled during her term as

---

[1] Report of the assembly of provincials, Chile, 1997: "We have seen the urgency of establishing a more evangelical government at the service of the life and growth of the body in fulfilling its vocation."

superior general,[2] a new Society of the Sacred Heart was in the process of appearing, one that would be led to look at the world and take our place in it differently, "more inserted, more in solidarity with the sufferings and hopes of humanity." This change required moving "from a conventual to a more open community life for apostolic reasons. It was no longer a question of waiting for people to come to us, but rather of going in search of them."[3] In relation to the past, this change was so radical that after 1970 Mother Bultó thought that the Religious of the Sacred Heart had not only to become aware of it, but to decide whether or not they wished to take it on.[4]

The Society of the Sacred Heart was already largely international in 1865. An ambitious policy of foundations, of responses to unexpected situations like the "expulsions," to occasional appeals, to evolution in the state of the world and to awareness of new ways of thinking had taken it to all the continents. In the long run, the intermingling of peoples, the openness to new civilizations and cultures could not continue without both successes and repercussions attaching to its image, the one the public had of the Society or the one it had of itself.

Historians and sociologists have recently become interested in the multiple identities of human beings determined by the milieu in which they live, formed by influences coming from the family, education, civil society and the sources of information. Religious life offers a good example of this intertwining of identities. It brings together, in the case we are considering, women united by their desire to follow Christ and glorify his Heart in the same way; women who form part of an international family, that of the Sacred Heart, which they entered at the time of their final commitment, as women by marriage enter into a new family. Ursula Bugembe remarked:

> Lacking a better expression, I use the term marriage to express the fact that I believe that in becoming a Religious of the Sacred Heart, I had to mature in a new family and learn new ways to live and form relationships.

---

[2] Testimony of I. Aranguren.

[3] P. García de Quevedo: "The Process of Refounding the Charism of the Society of the Sacred Heart across Its Various Cultures," 26 November 1998. She adds, "We will never again be very numerous. Ours is a form of religious life for the few, because it demands an unusual combination of strength and weakness. It requires as well a certain vulnerability in order to be ready to collaborate in the building of the Kingdom."

[4] Shortly after the Chapter of 1970, Mother Zurstrassen responded to one who posed the question: "Are not all these changes disconcerting for you who have worked for twenty-five years forming young religious according to totally different methods?" Her answer: "I see another type of Religious of the Sacred Heart coming, and I am full of confidence in the future."

I came to it with all the values of my culture. Some of them have been enriched, others, without being rejected, have been called into question; all have been unified. In my way of thinking and acting, I have had to meet other cultures and allow them to be themselves and at the same time to be challenged."

Going back over her experience of community life in the very international province of Uganda/Kenya, then on the general council, she added,

We always had the possibility of asking each one to explain in the simplest terms, even to use other words or symbols. The new community we were forming in order to work together very closely was in agreement about accepting each one's gifts. Acting thus, we allowed her to contribute to the common work from her own interior resources. As an African, Ugandan, Muganda, who at that time was "married" for twenty-two years in the family of the Sacred Heart and such as I had become, I took my part. I do not think my culture crushed me. At certain moments it took time for me to ask a question or to give a response because of language, for we were not using my own; but I think that if I felt I was not understood, I had the opportunity to say so, and we went back over the discussion. Even when it was time for us to conclude, I could always express a "but." I never felt that I was strange because I was Ugandan. My viewpoint was welcomed because it contributed something.

As this testimony aptly and profoundly shows every Religious of the Sacred Heart is characterized by her membership in the Society, taken on in respect for others and in solidarity with a body into which she is inserted freely and which also provides an easily recognizable identity. The *Cor unum* is always fundamental, therefore, even though it is realized and lived in different contexts.[5] In the same way that the Society of the Sacred Heart and its spirituality have been enriched by contributions from Asia, Africa and Latin America, the identity of the Religious of the Sacred Heart has been remodeled by a new way of formulating the mission, uniting it to the service of education by uncoupling community life and ministries, by new relationships with colleagues at work, alumnae/i and Associates, by the social and political conditions of the country where they live: "The conviction that 'the pierced Heart of Jesus opens us to the depths of God and to the distress of humanity and draws us into its movement of

---

[5] M.C. Chandler, p. 198. In the United States in 1999, 72.1% of the religious thought it was necessary to strengthen it.

adoration of the Father and of love for all, especially the poor,"[6] is the motive that stimulates us and gives us apostolic energy. We feel the urgency to be women of communion, of compassion, of reconciliation to nourish life and make it grow."[7] Symbolically in 2000 the members of the new general council were given a Bible and a newspaper.

A charism – that of a congregation and that of its founder – draws people into an institute and gives them the desire to persevere; it is enriched by successive contributions of its members, and in becoming more complex while keeping the same aim, it reinforces its unified character. The Society of the Sacred Heart had a new experience of this when in November 1994 another congregation took steps toward an eventual merger with it. It was a French institute founded in the first third of the nineteenth century also for the service of education in the Church. Three years later it decided not to pursue this path; but the process that developed in the meantime had allowed the general council and the religious of the French province – who were the most concerned – to talk about their charism, their spirituality, their life style, their government, internationality, their institutions, their relationship to material goods and their juridical status.

> In the course of these exchanges it seemed to us RSCJ that our charism and spirituality were so marked by reference to the Heart of Christ that it would be difficult for someone who did not have the vocation of a religious of the Sacred Heart to assume them. Education was viewed differently by the two congregations. It seemed to us that for them education was their charism. However, as far as the expression of the educational mission goes, it seemed to us that the two congregations had experienced the same evolution. To the Sisters of Sainte Clotilde, our life style and community life seemed to be notably influenced by our conventual past. It seemed to us that internationality was not very apparent among them. Our sense of internationality certainly attracted them, but it is likely that they had not grasped the consequences of it.[8]

This commentary presented at the Chapter of 2000 shows how rootedness in the past holds so much meaning for a congregation and colors its evolution. At its origin the Society of the Sacred Heart developed in France

---

[6] Constitutions of 1982, § 8.
[7] P. García de Quevedo, *Lettres...*, p. 149. She alludes to one of the convictions of the Chapter of 1994. In the United States in 1999, 96.6% of the religious believed that to be women of prayer was the fundamental element of their identity (M.C. Chandler, p. 198).
[8] Report to the General Chapter 1994-2000, p. 34. This congregation had no structure of government by provinces.

and elsewhere by absorbing some older religious congregations. But there comes a moment when it is difficult for an institute to enter into another religious body because of characteristics that its history and the expression of its charism have given it.

In this regard the sixties and seventies constituted a crucial stage in the evolution of the Society. By virtue of the experiences in the provinces and the decisions of the general chapters, the fundamental characteristics of religious life in a body that redefined itself as an apostolic congregation were revisited. The balance between interior life and the mission was sometimes hard to maintain, both being present in the charism of Saint Madeleine Sophie but now lived out in full view. But the Society of the Sacred Heart was able to go through the storms and, endorsing its restructuring, find new fruitfulness in relying on its new Constitutions. It gave proof then of a real capacity to bounce back and showed that, by taking into account the changes that affected the world and the Church, it was still able to discover and manifest the love of God, of which the Heart of Christ is the symbol. It was surely from this center that it could accomplish its mission and contribute to education in surroundings that were themselves highly diversified, in cultures that were becoming aware of themselves and the development of both adults and children. It was really a refoundation by means of a return to the sources, which had taken place in the last thirty years of the twentieth century, by attentiveness "to the Holy Spirit to render living the love of God revealed in Jesus Christ in his pierced heart,"[9] by a fidelity that from then on called for change, discernment, mobility and, in a word, conversion.

The tradition had proved in the long term that the message of the charism, though expressed differently, was the same one declared beginning in 1800. The Society of the Sacred Heart had changed, but it was still rooted in the vision and intuition of Madeleine Sophie Barat; and from one end of the world to the other, in new places and social milieus or in the same ones as before, it sought to glorify the Heart of Christ and to make it known to the greatest number of people.

---

[9] P. García de Quevedo, *Lettres...*, p. 129.

Sources and Bibliography

Sources

Archives of the Society of the Sacred Heart

General Archives (Rome)
Series A: The Society of the Sacred Heart, canonical institute
Series C: Internal history of the Society
    C I: Central government
        C I A: Generalates. Dossiers
            2, Joséphine Goetz (1865-1874)
            3, Adèle Lehon (1874-1894)
            4, Augusta von Sartorius (1894-1895)
            5, Mabel Digby (1895-1911)
            6, Janet Erskine Stuart (1911-1914)
            7, Marie von Loë (1914-1928)
            8, Manuela Vicente (1928-1946)
            9, Marie-Thérèse de Lescure (1946-1957)
            10, Sabine de Valon (1958-1967)
            11, María Josefa Bultó (1967-1970)
            12, Concepción Camacho (1970-1982)
            13, Helen McLaughlin (1982-1994)
            14, Patricia García de Quevedo (1994-2000)
        C I C: General Congregations and Chapters
    C III: History of the provinces of the Society
    C IV: History of the institutions
    C V: Formation of the members of the Society
    C VI: Spirituality of the Society

Monique Luirard

Archives of provinces and of houses
Archives of the Provinces of England/Wales (Roehampton), of Belgium/Netherlands (Brussels), of Canada (Montréal), of Egypt (Cairo), of the United States (Saint Louis, Missouri), of Ireland/Scotland (Dublin), of France (Poitiers), of Japan (Tokyo), of Mexico/Nicaragua (Guadalajara). Archives of the Trinità dei Monti (Rome)

Printed Sources
Constitutions et Règles de la Société du Sacré-Cœur, Lyons, 1852.
Constitutions. Society of the Sacred Heart, Apostolic Institute of Pontifical Right, Rome, 1987.
Acts of the General Chapters of 1967, 1970, 1976, 1988, 1994.
Lettres annuelles de la Société du Sacré-Cœur. They contain accounts from the houses, institutions and works and the death notices of members of the Society.

Reviews
Mitte me, Societas Sacratissimi Cordis Jesu, from 1961 to 1966.
Connections. International review of the Society of the Sacred Heart, 3 vols. 1991, 1992, 1993.
Religious of the Sacred Heart, Strasbourg, 1999.

Circular Letters and Conferences of the Superiors General
Lettres et circulaires de notre T.R. Mère Joséphine Gœtz, supérieure générale de la Société du Sacré-Cœur, n.d.
Lettres circulaires de notre T.R. Mère Adèle Aimée Thérèse Lehon et *Lettres circulaires de notre T.R. Mère Augusta Huberta de Sartorius*, Roehampton, 1914.
Lettres circulaires de notre T.R. Mère Marie Joséphine Mabel Digby et *Lettres circulaires de notre T.R. Mère Janet Erskine Stuart*, Roehampton, 1914 et 1915.
Lettres circulaires de notre T.R. Mère Marie de Loë, Roehampton, 1929.
Lettres circulaires de notre T.R. Mère María Manuela Vicente, Rome, 1947.
Lettres circulaires de notre T.R. Mère Marie-Thérèse de Lescure, Rome, 1958.
Lettres circulaires de notre T.R. Mère Sabine de Valon, Rome, 1967.
Lettres circulaires de Mère María Josefa Bultó, supérieure générale de la Société du Sacré-Cœur, Rome, 1991.
Concepción Camacho, RSCJ, Superior General of the Society of the Sacred Heart of Jesus, *Letters to the Society*, Rome, 1992, and *Conferences*, Rome, 1993.

Helen McLaughlin, RSCJ, Superior General of the Society of the Sacred Heart of Jesus, *Letters to the Society* and *Conferences*, Rome, 2006.

Patricia García de Quevedo, RSCJ, Superior General of the Society of the Sacred Heart of Jesus, *Letters and Conferences*, Rome, 2006.

Works on Spirituality

Un *Appel à l'amour. Le message du Cœur de Jésus au monde et sa messagère, Sœur Josefa Menéndez, Religieuse coadjutrice du Sacré-Cœur de Jésus 1890-1923*, Toulouse, 1944.

Cum clamore valido. Appel du Rédempteur aux âmes consacrées, Paris, 1943.

Consacrés. Cum clamore valido, Paris, 1946.

Un *Itinéraire spirituel. Religieuses du Sacré-Cœur*, 20 octobre 1999-21 novembre 2000, Rome, 1999.

Works on the History of the Society of the Sacred Heart

Histoire Abrégée de la Société du Sacré-Cœur, Rome, 1926.

Jeanne de Charry, *Histoire des Constitutions de la Société du Sacré-Cœur. Première partie: La formation de l'institut*, 2 vols. Rome, 1975.

Helen McLaughlin, Francisca Tamayo, Hannelore Woitsch, *Process of Approbation of the Constitutions: Society of the Sacred Heart of Jesus, 1982-1987*, Rome, 2007. For Religious of the Sacred Heart only.

Clotilde Maguire, *Two Messages of Love. A Comparative Study of Some Aspects of the Revelation of the Sacred Heart of Jesus to Margaret Mary Alacoque and to Sister Josefa Menéndez*, Manhattanville, 1957.

Mary H. Quinlan, *The Society of the Sacred Heart, 1914-1964*, U.S. Province, 1995.

Dominique Sadoux et Pierre Gervais, *La Vie religieuse. Premières Constitutions des Religieuses de la Société du Sacré-Cœur. Texte et commentaire*, Paris, 1986.

Janet Erskine Stuart, *The Society of the Sacred Heart*, London, 1924.

Marie-Thérèse Virnot, *Le Charisme de sainte Madeleine Sophie*, Poitiers, 1975.

Margaret Williams, *The Society of the Sacred Heart: History of a Spirit: 1800-1975*, London, 1978.

Works on Houses or Provinces of the Society of the Sacred Heart

Yves Bruley et Alain Rauwel, *La Trinité des Monts. Cinq cents ans de présence française à Rome*, Rome 2001.

Cor unum et anima una, Canada, 1842-1992, no place, date.

25 años en Nicaragua 1980-2005. Sociedad del Sagrado Corazón, Provincia México-Nicaragua, n.d.

50 years on. Part I. The Province Remembers: The Journey of Evacuation. A SHOC Supplement, London, 1990.

Les Religieuses du Sacré-Cœur à la Trinité des Monts. 178 ans de présence à Rome, Rome, 2007.
Marthe Baudouin, *The Religious of the Sacred Heart in Canada 1842-1880*, Montréal, 1981.
Marguerite Benziger, *Austria Nazified, Years of Terror*, 1938-1955, U.S. Province, n.d.
Geneviève Bovagnet, *Trente ans au Tchad*, Lyons, 2002.
Louise Callan, *The Society of the Sacred Heart in North America*, New York, 1937.
Mary Charlotte Chandler, *Supporting the Social Identity of Women Religious: a Case Study of One Apostolic Congregation of Women Religious in the United States*, Graduate Theological Union, Berkeley, 2001.
Catherine A Carroll, *A History of the Pius X School of Liturgical Music*, Saint Louis, 1989.
Madeleine Chi, *Shanghai Sacred Heart: Risk in Faith, 1926-1952*, Saint Louis, 2001.
Amparo Guerrero, *Apuntes para la historia de la Sociedad del Sagrado Corazón en España*. t. 2: *El Mundo como horizonte*, Madrid, 1999.
María Teresa Guevara, *Historia de la Sociedad del Sagrado Corazón en Iberoamerica*. n.d.
Grace Hammond, *The History of the England-Malta Province with Ireland and Scotland, 1842-1982*, London, n.d.
V.V. Harrison, *Changing Habits: a Memoir of the Society of the Sacred Heart*, New York, Doubleday, 1988.
Histoire de la Société du Sacré-Cœur en Colombie, n.d.
Histoire de la Province du Mexique-Nicaragua, (en cours).
Monique Luirard, *Les Religieuses du Sacré-Cœur à la Trinité des Monts*, Rome, 2000.
Frances Makower, *Towards Tomorrow. The Society of the Sacred Heart*, London, 2000.
Marie Louise Martinez: *"Southward, Ho!" The Society of the Sacred Heart Enters "Lands of the Spanish Seas," 1853...*, Saint Louis, 2003.
Clotilde Meeûs, *Histoire de la Province du Congo, 1927-2000*, Bruxelles, 2000.
Alina Merdas, *Histoire de la Société du Sacré-Cœur en Pologne*, n.d.
Isobel Page, *College Street Remembered*, n.d.
Luc Pelletier, *Histoire de l'école Sophie Barat, 1858-1996*, Montréal, 1997.
Raquel Pérez: *Religiosas del Sagrado Corazón en Cuba*, La Habana, 1997.
Margarita Recavarren Elmore: *Raíces y horizonte. Apuntes para una historia. Religiosas del Sagrado Corazón*, Lima, 2003.
Margaret Williams: *The Society of the Sacred Heart in the Far East 1908-1980*, Tokyo, 1982.

Prudence Wilson: *My Father Took Me to the Circus. Religious Life from Within*, London, 1984.

Studies of Sacred Heart Education
Germaine Bourgade: *Contribution à l'étude d'une histoire de l'éducation féminine à Toulouse de 1830 à 1914*, Toulouse, 1980.
Patricia Byrne, "A tradition of Educating women: the Religious of the Sacred Heart in Higher Education," *U.S. Catholic Historian*, vol. 13, N° 4, 1995, p. 49-79.
Marie-France Carreel, *Le Plan éducatif fondateur de la Société du Sacré-Cœur et ses formes actuelles*, Lyons, 2001.
Mona Latif-Ghattas, *Les Filles de Sophie Barat*, Ottawa, 1999.
M. O'Leary, *Education with a Tradition*, London, 1936.

Various Works
Odile Arnold, *Le Corps et l'âme. La vie des religieuses au XIXe siècle*, Paris, 1984.
Patrick Cabanel et Jean-Dominique Durand (éd.), *Le Grand exil des congrégations religieuses françaises 1901-1914*, Paris, 2005.
Jacqueline Lalouette et Jean-Pierre Machelon (éd.), *1901, les congrégations hors la loi? Autour de la loi du 1er juillet 1901*, Paris, 2002.
Claude Langlois, *Le Catholicisme au féminin. Les congrégations françaises à supérieure générale au XIXe siècle*, Paris, 1984.
Guy Laperrière, *Les Congrégations religieuses. De la France au Québec.* t.2: *Au plus fort de la tourmente, 1901-1904*, Québec, 1999.
Jean-Marie Mayeur, Charles et Luce Pietri, André Vauchez, Marc Venard (éd.), *Histoire du Christianisme*, t. XI: Libéralisme, industrialisation, expansion européenne (1830-1914), t. XII: Guerres mondiales et totalitarismes (1914-1958), t. XIII: Crises et renouveau (de 1958 à nos jours), Paris, 1990, 2000, 2001.
Françoise Mayeur, *L'Education des filles en France au XIXe siècle*, Paris, 1979.
Christian Sorrel, *La République contre les congrégations. Histoire d'une passion française, 1899-1914*, Paris, 2003.
Yvonne Turin, *Femmes et religieuses au XIXe siècle. Le féminisme «en religion»*, Paris, 1989.
Les congrégations religieuses et la société française d'un siècle à l'autre, Paris, 2004.

Biographies of the Superiors General of the Society of the Sacred Heart
Phil Kilroy, *Madeleine Sophie Barat. A Life*, Cork, 2000.
Monique Luirard, *Madeleine-Sophie Barat (1779-1865). Une éducatrice au cœur du monde, au cœur du Christ*, Paris, 1999.

Vie de la T.R. Mère Marie Joséphine Gœtz, seconde supérieure générale de la Société du Sacré-Cœur, Roehampton, 1895.
Margaret Williams, *Josephine Gœtz, a Woman of Reflection*, Washington, n.d.
Pauline Perdrau, *Les Loisirs de l'Abbaye*, 2 vols. Rome, 1934 et 1936.
Vie de la T.R. Mère Adèle Lehon, troisième supérieure générale de la Société du Sacré-Cœur, Roehampton, 1895.
Vie de la T.R. Mère Marie-Augusta de Sartorius, quatrième supérieure générale de la Société du Sacré-Cœur, no place, 1899.
Vie de la T.R. Mère Janet Erskine Stuart, 1857-1914, Roehampton, 1921.
Mary H. Quinlan, *Mabel Digby, Janet Erskine Stuart, Superiors General of the Society of the Sacred Heart, 1895-1914*, no place, 1982.
E. Delpierre-Delattre, *De l'Anglicanisme au Sacré-Cœur, Janet Stuart, sixième supérieure générale de la Société du Sacré-Cœur*, Avignon, 1955.
Maud Monahan, *Life and Letters of Janet Erskine Stuart*, London, 1931.
Vie de la T.R. Mère Marie de Loë, septième supérieure générale de la Société du Sacré-Cœur 1857-1928, Rome, 1932.
Vie de la T.R. Mère Manuela Vicente, huitième supérieure générale de la Société du Sacré-Cœur 1862-1946, Rome, 1950.
Vie de la T.R. Mère Marie-Thérèse de Lescure, neuvième supérieure générale de la Société du Sacré-Cœur, 1884-1957, Rome, 1961.
Monique Luirard, *Sabine de Valon (1899-1990), dixième supérieure générale de la Société du Sacré-Cœur (1958-1967)*, Rome, 1997.

Biographies of Religious of the Sacred Heart
Enfants de Marie du Sacré-Cœur, 2 vols. Paris, 1932.
Religieuses du Sacré-Cœur, 3 vols. Paris, 1927 et 1931.
Sœurs coadjutrices du Sacré-Cœur, Montauban, 1927.
April O'Leary, *Sister Frances Allpress, 1907-1994*, n.d.
Sara Grant, *Life of R.M. Catherine Andersson*, Bombay, n.d.
The Life and Times of Winifred Theodosia Archer Shee, 1882-1972, n.d.
Frances Allpress, *Sister Eleonora Bennett, RSCJ. 1891-1984*, n.d.
Mary H.Quinlan, *Ursula Benziger*, Cambridge, 1984.
Life of Mother Gertrude Bodkin, n.d.
Vie de la R.M. Césarine Borget, assistante générale de la Société du Sacré-Cœur, 1827-1917, Rome, 1939.
La R.M. de Brocard, 1842-1923, Toulouse, 1926.
Odile Biolley, *Une âme d'élite, la M. Hélène de Burlet, religieuse du Sacré-Cœur, 1872-1950*, Bruges, 1964.
Notice sur la R.M. Marie Adélaïde Cahier, assistante générale de la Société du Sacré-Cœur, n.d.

Vie de la R.M. Giulia Datti, assistante générale de la Société du Sacré-Cœur, 1868-1954, Rome, 1956.
Vie de la R.M. Juliette Desoudin, assistante générale de la Société du Sacré-Cœur, Roehampton, 1904.
Vie de la R.M. Jeanne Dupont, assistante générale de la Société du Sacré-Cœur, 1855-1945, Rome, 1949.
Mère Madeleine Drujon, assistante générale de la Société du Sacré-Cœur, 1899-1969, n.d.
Mary Coke, *Sister Dorothy Eyre, RSCJ, 1903-1994*, London, 1997.
Ruth Cunningham, *Helen Fitzgerald, RSCJ, 1895-1982*, New York, 1983.
Vie de la R.M. Clémence Fornier de Mairard, assistante générale de la Société du Sacré-Cœur, Roehampton, 1896.
G.L Sheil, *Mother F.A. Forbes, RSCJ*. London, sd.
Amélie de Gibergues, professe de la Société du Sacré-Cœur, 1870-1941, n.d.
Vie de la R.M. Guiraudet, 1826-1895, Alais, 1897.
Ruth Cunningham, *First American Daughter: Mary Aloysia Hardey, RSCJ*, Kenwood, 1981.
Vie de la R.M. Mary Ann Aloysia Hardey, assistante générale de la Société du Sacré-Cœur, Paris, n.d.
Helen McHugh: *Life of R.M. Rosalie Hill: The Founders Tale*, n.d.
Elizabeth Basset, *Sister Barbara Hogg, 1901-1993*, n.d.
Life of R.M. Mary Hughes, Vancouver, n.d.
April O'Leary: *Sister Mary Kehoe, RSCJ, 1900-1993*, n.d..
Guxi Cao et Yu Hao (ed.) et Shilong Deng: *A giving tree. Biography of Brigid Keogh*, Xian, 1995.
Vie de la R.M. Elizabeth Lamb, assistante générale de la Société du Sacré-Cœur, 1868-1929, Rome, 1935.
Vie de la R.M. Jeanne de Lavigerie, assistante générale de la Société du Sacré-Cœur, 1851-1932, Rome, 1935.
Vie de la Digne Mère Marie Le Baïl, secrétaire générale de la Société du Sacré-Cœur, 1852-1920, Roehampton, 1924.
Esperanza Medina y Gestoso, 1920-2004, n.d.
Marie Barberen, *Vie de Sœur Josefa Menéndez, sœur coadjutrice de la Société du Sacré-Cœur*, Rome, 1928.
Vie de la R.M. Catherine de Montalembert, assistante générale de la Société du Sacré-Cœur, 1841-1928, Rome, 1930.
Vie de la digne Mère Henriette de Montlivault, économe générale de la Société du Sacré-Cœur, 1865-1949, Rome, 1953.
Sœur Barbara Napier, 1904-2004, Bruxelles, n.d.
Vie de la R.M. Mathilde Nerincx, assistante générale de la Société du Sacré-Cœur, 1845-1919, Roehampton, 1924.
Joan Faber, *Sister Rebecca Ogilvie Forbes, 1895-1995*, n.d.

Notice de Gabriele Paradeis, 1909-1991, n.d.
Le Peintre de Mater admirabilis et le chantre de l'Enfant Jésus [Pauline Perdrau], Montauban, 1927.
Vie de la R.M. Constance Perry, assistante générale de la Société du Sacré-Cœur, 1867-1950, Rome, 1954.
Vie de la R.M. Marthe de Pichon, assistante générale de la Société du Sacré-Cœur, Roehampton, 1916.
Helen Tichenor, *Mother Eleanor Reagan*, Omaha, 1961.
Madeleine d'Ernemont, *La Vie voyageuse et missionnaire de la R.M. Anna de Rousier*, Paris, 1932.
Vie de la R.M. Helen Rumbold, assistante générale de la Société du Sacré-Cœur, 1847-1921, Roehampton, 1925.
Frances M. Gimber, *Woman of the Word. A Life of Marie Louise Schroen, Religious of the Sacred Heart, 1909-1991*, Saint Louis, n.d.
Vie de la R.M. Anna Josephine Shannon, religieuse du Sacré-Cœur, Roehampton, 1920.
O. Thoreau, *Vie de la R.M. Adèle Symon, assistante générale de la Société du Sacré-Cœur, 1871-1941*, Paris, 1950.
Mémoires de la R.M. Maria Stanislas Tommasini, Religieuse du Sacré-Cœur, 1827-1913, Roehampton, 1918.
Maria del Pilar de Veragua, religieuse du Sacré-Cœur, Paris, 1875.
Notice de la R.M. Paula Werhahn, n.d.
Winifred Wilson, *Memoir 1906-1997*, n.d.
Vie de la R.M. Elena Ytturalde, assistante générale de la Société du Sacré-Cœur, 1879-1958, Rome, 1962.
Vie de la digne Mère Maria Zaepffel, religieuse du Sacré-Cœur, 1832-1910, Rome, 1925.
Mère Elisabeth Zurstrassen, 1888-1971, à travers sa vie, à travers sa correspondance, n.d.

INDEX

A

Ahern, Mollie 620, 656, 660
Aldeguer, Sonia 636, 675
Amarante, Elizabeth 594, 595
Amette, Cardinal 259
Andersson, Catherine 312, 750
Antoncich, Ricardo 698

B

Baillot, Louise 412
Bakewell, Nancy 170
Barat, Madeleine Sophie xv, xvii, 3, 6, 29, 53, 99, 312, 343, 440, 676, 692, 720, 743, 749
Basset, Elizabeth 577, 751
Baternay, Agota 671, 698
Belón, Gabriela 487, 502, 521, 537, 599
Benedict XV 29, 251, 260, 282, 443
Bennett, Eleonora 312, 750
Benziger, Ursula 414, 750
Bernard, Louise 423
Best, Agnes 384
Blaire, Charlotte 471, 667
Blanes, María Antonia 666
Bodkin, Gertrude 58, 137, 154, 182, 183, 750
Bodman, Jeanne de 520
Bofarull, Guadalupe de 223
Boland, Doreen 406, 469, 540, 541, 559, 567, 622, 625, 627, 629, 658, 659, 660, 726
Borget, Césarine 160, 196, 750
Boudreau, Susannah 63
Bovagnet, Geneviève 182, 407, 471, 472, 748
Bowman, Vivien 492, 493, 540, 541, 684, 685
Braganza, Mary 460, 492, 510, 514, 521, 544, 579, 580, 584, 622, 725
Braun, Françoise 306, 459
Bremer, Margot 710
Brennan, Beatrice 575
Brolac, Madeleine de 245
Bugembe, Ursula 675, 708, 711, 721, 740
Buhet, Adrienne 245
Bultó, María Josefa 745, 746
Burlet, Hélène de 255, 750

C

Cabanous, Marie de 148
Calabuig, Esperanza 589, 594
Camacho, Concepción 521, 555, 570, 745, 746
Campbell, Pauline 469, 655, 658
Caracciolo, Teresa 510, 641
Carloni, Eleonora 525, 641
Caro, Juana Luisa 472

Carré, Marie-Thérèse 513, 586, 633
Casey, Mary 228
Catelani, Anna Maria 690
Charley, Marion 489
Charry, Jeanne de 32, 71, 129, 559, 667, 670, 677, 747
Chazottes, Christiane 576, 590
Chélas, Sophie du 162
Chlapowska, Helena 378
Cleary, Marguerite 469
Clock, Chantal de 16, 590
Coke, Mary xiii, 286, 489, 494, 526, 579, 751
Collins, Catherine 665, 682
Condon, Helen 374, 529, 530, 606, 609, 611
Conroy, Ann 488, 536, 575, 585
Conroy, Margaret 656

D

Dammann, Grace 285
d'Apice, Mary 519
Datti, Giulia 367, 751
Davidson, Honor 604
Depret, Juliette 162, 210
Desmarquest, Félicité 177
Desoudin, Juliette 80, 751
Deydier, Marie 233
Dhalla, Gool Mary 313, 544, 573
Díaz-Varela, Dolores 574
Digby, Mabel 44, 53, 80, 158, 204, 745, 746, 750
Donnelly, Moira 489, 671
Drujon, Madeleine 448, 527, 528, 551, 553, 751
Duchesne, Philippine xviii, xix, 6, 9, 46, 47, 173, 174, 302, 370, 443, 450, 463, 476, 553, 595, 667, 704, 732, 733
Duff, Elizabeth 426
Dupont, Jeanne 751

Duret, Bishop 226
Dusaussoy, Stanislas 173

E

Eechoud, Marijke van 472
Elió, Gloria 331
Eyre, Dorothy 490, 527, 544, 751

F

Faber, Joan 481, 489, 490, 493, 504, 544, 574, 602, 652, 751
Fabre, Marie-Louise 550, 585
Fabre, Monique 684
Finocchiaro, Maria 691
Fitzgerald, Helen 477, 512, 549, 751
Fitzgerald, Sadie 426
Flynn, Carmel 659
Forbes, Alice 183
Ford, Jean 489, 497, 666, 675, 701, 712, 714
Francs, Bernadette des 562, 581, 610, 611, 656, 666, 677
Frey, Antonia 125
Fühles, Margret 701

G

García de Quevedo, Patricia xiii, 323, 630, 675, 691, 711, 734, 745, 747
García, Shona 665, 682
Gazelli, Christine 14
Gibergues, Amélie de 442, 450, 751
Gimber, Frances xiii, 508
Gœtz, Joséphine 3, 29, 746, 750
Günther, Zofia 368
Gutzwiller, Hildegarde 394

H

Hanquet, Marguerite-Marie 596
Hardey, Aloysia 55, 751
Hartigan, Catherine 134

Hensgens, Magdalena 472
Heydon, Bridget 228, 229
Hill, Rosalie 288, 751
Hinde, Mary 582, 605, 668, 675, 711, 719, 729
Hirata, Madame 229
Hornedo, Carmen 653, 654, 737
Hurtado, Margarita 590, 666

Le Baïl, Marie 751
Lehon, Adèle 745, 750
Le Mintier de Léhélec, Anne-Marie 442
Leo XIII 21, 25, 29, 52, 104, 121, 174, 227, 295
Leplat, Marie-Louise 562, 565, 598, 600
Levis, Jean 411
Loë, Mathilde von 339

I

Iwashita, Kiyoko 301

M

Mackie, Anna 469, 474
Mallet, Alice 450
Mallia, Patrick 671
Mankowska, Maria 388
Marie-José, Princess 294
Martin, Anne-Marie 103
Martínez, Fanny 492, 544, 549, 597
Mattos, Odette 710
Mawete, Anne 559, 726
McAghon, Ursula 654
McCaffrey, Katherine 512
McGourty, Annie 469
McLaughlin, Helen 471, 473, 569, 630, 644, 656, 658, 661, 666, 670, 671, 675, 677, 745, 747
Medina, Esperanza 482, 483, 559, 596, 617, 634, 751
Meeûs, Clotilde xiii, 305, 460, 473, 522, 748
Menéndez, Josefa 443, 444, 445, 446, 447, 448, 450, 747, 751
Merle, Marguerite du 446, 463, 592, 667
Meylan, Andrée 492, 512, 519, 520, 579, 580, 582, 598
Miller, Margaret Mary 492, 537, 542, 559
Montalembert, Catherine de 208, 218, 267, 751
Moriarty, Betty 482, 597

J

Jacobs, Louisa 331
Jacobs, Marthe 502, 514, 515, 522, 526, 596
Jiménez, Marta 675, 702, 711, 713, 729, 730
John XXIII 450, 455, 462, 475, 556
Jordis, Maria von 257, 280, 287, 384

K

Karam, Rita 675
Kennedy, Kathleen 469
Keogh, Brigid 301, 400, 409, 413, 428, 438, 466, 484, 534, 727, 751
Keraly, Maryvonne 626, 675, 708, 711, 713, 723, 727, 729
Kerguiffinec, Charlotte de 231
Kerr, Henrietta 66, 100, 120
Killeen, Winifred 468, 469, 474, 655
Kilroy, Phil xvii, 6, 537, 737, 749
Kinlen, Aideen 270
Kömstedt, Anna 340
Krupa, Maria 412

L

Lataste, Marie 203
Lavigerie, Jeanne de 41, 54, 61, 230, 751

N

Napier, Barbara 380, 527, 751
Nerincx, Mathilde 751
Nicholls, Barbara 527
Nieuwland, Betzy 206
Nourry, Conchita 303, 400

O

Ogilvie Forbes, Rebecca 481, 497, 502, 512, 751
O'Leary, April 489, 750, 751
Olivella, Asunción 114
O'Meara, Virginia 723
O'Neil, Anne 612, 710

P

Paul VI 479, 535, 555, 691
Perdrau, Pauline 5, 7, 15, 169, 667, 750, 752
Pérez, Raquel 702, 748
Perry, Constance 414, 752
Pichon, Marthe de 187, 752
Pius IX 10, 11, 15, 23, 24, 25, 26, 27, 28, 29, 81, 118, 123, 153, 158, 171, 181
Pius XII xvi, 357, 366, 377, 418, 434, 441, 442, 462
Poncelet, Anne 596

Q

Quinlan, Mary 44, 53, 220, 447, 448, 648, 667, 677

R

Raynaud de Lage, Henriette 580
Repullés, Pilar 662, 710
Rousier, Anna de 14, 752
Roussin, Joséphine 232

Rumbold, Helen 41, 223, 752
Ryan, Oonah 612

S

Saade, Maria Luiza 222, 438, 440, 510, 528, 546, 570, 622, 625, 629, 710
Saint-Germain, Ines 304
Salmon, Amélie 248
Salm-Salm, Marie zu 375
Sartorius, Augusta von 745
Scarlatta, Giovanna 579
Schaffgotsch, Marie-Anne von 263
Schröder, Felicitas 397
Schroen, Marie Louise 369, 508, 727, 752
Schulten, Amélie 232
Scroope, Mary 228
Seidel, Victoria 612
Serres, Nathalie de 160, 165
Shanahan, Mary 499, 569, 622, 625
Shoda, Michiko 301
Simon, Madeleine 369
Sobota, Katarina 398
Sproule, Elizabeth 228
Stacpoole, Anne de 469
Stecka, Maria 702
Strözyk, Helena 472
Stuart, Janet Erskine 12, 23, 44, 217, 745, 746, 747, 750
Sullivan, Eleanor 296
Sweeney, Elizabeth 512
Symon, Adèle 255, 752

T

Tamayo, Francisca xiii, 463, 666, 675, 678, 688, 747
Thunder, Rose 38, 134, 180
Tobin, Mary Elizabeth 512
Tommasini, Stanislas 49, 752
Tournély, Léonor de 5

U

Ustara, María Josefa 524

V

Valle, Manuela 702
Valon, Sabine de 21, 449, 451, 508, 537, 745, 746, 750
Vercruysse, Fébronie 53
Verges, Pilar 332
Vicente, Manuela 745, 746, 750
Vié, Marie-Josèphe 546, 653, 667
Villalonga, Rosario 331
Virnot, Marie-Thérèse 441, 545, 559, 566, 568, 667, 747

W

Wakamatsu, Kiyoko 527
Walchnowska, Elzbieta 388, 412
Waldeck-Rousseau, Pierre 196
Ward, Ita 469
Wawra, Jadwiga 412
Werhahn, Paula 268, 382, 752
Willoquet, Marthe-Marie 472
Wilson, Winifred 277, 279, 370, 752
Wyszynski, Stefan 415

X

Xerri, Salvina 426

Y

Yanez, Leonor 492, 577

Z

Zaufal, Leonilda von 264
Zurstrassen, Elisabeth 366, 439, 457, 477, 481, 752

Printed in the United States
By Bookmasters